PERSONALITY

STRATEGIES AND ISSUES

Seventh Edition

Robert M. Liebert
(Ph.D., clinical psychology, Stanford University) is currently Professor of Psychology at the State University of New York at Stony Brook. He has published widely in the fields of personality, social development, and methodological issues and is coauthor of *Science and Behavior* and *The Early Window*, as well as many other books and articles. He also has strong avocational interests in poetry and philosophy.
Photo by Lynn

Michael D. Spiegler
(Ph.D., clinical psychology, Vanderbilt University) is Professor of Psychology at Providence College. His research interests range from the psychology of optimal experience and observational learning to the nature and treatment of obesity, anxiety, and chronic psychiatric disorders. He is coauthor of *Contemporary Behavior Therapy* and *The Community Training Center*. Professor Spiegler is well known for his innovations and training in active learning. When he is not engaged in professional activities, he may be found flying, sailing, running, skiing, enjoying early music and fine wine, and delighting in his family.

PERSONALITY
STRATEGIES AND ISSUES

Seventh Edition

Robert M. Liebert
State University of New York at Stony Brook

Michael D. Spiegler
Providence College

BROOKS / COLE PUBLISHING COMPANY
PACIFIC GROVE, CALIFORNIA

 The trademark ITP is used under license.

Brooks/Cole Publishing Company
A Division of Wadsworth, Inc.
© 1994 by Wadsworth, Inc., Belmont, California 94002.

Printed in the United States of America

10 9 8 7 6 5 4 3 2 1

Library of Congress Cataloging-in-Publication Data
Liebert, Robert M., 1942–
    Personality : strategies and issues / Robert M. Liebert, Michael D. Spiegler. — 7th ed.
      p.   cm.
    Includes bibliographical references and index.
    ISBN 0-534-17580-5
    1. Personality.   I. Spiegler, Michael D.   II. Title.
BF698.L465   1993
155.2—dc20
                                         93-36565
                                            CIP

Sponsoring Editor: Marianne Taflinger
Production Coordinator: Joan Marsh
Editorial Assistant: Virge Perelli-Minetti
Editing and Production: Graphic World Publishing Services
Interior Design: Graphic World Publishing Services
Cover Design: Cheryl Carrington
Cover Photo: Jody Dole
Interior Illustration: John Odam, Julie Walter
Section-Opening Illustrator: Karl Nicholason
Typesetting: Graphic World, Inc.
Cover Printing: Phoenix Color Corporation
Printing and Binding: R. R. Donnelley & Sons

Writing the seventh edition of *Personality: Strategies and Issues* has been a stimulating experience for us. Personality theorists and researchers have been extremely active in recent years, and the present edition has been substantially rewritten to reflect important changes in the field. We also have made organizational changes and enhanced several new pedagogical features, in keeping with our desire to have *Personality* be the best possible teaching book.

Our fundamental goal has always been to present the technical concepts and procedures of personality psychology in clear terms that students can grasp quickly and retain beyond the final exam. We have written expressly for students, which has meant avoiding jargon and translating often cumbersome theoretical terms into simple, concrete language that students can readily understand. We also have structured the book in a way that organizes the diverse material with which personality psychologists work into a single, overarching framework. This framework uses conceptual strategies and fundamental issues to explain the basic ideas behind personality psychology.

Within this framework, we examine four basic conceptual strategies that psychologists use in their study of personality: the *psychoanalytic, dispositional, phenomenological,* and *behavioral*. Each of these strategies is presented in a positive light and in the tone and format that its adherents would use. Our presentation of each strategy section begins with a short introductory chapter that lays out the major assumptions of the approach. Then, after a more detailed presentation of the specific theories, research, and applications that fall within the strategy, we conclude with a concise chapter on the strategy's liabilities, voiced in the negative terms most likely to be used by its harsher critics.

All strategies for the study of personality must come to grips with the same four major issues: a clear *theoretical statement,* a set of guidelines for *personality assessment,* a systematic body of *research,* and an explicit basis for understanding and implementing *personality change*. We view the scientific investigation of personality as the critical interplay of these four fundamental issues within each of the four basic strategies. We have been using this organizational framework in our teaching of personality for 25 years and have found it to be a highly effective way to orient students surveying the field for the first time. Our aim is to structure the material logically in order to clarify and highlight differences and similarities among the various viewpoints. In this way, our survey of personality theories does not come across as an incomprehensible hodgepodge of arbitrary approaches.

As in the preceding editions of *Personality*, we have not tried to give complete coverage of every individual theory and viewpoint. Even if that were possible (which is highly doubtful), we do not believe that an encyclopedic presentation is a prudent way to introduce students to the field of personality. Instead, our emphasis continues to be on presenting enduring principles and contemporary issues and illustrating them with selected examples rather than exhaustive lists.

The seventh edition of *Personality* has been thoroughly updated to reflect the most current developments in the field. Among the changes are a fuller discussion of the nature of theory; an expanded treatment of object relations theory and therapy; a comprehensive discussion of recent research generated by the five-factor model of personality; increased coverage of the assessment of self-actualization and application of personal construct theory; the addition of contemporary theory and application of classical conditioning and a discussion of paradigmatic behaviorism; and increased coverage of locus of control, self-efficacy, and cognitive-behavioral interventions. We have attempted to weave this new material carefully into the fabric of the core presentation.

A number of the book's features are specifically designed to make learning easy and enjoyable for the student. Each chapter begins with an overview in outline form and ends with a point-by-point summary. Key terms are in boldface type at the point where they are defined in the text and also appear in an expanded glossary at the end of the book for quick reference.

Personality courses are among the most popular offerings in psychology, but they are often disappointing to students who want information that bears on their own lives. To serve this legitimate need, we have illustrated concepts and principles through examples that are relevant to college students. We also have expanded a feature of previous editions that capitalizes on and stimulates college students' intellectual inquisitiveness and skepticism. Periodically, the reader is invited to perform easily implemented *Demonstrations* that examine the validity of various propositions discussed in the text. We have used these "personalized studies" repeatedly in our teaching and have regularly revised them on the basis of student feedback. Demonstrations appear throughout the book. One is included in each strategy's introductory chapter to provide an additional avenue through which the student can experience the "way of thinking" that is characteristic of each strategy. The remaining Demonstrations provide students with an opportunity to learn firsthand about specific aspects of personality. This edition includes a number of new and simplified Demonstrations. Additionally, a Demonstration Materials section at the end of the book contains work sheets on perforated pages, making the Demonstrations easy and inviting to carry out.

We believe that visual illustrations are appropriate to the extent that they have legitimate instructional value. Our illustration program therefore was created to be visually stimulating and purposeful—intended to elucidate, not decorate. The seventh edition of *Personality* contains more of such illustrations, including new photographs (some specifically shot for the book) that succinctly make a point or clarify an idea and consequently enhance students' understanding and retention.

We are most interested in our readers' reactions, opinions, and advice. Accordingly, there is a brief comment form provided on the last page of the book. It can be easily removed and returned to us postage-free. Please write us using this form or a letter.

We wish to thank the following reviewers, whose comments and criticisms helped our work on the seventh edition: Barry Fritz, Quinnipiac College; Susan B. Goldstein, University of Redlands; A.E.M. Jastrebske, University of Saskatchewan; James J. Johnson, Illinois State University; Richard Kolotkin, Moorhead State University; David L. Novak, Lansing Community College; Augustine Osman, University of Northern Iowa; Phillip L. Rice, Moorhead State University; Ed Sadalla, University of Arizona; Brian Stagner, Texas A & M University; and Teddy D. Warner, Iowa State University.

We have a continuing debt to the many undergraduates in our personality courses over the past 25 years whose comments, questions, and challenges have provided critical input that has allowed us to shape successive editions to meet their needs. We want to express our appreciation to Patricia Engler for her help with reference materials, Karen Cawley and George Raymond for helping to develop new Demonstrations, and Jennifer Lewis for her exceptionally competent handling of a myriad of tasks in the production phase. Michael Spiegler is grateful for the constant help he receives from Annmarie Mullen. And he is especially appreciative of his family's support, including his wife Margi's concocting palatable malteds from bitter ingredients and his daughter Heather's counsel regarding the plights faced by Hansel and Gretel and by the three little pigs.

Robert M. Liebert
Michael D. Spiegler

Contents

INTRODUCTION

Introduction

In the theater of ancient Rome, actors wore a mask, called a persona, to indicate the personality characteristics of the roles they played.

n ancient Rome, actors used no makeup. Instead, each player wore a persona, a full-face mask, which told the audience to expect a particular set of attitudes and behaviors. Various *personae* came to refer not only to the masks but also to the roles they implied (Burnham, 1968).

Although *persona* is the source of the English word *personality*, the concept of personality as we use it today did not emerge until the 18th century. Sampson (1989) traces the term to the modern idea of a "real person."

> Unlike our current understanding, which distinguishes between real persons and the roles they must play, in premodern society, roles were the elements that constituted the person as such. Roles were not appended to the "real" person who somehow continued to dwell authentically behind them. There was no stepping outside one's community and one's roles within it in order to act differently. . . . To be outside was in effect to be nonexistent, a stranger, or dead. (p. 915)

Sampson concludes that it was only with the emergence of the concept of personality 200 years ago that "seeking to understand the individual became a highly cherished cultural project" (1989, p. 916).

This book is an introduction to the psychological study of personality. It deals with the issues involved in developing a scientific approach to understanding ourselves and others. We have stressed the major ideas psychologists have followed in conceptualizing human personality. Our goal is to give you a general picture of the diversity of existing theories, the points these theories emphasize, the assumptions they make, and the nature of the evidence they consider. In this way, we have tried to explain the ideas underlying major groups of theoretical positions and, at the same time, summarize the questions they have answered and the ones they are still asking.

We refer to the broad approaches to personality psychology as **strategies**. Four major strategies can be identified: *psychoanalytic, dispositional, phenomenological,* and *behavioral*. All these strategies address the same four underlying **issues**: (1) a *theory* of personality; (2) an approach to the *assessment* (or measurement) of personality; (3) *research* procedures for testing hypotheses (or implications derived from the theory); and (4) methods of personality *change* (i.e., psychotherapy). However, the strategies differ in how they handle these issues.

There is considerable overlap in the roles played by each issue. Theories suggest ideas or *hypotheses* that are then tested in research. At the same time, the nature of the research is determined by what the particular theory leads the researcher to expect. To conduct research, the aspects of personality that are of interest must be measured. But first, assessment techniques that conform to the theory's assumptions about personality must be developed. The success of personality-change techniques serves to partially validate the therapeutic principles derived from the theory. In sum, theory, assessment, research, and personality change are intricately linked parts of every strategy.

In fact, it becomes difficult to talk about one issue without referring to one or more of the other three (Tjeltveit, 1989).

THE NATURE OF PERSONALITY PSYCHOLOGY

Modern psychology is a very broad field, comprising many specialized areas. Interest in interpersonal relations, attitude change, and the influence of social forces is typically the domain of *social psychology*. *Developmental psychology* emphasizes the historical antecedents of a person's behavior; it is concerned with the interplay of maturational and social influences as people advance from childhood to adulthood to old age. When someone's behavior is markedly different from the usual norms of society, especially when those differences are maladaptive for the person or others, the phenomena are of particular interest to *abnormal psychology*. This field includes the theoretical and experimental work of *psychopathology* and the applied work of *clinical psychology*.

Specific human enterprises are the focus of fields such as *health psychology, industrial and organizational psychology, environmental psychology, educational psychology,* and *school psychology. Experimental psychology* involves the study of single aspects of the organism, such as sensation, perception, learning, and emotion. *Cognitive psychology* concentrates on how human beings think and process information.

In many ways, **personality psychology** is at the crossroads of these other fields. One personality psychologist gives this view of the "big picture."

> To me, the most fruitful definition of the goal of scientific psychology is to understand and explain why individuals think, feel, act, and react as they do in real life. The special contribution of *personality psychology* to this effort is to develop theories and conduct empirical research *on the functioning of the individual as a totality.* (Magnusson, 1989, p. 1)

Defining Personality

Can we define the term *personality* more precisely? In fact, personality psychologists use many definitions. Which definition a particular psychologist selects depends on his or her theoretical orientation. Because of the diversity of definitions, there is little point in searching for a single definition of personality. And, as we will see repeatedly, a complete definition of personality always implies at least a partial theory of personality as well. To fully understand what a particular psychologist means by *personality*, we must examine his or her theoretical approach. Thus, definitions differ, mainly along theoretical lines, from one personality psychologist to another.

RECURRING QUESTIONS

Five recurring questions are embedded in the psychological study of personality.

Free Will versus Determinism

Do we have free choice, or are our actions and thoughts determined by forces and factors that are out of our control?

This is a fundamental matter on which personality psychologists are divided. Sappington (1990) argued that the question of free will versus determinism is actually a continuum, ranging from hard determinism to free will, with soft determinism falling in between.

Proponents of *hard determinism* say that human behavior is entirely determined by factors outside the person. They assume that all phenomena in the universe are determined by immutable "laws" and that "the mind is governed by the same laws that govern billiard balls or fish" (Sappington, 1990, p. 1). This is the position of the famous behaviorist, B. F. Skinner, who argued that all our actions result from environmental factors and our prior experience (or learning history).

Advocates of *soft determinism* take a different tack. They assume that free will and determinism are not really incompatible. Phenomenological theorist Carl Rogers subscribes to this view. Rogers argues that human behavior can be seen as either free or determined, depending on the purpose of our analysis.

Rogers (1959) likened his position to the approach modern physics has taken to the question, "Does light travel in the form of particles or in the form of waves?" For decades, physicists treated this as an either/or issue—and got nowhere. Quantum physics "solved" the problem by concluding that both views can be useful. Likewise, says Rogers, human behavior can be viewed as either completely free or completely determined, depending on how we look at it.

At first glance, soft determinism may appear to be an impossible position. However, it is closely related to the principle of relativity that made Albert Einstein famous. Einstein was concerned with the relationship between events and time. Before Einstein presented his theory, it was considered meaningful to say that two events occurred simultaneously, that is, at exactly the same time. But Einstein pointed out that to "operationalize" this idea, to *see* if two events occur simultaneously, one must look from *somewhere*. From some vantage points, the two events will be simultaneous; from other vantage points, they will not. There is no way to go from here. There is no higher authority. Our conclusions always depend on our vantage point. This is true regardless of whether our interest is in the movement of light or in human nature.

Finally, at the other end of the continuum, the *free will* position asserts that we control our own destinies. Free will implies that human beings are a special case, unique in nature because of our potential for self-determination. Humans, alone of nature's creatures, are seen as able to generate their own alternatives, set their own goals, and gauge their own performances. This is the view taken by personality theorist Albert Bandura, who wrote: "The capacity to exercise control over one's thought processes, motivation, and action is a distinctly human characteristic" (1989a, p. 1175).

Objective versus Subjective Aspects of Personality   Philosophers have long understood that we can never know directly what is "inside" another person; we cannot observe another's subjective experiences for ourselves. For example, people may say that Tom is happy in order to provide a summary label for his smiles, his jokes, or his invitation to take

Some personality psychologists have argued that subjective experiences are more important than objective appearances for assessing personality. The ever-smiling Marilyn Monroe committed suicide at the age of 36.
© Eve Arnold/Magnum Photos

everyone out for a beer. But they are speaking of his overt behavior and not necessarily of any private, internal state that he is experiencing.

Some personality psychologists hold that psychology's sole concern should be with observable behavior. They argue that the scientific study of personality must rest entirely on objective evidence. However, most personality psychologists argue that personality psychology must acknowledge and explain private, subjective experiences as well. Although Tom *appears* happy, he may, in fact, be miserable. Marilyn, who seems to be self-assured and "put together," may actually have numerous doubts and fears about her adequacy and competence. In general, outward appearances may not reflect a person's "real" personality. Which view is right? That depends on how personality is defined in the first place.

The Person versus the Situation

To what extent are people consistent in the way they think, feel, and act in various situations? One often hears descriptions such as "John is quiet" or "Sharon is irresponsible." People speak as though these are properties of individuals, rather like the color of their eyes, which is always apparent and virtually unchangeable. But personality is plainly not as consistent as eye color. John, the "quiet one," may be very outspoken about his hobby, stamp collecting. Sharon, the "irresponsible one," may be very careful in keeping her club's records (although she has not finished a single class assignment on time in 3 years). Definitions and theories of personality differ in the way they deal with the inconsistencies that may be observed in a person's behavior in different situations or at different times. Some theorists have minimized the importance of such inconsistencies, whereas others have emphasized their significance (Emmons & Diener, 1986).

Human Nature and Individuality

Henry Murray, a personality psychologist whose work we will discuss in Chapter 11, noted that there are three levels to the question of human nature and individuality. The modern version of "Murray's dictum" is as follows:

In some ways each person is like all other persons.
In some ways each person is like some other persons.
In some ways each person is like no other person.
(cf. Kluckhohn & Murray, 1953; Runyan, 1983)

Personality theories differ in the degree to which they address each of these three levels. Statements at the first level relate to *universals* in human nature. In psychoanalysis, for example, every human being is presumed to be driven by the same underlying forces and to pass through the same sequence of stages in the development of personality. In a parallel fashion, behaviorists believe that we are all shaped by the rewards and punishments doled out by our cultures and environments.

At the second level, we try to *categorize people* according to the type of personality or array of personality traits they possess. Thus, psychoanalysts speak of an *anal triad* of personality characteristics occurring in those who were especially stressed by toilet training, whereas dispositional theorists distinguish groups such as *introverts* or *neurotics*.

Only at the third level do we confront the idea of uniqueness in personality. Personality psychologists generally agree that every human being is unique in some way. But there is great controversy over the implications of this uniqueness for the study of personality. One view is that each person is so distinctive that he or she can be understood only in terms of his or her particular life and experiences. Comparison with others, according to this approach, is really not meaningful. This view, called the **idiographic** approach (from the Greek *idios*, meaning "personal"), has inspired extensive studies of the lives of individuals with the aim of achieving a unique understanding of each person (Hermans, 1988).

The alternative view is the **nomothetic** [no-mo-THET-ik] approach, which assumes that each person's uniqueness is a product of general biological and psychological laws (*nomos* is the Greek word for "law"). According to this approach, each person is a unique combination of "ingredients." Each ingredient, though, is a product of *general* processes. The processes can be understood by investigating specific aspects of personality in a wide variety of individuals, in order to formulate laws of behavior that hold for people in general.

Prediction, Control, and Understanding: Goals of Personality Psychology

The goals of personality psychology are *prediction*, *control*, and *understanding*. **Prediction** is the ability to accurately *anticipate* a person's behavior. **Control**, as used in psychology, means *influencing* a person's behavior. Suppose a theory indicates that people with a high need for achievement tend to take moderate risks. If we know that Barbara has a high need to achieve, we would predict that she will prefer a bet with 4 to 1 odds over a bet with either 2 to 1 or 20 to 1 odds. And we could control (influence) her betting behavior by changing the odds of the available bets.

Prediction and control are more or less straightforward ideas. The meaning of *understanding* is elusive and ambiguous. **Understanding** usually refers to comprehension of the process involved and the ability to give an *explanation* of some sort. But the level of comprehension and explanation sufficient for a person to say "I understand" varies from individual to individual. For most automobile drivers, it is enough to know that the car won't start because of a short in the ignition. But mechanically inclined drivers may not be satisfied until they know where the short is and what caused it. Understanding can thus mean different things to different people.

THEORIES OF PERSONALITY	We have already used the word *theory* on several occasions. Now the time has come to take a closer look at this term.
Scientific Theory	A scientific theory is an explanation, but not all explanations are scientific theories (Hesse, 1963). Scientific theories have two components: *theoretical constructs* and *relational propositions*.

Theoretical Constructs

The basic terms and building blocks of a theory are its *theoretical constructs* (CON-structs). Energy is a theoretical construct in physics; oxidation is a theoretical construct in chemistry; and natural selection is a theoretical construct in evolutionary biology. Personality psychologists use a wide variety of theoretical constructs; among the more familiar are anxiety, self-concept, extraversion, and ego.

One characteristic distinguishes all **theoretical constructs**; they have been *invented* to describe and explain observations. Thus, theoretical constructs do not actually exist; they cannot be seen, touched, or heard.

Why are theoretical constructs desirable or even necessary? A major reason is that they economically tie together meaningful relationships among observations that would otherwise soon become a hopeless quagmire of raw facts. Figure 1-1 illustrates the advantage of using the theoretical construct *anxiety* to link various events and observations. Even in the case of only three events and three observations, a single concept that unites each of the three events with the three observations (Figure 1-1*B*) is more economical, manageable, and comprehensible than describing nine separate relationships (Figure 1-1*A*).

Relational Propositions

The constructs of a scientific theory are related to one another by statements (sometimes called *laws*) that describe the relationships among the constructs. These are the theory's **relational propositions**. For example, Einstein's famous theory uses (among others) the constructs energy (*E*), mass (*m*), and a constant (*c*) which is the speed of light. The best-known relational proposition of the theory is $E = mc^2$.

Personality theories contain many relational propositions, although they are rarely quantified in the precise way they are in physics. Psychoanalytic theory, for example, tells us that frustration leads to aggression; dispositional theory tells us that similarity in genetic makeup leads to similarity in personality; and behavioral theory tells us that a response that has been reinforced occasionally will be more difficult to extinguish (eliminate) than one that has been reinforced continuously.

Functions of Theory

Theory serves three general purposes in science: (1) to organize and clarify observations, (2) to provide a sense of understanding of the subject matter, and (3) to guide future research.

Organizing and Clarifying Observations

The classic example of how a scientific theory can organize and clarify observations is Nicholas Copernicus' *heliocentric theory* of the solar system, which posits that the Sun (not the Earth) is the center of our planetary system. Copernicus considered the whole set of observations that had been made about the positions of the planets and stars in the sky, the diurnal cycle of the sun, the changing of the seasons, and so on, and found them a confusing hodgepodge. The then prevailing *geocentric theory* (that the Earth was the center of the Universe) seemed only to add to the confusion. By postulating the heliocentric theory, Copernicus brought a new order to these observations.

Similarly, Freud's theory that acts of forgetting, slips of the tongue, and other everyday mistakes that people make are the result of unconscious impulses gave meaning and order to what otherwise seemed common but inexplicable accidents.

Providing a Sense of Understanding

Freud's theory of transference illustrates how theories can provide a sense of understanding. We often notice that a person shows an immediate attraction or repulsion to someone he or she has never met before. Freud's notion is that

Figure 1-1
An illustration of the advantages of using *anxiety* as a theoretical construct, operating differently in a number of circumstances (B), over a mere listing of observed, separate relationships (A).
Source: Modified from "Liberalization of Basic S-R Concepts: Extensions to Conflict Behavior, Motivation, and Social Learning" by N. E. Miller, 1959, in S. Koch (Ed.), *Psychology: A study of a science* Vol. 2, New York: McGraw-Hill.

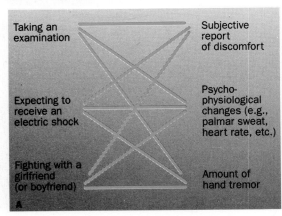
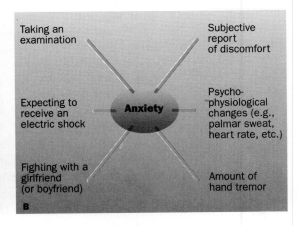

these feelings have been transferred from a person in the patient's past (such as the patient's mother) to the new person because of some similarity between the mother and the stranger.

Guiding Future Research

Finally, the way in which theories can generate intriguing new research is found in Leon Festinger's (1957) theory of cognitive dissonance. Festinger claimed that when we do something that seems to us not fully justified by the situation, a state of imbalance (dissonance) is created in our mind. To restore the balance, the person tries to justify his or her own behavior.

This proposition led to hundreds of experiments demonstrating such results as: (1) when people are underpaid for serving as research subjects, they evaluate the research project they are working on more highly than if they are adequately paid; or (2) when fraternity pledges are treated harshly, they place higher value on the fraternity's membership than when they are treated with more respect.

Criteria for Evaluating Theories

We can identify seven major criteria for evaluating a theory: empirical validity, parsimony, comprehensiveness, internal consistency, testability, usefulness, and acceptability. A theory may fulfill any of these criteria to a greater or lesser degree. No theory is likely to fulfill all the criteria equally well. Even the "best" theories are imperfect.

Empirical Validity

Empirical validity is the degree to which a theory is supported by evidence derived from observations. Theories are not themselves directly proved or disproved by research. Rather, more specific propositions, referred to as **hypotheses,** are derived from the general theory. These specific hypotheses may then be put to empirical test through research. Technically, even hypotheses cannot be proved or disproved absolutely. Rather, research may either *support* or *fail to support* a particular hypothesis derived from a theory. When research provides regular support for the hypotheses derived from a particular theory, scientists tend to accept the theory as useful. In contrast, theories that generate hypotheses that research consistently fails to support tend to be discarded.

Parsimony

Any phenomenon can be described and explained in different ways. Theories concerning the same phenomenon differ in the complexity and in the number of fundamental assumptions they make. When everything else is equal, theories that involve simpler explanations and fewer assumptions are considered better—they are more **parsimonious**.

The so-called *law of parsimony* is associated with a 14th century English Franciscan friar, William of Occam. Although he was not the first to invoke the idea, William used it so often and so sharply that the principle of choosing simpler explanations over more complicated ones came to be known as **Occam's razor**.

Comprehensiveness

Comprehensiveness refers to the breadth of the phenomena that the theory can encompass. All other things being equal, the more phenomena a theory accounts for, the better the theory is. The more comprehensive a theory, the greater the scope of the research efforts it inspires. In contrast, restricted theories tend to be restrictive theories. They exclude important phenomena and problems with which they are unable to deal.

Even a good theory of personality doesn't explain the whole range of psychological and social functioning. Thus, most of the personality theories we will discuss only deal with some aspects of personality functioning. The reason we have many *theories* is that no one theory has yet been able to encompass the breadth of the field.

Internal Consistency

A theory has **internal consistency** to the degree that its propositions and assumptions are consistent and fit together in a coherent, larger explanation. In other words, a theory should be free of internal contradictions. Some theories are such a loose confederation of ideas and concepts that the parts do not mesh. When this happens, the theory loses some of its explanatory power.

Testability

Testability refers to how well and how easily a theory can be supported or refuted. Testability is enhanced when a theory's concepts are so clearly defined that hypotheses derived from the theory can be stated precisely and unambiguously.

Until well into the 20th century, it was assumed that scientific propositions were testable to the extent they could be *verified*. Philosopher of science Karl Popper (1959) took issue with this so-called *principle of verification*, complaining that it is too easy to obtain verifications for a theory. Confirmations, argued Popper, are only impressive when they arise from "risky" predictions.

Suppose, for example, that a meteorologist has a theory that explains rainfall on the basis of the buildup of moisture in the soil. On the basis of this theory, the meteorologist predicts that it will rain in Seattle tomorrow—and it does. But inasmuch as it rains on most days in Seattle, this verification is not very impressive. The theory has predicted an outcome that might well have been true even if the theory is all wet. In short, this is *not* a risky prediction.

Now suppose instead that the theory predicted tomorrow's rainfall in Seattle will be exactly 3.2 inches. This is a rare occurrence, and thus a risky prediction. So, if tomorrow's rainfall in Seattle is exactly 3.2 inches, we are impressed. In other words, it is the *potential for falsification* that makes a theory testable.

Usefulness

"Theory," wrote the Irish poet James Stephens, "is but the preparation for practice." Scientists may balk at public demands for practical applications of their ideas, but theories that survive often lead to important practical applications, at least in the long run. Methods of personality assessment and techniques for inducing personality change provide a measure of the practical usefulness of personality theories.

Acceptability

To be influential, a theory must be known and taken seriously by others. This does not mean the theory must be popular or trendy. Yet theories proposed before or after "their time" do not fare well. A theory must have some acceptability among scientists if it is to be tested through research and applied in practice. Public tolerance and funding of research require a belief in the theory's worth. The most brilliant theory cannot thrive in a social climate that does not find it acceptable and plausible.

For example, as early as the 3rd century B.C., some Greek philosophers had suggested that the Sun rather than the Earth was the center of the universe (Oldroyd, 1986). But their idea could not gain acceptance then and had to lie dormant for almost two millennia until Copernicus proposed his theory.

On the Correctness of a Theory

Theories are theories. That is, they are *speculations* about the nature of phenomena. Facts (actual observations) are used to generate and substantiate theories. But theories are not facts. Therefore, strictly speaking, theories cannot be "right" or "wrong." They can, however, be more or less "useful," depending on their intended purposes. Thus, correctness is *not* one of the accepted criteria for evaluating theories.

Implicit Theories of Personality

As you read this book, you are likely to find some theoretical propositions that you immediately agree with; others will seem wrong to you. These reactions occur because you already have a set of ideas about how your own personality and the personalities of others work. You have an **implicit theory of personality** (Kemp, 1988). Implicit personality theories differ from the theories developed by personality psychologists. The theories we will examine are formal and have been communicated to others. In contrast, implicit theories of personality are not formalized and often are not communicated to others (Furnham, 1988).

PERSONALITY ASSESSMENT

Modern psychology is said to have begun in 1879. In that year, Wilhelm Wundt established a psychological laboratory at the University of Leipzig. Only 5 years later, Francis Galton proposed formal personality measurement. Galton (1884) wrote: "The character which shapes our conduct is a definite and durable 'something,' and therefore . . . it is reasonable to attempt to measure it" (p. 179). Toward this end, Galton made a number of specific proposals about how to assess personality, including ratings by teachers and peers and direct observation of the person in social situations.

Modern personality psychologists use many sources of information—

Projective techniques are indirect methods of personality assessment in which the subject responds to an ambiguous stimulus. Here the subject is making up a story based on a Thematic Apperception Test (TAT) picture. The examiner writes down the subject's story and later scores and interprets it.
Photo by Christopher O'Keefe and Michael D. Spiegler

such as self-reports, direct observations of behavior, impressions of others, and personal histories and life records—to draw inferences about personality. They then look for *converging lines of evidence* to show that the same conclusion can be reached from several different sources.

Self-Reports: Interviews and Questionnaires

One way to find out something about a person is to ask the person directly, either through an interview or a questionnaire or through a combination of the two. Such *self-report data* have been widely used in studies of personality. They have the advantage of providing information quickly. Moreover, they are our only access to the person's subjective experiences (e.g., "How are you feeling today?").

Despite their appeal, self-reports alone provide an incomplete picture. What people say about themselves is subject to memory lapses, misunderstandings, and a variety of distortions. This is especially true when "sensitive" content is involved. If it seems that direct self-reports may be invalid or inaccurate, indirect assessment techniques are used. In most cases, these techniques are "disguised" so the person being assessed cannot easily distort the measurement. However, as we will see, the difficulty with disguised test methods is that responses must be interpreted. Psychologists may disagree on how to interpret what a person reports, such as what the person sees in an inkblot.

Direct Observations of Behavior

A second way to learn about people is to observe them directly in particular situations. The situations may be simulated or natural.

For example, in some well-known studies of aggression, the test situation involved leading subjects to believe they were "teachers" in an experiment on the effects of punishment on learning. Subjects administered electric shocks to a "learner." (In fact, the learner was a confederate of the experimenter and no shock was given.) The severity of shock that subjects administered served as the measure of aggression.

In contrast, a psychologist interested in aggression might simply observe children on a playground, noting and recording the nature, severity, and circumstances of various acts of aggression that occur spontaneously. Such naturalistic observation (whether by a clinician or a researcher) may have more credibility than interviews or questionnaires. But naturalistic observation is often expensive or otherwise impractical; observation of even a single individual in more than a small number of situations is usually out of the question for personality assessment. Thus, direct observations usually provide only part of the information needed for a full assessment of personality.

Impressions of Others

Sociologist Erving Goffman (1959) suggested that personality includes both how people express themselves and how others are *impressed* by them. How people are seen by others, including friends, family, and employers, is an important part of who they are. Using the impressions of others to judge personality has a subtle implication: it blurs the line between objective judgment and mere opinion. Psychiatrist Thomas Szasz (1960), for example, has argued that terms such as *mental illness* and *abnormal personality* are really value judgments. They are used to describe persons whose values, thoughts, and actions simply differ from those of most other people.

Personal Histories and Life Records

Finally, much information can be found in a person's history and life records. Educational, employment, and marital histories as well as personal accomplishments can reveal a great deal about a person. Such data have the advantage that they can be obtained or confirmed objectively, such as by consulting school records.

Bogus Personality Assessment

So far, our discussion has focused on personality assessment from the assessor's viewpoint. An equally interesting aspect is the point of view of the person being assessed.

Popular "personality" assessment techniques include everything from horoscopes to handwriting analyses. These techniques have never been shown to be scientifically valid, yet they enjoy many enthusiastic endorsements.

Demonstration 1-1[1] illustrates how personality assessments may seem to be "true" to the person who is offered them when, in fact, like cotton candy, they have very little real substance. Demonstration 1-1 will also allow you to try your hand at some research, the next issue we will consider in this chapter.

---

[1] This book contains a number of Demonstrations that will allow you to experience both the principles and the problems associated with the study of personality. (Many of the Demonstrations require you to complete specialized forms, which are located at the back of the book in the Demonstration Materials section.)

■ *Demonstration 1-1*
THE CREDIBILITY OF BOGUS PERSONALITY ASSESSMENTS

Most people have read horoscopes in the newspapers and commented that it is difficult to imagine anyone being taken in by these overly general descriptions and predictions. It is possible, however, that a more sophisticated version of the same kind of generalized description can be extremely convincing and can even lead a person to believe that it is a unique description of his or her personality.

Testing this hypothesis, Ulrich, Stachnik, and Stainton (1963) asked students in psychology classes to take two personality tests. A week later, the students were given a written interpretation of their test scores. The interpretation was presented as the careful efforts of the professor. As a second part of the study, other students were taught how to administer the same two personality tests to a friend. For both phases of the study, the people whose personalities were being "interpreted" were asked to rate the accuracy of the "interpretation" (on a scale ranging from excellent to very poor) and to comment on it. Despite the individualized appearance of the personality description, all persons were given exactly the *same* "interpretation" (although the order of the statements varied), and, in fact, no actual interpretations of the tests were made. The "interpretation" read:

> You have a strong need for other people to like you and for them to admire you. You have a tendency to be critical of yourself. You have a great deal of unused capacity which you have not turned to your advantage. While you have some personality weaknesses, you are generally able to compensate for them. Your sexual adjustment has presented some problems for you. Disciplined and controlled on the outside, you tend to be worrisome and insecure inside. At times you have serious doubts as to whether you have made the right decision or done the right thing. You prefer a certain amount of change and variety and become dissatisfied when hemmed in by

restrictions and limitations. You pride yourself as being an independent thinker and do not accept others' opinions without satisfactory proof. You have found it unwise to be too frank in revealing yourself to others. At times you are extroverted, affable, and sociable, while at other times you are introverted, wary, and reserved. Some of your aspirations tend to be pretty unrealistic. (p. 832)

Virtually all the students who had been administered the personality tests by the professor rated the "interpretations" as good or excellent. In the second phase of the study, approximately 75% of the subjects tested by admittedly inexperienced students also rated the assessments as good or excellent. Furthermore, the subjects' comments clearly indicated an acceptance of these "interpretations" as accurate and individualized descriptions of their own personalities. One subject who had been given the tests and "interpretation" by the professor said: "On the nose! Very good. I wish you had said more, but what you did mention was all true without a doubt. I wish you could go further into this personality sometime." A subject who had been given the tests and "interpretation" by a student commented: "I believe this interpretation fits me individually, as there are too many facets which fit me too well to be a generalization" (p. 833).

Snyder and Larson (1972) replicated this study, extending it to show that college students accept these global evaluations as relevant, regardless of whether they are presented by a psychologist in an office or a graduate student in the laboratory. Indeed, even among students who had been led to believe that their tests had been scored by a computer (rather than evaluated by a human scorer), most rated the statements as between good and excellent. From their own and earlier experiments of this sort, Snyder and Larson concluded that the evidence provides

> an object lesson for the users of psychological tests. People place great faith in the results of psychological tests, and their acceptance of the results as being true for them is fairly independent of test setting, administrator, and scorer. Furthermore, it must be realized that presentation of the results of psychological tests, typically presented to the individual as being for him personally, maximizes the acceptance of the psychological interpretation. Thus, the individual's acceptance of the interpretation cannot be taken as a meaningful "validation" of either the psychologist or his tests. (p. 388)

To replicate this experiment for yourself, tell a friend that you are learning how to use personality tests in class. Ask the person to make two different drawings for you: (1) a picture of herself or himself, and (2) a picture as he or she would like to look. (The Draw-a-Person Test is a projective technique used to assess personality; we will have more to say about projective techniques in Chapter 6.) Then, in your own handwriting, copy the "interpretation" quoted earlier in the Demonstration on page 16. About a week later, offer this assessment to your friend. After he or she has had an opportunity to read it, ask your friend to rate the "interpretation" using one of five adjectives: *excellent, good, average, poor,* or *very poor.* Then ask for some feedback as to how well you are doing as a "psychological examiner."

Finally, after obtaining the feedback, it is important that you tell your friend the real nature of the Demonstration. Complete explanation of the deception, called *debriefing,* should remove the possibility that permanent misconceptions about psychological testing will result. It also may evoke further comments of interest.

THE IMPORTANCE OF RESEARCH

A strategy for studying personality includes theory, assessment, research, and personality change. The importance of theory and assessment, introduced briefly earlier, is obvious to most beginning students of personality. We all have implicit personality theories, and we have informally assessed other personalities (and our own) long before studying personality psychology. Often, the importance of research seems less obvious.

Until about 100 years ago, the formal study of personality was rooted in philosophy; it proceeded almost entirely on *rational* grounds. Discussion, argument, the opinions of various authorities, and a general appeal to "reason" were the basis for settling disputes among adherents of differing viewpoints. But people often cannot agree on what is reasonable; so the rational approach to the study of personality, by itself, offers no solid way of resolving differences of opinion. What one person regards as a great insight may seem to be a preposterous fantasy to someone else.

An alternative to the rational approach is the *empirical* approach, which can be traced at least to the 17th century and John Locke. According to the empirical approach, disputes can be settled by admitting as "fact" only what is verifiable by direct observation. Thus, the empirical approach demands objectively verifiable data rather than circumstantial or subjective evidence. Rational considerations may give rise to theories, but they are not strong enough to validate theories.

Empirical research involves systematic attempts to gather evidence through observations and procedures that can be repeated and verified by others. The four strategies we will consider (psychoanalytic, dispositional, phenomenological, and behavioral) are all committed to supporting the validity of their theories, assessment procedures, and personality-change techniques through empirical research. This commitment to research distinguishes the scientific approach to knowledge from other approaches (Neale & Liebert, 1986).

Scientific personality research is not a stereotyped or rigid enterprise, however. There are many scientifically legitimate ways of investigating personality. In Chapter 2, we will consider three basic methods of investigation: experimental, correlational, and case study.

We will also see, throughout this book, how research has helped to dispel an "obvious" but incorrect idea or establish a nonobvious principle or process that seemed implausible until the evidence was obtained. Empirical demonstration is never superfluous.

PERSONALITY CHANGE	The fourth issue that personality psychologists deal with is personality change. *Change* in personality actually has two meanings: (1) naturally occurring developmental changes over time, and (2) planned changes when personality "problems" arise. Natural changes, or *personality development*, will be covered as we discuss theories. In this book, the term *personality change* refers only to *planned* personality change. For the most part, this term is synonymous with *psychotherapy*.

Personality psychology, as distinguished from abnormal psychology, primarily deals with normal personality. However, normal and abnormal personality are closely related, and personality theorists often link the two. In fact, many personality theorists began their professional careers as psychotherapists. Their theories arose from observations of their patients or clients and dealt with the development and treatment of abnormal personality. These psychologists then used the insights they had gained from dealing with clients in psychotherapy to better understand human personality in general. Finally, personality change has a uniquely important place in the field of personality psychology because it is its single most significant application.

PLAN OF THIS BOOK	This book is divided into five sections. Section One includes this introductory chapter and Chapter 2, which deals with methods of personality research that will be illustrated throughout the book. The remaining four sections are devoted to descriptions of the *theories*, *assessment techniques*, *research methods*, and *personality-change procedures* characteristic of each of the four strategies for the study of personality: *psychoanalytic*, *dispositional*, *phenomenological*, and *behavioral*. Thus, we present the study of personality in terms of a 4×4 matrix, as illustrated in Figure 1-2.

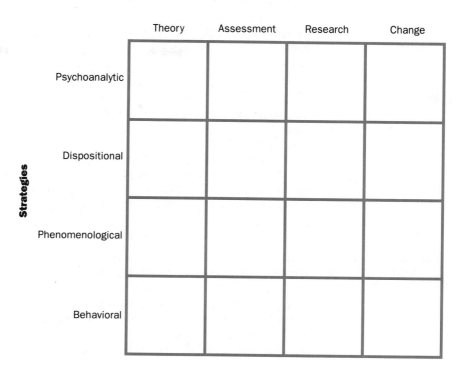

Figure 1-2
Personality can be studied from the perspective of four different strategies, each of which is concerned with four issues.

Each strategy section begins with a brief introductory chapter. This chapter should be read first. You may also want to reread it after you finish the section to help integrate what you've learned about the strategy.

Our aim is to convey a sense of the nature of these strategies. The formats, emphases, and writing styles of Sections Two through Five vary somewhat to be consistent with the "flavor" and "customs" of each strategy. Each strategy is written in a generally positive light that emphasizes its assets. In essence, each strategy is presented from the viewpoint of its proponents. We believe that this is the best way to learn about the strategy.

The last chapter in each strategy section deals with the strategy's liabilities according to its critics. In these chapters, we adopt the stance of a harsh critic to highlight each strategy's weaknesses. This complements the positive light in which each strategy was presented in earlier chapters. The liabilities chapters are not intended as complete critiques or even-handed evaluations; rather, they illustrate the range of limitations and problems each strategy encounters when applied to the full scope of the study of human personality. Overall, our aim is to give readers an opportunity to evaluate the merits and limitations of each strategy, thereby providing an optimal introduction to the scientific study of personality.

SUMMARY   1. The modern idea of personality is only about 200 years old.

2. There are four broad strategies for the study of personality: psychoanalytic, dispositional, phenomenological, and behavioral. Each of these deals with the same four issues: theory, assessment, research, and personality change.

3. Personality psychology is the study of the total functioning of the individual; a more specific definition of personality depends on theoretical considerations.

4. The question of free will versus determinism divides personality theorists. Personality psychologists also differ in the degree of emphasis they put on the subjective and objective aspects of human functioning; on the relative emphasis they place on the person versus the situation; and on their views of individuality (nomothetic or idiographic). Finally, they differ on whether prediction and control are the only goals of personality psychology or whether understanding should be a major goal.

5. The basic terms used by a theory are its theoretical constructs and relational propositions, which help pull together various observations and outcomes.

6. Theory serves three general purposes: (1) to organize and clarify observations, (2) to provide a sense of understanding of the subject matter, and (3) to guide future research.

7. Evaluation of theories involves seven major criteria: empirical validity, parsimony, comprehensiveness, internal consistency, testability, usefulness, and acceptability.

8. Theories cannot be considered correct or incorrect; they are only more or less useful.

9. Most people have their own implicit theories of personality, which are typically informal and are not communicated to others.

10. There are four broad methods of personality assessment: self-reports (including interviews and questionnaires), direct observations of behavior, impressions of others, and personal histories and life records. Bogus personality assessments, though highly general in their content, are often accepted as correct.

11. Empirical research is the hallmark of the scientific study of personality. Such research involves systematic attempts to gather evidence through observations and procedures that can be repeated and verified by others.

12. Personality change can refer to naturally occurring developmental changes or to changes produced intentionally (through psychotherapy); in this book we use the term only in the latter sense. Many personality theorists developed their ideas through observing the clients they saw in psychotherapy.

Chapter Two

Asking and Answering Questions About Personality: Research

ersonality research involves asking and answering questions about why people act, feel, and think as they do. In this chapter we will describe how psychologists carry out this task. In the remaining chapters of the book, you will see many examples of research studies designed to provide evidence for the validity of personality theories.

THREE BASIC APPROACHES TO PERSONALITY RESEARCH: OVERVIEW

Three major research methods have been used to gather information about personality: case-studies, correlational studies, and experiments. *Systematic observation* of behavior is the element that the three methods have in common. The major differences are (1) the types of observations made; (2) the circumstances in which the observations are made; and (3) how the data from the observations are examined.

A **case study** involves a detailed *qualitative description* of the behavior of a single individual. Case studies yield a depth and richness of information that cannot be obtained with correlational studies and experiments. A **correlational study** examines the *quantitative relationship* between two or more events for a group of people observed under the *same* conditions. An **experiment** looks at the *quantitative relationship* between conditions that are systematically varied and are expected to *cause* specific changes in people's behavior. (Note that the terms *experiment* and *experimental* refer only to experiments and not to research in general.)

In principle, most questions can be answered using any of the three basic methods. How the research questions are stated and the type of answers desired determine the method employed. In addition, considerations of feasibility and economy also may influence the method chosen.

Before examining each of the methods in detail, we will take a single, broad question—*Does viewing violence on television affect the aggressive behavior of children?*—and see how it has been investigated using each method. This comparison will show that the same basic question can be studied in different ways.

Television Violence and Aggression: Case Studies

The earliest investigations of TV violence and children's aggressive behavior were case studies of individual youngsters who had apparently become more aggressive by imitating what they had seen on television. The following are two excerpts from case studies involving TV violence and aggression (Schramm, Lyle, & Parker, 1961).

> In Los Angeles, a housemaid caught a seven-year-old boy in the act of sprinkling ground glass into the family's lamb stew. There was no malice behind the act. It was purely experimental [not in the scientific sense!], having been inspired by curiosity to learn whether it would really work as well as it did on television. . . . (p. 161)

> A 13-year-old . . . boy, who said he received his inspiration from a television program, admitted to police . . . that he sent threatening notes to a . . . school teacher. [The idea] for the first letter came while he was helping the pastor of his

church write some letters. When the minister left the office for an hour, the boy wrote his first poison-pen letter. "I got the idea when I saw it happen on TV," he told Juvenile Sergeant George Rathouser. "I saw it on the 'Lineup' program." (p. 164)

Such reports are of isolated incidents, but they certainly raise the possibility that TV violence is related to aggressive acts. More children must be examined in a systematic manner to determine whether such a relationship exists for the general population and not just for the few children in the case studies. Further, if researchers want to know *how much* of a relationship exists between TV violence and aggression among children, they need *quantitative* data (numbers) to supplement the qualitative descriptions that case studies yield. The correlational method satisfies these additional requirements.

Television Violence and Aggression: Correlational Studies

Numerous correlational studies have provided quantitative evidence of a relationship between viewing TV violence and aggression for children in general (Centerwell, 1989; Liebert & Sprafkin, 1988). For example, one study correlated the viewing habits and antisocial behaviors of 2300 junior and senior high school students in Maryland (McIntyre & Teevan, 1972). First, the students were asked to list their four favorite TV programs, "the ones you watch every time they are on the air." A numerical rating of violence was assigned to each program, and an average violence score was computed for each subject. Second, the students completed a self-report checklist of various antisocial behaviors (such as serious fights at school). The subjects indicated how often they engaged in each behavior using a simple numerical scale (0 = never, 1 = once, 2 = twice or more).

The researchers now had two numerical scores for each of the 2300 students. One score was the degree of violence in their preferred TV programs; the other score was the extent of their antisocial behavior. It thus was possible to statistically examine the nature of the relationship (correlation) between these two sets of scores. This correlation would show whether the scores were systematically related and, if they were, the nature of their association. The results indicated a direct relationship between the antisocial behavior and program violence ratings—the more violent the programs watched, the greater was the incidence of antisocial behavior.

Television Violence and Aggression: Experiments

Although the correlational evidence is impressive, it does not indicate that television violence *caused* the aggressive behavior. All it tells us is that the amount of TV violence watched is *related* to the frequency of exhibiting deviant behaviors. It is possible that performing deviant behaviors makes youngsters more interested in watching violent TV programs, rather than vice versa.

Cause-and-effect relationships can be demonstrated most clearly using the experimental method. For example, Liebert and Baron (1972) hypothesized that children who saw violent TV programs would be significantly more willing to hurt other children than would children who saw nonviolent programs. To test this hypothesis, boys and girls ages five through nine initially were left alone to watch television. The episodes they saw came from actual television shows. Half of the children saw an episode with a chase, two fistfights, two shootings, and a knifing. The other half of the children saw an exciting sports episode of equal length.

After watching television, each child was brought to another room and seated in front of a large box with wires leading into the next room. On the box were a green button, labeled HELP, and a red button, labeled HURT. Over the two buttons was a white light. The experimenter explained that the wires were connected to a game a child in another room was going to play. The game involved turning a handle; each time the child started to turn the handle, the white light would come on. The experimenter explained that, by pushing the buttons, the subject could either help the other child by making the handle easier to turn or hurt the other child by making the handle hot. The subjects were told that the longer they pushed the buttons, the more they helped or hurt the other child. Finally, the experimenter said that they had to push one of the two buttons every time the light came on. The experimenter then left the room and the light came on 20 times. (In fact, there was no other child, so the subjects' responses had no effect on anyone.)

How long a child pushed the HURT button was the measure of aggression. The investigators found that children who had seen the violent programming were significantly more willing to hurt another child than were those who saw the sports episodes. As Figure 2-1 shows, this finding appeared for boys and girls in both age groups. Because the only difference between the two groups of children was the TV episode they saw, it is possible to

Figure 2-1
Mean total duration of aggressive responses in Liebert and Baron's (1972) experiment.
Source: "Some Immediate Effects of Televised Violence on Children's Behavior" by R. M. Liebert and R. A. Baron, 1972, *Developmental Psychology, 6,* pp. 469–475.

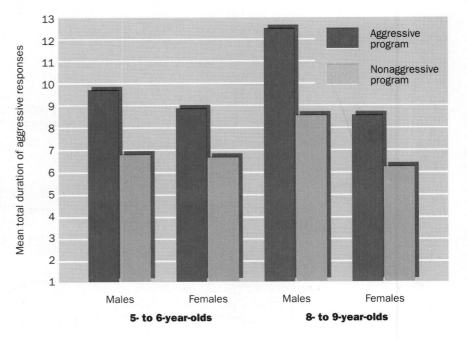

conclude that watching the violent TV episodes caused the greater willingness to hurt other children.

We now turn to a detailed examination of each of the three major research methods. Bear in mind that the same basic question can be approached using different methods of research, as you've just seen. Each strategy for the study of personality favors particular types of research, although all three basic research methods are used in each strategy.

THE EXPERIMENTAL METHOD

The experimental method requires that two conditions be met: (1) a factor that is hypothesized to cause the behavior being studied is systematically varied, while (2) all other possible causative factors are held constant.

In an experiment, the condition that is varied systematically is called the **independent variable**. In our previous example, TV violence was the independent variable; it was varied by being either present (for experimental subjects) or absent (for control subjects).

The behavior that is to be observed is called the **dependent variable**, because it is expected to be caused by, or *depend on*, the independent variable. Total time pressing the HURT button was the dependent variable in our example.

In the simplest experiment, two groups of subjects are employed. Subjects in an **experimental group** are exposed to the independent variable (the hypothesized causal factor), and subjects in a **control group** are not. In all other respects, the groups are treated alike. If the two groups differ on the dependent variable (the behavior being measured), the difference must be due to the independent variable. In our example, the experimental group saw violent TV episodes and the control group did not. The only difference between the two groups was the television episodes they watched.

Suppose the experimental group happened to have a higher proportion of "naturally aggressive children" than the control group. If that were the case, the greater aggression observed in experimental subjects might have been due to a difference in the characteristics of the subjects rather than to the violent TV episodes they watched.

To eliminate the possible effects of such *confounding variables*, groups in an experiment must be equivalent in subjects' personal characteristics relevant to the experimental hypothesis. Usually, this is done by *randomly* assigning subjects to the groups. *Random assignment* means that every subject has an equal chance of being placed in each group. The usual result is that subjects' personal characteristics, such as "natural aggressiveness," tend to equalize across groups. Thus, no group has a disproportionate number of subjects with a particular characteristic.

Matching is another method of ensuring that subjects' personal characteristics are equally distributed in each group. Subjects' characteristics that may cause changes in the behavior being studied are assessed before the subjects are assigned to groups. Then, subjects are paired so that each member of a pair has the same value of the characteristic. Finally, one member of each pair is randomly assigned to each group.

The experimental method controls conditions so that cause-and-effect relationships can be assessed. **Control** in psychological research refers to systematically varying, randomizing, or holding constant the conditions under which observations are made. Such procedures make it possible to conclude that the variable under study—and not some other factor—caused the observed effect.

In studies that employ groups of subjects, *average performance* is examined. Liebert and Baron found that on the average, children exposed to a violent TV program were more aggressive than children who were exposed to a nonviolent sports program. However, the amount of aggression among subjects in each group varied. Thus, some experimental subjects may have exhibited less aggression than some control subjects.

Experiments can have more than two groups, and a control group is not always required. Instead of just having the independent variable present or absent, different amounts or levels of the independent variable can be examined. For example, a logical next step to Liebert and Baron's experiment might be to examine the hypothesis that the more TV violence children observe, the more aggression they will exhibit. Testing this hypothesis would require several experimental groups, each watching a different amount of TV violence (e.g., 10, 30, and 60 minutes). In this experiment, comparisons would be between groups exposed to different amounts of TV violence. No control group is necessary because the hypothesis only concerns varying degrees of TV violence. However, as with the simpler experiment, it would be necessary to assign children to groups randomly, so that the only difference among the groups was the independent variable (amount of TV violence watched).

Evaluation of the Experimental Method

The major advantage of the experimental method is that it can be used to demonstrate cause-and-effect relationships. Changes in the dependent variable can be causally linked to the independent variable when all other relevant variables (influences) are controlled.

Experiments often are conducted in a psychological laboratory where tight control over conditions is possible. However, the price paid for such control may be artificiality because the context is different from real life. For example, watching TV in a psychology laboratory is not exactly the same as watching TV at home. Similarly, pushing a HURT button is different from physically assaulting another child on the street. The experimental conditions must be similar enough to the real-life circumstances that it is legitimate to generalize from what is found in the experiment to real life.

Control in experiments allows us to obtain more precise and reliable information about specific aspects of a question. However, in experiments we obtain less total information about the overall question. As you will see, the correlational and case-study methods involve less control over relevant variables; but they preserve more naturalness.

THE CORRELATIONAL METHOD

Correlational studies answer questions about the relationship between variables. *Correlation* means co- or joint relationship. Questions of relationship are frequently asked about personality. (Is late toilet training related to compulsiveness in adulthood? Is the frequency of dating in college related to marital happiness?) Using the correlational method, observations of all subjects are made under the *same conditions*. Note the contrast with the experimental method, in which the conditions under which subjects are observed are systematically varied.

In a correlational study, a pair of observations is collected for each member of a group of subjects. Suppose Professor Curious is interested in whether a relationship exists between how close students sit to the front of the classroom and how well they do in the course. The professor could list the number of the row in which each student chose to sit at the beginning of the semester and each student's final grade in the course, as in Table 2-1. These data could be used to correlate seating and final grade. Notice that all the subjects in this correlational study were observed under the same conditions.

Knowing that two variables are correlated is not sufficient. It is essential to know the strength of the relationship and the way in which the variables relate. The *magnitude* (strength) of a correlation tells us how well one variable can predict the other variable. The stronger the correlation, the more accurate the prediction.

Two variables can be related directly or indirectly, which is referred to as the *direction* of the correlation.[1] A direct or **positive correlation** between variable X and variable Y means that high scores on X tend to be associated with high scores on Y, and low scores on X tend to go with low scores on Y.

[1] *Direction* can be a misleading label. The direction of a correlation refers only to whether the relationship is direct or inverse. It has nothing to do with which variable is causing the other.

Table 2-1

Data from a hypothetical study of the relationship between how close a student sits to the front of the classroom and final course grade

SUBJECT	ROW	FINAL GRADE	SUBJECT	ROW	FINAL GRADE
Andy	2	76	Linda	5	71
Ann	5	60	Mary	1	95
Bill	4	79	Pam	1	87
Bob	3	67	Pat	3	80
Eric	1	82	Polly	3	75
Howie	2	91	Robert	4	81
Jerry	2	86	Sam	2	82
Joan	5	64	Sheila	5	55
John	4	62	Shelley	3	90
Ken	4	66	Steve	1	99

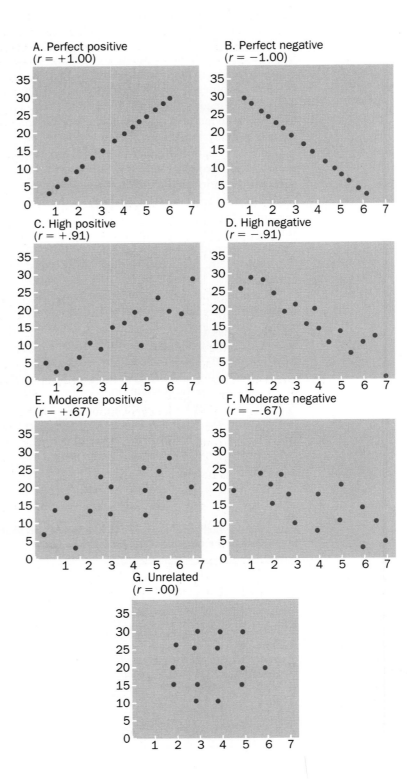

Figure 2-2
Scatter diagrams showing various degrees of relationship between two variables.

For example, a positive correlation is regularly found between the IQs of parents and children; generally, brighter parents have brighter children.

In contrast, with an inverse or **negative correlation**, high scores on *X* are associated with low scores on *Y*, and low scores on *X* go with high scores on *Y*. Age and quickness of reflexes are negatively correlated; the older people are, the slower are their reflexes.

The correlation between two variables can be estimated by plotting the scores to make a **scatter diagram**. Look at the scatter diagrams in Figure 2-2. One variable is plotted on the horizontal axis and the other on the vertical axis. Each point represents one subject's scores on the two variables.

The magnitude of the correlation is estimated by how closely the points in the scatter diagram conform to a straight line, the *line of perfect correlation*. With a *perfect correlation*, all the points fall on a straight line (Figures 2-2A and 2-2B). Knowing a person's score on one of the variables (it makes no difference which one) enables a researcher to predict perfectly the person's score on the other variable (as Figure 2-3 depicts). Unfortunately, perfect correlations between psychological variables do not exist.

With a high or strong (but not perfect) correlation, there is some "scatter" (deviation) around the line of perfect correlation (Figures 2-2C and 2-2D). But the points tend to fall within a narrow ellipse, making prediction of one variable from the other reasonably accurate. The lower or weaker the correlation, the more scatter there is. Figures 2-2E and 2-2F show a moderate correlation. Where there is no systematic relationship between the variables, the points are scattered all over, making it impossible to predict one variable from the other (Figure 2-2G).

The direction of the correlation is determined by the way the points are oriented. If the points generally converge around a line that goes from bottom left to top right, the correlation is positive or direct (Figures 2-2A, 2-2C, and 2-2E). If the points travel from bottom right to top left, the correlation is negative or inverse (Figures 2-2B, 2-2D, and 2-2F).

The data from Professor Curious' study of the relationship between where students sit in class and their grades (Table 2-1, p. 27) are plotted in Figure 2-4 (p. 30). Most of the data points fall in a narrow ellipse, indicating

Figure 2-3

In a scatter plot of correlational data, the intersection of the line of perfect correlation of two lines drawn at right angles to each axis allows prediction of one variable from another. For example, a person obtaining a score of 4 on variable X would obtain a score of 22 on variable Y.

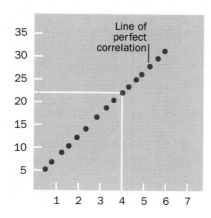

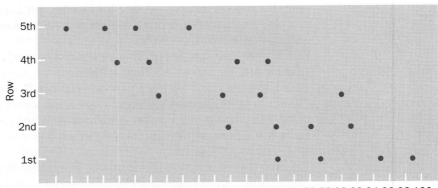

Figure 2-4
Scatter diagram of data (presented in Table 2-1) from a hypothetical study of the relationship between how close a student sits to the front of the classroom and final course grade ($r = -.79$).

a high correlation or strong relationship. The points are oriented from lower right to upper left, indicating a negative correlation. Thus, there is a general tendency for students who sit close to the front of the room (i.e., lower row number) to earn higher grades.

The **correlation coefficient** (abbreviated r) is a numerical index of the correlation between two variables. It is calculated by means of a mathematical formula. Correlation coefficients range from $+1.00$ to -1.00. The direction of the correlation is indicated by the algebraic sign, plus for a positive correlation and minus for a negative correlation.

The magnitude of a correlation is indicated by the absolute numerical value of the correlation coefficient, whether it is positive or negative. A correlation coefficient of 1.00 ($+$ or $-$) would indicate a perfect correlation, so that either variable can be *exactly* predicted from the other. As the coefficient decreases in absolute value from 1.00 to zero, the ability to predict one variable from the other decreases. In the extreme, a correlation of zero indicates that the variables are totally unrelated; with a zero correlation, knowledge of one variable would not assist at all in predicting the other.

Note that how closely two variables are related depends only on the absolute size of the correlation coefficient. Thus, correlation coefficients of $+.60$ and $-.60$ are equivalent in their ability to predict one variable from the other. The correspondence between correlation coefficients and scatter diagrams can be seen in Figure 2-2 (p. 28), where the correlation coefficient is given in parentheses.

Evaluation of the Correlational Method

The correlational method involves making observations without controlling the subjects' behaviors or varying the circumstances under which the subjects are observed. Thus, the naturalness of the situation is preserved. This may bring the research closer to real life than is possible with the experimental method.

Generally, the correlational method has four advantages over the experimental method. First, some variables of interest to personality researchers are difficult or impossible to vary systematically. A researcher simply cannot vary sex, age, and birth order, for example. And it would be unethical to induce traumatic experiences such as rape and kidnapping to study their effects on people.

Second, collecting data on a variable as it naturally occurs—as is done in correlational studies—may let a researcher examine the variable over a broader range than is possible with experiments. For instance, in studying the effects of stress, it is not ethical to induce more than brief, mild stress in research subjects. But, in naturally stressful situations, psychologists can collect data that may help them learn what factors are associated with severe and prolonged stress.

One such correlational study was carried out during a massive power failure that encompassed much of the Eastern Seaboard of the United States on November 9–10, 1965. The blackout occurred in New York City at about 5:30 P.M., the height of rush hour. Thousands of people on their way home from work had to spend the night in public facilities. In the early morning hours, a team of psychologists collected data from people in a bus terminal and a hotel lobby, both of which were illuminated by emergency power (Zucker, Manosevitz, & Lanyon, 1968). They asked people to complete a questionnaire asking for their birth order, their feelings about being stranded for the night, their level of anxiety, and their preference for being alone or with other people. Additionally, before approaching a subject, the investigators noted whether he or she was talking to or standing with someone else.

Previous laboratory experiments that created mild stress in subjects had indicated that firstborn persons tend to show more anxiety and a greater preference to be with other people when confronted with stress-inducing conditions than do persons lower in birth order. The data collected during the blackout generally confirmed the previous findings and extended them to a broader range of stress in a real crisis situation.

A third advantage of correlational investigations over experiments is that correlational studies allow researchers to examine a large number of variables simultaneously. This is important because, in real life, people's behaviors invariably are influenced by multiple factors. In experiments, the number of independent variables usually is limited to one or two.

A fourth advantage is that correlational studies are often more economical in terms of time, effort, and expense. Correlational data frequently are collected under conditions that already exist, so there is no need to "set up" situations.

Correlation and Causation

The major limitation of correlational research is that conclusions about *cause-and-effect* relationships often cannot be drawn. Knowing that two variables are correlated does not tell a researcher which is the cause of the other; this dilemma is known as the **directionality problem**.[2] Consider the

---

[2] The directionality problem has nothing to do with whether a correlation is positive or negative.

positive correlation between grades and attending class. One possible explanation is that better attendance increases the amount learned and thus results in higher grades. A second, equally plausible interpretation is that good grades lead students who earn them to attend class more often.

In many correlational studies, the problem of directionality cannot be resolved. There are exceptions, however. Some relationships can be logically conceptualized in one direction only. For instance, there is a negative correlation between the amount of alcohol consumed and the speed of one's reflexes. Obviously, this relationship only makes sense in one direction; the speed of your reflexes is not likely to influence how much you drink (unless you are in a drinking contest).

■ *Demonstration 2-1*
CORRELATION: IT'S A PLOT

The best way to gain an understanding of the basics of correlational research is to do some yourself. This is easier than it might sound.

Correlational data consist of pairs of observations gathered from a number of subjects. You can quickly gather such data by asking 15 (or more) people of the *same sex* for their height and weight.

Once you have collected 15 or more observation pairs, the next step is to make a scatter diagram of them. Remove the graph for Demonstration 2-1 from the Demonstration Materials section at the back of the book (or use a piece of graph paper). Looking at your data, determine the range of weights, by finding the highest and lowest. Make these the endpoints of the horizontal axis. Then divide the axis into equal units. Next, find the range of heights *in inches* and set up the vertical axis in the same way.

Now plot a point to represent each person's height and weight.

Finally, examine the scatter diagram of your points to determine the nature and strength of the correlation. How are the points oriented? You will find that they go from bottom left to top right, which indicates a positive correlation (taller people generally are heavier). The points should roughly fall in the shape of an ellipse. Compare your scatter diagram to Figure 2-2C (p. 28). If the points make a tighter (flatter) ellipse than that shown in the figure, then you may have obtained a strong correlation. If the points make more of a circle (as in Figure 2-2G) than an ellipse, you need to collect more data. Adding five to ten more points should make your scatter diagram more ellipselike. (If most of the points fit with an ellipse and there are just a few points that are clearly out of the bounds of the ellipse, you can safely ignore the "outliers.")

It also is possible that both variables could be caused by some other factor, which is called the **third-variable problem**. Consider the positive correlation between the number of churches in a city and the number of crimes committed in that city; the more churches a city has, the more crimes are committed in it. Does this mean that religion fosters crime? Probably not. That crime fosters religion? Unlikely. The relationship is due to a third variable—population. The higher the population, the greater are the number of churches *and* the number of crimes.

When causation cannot be inferred directly from correlational evidence, this does not mean a cause-and-effect relationship does not exist. It merely means that the correlational method by itself does not permit the identification of the nature of the causal relationship.

Sometimes it is *not* necessary to know whether one variable causes the other or whether a third variable is responsible. This frequently is the case in applied areas of psychology in which only prediction of a criterion is required. For instance, college admissions committees use high school grades as one criterion to predict success in college. Typically, there is a moderate to high positive correlation between grades in high school and academic achievement in college. Thus, admissions committees can do their jobs effectively without being concerned with the causes of college achievement.

STATISTICAL SIGNIFICANCE AND PRACTICAL IMPORTANCE	In an experiment or correlational study, a small group of people (subjects), called a **sample**, is selected from a much larger group of people, called a **population**. Personality researchers study a sample—a subset of the relevant population—because it is not feasible to deal with an entire population, such as all children who watch television.

However, the researcher usually wants to be able to draw conclusions about the population, not just about the particular sample. To do this, the researcher makes *inferences* about the population from the sample. For the inferences to be meaningful, the findings from the sample must be *reliable*. In other words, the researcher must be able to count on the findings occurring again, with a different sample from the same population.

Statistical significance is the standard of reliability of quantitative research findings. It is computed mathematically by *statistical tests*, which provide the researcher with an estimate of the *probability that the finding from a sample is due to chance alone*. The lower the probability, the more reliable the finding is. In psychological research, a finding is considered *statistically significant* if the odds are less than 5 in 100 that it is due to chance alone. This is written "$p < .05$" and is read "probability less than 5% (or, 5 in 100)." Statistical significance can be computed for either experimental or correlational findings.

Statistical significance refers only to the reliability of a finding; it does *not* imply that the finding is important, socially relevant, or practically meaningful.[3] It is possible that a highly reliable (statistically significant) finding may have little or no practical import. To use a somewhat whimsical example, suppose a sample of able-bodied people were randomly assigned to an experimental group in which subjects had their feet tied together and a control group in which they did not. Both groups are asked to climb three

---

[3] This point sometimes is confusing because when the results of psychological research are reported, the word *statistically* often is omitted, as in: "A significant difference was found between the experimental and control group."

flights of stairs as fast as they can. Not surprisingly, the experimental group is found to climb significantly slower than the control group. Clearly, this *statistically significant* finding has little practical importance.

THE CASE-STUDY METHOD   Case studies provide rich, detailed accounts of significant events in an individual's life. You can see this in the excerpt from Oscar Lewis' (1961) classic case study of family life in a Mexico City slum, *The Children of Sanchez*; the study is based on extensive interviews in which the then-grown children were asked to relate their life histories.

> Manuel, the eldest son, came closest to the pattern of traits held to be typical in a disorganized slum environment. He recalled little about his home life, though his brother and sisters remembered all too well his crude assertions of authority when father was not at home. Having an "aversion to routine," as he put it, he remembered only "the exciting things," and these occurred mainly with his gang of friends who soon became the most important part of his life. Stocky and strong, he was from the first a good fighter and earned the other boys' respect. One of his fiercest fights, started to defend his brother, led oddly to a firm friendship; he and his new companion became inseparable, exchanged many confidences, and for years supported each other during emotional hard times. Manuel did poorly in school, which after the sixth grade he gladly gave up in favor of jobs, pocket money, and girls. At 13 he was inducted into sexual intercourse, after which "the fever, this sex business," got hold of him "in such a way that all I did was to go around thinking about it. At night my dreams were full of girls and sex. I wanted every woman I saw." Presently he fell into the grip of another fever, gambling at cards. "If a day passed without a game," he said, "I was desperate." This fever soon mounted to a point where he would bet a whole week's pay, but when he won he would go out with his friends and "throw it all away." Regretfully he recalled that he "never did anything practical" with his winnings.
>
> There is a certain charm about Manuel. His narrative is full of vitality and drama, and he sometimes reveals generous impulses, especially toward male friends. On one occasion he took over a sick friend's job to hold it for him, thereby sacrificing a much better job of his own. On another occasion, he set up in a small business making shoes, he paid his three helpers so well that he went bankrupt. This mishap extinguished an already feeble spark: "I lost the little confidence I had in myself and lived just from day to day, like an animal. I didn't have the will power to carry out plans." At 15 he started a family and presently had four children. He never provided a home for his family, which finally became part of his father's household, and he increasingly neglected his wife, staying away and having a torrid affair with another woman. When his wife died he was grief-stricken. With his boyhood companion he departed for some months to work and gamble elsewhere, leaving the children to his father's support. No doubt this behavior contained some element of revenge for the humiliations and belittlements received from his father, but there was a strong undertone of shame and sadness in Manuel at having led a life "so sterile, so useless, so unhappy." (White, 1976, pp. 132–133)

The case study is mainly descriptive, and its data are qualitative. It is the least systematic and least controlled research method. As we will discuss shortly, this characteristic has both advantages and disadvantages.

Many case studies deal with abnormal personality, where they are used to present data concerning unusual cases. "A Case of Multiple Personality" is well-known account of a 25-year-old married woman, "Eve White," who displayed three very distinct personalities (Thigpen & Cleckley, 1954, 1957). Eve White had been in psychotherapy for several months because of severe headaches and blackouts. Her therapist described her as "retiring and gently conventional." One day during an interview:

> As if seized by a sudden pain she put both hands to her head. After a tense moment of silence, her hands dropped. There was a quick, reckless smile and, in a bright voice that sparkled, she said, "Hi there, Doc!" The demure and constrained posture of Eve White had melted into buoyant repose. . . . This new and apparently carefree girl spoke casually of Eve White and her problems, always using *she* or *her* in every reference, always respecting the strict bounds of a separate identity. When asked her own name she immediately replied, "Oh, I'm Eve Black." (p. 137)

Following this startling discovery, Eve was observed over a period of 14 months in a series of interviews totaling approximately 100 hours. During this time, a third personality emerged. Later, she exhibited other personalities, 22 in all (Sizemore & Huber, 1988). This case study was especially valuable because, 40 years ago, it was one of only a small number of well-documented cases of a rare phenomenon, a true multiple personality (Comer, 1992). In the past 15 years, the prevalence of multiple personality has increased dramatically, which has lead to increased interest in the study of this fascinating phenomenon (e.g., Kluft, 1991; Ross et al., 1990).[4]

Case studies are sometimes used to test hypotheses and support theories. Psychoanalysts use case studies extensively to support their theoretical claims. But because case studies are basically uncontrolled, using them in this way is questionable.

However, case studies can sometimes be helpful in *disconfirming* the implications of a theory. For instance, when a theory purports to be *universally* true, case studies can provide negative instances. A single negative instance—a relevant example that does not conform to the theory—is sufficient to disprove universality. Consider Freud's hypothesis that all male children experience an Oedipus complex (sexual attraction to their mothers; see Chapter 4). Anthropological case studies, however, have revealed non-Western cultures in which young boys do not exhibit the Oedipus complex (Malinowski, 1927). These case studies cast serious doubt on Freud's original hypothesis. (A more restricted theory might still be tenable, such as limiting the Oedipus complex to Western societies.)

---

[4] It is not clear why the prevalence of multiple personality disorder has increased. One possibility is that the disorder is being more accurately diagnosed in recent years (e.g., Putnam, Guroff, Sliberman, Barban, & Post, 1986; Ross et al., 1990). Another explanation is that the prevalence is artifically inflated by an increased interest in the disorder as a result of attention in the popular media (e.g., Bass & Davis, 1988). It also is possible that some as yet unidentified factor is producing an actual dramatic increase in the number of cases.

Evaluation of the
Case-Study
Method

As a method of personality research, the case study has several advantages. It is an excellent way of examining the personality of a single individual in great detail. A closely related advantage is that the case study allows an individual's idiosyncrasies and contradictions to show up. No matter how general the laws of human behavior are, each person is unique.

Case studies can reflect the richness and complexity of personality, which makes them a fertile source of hypotheses about human behavior. Hypotheses formulated from case-study material then can be tested using more controlled and rigorous methods.

Because the case study allows circumstances to vary naturally, it offers greater potential for revealing new and surprising findings. With the other research methods, the variables measured are specified in advance, and only those variables are assessed. As a result, the investigator may miss some vital observations. In contrast, the case study does not specify the observations to be made; instead as much as possible of the entire situation is recorded.

Another advantage of case studies is that they typically deal with people in their natural environments, not in artificial laboratory settings. In the final analysis, theories of personality are intended to explain behavior in real life. Case studies therefore directly examine the phenomena of ultimate interest.

The case-study method has five important limitations. First, because case-study observations are not made under controlled conditions, they cannot be directly repeated by independent investigators. Replication of research is essential in science.

Second, as with correlational studies, it is impossible to make definitive statements about cause-and-effect relationships from case studies. This is because there is no control over variables that may influence the behavior being studied.

Third, the data for case studies usually come from *retrospective* reports by the subject and other people, such as family members. With retrospective reports, observers (the subject and others) tend to forget what happened and how they felt. Moreover, with the passage of time, observers may see events in a different perspective, as memories become mixed with present thoughts and feelings. (The case of Eve White/Black is an example of a *non*retrospective case study and is an exception; the data were systematically collected as Eve White/Black was exhibiting her multiple personalities.)

Fourth, the data from case studies are usually qualitative rather than quantitative. Qualitative data provide less precise descriptions of behavior than quantitative data.

Finally, it is difficult to generalize from a case study to people in general because the data come from a single individual.

Whether the disadvantages of the case-study method outweigh its advantages depends on the purpose of the investigation. At the very least, it is reasonable to employ the case study in preliminary research that generates intriguing hypotheses. The validity and generality of such hypotheses then can be tested in correlational studies and experiments.

**LOOKING AHEAD:
ADVICE TO THE
TRAVELER** Learning about personality in terms of the four strategies is analogous to visiting four very different countries. Your tour of each strategy begins in an introductory chapter. You may become aware of the strategy's unique structure almost immediately, just as you would notice the landscape of a new country as your plane comes in for a landing and your tour guide previews what you will be seeing. As you enter the strategy, you will become aware of its distinctive language. You will have to acquaint yourself with new terminology and with common words that are used in novel ways. Moreover, the personality psychologists in each strategy express themselves in a unique style. The presentation style itself can tell you much about the approach to personality.

Foreign travelers are advised to immerse themselves in a new culture, leaving behind their own customs and even assumptions and values. Your understanding and appreciation of each strategy will be enhanced if you temporarily adopt its approach. This includes suspending your critical evaluation until you are leaving the strategy. In this way, you will be able to put the frequently voiced criticisms discussed in the liability chapter in perspective.

Travel is educational because it exposes the traveler to new ideas about human existence, thought, values, and behavior. You will have a similar experience in learning about personality through the perspective of four diverse approaches to the same phenomena. Your journey begins in the birthplace of the scientific study of personality, the psychoanalytic strategy. Bon voyage!

SUMMARY   1. All methods of personality research involve observation of behavior. The methods differ in the types of observations made, the circumstances in which they are made, and the manner in which the data are examined.

2. In the experimental method, an independent variable hypothesized to be causing the behavior being studied (dependent variable) is systematically varied while all other possible causative factors are controlled. This involves comparing an experimental group in which the independent variable is present with a control group in which the independent variable is absent. When the two groups are equivalent except for the presence of the independent variable, differences between the groups (on the dependent variable) can be attributed to the independent variable.

3. Experiments allow cause-and-effect relationships to be established. However, the controls that must be exerted to provide such information make experiments narrow in scope and limit our ability to generalize from the results.

4. Correlational studies examine the degree to which two variables are related. The data consist of a pair of observations collected from each of a group of subjects under the same conditions. Correlations may be positive or direct (the variables change in the same direction) or negative or inverse (the

variables change in opposite directions). The magnitude (strength) of the correlation indicates how accurately one variable can be predicted from the other. The higher the correlation, the more accurate is the prediction.

5. Correlations can be plotted on a scatter diagram. The direction of the points indicates whether the correlation is positive or negative. The degree of deviation of the points from the line of best fit indicates the magnitude of the correlation. Correlation coefficients are mathematically determined indexes of the direction and magnitude of a relationship; their values range from zero (no correlation) to ±1.00 (perfect correlation).

6. Correlational research allows observations to be made in existing, natural situations because the variables are just measured and not systematically varied. Definitive cause-and-effect relationships usually cannot be determined from correlational data alone. Either variable may cause the other, or a third variable may cause both variables.

7. Statistical significance is an estimate of the reliability of a quantitative finding. Statistical significance is expressed as the probability that the results are not due to chance and therefore will occur again.

8. Case studies involve qualitative, detailed descriptions of single individuals. They can provide a picture of the richness and complexity of personality that neither the experimental nor the correlational method can.

9. Problems with case studies are: they cannot be replicated; cause-and-effect statements cannot be made from them; they are usually retrospective; they are qualitative rather than quantitative; and generalizations to other people are tenuous.

THE PSYCHOANALYTIC
STRATEGY

Chapter Three

Introduction to the Psychoanalytic Strategy

efore reading any further in this chapter, try something. Write down the words or phrases you think of when you hear the word *psychoanalysis*.

What did you come up with? You may have thought of Freud, unconscious, sex, libido, Oedipus complex, repression, id, ego, superego, defense mechanism, dreams, couch. Most people know more about the psychoanalytic strategy than the other three personality strategies. Psychoanalytic concepts have become part of our popular culture as well as part of a variety of academic disciplines other than psychology, such as literary and art criticism, philosophy, and history (Arlow & Brenner, 1988; Elms, 1988; Runyan, 1988).

WHAT IS PSYCHOANALYSIS?

Psychoanalysis has three different, yet interrelated meanings: a theory ofpersonality, an approach to studying personality, and procedures for changing personality (Freud, 1961b*; Michels, 1988). Psychoanalytic personality theory emphasizes the roles of (1) intrapsychic events (processes occurring in the mind), (2) unconscious drives, and (3) early childhood development. To study these phenomena, psychoanalysis examines a person's thoughts, dreams, mistakes, and other behaviors to discover their underlying meaning or significance for the individual. These same procedures are used to bring about personality change in psychoanalytic psychotherapy.

The four basic issues in personality psychology—theory, assessment, research, and personality change—are highly intertwined in the psychoanalytic strategy. Most psychoanalysts are therapists and are directly involved with *personality change*, which requires *assessment* of people's intrapsychic processes. Observations made in psychoanalytic therapy form both the basis of personality *theory* and the *research* evidence for the theory's validity.

The psychoanalytic strategy has been dominated by the work and writings of a single individual: Sigmund Freud. He was not only the founder of psychoanalysis (theory, research methodology, and psychotherapy) but also the first modern personality psychologist. All psychoanalytic thinking is based on Freud's ideas. It may be an outgrowth of his ideas, a variation on or expansion of them, or a direct contrast with them—to the point of being anti-Freudian. Accordingly, our discussion of the psychoanalytic strategy will draw heavily on Freudian conceptualizations and practices. However, we will also consider ego psychology and object-relations viewpoints and describe the most recent trends within the strategy.

Psychoanalytic theorists fall into three broad camps: **Freudians**, who closely subscribe to Freud's ideas; **ego psychologists**, who focus more on adaptation and the potential for personality development beyond childhood; and **object-relations theorists**, who emphasize interpersonal issues and the

Sigmund Freud
(1856-1939)
founded psychoanalysis. He introduced the idea of unconscious motivation and offered descriptions of the organization and development of personality.
Courtesy of National Library of Medicine, Bethesda, Maryland 20014

* The dates used in this book refer to the actual references used (sometimes translated or reprinted editions); thus they do not always correspond to the original publication date of the work.

concept of self. Ego psychologists and object relations theorists are both considered **post-Freudians**.

PSYCHOANALYTIC PERSONALITY THEORY

Freud's theory of personality actually consists of a number of separable but interrelated minitheories, which he revised a number of times over the course of some 45 years of theorizing that began in the mid-1890s (Gay, 1988).

The second half of the 19th century was a period of great intellectual excitement. In particular, two daring ideas were advanced during this time that influenced Freud's thinking. The first was that *human beings are a natural result of evolution and therefore not fundamentally different from other animals*. Charles Darwin (1809–1882) reached this conclusion in 1871. He believed that humans gradually evolved from other life forms through random variation and environmental selection. Darwin's theory accounts for the appearance, disappearance (extinction), and evolution of species. Darwin claimed that all life forms are motivated by two forces: the will to survive and the urge to reproduce. Darwin stopped short of providing a scientific analysis of the mind; but he set the stage for this task, and Freud accepted the challenge.

The other revolutionary idea affecting Freud's thinking was that *unconscious, irrational, and primitive forces play a central role in human motivation*. Philosophers Arthur Schopenhauer (1788–1860) and Friedrich Nietzsche (1844–1900) observed that human behavior is often driven by unconscious and irrational forces. Both emphasized how easily the intellect can be self-deluding. Schopenhauer considered sex to be the most important human instinct. Nietzsche suggested that people forget certain memories, turn aggression inward to become a basis for ethics and conscience, and derive their ultimate strength from the most primitive part of themselves. By the late 19th century, these ideas held sway among many intellectual Europeans (Ellenberger, 1970; Kern, 1973; Sulloway, 1979). There is little doubt that the 19th century provided the bedrock out of which Freud's ideas were formed (Sand, 1988).

Major Themes in Psychoanalytic Theory

Four adjectives characterize psychoanalysis: deterministic, dynamic, organizational, and developmental.

Deterministic

According to Freud, all behavior is determined, or caused, by some force within the person. Thus, all behavior has meaning; no behavior occurs by chance. Even the simplest examples of human behavior can be traced to complicated psychological factors of which the person may be totally unaware. Perhaps the best-known occurrences are so-called **Freudian slips**—errors made in speech, writing, and reading that presumably reveal something about the person's "inner" thoughts, or "real" intents. Here are three simple examples:

> A psychologist was preparing an article condemning Freud's ideas. She began by writing: "Fraud's theory. . . ."

> A man was examining the centerfold of *Playboy* magazine. A friend asked what magazine he was reading. He responded, "Playbody."

> A student told her boyfriend that she was "getting rid of" a statistics exam when she meant to say "getting ready for" the exam.

Other examples of Freud's (1963) thoroughgoing determinism relate to "accidentally" forgetting something or losing an object:

> If anyone forgets a proper name which is familiar to him normally or if, in spite of all his efforts, he finds it difficult to keep it in mind, it is plausible to suppose that he has something against the person who bears the name so that he prefers not to think of him. . . . (p. 52)

> We lose an object if we have quarreled with the person who gave it to us and do not want to be reminded of him; or if we no longer like the object itself and want to have an excuse for getting another and better one instead. The same intention directed against an object can also play a part, of course, in cases of dropping, breaking, or destroying things. . . . (p. 54)

> Here [says Freud] is the best example, perhaps, of such an occasion. A youngish man told me the following story: "Some years ago there were misunderstandings between me and my wife. I found her too cold, and although I willingly recognized her excellent qualities, we lived together without any tender feelings. One day, returning from a walk, she gave me a book she had bought because she thought it would interest me. I thanked her for this mark of 'attention,' promised to read the book, and put it on one side. After that I could never find it again. Months passed by, in which I occasionally remembered the lost book and made vain attempts to find it. About six months later my dear mother, who was not living with us, fell ill. My wife left home to nurse her mother-in-law. The patient's condition became serious and gave my wife an opportunity of showing the best side of herself. One evening I returned home full of enthusiasm and gratitude for what my wife had accomplished. I walked up to my desk, and without any definite intention but with a kind of somnambulistic certainty opened one of the drawers. On the very top I found the long-lost book I had mislaid." (p. 55)

Freud analyzed and interpreted incidents like these to understand facets of personality that would not otherwise be accessible. He first wrote about them in *The Psychopathology of Everyday Life* (1963), from which the preceding excerpts are taken. (The book is easy to read and is available in paperback.) Freudian slips and related phenomena are particularly appealing ideas because they make psychoanalytic concepts part of daily life (Turkle, 1988).

These examples are also noteworthy because they imply that some of our feelings can be hidden from consciousness. Slavin (1990) commented:

> The underlying notion that there is some important set of desires or perceptions missing from the central conscious personality is, almost by definition, a universal psychoanalytic observation. (p. 308)

Dynamic

Dynamic, as applied to psychoanalytic theory, refers to the exchange and transformation of energy within the personality. Like most other personality theorists, Freud believed that understanding the *motivation* for human actions is essential. For Freud, the source of human motivation was **psychic energy**. He theorized that people have a *fixed amount* of psychic energy that is used for all psychological functions. Thus, if a large amount of psychic energy is being used for one activity (such as work), little will be available for other activities (such as social life). But psychic energy can be refocused, and the movement of psychic energy from one object to another plays an important role in personality functioning.

Organizational

Freud organized personality in two different ways. His early theory held that personality operates at three levels of awareness: unconscious, preconscious, and conscious. Later, he divided personality into three basic functions: id (primitive, pleasure-seeking impulses), ego (rational self), and superego (internalized values of society). According to Freud, natural biological instincts (id), such as the need for food, elimination, and sexual gratification, are inevitably in conflict with the restraints of reality (ego) and the rules of society (superego). These conflicts determine an individual's specific actions.

Freud emphasized the unconscious and the id in personality development and functioning. Many ego psychologists compensate by stressing rational, conscious ego processes. Ego psychologists also disagree with Freud about the central role of *conflict* in understanding personality; they concentrate more on conflict-free personality functions.

Developmental

The importance of early childhood development in determining adult personality is a cornerstone of Freud's theory. In fact, Freud believed that adult personality is established by about the age of five. In Freud's own words, "The little creature is often completed by the fourth or fifth year of life, and after that merely brings gradually to light what is already within him" (quoted by Roazen, 1975, p. 106). All psychoanalysts agree that early childhood experiences are important. But ego psychologists consider later experiences to be equally important in determining personality. Object-relations theorists, on the other hand, argue that the first five or six *months* of life may be critical for healthy personality development. But object-relations theorists, like ego psychologists, are optimistic about the ability of therapy to restore healthy personality in adulthood.

Freud theorized that personality development follows a more or less set course from birth. He divided development into a series of discrete stages through which every human being passes. Most post-Freudians agree with

Freud that personality development follows a course of discrete stages. However, they have suggested a variety of sets of stages that differ as to when they occur and what transpires in them.

Intention and the Search for Meaning

Every day, we form judgments about other people and their behavior by evaluating their intentions. We are curious about people's intentions, which prompts us to ask questions such as: "Why did Margaret want to buy me a present—because she likes me or because she felt she owed me something?" We are also interested in having others know about our (usually good) intentions. Thus, we often explicitly tell others the reasons (intentions) behind our actions. Sometimes, however, it is advantageous to conceal our intentions. For example, a student who does extra reading for a class in the hope of getting on the teacher's good side might tell the teacher, "I'm very interested in the topic."

The significance of intentions in our culture is evident in the criminal justice system, which places great emphasis on premeditation. For instance, a person will be sent to jail for as little as a year for killing someone if intent to murder cannot be shown; but if intent is clearly established, the penalty can be life imprisonment or even death.

The concept of intention is learned early in Western societies. Jean Piaget, the famous Swiss developmental psychologist, found that children as young as seven acknowledge that a small amount of intended damage is "naughtier" than a great deal of damage resulting from ignorance, oversight, or accident. In our culture, high status is given noble intentions, even when the outcome is undesirable. It is not the gift that is important; it is the *thought* (the giver's intent) that counts. Parents may punish children severely because "they love them."

Intention is a complex concept. For example, when you tell someone you will do something (state an intention), you must not only remember what you have committed to do but also remember that you have made the commitment (Kvavilashvili, 1987). Intention also is an elusive concept, especially because it is always *inferred* from behavior (as are all theoretical constructs). We never have direct access to others' intentions. All we can know is what we see them do and what we hear them tell us about why they acted as they did.

The psychoanalytic strategy stresses questions of motivation and intention for understanding personality. These issues relate to other emphases of the strategy. For example, as implied by words such as *really*, individuals may not always be aware of their own intentions and motivations; some of the most important aspects of an individual's personality may be unconscious. Therefore, these aspects are the products of motivations of which the person is entirely unaware.

People vary in how they use behavior to evaluate interpersonal interactions and in the extent to which they go beyond behavior to infer intentions. Demonstration 3-1 allows you to explore your own use of behavior and intentions to evaluate personal interactions.

■ *Demonstration 3-1*
INTENTION VERSUS BEHAVIOR

In our daily lives, we interact with many people: roommates, salespeople, friends, teachers, bus drivers. In each interaction, we have certain expectations, either explicit or implicit, about what should take place. For example, the bus driver is supposed to get us to work on time, a teacher must assign grades, and a friend should listen sympathetically to our problems. Some of our expectations are doubtless satisfied (teachers almost never forget to give grades), whereas others are not satisfied (friends are not always eager to hear about our frustrations). When our expectations about how another person is supposed to act are not met, our reactions and feelings about that person are based on two sources of information: the person's *behavior* (what he or she has done or failed to do) and the person's *intent* (what he or she meant to do).

Suppose that a bus driver fails to stop at your corner. You might be very annoyed if this behavior results in your being late for an appointment. It would make little difference to you if the driver "meant" to stop. The driver's intent and behavior are at odds; your reaction of annoyance is based on the bus driver's *behavior* of going past your corner, not on the driver's intent.

In this instance, the driver has not explicitly stated an intention to stop, but the intention is implicit (drivers are expected to stop at designated locations). In other situations, the person's intention is explicitly stated. Suppose you meet your friend Dave at lunch, hoping to share with him the events of your frustrating morning. Dave says he wants to listen (intent) but has to rush off (behavior) to study for a physics test scheduled for that afternoon. You appreciate Dave's desire to listen to you and wish him well on his exam. Once again the person's intent and behavior are inconsistent. But in

this situation, you evaluate the interaction in terms of Dave's *intention* to listen rather than his behavior of rushing off.

A third way of reacting to an inconsistency between intention and behavior takes both factors into account. If Dave were leaving to play tennis, you would feel less good about your interaction with him than if he left for an exam. You would understand that Dave had planned to play tennis, yet you might think that he could have given your feelings and needs a higher priority. By considering both behavior (Dave's playing tennis) and intention (his wanting to listen to you), you would view the situation differently than if you took into account only his intention or only his behavior.

The purpose of this Demonstration is to sensitize you to the role played by other people's intentions and behavior and the relation between the two in some of your daily interpersonal transactions. You will first compile a list of people with whom you have dealt recently and whom you know very well or with whom you merely have a passing acquaintance. Then you will consider interactions you have had with these people in which their intentions and behavior were inconsistent.

PROCEDURE

1. First, make a list of the people with whom you have interacted over the past few weeks. Try to include as many people as you can.

2. Next, divide the people on your list into three categories:

Close: People you know well, interact with frequently and regularly, think about, and so on (such as roommates, good friends, and parents)

Distant: People you do not know well, interact with infrequently and irregularly, may have met only once or twice, or have only brief business-type dealings with (such as salespeople and teachers with whom you have minimal contact)

Other: people who do not fit into either the "close" or the "distant" category—those whom you would not consider intimate acquaintances but with whom you have had more than just a brief encounter (such as many classmates, people who live in your dorm, your mail carrier). The people in this category will *not* be used in the Demonstration.

Keep in mind that the object of this preliminary step is to provide you with a list of people with whom you have recently interacted and whom you would consider either "close" or "distant." Thus, if you are having difficulty coming up with at least six people in each of the two categories, your criteria for either close or distant relationships may be too stringent. If this seems to be the case, adjust your criteria accordingly.

3. Having compiled a sizable list of people you would construe as close and distant, you are ready to proceed with the major part of the Demonstration. This step involves identifying as many interactions as you can with the individuals on your close and distant lists *in which the persons' intentions and behaviors were somehow inconsistent.* Certainly not all your interpersonal interactions will meet this requirement. Your goal should be to come up with at least four instances of intention-behavior discrepancies for each of the two categories of people (that is, four for close and four for distant).

4. From the Demonstration Materials section at the end of the book, remove Work Sheet 3-1. Note that the top half of the work sheet is designated for interactions with close acquaintances and the bottom half for interactions with distant acquaintances. Figure 3-1 contains examples of the type of information you should enter on the work sheet. (The examples are taken from the cases described

		I Other person	II Nature of interaction	III Other's behavior	IV Other's intention	V Your evaluation	VI Basis for evaluation
Close relationships		Dave	Met Dave after having rough morning	Went to study	Wanted to talk with me	Understood why he couldn't talk and felt okay about it	I
		Dave	Met Dave after having rough morning	Went to tennis game	Wanted to talk with me	Appreciated that he had a tennis date but was a bit angry with him	B and I
Distant relationships		Bus driver	On bus going to appointment	Drove past my stop	To stop	Annoyed at the driver making me late for my appointment	B

Figure 3-1
Sample work sheet for Demonstration 3-1.

earlier in this Demonstration.) For each interaction in which intention and behavior were inconsistent, record the following information in the appropriate columns.

Column I: Write the *name* of the person with whom you had the interaction.

Column II: Write a brief description of the *interaction*.

Column III: Write a brief description of the other person's *behavior*.

Column IV: Write a brief description of the other person's *intention*.

Column V: Write a brief description of how you *evaluated* the incident—that is, how you felt about and reacted to the other person and to the outcome of the incident.

Column VI: Indicate whether the basis for your evaluation in Column V was primarily the other person's behavior (B), primarily the other person's intention (I), or a combination of the two (B and I).

DISCUSSION

After completing Demonstration 3-1, you should know more about the differences between intention and behavior. This is an essential distinction in the psychoanalytic strategy. It also bears on our daily lives. We rarely distinguish between intention and behavior when the two are consistent with each other. However, when they are discrepant, we try to distinguish between them. Such a distinction allows us to evaluate the situation in terms of the person's intent, the person's behavior, or some combination of the two.

The Demonstration should give you a sense of how you typically use intention and behavior in situations where they are inconsistent. Is there any pattern in your reliance on intention versus behavior? There are many relevant factors. One has been built into the Demonstration. Compare your Column VI entries for close relationships with those for distant relationships. You may find that you rely on intention with one of these groups, and behavior for the other. Clearly, this is an individual matter. The more interactions you considered, the greater the likelihood that a pattern will emerge.

Look at your use of intention and behavior in relation to other factors, such as the importance of the interaction, the sex of the other person, and whether your evaluation of the other person's intention-behavior discrepancy had direct consequences for the person.

You might also find it interesting to examine instances in which your own intentions and behaviors have been inconsistent. How did you evaluate such situations? How did others react in terms of the emphasis they placed on your intention versus your behavior?

PSYCHOANALYTIC ASSESSMENT Psychoanalytic theory assumes that our motivations are often unconscious. That is, we are often unaware of why we act the way we do. Assessing motives that you are partially or completely unaware of is complex and difficult. To appreciate the complexity, ask yourself the following questions:

1. Why am I going to college?
2. Why do I like (dislike) my roommate (friend, relative)?
3. Why do I enjoy my favorite activity?

If the answers to these questions seem obvious at first, try inserting the word *really* in front of the words *going, like (dislike),* and *enjoy*. Does this make answering the questions more difficult?

Psychoanalytic personality assessment is *indirect* in two respects. First, because unconscious phenomena cannot be observed directly by others, they must be assessed by indirect methods. Second, according to psychoanalytic theory, personality characteristics appear as either direct or indirect expressions of underlying drives. We normally expect direct expression. For example, we expect an individual who feels hostile to attack another person, either physically or verbally. It is also possible that underlying motives will be expressed indirectly. Thus, hostility may be disguised, such as by ignoring others. The most indirect way to express a motive is as its opposite. Hostility may come out as friendly and loving acts. The more socially unacceptable a motive, the more likely it is to be expressed indirectly. Indirect expression gives unacceptable motives an outlet without the person feeling the anxiety or guilt normally associated with socially unacceptable motives.

PSYCHOANALYTIC RESEARCH

Freud relied entirely on the case-study method. He gathered extensive information about the patients in his clinical practice. Then he used these observations both as the source of his personality theory and as evidence for the theory.

Psychoanalytic case studies include more than just a detailed description of the patient/subject's behavior. The observations are *interpreted*. These interpretations become an integral part of the case study (Steele, 1986). Any behavior occurring during the psychoanalytic session, including the patient's reports of behavior outside the session, may be interpreted. Psychoanalysts interpret their patients' free associations and dreams, which are assumed to be valuable sources of unconscious material that have become conscious in disguised or symbolic form.

Before making an interpretation, the analyst waits until a similar observation is made several times, so that a theme is established. An interpretation is validated partially by the degree to which the patient accepts it as true and partially by whether it leads to changes in the patient's behavior.

Many psychoanalysts believe that psychoanalytic concepts can be validated only through analysis and interpretation of material obtained from case studies. Freud wrote to some researchers who had attempted to validate psychoanalytic concepts through experiments:

> I have examined your experimental studies for the verification of psychoanalytic assertions with interest. I cannot put much value on these confirmations because the wealth of reliable observations on which these assertions rest make them independent of experimental verification. Still, it can do no harm. (quoted by MacKinnon & Dukes, 1962, p. 702)

Case studies, more than any other research method, allow psychologists to explore the richness and complexity of human personality. Interpretative case studies are still the main method of research in the psychoanalytic strategy (Langs, 1987, 1988). However, post-Freudians have increasingly used correlational and experimental methods to test psychoanalytic propositions (e.g., Fisher & Greenberg, 1977; Kline, 1972; Masling, 1983, 1985a).

PSYCHOANALYTIC PERSONALITY CHANGE

Psychoanalytic theory, assessment, and research began with attempts to change abnormal personality. Even today, most psychoanalysts are psychotherapists ("personality changers") first and theorists, assessors, and researchers second (Michels, 1988).

Psychoanalytic personality change (psychotherapy) involves indirect methods, just as psychoanalytic assessment does. These methods are used because the conflicts causing patients' problems are primarily unconscious. A major aim of psychoanalytic personality change is to make patients aware of their unconscious processes and motives—that is, making conscious what is unconscious.

Personality change comes about primarily through the lengthy process of patients' discovering and understanding the underlying causes of their behavior. This process is sometimes accompanied by intense emotional release. Patients frequently discover, in the course of psychoanalysis, that their present behaviors and motives are based on early childhood adjustment problems and conflicts. They must learn that such factors are no longer relevant to their lives and are therefore unrealistic guides for their present behavior.

SUMMARY

1. Psychoanalysis refers to a theory of personality, an approach to research, and procedures for changing personality. Freud was the originator of psychoanalysis, and his ideas dominate the psychoanalytic strategy.

2. Psychoanalytic theorists fall into three broad camps: Freudians, ego psychologists, and object-relations theorists.

3. Psychoanalytic theory holds that behavior (1) is determined by forces within the person and (2) has meaning for the person. No behavior is purely accidental. Freudian slips are examples of this strict determinism.

4. Psychoanalytic theory posits that personality is a dynamic system, involving continuous exchanges of psychic energy.

5. Freud organized personality in two ways: levels of awareness (unconscious, preconscious, and conscious) and functions of personality (id, ego, and superego).

6. Psychoanalytic theory is developmental. Early childhood experiences are critical in determining adult personality. Psychoanalysts have identified discrete, universal stages of development.

7. A person's intentions are more central to the psychoanalytic view than is behavior.

8. Psychoanalytic personality assessment uses indirect methods because personality operates primarily at an unconscious level.

9. Case studies, usually of patients in psychoanalysis, are the primary research method in this strategy. Case studies provide the major source of evidence for psychoanalytic personality theory.

10. Most psychoanalysts are practicing psychotherapists. Psychoanalysis is usually a long process in which the patient is made aware of the underlying, often unconscious determinants of his or her behavior and personality.

Chapter Four

Origins and Development of Personality

In this chapter we will explore the development of personality from the psychoanalytic perspective. The psychoanalytic strategy describes in great detail how personality develops, especially in early childhood. We begin by discussing the forces that lie behind its development.

DRIVES AND LIBIDO

A **drive** in psychoanalysis is an inborn, intrapsychic force (Vermorel, 1990). When operative, a drive produces a state of excitement or tension. In Freud's early theory, there were two classes of drives: self-preservative and sexual. *Self-preservative drives* satisfy physical needs, including breathing, hunger and thirst, and excretion.

When our drives are not satisfied, we experience tension. For example, when a person holds her breath, she feels a tightness in her chest; when an individual has not eaten in some time, he feels hunger pangs. Under unusual circumstances, a drive such as hunger can become abnormally strong and can exert a powerful influence on behavior. In October 1972, a plane carrying a Uruguayan rugby team and its supporters crashed in the Andes. The passengers and crew were given up for lost. Miraculously, 16 men survived for 73 days in subfreezing temperatures with no fuel and only enough food for 20 days. The survivors remained alive by eating parts of the bodies of those who had died. (A popular book, *Alive: The Story of the Andes Survivors* [Read, 1974], and two movies, *Survive* and *Alive,* are based on this incident.)

The second group of drives relates to *sexual urges*. Freud used the term sexual to refer to all pleasurable actions and thoughts, including, but not confined to, erotic ones. The psychic energy of sexual drives is called **libido**. Libido is also the energy for all mental activity, including thinking, perceiving, imagining, remembering, and problem solving.

Freud initially believed all human motivation was sexual; in other words, all human behavior is motivated by the wish to bring ourselves pleasure. Yet societies place obstacles in the way of completely or even predominantly satisfying pleasure-seeking drives. In capsule form, Freud's theory of personality deals with how people handle their sexual needs in relation to society, which usually prevents the direct expression of those needs. Each individual's personality is therefore a result of a unique compromise between satisfying sexual drives and conforming to society's restraints.

Around 1920, shortly after World War I, Freud revised his theory of motivation to include the **aggressive drive**. (Freud also called the aggressive drive the *death drive, death instinct*, or *Thanatos;* this is in opposition to the life drive, or *Eros*.)

The aggressive drive accounts for the destructive aspects of human behavior, and has its own kind of psychic energy. However, Freud did not give a specific name to this energy. The development and function of the aggressive drive and the sexual drive are parallel. Freud's **dual theory of drives** assumes that both the sexual and the aggressive drives are involved in motivating behavior.

The contributions of the two drives are not necessarily equal. Freud did not describe the aggressive drive as fully or clearly as the sexual drive. Despite his recognition that human motivation is more than sexual, Freud always considered the sexual drive to be paramount. Accordingly, our discussion will focus on the sexual drive.

Dynamics of the Mind

Freud's psychic energy system is a *closed* system; that is, energy cannot be added to the system, and no existing energy can escape or be permanently depleted. Each person has a fixed quantity of psychic energy that is invested in (devoted to) various behaviors, people, and ideas. An investment of psychic energy is known as a **cathexis** (*cathexes* is the plural form); **cathect**, the verb form, is the process of investing psychic energy.

Psychic energy cannot actually be invested in (attached to) people or activities. But in the mind, psychic energy can be cathected to mental representations in the form of thoughts, images, and fantasies. The strength of a cathexis, or the amount of energy invested, indicates the importance of the focus of energy. Because each of us possesses a *fixed* amount of psychic energy, the greater the amount of energy given to one cathexis, the less psychic energy is available for other cathexes and mental activities. A young man who is constantly thinking of a woman friend has difficulty doing other things, such as reading an assignment in his personality textbook. Cathexes are not permanent. When we turn our attention to another activity or person, the energy transfers to the new focus.

You may be wondering whether some people have more psychic energy than others. The concept of psychic energy has never been quantified, so the question cannot be answered. What is important is that each person has a fixed amount of psychic energy, which places limits on actions, thoughts, and feelings.

Freud used an analogy to explain the nature of psychic energy: the pressure of psychic energy builds in the same way water pressure builds. Take, for example, a series of water-filled pipes, in which the external valve is closed. If pressure increases and there is no outlet for the water, the pipe will burst at its weakest point. Reduction of psychic tension is necessary for a person to be able to function. Because tension is unpleasant or painful, reducing tension produces a highly pleasurable experience. The tendency to reduce tension is known as the **pleasure principle**. If the individual's psychic energy does not have an opportunity to discharge in normal or socially acceptable ways, the pressure will increase. Finally, as in the water-pipe analogy, the pressure will burst out violently at the weakest point in the personality.

ALTERNATIVE VIEWS OF THE BASIC HUMAN MOTIVE: JUNG AND ADLER

Mention Freud, and many people's initial association is *sex*. Freud's insistence on the preeminence of the sexual drive in human motivation ultimately made his views unacceptable to many. This included two of his ardent followers, Carl Jung and Alfred Adler. Early in their relationship, Jung (pronounced YOONG) wrote Freud to ask:

Carl Jung
(1875-1961)
challenged Freud's
emphasis on the sexual
drive. He later
introduced the idea of a
collective unconscious
furnished with archetypes
from our ancestral past.
Courtesy of National Library
of Medicine, Bethesda,
Maryland, 20014

Is it not conceivable, in view of the limited conception of sexuality that prevails nowadays, that the sexual terminology should be reserved only for the most extreme forms of your "libido," and that a less offensive collective term should be established for all the libidinal manifestations? (Freud & Jung, 1974, p. 25)

Jung believed that the sexual drive is an important source of motivation, but not the only source.

Adler's disagreement with Freud over the importance of the sexual drive is sharper. Adler believed the fundamental human motive is **striving for superiority**, as compensation for feelings of inferiority. Adler's own life was the basis of the idea. As a child, Adler was continually sick and weak. He suffered from rickets (a disease that softens the bones), which made engaging in physical activities with his peers very difficult. In later years, Adler recalled his feelings of inferiority:

I remember sitting on a bench bandaged up on account of rickets, with my healthy elder brother sitting opposite me. He could run, jump, and move about quite effortlessly, while for me, movement of any sort was a strain and an effort. (quoted in Bottome, 1957, pp. 30–31)

Adler had twice been run over in the street, and he almost died from pneumonia (Orgler, 1963). As a consequence, he decided early in life to become a physician in an effort to overcome death and his fear of death (Ansbacher & Ansbacher, 1956).

Adler practiced general medicine before turning to psychiatry. In 1907, he presented the intriguing theory that people develop a disease or malfunction in their weakest organ or body part. Further, Adler believed that people deal with such weakness by compensating and even *over*compensating. For example, a person born with weak legs might spend many hours developing the leg muscles (compensation). As a result, the individual might eventually become a long-distance runner (overcompensation).

When Adler began to practice psychiatry, he broadened his theory to all feelings of inferiority, including those arising from psychological or interpersonal weaknesses. The individual's perceived inferiority—be it biological, psychological, or social—leads to *striving for superiority* as a form of compensation. Adler (1964) believed that all people are motivated by two forces: (1) the need to overcome inferiority and (2) the desire to do so by becoming superior. In normal development, striving for superiority compensates for feelings of inferiority. In the resulting compensatory life-style that the individual adopts, feelings of inferiority, which are most prominent in childhood, may be forgotten.

When feelings of inferiority and/or strivings for superiority become exaggerated, abnormal behavior (neurosis) can occur. **Inferiority complex** was Adler's term for such an exaggerated, neurotic reaction. Current thinking among Adlerians has further refined the concept of inferiority complex as having three features:

1. It develops in early childhood and forms the foundation of an emerging life-style.

Alfred Adler
(1870-1937)
claimed that the primary
human motivation is
striving for superiority in
an effort to compensate
for feelings of inferiority.
AP/Wide World Photos

2. It is a subjective perception of the self which results from a comparison of beliefs about others in one's primary group, most notably siblings.
3. The comparison is made regarding three sets of characteristics—physical, social, and goals and standards. The inferiority (and the comparisons) may not be consciously experienced. (Strano & Dixon, 1990, p. 29)

Other psychoanalysts emphasize different nonsexual sources of motivation. Many consider social factors critical in the development of personality. We will explore these "social alternatives" later.

ISSUES IN THE PSYCHOANALYTIC THEORY OF PERSONALITY DEVELOPMENT	Precisely *how* personality develops is critical in psychoanalytic theory. Most psychoanalysts divide personality development into a number of discrete stages that are considered to be *universal*, or relevant to all people. There is considerable controversy, however, about the nature of the stages.

One controversy involves the role of biological factors versus social factors in development. Freud believed that biological factors are paramount. His developmental stages are biologically determined. Many contemporary psychoanalysts emphasize social factors and minimize the role of biology; the developmental stages they propose are based primarily on social phenomena.

Another controversy concerns the extent to which early experience determines adult personality. All psychoanalysts consider early experience important. Freud believed that adult personality is relatively fixed by about age 5. Many post-Freudians agree that early experiences can have a profound impact on later personality, but they think that later experiences can also have important effects. These post-Freudians have pursued the fascinating questions of when and how underlying personality changes occur after childhood.

FREUD'S STAGES OF PSYCHOSEXUAL DEVELOPMENT	Freud's stages of personality development are called **psychosexual** because they are concerned with the psychological manifestation of the sexual (pleasure) drive. At particular times in the development sequence, one body area—specifically, the mouth, anus, or genital region—is particularly sensitive to erotic stimulation. These areas are called *erogenous zones*.

While in a given psychosexual stage, much of the individual's libido is invested in behavior involving the primary erogenous zone. To progress to the next stage, the libido must be freed from the primary erogenous zone of the stage it is in and be reinvested in the primary erogenous zone of the next stage. This is necessary because each individual has only a fixed amount of libido.

The ability to transfer libido from one stage to the next depends on how well the individual has resolved the developmental *conflict* associated with each psychosexual stage. *The conflict is always between free expression of biological impulses and parental constraints.* Freud used the analogy of military troops on the march to explain this process. As the troops march, they are met by opposition (conflict). If they are highly successful in winning the battle (resolving the conflict), virtually all the troops (libido) will be free to move on. (Thus, there will be ample libido available to deal with the conflict of the next stage.) If the troops experience difficulty in winning the battle, more troops will be left behind and fewer troops will be available to move on. (In other words, less libido will be available to cope with the next conflict.)

People have difficulty leaving one stage and proceeding to the next when they have been either frustrated or overindulged in the present stage. *Frustration* occurs when the person's needs relevant to the psychosexual stage have not been met. *Overindulgence* occurs when relevant needs have been so well satisfied that the person is reluctant to leave the stage. In both cases, a portion of libido remains permanently invested in a previous developmental stage; this is known as **fixation**. Inevitably, *some* libido is fixated at each psychosexual stage. The more difficult it is for a person to resolve the conflict of a given stage, the more libido remains fixated at that stage.

Fixation, which occurs in childhood, influences adult personality. If there is little fixation, then only vestiges of earlier ways of obtaining satisfaction are seen in later behavior. If the fixation is strong (a substantial amount of fixated libido), the individual's adult personality is dominated by ways of obtaining satisfaction that were used in the stage. As a result, the individual develops an adult **character type** (such as an *anal character*) reflecting the poorly resolved conflict (Freud, 1959). Once formed, character types are believed to be quite stable and to greatly influence one's choice of mate and occupation (Baudry, 1988).

Oral Stage

During the first year of life, the mouth is the most important source of tension reduction (e.g., eating) and pleasure (e.g., sucking). This is the **oral stage**. Weaning is the crucial conflict. The more difficult it is for the child to leave the mother's breast (or bottle) and its accompanying sucking pleasure, the more libido is fixated at the oral stage. Freud focused on the biological ramifications of the oral stage. Post-Freudians emphasize the psychological aspects. As Strupp (1967) put it:

> The focal point of the child's personality organization at this period is not necessarily the mouth per se but *the total constellation of immaturity, dependency, the wish to be mothered, the pleasure of being held, the enjoyment of human closeness and warmth.* (p. 23)

Karl Abraham (1927) divided the oral stage into two phases. The early phase is **oral eroticism**, characterized by the pleasure of sucking or taking things in through the mouth (*oral incorporation*). The later phase is **oral sadism**, which begins as teeth emerge and represents the development of the aggressive drive. The child is now capable of biting and chewing—and therefore of behaving aggressively and destructively.

The Oral Character

Fixation at the oral stage results in an **oral character** (Abraham, 1927). Some of the major characteristics of the oral character are:

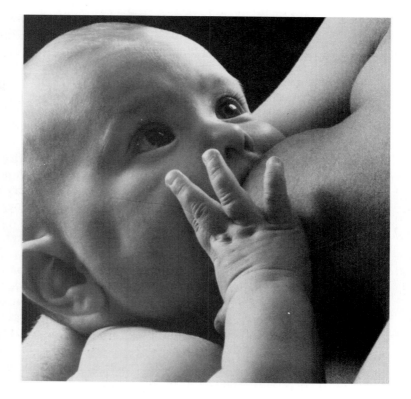

Gratification through the mouth, especially nursing, is the focus of the oral stage.
Dag Sundberg/The Image Bank

1. Preoccupation with issues of giving/taking.
2. Concern about dependence/independence and passivity/activity.
3. Special attitudes about closeness and distance to others—being alone versus attachment to the group.
4. Extremes of optimism/pessimism.
5. Unusual ambivalence [especially true of the oral sadistic character].
6. Openness to novel experience and ideas, which involves enhancing curiosity and interest in investigating nature.
7. A hasty, restless, impatient orientation—wanting to be "fed" with events and things.
8. Continued unusual use of oral channels for gratification or . . . [coping with frustration] (for example, overeating, not eating enough, smoking, excessive talking). (Fisher & Greenberg, 1977, p. 88)

These characteristics are general. The specific group of traits a person manifests depends on two factors: (1) whether the person is fixated at the oral erotic or oral sadistic phase and (2) whether the fixation is due to frustration or overindulgence.

How might the general characteristics be manifested differently? Consider *optimism/pessimism* as an example. People who were frustrated would be expected to be pessimistic; those who were overindulged would be expected to be optimistic. The specific form of optimism or pessimism could be broadly passive or active, depending on whether the individual was fixated early (erotic phase) or late (sadistic phase) in the stage. The four possible outcomes are shown in Table 4-1.

Joseph Masling and his associates have correlated a variety of behaviors with oral fixation (Masling, 1985). They measured oral fixation using Rorschach inkblots—ambiguous figures that look like spilled ink (see Chapter 6 for a detailed description). Subjects were asked to say what they saw in the blots. Examples of Rorschach responses that are taken to indicate oral-dependent behavior appear in Table 4-2.

One direct prediction from Freud's theory is that people fixated at the oral stage will tend to eat and drink excessively. A positive correlation has been found between subjects' reporting oral imagery in Rorschach inkblots and both obesity and alcoholism (Bertrand & Masling, 1969; Masling, Rabie, & Blondheim, 1967).

Dependency is a central trait of the oral character. One study found that college students who depend on others to make decisions for them in ambiguous situations report more oral imagery than do students who make their own decisions (Masling, Weiss, & Rothschild, 1968).

Complying with rules is another indication of dependency on others (authorities) for approval. A positive correlation has repeatedly been found between oral fixation and compliance (Bornstein & Masling, 1985; Ihilevich

Table 4-1
Development of optimism/pessimism as an oral character trait

TIME OF FIXATION	CAUSE OF FIXATION	
	OVERINDULGENCE	FRUSTRATION
	PASSIVE OPTIMISM	PASSIVE PESSIMISM
ORAL EROTIC (EARLY)	Believing the world will always provide for one's needs, no matter what one does	Behaving as if there were nothing one can do to improve one's lot in life
	Example: Student doesn't study because he/she expects tests will be easy, teacher will understand	*Example:* Student doesn't study because he/she feels it is no use; nothing can help; will inevitably do poorly
	ACTIVE OPTIMISM	ACTIVE PESSIMISM
ORAL SADISTIC (LATE)	Aggressively taking (in) from the world to provide for one's needs	Behaving cynically and hostilely toward perceived harsh world; striking out at others indiscriminately
	Example: Student studies hard; seeks extra help; does additional reading, assignments	*Example:* Student devotes time to criticizing teachers, classes, exams; bad grades attributed to system

Table 4-2
Examples of oral-dependent Rorschach responses

CATEGORY	SAMPLE RESPONSES
Food and drink	Milk, whiskey, boiled lobster
Food providers	Waiter, cook, bartender
Food organs	Mouth, stomach, lips, teeth
Oral instruments	Lipstick, cigarette, tuba
Nurturers	Jesus, mother, father, doctor, God
Good luck objects	Wishbone, four-leaf clover
Oral actvitiy	Eating, talking, singing, kissing
"Baby talk" responses	Patty-cake, bunny rabbit, pussy cat
Negations of oral percepts	No mouth, not pregnant, woman without breasts

Source: Based on "Orality and Latency of Volunteering to Serve as Experimental Subjects: A Replication" by R. F. Bornstein and J. Masling, 1985, *Journal of Personality Assessment, 49,* p. 307.

& Gleser, 1986; Masling, O'Neill, & Katkin, 1981). People who seem focused on the mouth and themes of incorporation on various projective measures also appear to show a special motivation for closeness and support from others (Fisher & Greenberg, 1977). These and other correlational findings are consistent with the concept of the oral character. It is important to note, however, that little evidence shows that the character type originates from fixation in the oral stage.

Post-Freudian Extensions of the Oral Stage

Erich Fromm believed that character types develop from the social interactions between children and parents. Like Abraham, Fromm (1947) distinguished two basic oral types. He theorized that individuals reared in environments that fostered an attitude of *expecting to receive* become **receptive characters** (Abraham's oral-erotic characters). The idea is that the demands of the home situation were best dealt with by being receptive, friendly, and pleasing. In contrast, when home circumstances are frustrating, children develop the attitude that they must *take to receive* (Thompson, 1957). Such persons become **exploitative characters** (Abraham's oral-sadistic characters). It is noteworthy that Abraham and Fromm observed the same two types of personality but interpreted them somewhat differently.

Another extension of the basic Freudian notion of the oral character was made by Harry Stack Sullivan. Sullivan believed that the critical aspect of the first year is the social interaction between child and mother. The child learns to evaluate and discriminate the mother's emotions. This ability to "read" the mother's feelings is the basis for accurately perceiving and predicting other people's behavior. Partial support for this idea comes from a correlational study (Masling, Johnson, & Saturansky, 1974). High-oral college students were better than low-oral students at predicting the responses of other

Erich Fromm
(1900-1980)
argued that different early environments lead to distinctive character types.
© René Burri/Magnum Photos

Harry Stack Sullivan
(1892-1949)
emphasized the
importance of being able
to "read" others' feelings
as a basis for adequate
social adjustment.
Courtesy of William Alanson
White, Psychiatric
Foundation, Inc.

students on a personality test. This finding was also obtained with another group of college students who knew each other well and were all enrolled in a Peace Corps orientation. The investigators correlated the measures of oral dependence and interpersonal perception with a measure of success in the Peace Corps. Obviously, accurate perception of others would be essential to working well with people in foreign cultures. Both accurate interpersonal perception and oral dependence were found to be positively correlated with success in the Peace Corps.

Bruno Bettelheim (1976) presented an interesting extension of the oral stage. He considered the story of Hansel and Gretel to be a tale of oral sadism. Hansel and Gretel are sent into the woods because they have been careless with milk (an oral symbol). In the woods, they greedily devour part of the witch's gingerbread house. Like their mother, the witch gratifies their needs at first. Soon, however, the witch reveals her intention to eat the children. The children resolve their dilemma by abandoning their strictly oral impulses in favor of using reason. They outwit and kill the witch, returning home as more mature children. Bettelheim believed the story is popular with children precisely because it helps them deal with their oral conflicts. Consistent with this view, modern psychoanalysts claim that fairy tales are a useful way of eliciting and reducing anxiety in young children (Lubetsky, 1989).

Anal Stage   When a child is weaned, libido shifts from the mouth to the anus. Pleasure is obtained at first from expelling feces—the **anal sadistic phase**. Later, pleasure comes from retaining feces—the **anal erotic phase**. This is not to say that the child did not derive similar pleasure during the oral stage. However, during the second and third years of life, anal pleasure predominates, just as oral pleasure did in the first year.

Parents make few demands on children in the first year of life. Starting in the second year, however, parents in most Western cultures begin to place restrictions on their offspring's behaviors, especially regarding bladder and bowel control. The conflict in the anal stage pits the sexual drive for pleasure—from the tension reduced by elimination of bodily wastes—against the social expectation that children develop self-control with respect to urination and defecation.

Muscle control becomes the prototype for self-control in general, just as weaning is a prototype for dependency. If children easily accede to their parents' toilet-training demands, they will develop the basis for successful self-control. A child who has difficulty developing control and meeting parental demands will become (to some degree) an **anal character**, a person who is *orderly*, *stingy*, and *stubborn* (Freud, 1959).

The Anal Character

When children find their parents' demands for toilet training difficult, they will show resistance. Resistance can be either active or passive.

Active resistance entails *direct opposition* (a "you can't make me do that" attitude). For instance, there may be attempts to counterattack by defecating at especially inopportune moments, such as immediately after being taken off

In the anal stage, toilet training is the critical conflict.

Photo by Michael D. Spiegler and Nursher Associates

the potty. Children who discover that direct opposition is a successful means of social control will adopt it as a strategy for handling frustration in general. This results in the development of an **anal expulsive character**. Anal expulsives are fixated at the anal sadistic phase. They are expected to rebel or to express anger by becoming wasteful, disorderly, or messy. It is interesting that our colloquial statements of extreme anger and hostility—"Piss on it" or "Oh, shit," for example—often refer to elimination.

Passive resistance to toilet training demands involves *retaining feces*. Gentle pressure against the intestinal walls is pleasurable. Furthermore, children can indirectly strike back at their parents by simply not having bowel movements (which can be a serious danger to a child's health). When this tactic is successful, it may set the stage for retentive behavior patterns in later life. This pattern leads to the development of an **anal retentive character**. Anal retentives are fixated at the anal erotic phase. They are neat, careful, systematic, and orderly. They may be upset or even revolted by a mess of any kind, including a room in disarray or poorly organized plans that lead to confusion and uncertainty.

Anal expulsiveness and anal retentiveness are two sides of the same fixation; both are responses to being controlled and forced. Examples of behaviors that epitomize the two anal character types are presented in Table 4-3.

Many correlational studies have examined whether the three basic anal retentive character traits—orderliness, stinginess, and stubbornness—tend to occur together (Fisher & Greenberg, 1977). The evidence largely supports

Fixation at the anal stage can result in two contrasting character types: the anal expulsive and the anal retentive character. Can you tell which office goes with each type?

Photos by Michael D. Spiegler

Freud's "anal triad." The strongest direct association is between orderliness and stinginess. For example, people who are overly neat also tend to be excessively cheap.

Evidence for the anal character also comes from some cleverly designed experiments. In one study, male college students identified geometric forms under two conditions: while their hands were immersed in a smelly, fecal-like substance and while they were immersed in clean water (Rosenwald, 1972). Comparison of performance in the two conditions was used as a measure of anal anxiety; the greater the difference in performance, the greater the anal anxiety. Men who had the most difficulty in the fecal-like material tended to be the most stubborn and the neatest.

Studies of the origin of the anal character have failed to support the idea that it is related to difficulty in toilet training (Fisher & Greenberg, 1977). Thus, empirical evidence does not support Freud's hypotheses that fixation causes either the anal or oral character. This does not mean that the concept of an anal or an oral character is not valid. Freud's observations of certain

Table 4-3
The anal character

CHARACTER TYPE	EXAMPLES OF ADULT BEHAVIOR
Anal expulsive	Messy; disorderly; disorganized; careless Wasteful; extravagant; reckless; tardy Defiant; aggressive
Anal retentive	Neat; orderly; organized; careful Parsimonious; hoarding; precise; prompt Withholding; passive-aggressive

basic traits associated with various adult behaviors may be accurate. However, his theory (inference) that character type is caused by fixation at a psychosexual stage may be inaccurate.

Phallic Stage

During the fourth and fifth years of life, the libido is centered in the genital region. Children at this age are frequently observed examining their genitals, masturbating, and asking questions about birth and sex. According to Freud, the conflict in the **phallic stage** is the last and most crucial conflict with which the young child must cope. The conflict involves *the child's unconscious wish to possess the opposite-sexed parent and at the same time to do away with the same-sexed parent*. Freud called this situation the **Oedipus complex** (pronounced ED-ipus). The name is derived from the Greek myth in which the hero, Oedipus, kills his father and marries his mother. Freud, incidently, was well read in classical mythology (Glenn, 1987), and the Oedipus myth seems to have been particularly salient for him (Rudnytsky, 1987).

The Oedipus Complex

The Oedipus complex operates somewhat differently for males and females. We will address the male Oedipus complex first.

The boy's first object of love is his mother. As the libido centers in the genital zone, his love for his mother becomes erotically tinged and therefore incestuous. Naturally, the boy's father stands in the way of this sexual desire for his wife. Thus, the boy sees his father as his rival, someone he would like to eliminate. These aggressive desires make the boy afraid that his father will retaliate. The fact that the little boy knows from casual observations that women lack penises suggests to him that his father may retaliate by castrating him (which is what he thinks happened to women). Because **castration anxiety** is stronger than the boy's desires for his mother, the boy gives up his wish to possess her.

Resolution of the Oedipus complex entails two processes: repression of his incestuous desires and defensive identification with his father. **Repression** is putting a thought or feeling completely out of consciousness. **Defensive identification** involves becoming like a threatening person ("if you can't beat him, join him"), sometimes known as *identification with the aggressor* (Porder, 1987). The boy unconsciously "reasons": "I cannot directly possess my mother, for fear of being castrated by my father. I can, however, possess her vicariously. I can get some of the joy of possessing my mother *by becoming like my father*." The boy resolves his conflict by identifying with his father's behavior, attitudes, and values. Defensive identification allows the boy to (1) possess his mother vicariously; (2) eliminate his castration anxiety; and (3) assimilate appropriate sex-role behavior. This identification also forms the rudiments of conscience.

Just as Bettelheim linked children's stories to oral conflicts, Ainslie (1989) has suggested that the play of 5-year-old boys reflects their efforts to deal with Oedipal conflicts. This is why "action figures" with exaggerated masculine characteristics, such as *The Masters of the Universe,* are so popular among boys of this age.

The female version of the Oedipus complex is called the **Electra complex** or the *female Oedipus complex*. (In Greek mythology, Electra persuades her brother to murder their mother and their mother's lover, who together have killed their father.) The Electra complex is considerably more complicated and less clear than the Oedipus complex (Ogden, 1987).

The little girl's first object of love is also her mother. However, during the phallic stage, the little girl is likely to discover that her father and other males have penises. But she and her mother (and other women) do not. She reasons that she must have had a penis at one time, and she blames her mother for her apparent castration. These feelings, along with other inevitable disappointments in her mother, lead to some loss of love for her mother and increased love for her father. Her love for her father is erotically tinged as well as envious because he has a penis.

Freud considered **penis envy** the counterpart of castration anxiety. But penis envy carries no threat of retaliation, whereas castration anxiety is very threatening and motivates the boy to renounce his incestuous desires. However, the little girl fears *loss of her mother's love*, which motivates her to resolve the Electra complex.

Freud was vague about how the Electra complex is resolved. He did state that the resolution occurs later in life than for males and is never complete. (This implies that women always remain somewhat fixated at the phallic stage.) The mother does not hold the threat of castration over her daughter. However, she would not tolerate incestuous relations between her husband and daughter.

Presumably, the impracticality of fulfilling her Oedipal wish causes the girl to repress her desires for her father and defensively identify with her mother. This protects the girl from losing her mother's love. It also allows her to possess her father vicariously. We should note that Freud's concept of penis envy and its supposed role in female psychosexual development are among his *least* accepted ideas today (Wilkinson, 1991).

We have presented the general formula for the Oedipus complex. The exact pattern for each individual depends on development in the prephallic stages and on specific family circumstances during the phallic stage. For example, if one parent is absent, the child will substitute a surrogate, such as an aunt or uncle.

Freud considered resolution of the Oedipus complex the single most critical aspect of personality development. Normal adult personality requires a successful resolution. Unsuccessful resolution inevitably leads to psychopathology. The phallic stage is also important because the child's moral principles (conscience) develop through identification with parents at this stage.

Fixation at the phallic stage results in a **phallic character type**. The phallic character is *reckless, resolute,* and *self-assured* (Fenichel, 1945); there is also a narcissistic element, involving *excessive vanity and pride*. Phallic characters have not successfully resolved their Oedipus complexes. Because they still suffer from castration anxiety, they tend to be afraid of closeness and love. They also appear courageous and are prone to show off; these behaviors serve as a partial defense against castration anxiety.

Freud's concepts of infantile sexuality and the Oedipus complex are difficult for people to accept. This was true at the beginning of the century, when Freud introduced his revolutionary theory; it is equally true today for students being introduced to these notions. Most people can accept the conflicts of the oral and anal stages. We may not recall being weaned and toilet trained, but there is strong evidence in our present behavior that we were! In contrast, it is unclear that we once had incestuous desires toward our opposite-sexed parent. The very idea is contrary to our morality. Indeed, most people would assert: "I never went through an Oedipus complex!" Freud, believing that all people have experienced the Oedipal situation, might have responded to such an allegation as follows: The taboo against incest is very strong; because of the anxiety created by incestuous desires, you have repressed memories of your Oedipus complex.

Evidence for the Oedipus Complex

Freud's theory of the Oedipus complex is actually a collection of minitheories concerned with various aspects of socialization (such as directing erotic drives and adopting sex roles) and a number of theoretical constructs (such as castration anxiety and penis envy). Case studies have focused on validating the overall concept of the Oedipus complex (such as the case of "Little Hans," which we will discuss in Chapter 5). Correlational and experimental studies have concentrated on validating specific aspects of the Oedipus complex. We will examine two of these studies.

Hall and Van de Castle (1963) analyzed the dreams of 120 college students for indications of castration anxiety and penis envy. Dream content taken to indicate castration anxiety included the dreamer's inability to use either his penis or a *phallic symbol* (e.g., a pen or a gun). Acquiring a penis or a phallic symbol and changing into a man in the dream were regarded as evidence for penis envy. The results were consistent with the theoretical differences between the Oedipal situation for males and females. Men had more dreams of castration anxiety than women; women had more dreams of penis envy and the wish to be castrated. (The wish to be castrated is related to penis envy because the wish assumes one has a penis.)

In a very different type of investigation, Sarnoff and Corwin (1959) studied the relationship between castration anxiety and fear of death. Psychoanalysts consider death (and bodily harm) to be a symbol of castration. Sarnoff and Corwin hypothesized that the greater a male's underlying castration anxiety, the greater should be his fear of death when castration anxiety is aroused. They measured male undergraduates' fear of death before and after purposely arousing castration anxiety. In the first part of the experiment, subjects indicated their agreement with statements about death (e.g., "I am disturbed when I think of the shortness of life") on a brief Fear of Death scale. Castration anxiety was assessed using a test in which subjects had to choose appropriate descriptions of a cartoon presumed to depict castration. On the basis of this test, subjects were divided into high-castration-anxiety and low-castration-anxiety groups.

Subjects returned 4 weeks later for the second part of the experiment.

Ostensibly they were to rate the aesthetic value of some pictures. Half the subjects in each of the castration-anxiety groups rated pictures of nude women (high-sexual-arousal condition); half rated pictures of fully clothed fashion models (low-sexual-arousal condition). Then the subjects again completed the Fear of Death scale.

As predicted, under conditions of high sexual arousal (which were presumed to arouse castration anxiety), high castration–anxiety subjects showed significantly greater increases in fear of death than did low castration–anxiety subjects. No differences were found when sexual arousal was low. Assuming that fear of death is an indication of castration anxiety, this study lends support to the important psychoanalytic concept of castration anxiety.

Alternative Views of the Oedipus Complex: A Feminist Perspective

There is little doubt that children around the age of 5 appear to experience jealousy, rivalry, and ambivalent feelings of love and hate for their parents. Freud was the first to draw widespread attention to this phenomenon, which he explained in terms of the Oedipus complex. Many psychologists, including some psychoanalysts, are skeptical of the sexual interpretation Freud placed on the 5-year-old's feelings and behaviors (Chodorow, 1990).

Psychoanalyst Karen Horney (pronounced HORN-eye), for example, reinterpreted the Oedipus complex in terms of interpersonal dynamics.

> The typical conflict leading to anxiety in a child is that between dependency on the parents . . . and hostile impulses against the parents. Hostility may be aroused in a child in many ways: by the parents' lack of respect . . . ; by unreasonable demands and prohibitions; by injustice; by unreliability; by suppression of criticism; by the parents dominating . . . and ascribing these tendencies to love. . . . If a child, in addition to being dependent on . . . parents, is grossly or subtly intimidated by them and hence feels that any expression of hostile impulses against them endangers security, then the existence of such hostile impulses is bound to create anxiety. . . . The resulting picture may look exactly like what Freud describes as the Oedipus complex: passionate clinging to one parent and jealousy toward the other or toward anyone interfering with the claim of exclusive possession. . . . *But the dynamic structure of these attachments is entirely different from what Freud conceives as the Oedipus complex. They are an early manifestation of neurotic conflicts rather than a primarily sexual phenomenon.* (1939, pp. 81–83; italics added)

Karen Horney
(1885-1952)
challenged Freud's claim that women experience penis envy and introduced the feminist perspective in psychoanalysis.
Jerry Soalt/Zwerling Soalt Associates

Horney, unlike Freud, theorized considerably about women. She challenged Freud's use of penis envy to explain feminine inferiority and disputed Freud's claim that motherhood's greatest psychological importance for women is as a means of compensating for that inferiority. Horney believed that Freud's image of women was distorted and biased because he based it exclusively on observations of neurotic women.

Horney was the first feminist voice in psychoanalysis (dating back to the 1920s). More recently, feminist perspectives in psychoanalysis have become quite prominent (Chodorow, 1990; Sayers, 1991). For example, psychoanalyst Esther Shapiro noted that Freud's concept of penis envy needs a complementary concept of *womb envy*:

> Freud saw only part of what happens in the formation of sexual identity. While little girls may wish they could have what their fathers have, little boys at four or five years of age wish they could have what their mothers have. They have a fascination with childbirth and envy their mothers' ability to have children. It has been called "womb envy." (quoted in Buie, 1989b, p. 19)

Further, Shapiro pointed out that the traditional masculine psychoanalytic view of ego development, with its emphasis on autonomy and separation, lacks the feminist perspective that emphasizes attachment and relationships. Clearly, both perspectives would make for a more balanced view.

Latency Period

Following the resolution of the Oedipus complex, children pass into a period known as **latency**. Latency is *not* a stage of psychosexual development because the sexual drive does not continue to develop during this time. (The term *latency* refers to the fact that the libido remains dormant.)

According to Freud, latency involves massive repression of sexual as well as oral and anal impulses. Libido is rechanneled from sexual pursuits to activities such as school and cognitive development, friendships with children of the same age and gender, sports, and hobbies (Sarnoff, 1976). Post-Freudians who focus on social and cognitive aspects of development and deemphasize sexual aspects consider the latency period to be critical in the child's development (e.g., Erikson, 1963, 1968; Sullivan, 1953).

Genital Stage

Freud's final stage of psychosexual development begins at puberty, when the young adolescent starts to mature sexually, and lasts through adulthood. In the **genital stage**, libido is again focused in the genital area. Now, however, it is directed toward heterosexual, rather than autoerotic (masturbatory), pleasure. The greater an individual's success in reaching the genital stage without large amounts of libido fixated in pregenital stages, the greater will be the person's capacity to lead a "normal" life, free of neurosis, and to enjoy genuine heterosexual relationships.

People spend most of their lives in the genital stage. Yet Freud had little to say about adulthood. This is consistent with his belief that the first 5 years of life are paramount in determining personality. Other psychoanalysts, such as Freud's daughter, Anna, have theorized more about the genital stage. Anna Freud was among her father's most devoted colleagues and his constant companion in his later years. She continued to work within her father's classic psychoanalytic framework until her death.

Anna Freud (1958) observed that adolescence brings an onslaught of sexual and aggressive impulses. Indeed, she wrote that "there are few situations in life which are more difficult to cope with than an adolescent son or daughter during the attempt to liberate themselves" (p. 323). (Ask your parents if they would agree.) Anna Freud identified two major strategies that adolescents use to gain a sense of control. One is *asceticism*, in which the

Anna Freud
(1895-1982)
extended her father's
work to the examination
of the adolescent years.
The Bettman Archive

adolescent tries to abandon physical pleasure, such as through strict diets or vigorous exercise. The other strategy adolescents use to cope is *intellectualization*, in which they develop personal theories about the nature of love or of life.

JUNG'S CONCEPT OF THE MIDLIFE CRISIS

Jung (1933) targeted middle age (beginning in the late 30s, early 40s) as a critical period in a person's life, and a number of modern writers have agreed (Levinson, Darrow, Klein, Levinson, & McKee, 1978; Sheehy, 1976, 1981; Vaillant, 1977). Jung described this period as a time when people undergo a major transition: from youthful impulsiveness and extraversion to thoughtfulness and introversion; from interests and goals that have their roots in biological urges to interests and goals that are based on cultural norms. The person's values become more social, civic-minded, and philosophical or religious. In short, the middle-aged individual develops into a spiritual being.

These changes precipitate what Jung referred to as a **midlife crisis**. The crisis occurs even among quite successful people as they realize many of their goals have been set for them by others. "The achievements which society rewards are won at the cost of diminution of personality. Many—far too many—aspects of life which should have been experienced lie in the lumber room among dusty memories" (Jung, 1933, p. 104).

Jung believed that if the transformation of energy during midlife does not occur smoothly, the personality may be seriously and permanently crippled. Jung was very successful in treating individuals who were having difficulties with this transition. He believed that the midlife crisis can only be resolved through *individuation*, or finding one's own way. The process begins by "turning our energy away from the mastery of the external world . . . and focusing on our inner selves. We feel inner urgings to listen to the unconscious, to learn about the potentials we have so far left unrealized. We begin to raise questions about the meaning of our lives" (Crain, 1980, p. 194).

An interesting aspect of Jung's theory is that it may explain why so many people experience "burnout" at middle age. It also suggests that burnout can be viewed as a positive rather than a negative development (Garden, 1991). Recent evidence suggests that, consistent with Jung's idea, as the midlife crisis is resolved both men and women experience an increase in positive emotions and renewed enthusiasm for their careers (O'Connor & Wolfe, 1991).

ERIKSON'S EIGHT STAGES OF PSYCHOSOCIAL DEVELOPMENT

The best-known alternative to Freud's psychosexual stages has been proposed by Erik Erikson, who was a student of Anna Freud. Erikson did not discount biological and psychosexual influences on the developing individual. But he emphasized the influence of society and culture. Thus, Erikson considered Freud's latency period to be a time of growth rather than stagnation, and he viewed adult development as important.

Erik H. Erikson
(1902-   )
introduced a lifespan
perspective in personality
development, which
encompasses eight
stages from infancy to
old age.
Harvard University Archives

Erikson (1963, 1968) believed that there are eight critical developmental issues in life. Each issue becomes the central focus of attention at a specific period, leading to eight stages of psycho*social* development. Each stage is named for the central issue at that period of life. Each issue involves conflict between an adaptive and a maladaptive way of handling an issue, such as between basic trust and mistrust. A conflict must be successfully resolved in the period in which it predominates in order for the person to be fully prepared to deal with the conflict that predominates next. Successful resolution is relative and involves developing a "favorable ratio" between the adaptive and maladaptive alternatives (such as more trust than mistrust).

In contrast to Freud's concept of psychosexual stages, Erikson's eight issues are present at birth and remain throughout the life span. For example, during the first year of life (Erikson's first stage), the child's major problems center on developing basic trust. However, the child is also struggling to develop autonomy—the central issue in Erikson's second stage—as when it wriggles to be set free if held too tightly. Similarly, adolescents are primarily concerned with identity, but they also encounter conflicts with autonomy when they struggle to be confident rather than self-conscious.

Erikson's concept of development is illustrated in Figure 4-1, a diagram of Erikson's psychosocial stages plotted against periods of physical and/or psychosexual development. Each vertical column represents one of the eight developmental issues. The period in life when that issue becomes the central conflict is highlighted in a darkly shaded box. The darkly shaded boxes form the diagonal of the diagram. To understand the form of one developmental issue—*identity versus role confusion*—in other periods of development, follow the fifth vertical column up from the oral-sensory period to maturity. The nature of each of the other seven developmental issues (that are not the central conflict during puberty and adolescence) is shown in the fifth horizontal row in the lightly shaded boxes.

Erikson's description of his eight stages of psychosocial development focuses on the way the person deals with the issue that is the central conflict of the stage.

Basic Trust versus Mistrust

Initially, an infant must develop sufficient trust to let his or her mother, the provider of food and comfort, out of sight without experiencing anxiety or rage. Such trust involves not only confidence in the predictability of the mother's behavior but also trust in oneself. This conflict occurs during Freud's oral stage.

Autonomy versus Shame and Doubt

Next, the child must develop a sense of autonomy, which is originally accomplished with respect to bladder and bowel control. This stage, not surprisingly, parallels Freud's anal stage. If the child fails to meet parental expectations for bladder and bowel control, shame and doubt may result. The shame of being unable to demonstrate the self-control demanded by parents becomes the basis for later problems with independence. In contrast, the

Developmental period

	1	2	3	4	5	6	7	8
VIII Maturity					Objective view of accomplishments vs. Distorted view of accomplishments*			Ego integrity vs. Despair
VII Adulthood					Role diversity vs. Burnout*		Generativity vs. Stagnation	
VI Young adulthood					Role acceptance vs. Role rejection*	Intimacy vs. Isolation		
V Puberty and adolescence	Temporal perspective vs. Time confusion	Self-certainty vs. Self-consciousness	Role-experimentation vs. Role fixation	Apprenticeship vs. Work paralysis	Indentity vs. Role confusion	Sexual polarization vs. Bisexual confusion	Leader- and followership vs. Authority confusion	Ideological commitment vs. Confusion of values
IV Latency				Industry vs. Inferiority	Task identification vs. Sense of futility			
III Locomotor-genital			Initiative vs. Guilt		Anticipation of roles vs. Role inhibition			
II Muscular-anal		Autonomy vs. Shame and Doubt			Will to be oneself vs. Self-doubt			
I Oral-sensory	Basic trust vs. Mistrust				Mutual recognition vs. Autistic isolation			

Psychosocial stages

Figure 4-1

Erikson's diagram of the eight stages of psychosocial development.

*Conflict conceptualized by authors, extrapolating from Erikson's theory.

Source: Adapted from *Childhood and Society* by E. H. Erikson, 1963, New York: W. W. Norton; and *Identity, Youth, and Crisis* by E. H. Erikson, 1968, New York: W. W. Norton.

experience of attaining adequate self-control with respect to toilet training results in feelings of autonomy in later life. Erikson (1963) noted:

> This stage . . . becomes decisive for the ratio of love and hate, cooperation and willfulness, freedom from self-expression and its suppression. From a sense of self-control without loss of self-esteem comes a lasting sense of goodwill and pride; from a sense of loss of self-control and of foreign overcontrol comes a lasting propensity for doubt and shame. (p. 254)

Initiative versus Guilt

Initiative versus guilt is the last conflict experienced by the preschool child. It occurs during Freud's phallic stage. The child must learn to control feelings of rivalry for the mother's attention and develop a sense of moral responsibility. At this stage, children initially indulge in fantasies of grandeur, but they may actually feel meek and dominated. To overcome the latter feelings, the child must learn to take role-appropriate initiative by finding pleasure in socially and culturally approved activities, such as creative play and caring for younger siblings.

Industry versus Inferiority

The conflict between industry and inferiority begins with school life. If children are to emerge as healthy individuals, at this stage they must apply themselves to their learning, begin to feel competent relative to peers, and face their own limitations. Note that these important developments occur during the time when, from Freud's point of view, the child is in a period of latency.

Identity versus Role Confusion

With the advent of puberty, the adolescent's attention turns to developing a sense of identity. For Erikson, **identity** refers to confidence that others see us as we see ourselves. The selection of an occupation or career is particularly important for identity. If an identity is not formed, **role confusion** may occur; it is characterized by an inability to select a career or to further educational goals and by overidentification with popular heroes or cliques. Today, role confusion often extends beyond adolescence and well into young adulthood (Cote & Levine, 1989). And even by young adulthood, identity formation is by no means complete. Rather, as predicted by Erikson's theory, it has been shown to be continually refined and expanded over the entire life span (Berzonsky, 1990).

Intimacy versus Isolation

For Erikson, **intimacy** is the capacity to commit to a relationship without losing one's own identity (Prager, 1986). By young adulthood, people are expected to be ready for true intimacy. They must develop cooperative social and occupational relationships with others and select a mate. If they cannot develop such relationships, they will remain isolated (cf. Storr, 1988).

There is evidence consistent with Erikson's claim that identity must *precede* intimacy. Adolescents and young adults without a firm sense of self have been found unable to commit to another person (Dyk & Adams, 1990).

Erikson (1963, p. 265) noted that when Freud was asked what a healthy person should be able to do well, he curtly answered: *"Lieben und Arbeiten"* (love and work). Erikson believed that this simple formula gets deeper as you think about it. For when Freud said "love" he meant *genital* love . . . ; when he said . . . work, he meant a general work-productiveness which would not preoccupy the individual to the extent that . . . [the individual loses the] right or capacity to be a genital and a loving being. . . . We cannot improve on the doctor's prescription for human dignity—and for democratic living.

Generativity versus Stagnation

According to Erikson, a mature person must do more than establish intimacy with others. The individual "needs to be needed" and to assist younger members of society. **Generativity** involves guiding the next generation; if it is not done, the individual may feel stagnant and personally impoverished.

Ego Integrity versus Despair

Despair in later life results from not suitably handling the preceding conflicts. When this occurs, people feel disgusted with themselves, and correctly realize that it is too late to start another life. Such individuals remain in a state of incurable remorse for the rest of their lives. In contrast, developing adaptive qualities in the other seven stages leads to becoming psychosocially adjusted and having a lasting sense of integrity. Erikson believed that everyone, regardless of capabilities, can achieve such adjustment.

A Paper-and-Pencil Measure of Psychosocial Development

The Inventory of Social Balance (ISB) is a recently published paper-and-pencil measure of the degree to which a person has resolved the eight Eriksonian conflicts (Domino & Affonso, 1990). Sample items from the ISB are shown in Table 4-4, which serves as an overview and summary of Erikson's theory.

Erikson believed that mature people must seek generativity, which involves concern for the development of the young.
Margaret W. Peterson/The Image Bank

Table 4-4
Sample items from the Inventory of Social Balance (ISB)

TASK	SAMPLE ITEM*
Trust	"I can usually depend on others."
Autonomy	"I am quite self-sufficient."
Initiative	"When faced with a problem, I am very good at developing various solutions."
Industry	"I genuinely enjoy work."
Identity	"In general, I know what I want out of life."
Intimacy	"I have experienced some very close relationships."
Generativity	"I derive a great deal of pleasure from watching a child master a new skill."
Ego Integrity	"Life has been good to me."

*Responses are made on a five-point scale, from strongly agree to strongly disagree.
Source: Domino & Affonso, 1990, p. 580.

OBJECT RELATIONS THEORIES

Since the 1950s, there has been a marked shift in psychoanalytic theorizing. The shift has been away from drives, and toward the patterns of thought and feeling that underlie interpersonal behavior. Such theorizing focuses on what psychoanalysts call *object relations*. In psychoanalysis, the term **object** generally refers to persons, not things. **Object relations** is currently seen as "a set of cognitive and affective processes that mediate interpersonal functioning in close relationships" (Westen, 1991a, p. 211).

The principal claim of object relations theories is that people develop internal working models of self and others. In turn, these models govern feelings and reactions toward the self (such as self-esteem) and feelings and reactions toward other people. The cognitive representations of particular people are called **object representations**.

A number of object relations theories exist, but none is complete. Current thinking about object relations can be traced to a variety of psychoanalysts, spanning a period of more than 50 years (Westen, 1991b). Our major aim has been to synthesize the work of a number of theorists into a coherent whole.

Two major differences between object relations theories and Freudian theory can be distinguished. One difference concerns the basic nature of human motivation. Instead of believing in drive reduction, object relations theorists hold that human beings are primarily motivated by the need to establish and maintain relationships with others. In other words, the primary need is for human contact (Cashdan, 1988). The second major difference is that all object relations theories focus on the early mother-child relationship

Melanie Klein
(1882-1960)
founded object relations
theory, focusing
attention on internal
representations of self
and others.
Wellcome Institute Library,
London

as the key to psychological growth (Sayers, 1991). In contrast, Freud emphasized the role of the father and thought that the major turning point in development occurred during the Oedipal years.

The first psychoanalyst to discuss object relations was Melanie Klein (1882–1960), an English psychiatrist and Freud's contemporary. Whereas Freud's ideas about children's development were based almost entirely on the recollections of his adult patients, Klein worked directly with children. Her clinical observations led her to the conclusion that children spend more energy on constructing their interpersonal worlds than they do trying to control libidinal impulses. Klein has been called "the mother of object relations" for her claim that the inner object world forms the basis for the human psyche (Cashdan, 1988).

Klein's ideas were picked up by W. R. D. Fairbairn. Fairbairn believed that *dependency on others* was the key to personality development. He suggested that there are three stages of dependency. During the first stage, *infantile dependence*, the child is "merged" with the mother. The middle or *transitional stage* is the bridge between stage one and stage three and is considered a lifelong process. It involves gradually breaking away from one-way dependence and moving toward *inter*dependency with others. During the third stage, *mature dependency*, the person's relationships with others are characterized by mutual exchange.

**Development of
the Self: Mahler's
Theory**

Margaret Mahler took a major step in advancing our understanding of object relations. Mahler, a pediatrician, became interested in the very close relationship between mother and child, which led to her becoming a psychoanalyst. She relied primarily on naturalistic observations to collect data about early childhood experiences to develop her theory. The observations were made in a large indoor playroom where children were free to use various toys. The room was divided by a low, fencelike barrier. Mothers sat and watched their children from the other side of the barrier. Research assistants interacted with both children and mothers and later made detailed records of their observations (Bergman & Ellman, 1985).

Mahler believed that personality begins in a state of fusion with other people, especially with the mother. Newborn infants do not appear to make a distinction between themselves and others. They consider *self* ("me") and *nonself* ("not me") the same. For example, infants appear to view their mothers as part of themselves. Mahler's theory focuses on the process by which the infant assumes its own physical and psychological identity, as distinct from that of other people (Mahler, 1968; Mahler, Bergman, & Pine, 1975). Development of the self involves separating from this fusion and becoming an individual independent of others.

Margaret Mahler
(1897-1985)
provided a detailed
analysis of object
relations development.
From the archives of the
American Psychiatric
Association, Washington,
D.C.

Mahler divided the child's development into three phases (stages): (1) normal autism, (2) normal symbiosis, and (3) separation-individuation. These phases are summarized in Table 4-5. The manner in which the child "negotiates" each of these phases determines to a great extent the nature of his or her interpersonal relations as an adult. This aspect is similar to Freud's scheme, in which the degree of success in getting through psychosexual stages

Table 4-5
Mahler's stages of object relations development

PHASE	APPROXIMATE TIME FRAME	DEVELOPMENTAL PROCESSES
Normal autism phase	Birth — 1st month	Completely within self; unresponsive to external stimuli
Normal symbiosis phase	2nd–3rd month	Undifferentiated self and onself; fusion with mother; vague awareness of need-satisfying objects
Separation-individuation phase		
Differentation subphase	4th–8th month	Initial attempts at separation; sensory exploration of external environment; frequent checking back to mother
Practicing subphase	9th to 15th–18th month	Locomotion allows further exploration of world; increased temporary separation from mother
Rapprochement subphase	15th–18th to 24th month	Conflict between independence and dependence; child wants to be with mother yet fears being engulfed by her; critical period for future development
Individuality and emotional object constancy subphase	24th month on	Development of permanent sense of self and permanent emotional and mental representations of others

of development influences later personality. The major difference is that, for Freud, personality development involves channeling sexual energy toward pleasurable goals. For Mahler, development involves the investment of psychic energy in relations with other people.

Normal Autism Phase
The first phase takes place in the first month of life. The infant is in a phase of **normal autism**—completely within itself, oblivious to an external world. The infant evaluates all experiences in terms of a simple instinctual dichotomy: pleasurable/good versus painful/bad. The infant's task in this totally narcissistic condition is to establish a homeostatic equilibrium in a new external environment (Goleman, 1988).

Normal Symbiosis Phase
During the second through fourth months of life, the infant enters the **normal symbiosis** phase. (*Symbiosis* refers to two different organisms living together in intimate association.) The infant is still in an undifferentiated state, fused

with its mother, and does not yet distinguish between self and nonself. However, the child is vaguely aware of the need-satisfying object—the mother. It is critical for later development that the infant derive satisfaction from the symbiotic relation with her. This temporary fusion serves as the basis for the process of becoming different and separating from the mother. The latter process cannot fully occur without prior satisfaction in normal symbiosis.

The normal autistic and normal symbiotic phases do not involve object relations per se. What the infant experiences in these phases are the prerequisites for the development of object relations. How the infant has fared in them affects the critical separation-individuation process.

Separation-Individuation Phase

The development of true object relations takes place during the **separation-individuation** phase. This third and final phase of the developmental sequence begins about the fifth month and in some sense continues throughout one's life. It reflects every person's conflict between the desire for autonomy and the desire to be linked with others.

Separation-individuation involves two developmental processes that are closely related and occur simultaneously. **Separation** is the process whereby the child achieves *intrapsychic* distinctiveness from the mother. In other words, the child comes to clearly differentiate intrapsychic *representations* (as opposed to the actual objects) of the self and others (Tuttman, 1988). **Individuation** is an early stage of identity. "To be individuated is a feeling *that I am*—an early awareness of a sense of being, of entity—while identity is the later awareness of *who I am*" (St. Clair, 1986, p. 106). Mahler divided the separation-individuation phase into four subphases: differentiation, practicing, rapprochement, and individuality and emotional object constancy.

Differentiation subphase

Beginning in the fourth or fifth month through about the eighth month, the infant begins the separation-individuation process in the first subphase, **differentiation**. Here "infants take their first tentative steps toward breaking away, in a bodily sense, from their hitherto completely passive . . . stage of dual unity with the mother" (Mahler et al., 1975, p. 55). Infants who experienced optimal satisfaction in the symbiotic phase will freely explore their environment. This exploration includes being curious and fascinated with other people, rather than experiencing anxiety around strangers. Children are not completely independent of their mother, however. They can be observed periodically checking to see whether mother is nearby as they tentatively venture into the external world.

Practicing subphase

The next subphase—**practicing**—takes place from about 9 months to about 15 to 18 months. Here, children expand their horizons even more. They become physically able to explore the external environment as they begin to locomote, first by crawling and climbing, and finally by walking upright. During this period, the child "appears to be at the peak point of his belief in his own magic omnipotence, which is still to a considerable extent derived from his sense of sharing his mother's magic powers" (Mahler, 1968, p. 20). The child begins to venture farther and farther away from his or her mother but occasionally returns for a boost of emotional support.

Rapprochement subphase   The third subphase, **rapprochement**, begins at about 15 to 18 months and ends at about 24 months. It is characterized by ambivalence about separating from the mother—a struggle between still wanting to be close to her and being afraid of being engulfed by her. As the child becomes more aware of separation and experiences greater separation anxiety, he or she has an increased desire to be with the mother, share with her, and experience her love. The child alternately "shadows" the mother and flees from her. Mahler considered this subphase to be critical for future personality development. The child must develop a *rapprochement* (a coming together) between the need for independence and dependence. To develop rapprochement, however, requires that the mother continue to provide needed emotional support while allowing the child to be independent. Failure to permit independence often results in the child's remaining attached to the mother, unable to become interested in activities or other people (Eagle, 1984).

Individuality and emotional object constancy subphase   The fourth and final subphase of separation-individuation—**individuality and emotional object constancy**—begins around the third year of life. To some degree, it continues during later development because the process of developing an independent identity is never fully completed. In this subphase, the child achieves a defined lifelong individuality and sense of object permanency, which involves developing mental representations of people (especially the mother) so that they are constantly with the child *symbolically*. Because the mother's love and approval have been internalized, the child can be away from the mother without having to give up a healthy degree of emotional dependence on her love and approval. For example, while at nursery school, a child may help another child and feel good about doing so. This good feeling comes from the mental image of the mother approving of such behavior.

Splitting   The concept of *splitting* plays a central role in several object relations theories (Cashdan, 1988; Fairbairn, 1952; Winnicott, 1971) and also helps to put Mahler's theory in a larger perspective. **Splitting** is the mental separation of objects into their "good" and "bad" aspects.

The first splitting occurs because the mother is experienced as inconsistent. Sometimes she is "good," meeting all the infant's needs. Sometimes she is "bad," by failing to respond as completely or as quickly as the infant wishes. The infant is not mentally equipped to think of the same person as good *and* bad, and is thus faced with a dilemma. The dilemma is resolved by dividing the mother into good and bad components, and *mentally splitting one from the other*. In this way, infants are able to maintain their dependent ties without constantly feeling threatened.

Splitting is not by itself abnormal, nor is the process limited to the mother or to early childhood. Rather, carving experience up evaluatively, into *good versus bad*, is a pervasive way of processing information for adults as well as children (Osgood, Suci, & Tannenbaum, 1957). Thus, the critical question is not whether there is splitting—there invariably is. The question is, "How is initial splitting resolved in later development?"

Reintegration versus Fragmentation

When the beliefs of several object relations theorists are integrated, the resultant developmental path of splitting is an eight-stage process. The stages are diagrammed in Figure 4-2.

Stage I. This is Mahler's normal autism phase. Experience is undifferentiated. This is presumed to be the original state.

Stage II. Vague awareness of a possible differentiation of experience begins by the second month. This is Mahler's normal symbiosis phase.

Stage III. There is a dramatic split of experience between "self" and "other."

Stage IV. The "other," mainly composed of mother at this stage, is split into good and bad. This is the "good mother"/"bad mother" split referred to by many object relations theorists.

Stage V. "Self" is also split into good and bad, as a result of mother having been partly "incorporated" into the self.

Stage VI. This is the critical juncture for all later object relationships. Essentially there are two ways to go.

> VI*a*. Mothering has been "good enough." The individual begins to fuse (co-accept) both aspects of mother.

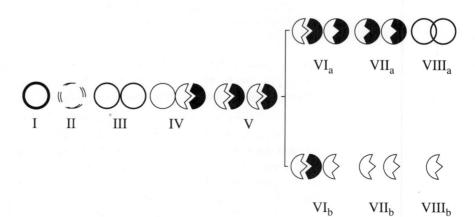

Figure 4-2
Stages of splitting.

VI*b*. If the mother is very rejecting or extremely *un*gratifying, then it becomes necessary to push the bad mother completely out of awareness. Should this happen, the individual will have trouble dealing with self-splitting, and is in for considerable trouble in all of his or her future relationships (Kernberg, 1975, 1976; Kohut, 1977, 1984).

Stage VII. The path is now set toward (*a*) integration or (*b*) complete fragmentation.

VII*a*. Acceptance of mother's dual nature permits acceptance of one's own dual nature.

VII*b*. Bad mother and bad self are now both repressed (pushed out of awareness).

Stage VIII. This is the terminal condition of each path.

VIII*a*. The person is now capable of relationships characterized by mutual interdependence. This is psychological maturity.

VIII*b*. The person is unable to deal with others in cooperative, sustaining ways. Neither self nor any other can be accepted. The individual is prone to *projective identifications* (which will be discussed in Chapters 5 and 6).

SUMMARY   1. Freudian theory holds that human beings are primarily motivated by the sexual drive and secondarily by the aggressive drive. For Freud, "sexual" is synonymous with pleasure.

2. People have a fixed amount of psychic energy that they cathect (invest) in the mental images of people, things, or activities. Psychic energy builds up within the personality and is experienced as tension that periodically must be released. Tension release is pleasurable.

3. Many psychoanalysts disagree with Freud's emphasis on the sexual drive. Adler considered strivings for superiority to be the dominant human motive.

4. Personality development is a central issue in psychoanalysis, although psychoanalysts differ in the importance they place on biological versus social factors and early versus later experiences.

5. Freud described four basic stages of psychosexual development. The stages are named after the erogenous zone that predominates at various ages. At each stage, one erogenous zone is the focus of the libido (sexual energy). Each stage has a conflict that must be successfully resolved in order to proceed to the next stage. When people have difficulty moving to the next stage (because of frustration or overindulgence in the present stage), they leave some libido fixated at that stage. Fixation results in adult character types.

6. In the oral stage (the first year of life), pleasure is derived from sucking, eating, and biting. The conflict is weaning. The oral character centers on dependency. Post-Freudians have broadened Freud's theoretical ideas about the oral stage to focus on its social aspects.

7. In the anal stage (second and third years), pleasure focuses on the retention and expulsion of feces. Toilet training is the conflict. The anal character involves three basic traits: orderliness, stinginess, and obstinacy.

8. In the phallic stage (ages 4 and 5), pleasure focuses in the genital region. The Oedipus complex, the conflict in the phallic stage, involves the child's sexual attraction to the opposite-sexed parent. Freud considered resolution of this conflict to be critical for normal personality development. Horney, among other psychoanalysts, provided alternative (less sexual) explanations for the child/parent rivalries observed during the phallic stage.

9. Between the phallic stage and puberty, the child enters a period of latency that involves no psychosexual development. Post-Freudians stress important social developments that occur at this time.

10. The genital stage begins at puberty and lasts through adulthood. Again the libido is focused in the genital area, but now it is directed toward heterosexual rather than autoerotic pleasure.

11. Erikson's eight psychosocial stages provide an alternative to Freud's developmental scheme.

12. The term "object relations" refers to one's relationships with persons, not things. Object relations are mediated by intrapsychic images of ourselves and significant others. This idea was first introduced by Melanie Klein.

13. Mahler elaborated in detail the process of the child's separation from the mother.

14. According to several object relations theories, splitting (separating of good and bad components of objects) invariably occurs. Whether splitting ultimately leads to reintegration or complete fracturing will greatly influence the person's later relationships.

The Organization of Personality

It is a shattering experience for anyone seriously committed to the Western tradition of morality and rationality to take a steadfast, unflinching look at what Freud has to say. It is humiliating to be compelled to admit the grossly seamy side of so many grand ideals . . . To experience Freud is to partake a second time of the forbidden fruit. (Brown, 1959, p. xi)

In Chapter 4, you were treated to a taste of "forbidden fruit": Freud's ideas about basic pleasure-seeking motives in general and infantile sexuality in particular. In this chapter, our exploration of the irrational and even immoral aspects of human personality continues. We begin by discussing the central concept of unconscious motivation.

Freud was not the first to suggest the unconscious; the idea goes back to at least the 13th century (Vermorel, 1990). But Freud's emphasis on aspects of personality of which people are unaware has had an enormous influence on the scientific study of personality. It has also affected everyday ideas about the human condition.

Freud noted that humans had suffered three blows to their egocentrism. The first blow was dealt by Copernicus, who declared that the Earth is not the center of the universe. Next, Darwin said that humans are merely animals among animals. Finally, Freud himself revealed the unconscious part of the mind; he made people aware of how much they are influenced by hidden internal forces that may be beyond their control.

THREE LEVELS OF CONSCIOUSNESS

Freud divided the mind into three levels of awareness: conscious, preconscious, and unconscious. The **conscious** includes what we are aware of at a given point in time. This definition is close to the everyday use of the term. However, Freud contended that only a small portion of a person's thoughts, images, and memories is conscious. The Freudian mind, like an iceberg, is nine-tenths below the surface.

The **preconscious** includes thoughts of which we are not immediately aware (conscious) but that can easily be brought to awareness. You may have had the experience of concentrating on a topic, as in an intense conversation, and suddenly finding yourself thinking about a completely unrelated topic. These unrelated thoughts have been in your preconscious.

Finally, there is the **unconscious**, the dominant part of the mind. According to Freud, most behavior is motivated by forces of which the person is totally unaware. They are kept out of consciousness. These unconscious thoughts enter consciousness only in disguised or symbolic form.

JUNG'S DIVISION OF THE PERSONALITY

Jung also divided the personality into three levels of consciousness: conscious ego, personal unconscious, and collective unconscious. The **conscious ego** includes perceptions, thoughts, feelings, and memories of which a person is aware. It is essentially equivalent to Freud's conscious.

The **personal unconscious** contains some mental images that we are not immediately aware of but that can readily become part of the conscious ego.

In some cases, we are unaware of this unconscious material because we are attending to other matters. In other cases, images in the personal unconscious are actively repressed because they are threatening to the conscious ego.

Jung's personal unconscious has features similar to Freud's preconscious and unconscious. However, Jung's ideas about the personal unconscious diverge from Freud's in three important ways. First, Jung rejected the idea that the unconscious is "monstrous" (Roazen, 1975). Second, Jung believed that the personal unconscious not only stores past experiences but also anticipates the future. Third, Jung argued that the personal unconscious serves an adaptive function by balancing out conscious attitudes that lean too heavily in one direction. This adjustment is accomplished by allowing the appropriate opposite tendency to occur in dreams and fantasies (Jung, 1969).

Jung believed that personality is more than just a product of personal experiences and memories. Individuals also think and act in ways shaped by experiences common to all humans throughout the evolution of the species. Jung called the part of personality containing these ancestral memories the **collective unconscious**. Jung considered the collective unconscious to be the dominant aspect of personality. This concept has no direct parallel in Freud's theory and is Jung's most original and controversial idea (Badalamenti, 1988).

The collective unconscious contains **archetypes**, or predispositions to think and act in particular ways. Archetypes are inherited, general tendencies to form representations of mythological themes. The specific content of each theme (archetype) varies considerably according to time and place but always retains its fundamental pattern. How a person's thoughts and actions are influenced by any given archetype depends on where and when the person lives. The *Hero* archetype, for example, could assume the form of a medieval knight, a Chinese warlord, an explorer, a basketball player, a civil rights leader, or an astronaut. The Hero archetype can be considered a flexible mold underlying the idea of hero; the archetype requires a culture to fill it with a myth (Storr & Kermode, 1973).

Jung devoted much of his career to discovering the archetypal images that frequently appear in myths from diverse cultures, in dreams and fantasies (including his own), and in art. We have already mentioned the Hero archetype. It embodies the generally agreed upon meanings of heroism: courage, vanquishing evil or the unknown, and serving noble ends, often for the good of others.

Mother is an archetype that may be elicited by any "mothering" figure. This includes real people, such as one's mother or grandmother, and mother symbols, such as the Virgin Mary, one's alma mater (Latin for "other mother"), the Church, and Mother Earth. The Mother archetype has a dual nature: positive (good, light) and negative (evil, dark). The Evil Mother often appears in myths and fairy tales as the Wicked Witch (Ulanov & Ulanov, 1987).

The *Shadow* archetype represents the "dark side" of personality, the side people do not like to acknowledge in themselves. It is the model for people's animal instincts and for evil and unacceptable ideas. Shadow images appear in myths as evil, the devil, monsters, and demons (Bly, 1988).

Animus is the archetype of the "masculine" aspects of women; *Anima* is the archetype of the "feminine" aspects of men. (Jung, like Freud, believed in the bisexuality of human personality.) The difference between Animus and Anima is that Animus produces *opinions* (solid conviction) in women: Anima produces *moods* (often expressed in sudden changes) in men.

Persona is the archetype for the public mask. It is the "front" an individual presents to others. The danger of Persona exerting too strong an influence on one's personality is seen when people actually believe they are who they pretend to be.

Jung's ideas about archetypes and the collective unconscious came from his extensive study of universal myths and symbols. He and others found that there are indeed common themes in myths and fairy tales across cultures separated geographically and temporally (Campbell, 1988).

One source of indirect support for Jung's idea is related to the development of phobias (irrational fears). Martin Seligman (1971) noted that certain phobias seem to be learned quickly and are difficult to eliminate. Further, people are phobic only about a limited number of things, including fear of the dark, snakes, insects, high places, and open spaces (Spiegler & Liebert, 1970). These stimuli are not, under normal circumstances, objectively threatening, yet people often report being afraid of them. In contrast, Seligman (1971) pointed out that "only rarely, if ever, do we have . . . electric

Star Wars is a mythical tale in which each of the main characters represents an archetype. Darth Vader represents the *Shadow* and Ben Kenobi represents the *Wise Old Man.*
20TH Century-Fox Film Corporation/Photofest

outlet phobias, or hammer phobias, even though these things are likely to be associated with trauma in our world" (p. 312). Possibly, the events that give rise to phobias are "related to the survival of the human species through the long course of evolution" (p. 312). Humans may be *prepared* to fear such species-survival–based events. This conclusion bears on Jung's notion of a collective unconscious.

> Does preparedness range beyond simple symbolic associations? Are there ways of thinking in which humans are particularly prepared to engage? . . . Are there stories that . . . [humans are] prepared to formulate and accept? If so, a *meaningful version of the . . . [collective unconscious] lurks close behind"* (pp. 317-318; italics added).

ID, EGO, AND SUPEREGO: THREE FUNCTIONS OF PERSONALITY

Initially, Freud organized personality in terms of levels of consciousness, emphasizing the unconscious. Later, around 1920, he revised his theory, providing another division of personality: id, ego, and superego. Functions formerly relegated to the unconscious were primarily taken over by the id, which Freud saw as operating totally at the unconscious level. He proposed that the ego and superego function at all three levels of awareness, but mainly at the unconscious level. The three personality functions in relation to the three levels of awareness are shown schematically in Figure 5-1.

The id, ego, and superego can be viewed three ways. First, they are theoretical constructs; they do not physically exist within the brain. (Freud did believe that all mental functions would be ultimately tied to neural structures, but his theory does not depend on discovering specific structures.)

Figure 5-1
The relationship of Freud's personality functions to the levels of awareness.

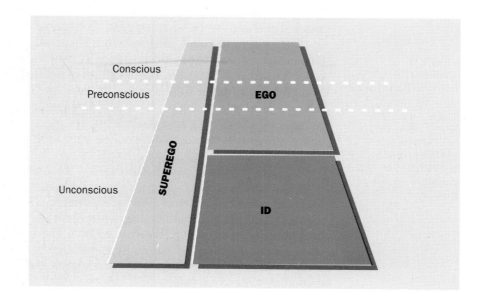

Second, although the id, ego, and superego are often referred to as structures, it is more useful to think of them as *functions* or *aspects* of the personality. They represent the desiring/pleasure-seeking (id), realistic/rational (ego), and moral/ideal (superego) parts of human behavior.

Third, the three personality aspects are often discussed *anthropomorphically* — that is, by giving them human capabilities. For example, "The id *demands* immediate gratification" and "The superego *inhibits* the id's *desire* for immediate gratification." Psychoanalysts do not actually view the id, ego, and superego as little people inside us, but it is easy to talk and write about them *as if* they were little people (as you will see in the next few pages). Id, ego, and superego are merely convenient ways of conceptualizing complex psychological functions.

Id   The term *id* (which rhymes with *kid*) comes from the German word *es*, meaning "it." The **id** is the original system of personality; it contains all psychological aspects present at birth. The id is a reservoir for all drives and derives power directly from bodily needs and processes. As bodily needs, such as hunger and thirst, build up, they have to be satisfied. The resulting increase in tension must be discharged. When the id governs this discharge, gratification is *immediate*. The id cannot tolerate any delay in gratification. The id is regulated by the **pleasure principle**, which demands immediate tension reduction — in other words, instant pleasure and no pain.

The id uses two basic techniques to reduce tension: *reflex action* and *primary process*. At its most primitive level, the id works by reflex action. It reacts automatically and immediately to internal and external irritants to the body. Tension or distress from the irritants is thus quickly removed. Reflex actions include inborn mechanisms such as sneezing, blinking, and coughing.

The id cannot tolerate any delay of gratification or any tension. Thus, we would expect very young children to "cry" the instant an appetite or need arises. This seems to be what happens. (Infants, of course, can satisfy some of their own needs, such as urination.) The child may require something tangible from the outside world, such as food or water. If the needed object is not immediately available, the id's **primary process** forms a *mental image* of it. When the infant is hungry, for instance, the id's primary process can instantly produce an image of food. This experience is called **wish fulfillment** because, for the moment, the desire is fulfilled. Adult dreams in which a fond desire is met (such as a sexual encounter with a movie star) are remnants of infant wish fulfillment.

Primary process is a crude mechanism. No distinction is made between what is actually required and a mere mental image of what is required. Thus, food and a mental picture of food are equivalent. The id is satisfied with the image, but the image obviously does not actually reduce tension. One cannot long survive on mental pictures of food. If the infant's needs were met immediately, as they were before birth, primary process would be satisfactory. But inevitably, gratification must be delayed. No mother can be available constantly to feed her baby.

Infants' capacities to tolerate delay of gratification develop as they become aware of a separate external world. Children grow aware of something that is "not me" that must be taken into account and considered apart from, but interrelated with themselves. This occurs with the development of the second aspect of personality, the ego.

Ego   The **ego** "borrows" some of the id's psychic energy for its own functions. At birth, all the child's psychic energy is contained in the id, where it is used for primary processes. Therefore, the energy for ego functions must come from the id. Because there is only a limited amount of psychic energy, transfer of psychic energy to the ego means that less energy remains for id functions. One consequence is that the child becomes more willing to wait for gratification.

In contrast to the id's pleasure principle, the ego is governed by the **reality principle**. This principle postpones the discharge of energy until an appropriate situation or object in the real world appears. The ego does not challenge the id's pleasure-seeking motivation. Instead, it temporarily *suspends pleasure for the sake of reality*.

The ego is the representative of the external world. Whereas the id's primary process identifies the object or situation necessary to satisfy a particular need (such as an image of food), the ego's **secondary process** creates a *strategy* for obtaining the object or situation (such as going to the cookie jar). The ego, then, is characterized by realistic thinking and problem solving. It is the seat of intellectual processes. Daydreaming is an example of a secondary process and illustrates the reality-bound nature of the ego. People enjoy the pleasurable fantasy of a daydream, but they do not mistake the fantasy for reality as they do with a nocturnal dream (which is a primary process).

Human beings function both as individuals and as members of society. To do so, they must learn not only to deal with the direct constraints of *physical reality* but also to follow *social norms and prohibitions*. Further, they must conform to society's "laws," even in the absence of external monitors or threats of apprehension, punishment, or failure. Around age three or four, children begin to evaluate their own behavior independently of immediate threat or reward. This is the function of the third aspect of personality, the superego.

Superego   The **superego** is the internal representative of the values of parents and society. It strives for the *ideal* rather than the real. The superego judges an act as right or wrong, as consistent or inconsistent with moral values, independent of its usefulness.

When our actions and thoughts are acceptable, we experience pride, satisfaction, and worthiness. When our behavior is unacceptable, we experience guilt.

Superego functions can be divided into two spheres: conscience and ego ideal. The **conscience** fosters morally right behavior. It does so in two ways:

(1) by inhibiting id impulses for pleasure and (2) by persuading the ego to attend to moral rather than realistic goals. The **ego ideal** promotes idealistic and perfectionistic goals (Edwards, 1987).

Until this century, ethical or moral behavior was generally presumed to come from a "still, small voice" provided by God (Brown, 1965). In contrast, Freud argued that moral conscience is acquired after birth. The superego develops through the process of **incorporation**: "taking in" the values of parents in a manner analogous to the way we take in food. Incorporation begins about the fourth year of life and is closely related to the resolution of the Oedipus complex. Through defensive identification, the child acquires the moral values of the same-sexed parent. Children also come to value both parents because of the love, warmth, and comfort the parents provide. By association, they also come to value their parents' standards and ideals.

Interaction Among the Id, Ego, and Superego

To summarize the Freudian view of development, at birth only the id exists. Later, in response to the demands of reality, the ego develops. Finally, the superego emerges as the societal representative in the personality. When all three aspects have developed, the psychic energy that once belonged solely to the id is divided among the id, ego, and superego and fluctuates among them. The ego serves as a mediator among three basic forces: (1) the demands of the id, (2) the requirements of reality, and (3) the limitations imposed by the superego (Figure 5-2). The ego ensures that instinctual needs are met in a realistic and socially approved manner.

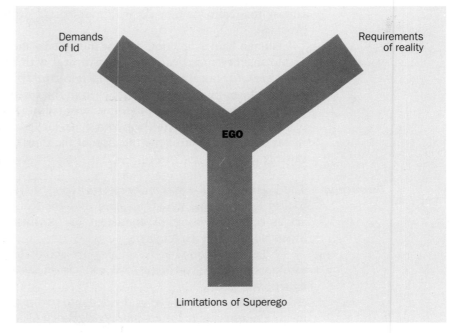

Figure 5-2
The ego as the mediator of personality.

Table 5-1
Possible conflicts among the aspects of personality

CONFLICT	EXAMPLE
Id versus Ego	Choosing between a small immediate reward and a larger reward that requires some period of waiting (i.e., delay of gratification)
Id versus Superego	Deciding whether to return the difference when you are overpaid or undercharged
Ego versus Superego	Choosing between acting in a realistic way (e.g., telling a "white lie") and adhering to a potentially costly or unrealistic standard (e.g., always telling the truth)
Id and Ego versus Superego	Deciding whether to retaliate against the attack of a weak opponent or to turn the other cheek
Id and Superego versus Ego	Deciding whether to act in a realistic way that conflicts with both your desires and your moral convictions (e.g., the decision faced by devout Roman Catholics regarding use of contraceptive devices)
Ego and Superego versus Id	Choosing whether to act on the impulse to steal something you want and cannot afford; the ego would presumably be increasingly involved in such a conflict as the probability of being apprehended increased

Intrapsychic conflict arises when the aims of one aspect of personality are at odds with the aims of one or both of the other aspects. Most often, intrapsychic conflict erupts because of id demands pressing for immediate satisfaction. But the aims of all three aspects of the personality can be in conflict (Rangell, 1988). Examples appear in Table 5-1.

How are intrapsychic conflicts resolved? Logically, three possibilities exist: (1) completely eliminating the drive, (2) directly expressing the drive, or (3) redirecting the drive. It is assumed that a drive can never be completely eliminated; it can be banished from consciousness but not from the total personality. Direct expression rarely occurs; if an id drive were allowed total expression, the ego would be overwhelmed with excitation and the person would feel intense anxiety. (The defensive processes the ego uses to prevent this anxiety will be discussed shortly.) Therefore, most intrapsychic conflicts are dealt with by redirection of a drive. This entails a *compromise* between the personality functions involved. For instance, in an id-ego conflict over the desire to hit someone with whom you are angry, you may choose to say something nasty to the person.

Intrapsychic conflicts are part of normal personality functioning. Their resolution is a defensive process performed by the ego, which requires psychic energy. The more successfully the ego minimizes intrapsychic conflicts, the more energy is "left over" for the ego's higher mental functions, such as problem solving and creative endeavors.

EGO PSYCHOLOGY: EXPANDING THE FUNCTIONS OF THE EGO

According to Freud, the id is the dominant force in personality. A major role of the ego, and to some extent of the superego, is ensuring that id impulses are held in check. Without the ego, personality would be overwhelmed by instinctual desires.

As psychoanalysis developed, the id-dominated view of the dynamics of personality began to fade. A conflict-ridden personality was a reasonable explanation of the development of psychopathology, but it was inadequate to explain normal, adaptive personality. From this perceived deficit, **ego psychology** arose as a new branch of psychoanalysis (Blanck & Blanck, 1974).

Ego psychology emphasizes (1) *adaptive control* rather than defense; (2) *general motives*, such as mastery and competence, rather than limiting itself to sexual and aggressive drives; and (3) *conscious determinism* rather than unconscious determinism (Klein, 1976; Levine & Slap, 1985).

Heinz Hartmann is considered the founder of ego psychology. He believed that the ego develops partially independent of the id and remains so. Hartmann (1958, 1964) acknowledged the existence of and necessity for conflict between the ego and the id and acknowledged the defensive operations of the ego. But he believed that there is also a "conflict-free ego sphere." This part of the ego is not at odds with the id, the superego, or external reality.

Ego psychology is concerned with how the ego adaptively deals with reality through perception, thinking, language, creative production, attention, and memory. In this regard, ego psychology comes closer to mainstream psychology than classical psychoanalytic theory. It also provides a more complete account of the full range of psychological processes (Friedman, 1989; Loewenstein, Newmann, Schur, & Solnit, 1966; Siskind, 1987).

Hartmann (1951) believed that ego psychology should investigate "how psychological conflict and 'peaceful' internal development mutually facilitate and hamper each other" (p. 368). The emphasis in ego psychology is clearly on the *conscious, normal, coping* functions of personality. This contrasts with the emphasis in classical, id-dominated Freudian psychoanalysis on unconscious, abnormal functions.

Heinz Hartmann (1894-1970) emphasized the adaptive functions of the ego in the normal personality.
UPI/Bettmann Newsphotos

Fantasy, for example, is a secondary process that can have definite adaptive features. Hartmann (1951) contended that "fantasy can be fruitful even in scientific thinking, which is the undisputed domain of rational thinking" (p. 372). Other ego psychologists, such as Ernest Kris (1950), had

Robert White
(1904-   )
focused on competence
as opposed to drive
reduction within the
framework of ego
psychology.
Photo by Paul Koby

an additional idea. They argued that the role of fantasy in creative and artistic thinking can be fully explained *only* if the ego is considered an autonomous part of the personality that can freely make and relinquish its own cathexes (investments).

Robert White developed an ego psychology theory in which *competence*, not drive reduction, is the major motivation. Sex and aggression, the primary drives in Freudian theory, are satisfied by drive reduction. In contrast, competence drives are satisfied by *stimulation* of the drive. **Competence** means an organism's "fitness or ability to carry out those transactions with the environment which result in its maintaining itself, growing, and flourishing." White (1959, 1963) buttressed his ideas with research showing the importance of motives like exploration, manipulation, and curiosity in human behavior.

The difference between White's ego psychology and Freud's "id psychology" is illustrated by White's reconceptualization of Freud's psychosexual stages. White (1960) traced the development of competence, in its various forms, just as Freud did with the sexual drive. Table 5-2 summarizes White's view of development. Note the similarities with the psychosocial stages described by Erikson, who is also considered an ego psychologist (see Chapter 4).

LEVELS OF OBJECT RELATIONS

Object relations theorists believe that people can be understood in terms of the *level of object relations* they have reached (Blatt & Lerner, 1983; Hamilton, 1989: Westen, 1991b). Recall from Chapter 4 that the basic idea behind object relations theories is that we have internal working models of self and others; these internal "objects" greatly influence our feelings about ourselves and our dealings with other people. The more advanced one's level of object relations development, the better will be both one's self-concept and one's interpersonal relationships. Consistent with this view, the level of adults' object relations has been shown to be a good predictor of their interpersonal functioning (Mayman, 1967; Piper et al., 1991).

Westen (1991b) has suggested that a person's level of object relations has four aspects: (1) complexity of representations, (2) emotional tone, (3) capacity for emotional investment, and (4) understanding of social causality. Westen's scheme involves five levels, as shown in Table 5-3 (pp. 96-97). Note how, at any given level, the four components fit together as a coherent whole. Also note that very few people are likely to operate at level 5—at least not all the time.

One appealing feature of this object relations model is that it can map level of object relations to the type of psychopathology to which a person may be susceptible. Individuals at level 1 are likely to be autistic or schizophrenic. Individuals at level 2 have borderline personality disorders. Those at level 3 will tend to have anxiety disorders. Those at levels 4 and 5 are functioning without interpersonal psychopathology.

Table 5-2
White's reconceptualization of Freud's psychosexual stages

FREUD'S STAGE	FREUD'S THEME	WHITE'S THEME (COMPETENCY)	EXAMPLE OF COMPETENCY
Oral stage	Feeding	*Coping with environment*	Infant playing with any and all objects it comes in contact with
Anal stage	Elimination	*Independence*	Two- to three-year-olds' negativism: not wanting to do what they are told and wanting to do things on their own
Phallic stage	Oedipal situation	*Locomotion*	Moving about freely and at will
		Language	Communicating needs verbally and influencing other people through language
		Imagination	Taking on imaginary roles, especially those of adults
Latency period	No psycho-sexual development	*Social skills*	Making and keeping friends; coping with social rejection
		Meeting realistic challenges	Doing well with schoolwork and athletics
Genital stage	Heterosexual behavior	*Sense of identity*	Defining oneself in terms of strengths and weaknesses and developing self-confidence
		Life skills	Developing intellectual skills that will be used in lifelong pursuits

ANXIETY AND DEFENSE

Anxiety is all too familiar to each of us. In his early theorizing (in the 1890s), Freud suggested that repressed libido is transformed into anxiety. Some 30 years later, Freud changed his focus and stated: *anxiety leads to repression*. This latter view is held by most psychoanalysts today. As one contemporary analyst put it: "Anxiety . . . is generally assumed to represent the ego's response to the threatened breakthrough of unacceptable impulses or an anticipated loss of an object necessary for the maintenance of inner stability" (Cooper, 1985, p. 1397).

Put in a slightly different way, anxiety can be viewed as a *signal* of impending danger. The source of the danger can be either external or internal. But, as you probably can guess by now, Freud thought that anxiety is usually the result of an id impulse seeking expression. Why is this dangerous?

When the infant is incapable of delaying gratification—before the ego develops—he or she is occasionally overwhelmed by the tension created by an id impulse. This may occur when there is no one around to satisfy a basic drive (such as hunger). Such trauma is accompanied by an intense feeling called **primary anxiety**. Children later learn to anticipate the danger and to react with *signal anxiety*. **Signal anxiety** is less intense than the primary anxiety that accompanied the actual traumatic experience (no food). It warns (signals) the ego to somehow prevent the recurrence of the trauma and the accompanying intense stimulation. The ego is "motivated" to deal with the danger because anxiety is unpleasant.

Freudian theory distinguishes three types adult anxiety:

1. **Neurotic anxiety** results from an id-ego conflict. The id seeks to discharge an impulse, and the ego tries to impose reality restraints on the impulse. An example would be fending off your impulse to respond angrily when a professor criticizes you in class.
2. **Moral anxiety** is generated by an id-superego conflict. Here the id impulse (such as to shoplift) is in opposition to the moral and ideal standards of society ("Thou shalt not steal") and is experienced by the individual as *guilt* or *shame*.
3. **Objective anxiety** is produced when a realistic, external threat is present, such as a fire or a mugger.

In each case, anxiety signals impending danger. In objective anxiety, the danger is external. It can be dealt with by taking realistic steps to eliminate or reduce the actual threat. Neurotic and moral anxiety are due to an impending *intrapsychic* danger. They must be coped with by internal means — namely, the defense mechanisms of the ego.

Ego Defense Mechanisms

Defense mechanisms are *unconscious* ego processes that keep disturbing and unacceptable thoughts from being directly expressed. *What* is being defended against can be an impulse, an object loss, or a failure experience (Cooper, 1988). In learning about defense mechanisms, it is helpful to examine them separately. Bear in mind, though, that people rarely defend themselves against anxiety with a single mechanism; typically, defense mechanisms operate in combination. Further, as will become apparent, there is considerable overlap in the way defense mechanisms protect the ego from overwhelming anxiety.

Repression

Repression involves actively and totally excluding threatening thoughts from consciousness. This does not mean that the thoughts are no longer influencing the individual. Quite the contrary. Repressed thoughts exert a powerful influence on behavior, as do all unconscious impulses. However, because they are unconscious, the person is not directly aware of them. Repression is characterized by a continual struggle to contain primitive desires.

Like all defense mechanisms, repression may occur in "healthy" or normal individuals. A price is always paid when defense mechanisms are operative, however. Psychic energy used to defend the ego is unavailable for more adaptive functions such as intellectual and social pursuits. In the case of repression, the price is particularly severe. Repressed impulses may be

Table 5-3
Five levels in the development of object relations

	COMPLEXITY OF REPRESENTATIONS OF PEOPLE	EMOTIONAL TONE OF REPRESENTATIONS OF PEOPLE
LEVEL 1	People are not clearly differentiated; confusion of points of view.	Malevolent representations: gratuitous violence or gross negligence by significant others.
LEVEL 2	Simple, unidimensional representations; focus on actions; traits are global and univalent.	Representation of relationships as hostile, empty, or capricious but not profoundly malevolent; profound loneliness or disappointment in relationships.
LEVEL 3	Minor elaboration of mental life or personality.	Mixed representations with mildly negative tone.
LEVEL 4	Expanded appreciation of complexity of subjective experience and personality dispositions; absence of representations integrating life history, complex subjectivity, and personality processes.	Mixed representations with neutral or balanced tone.
LEVEL 5	Complex representations, indicating understanding of interaction of enduring and momentary psychological experience; understanding of personality as system of processes interacting with each other and the environment.	Predominantly positive representations; benign and enriching interactions.

Source: Modified from Westen (1991b)

healthy or adaptive, yet they may be permanently excluded from the development of the personality. For example, exclusion of all aggressive impulses is likely to result in an overly passive person.

Repression is the most fundamental defense mechanism. It is also the crudest. In Freud's early writings, he used *repression* as a general term, synonymous with ego defense. In a sense, other defense mechanisms could be viewed as types of repression.

Repression should not be confused with **suppression**, which refers to *conscious* forgetting of unpleasant events or threatening thoughts. Suppres-

CAPACITY FOR EMOTIONAL INVESTMENT	UNDERSTANDING OF SOCIAL CAUSALITY	PSYCHIATRIC APPEARANCE
Need-gratifying orientation: profound self-preoccupation.	Noncausal or grossly illogical depictions of psychological and interpersonal events.	Autism/ schizophrenia
Limited investment in people, relationships, and moral standards; conflicting interests recognized, but gratification remains primary aim; moral standards immature and unintegrated or followed to avoid punishment.	Rudimentary understanding of social causality; minor logic errors or unexplained transitions; simple stimulus-response causality.	Personality disorders
Conventional investment in people and moral standards; stereotypic compassion, mutuality, or helping orientation; guilt at moral transgressions.	Complex, accurate situational causality and rudimentary understanding of the role of thoughts and feelings in mediating action.	Anxiety disorders
Mature, committed investment in relationships and values; mutual empathy and concern; commitment to abstract values.	Expanded appreciation of the role of mental processes in generating thoughts, feelings, behaviors, and interpersonal interactions.	Adequate functioning
Autonomous selfhood in the context of committed relationships; recognition of conventional nature of moral rules in the context of carefully considered standards or concern for concrete people or relationships.	Complex appreciation of the role of mental processes in generating thoughts, feelings, behaviors, and interpersonal interactions; understanding of unconscious motivational processes.	Superior functioning

sion is *not* considered an ego defense mechanism because it functions on a conscious level.

Experimental investigation of repression   The existence of repression has been the subject of experimental investigation for more than 50 years. Many experimenters have used the paradigm outlined in Table 5-4 (e.g., D'Zurilla, 1965; Worchel, 1955; Zeller, 1950, 1951). The experiments involve three phases. In the first phase, experimental and control subjects memorize a list of words. They are then tested for their recall of the words (Recall

Table 5-4
Experimental paradigm for demonstrating the existence of repression

	EXPERIMENTAL SUBJECTS	CONTROL SUBJECTS	PREDICTION	INTERPRETATION
	PROCEDURES			
Phase 1	Learn list of words Recall Test 1	Learn list of words Recall Test 1	No differences between experimental and control subjects	Groups have been treated identically
Phase 2	Ego-threatening task Recall Test 2	Neutral task Recall Test 2	Experimental subjects recall less than control subjects	Ego threat and resultant anxiety lead experimental subjects to repress words associated with threat
Phase 3	Debriefing (threat removed) Recall Test 3	Debriefing Recall Test 3	No differences between experimental and control subjects	When threat is removed, repression is lifted and memory of repressed words become conscious again

Test 1). Because subjects have been treated in the same way up to this point, no difference between the recall of experimental and control subjects is expected.

During the second phase, experimental subjects are exposed to an *ego-threatening situation*. An example is taking a personality test and getting negative feedback, such as "The test indicates that you may be prone to spells of anxiety." The control subjects are exposed to a similar, but nonthreatening, situation. They may take a personality test but get neutral feedback, such as "The results are in the normal range."

Next, subjects' recall of the words is reassessed (Recall Test 2). Now, experimental subjects who have been ego threatened are expected to recall fewer words than control subjects. The words are assumed to be associated with the ego threat for the experimental group because both occurred at the same time and in the same situation. Consequently, the words that elicit anxiety because of the threat are repressed.

In the third phase of the study, subjects are debriefed. That is, they are told that they were given *false* feedback. Then their recall of the words is tested once more (Recall Test 3). According to the theory of repression, if the threat has been removed and anxiety thereby reduced, the repressed material should return to consciousness. Thus, no difference in recall between the experimental and control subjects is expected.

In general, the results of experiments using this design have been consistent with the predictions based on psychoanalytic theory. Ego threat leads to lowered recall in Test 2; removal of the threat restores recall to prethreat levels in Test 3. These results have been interpreted as supporting the concept of repression.

The experimental model just described has an important limitation, namely, the threat to subjects is explicit and therefore *not* unconscious. To overcome this difficulty, Lloyd Silverman (1983) and his colleagues have used the method of *subliminal psychodynamic activation* to study repression. Subjects are exposed to experimental and control stimuli for a very brief period (4 milliseconds) so that recognition can only be unconscious. The experimental stimuli consist of words or pictures designed to activate repressed wishes, fears, and fantasies. An example would be the phrase "Loving Daddy Is Wrong" accompanied by a picture of a nude woman and man in a suggestive pose (Geisler, 1986). Control stimuli are neutral words and pictures. As in the earlier experimental paradigm, the dependent variable is subjects' recall of the experimental stimuli.

The subliminal psychodynamic activation method has yielded an impressive number of studies providing support for psychoanalytic theory (Kline, 1987; Shulman, 1990). In one interesting line of research, psychiatric patients were exposed to stimuli designed to intensify conflicts that psychoanalytic theory predicts are central to the patients' particular disorders (Silverman, 1983). For example, psychoanalysts consider depression to be based on oral conflicts. When depressed patients were exposed to subliminal stimuli reflecting oral aggression (e.g., a picture of a snarling man with a knife or a verbal message "Cannibal Eats Man"), the patients reported increased feelings of depression. Similarly, psychoanalysts believe that stuttering is caused by anal conflicts, and stutterers showed increased speech difficulties when they were exposed to subliminal anal stimuli.

Studies in which subjects are tested for their recall of words or images are all vulnerable to one basic criticism. Despite their experimental rigor, the laboratory tasks lack *external validity*. They are far removed from the concept of repression. For instance, repression occurs to defend against *actual* painful memories.

In light of this criticism, Davis and Schwartz (1987) devised a more realistic setting to study repression. They asked undergraduate women to recall personal experiences from childhood associated with specific emotions (happiness, sadness, anger, fear, and wonder). The women were classified as "repressors" (based on test scores indicating low anxiety and high defensiveness), as high anxious, or as low anxious. Repressors recalled fewer negative memories than either high-anxious or low-anxious subjects. Repressors were also substantially older at the time of their earliest recalled negative memories. Thus, in a more realistic situation, the idea that repression is a process that limits access to negative affective memories was supported.

It should also be noted that repression can be used to cope with negative emotions other than anxiety. For example, cancer patients who repress pain experience fewer and less severe side effects from medication than do nonrepressors (Ward, Leventhal, & Love, 1988).

Denial

Denial of painful experiences and thoughts is one of the earliest defense mechanisms a person develops (Cramer, 1987; Cramer & Gaul, 1988). Sometimes denial reaches frightening proportions, as when a bereaved person believes that a deceased person is still alive. A more common form of denial involves fantasy or play, which most of us engage in from time to time (Cohen, 1987). People find temporary relief from reality by daydreaming about how their lives might have been different if some unpleasant event had not occurred. Children deny feelings of inferiority through play, as when a young boy becomes a strict father while playing "house."

Regression

Regression is engaging in behavior associated with the pleasure and satisfaction of an earlier developmental period. Common examples of regression include fingernail biting, using baby talk, overeating, and losing one's temper.

Undoing

Undoing involves making symbolic retribution for an unacceptable impulse or act. Suppose a woman has been unscrupulous in business dealings. She could undo this behavior by being active in civic and charitable organizations. Undoing frequently involves a ritual act that symbolically compensates for an id impulse that is threatening the ego. A classic example is Lady Macbeth

Denial is a powerful defense mechanism that protects us from becoming aware of disturbing events.
© 1985 Jan Lukas/Photo Researchers

Fingernail biting is an example of the defense mechanism called regression. To deal with anxiety or frustration, the person reverts to a mode of behavior that was comforting at an earlier stage of psychosexual development—in this photograph, the oral stage.
Photo Source Inc./St. Louis

compulsively washing her hands as if to cleanse herself of the blood spilled in Duncan's murder.

Reaction Formation

One way of warding off an unacceptable impulse is to overemphasize its opposite in both thought and behavior. Thus, a man who is threatened by his desire to dominate and be aggressive in social situations may think of himself as timid and shy and act passively. Timidity and passivity would be a **reaction formation** against a strong aggressive drive.

It is often difficult to tell whether an act is a manifestation of an impulse or of its opposite. An important hallmark of reaction formation is the *persistence* or *excess* of the behavior (going overboard). As Shakespeare's Hamlet observed, "The lady doth protest too much." In this view, the apparently puritanical person, particularly one who responds to sexual advances with exaggerated alarm, may well be seething with erotic desire. Similarly, an individual's avowed love for a sibling or spouse may sometimes indicate profound, but disguised, hate.

Defensive Projection

Defensive projection is attributing one's own unacceptable impulses or wishes to someone or something else. Freud used the example of the jealous husband who called his wife unfaithful. In fact, it was the husband who wanted to have an affair but could not face it in himself. Defensive projection involves three steps: (1) repressing the threatening impulse, (2) projecting the impulse onto another person, and (3) distancing oneself from the other person (Kernberg, 1987).

Note that defensive projection occurs when an individual *is unaware of* having a negative characteristic. To defend against becoming aware, the person attributes the characteristic to someone else, usually someone whom the person dislikes. Scapegoating is an example of defensive projection on a mass scale.

Attributive projection, in contrast, involves projecting a characteristic one *is aware of* onto another individual. Attributive projection is not a psychoanalytic defense mechanism because it is a conscious process (Holmes, 1978).

Research over several decades has shown that defensive projection does occur in some circumstances (Bramel, 1963; Halpern, 1977; Shulman, 1990). In one study, undergraduate men and women completed a questionnaire designed to tap their sexual defensiveness (Halpern, 1977). The questionnaire required true or false responses to simple statements such as "I never have sexual fantasies" and "I never have dreams with sexual content." Most people have sexual fantasies and dreams. Thus, subjects responding "true" to a large number of such statements were presumed to be relatively sexually defensive. Next, subjects looked at six photographs of college students. They ranked the photographs from most favorable to least appealing.

At this point, subjects assigned to the experimental group were shown a set of pornographic pictures to heighten sexual arousal. Control subjects were not shown any pictures. Then, as a final measure, all subjects used a personality scale to rate themselves and the person they had picked from the photographs as least appealing. The scale included a rating of lustfulness.

Psychoanalytic theory would predict that subjects who were highly sexually defensive would deny the feelings aroused by sexually stimulating material by projecting them onto the unappealing other. This prediction was borne out. In the experimental group, high-defensive subjects projected more lust onto the disliked other than did low-defensive subjects. In the control group, there was no difference between high-defensive and low-defensive subjects.

In another study, female undergraduates were given false feedback indicating that they had a tendency toward "neuroticism" (Sherwood, 1979). The women then rated both a favorable and an unfavorable target person on neuroticism. As the theory of projection would predict, women who denied the higher level of neuroticism in themselves tended to attribute neuroticism to the unfavorable target person; those who accepted the psychologist's claim that they were neurotic tended to attribute neuroticism to a favorable other. This study demonstrates the operation of both defensive and attributive projection.

Displacement

Displacement involves shifting an impulse provoked by an unacceptable, threatening object toward a more acceptable, less threatening object. A common example is the person who is criticized at work by a superior and later gets angry at a family member at home for no apparent reason. Expressing hostility toward the superior is obviously a threatening and unadaptive strategy. Consequently, the person redirects the anger toward a family member who is less likely to retaliate. All this is said to go on outside one's conscious awareness.

According to psychoanalysis, displacement is the primary mechanism in phobias. A phobia starts with a fear (realistic or unrealistic) of someone or something that is difficult to avoid. Repeated contact with the feared stimulus induces intense anxiety. To reduce it, the person displaces the fear to another target that (1) can easily be avoided and (2) is symbolically related to the feared stimulus. Freud's (1957b) famous case of "Little Hans" involved a 4-year-old boy who became fearful of horses. He was actually afraid of his father, someone he could not avoid. Hans displaced his fear onto horses, a symbol for a strong, masculine figure. This displacement lowered Hans's

Fido is the innocent victim of displaced aggression.
Courtesy of Lynn L. Liebert

anxiety because he *could* avoid horses, which had become the anxiety-evoking stimuli.

Rationalization

A person who performs an unacceptable act or thinks a threatening thought may get rid of the anxiety or guilt by finding a "perfectly reasonable" excuse for the impulse. This defense mechanism is called **rationalization**. People often use it to maintain their self-esteem. If you are stood up by a date, you may tell yourself and friends that you "really didn't want to go out with that loser." Such rationalization is known as *sour grapes*, after the fable of the fox who, unable to reach some grapes, concluded that they must be sour. Rationalization is an *unconscious* process, as are all the ego defense mechanisms; it is not the same as consciously making excuses.

Defensive Identification

We have already discussed defensive identification as a fundamental process in the development of superego functions as part of the resolution of the Oedipus complex (Chapter 4). *Defensive identification* is taking on other people's characteristics in order to reduce one's anxiety and other negative emotions.

Defensive identification is a common way that people deal with envy (Rosenblatt, 1988). For example, a younger child identifies with an older sibling in order to defend against hostile envy. This identification eliminates envy because the younger child now "possesses" the personal characteristics of the older sibling and no longer feels inadequate. Similarly, the envy of college students toward star athletes can be alleviated by identifying with team members. How often do we hear someone say, "Didn't 'we' play great tonight?" when in fact the speaker is not a member of the team and so cannot actually claim "we." Identifying with others in this way gives people feelings of pride.

Projective Identification

Melanie Klein, the "mother of object relations theory," introduced the defense mechanism called *projective identification*. The idea was subsequently developed by other theorists (Cashdan, 1988; Ogden, 1982).

Contemporary analysts view **projective identification** as a three-stage process (Ogden, 1982). In the first stage, the individual has a wish to get rid of a "bad" part of the self and so projects it onto another person. In the second stage, the individual pressures the recipient to behave in ways that conform to the bad self, that is, to *identify* with the bad self. In the third stage, the recipient responds to the pressure by acting as if the bad self were part of him or her.

Consider the example of projective identification of *dependency*. This phenomenon has its roots in the parenting style in which the parent conveys to the child, "If I can't take care of you, I won't love you." According to object relations theory, repeated exposure to this message causes a *split* (see Chapter 4, p. 79) between the side of the child that feels "I can't survive" and the side of the child that says "I *can* survive; I *can* take care of myself." The side of the child that says "I can't survive" is consistent with the parent's demand for dependency and becomes the displayed *good self*.

But the other, "I *can* take care of myself" side is repressed because it threatens the loss of parental love. This is the *bad self*. In subsequent relationships, the bad self will be projected on significant others. Instead of acknowledging "I want to take care of me," the person projects on the other: "*You* want to take care of me." The projector then endeavors to force the other into the role of caretaker, so as to mesh with their own "good" (dependent) side.

Almost any overbearing parental demand can lead to later projective identification, but Cashdan (1988) claims that four forms are common: dependency, power, sex, and ingratiation. The origin and manifestations of each of these forms, and the splits on which they are based, are shown in Table 5-5.

Sublimation

Sublimation alters unacceptable impulses by channeling them through completely acceptable, even admired, outlets. Sublimation allows an impulse to be expressed *directly* because the expression is socially acceptable and therefore nonthreatening (Vaillant & Vaillant, 1990). Freud considered religion, science, and art to be the major avenues of sublimation (Muller, 1987).

Creative endeavors, such as painting and writing poetry, are common sublimations of the sex drive; playing, or even watching, contact sports like football and boxing are common sublimations of aggression (Golden, 1987). Freud believed our highest virtues are sublimations of our basest

Table 5-5
The four forms of projective identification

PROJECTIVE IDENTIFICATION	PARENT HAS CONVEYED TO CHILD:	DISPLAYED GOOD SELF	PROJECTED BAD SELF
Dependency	"If I can't take care of you, I won't love you."	"I can't survive."	"You want to take care of me."
Power	"If you can't take care of me, I won't love you."	"I want to make all the decisions."	"You don't want to make any decisions."
Sex	"If you can't gratify me sensually, I won't love you."	"I will fulfill you sexually."	"You find me sexy."
Ingratiation	"If you don't appreciate all I've done for you, I won't love you."	"You owe me."	"You are not sufficiently appreciative."

Source: Based on Cashdan (1988)

 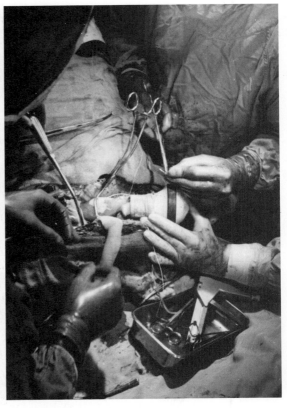

According to psychoanalytic theory, artistic work is a sublimation for the sexual drive, and surgery is a sublimation of the aggressive drive. Both are socially acceptable ways of expressing id impulses.
Left: Photo by Christopher O'Keefe and Michael D. Spiegler; right: Owen/Black Star

characteristics. The surgeon, for example, has found a socially acceptable outlet for aggressive impulses; the movie censor is expressing sublimated sexual drives.

Sublimation is the only truly *successful* defense mechanism because it succeeds in permanently redirecting undesirable impulses. All other defense mechanisms are to some degree *un*successful. They require continually warding off the threatening impulses. This requires expenditure of psychic energy that is no longer available for other functions.

Choice of Defense Mechanisms

Many factors combine to determine which defense mechanisms a person will use to fend off anxiety. Age is an important factor (A. Freud, 1966; Valliant, 1971, 1977). Early in life, people develop primitive or "immature" defenses, such as denial and repression. Later, they develop more complex and "mature defenses," such as defensive identification and rationalization.

Cramer (1987) provided empirical evidence for a developmental hierarchy of defense mechanisms. Four age groups were studied: preschool, elementary school, early adolescence, and late adolescence. Subjects' use of three different defense mechanisms—denial, projection, and defensive identification—was assessed from stories they made up about two ambiguous pictures from the Thematic Apperception Test (TAT). (See Chapter 11 for a description of the TAT.) It was predicted that denial would be the most primitive defense and identification the most mature; projection was predicted to be intermediate. As Figure 5-3 shows, the results of the study were consistent with the predicted pattern.

Adults tend to have characteristic ways of defending themselves. These "defensive habits" develop in early childhood when instinctual conflicts first arise. Three factors appear to account for a person's characteristic defense mechanisms: (1) the nature of the original conflicts, (2) the time in the developmental sequence at which the conflicts occur, and (3) the particular circumstances surrounding the original conflicts (Fenichel, 1945). Most impulses can be defended against by any number of defense mechanisms, as the example in Table 5-6 (p. 108) illustrates.

Defense Mechanisms as Adaptive Functions

According to Freud, the main purpose of ego defense mechanisms is to defend the ego from id impulses. Ego psychologists believe that defense mechanisms can also play a more positive, adaptive role. For instance, indefinitely putting off studying for a final examination is far from adaptive.

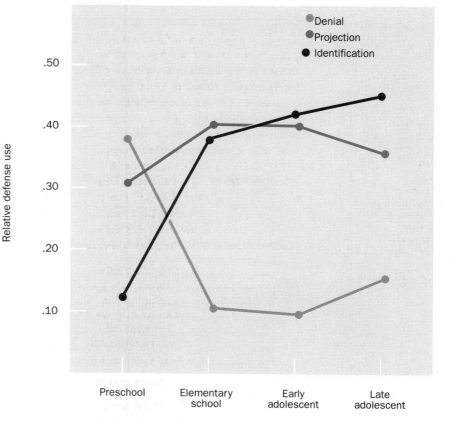

Figure 5-3
The relative use of three defense mechanisms—denial, projection, and identification—among children of four age groups.
Source: Data from *The Development of Defense Mechanisms* by P. Cramer, 1987, *Journal of Personality,* 55, p. 607. Copyright by Duke University Press.

Table 5-6
How the same unacceptable impulse can be defended against by different defense mechanisms

UNACCEPTABLE IMPULSE: NEGATIVITY	
DEFENSE MECHANISM	EXAMPLES OF ITS USE
Sublimation	Being a movie or restaurant critic; reviewing scientific studies for publication
Reaction formation	Expressing optimism and finding worthwhile aspects in any situation
Projection	Being sensitive to negativity in others
Rationalization	Believing that the world is in a dismal state and therefore negativity is "legitimate"
Undoing	Working for positive, optimistic causes (e.g., a world peace organization)
Regression	Doing sloppy work or sulking
Denial	Not being aware of one's negativity

But it may be useful to *temporarily* forget the upcoming test (denial) in order to clear one's mind.

Nesse (1990) has suggested that the defense mechanisms are an adaptive feature in the human species, shaped over time by natural selection. The heart of his argument is that it is often in our best interest to conceal our true motives — even from ourselves.

> Being aware of one's own motives might make it difficult to hide them adequately . . . the capacity for repression may, therefore, offer a selective advantage by increasing the ability to deceive others about the pursuit of covert selfish motives. . . . (p. 263)

> A man who believes that he will do anything for his new love and who can sincerely promise her his undying devotion will be far more likely to garner sexual favors than a man who says the same things without believing them. A person who hates an exploiting superior, but experiences only admiration and feelings of inadequacy, will have a considerable advantage over someone who is aware of rage and competitive feelings. We tend to assume that the brain has been shaped for accurate perception of reality, but it is evident that, in some situations, distorted perceptions of reality may enhance fitness, and selection will tend to favor those tendencies to distortion. (p. 274)

The use of defense mechanisms is therefore part of normal personality functioning. No problem arises as long as the defensive processes do not radically distort one's perceptions of the world or preclude effective action in dealing with the source of anxiety. When distortion is too extreme, there is a problem. Persons with extremely distorted perceptions are likely to exhibit abnormal behavior.

TRENDS IN THE EVOLUTION OF PSYCHOANALYTIC THEORY

Psychoanalytic theory has been evolving ever since Freud and his early followers first charted its course. This evolution has taken five broad directions.

First, there has been increasing recognition of social determinants of personality. This approach contrasts with the predominant role assigned to biological drives and instincts in classical psychoanalysis. Further, whereas classical psychoanalysis is a "one-person psychology," more recent psychoanalytic approaches have been "two-person psychologies," in the sense of assuming that individuals can be understood only in the context of another person (e.g., Modell, 1984). Object relations theories are prime examples of this growing recognition among psychoanalysts (Leichtman, 1990).

Second, the time frame of personality development has been expanded and elaborated. Many psychoanalysts view personality development as a lifelong process rather than as one that is, as Freud believed, virtually completed by age 5. "Whereas the formation of psychic structure in a child is like broad strokes painted on a bare canvas, the evolution of psychic structure in adulthood is equivalent to fine, nearly invisible strokes on a complicated background" (Colarusso & Nemiroff, 1979, p. 62). This broader concept of personality has implications for personality change (Gedo, 1979). "The analytic patient, regardless of age, is considered to be still in the process of ongoing development as opposed to merely being in possession of a past that influences . . . present conscious and unconscious life" (Shane, 1977, pp. 95–96).

Third, many psychoanalysts, particularly ego psychologists, consider conscious aspects of personality to be important (Robbins, 1989). This view contrasts with the almost exclusive role given the unconscious in Freudian theory. It is still true, however, that psychoanalysis emphasizes unconscious motives and conflicts more than any of the other three strategies.

Fourth, contemporary psychoanalysis emphasizes normal personality more than does classical psychoanalysis. This is true in terms of devoting more study to normal personality functioning, as ego psychologists do; it is also true in terms of viewing normal personality as worthy of detailed analysis. Classical psychoanalytic theory focuses on intrapsychic conflict, anxiety and defense, and psychopathology. Ego psychologists examine the other side of the coin: the conflict-free sphere of personality. This part of personality allows people to remain relatively healthy by coping successfully with the inner and outer forces that shape their personalities. Still, psychoanalysis remains a strategy that tends to proceed from abnormal personality to normal personality. This is the case because most psychoanalytic theorists and researchers are psychotherapists by training and profession.

Fifth, psychoanalysis has increasingly been related to basic theory and research in mainstream psychology. Psychoanalysis began outside traditional academic circles, in Freud's private psychoanalytic sessions. The methods of psychoanalysis — dream analysis, free association, interpretation of mistakes and symbolism — are not those considered acceptable to many academic psychologists. Since the 1930s, however, numerous attempts have been made to relate psychoanalysis to theories and research in the mainstream of academic psychology and to try to empirically validate psychoanalytic concepts through correlational and experimental research. There also has been an effort to relate psychoanalysis to one of the most talked-about recent developments in physics, chaos theory (Moran, 1991).

Interest in cognitive processes is at the forefront of contemporary academic psychology, and a number of psychologists are vigorously pursuing the possible ties between cognitive psychology and psychoanalysis. One link is in the conclusion of cognitive psychologists that humans systematically process and "edit" environmental input or stimuli through unconscious but nonetheless highly active processes (Erdelyi, 1974; Motley & Baars, 1978; Neisser, 1976; Nisbett & Wilson, 1977; Posner, 1973). Psychoanalysts have been insisting on the importance of unconscious editing processes for almost 100 years.

SUMMARY   1. Freud divided the mind into three levels of awareness: conscious, preconscious, and unconscious. Personality functioning is dominated by the unconscious.

2. Jung proposed an alternative division: conscious ego, personal unconscious, and collective unconscious. Jung emphasized the influence of the collective unconscious, which contains archetypes that are universal predispositions to think and act in common ways.

3. Freud divided personality according to three basic functions. The id is concerned with pleasure seeking and is the reservoir of biological drives. It operates through the pleasure principle, which requires immediate gratification of needs. This gratification is accomplished through primary process, in which memory images of goals are formed.

4. The ego is the rational aspect of personality and operates according to the reality principle — the gratification of needs is delayed until an appropriate actual goal can be obtained. This gratification is accomplished through secondary process, which involves problem solving and other intellectual functions.

5. The superego is the moral aspect of personality. It is the internal representative of the values of society and guides the individual toward ideals.

6. The ego serves as a mediator among the pleasure demands of the id, the moral limitations of the superego, and the requirements of the real world. Intrapsychic conflicts among the id, ego, and superego play a major role in determining one's personality.

7. Ego psychologists emphasize ego functions, including conflict-free adaptive functions, general motives (such as competency), and conscious determinism.

8. Object relations theorists believe that adults differ in the level of object relations they have achieved.

9. Anxiety is a central Freudian concept. Freud distinguished three types: neurotic anxiety (from an id–ego conflict), moral anxiety or guilt (from an id–superego conflict), and objective anxiety (from actual external dangers).

10. Unconscious ego defense mechanisms keep people from being overwhelmed by unacceptable impulses that are the basis for neurotic and moral anxiety. Repression, in which unacceptable impulses are totally excluded from one's consciousness, is the most fundamental defense mechanism. Other defense mechanisms include denial, regression, undoing, reaction formation, defensive projection, displacement, rationalization, and defensive identification.

11. Projective identification, a term introduced by object relations theorists, involves repressing an undesirable aspect of the self (the "bad self"), projecting the repressed aspect onto another person, and attempting to control the repressed element in the other person.

12. Sublimation involves the channeling of unacceptable impulses into socially acceptable endeavors; it results in a permanent solution to dealing with unacceptable impulses. All other defense mechanisms require a continual defensive process to ward off unacceptable impulses.

13. The use of defense mechanisms is part of normal personality functioning and can be adaptive. But when defenses are excessive, abnormal behavior results.

14. Five ongoing trends in psychoanalytic theory can be identified: (1) recognizing social factors; (2) considering present influences on behavior; (3) emphasizing conscious personality functioning; (4) emphasizing normal personality functioning; and (5) relating psychoanalytic theory to basic psychological research and theory.

Assessment and Personality Change

n Chapters 4 and 5, we explored the major theoretical ideas of psychoanalysis. Now we will look at psychoanalytic personality assessment and change. Most psychoanalytic personality assessment procedures are indirect because they are designed to assess unconscious processes that cannot be directly observed. We will discuss two indirect assessment methods: dream interpretation and projective techniques. Psychoanalysis as psychotherapy, the final topic of the chapter, involves both personality change and assessment. This is because psychoanalysts consider uncovering what is in the patient's unconscious central to the therapy process.

DREAMS: THE ROYAL ROAD TO THE UNCONSCIOUS

We spend one-third of our lives sleeping, and as we sleep we often dream. Humans have always been intrigued by their dreams and wondered what they meant. One ancient view is that every dream has a secret meaning that can be interpreted by an expert. Joseph, in the Bible, was considered such an expert. A second ancient view is that dreams represent wishes in disguised form. Finally, it has long been suspected that dreams result from experiences and ideas in waking life.

What is a dream? Technically, a **dream** is a mental experience during sleep that involves mainly visual images. The images are often vivid and are considered "real" when they occur (Hobson & McCarley, 1977). They have been called *cinematographic* because they are like movies that pass through one's mind while asleep (Shannon, 1990).

Psychoanalytic Dream Theory

Freud was not the first to call attention to the psychological meaning of dreams (Resnik, 1987). But Freud's theory was the first comprehensive account of dreaming (Freud, 1961a). Freud believed that dreaming obeys the same underlying psychological laws as all other mental functions. He considered *The Interpretation of Dreams*, first published in 1900, his most significant work, and many commentators agree with his evaluation. Freud revised this book a number of times and it has been translated into many languages (Bloom, 1987; Porter, 1987).

Freud's dream theory is largely based on his analysis of his own dreams. In fact, the germ of many of Freud's ideas came from his self-analysis, which he began in 1897 by examining a dream. Freud continued self-analysis throughout his lifetime, usually the last thing he did each day (Jones, 1953).

Freud believed that dreams are highly significant mental products. They result from the dynamic interaction of (1) unconscious wishes, (2) the censoring mechanisms of the ego, and (3) events in waking life. Although the dream itself occurs in sleep, the origins and preparation of the dream reflect all aspects of the dreamer's psychological experience.

Dreams, for Freud, are carefully constructed camouflages; there is always a concealed wish and a true meaning to be found. Dreams are subtle and profound reflections of intrapsychic processes. Freud likened a dream to a fireworks display "which takes hours to prepare but goes off in a

Henri Rousseau's "The Dream" (1910) depicts the rich visual imagery in dreams.
Oil on canvas, 6'8½ x 9'9½. Collection. The Museum of Modern Art, New York. Gift of Nelson A. Rockefeller.

moment." He considered dreams the single best source of information about a person's unconscious—in fact, he called dreams "the royal road to the unconscious."

Jung's unique contribution to dream theory is his focus on unusual dreams with mythical symbolism. These he called **archetypal dreams**. He was convinced that mythical motifs occur spontaneously in the dreams of modern people who have never been exposed to ancient myths in their conscious lives. For example, Jung placed great significance on the fact that pregnant women are considerably more likely than other women to have dreams involving twins. This is interesting because of the ancient myth that every individual has a prenatal twin (Robert, Jansson, & Wager, 1989).

Manifest versus Latent Content of Dreams

Freud distinguished two levels of dream content. **Manifest content** is what a person can remember about a dream. **Latent content** is the set of underlying intrapsychic events that led to the manifest content. The latent content is composed primarily of unconscious thoughts, wishes, fantasies, and conflicts, which are expressed in translated or disguised form in the manifest content.

The relation of manifest and latent dream content is like a rebus, such as the one in Figure 6-1. In these puzzles, pictures suggest the sounds of words or syllables they represent. Latent meaning cannot directly enter consciousness because it is threatening; it can, however, be disguised. Manifest content is the "dressed-up" version of the threatening determinants of the dream. Like the symbols in a rebus, the images in manifest content "stand for" something else. Latent content becomes manifest through two basic processes: dream work and symbolization.

Dream Work

Dream work refers to the processes by which latent dream content is transformed into manifest content. Freud believed that *condensation* and *displacement* are the major processes in dream work. He also identified two other processes: visual representation and secondary revision.

Condensation combines and compresses separate thoughts. The resulting manifest content is a much abbreviated version of the latent content. An example would be a man dreaming of being affectionate with a woman who looked like his wife, who acted like his ex-wife, and whom he believed in the dream to be his mother. The wife, ex-wife, and mother are condensed into a single person. One implication of condensation is that all elements in the dream result from more than one latent source. Thus, dreams are *multiply determined*; they are the product of many sources. Condensation, like all forms of dream work, disguises threatening latent content. Thus, its threat is not apparent in the manifest dream.

Displacement involves shifting emphasis. This often means that an important element of the dream is changed to an unimportant element. Consider the example of a woman who received a telegram saying that her son had been killed. That night she dreamed of receiving a telegram stating that her son would not be coming home for the weekend. In this dream, a critical aspect of the latent content appears as a trivial aspect of the manifest content.

Abstract wishes, urges, and ideas that make up latent content may be translated into concrete pictures or images by the dream-work process known as **visual representation**. A rebus (see Figure 6-1) is a crude example of visual representation. A more sophisticated example would be representing the concept of possession by the act of *sitting on an object*, much as children actually do to keep other children from having a prized toy. Note the similarity between displacement as dream work and displacement as a defense mechanism. Both dream work and defense mechanisms keep individuals from becoming conscious of unacceptable and threatening material.

Figure 6-1

An example of a rebus in which the pictures depict the syllables of a word. If you are unable to decipher the word that is visually represented, see the first page of this book on which the word appears.

When we awaken after dreaming, we often try to reconstruct our dream. Such attempts at reconstruction often lead to the discovery that the parts of the dream do not logically fit together. This is not surprising. The meaning of the dream (latent content) has been distorted and disguised through condensation, displacement, and visual representation. "Dreams, like symptoms," said one contemporary analyst, "are compromises simultaneously expressing wish and resistance, subjective need and its repression" (Gallego-Mere, 1989, p. 97).

Because manifest content often is confusing, we attempt to fill in the missing elements to create a coherent overall picture of the dream. For example, a college student dreamed that he was sitting in his room talking to friends, and the next moment he was asking a question in one of his classes. The instantaneous change of location did not make sense. So, in describing his dream, the student added that *he left his room and walked to class*, which was not part of the dream itself. This process, known as **secondary revision**, further distorts the dream. However, according to psychoanalysis, secondary revisions contain significant information about the person. Accordingly, they are part of the data that the psychoanalyst analyzes.

Symbolization

Dream work changes unacceptable latent content into acceptable manifest content. **Symbolization** allows latent content to become part of the manifest content directly, but in an unrecognizable and, therefore, nonthreatening form. *Symbols* are objects or ideas that stand for something else. Freud believed that some symbols have universal meanings and therefore represent the same thing in all dreams.

Examples of symbols and their meanings according to psychoanalytic theory appear in Table 6-1. Symbols do not occur only in dreams; they also appear in myths, fairy tales, literature, and other aspects of mental life. For example, one of Freud's patients hallucinated that his finger had been severed; Freud took this to be a sign of castration anxiety (Schmukler & Garcia, 1989).

A quick look at Table 6-1 shows that most of the symbols refer to sexual objects and activities. This is consistent with the central Freudian idea that human motivation is primarily sexual. Freud believed that although there are many symbols, only a few concepts are symbolized.

What evidence exists for sexual symbolism? Do people connect sexual symbols with sexual objects, as psychoanalysis proposes? One line of research has had people classify psychoanalytic symbols of male and female genitals as either masculine or feminine. In general, these studies show that adults, and sometimes children, can group sexual symbols according to the gender predicted by psychoanalytic theory at a better-than-chance level (Kline, 1972). For example, fruit is considered feminine and snakes masculine. However, people may use cultural associations to make the classification even though their responses are consistent with psychoanalytic theory. For instance, a gun is a masculine symbol both in our culture and in psychoanalysis.

Table 6-1
Common psychoanalytic symbols and their latent meanings

SYMBOL	LATENT MEANING
House	Human body
Smooth-fronted house	Male body
House with ledges and balconies	Female body
King and queen	Parents
Little animals	Children
Children	Genitals
Playing with children	Masturbation
Beginning a journey	Dying
Clothes	Nakedness
The number three	Male genitals
Elongated object (e.g., snake, gun, necktie)	Penis
Balloon, airplane	Erection
Woods and thickets	Pubic hair
Room	Woman
Suite of rooms	Brothel or harem
Box	Uterus
Fruit	Breast
Climbing stairs or ladder	Sexual intercourse
Baldness, tooth extraction	Castration
Bath	Birth

Lessler (1964) found that whether psychoanalytic or cultural stereotypes were used to classify so-called sexual symbols depended on the context. When the symbols had cultural referents, subjects used cultural stereotypes to assign gender. Where no cultural bias existed, subjects classified the symbols according to psychoanalytic theory. Lessler argued that these findings are consistent with the theory's expectations. Sexual objects are usually threatening. Thus, if a cultural gender referent for the symbol exists, people will choose it (because it is nonthreatening) over the psychoanalytic sexual meaning. An example is calling a rolling pin (a phallic symbol) feminine. If no cultural gender meaning is obvious, then people "must" use the psychoanalytic sexual meaning (such as classifying a cane as masculine).

There is indirect support for the sexual symbolism predicted by psychoanalytic theory from comparisons of the dreams of men and women. An example is Hall and Van de Castle's (1963) study of the differences in the Oedipal symbolism in dreams of men and women described in Chapter 4 (p. 67). Contemporary psychoanalysts do not agree that all symbolism is sexual. For example, Turkel (1988) believes that dreaming about money is symbolic of internal conflicts over dependency, responsibility, exploitation, and pride. This is considerably different from Freud's original view that money almost always symbolizes feces and the "anal pleasure" of bowel movements.

Freudian Dream Interpretation

Freud's method of dream interpretation begins with the person's report of the dream (the manifest content). The person is then asked to make associations to the dream (e.g., Smith & Andresen, 1988). Dream reports are often relatively short, but the associations to them are generally quite extensive. In the final step, the psychoanalyst uses the principles of dream work and symbolization to interpret the latent meaning of both the manifest content and the associations. The interpretation also takes into account information the analyst has about the individual, such as events in the person's life that appear to be related to the dream.

Thus, Freudian dream interpretation involves analysis of more than just the dream and is admittedly subjective. Its validity cannot be judged against any objective standards of right or wrong. The validity of an interpretation is more a matter of how *useful* it is in providing the psychoanalyst with information about the individual's personality. Thus, there may be more than one "correct" (useful) interpretation of a dream (Fosshage, 1987; Warner, 1987).

The following dream interpretation by Freud (1961a) illustrates the use of condensation, displacement, and symbolization to understand the latent meaning of the dream. The dreamer was one of Freud's patients. Although the woman was still quite young, she had been married for a number of years. She had recently received news that a friend, Elise L., who was about the same age, had become engaged. Shortly thereafter, she had this dream:

> She was at the theater with her husband. One side of the stalls [theater boxes] were completely empty. Her husband told her that Elise L. and her fiancé had wanted to go too, but had only been able to get bad seats—three for one florin fifty kreuzers—and of course, they could not take those. She thought it would really not have done any harm if they had. (p. 415)

Freud began his interpretation of this rather brief dream by analyzing the symbolic meaning of the monetary units. This particular symbol was in part determined by an unimportant event of the previous day. The dreamer had learned that her sister-in-law recently had been given a gift of 150 florins (exactly 100 times the amount dreamed of) and had quickly spent this gift on jewelry.

Freud noted that *three* tickets were mentioned in the dream. Elise L. and her fiancé would only have needed two tickets for themselves. Examination of previous statements made by the dreamer revealed a connection: "her newly engaged friend was the same number of months—*three*—her junior" (p. 415).

That one side of the theater boxes was entirely empty is significant. Recently, the patient had wished to attend a play. She had rushed out to buy tickets days ahead of time. In doing so, she had incurred an extra booking fee. When the patient and her husband arrived at the theater, they found that only half the seats were taken. This bit of information accounts in part for the appearance of the "empty stalls" in the dream.

More important in terms of psychoanalytic theory is the underlying meaning of the empty stalls. The patient's actual experience with the theater tickets could clearly lead to the conclusion that she had been too hasty about running out to buy tickets and therefore had to pay an additional, unnecessary price. Freud assumed that she might have had the same hidden feelings concerning her own marriage; in symbolic form, these feelings are revealed by the dream. Thus, Freud offered the following summary interpretation of the dream:

> "It was *absurd* to marry so early. There was *no need for me to be in such a hurry*. I see from Elise L.'s example that I should have got a husband in the end. Indeed, I should have got one *a hundred times* better" (a *treasure*) "if I had only *waited*" (in antithesis to her sister-in-law's *hurry*). "My money" (or dowry) "could have bought *three* men just as good" (p. 416).

The Functions of Dreaming

Why do people dream? Freud discussed three interrelated functions of dreaming: (1) *wish fulfillment*, (2) *the release of unconscious tension*, and (3) *preservation of sleep*. He believed that every dream is an attempt to fulfill a wish. The wish may be a conscious desire that is not fulfilled during the day (e.g., wishing to be skiing rather than studying). Or it may be an unconscious desire that is an expression of a repressed impulse (e.g., to hurt a friend). Most dreams represent a combination of the two. Further, events and thoughts that occur while awake, called day residues, combine with unconscious impulses to produce the dream. In effect, the unconscious impulses provide the psychic energy for enactment of the day residues in the form of a dream. The result is that each of the three functions of dreaming is satisfied.

First, the wish is fulfilled in the dream. Dreams are a primary process. Therefore, the mental representation of the behavior needed to satisfy a wish is not distinguished from the actual behavior. When a wish "comes true" in a dream, it is as if the wish were actually fulfilled. While dreaming, we usually believe that the events are really happening, which is why nightmares can be so frightening.

Second, the unconscious impulse is allowed expression. However, this expression is in a disguised and acceptable form, due to dream work and symbolization. Thus, dreams allow the release of tension that has built up in the unconscious.

Third, the individual remains asleep even though unconscious threatening impulses are becoming conscious in the manifest dream. If threatening impulses begin to enter consciousness during waking periods, anxiety is generated. If such anxiety were present while dreaming, the dreamer would wake up. However, through dream work and symbolization, the threatening aspects of the latent material are removed. The result is that anxiety is not generated, and the person can continue sleeping.

The Physiology of Sleep and Dreaming

Freud was well aware that his study of dreams was subjective. Even if he had wanted to use more objective methods, more than 50 years would pass from the publication of *The Interpretation of Dreams* to the advent of the remarkable techniques for studying dreams that are employed today. Modern methods are based on continuously recording brain-wave patterns and the parallel eye movements of sleeping subjects (Horne, 1988). Volunteers sleep in a sleep laboratory, and their physiological functions are monitored. They are occasionally awakened and questioned about their dreams.

Monitoring Physiological Functions During Sleep

Brain waves are recorded by an instrument called an **electroencephalograph** (e-LEK-tro-en-CEF-a-low-graph), which produces an **electroencephalogram** **(EEG)**, a tracing, plotted against time, of the frequency and potential (voltage) of electric currents emitted by the brain (Figure 6-2). The frequency of electric currents from the brain is measured horizontally on the EEG; the closer the tracings, the higher the frequency. Electrical potential is measured vertically on the EEG; the greater the amplitude, or height, of the tracings, the greater is the electrical potential. Electroencephalograms are made by placing electrodes directly on the scalp. The procedure is painless and does not disturb sleep.

Eye movements are measured during sleep by placing small electrodes around the orbits of the eyes. Differences in electrical potential produced by displacement of the eyeballs are measured. Figure 6-3 shows a subject wearing both brain-wave and eye-movement electrodes while sleeping.

Stages of Sleep and Dreaming

Sleep is not a uniform state. Instead, it consists of various stages. Electroencephalograms reveal four basic stages of sleep. As sleep progresses

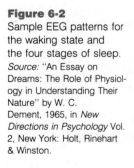

Figure 6-2
Sample EEG patterns for the waking state and the four stages of sleep.
Source: "An Essay on Dreams: The Role of Physiology in Understanding Their Nature" by W. C. Dement, 1965, in *New Directions in Psychology* Vol. 2, New York: Holt, Rinehart & Winston.

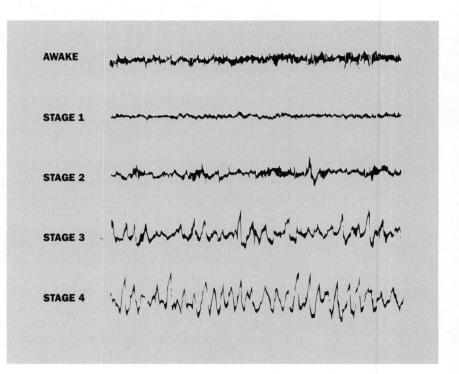

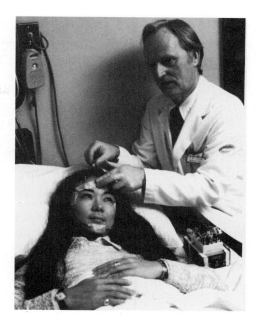

Figure 6-3
A sleeping subject with
EEG and eye-movement
electrodes.
© Robert McElroy/Woodfin
Camp & Assoc.

from stage 1 to stage 4, high-amplitude, low-frequency waves develop (see Figure 6-2). Originally, these waves were thought to be correlated with reduction in neural activity and responsiveness as the person went from "light sleep" in stage 1 to "deep sleep" in stage 4. The stages of sleep *can* be roughly placed on a quantitative continuum of depth. However, there is a very important exception that occurs during Stage 1 sleep. It is so striking that it has been the primary focus of researchers for almost 50 years (Gackenbach, 1987).

In 1953, Eugene Aserinsky and Nathaniel Kleitman at the University of Chicago were studying the sleep patterns of infants. They inadvertently discovered occasional periods of very quick movements of the eyes during sleep. Such **rapid eye movement, or REM**, only occurs during stage 1 sleep. Rapid eye movement occurs in all stage 1 sleep with the exception of the initial period when the person is first falling asleep.

Much research has examined the characteristics of REM sleep. During this phase, there is a considerable amount of neural activity in the cerebral cortex of the brain, similar to that in the waking state. The autonomic nervous system is activated, as indicated by irregular heartbeat, irregular breathing, and genital arousal (Figure 6-4). These physiological correlates of REM sleep give the impression of "light sleep." At the same time, REM sleep is associated with considerable muscular relaxation. People in REM sleep are relatively insensitive to external stimulation; when they are awakened, they frequently report having been in "deep sleep."

Is REM sleep "light" or "deep"? The best available answer seems to be that it is both, which is why it is called **paradoxical sleep** (Chase & Morales, 1990). REM sleep is a unique neurophysiological stage that is qualitatively

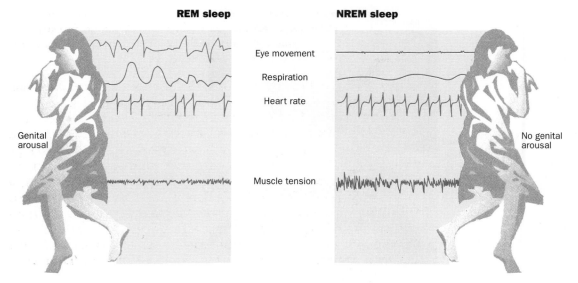

Figure 6-4

Rapid eye movement
(REM) sleep is paradoxi-
cal in that it consists of
elements of both light
sleep and deep sleep.
There is rapid eye move-
ment, irregular heartbeat
and breathing, and
genital arousal. But there
is also skeletal muscle
relaxation, and it is
difficult to awaken the
sleeper.

different from the other sleep stages. It occurs in humans of all ages and in other mammals ranging from the opossum (Snyder, 1965) to the monkey (Weitzmann, 1961). The proportion of REM sleep decreases with age— about 50% of total sleep time in infants, 30% in adolescents, and 20% in adults. REM sleep occurs in regular cycles of approximately 90 minutes each (Figure 6-5). Successive REM periods become progressively longer. The final period lasts from 25 to 60 minutes (Webb, 1982). Of course, these are only average figures; they vary somewhat from individual to individual and from night to night.

What makes REM sleep important psychologically is that most dreaming occurs during REM. When Aserinsky and Kleitman discovered REM, they believed that it might be related to dreaming. To test this, they awakened adults during both REM and **nonrapid eye movement (NREM)** periods and asked whether they had been dreaming. Of the subjects awakened from REM sleep, 74% said that they had been dreaming. Only 7% of those awakened from NREM sleep said that they had been dreaming (Aserinsky & Kleitman, 1953).

For the first time, a reliable relationship had been found between an objective measure of a sleep variable (REM) and recall of dreams. The percentage of dream recall for REM and NREM has varied in different studies. But generally, REM periods are associated with substantially more dreaming than NREM periods (Rotenberg, 1988; Van de Castle, 1971).

If dreams actually occur during REM sleep, then the subjective duration of the dream should be proportional to the duration of REM observed before the subject wakes up. This hypothesis received strong support in studies by William Dement (1965).

In one series of trials, subjects were awakened either five minutes or fifteen minutes after the onset of REM and were asked to choose the correct interval on the basis of whatever dream material they recalled. A correct choice was made in 92 of 111 instances. In another series, high correlation coefficients were obtained between the number of words in the dream narratives and the number of minutes [of REM] preceding the awakenings. [p. 172]

Researchers use the presence of REM sleep to indicate dreaming. Observation of REM also yields information about some general aspects of the content of dreams. People apparently scan their dream images in much the same way that they visually scan similar events when they are awake, and their eyes move accordingly. For example, more frequent eye movements are associated with reports of active dreams, such as running; less-frequent eye movements are related to reports of passive dreams, such as staring at a distant object (Berger & Oswald, 1962; Dement & Wolpert, 1958). Further, when their eyes move up and down, people tend to report dreams of vertical movement, such as looking up and down a flight of stairs; when people's eyes move from side to side, their dream reports tend to contain horizontal images, such as two people throwing a ball back and forth (Dement & Kleitman, 1957).

Freudian Dream Theory in the Light of Recent Evidence

To what degree does contemporary dream research support Freudian dream theory? Let us first look at the three functions of dreams that Freud identified in the light of modern physiological research.

Functions of Dreaming

Freud stated that "wish fulfillment" is the basis for all dreams. However, it is quite possible that Freud actually meant by this that dreams portray unconscious impulses (Fisher & Greenberg, 1977). Freud (1953) said that "the reason why dreams are invariably wish fulfillments is that they are products of the . . . unconscious, whose activity knows no other aim than the fulfillment of wishes and which has at its command no other forces than wishful impulses" (p. 568). If one assumes that wish fulfillment and the expression of unconscious impulses are equivalent, then two of the three functions of dreaming that Freud identified—wish fulfillment and release of unconscious tension—also become one and the same.

Regarding the release of repressed psychic energy through dreaming, if this outlet is not provided, the individual should show signs of abnormal behavior. Studies of *dream deprivation* are related to this issue. Subjects in a

Figure 6-5
Sleep cycles as they relate to stages of sleep.

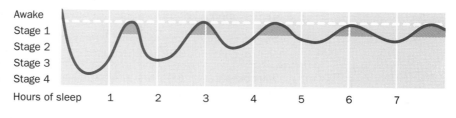

Awake
Stage 1
Stage 2
Stage 3
Stage 4
Hours of sleep   1   2   3   4   5   6   7

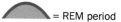 = REM period

sleep laboratory are awakened just as they are entering a REM period and then allowed to go back to sleep. Thus, the subjects are not deprived of all sleep—just REM sleep. Two general findings have emerged from these studies. First, there are large individual differences in responses to dream deprivation (Cartwright & Ratzel, 1972); any general statements about the effects of not dreaming must be viewed cautiously. Second, "there is a discernible average trend for signs of disturbance to a person following limitation of dreaming that fit in with the [Freudian] idea that dreams somehow serve as an outlet or channel for tension reduction" (Fisher & Greenberg, 1977, p. 61).

Contemporary physiological research generally does *not* support Freud's third function of dreaming: preserving sleep. As we have seen, dreaming occurs at regular intervals and is therefore unlikely to be caused by threatening impulses that occur at irregular times. Further, more than half of all REM periods, when dreaming is known to occur, include short periods of wakefulness (Dement, 1964). The only sense in which REM periods can be said to preserve sleep is that people are relatively insensitive to external stimulation during REM periods.

The Importance of Manifest Content

An essential element of Freud's dream theory is the importance placed on the latent content relative to the manifest content. Indeed, Freud considered manifest content important only insofar as it reveals latent content. Contemporary psychoanalytic researchers do not deny the significance of the latent content, but they have found manifest content itself to be rich with psychological meaning. Dream reports clearly indicate that people tend to dream about matters that concern them (McCann, Stewin & Short, 1990).

Here is a poignant dream of a still grieving widow:

> I dreamt that I wanted to tell my husband something but there is nobody there. I was somewhere and I was looking for him, but could not find him. So many people were around and still he was not there. I was very upset, astonished that everyone was there, but he was not. (Prince & Hoffman, 1991, p. 5).

Consider a few other examples of the effects of everyday life on dreams from a wide array of findings (Fisher & Greenberg, 1977; Zayas, 1988):

> Pregnant women are significantly more likely than other women to report dreams involving babies or children.

> Men are more likely than women to report dreaming about aggression.

> Women are more likely to report dreams relating to sex or hostility during their menstrual periods than at other times.

> Older people (over 65) are more likely than younger individuals to report dreams involving loss of resources and strength or death-related topics.

> Expectant fathers tend to dream about loneliness and exclusion.

In a study in Germany, subjects were shown either a film depicting violence, humiliation, and despair or a neutral film (Lauer, Riemann, Lund, & Berger, 1987). Subjects who had seen the disturbing film reported dreams with considerably more manifest aggressive and anxious content than subjects who had viewed the neutral film. Further, a third of the initial dreams of the subjects exposed to the upsetting film included specific content from the film itself. Not only does this study indicate the significance of manifest content, but it also indicates that the manifest content of dreams can be influenced by our experiences while awake.

Dreaming as Problem Solving

In ancient Greece, troubled "patients" were treated by priests. Part of the treatment involved administering drugs to induce dreams that were expected to provide the solutions to problems (Marcus, 1988). Many post-Freudian analysts think that dreaming can serve to solve problems, particularly interpersonal problems, and to plan future actions (e.g., Adler, 1973; Erikson, 1954; French & Fromm, 1964; Miller, 1989; Resnik, 1987; Winson, 1985). For example, dreaming may "integrate current stressful experiences with similar experiences from the past, thus enabling the individual to use . . . basic coping mechanisms (defenses) to deal with the current stressful situation" (Grieser, Greenberg, & Harrison, 1972, p. 281).

This idea was tested in an experiment in which college students solved anagrams (words formed by reordering letters of another word) (Grieser et al., 1972). The students were told which anagrams they had solved and which they had failed to solve. Failure was made ego threatening by telling the subjects that the anagrams were a test of intelligence on which the average college student did quite well. It was predicted that subjects who were permitted to dream following the task would remember the failed anagrams better than subjects who were prevented from dreaming. This hypothesis follows from the idea that dreaming is a period in which people cope with stressful situations, such as failure. Presumably, coping with failure makes the failure less threatening. This reduces the need to repress the events leading to the failure (the unsolved anagrams) and makes it more likely that the events will be remembered.

Subjects who were awakened during NREM periods recalled significantly more failed anagrams than subjects who were awakened during REM periods. The greater recall with NREM awakenings is presumably because the subjects' dreaming was not disturbed (as it was with REM awakenings). These results support the view that dreaming enables the dreamer to cope with threatening material.

Freud's dream theory and the post-Freudians' problem-solving theory are psychological accounts of why people dream, and they relate dreaming to emotional factors. There are also physiological theories of dreaming that essentially ignore the role of emotions. For example, one theory proposes that dreams are by-products of spontaneous brain activity (Hobson & McCarley, 1977; Lavie & Hobson, 1986).

PROJECTIVE TECHNIQUES

Projective techniques are another method of indirect personality assessment. Subjects are given ambiguous stimuli and asked to impart meaning to them. By doing so, the subject reveals unconscious motives, ideas, and feelings.

The Nature of Projective Techniques

Projective techniques are based on the **projective hypothesis**: when individuals must impose meaning or order on an ambiguous stimulus, their responses will project or reflect their feelings, attitudes, desires, and needs. (This process has some obvious parallels with projection as an ego defense mechanism.) Some projective techniques appear similar to a test, but calling them *techniques* or *methods* is more accurate. Most projective techniques do not meet the generally accepted criteria for tests, such as being standardized and having norms (Anastasi, 1988a).

There are a number of different types of projective techniques. They vary in the nature of the stimulus presented to subjects and the nature of the response required. Most projective techniques fall into one of four categories:

1. *Association*, such as to inkblots or words.
2. *Construction* of stories about pictures that are open to a variety of interpretations (e.g., the Thematic Apperception Test).
3. *Completion* of sentences (e.g., "I often feel. . . .") or stories.
4. *Expression* in drawings (e.g., Draw-a-Person Test) or through acting out a loosely specified role (e.g., in psychodrama).

All projective techniques share five important characteristics:

1. The stimulus is relatively unstructured and ambiguous, which forces the subject to impose order or structure.
2. The purpose of the test or how responses will be scored or interpreted is not disclosed.
3. The subject is told that there are no correct answers.
4. Each response is assumed to reveal something valid and significant about the subject's personality.
5. Scoring and interpretation are generally lengthy and relatively subjective procedures.

We will first describe the most common projective technique, Rorschach inkblots, and then contrast it with the Holtzman Inkblot Technique. Another widely used projective technique, the Thematic Apperception Test (TAT), is discussed in Chapter 11.

The Rorschach Inkblots

The use of inkblots to reveal something about an individual, such as imagination, was not a new idea when Hermann Rorschach began his experiments in the early part of the 20th century. But Rorschach, a Swiss psychiatrist, was the first to systematically use a standard set of inkblots to assess personality. In 1921, Rorschach published the results of his work. His monograph, *Psychodiagnostik*, bore the informative subtitle *Methodology and Results of a Perceptual-Diagnostic Experiment (Interpretation of*

Accidental Forms). A year later Rorschach died, and it was left to others to elaborate on the basic procedures he had outlined.

Description of the Inkblots

There are 10 nearly symmetrical **Rorschach inkblots;** five have some color and five are black and white. The blots are printed on white cardboard (about 7 × 10 inches). Figure 6-6 shows inkblots similar to those used in the Rorschach. The blots were originally made by spilling ink on a piece of paper and then folding the paper in half (something you might enjoy trying yourself).

Administration

The Rorschach inkblot technique, or *the Rorschach* as it is commonly called, is administered individually in two phases. The first is *performance proper*, which begins with simple instructions from the examiner: "I am going to show you a number of inkblots, and I want you to tell me what you see in each of them." The examiner records exactly what the subject says about each blot (e.g., "That reminds me of a rabbit running").

When the subject has responded to all 10 inkblots, the second phase—*inquiry*—begins. Starting with the first card, the examiner reminds the subject of each response made. The examiner asks the subject where on the inkblot the response was seen ("Where did you see a rabbit running?") and what made it look like that ("What about the inkblot made it look like a rabbit running?").

Scoring and Interpretation

There are a number of different systems for scoring and interpreting Rorschach responses. In one of the most widely used systems, each response is scored for five characteristics that focus on how the response was generated (Klopfer & Davidson, 1962):

1. *Location*—where on the card the concept was seen.
2. *Determinant*—the qualities of the blot that led to the formation of the concept (such as shape, color, and apparent movement).
3. *Popularity-originality*—the frequency with which particular responses are given by people in general.
4. *Content*—the subject matter of the concept.

Figure 6-6
Inkblots similar to those used by Rorschach.

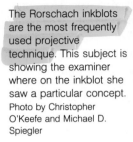

The Rorschach inkblots are the most frequently used projective technique. This subject is showing the examiner where on the inkblot she saw a particular concept.
Photo by Christopher O'Keefe and Michael D. Spiegler

5. *Form-level*—how accurately the concept is seen and how closely the concept fits the blot.

Interpretation of the Rorschach requires extensive knowledge of psychoanalytic concepts (Jaffee, 1988). The interpreter looks for patterns of responses or consistent themes rather than interpreting single responses. Rorschach interpretations are admittedly subjective. Table 6-2 presents examples of possible interpretations.

The Holtzman Inkblot Technique

Projective techniques have been criticized for not adhering to the same psychometric standards as other personality assessment methods. Aware of this limitation, Wayne Holtzman and his associates developed "a completely new approach to inkblot testing, one which is designed from its inception to meet adequate standards of measurement while preserving the uniquely valuable projective quality of the Rorschach" (Holtzman, Thorpe, Swartz, & Herron, 1961, p. 10). They tested a large number of inkblots with samples of normal college students and psychiatric patients. Inkblots were then evaluated and selected on the basis of two additional criteria: (1) the ability of an inkblot to reliably differentiate between the normal and abnormal samples, and (2) maximum **interrater reliability** (agreement among scorers) on the categories for which the inkblots were being scored.

Two equivalent sets of 45 inkblots were selected for the final version of the Holtzman Inkblot Technique. With two sets of inkblots, a psychologist can administer the technique twice to the same subject without the second responses being "contaminated" by previous exposure to the same set of inkblots. The equivalent sets also make it possible to assess **retest reliability**, which measures the stability of a test over time.

With the Holtzman inkblots, subjects are asked to give *one* response to each of the 45 inkblots. The total number of responses made is therefore constant for all subjects. As a result, it is easier to compare subjects' responses and to develop norms. Each response is scored for 22 variables, including all the variables for which the Rorschach is scored and other variables such as anxiety and hostility. Research over 30 years shows that the Holtzman Inkblot Technique and a new, shorter form with 25 inkblots are highly reliable (Holtzman, 1988).

| **PSYCHOANALYTIC PSYCHOTHERAPY** | For Freud, the practice of psychotherapy was more than just a way to help his patients. His clinical cases provided both the data and the evidence for his theory of personality. Based on what he learned from his patients, Freud formulated his theory. He then gathered support for the theory from further |

Table 6-2

Examples of scoring and interpreting the Rorschach inkblots

SCORING CHARACTERISTIC	EXAMPLES OF SCORING CATEGORY	SAMPLE RESPONSES	EXAMPLES OF INTERPRETATIONS*
Location	Whole	Entire blot used for concept	Ability to organize and integrate material
	Small usual detail	Small part that is easily marked off from the rest of the blot	Need to be exact and accurate
Determinant	Form	"The outline looks like a bear"	Degree of emotional control
	Movement	"A flying hawk"	Level of ego functioning
Popularity-originality	Popular	Response that many people give	Need to be conventional
	Original	Response that few people give (and that fits blot well)	Superior intelligence
Content	Animal figures	"Looks like a house cat"	Passivity and dependence
	Human figures	"It's a man or a woman"	Problem with sexual identity
Form-level	High form-level	Concept fits blot well	High intellectual functioning
	Low form-level	Concept is a poor match to blot	Contact with reality tenuous

*Interpretations would be made only if the type of response occurred a number of times (not just once). See text for further precautions regarding interpretations of Rorschach responses.

clinical observations. The result is psychoanalytic personality theory and psychoanalytic psychotherapy. In the following discussion, the term *psychoanalysis* refers to therapy (as opposed to personality theory).

Most of Freud's patients suffered from *hysteria* (more commonly known today as *conversion disorder*) — a psychological disorder characterized by a physical ailment, such as paralysis of the legs, with no physiological cause. Hysteria was quite common at the end of the 19th century, but physicians had little success treating it. For example, Jean Charcot, a neurologist in Paris with whom Freud studied, hypnotized his hysteric patients and then directly instructed them to renounce their symptoms. This hypnotic suggestion was generally effective as long as the patient remained hypnotized. But when the patient awoke, the symptoms almost invariably returned.

Shortly after studying with Charcot, Freud opened his private medical practice in Vienna and became associated with Josef Breuer, a prominent Viennese physician. Breuer also used hypnosis in treating hysteria. Breuer, however, did not tell his hypnotized patients to make their symptoms disappear. Instead, he asked the patient to vividly recall the traumatic experience that had first led to the hysterical symptom. The patient's recall of the trauma was accompanied by a great emotional release (*catharsis*), which seemingly led to a cure. In contrast to Charcot, Breuer obtained changes that lasted after the patient awakened.

Breuer and Freud (1955) concluded that hysterical symptoms arise from painful memories and emotions that have been repressed. This explains why the patient's symptoms go away when the repressed memories and associated painful emotions are finally permitted expression. Freud later generalized the theory to all neuroses. **Neuroses** (plural of *neurosis*) are psychological disorders characterized by anxiety and abnormal behavior, such as phobias, obsessions, and physical complaints without a physical basis. Freud believed that neuroses always reflect unresolved repressed conflicts, which must be resolved for the neuroses to be fully cured.

The Process of Psychoanalysis

The basic aim of psychoanalysis is, in a nutshell, to *make what is unconscious, conscious*. More specifically, the patient must become aware of unconscious desires and the conflicts that result from them. Four fundamental processes are involved: *free association*; *resistance*, including transference; *interpretation*; and *insight*. The patient talks and freely associates to anything that comes to mind. The therapist listens and at the appropriate time, interprets what the patient has said (e.g., Spiegler & Davison, 1989). The patient is expected to gain insight about the causes of the problems from these interpretations. This is possible when the patient's inevitable resistance to gaining insight (and being cured) is overcome (Figure 6-7).

Free Association

When Freud first began his practice, he hypnotized his patients to help them recall events that might have been related to the onset of their disorders. Soon, however, Freud began to urge patients to recall repressed events without hypnosis. He found that, given sufficient freedom, patients

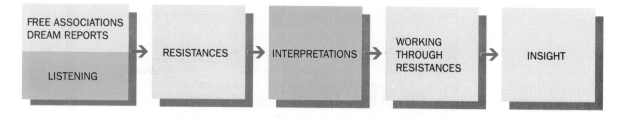

Patient's role/behavior

Analyst's role/behavior

→ Direction of process

Figure 6-7
Steps in the process of psychoanalytic psychotherapy.

wandered in their thoughts and recollections, which allowed him to understand their unconscious conflicts. This free-association technique became the cornerstone of psychoanalysis.

In **free association**, the patient says whatever comes to mind regardless of social convention, logic and order, seeming importance, or feelings of embarrassment. Freud had his patients free associate while lying on a couch. The reclining position is reminiscent of sleep, which brings the patient closer to unconscious processes. Freud sat behind the couch, out of the patient's view (Figure 6-8). Free association is easier for the patient when the patient is not constantly reminded of the therapist's presence. (But free association is not easy. You can demonstrate this for yourself by trying to tell a friend or even just a tape recorder everything and anything that you are thinking of for 5 minutes.)

Resistance

Freud's patients sought treatment for their neuroses. But they often seemed to resist being cured (e.g., Finell, 1987). **Resistance** refers to anything that impedes the progress of therapy. Resistance can be conscious or unconscious (Strean, 1985). *Conscious resistance* occurs when the patient is aware of impeding the progress of the analysis. A patient may have a disturbing dream and decide not to tell the analyst about it. Or a patient might deliberately miss a therapy session. In *unconscious resistance*, the patient is not aware of "fighting" the treatment; thus, unconscious resistance is more difficult to overcome than conscious resistance. Unconscious resistance is also more significant because it indicates the patient's unconscious strivings and thereby provides the analyst with clues about the patient's personality (e.g., Thompson, 1987). Resistance always has a dual nature: (1) it interferes with treatment, and (2) it is a source of information (e.g., Levenson, 1988).

Transference: A Special Form of Resistance

The patient's inappropriate feelings toward the psychoanalyst are called **transference**. These feelings are *distorted displacements* from significant figures in the patient's life (usually in the past) to the analyst. For example,

patients may act as if the analyst were their father or mother. Transference can be positive (e.g., love, respect, and admiration) or negative (e.g., hatred, jealousy, and disgust). Transference is considered the most important form of unconscious resistance (Grubrich-Simitis, 1987; Singer, 1985; Stolorow, 1988). Moreover, the development of transference in a patient is taken as evidence that the psychoanalytic process is underway (Renik, 1990).

Here is an example of transference, recently published in the psychoanalytic literature (Mendelson, 1991). The patient is a single professional woman who had just gone through a painful relationship with an "unavailable" man. So far, the analyst's efforts to get her to free associate had been relatively unsuccessful; the patient simply remained silent after the request to speak openly. The analyst again commented on her silence.

> To this she promptly replied that she had used fully with me the technique that had greatly frustrated her mother, namely, silence. She knew it had been provocative. In childhood, she challenged her mother to get angry, and own up to her rejecting attitude. The same applied to me: she wanted to goad me into admitting that I too did not want her and found her arrival at each session unwelcome: "Oh, her again?" While I did not have that reaction, there were times when I wondered when—or if—she would ever be able to emerge from the sullenness that was usually evident when I greeted her. I had adapted myself, until I became clearly aware of it, to a routine of expecting to be turned to when she felt in need, and at the same time to be viewed as a feared and resented enemy. In effect, I had gone along with her as her mother did, in partial compliance with her provocativeness. (pp. 190–191)

Are all feelings that a patient has about the psychoanalyst instances of transference? Is it possible for a patient to like or dislike the analyst as a person rather than as a representation of a significant other in the patient's life? Some psychoanalysts would say no. But others would say that transference distinguishes itself from "real" feelings by inappropriateness and repetition of the past (Schimek, 1983). One of the keys to identifying transference is the intensity of the patients emotions: " . . . transference is not a slice of life; it is a highly intensified . . . version of what the patient is exploring" (Levenson, 1988, p. 14).

Transference is an impediment to psychoanalysis because it is an inappropriate reaction. For instance, although the analyst is not the patient's father, a patient who had a strict father may respond to the analyst's interpretations as if they were criticisms. This reaction would make it more difficult for the patient to accept interpretations.

Transference can also facilitate the therapeutic process. Analysts use such inappropriate behavior to point out to patients the nature of their relationships to significant people in their lives. The interpretation of transference is an integral part of psychoanalysis. Indeed, Freud believed that the patient has to experience transference toward the analyst and work through it if psychoanalysis is to be successful (Osman & Tabachnick, 1988).

Psychoanalysts may experience distorted displacements toward their patients (Gorkin, 1987). This **countertransference** may adversely affect the critical patient-analyst relationship, such as by reducing the analyst's objectivity. Two major controls have been established to deal with countertransference. First, psychoanalysts themselves must undergo psychoanalysis as part of their training. Having insight into their own unconscious processes and conflicts helps analysts recognize and deal with countertransference (e.g., Marcus, 1988). Second, analysts regularly review their cases with a supervising analyst who may notice countertransference that the analyst overlooked and help the analyst deal with it (e.g., Novick, 1987).

Like transference, countertransference can be therapeutically beneficial (e.g., Drell, 1988). Analyzing the countertransference can provide the analyst with useful information about the patient. For example, when some aspect of the patient's behavior triggers an emotional response in the analyst, it is likely that the patient also affects other people in a similar way. Thus, the countertransference reflects the patient's social interactions with others. Countertransference is considered particularly important by object relations therapists (Cashdan, 1988).

Transference is not limited to therapeutic relationships (e.g., Singer, 1985); it can occur in any relationship, as the following incident shows:

> A young woman, Heather, was living in her fiancé's apartment while he was away for several months. When Heather and a male friend were walking out of the apartment one day, they met the landlord. The landlord remarked, "When the cat's away, the mice will play." In fact, the relationship between Heather and her male friend was totally aboveboard. But Heather was extremely upset by the landlord's implied accusation. She continued to be upset the next day, which surprised her because she clearly "didn't give a damn what the landlord thought." Sometime later she realized that it was not her landlord's disapproval that bothered her, but her father's. (Spiegler, 1989)

Interpretation

Patients provide the analyst with a wealth of information, but the meaning of what they report is often not immediately apparent. Unconscious material becomes conscious only in disguised or symbolic form (e.g., Shear & Kundrat, 1987). Thus, the analyst's job is to discover the hidden meanings of what the patient talks about and what the patient does, including symptoms and forms of resistance. The analyst then communicates these meanings to the patient as **interpretations.** The interpretations help patients understand how their neurotic behavior developed by reconstructing childhood experiences that led to the conflict producing the neurosis. Freud likened this process to the excavation and reconstruction of an archaeological ruin. (Freud was fascinated by archaeology, as you might guess from the works of art in his consulting room; see Figure 6-8, p. 132.)

Schwaber (1990) has distinguished two kinds of interpretations used by contemporary analysts. One type of interpretation is aimed at helping patients understand and acknowledge something about themselves that the analyst already understands. The other is aimed at stimulating patients conscious and unconscious thoughts about a question to which the analyst does not yet have an answer.

Interpretations cannot be forced on a patient. It is important that the analyst does not advance an interpretation until the patient is "ready" to hear it. The patient often must work through resistances to be able to accept an interpretation as personally meaningful.

Insight

Analysts' interpretations help patients gain insight into the nature and origin of their neuroses. **Insight** involves more than an intellectual understanding; it also requires *emotional* acceptance. The patient must think and feel that the new self-knowledge is personally "right" or that it "fits." This sort of understanding and acceptance develops gradually and often painstakingly. Insight is the final goal of psychoanalysis and is expected to bring about a cure.

The Practice of Psychoanalysis

At the beginning of the 20th century, psychological problems were treated almost exclusively by physicians. (Psychiatry did not yet exist as a specialty.) Freud himself believed that psychoanalysts did not need to have medical training. (Anna Freud, for one, did not.) Nonetheless, most early analysts were physicians.

Today, the majority of practicing psychoanalysts are still psychiatrists, medical doctors trained in the treatment of psychopathology. However, this state of affairs is changing rapidly. As the 1980s came to an end, four psychologists filed an antitrust law suit against several psychoanalytic organizations (mainly, the American Psychoanalytic Association). The suit charged that psychologists were being excluded from psychoanalytic training and membership in psychoanalytic societies. In an out-of-court settlement, the psychoanalytic organizations agreed to admit more psychologists and other nonmedical professionals into their training institutes and as members of psychoanalytic societies (Buie, 1988, 1989a).

At the same time, psychoanalysis is becoming less important to general academic psychiatry (Reisner, 1989). The resulting trend is that psychoanalytic practice is fast becoming "demedicalized" (Cooper, 1990).

Modifications of Psychoanalytic Psychotherapy

Post-Freudian psychoanalysts have made changes in psychoanalytic psychotherapy that are consistent with their modifications in personality theory. Although there are many forms of post-Freudian therapy, some overall themes can be abstracted.

The most general of these themes is that post-Freudian analysis is *more flexible* and *broader* than Freudian analysis (Modell, 1988). This is manifested in many specific ways.

Post-Freudian psychoanalysis focuses on the present as well as the past. Post-Freudians consider it important to explore the ways the patient is functioning effectively as well as to analyze problem behaviors that bring the patient to therapy. The individual's strengths are used to devise a treatment plan. The patient's interpersonal relations are emphasized, and situational stresses are considered along with intrapsychic conflicts.

Analysts who do focus on the past are rethinking the purpose of this practice. Freud hoped to obtain historically true pictures from the memories of his patients (Bloch, 1989). Modern analysts measure the validity of reconstructions of the patient's past created in psychoanalysis by how convincing the reconstructions are to the patient and the analyst. Reconstructions are only *narratives*, a search for meaning in the present. This means, of course, that there is no *one* truth about a person's past. Multiple narratives are possible (Leichtman, 1990). What a good narrative truth must do is provide an "assured conviction," which is as therapeutic as a memory truly recaptured (Roth, 1991).

Interaction between therapist and patient is less formal and restrictive in post-Freudian analysis. The patient usually sits facing the therapist. The emphasis in therapy can be supportive as well as uncovering (e.g., Bemporad, 1988; Josephs, 1988; Wallerstein, 1989). The patient/therapist relationship is considered important independent of, but not excluding, transference. Post-Freudian analysts specifically attempt to foster a **therapeutic alliance**, that is, a stable, cooperative relationship between patient and therapist (e.g., Novick, 1987). It is considered a necessary (but not a sufficient) condition for effective therapy (Greenson, 1965, 1967; Hartley & Strupp, 1983; Zetzel, 1956). Fostering a therapeutic alliance is one example of the more active role post-Freudian analysts play. They also tend to talk more and to be more directive, including giving advice to their patients, which Freudians usually do not do.

Presently, there is a much wider range of psychoanalytic patients than in Freud's day (Rockland, 1989). Freud himself thought psychoanalysis was useful mainly for adult neurotics. Melanie Klein and Anna Freud were both instrumental in beginning the practice of child analysis, a specialty that is currently flourishing (Fonagy & Moran, 1990). Psychoanalysis is now considered adaptable to group and family therapy (McCallum & Piper, 1988; Scharff & Scharff, 1987), and has been expanded to treat disorders not usually treated by traditional psychoanalysis, such as substance abuse (Brickman, 1988). Also, traditional analysis typically requires three to five sessions per week over the course of 3 or more years. Post-Freudian therapy often is briefer, involving fewer sessions per week and fewer total sessions (Arlow & Brenner, 1988).

There are still other ways that post-Freudian approaches to therapy are more flexible than traditional psychoanalysis. The therapy often is individualized and less likely to follow standard procedures that guide the treatment of all patients (such as experiencing and successfully working through transference). Post-Freudian interpretations are likely to be (1) psychosocial as well as psychosexual, (2) more concrete and practical, and (3) less abstract and theoretical.

Finally, the purpose of psychoanalysis has expanded. Fromm went so far as to say that people should undergo psychoanalysis "not as a therapy but as an instrument for self-understanding. That is to say an instrument for self-liberation, an instrument in the art of loving" (quoted by Bacciagaluppi, 1989, p. 230).

Another major issue is how to think of countertransference. Freud believed that countertransference should be feared and avoided as an impediment to therapy. Many contemporary psychoanalysts feel they can use the countertransference for therapeutic purposes (Greenson, 1974; Hoffer, 1985). Object relations therapy, to which we turn next, actually makes countertransference the centerpiece of treatment.

Object Relations Therapy   Some psychoanalysts feel that contemporary object relations theory suggests a new approach to therapy (Arcaya & Gerber, 1990; Cashdan, 1988; Ogden, 1982). Recall that according to object relations theory, personality is thought to evolve out of human interactions rather than out of biologically derived tensions. Instead of tension reduction, human beings are primarily motivated by the need to establish and maintain relations with others.

> Relationships are not simply welcome additions to human existence. They are what existence is all about. If human beings hope to retain an ongoing sense of who they are and where they fit in the world, they need to form meaningful relationships with significant others. What's more, they need to ensure that these relationships endure.
>
> But what if people have grave reservations about their self-worths? What if they not only question their ability to form meaningful relationships but to sustain them? For such individuals, human relationships are at best tenuous affairs. They cannot assume that others will stay involved with them of their own volition. *They consequently search for means by which to ensure the significant figures in their lives remain bound to them.* The results are seen in patterns of adult object relations that fall under the rubric of "projective identifications." (Cashdan, 1988, p. 55)

Projective identification involves projecting a "bad" part of the self to another person and then pressuring the recipient to identify with the projected bad characteristic (see Chapter 5). This maladaptive means of relating to others is the focus of object relations therapy. In fact, patients' projective identifications actually are used for therapeutic benefit. Specifically, object relations therapists allow themselves to become the recipients of their patients' projective identifications.

> . . . the goal of treatment involves helping clients differentiate reality from projection and assisting them to recognize how their past representations of reality interfere with their apprehension of the present situation. . . .
>
> The object relations perspective maintains that the only way in which therapists can understand and begin to rectify their patients' distorted object representations is by permitting themselves to be affected by them. This process then allows the therapist to enter into the subjective world of the client by becoming an object of the patient's projective identification. . . .
>
> The basis of this therapeutic approach consists of the therapist's tactful, but insistent manner of bringing these disowned or unconscious images back into the patient's conscious awareness so that they can be altered or discarded by the client's rational self. . . .
>
> [Object relations therapy] is an experiential approach which teaches the client how to recognize and deal with those external situations which stimulate his or her own self-attacking feelings. (Arcaya & Gerber, 1990, pp. 621–622)

Cashdan (1988) sees the object relations therapy as a four-stage process: engagement, projective identification, confrontation, and termination.

Engagement

During **engagement,** the object relations therapist must become a significant person for the patient. The therapist is not just another professional, but is a person who empathizes with and can reflect the patient's emotions. This requires demonstrating interest in the details of the patient's life and *emotionally linking* these details to the patient's feelings. Here are four examples of phrases that object relations therapists use to demonstrate emotional linking:

> "It makes you *happy* when you talk about _____."
>
> "You seem *upset* whenever the subject of _____ comes up."
>
> "You're really *annoyed* at _____."
>
> "_____ makes you *embarrassed*."

Projective Identification

During this stage the patient engages in projective identification, targeting the therapist. The extent to which this is therapeutic for the patient depends on

> . . . the therapist's ability to receive the patient's projections, utilize facets of [the therapist's] own more mature personality system to process the projection, and

then make the ... projection available for [the patient's] reinternalization through the therapeutic interaction. (Ogden, 1982, p. 20)

Confrontation

During **confrontation,** the object relations therapist confronts the patient's pathology in a direct and forceful manner, while refusing to concede or conform to the parts of the self the patient has projected onto the therapist. At the same time, the therapist/patient relationship must be reaffirmed. The projective identification is being rejected, not the patient.

At first, this may lead to the patient's intensifying projective identification, blaming, or attempting to terminate therapy. But the therapist must "hang in there." Here is how the therapist confronted a patient whose projective identification was dependency.

Beth: Does it pay for me to keep coming?

Therapist: I'll be here next week ... same time, same place.

Beth: I'm not sure I'll be coming.

Therapist: You decide what's best. Just remember, this time is yours. I'll be here no matter what you decide.

(Cashdan, 1973, p. 89)

This interchange was highly significant. The therapist later explained: "Beth told me that the turning point occurred for her when she 'returned' to therapy and found I was waiting for her as I said I would. She said that from that moment on something changed in our relationship and she began to see herself differently" (Cashdan, 1988, p. 131).

Termination

During **termination,** the therapist provides information as to how the patient is perceived by others, drawing on what has happened "in the room." Cashdan (1988) says: "I reveal that my first impulse was to wash my hands of them" (p. 133). An example of what he said to one patient is: "Do you know that whenever you ask me something, there is a pleading quality in your voice?" (p. 134). Such candor "allows the patient to experience what it feels like to be in an open relationship with another human being" (p. 135).

It is difficult to convey the depth of this experience without getting maudlin or sentimental. But it is fair to say that patients who go through the process find it very powerful. They describe it as 'freeing' and even exhilarating. Patients who relinquish their projective ways of being in the world feel as if a millstone has been lifted from their necks. They begin to see human relationships in a different light and are able to consider options they have never before thought possible. (p. 136)

During this stage, the patient is encouraged to "let go," which

... means to forgive. It means being able to experience one's inner objects as fallible and to absolve them of their shortcomings. The patient needs to see his early caretaker(s) as flawed human beings who were incapable of engaging the patient in a nonmanipulative relationship because of their own shortcomings... Unless the patient forgives his inner objects, the patient will find it impossible to forgive himself. (p. 139)

The last act in termination is separating from the therapist. Cashdan says: "I make it a point to let my patients know that I am gratified that they have reached this juncture in their lives and saddened by the fact that they no longer will be an active part of mine" (p. 144).

SUMMARY

1. Freud considered dreams to be the most revealing source of information about personality. He believed that the manifest content—what we recall of the dream—is determined by a latent content that involves unconscious desires and conflicts.

2. Socially unacceptable latent content is transformed into acceptable manifest content through dream work, including condensation, displacement, visual representation, and secondary revision. Through symbolization, latent content becomes manifest content in disguised and nonthreatening forms. Freud emphasized sexual symbolism in dreams.

3. In Freudian dream interpretation, the manifest dream as well as the patient's free associations to it are analyzed. The psychoanalyst interprets both of these sources based on the principles of dream work and symbolism.

4. Freud posited three functions of dreaming: wish fulfillment, tension release, and sleep preservation.

5. The physiology of sleep and dreaming has been studied in the laboratory by measuring brain waves (EEG) and eye movements. Four basic sleep stages have been identified. Most dreaming occurs in rapid eye movement (REM) sleep. This sleep is paradoxical; the person is very relaxed as in deep sleep yet is mentally active as in light sleep. The physiology of dreaming provides some indirect support for Freud's dream theory.

6. Post-Freudians propose that dreaming serves other functions than those suggested by Freud, including problem solving and planning future actions.

7. Projective techniques present an ambiguous stimulus on which the subject must impose order or meaning; it is assumed that these projections are based on the subject's unconscious feelings, thoughts, and wishes. Projective techniques involve association (e.g., to words), construction (e.g., of stories), completion (e.g., of sentences), and expression (e.g., through drawing).

8. The Rorschach inkblots are the most common projective technique. The Holtzman inkblots provide a more standardized and more objective alternative.

9. In Freudian psychoanalysis, the patient talks about his or her problems and is encouraged to free associate about them. The psychoanalyst makes

interpretations of what the patient reveals, and the patient gains emotional and intellectual insight into the causes of the problems. Insight is possible only when the patient has worked through various resistances. Transference is a major form of resistance in which patients displace feelings about significant people in their lives onto the analyst.

10. Post-Freudian therapy places greater emphasis on the present and a therapeutic alliance between the patient and therapist. Besides making interpretations, post-Freudian analysts provide concrete suggestions for action. Post-Freudian analysis is often briefer than Freudian analysis (which tends to be quite lengthy).

11. Object relations therapy involves four steps: (1) engagement of the patient; (2) permitting the patient to develop a projective identification toward the therapist; (3) confronting the patient's projective identification; and (4) a termination process in which patients forgive their inner objects, including themselves, for previously repressed ("bad") characteristics.

Liabilities of the Psychoanalytic Strategy

ach strategy has strengths and weaknesses. In the preceding chapters, we have tried to present the substance and flavor of the psychoanalytic strategy primarily in terms of its strengths. In this "liabilities" chapter, we will discuss the strategy's major weaknesses. A parallel liabilities chapter concludes the discussion of each of the other three strategies.

Bear in mind that the criticisms we will discuss have been made mainly by proponents of other strategies. Also, as you will see, it is typical for a given liability to plague more than one strategy. Finally, it would not be surprising if some of these liabilities have already occurred to you.

We will consider eight of the most commonly voiced criticisms of the psychoanalytic strategy. They are: (1) many psychoanalytic concepts are poorly defined; (2) some psychoanalytic hypotheses are untestable; (3) psychoanalytic reasoning is prone to logical errors; (4) classical psychoanalytic theory is sex biased; (5) psychoanalytic assessment has low reliability and validity; (6) psychoanalytic case studies are unduly biased; and (7) psychoanalytic treatment does not recover historical truth. The last liability we will discuss is posed as a question: (8) Is psychoanalysis a science?

MANY PSYCHOANALYTIC CONCEPTS ARE POORLY DEFINED

Read Freud's writing closely and you will find that many psychoanalytic concepts are never defined. Instead, they are merely described, usually in vague, nonspecific, and ambiguous ways. This is apparent even within the contemporary psychoanalytic community. For example, writing in *The Psychoanalytic Review*, Shulman (1990) reported: "To some psychoanalysts the concept of orality may refer to an instinctual regression to the bodily zone, while to others this concept may refer to interpersonal dependence" (p. 256).

As a result, researchers who wish to test the claims of psychoanalytic theory have no concrete guidelines for determining when a phenomenon discussed by the theory is actually occurring. Consider the case of reaction formation. When does affection reflect underlying hate as opposed to love, for instance? According to psychoanalytic theory, persistence and excess are two possible signs that reaction formation is operating. How much love must a husband show a wife before his expressed feelings and actions are considered a reaction formation to his underlying hate?

The problem of imprecise definitions is even more serious for those psychoanalytic phenomena that are said to occur in varying amounts, such as fixated or cathected libido. Because the theory provides no way of actually quantifying libido, critical questions are unanswerable. For example, how much libido must be invested at the oral stage for a person to become an oral character? How much threat of castration must children experience to repress sexual desires for their opposite-sexed parent? Again, the problem has been recognized by research-minded analysts who have begun to call for the establishment of a quantitative tradition within psychoanalysis (Eagle & Wolitzky, 1985; Masling & Cohen, 1987; Shulman, 1990).

Because psychoanalytic theory does not specify how to operationalize its concepts, some investigators have tried to test the propositions of psychoanalytic theory by creating their own research definitions. This is to their credit. However, developing valid research definitions for most psychoanalytic concepts has proven extremely difficult. Valid definitions must be closely related to the theoretical concept so that research findings will have a bearing on the theory.

A study of penis envy illustrates the problem. The study tested the straightforward prediction that more women than men would exhibit penis envy (Johnson, 1966). Penis envy was operationally defined as "keeping a borrowed pencil" (a pencil is a phallic symbol). In fact, significantly more women than men did fail to return pencils that had been loaned to them. "Keeping a borrowed pencil" is an objective and reliable measure; the researcher has only to count the number of pencils loaned to each sex and the number returned by each sex. It could be argued, however, that pencil hoarding is not a *valid* measure of penis envy because it is too remote from the theoretical concept. This study shows that a reliable measure may not be a valid measure. It is easy to question whether the results validate the concept of penis envy.

SOME PSYCHOANALYTIC HYPOTHESES ARE UNTESTABLE

A fundamental requirement of any scientific theory is that its propositions must be testable, that is, open to verification or falsification through research (see Chapter 1). Critics of psychoanalytic theory claim that some of its most important propositions are not testable because the theory can be stretched to fit any outcome. For this reason, psychoanalytic theory is sometimes called a "rubber sheet" theory. As one analyst concedes:

> Psychoanalysis is hard to test because it allows for the existence of contraries [and because] the psychoanalytic model of mind asserts that there will be a variety of conflicting and complementary unconscious forces that, depending on their combinations and permutations, may result in very different observable manifestations. (Wallace, 1986, p. 381)

To illustrate the problem, suppose one investigates the hypothesis that people fixated at the oral stage are dependent in their relationships. If the results of the study show that oral characters are dependent, then obviously the hypothesis is supported. But suppose the results indicate that oral characters are independent. In this case, the hypothesis also would be supported because independence can be a defense, a reaction formation, against dependence. Finally, oral characters might be found to be both dependent and independent. The hypothesis would still be supported, because going back and forth between dependence and independence can be seen as a compromise between the drive and its defense.

Similarly, Freud postulated that all dreams fulfill a hidden wish. Yet dreams are often unpleasant and disturbing. It is difficult to understand how such dreams can be wish-fulfilling. Freud (1961a) explained that these are counterwish dreams that satisfy the dreamer's masochism. This type of reasoning led an early critic to comment that psychoanalysis "involves so many arbitrary interpretations that it is impossible to speak of proof in any strict sense of the term" (Moll, 1912, p. 190).

PSYCHOANALYTIC REASONING IS PRONE TO LOGICAL ERRORS	Psychoanalysts commit three logical errors in presenting research evidence for their theory. First, they *fail to distinguish between observation and inference.* Consider the Oedipus complex. Freud observed that at around age 4, boys are affectionate toward and seek the attention of their mothers; to some degree, they also avoid their fathers. To explain these observations, Freud conjectured that a boy's feelings for his mother are due to sexual desires; his feelings for his father are related to the rivalry due to this sexual attachment and the implicit threat of castration. This inference has the status of a hypothesis—it is one possible explanation and nothing more.

To say "4-year-old boys experience an Oedipus complex" is *to replace an observation with an inference.* It would be a different matter to say "4-year-old boys show behavior consistent with the Oedipus complex." Presenting inferences as observations when they represent only one possible explanation is a logical error. The seriousness of this error becomes even more salient because nonpsychoanalytic theories can sometimes provide equally good, and often better, explanations of the observed facts (e.g., Sears, 1943; Wolpe & Rachman, 1960).

A second logical error that psychoanalysts often commit is *confusing correlation and causation.* For instance, it is legitimate to report that during the first year of life infants engage in many behaviors involving the mouth (such as eating, sucking, and crying). Infants are also dependent on others for most of their needs. Thus, oral behavior and dependency occur together (at the same time), and one can legitimately say that they are *correlated.* However, one cannot legitimately conclude that dependency is *caused by* orality. It is entirely possible that a third variable accounts for both dependency and orality. (See Chapter 2 for a discussion of correlation and causation.)

Psychoanalysts frequently use analogies to describe their observations, and herein lies a third logical error. *Analogy is not proof.* An analogy may help to describe a new or complex concept, but it cannot be considered verification of the concept. For example, troops left in battle are used to help explain fixation. It is true that military troops may be permanently lost for future battles in a difficult skirmish. This fact, however, does not in any way validate the claim that libido is fixated at a stage in which the child had trouble resolving the relevant conflict.

CLASSICAL PSYCHOANALYTIC THEORY IS SEX BIASED	By today's standards, Freud's theory appears blatantly sexist (Frosh, 1987; Sagan, 1988; Sayers, 1991), and this is also true of much post-Freudian theorizing. The theories are based on males and then extended to females. For example, Freud attempted to make the Electra complex fit the model of

the Oedipus complex. The fit is none too snug (Person, 1988). Similarly, Freud's concept of castration anxiety follows from the notion that the little boy wants to have sex with his mother. Castration is obviously a fitting punishment. Freud considered penis envy to be the female counterpart of castration anxiety. But penis envy is not directly parallel, and it does not serve the same purpose as castration anxiety — namely, to prevent incest. This part of Freud's theory is poorly formulated because he used male personality development as the basis for female development. It is curious that Freud was not better at theorizing about females, since most of his early patients were women. It may be that Freud actually based much of his theory on his own self-analysis (Anzieu, 1986; Hardin, 1987, 1988a, 1988b).

Freud used male personality as a prototype and considered it the ideal. Quite bluntly, in Freud's view, women are inferior to men. He believed that the part of their personality that is different from men's comes from defending against and overcompensating for their inferiority. Consider three of Freud's ideas about female sexuality and personality:

1. *Females are castrated.* Obviously this concept assumes that women once had a penis, which implies the superiority of the male sexual anatomy. In Freud's (1964b) words: "Her self-love is mortified by the comparison with the boy's far superior equipment" (p. 126). There is no evidence that women feel inferior because they have a vagina rather than a penis or that a penis is in any way superior to a vagina.

2. *Females have more difficulty establishing a sex role than males.* Freud derived this proposition from the view that the girl has a more complicated Oedipal situation. Although the mother is the first object of love for both sexes, the girl must switch her love to her father, whereas the boy continues with his mother as his primary love object. The additional step for the girl could make her sex-role identification more troublesome. "But the empirical literature suggests that, if anything, the female has *less* difficulty than the male in the process of evolving a sex role" (Fisher & Greenberg, 1977, p. 220).

3. *Vaginal orgasm indicates sexual maturity.* Freud believed that a woman needs to relinquish her desire for a penis (penis envy) to successfully resolve her Electra complex and to function as a mature adult. According to Freud, the mature woman derives sexual pleasure primarily from penile stimulation of the vagina rather than the clitoris. Freud viewed the clitoris as a woman's penis. Therefore, "no longer deriving sexual pleasure from clitoral stimulation" means relinquishing penis envy. Although this is a minor aspect of Freud's theory, it has been widely accepted as fact. The existing evidence, however, contradicts it:

> Fisher (1973) obtained ratings from several different samples of married women with regard to the degree to which they prefer clitoral as compared to vaginal stimulation in the process of attaining orgasm. He found no indications that women with a clitoral orientation were especially inferior in their psychological adaptation. Surprisingly . . . it was not the clitorally-

oriented woman who was most anxious, as would be expected within the Freudian framework, but rather the vaginally-oriented one. (Fisher & Greenberg, 1977, p. 212)

Many of Freud's views of women have not been substantiated, which is not, in itself, an indictment. Theories are developed to be tested. The telling criticism of classical psychoanalytic views of women is that they assume men are the model for all human personality and women should strive to be like men.

Classical psychoanalytic views of women have not gone unchallenged. *Feminist analysis*, although not new, is very much a contemporary approach within psychoanalysis (Steele, 1985). Early feminist analysis (e.g., Horney, 1939; Jones, 1927; Thompson, 1941, 1942, 1943, 1950) primarily involved a critique and reformulation of classical psychoanalytic ideas. More recently, feminist analysis has gone beyond criticism of Freud's position to present a more balanced view of female personality (e.g., Buie, 1989b; Cantor & Bernay, 1988; Gilligan, 1982; Sayers, 1991). Mitchell (1974a, 1974b), for example, used classical psychoanalysis as a starting point. She argued that classical psychoanalysis need not be viewed as "a recommendation *for* a patriarchal society," but as "an analysis *of* one. If we are interested in understanding and challenging the oppression of women, we cannot afford to neglect it" (1974b, p. xv).

PSYCHOANALYTIC ASSESSMENT HAS LOW RELIABILITY AND VALIDITY

Several thousand studies have examined the reliability and validity of projective techniques (Buros, 1965, 1972). Interrater reliability (agreement among raters) and internal consistency (agreement among the items or stimuli used with a given technique) are usually low. Retest reliability (consistency over time) is equally poor when responses or the themes based on those responses are compared in two separate test administrations. For example, Lindzey and Herman (1955) gave the same subjects the TAT twice. For the second administration, they told the subjects to write different stories. If the TAT were effective in assessing the subjects' personality dynamics, then the *themes* of the stories would be the same for each subject in the two administrations, even though the specific stories were different. There was no support for this hypothesis.

The validity of projective techniques is also largely unsubstantiated by empirical research (Anastasi, 1988a; Cronbach, 1949). In one of the more common types of validity studies, experienced clinicians write personality descriptions about subjects based on responses to a projective technique such as the Rorschach. The judges are "blind" in terms of other information about the subjects. In such studies, agreement between the judges' descriptions has been low. Also, the judges' descriptions are often so general that they could apply to almost anyone. (The description would include statements like those appearing in Demonstration 1-1 on bogus personality testing.)

Another source of negative evidence casts doubt on the very basis of the techniques, namely, the projective hypothesis (Anastasi, 1988a). According to the hypothesis, responses to ambiguous stimuli will be projections of a person's enduring personality characteristics. Rather than assessing underlying personality dynamics and motivational dispositions, projective techniques may be measuring individual differences in perceptual and cognitive factors. For instance, suppose researchers could demonstrate a relationship between the number of sexual responses to an inkblot and frequency of sexual activity. This finding would not necessarily mean that they were measuring an underlying sexual drive and that this drive causes the sexual behavior. An equally plausible explanation of the relationship is that people who engage in more sexual behavior have more sexual thoughts (Epstein, 1966; Klinger, 1966).

Some problems with projective techniques stem from a lack of standardization of administration, scoring, and interpretation. Subtle changes in how a projective technique is presented to the subject, including the relationship between the examiner and the subject, can influence performance (e.g., Masling, 1960).

Subjectivity is another factor that may account for the low reliability and validity of projective methods. Scoring projective techniques requires at least some subjective judgment, even when scoring involves placing responses in pre-designated categories. Free interpretations of projective responses vary widely according to the skill and experience of the examiner. They also vary among examiners of comparable ability. Projective techniques may be as much a projection of the examiner's own biases, hypotheses, favorite interpretations, and theoretical persuasions as an indication of the characteristics of the subject (Anastasi, 1988a). Well-developed standards for scoring and interpreting projective techniques would certainly help increase their reliability and validity, but few adequate standards exist.

Despite their problems, projective techniques are used extensively in personality research and in applied clinical settings for assessment and diagnosis (Lubin, Wallis, & Paine, 1971). The theoretical basis for projective techniques is most often psychoanalytic. However, psychologists of different theoretical persuasions also use projective techniques in their research and clinical practice (e.g., Swan & MacDonald, 1978).

What accounts for this popularity, given the negative evidence for reliability and validity? The simplest explanation can be summarized in one word: Tradition! Compared with other methods of personality assessment, projective techniques have the longest history and have received the most attention. It is difficult to discard such a huge investment of time and effort. Moreover, projective techniques are used mainly to measure unconscious motives, conflicts, and thoughts. Few alternatives for assessing the unconscious have been developed.

Reliability and validity of dream interpretations are a related problem. For instance, different analysts looking at the same data should reach similar interpretations. As it turns out, such agreement is rare. The same dream report is likely to be interpreted in different ways by independent, highly competent psychoanalysts (Lorand, 1946; Schafer, 1950).

Psychoanalytic interpretations have low reliability partially because the data and interpretations are qualitative. If they were quantified, even in the basic sense of categorizing, greater agreement might be possible (Shulman, 1990).

PSYCHOANALYTIC CASE STUDIES ARE UNDULY BIASED

Case studies are considered the primary method of research in the psychoanalytic strategy (Freud, 1955; Levenson, 1988). These studies are almost invariably of patients undergoing psychoanalysis. The limitations of the case-study method were discussed in Chapter 2; here, some specific problems with psychoanalytic case studies will be addressed.

The psychoanalytic session is private. Yet it is during these sessions that the data for case studies are gathered. This situation raises a serious problem. Because of theoretical bias, the analyst may selectively recall certain aspects of the case while selectively forgetting other aspects (Grünbaum, 1984). This process, in turn, may result in the analyst's reconstructing earlier material based on later observations. "Thus, the psychoanalyst's theoretical commitment can influence both the patient's utterances themselves and the manner in which they are organized, written up, and interpreted" (Sherwood, 1969, p. 71).

Evidence suggests that analytically-oriented therapists may be more likely to succumb to observer bias than therapists of other orientations. In one experiment, psychoanalysts and behavior therapists interviewed people who were presented as either "patients" or "job applicants"(Langer & Abelson, 1974). The analysts were significantly more likely to vary their clinical observations based on the labels alone. They tended to find the "patients" more disturbed than the "job applicants."

Psychoanalytic case studies are also biased in the sense that they are based on a small, atypical sample. Freud's theorizing, which is the basis of all psychoanalytic theory, is highly susceptible to this criticism. A good deal of Freud's original theory is based on his own self-analysis (Gay, 1988). In all of his writings, Freud describes only 12 cases in detail.

Size alone, however, does not determine the suitability of a sample. The critical criterion is whether the sample is representative of the population to which the generalizations will be made. Freud believed that few people are suitable for analysis. His requirements for a suitable patient included maturity, courage, education, and good character, as well as the intellectual ability to understand the complexities revealed in analysis (Roazen, 1975).

Additionally, the subjects of published psychoanalytic case studies suffer almost exclusively from some form of psychopathology (Tuttman, 1988). How can one justify generalizing to normal personality from a sample characterized by abnormal personality? The restricted nature of Freud's sample makes it difficult to justify his sweeping generalizations to all humanity.

Contemporary psychoanalytic cases present the same problem. The samples from which generalizations about human personality are made are not representative. Today, patients in psychoanalysis are typically young or middle-aged white adults; they are above average in intelligence, highly articulate, and have relatively high incomes. (Psychoanalysis can easily cost $25,000 per year.) They are typically Jewish or Protestant, almost never Catholic. They are also unusually psychologically minded. In fact, many are workers in mental-health fields (Grünbaum, 1984; Knapp, Levin, McCarter, Wermer, & Zetzel, 1960; Masling & Cohen, 1987; Wallace, 1986).

Moreover, observation of this highly restricted sample is very limited. The subjects are observed in a psychoanalyst's office, sometimes stretched out on a couch, free associating about their dreams and early childhood memories for 50 minutes. How typical is that of human behavior? Thus, a well-known critic of psychoanalysis quipped: "We can no more test Freudian hypotheses on the (analytic) coach, than we can adjudicate between the rival hypotheses of Newton and Einstein by going to sleep under an apple tree" (Eysenck, 1963, p. 22).

PSYCHOANALYTIC TREATMENT DOES NOT RECOVER HISTORICAL TRUTH	Freud's good friend and faithful critic, Wilhelm Fliess, posed what is perhaps the most serious challenge of all, back at the turn of the century. It specifically dealt with psychoanalytic therapy, but it had implications for psychoanalytic theory, assessment, and research as well.

> During the summer of 1900, in a small resort in what was then western Austria, Wilhelm Fliess suggested to Freud that he [Freud] merely read his own thoughts into the minds of his patients. As Freud realized, the challenge put to him by Fliess in the Achensee was a serious one, striking at the very heart of psychoanalysis. It challenged the *therapeutic* claim that lasting and significant gains in psychoanalysis result from insight into the cause of the illness; moreover, it threatened the allied *diagnostic* claim that psychological disorders are rooted in repressed memories and desires. (Richardson, 1990, p. 668)

It is interesting how Freud answered Fliess's challenge.

Freud's clinical experience and that of his immediate followers led to the belief that psychoanalytic treatment is successful ("produces lasting and significant gains") in some, but not all, patients. Many of these patients had come in with *symptoms* (hysterical paralysis, phobias, impotence, and so on) *which Freud believed to have deep causes*. Thus, "successful" can be viewed in two different ways. One way is to ask if the symptoms are gone. (This is, after all, what the patient has come in for.) But the other way is to ask about underlying process: Have the intrapsychic causes of these symptoms been identified and exposed?

Freud believed a symptom might be banished merely by suggestion. He had seen Charcot order a hypnotized patient with hysterical paralysis to stand up and walk, whereupon she apparently did so. But such cures never lasted; when the patient was awakened from hypnosis, she was again paralyzed. So ridding the patient of the symptom would *not* be Freud's criterion. Rather, Freud was totally convinced that the analyst had to expose *the truth*; make the causes of the neurosis visible to the patient's conscious ego; and thereby release the underlying repression at the root of the patient's problems. This criterion is a good deal more problematic than determining the presence or absence of symptoms (Spence, 1984).

Fliess's challenge was to ask: In the practice of psychoanalysis, how do analysts know when they have discovered the truth? Freud's answer was that only the truth would be accepted by the patient as a basis for real insight to occur. An interpretation had to "tally" with the truth. Only a true interpretation would trigger the healing process. Here is the way Freud put his argument: "[The patient's] conflicts will only be successfully solved and his resistances overcome *if the anticipatory ideas he is given [by the analyst] tally with what is real in him*" (Freud, 1955, pp. 452–453).

Critics beginning with Fliess have suggested that psychoanalysis may offer little more than a good story to the patient. Such a story will have *narrative truth* (it will be coherent, convincing, and believable). But it will not have *historical truth* and it may be as much the analyst's invented yarn as anything else. As Siegert (1990), himself a psychoanalyst, recently argued

> free association is anything but free. . . . [I]n practice, analysts actually discourage truly free association. . . . What we listen for are stories or narratives, and relatively organized and edited associations to those stories, not to a random collection of disconnected words. . . . Our listening is always and inevitably shaped by what we expect to hear [and] one can only hear after one has a framework. . . . What we listen for is to a very great extent theoretically determined. That is why Freudians tend to hear oedipally, Kleinians tend to hear preoedipally, and Sullivanians tend to hear interpersonally. Our listening isn't unbiased. Our patients don't associate freely. And we do not listen without preconception. . . . In other words, when we believe we are reconstructing the past, we are actually creating or constructing a past that often has never occurred. (pp. 163–164)

IS PSYCHOANALYSIS A SCIENCE?

Defenders of psychoanalytic theory argue that psychoanalysts, as much as other personality psychologists, care passionately for the truth, but conceive of it in a different way (Langs, 1987). According to this view, different is not necessarily less valid. Objectivity and repeatability appear to be logical and even "right"; still, they are, in the end, as they were when they were adopted, arbitrary standards.

The goal of the psychoanalytic strategy also is different from the goal of mainstream psychology, which emphasizes prediction and control. Psychoanalysis is concerned mainly with understanding, which is subjective and often incomplete and ambiguous (Steele, 1979). It also is relevant that the primary researchers in the psychoanalytic strategy are analysts engaged in full-time psychoanalytic therapy. As such, they are more interested in helping their patients than in researching the theoretical foundations on which they base their clinical practice (Michels, 1988; Wallerstein, 1988).

The issue of the relation of psychoanalysis to science is as old as psychoanalysis itself. Freud often considered calling psychoanalysis *metapsychology* — meaning that it goes *beyond* psychology — thereby removing it from psychology defined as the science of behavior. In 1900, Freud wrote:

> I am not really a man of science . . . I am nothing but by temperament . . . an adventurer . . . with the curiosity, the boldness, and the tenacity that belongs to that type of being. Such people are apt to be treasured if they succeed, if they have really discovered something; otherwise they are thrown aside. And that is not altogether unjust. (quoted in Jones, 1953, p. 348)

SUMMARY

1. Many psychoanalytic concepts are defined in vague, nonspecific, and ambiguous terms. The inadequate definitions make measuring the concepts problematic.

2. Many psychoanalytic propositions are stated in a way that makes them incapable of being falsified.

3. Psychoanalysts often commit three logical errors in presenting evidence for their theories: (1) they fail to distinguish between observation and inference; (2) they confuse correlation and causation; and (3) they use analogy as proof.

4. Freud's theorizing is biased against women. Freud considered the male personality to be both a prototype and an ideal. Contemporary evidence does not support his views about the female personality.

5. Projective techniques generally have low reliability and validity. Nonetheless, they continue to remain popular as personality assessment procedures. The reliability of psychoanalytic dream interpretations also is generally low.

6. Psychoanalytic case studies may be unduly biased due to the highly private nature of the observations and because these case studies are based on small, atypical samples of people. Also, psychoanalysts may be more biased in their observations than other therapists.

7. It is questionable whether practicing psychoanalysts discover the historical truth about their patients, as Freud had supposed.

8. Psychoanalysis has been criticized as being unscientific. It may be that psychoanalysis should *not* be judged by the standards of mainstream scientific psychology.

Section Three

THE DISPOSITIONAL STRATEGY

Introduction To
The Dispositional Strategy

He had a special personal charm, a fine courage that dominated his physical weakness, great gifts as a conversationalist and a persistent gaiety that made for him warm friends. (Nisenson & DeWitt, 1949, p. 139)

This description gives us the feeling that we know something about the man described. There is a hint of the enduring qualities that set him apart from others. These qualities might help identify him or predict what he would do in various situations. The man described is the 19th-century Scottish author Robert Louis Stevenson. The description might, of course, apply to many other people as well. There is also much that it does not tell us. Still, a single sentence has provided a reasonable sense of Stevenson's basic characteristics and the way he usually was *disposed* to behave.

In this section, we will consider the dispositional strategy for understanding human personality. The major idea behind the strategy is found in the definition of a **disposition**: an enduring, stable personality characteristic. According to the dispositional strategy, people differ in the way they are generally *disposed* to act. Describing individuals, groups, and even nations in dispositional terms seems to almost "come naturally." Before proceeding further, you may wish to try Demonstration 8-1, in which you can explore some of your own dispositional notions about human behavior and personality. Most students find Demonstration 8-1 easy; this is because we are accustomed to thinking of others in dispositional terms. Dispositional labels serve as organizing concepts that may explain a person's behavior in a variety of situations. Stagner (1976) gives this example:

If a young man refuses an invitation to a party, drops a course that requires group discussion, and takes his vacation hiking alone in the mountains, we begin to get the idea that there is an inner consistency that involves the avoidance of situations that require close contact with other human beings . . . [The idea of a trait] makes sense as a unifying concept here . . . (p. 112)

■ *Demonstration 8-1*
DESCRIBING PEOPLE IN DISPOSITIONAL TERMS

We are accustomed to using dispositional notions in describing and attempting to explain one another's behavior. These notions usually take the form "So-and-so is a _____ person" or "So-and-so acts that way because he or she is _____." For example, one might say that "Harry is a meek person" or that "Susan acts that way because she is proud."

The purpose of this Demonstration is to give you an opportunity to describe people you know in dispositional terms. It will allow you to compare the way you use dispositions with the way personality psychologists use the dispositional strategy. The Demonstration also introduces some of the methods, predictions, and general findings of the strategy.

Procedure

1. Take six sheets of lined paper and write one of the letters A through F at the top of each sheet. Then remove Work Sheet 8-1, which you will find in the Demonstration Materials section at the back of the book. The work sheet will be used later in the Demonstration. (Table 8-1 provides a sample work sheet.)

2. For each of the categories below, designate a particular person of your own sex.

Table 8-1

Sample work sheet for Demonstration 8-1

RANK	NAME	NUMBER OF ADJECTIVES USED	PERVASIVENESS				PERCENTAGE OF SIMILARITY
			ALMOST ALWAYS 4	FRE- QUENTLY 3	OCCA- SIONALLY 2	RARELY 1	
	Self						%
Know best 1st							%
2nd							%
3rd							%
4th							%
Know least 5th							%
Σ = Sum (total)		Σ =	Σ =	Σ =	Σ =	Σ =	
M = Mean		M =	%	%	%	%	

Write each person's name at the top of the appropriate sheet of paper.

A. Your same-sexed parent or, if you have never known this person, a close biological relative of the same sex (a blood relative).

B. A close friend who is not related to you.

C. Someone not related to you with whom you are somewhat friendly (a more casual relationship than you have with person B).

D. Someone not related to you whom you know only in one specific context (such as a school teacher).

E. A historical figure whom you admire.

F. Yourself.

Write down as many or as few adjectives as seem necessary to fully describe your same-sexed parent (person A). (The order of the adjectives does not matter.) Repeat this pro-

cedure for the people in categories B through F, in that order.

Look over the adjectives you have listed for person A. Are any similar or redundant? (For example, *clumsy* and *awkward* have similar meanings.) If you are unsure of any of the definitions, double-check them with a standard dictionary. *Condense any redundant adjectives either by eliminating them or by combining them* (such as *clumsy-awkward*). Repeat this procedure for persons B through F, in that order.

Now rate each of the adjectives or adjective combinations according to the degree to which each characterizes person A. Use the following scale:

4 = *Almost always* characterizes the person.

3 = *Frequently* characterizes the person.

2 = *Occasionally* characterizes the person.

1 = *Rarely* characterizes the person.

Write the scale number that is most applicable next to each of the adjectives or adjective combinations. Repeat this procedure for persons B through F, in that order.

Rank persons A through E (excluding yourself) in terms of how well you know them. The person whom you feel you know best should be given the "first" rank, the person whom you feel you know second-best shouldbe assigned the "second" rank, and so on until the person whom you feel you know least well has received the "fifth" rank. Write the rank in the upper right-hand corner of each sheet.

In the first column of the work sheet, list the names of the five people *other than yourself* (persons A through E) in order of familiarity, that is, according to the rank you assigned them in step 6. The person whom you ranked "first" (the one you feel you know best) should be listed first, the person whom you ranked "second" should be listed next, and so on.

On the work sheet, in the "Number of Adjectives Used" column, put the total number of adjectives or adjective combinations you used to describe each person (A through F).

Next, at the bottom of the column, put the total number of adjectives or adjective combinations you used to describe all the people other than yourself (sheets A through E). Divide this total by 5 to obtain the mean number of adjectives you used to describe the other people, and enter this number in the appropriate space at the bottom of the work sheet.

In the "Pervasiveness" columns, record the number of adjectives for each person (A through F) that fall in each of the four categories. These are the numbers you wrote next to the adjectives in step 5.

At the bottom of the column, put the total number of adjectives in each of the four pervasiveness categories for the five persons *other than yourself*.

Compute and record at the bottom of the work sheet the percentage of adjectives that fall into each of the pervasiveness categories. To do this, divide the total number of adjectives for each category by the total number of adjectives used to describe the other persons (i.e., combined across all categories) and then multiply by 100.

Looking at all six sheets (A through F), check to see whether any of the adjectives are similar or redundant across persons. For example, if you described yourself as generous and your parent as giving, condense these adjectives into one term, either by changing *generous* to *giving* or vice versa or by hyphenating the two adjectives whenever they both appear (i.e., *generous-giving*). This step is similar to step 4, and you may find a thesaurus helpful. On sheets A through E (every sheet except yours) *circle each adjective or adjective combination that is the same as one you used to describe yourself* (on sheet F).

11. Compute the *percentage* of adjectives used for each of the other people (A through E) that corresponds to your own, and record it in the "Percentage of Similarity" column. (That is, divide the number of adjectives that are the same for you and the other person—the ones you have circled—by the total number of adjectives used to describe the other person, and then multiply by 100.)

Discussion

You may have already noticed a number of interesting features and patterns in your use of dispositional descriptions for others and yourself. We will mention a few of the findings of dispositional psychologists that are related to the Demonstration.

Number of Descriptive Adjectives Used

Gordon Allport (1937) was one of the first to examine the range of dispositional terms, or "trait names," that people use to describe others. He found that although people often use a large number of descriptive adjectives, many are synonymous and thus the total number can be reduced. To the extent that your own experiences in this Demonstration parallel Allport's findings, you would have been able to substantially reduce the size of your initial lists of descriptive adjectives.

After condensing redundant adjectives, Allport found that most people actually use a fairly small number of adjectives in describing others they know; the usual range is between 3 and 10. Does your mean number of adjectives fall within this range? How does the number of adjectives you used to describe yourself compare with the mean number of adjectives you used to describe other people?

Dispositions and Genetics   Dispositional psychologists who take a biological view have found evidence suggesting that certain dispositions are transmitted genetically. Evidence of genetic dispositions might show up in this Demonstration in the degree of similarity between you and your parent ("Percentage of Similarity" column on the work sheet). Is this similarity greater than the similarity between you and a close friend?

Relationship to People   Many people believe that the closer their relationship is to someone, the better they know that person. Yet psychological studies provide some evidence that an individual often feels more comfortable assigning dispositional adjectives to people whom he or she knows *less* well.

Examine the relationship between the number of adjectives you used to describe a person and how well you feel you know that person.

The five people other than yourself are listed on the work sheet in descending order of familiarity, so you can look down the "Number of Adjectives Used" column to see whether a pattern emerges. Is "secondhand" information, such as that which you used to describe the historical figure, sufficient to adequately characterize the person? How well were you able to describe the person you know in only a single context?

Pervasiveness   Allport and others have noted that dispositions vary in the degree to which they pervade a particular personality. Not many people have dispositions that pervade all that they do and dominate their entire personality ("Almost Always" category). Did any of the people on your list appear to have a highly pervasive disposition? Did most have a few dispositions that characterize them in many situations ("Frequently" category)?

Other Issues   You might find it interesting to consider some further analyses of your own. What are the qualitative differences among the adjectives you use to describe various individuals you know? What differences would you expect if you repeated the Demonstration, but described people of the *opposite* sex? Examining questions like these will help you understand the dispositional strategy. Save the Demonstration materials and inspect them again as you read the chapters in this section.

EARLY DISPOSITIONAL CONCEPTS   Dispositional concepts in one form or another have been used to organize and explain the actions of others for thousands of years. Early dispositional views assumed that people could be divided into a relatively small number of types, according to their personalities. By knowing an individual's type, you could predict the way that individual would behave in a variety of circumstances.

The ancient Hebrews used this perspective for what may have been the first formal personality assessment, shown in the following quotation from the Old Testament. The goal was to identify two types of people, those who should fight and those who should not.

> And the Lord said unto Gideon, The people that are with thee are too many for me to give the Midianites into their hands . . . Now therefore go to, proclaim in the ears of the people, saying, Whosoever is fearful and afraid, let him return and depart early from Mount Gilead. And there returned of the people twenty and two thousand; and there remained ten thousand.
>
> And the Lord said unto Gideon, The people are yet too many; bring them down unto the water, and I will try them for thee there . . . So he brought down the people unto the water: and the Lord said unto Gideon, Every one that lappeth of the water with his tongue, as a dog lappeth, him shalt thou set by himself; likewise every one that boweth down upon his knees to drink. And the number of them that lapped putting their hand to their mouth, were three hundred men: but all the rest of the people bowed down upon their knees to drink water. And the Lord said unto Gideon, By the three hundred men that lapped will I save you, and deliver the Midianites into thine hand: and let all the other people go every man unto his place. (Judges 7:2–7)

A second historic view, the *theory of the four temperaments*, is close to several contemporary theories and many everyday conceptions of personality. This view is based on the ancient Greek idea that the universe can be described in terms of four basic elements: air, earth, fire, and water. The Greek physician Hippocrates, the father of medicine, extended this argument to people. He suggested that the body is composed of four "humors"—blood, black bile, yellow bile, and phlegm—that correspond to the four elements. The Roman physician Galen later suggested that an excess of any of these humors leads to a characteristic temperament or "personality type": sanguine (hopeful), melancholic (sad), choleric (hot-tempered), or phlegmatic (apathetic).

This ancient theory of personality is no longer used today. But the theory of the four temperaments was gradually transformed into the idea that there are two major dimensions of personality, *extraversion* and *neuroticism* (Stelmack & Stalikas, 1991). These two dispositions play a central role in modern trait theory.

Clearly, one can distinguish many types of people. This fact was obvious even to the ancients, and extensive catalogs of types emerged. With few changes, identifying types of people continued to be popular for thousands of years. The most striking idea was that physical appearance indicated personality. In Shakespeare's play *Julius Caesar*, for example, Caesar advises Marcus Antonius:

> Let me have men about me that are fat;
> Sleek-headed men, and such as sleep o' nights.
> Yond Cassius has a lean and hungry look;
> He thinks too much: such men are dangerous.
>
> (act 1, sc. 2)

The belief advanced by Shakespeare's Caesar is still popular; for instance, many people believe that they can identify a "criminal type" by physical appearance.

THEORETICAL ASSUMPTIONS OF THE DISPOSITIONAL STRATEGY

Three major assumptions are common to all theories and viewpoints within the dispositional strategy:

1. Dispositions are relatively *stable* and *enduring* within the individual.
2. Dispositions have some *consistency* and *generality* for each person.
3. Differences between individuals arise from differences in the *strength*, *amount*, and *number* of dispositions each person has.

Relative Stability of Dispositions

If individuals are truly disposed to act in particular ways, then personalities should be fairly stable over time. However, dispositional psychologists often caution that this assumption must be understood in the light of several further distinctions.

Most dispositional psychologists conceptualize an individual's enduring dispositions as *traits* and distinguish them from temporary dispositions, or *states*. The latter result from temporary conditions like fatigue, stress, or sudden changes in fortune. The difference between these two types of dispositions can be seen with anxiety. Spielberger described trait anxiety as "the disposition to respond with anxiety to situations that are perceived as threatening." This is different from state anxiety, which is "a condition of the organism characterized by subjective feelings of apprehension and heightened autonomic nervous system activity" (Spielberger & Gorsuch, 1966, p. 33).

Note that trait anxiety is only a predisposition to be anxious. A person high in trait anxiety will not necessarily be anxious all the time. A person low in trait anxiety may exhibit state anxiety under highly stressful conditions. Research suggests that the trait/state distinction is valuable for clinical as well as for normal populations and for dispositions other than anxiety (Oei, Evans, & Cook, 1990). As would be expected, state measures vary more than trait measures from one situation to another (Zuckerman, 1983).

Dispositional psychologists also point out that a disposition is a general mode of functioning. The disposition may take different concrete behavioral forms as the individual matures. Thus, a psychologist must know what to look for before he or she can tell whether a person's behavior has been "stable" over time. Dispositions are not merely habits; instead, they reflect an inner consistency. However, discovering this consistency often takes more than a simplistic analysis of overt acts (Buss, 1989).

Pediatric psychologist Michael Lewis (1967) clearly illustrates this point in his article "The Meaning of a Response, or Why Researchers in Infant Behavior Should Be Oriental Metaphysicians." Briefly, Lewis was interested in the consistency of infants' responses to frustration, which he measured in a group of babies at 1 month of age and then again when they were 12 months old. At 1 month, the frustration involved removing a nipple from the infants' mouths for 30 seconds; at 12 months, a physical barrier blocked the youngsters from reaching either their mothers or some attractive toys. Crying was the measure of frustration.

Responses to the two situations were *negatively* correlated. That is, babies who cried at 1 month were *not* the ones who cried at 12 months. However, as Lewis pointed out, this behavior should not mask a deeper consistency. Specifically, some of the babies were consistently active and others were consistently passive in their responses. At 1 month, motor skills are not yet developed. Thus, the active baby can do nothing but cry—which he or she does. But at 12 months, crying is a relatively passive response. At this age, the active babies did not cry; rather, they took some physical action to change the situation.

Consistency and Generality of Dispositions

The second major assumption of the dispositional strategy is related to the first. Dispositions have some consistency and generality within a person. Consistency and generality refer to the extent to which a disposition affects behavior. A man who is ambitious in his work is also likely to be ambitious and striving in his recreational activities. He will probably have high ambitions for his children as well.

No disposition is expected to appear all the time or in every situation. One reason is that a person has many dispositions. Different demands and circumstances can bring a somewhat different set of dispositions into play.

Nonetheless, some aspects of behavior are quite consistent across situations (e.g., Diener & Larsen, 1984; Woodruffe, 1985) and time (e.g., Conley, 1984; Siegler et al., 1990; Staw & Ross, 1985). Woodruffe (1985), for instance, found a high degree of consistency across situations in the tendency to be outgoing or reserved. Conley (1984) showed that Introversion/Extraversion and Emotionality remain moderately consistent across a 45-year period. That would be over a substantial part of the adult lifespan!

Individual Differences

We have all noticed clear differences in abilities, interests, and social responses among adults we know. Even from birth, infants differ in the vigor and style of their responses to frustration and reward (Buss & Plomin, 1984). Clearly, every individual is unique, different from others. Describing and explaining *individual differences* is a major goal of the dispositional strategy. How does the dispositional strategy account for individual differences? The answer is found in the third major assumption of the strategy: *individual differences arise from differences in the strength, amount, and number of dispositions a person has.*

IDENTIFYING PERSONALITY DISPOSITIONS

Human behavior can be ordered and divided on a nearly infinite number of dimensions. An individual can be known as a happy person, an aggressive person, a person who needs to be loved, a benevolent person, a stingy person, and so on. Which of these dimensions is important? Which dimensions will most likely meet the theoretical assumptions of the dispositional strategy?

As Demonstration 8-1 reveals, most people describe themselves and others with a relatively small number of dispositions. But the total number of traits, types, motives, and needs suggested as human dispositions is vast. Therefore, modern dispositional psychologists have been searching for a set of underlying personality dimensions from which all other traitlike characteristics can be derived.

The search is akin to early efforts by psychologists interested in visual perception and color vision. These investigators wanted to identify the primary colors from which all other colors could be derived by appropriate combinations and mixtures. It is now common knowledge that just three colors of light—red, green, and blue—can produce any one of the vast array of colors that a normally sighted person can see. Many dispositional psychologists believe that personality can also be cast into a small set of primary, underlying dimensions from which all others can be derived.

A major task of dispositional psychologists is to identify important dimensions, or dispositions, that describe and explain human personality. To do this, it is essential that some fairly clear indicators, or criteria, exist that can be used to test whether a given dimension—a prospective psychological disposition—will be useful. One such indicator involves meeting the assumptions of consistency and generality. But consistency and generality are not sufficient. As we saw in Demonstration 8-1, the dimension must also clearly distinguish one person from another. If everyone were happy (or aggressive or ambitious), this dimension would be of little use as a psychological disposition; it could not be used to predict or explain any of the *differences* in people's behavior. Dispositional approaches are, in fact, very much psychologies of "amount." Dispositions that do not let us say that one person has more or less of some durable characteristic than another add little predictive power.

DISPOSITIONAL PERSONALITY ASSESSMENT

The dispositional strategy employs almost all the major personality assessment techniques. Interviews as well as projective and situational tests are used to identify various characteristics. However, *reporting* (as opposed to observing directly) plays a central role in most dispositional assessments. A wide range of "paper-and-pencil" self-report tests are used, as are "reputational" reports in the form of descriptions given by friends, acquaintances, and, sometimes, biographers.

Dispositions are theoretical constructs. It is therefore not possible to measure them directly. Instead, dispositional researchers must devise measures of behavior that yield indicators of various underlying dispositions. Most often these measures are self-report inventories or questionnaires. At the same time, it is presumed that there is no one absolute measure of a

disposition; in fact, there should be several different indexes. The dispositional psychologist

> explains the behavior of an individual by the values assigned him on dimensions
> considered relevant to the behavior in question. These values may be expressed
> numerically as scores on a test, or they may be represented by labels that stand
> for different positions on the dimension. A psychologist might, for example,
> explain an individual's pattern of deference to certain people and hostility to
> others in terms of authoritarianism, by saying that he is an authoritarian type of
> person. Or the psychologist might predict a person's success as a business
> executive from his scores on measures of intelligence, aggressiveness, and
> sociability. The use of these and other dimensions implies that the values
> obtained on them by individuals have consequences over a fairly wide realm of
> behavior and that these dimensions exist independently of any single method of
> measurement. Therefore, although a particular test may be the one most
> frequently used in the measurement of some dimension, it is assumed that there
> may be other, equally valid measures. Like other theoretical constructs,
> dimensions are inferred; their definition rests not on any single set of operations
> but on the convergence of a set of operations. (Levy, 1970, p. 200)

A related characteristic of dispositional personality assessment is the
assumption of *additivity*. The strength of any disposition is assumed to be the
"sum" of various individual response tendencies. Consider Sean, a student
who likes to meet strangers, easily approaches teachers to dispute grades on
examinations, *and* is often outspoken in class discussions. Sean would be
considered somewhat more extraverted (outgoing) than Marvin, another
student who likes to meet strangers and argue about grades but prefers not
to take part in class discussions.

A good example of "adding" behaviors to infer a disposition can be
seen in the work of Robins (1966), who used a combination of aggressive
symptoms in childhood to predict criminal behavior in adulthood. Robins
found that adding up all the early signs and symptoms suggesting a
disposition toward aggression predicted later criminal behavior considerably better than any single aggressive or delinquent act during childhood.

Two formal criteria have been adopted for measuring the adequacy of a
dispositional assessment procedure: convergent validity and discriminant
validity (Campbell & Fiske, 1959). Measures of presumably the same
disposition may have quite different forms—such as paper-and-pencil,
projective, and situational measures—but they should *converge* and thus
correlate highly with one another. In contrast, tests designed to measure
different dispositions should *discriminate* between them. Thus, they should
not be highly correlated.

Dispositional psychologists readily acknowledge that their tests are
imperfect. Every personality test score is assumed to include error, or
"noise," as well as true information about the disposition being measured. So
these tests probably *under*estimate the actual stability and generality of the
underlying dispositions.

**DISPOSITIONAL
RESEARCH**

Dispositional personality research has three major goals:

1. To identify the underlying dimensions of personality.
2. To discover the source of various individual differences. (This especially relates to inherited characteristics or those stemming from early life experiences.)
3. To examine the reliability, validity, and utility of various personality and ability tests.

Recall that the psychoanalytic strategy dictates that the predominant method of research must be the case study. The dispositional strategy also dictates that one method of research will predominate: the correlational method. The dispositional researcher is always interested in how closely various behaviors go together. Only when a number of different behaviors are related can one speak of an underlying personality disposition that may be influencing them.

**DURABILITY OF
DISPOSITIONS
AND
PERSONALITY
CHANGE**

Unlike the other strategies discussed in this book, the dispositional strategy is not associated with any form of psychotherapy. In fact, the dispositional strategy says little about personality change.

There are at least two reasons the dispositional strategy does not deal with personality change. First, the strategy emphasizes the stability of personality. It follows, therefore, that personality change would be difficult, if not impossible. Second, many dispositional psychologists have strong links with academic psychology rather than with clinical practice. The practical contributions of dispositional psychologists focus on measurement of personality rather than on personality change.

To help a person adjust, the dispositional psychologist looks for a life situation for which the person is already well suited by virtue of his or her enduring dispositions. This approach contrasts with psychotherapy, which tries to change the person to fit the situation he or she is in. For example, suppose a person is disposed to be very aggressive. It may be wiser to keep that person away from aggression-provoking situations than to try to change him or her into someone who "turns the other cheek."

Although the dispositional strategy per se has not been associated with efforts to change personality, some of the psychologists discussed in this section have been actively interested in personality change techniques based on other strategies. David McClelland, for example, has developed an imaginative program for altering one disposition, the need to achieve (as you will see in Chapter 11).

SUMMARY

1. A disposition is an enduring, stable personality characteristic. Most people find it "natural" to think about others and themselves in dispositional terms.

2. The concept of personality dispositions goes back thousands of years. Most of the early dispositional views simply divided people into a number of distinct types.

3. The major assumptions of the dispositional strategy are that dispositions are relatively stable over time and relatively consistent across situations. But dispositional psychologists do not expect a person's dispositions to manifest themselves all the time or in every situation.

4. A major task of the modern dispositional strategy is to identify the most important or central dispositions on which people can be compared.

5. The dispositional strategy relies heavily on self-reports and on the reports of others to assess personality. Assessment is usually additive, in the sense that the strength of a disposition is assumed to be the sum of all the individual's responses that are related to the disposition in question. Because there is error or "noise" in every measure of personality, dispositional psychologists believe that estimates of the stability and generality of personality dispositions are often underestimated.

6. Dispositional personality research involves identifying dispositions, exploring individual differences, and evaluating tests.

7. The dispositional strategy has less to say about personality change than the other three strategies, partly because it views personality as stable and partly because relatively few dispositional psychologists have been concerned with clinical endeavors.

Chapter Nine

The Assessment
Of Dispositions

Broadly speaking, there are two possible reasons for assessing a person's dispositions: To assist the person in the context of counseling or psychological treatment (*clinical applications*) and to provide assessment information as part of a research study (*research applications*).

In clinical applications, the person being assessed will almost certainly be interviewed as part of the procedure; thus, direct observations made by the counselor or therapist will be an integral part of assessment. For most research applications, though, the primary (or sole) source of assessment information is the self-report personality inventory. Thus, these inventories are a sufficiently important part of the dispositional strategy to be examined in some detail.

SELF-REPORT PERSONALITY INVENTORIES

A self-report personality inventory is, in essence, a specialized questionnaire, made up of statements that might or might not apply to any person. Taking a self-report inventory involves responding to a large number of such statements. The following statements are typical items:

I often get mad when things don't turn out as planned.

I enjoy music and dancing.

I am afraid of high places.

I have trouble falling asleep at night.

Respondents indicate whether each statement is generally true or false for them or the degree to which they agree or disagree with the statement. (Occasionally, there is a "cannot say" choice.) The statements are usually printed in a booklet with a separate answer sheet.

Self-report personality inventories are widely used; almost two-thirds of the United States population will be asked to take a personality inventory at some time in their lives. One reason for their popularity, of course, is convenience: You just give the person the questionnaire, he or she fills it out (typically without any supervision or assistance), and you then score the test—using answer keys provided by the test publisher.

Personality inventories are typically scored for a number of different dimensions or *scales*. Each scale involves some subset of the items on the inventory, so the overall inventory provides a set of scale scores that, taken together, reveal the pattern of dispositions of a particular individual.

The scale scores are interpreted by the application of *norms*, indicating the range of scores obtained by a large number of individuals who are demographically similar to the person being tested—the so-called **normative sample**. By consulting a table of norms, the researcher or clinician learns where the individual stands relative to other individuals in the population to which he or she is being compared.

In addition, most inventories are supported by reliability and validity data, provided by the creators or publishers of the inventory. **Reliability** refers to the degree to which the scales yield information that is consistent or stable over time, whereas **validity** refers to whether the scale measures what it purports to measure.

Hundreds of self-report inventories have been published over the past 50 years. Most of these never become popular. If an inventory has come to be widely accepted over the years, it typically is revised. Revisions may add new scales, improve the wording of items, and provide updated or extended norms. We will illustrate the nature of self-report inventories by describing two of the most widely accepted inventories, the MMPI and the NEO-PI.

The Minnesota Multiphasic Personality Inventory

Constructed in 1942 by S. R. Hathaway, a clinical psychologist, and J. C. McKinley, a neuropsychiatrist, the Minnesota Multiphasic Personality Inventory (MMPI) filled a need for a practical and valid test to screen patients for various psychiatric disorders. Hathaway and McKinley began with a pool of 1000 self-descriptive statements collected from various psychiatric examination forms and procedures, psychiatric textbooks, and previous inventories. The 1000 statements were given to groups of diagnosed psychiatric patients (who had been classified based on clinical judgments) and to groups of normal individuals. A tabulation was then made of how often subjects in each group agreed with each item. Only items that clearly differentiated between a diagnostic group and the normal group were retained. For instance, a statement became an item on the depression scale if, but only if, patients with a depressive disorder agreed (or disagreed) with the statement significantly more often than did normal persons. This method of choosing scale items is called **empirical keying**.

Still the most widely used personality inventory, the MMPI consists of over 500 statements about attitudes, education, general physical health, sex roles, mood, morale, vocational interests, fears, and preoccupations. A revision of the MMPI, the MMPI-2, appeared in 1982. It is scored for 4 validity scales and 14 basic clinical scales (University of Minnesota, 1982). Table 9-1 shows the scale names, their customary abbreviations, and a brief characterization of the disposition each scale appears to measure.

The validity scales provide information about the trustworthiness of responses on the clinical scales. For example, an elevated Lie (L) scale indicates that the respondent is trying to answer the items to present herself or himself in a favorable light.

Scoring the MMPI is straightforward. Scoring keys indicate the items that make up each scale and the direction (true or false) of each item. The test can be scored by hand in less than 10 minutes; scoring is even faster with a computer. Interpreting the scores is not as simple. Experience has shown that most of the scales cannot be interpreted literally; that is, a person who scores high on the schizophrenia scale is not necessarily schizophrenic. For this reason, the original scales are usually designated by code number (0–9) rather than by the names of psychiatric categories. (Note the numbers in parenthesis in Table 9-1.)

To reach a clinical diagnosis, the *pattern* of scores on the scales is examined and often graphed in a personality profile. An example is shown

Table 9-1
Validity and clinical scales of the Minnesota Multiphasic Personality Inventory

SCALE NAME	ABBREVIATION	INTERPRETATION
CANNOT SAY	?	One of four validity scales. It is the number of items in the "Cannot Say" category or that the respondent leaves blank.
LIE	L	The second validity scale. It measures the subject's attempt to put himself or herself in a favorable light (e.g., by answering *false* to items that are true for just about everyone, such as "I get angry sometimes").
FREQUENCY	F	The third validity scale; it is a measure of carelessness or confusion. One item scored on this scale, if the subject answers *true*, is "Everything tastes the same."
CORRECTION	K	The fourth validity scale; often taken as defensiveness.
HYPOCHONDRIASIS (1)	Hs	The tendency to complain of numerous physical symptoms. High scorers often have a defeatist attitude.
DEPRESSION (2)	D	The tendency to experience depression or pessimism.
HYSTERIA (3)	Hy	The tendency to express psychological conflict through unbased physical complaints.
PSYCHOPATHIC DEVIATE (4)	Pd	The tendency to be antisocial, rebellious, and impulsive.
MASCULINITY-FEMININITY (5)	Mf	The tendency to have attitudes or feelings often associated with the opposite sex (e.g., sensitivity in males or aggressiveness in females).
PARANOIA (6)	Pa	The tendency to be suspicious or place excess blame on others.
PSYCHASTHENIA (7)	Pt	The tendency to be rigid, phobic, and self-condemning.
SCHIZOPHRENIA (8)	Sc	The tendency to have peculiar thoughts or ideas.
HYPOMANIA (9)	Ma	The tendency to be energetic, optimistic, and flighty.
SOCIAL INTROVERSION/ EXTROVERSION (0)	Si	The tendency to be shy and self-effacing. Low scorers tend to be sociable and outgoing.
ANXIETY*	A	The tendency to become apprehensive.
REPRESSION*	R	The tendency to keep problems from conscious awareness.
EGO STRENGTH*	Es	The ability to maintain well-integrated responses under stress or when in conflict.
MACANDREW ALCOHOLISM SCALE*	MAC	The tendency to abuse alcohol or to become addicted to it.

*The scales were not part of the original MMPI but were incorporated into the latest revision.

in Figure 9-1. MMPI atlases assist in interpreting profiles; they contain typical profiles and descriptive information about samples of subjects producing each profile (e.g., Marks & Seeman, 1963). For example, the atlases list typical and atypical symptoms and behaviors for people with a given profile. They provide information about the most common diagnostic category for these people, their personal histories, and courses of treatment.

It is rare to find a perfect match of profiles; that is, identical scores on all the scales. Therefore, the atlases give criteria for determining whether two profiles can be considered similar. These criteria help the examiner find the profile in the atlas that is most like the respondent's profile. An updated set of norms, based on a large sample of subjects ranging in age from 18 to 99, is also available (Colligan, Osborne, Swenson, & Offord, 1984). The MMPI-2 has also been shown to be appropriate for use with college students (Butcher, Graham, Dahlstrom, & Bowman, 1990), and there are separate norms available for adolescents (Pancoast & Archer, 1988).

What about the reliability and validity of the MMPI? The MMPI seems to be more useful for adults than for teenagers, and college graduates reply in a more consistent fashion than those with less education (McFarland & Sparks, 1985). Nonetheless, a comprehensive review of more than 40 years

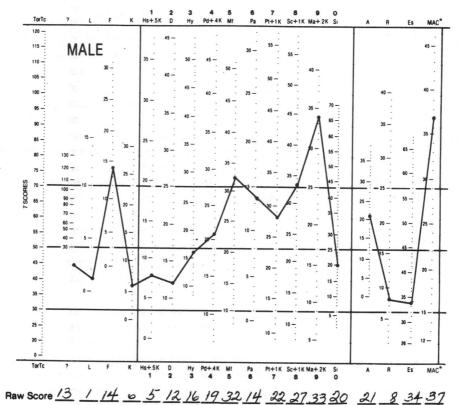

Figure 9-1
Sample MMPI profile.

of research suggests that, overall, the MMPI is an adequate instrument in terms of reliability and validity (Parker, Hanson, & Hunsley, 1988). To be sure, critics have found fault with the MMPI (Pancoast & Archer, 1989) and the MMPI-2 (Duckworth, 1991). But the MMPI and MMPI-2 continue to be widely used (Popham & Holden, 1991).

The MMPI has been employed in personality research to predict both undesirable and desirable behavior. Hathaway and Monachesi (1952), for example, predicted delinquent behavior using the MMPI. Harrell (1972) predicted subjects' speed of advancement in business and income 10 years after they had taken the MMPI. More recently, Goldwater and Duffy (1990) showed that the MMPI can be used to detect women who were abused, sexually as well as nonsexually, as children. And, interestingly, the MMPI can be used to predict marital satisfaction. Couples who have similar MMPI profiles are the most happily married (Richard, Wakefield, & Lewak, 1990).

There is also no doubt that the MMPI can still predict a variety of psychiatric symptoms (Kolotkin, Revis, Kirkley, & Janick, 1987; Walters & Greene, 1988). The MMPI scales can even be used to predict outcomes related to people's health as well as to their behavior. A 20-year longitudinal study of over 2000 men revealed that Depression scores on the MMPI predict the long-term likelihood of developing cancer. In fact, individual differences on the MMPI Depression scale predict the likelihood of getting cancer even after statistically removing the effects of other predictors including number of cigarettes smoked, alcohol intake, family history of cancer, and serum cholesterol (Persky, Kempthorne-Rawson, & Shekele, 1987).

A note of caution is in order here. When we say "predict," we mean make guesses about what a *group of people* will do (e.g., become juvenile delinquents or not become juvenile delinquents) at better-than-chance level. But critics have pointed out that MMPI scores or even combinations of scores are almost never accurate enough as predictors to make significant decisions about *particular individuals* (Colligan & Offord, 1987, 1988). The potential problem is illustrated by the story of the ill-fated MAC scale.

Secondary Scales Derived From the MMPI: The Case of the MAC

Because the MMPI has such a large and diverse item pool, there have been a number of efforts to derive *secondary scales* from it. Essentially, this involves identifying a theoretical personality construct to be measured and then finding a subset of MMPI items that discriminate between those with and without (or high and low on) the characteristic in question. Following this procedure, investigators have derived scales of anxiety (Taylor, 1953), alcoholism (MacAndrew, 1965), narcissism (Wink & Gough, 1990) and alexithymia[1] (Bagby, Parker, & Taylor 1991, among others).

Typically, these scales never come into wide use, but the MacAndrew Alcoholism scale (or MAC) is an exception. MacAndrew's (1965) scale was

---

[1]*Alexithymia* means limited emotional awareness, and is said to be related to the presence of psychosomatic disorders.

developed to discriminate between male alcoholic outpatients and non-alcoholic psychiatric outpatients. Over the course of 20 years, it came into wide clinical use as a technique for identifying alcoholics; in fact, the MMPI-2 actually incorporated the MAC as a new primary scale (see Figure 9-1). But recent research has shown that the MAC is not all it was cracked up to be.

One team of researchers scored the MMPIs of almost 15,000 men and women from a variety of backgrounds for the MAC, and then determined the alcoholic or nonalcoholic status of each person by independent means. Overall, the MAC correctly identified only 71% of the alcoholic men and a mere 38% of the alcoholic women. By way of contrast, the single MMPI item "I have used alcohol excessively" identified 95% of the men and 94% of the women alcoholics. (Davis, Colligan, Morse, & Offord, 1987).

Shortly thereafter, Gottesman and Prescott (1989) published a review of 74 studies on the MAC. Their conclusion was that

> only 15% of individuals identified by the [MAC] scale as alcoholics are correctly classified, while 85% of those called "alcoholic" are not actually affected. The data are so clear that we call for a suspension of the use of the MacAndrew Alcoholism scale outside of research settings. (p. 223)

The NEO Inventories

The NEO Personality Inventory (NEO-PI) and its successors, the NEO-PI-R and the NEO Five Factor Inventory (NEO-FFI) can in many ways be contrasted with the MMPI. The NEO inventories are relatively new, were originally designed for a normal population, and their basis for item selection was not empirical keying. What the NEO inventories do share with the MMPI is popularity; they are fast becoming one of the most popular inventories for research and clinical use.

The NEO personality inventories were developed by two psychologists, Paul Costa and Robert McCrae, in conjunction with their *five-factor model of personality*. The original NEO-PI was published in 1985. The current versions, the NEO-PI-R and the NEO-FFI, were published in 1992 (Costa & McCrae, 1992).

Briefly, the five-factor model states that there are five major domains of personality: Neuroticism (N), Extraversion (E), Openness (O), Agreeableness (A), and Conscientiousness (C).

We will discuss the theoretical background and history of the model in Chapter 10. For the moment, it is sufficient to know that the NEO Inventories were developed for the specific purpose of assessing the factors named in the model.

The NEO-PI-R

The *NEO-PI-R* is the current full inventory, having replaced the original NEO-PI in 1992. It consists of 240 items, each answered on a 5-point scale from "strongly agree" to "strongly disagree." Any given item is scored for only one domain, and each domain is covered by 48 items.

The items were selected on their ability to correlate with other measures of the factors (so-called *criterion validity*), as well as the criteria of plausibility and reasonableness (*content validity*). For most of the items, it is fairly obvious what they are intended to measure. For example, a typical Neuroticism item is "I am easily frightened." A typical Extraversion item is, "I am a warm and friendly person."

An important feature of the NEO-PI-R is that it assesses not only the major domains of personality, but also the narrower traits or *facets* that the five-factor model specifies for each domain. Thus, all together, a person gets 30 different scale scores from the NEO-PI-R—six facets within each of five domains. The domains and facets of the NEO-PI-R are shown in Table 9-2.

The NEO inventories were developed for use with normal populations. There are separate norms for males and females, and for college-age (17–20) individuals as well as adults. There are also two versions of the NEO-PI-R, one for self-reports and one to be filled out by a rater who knows the person well. Like the MMPI scores, NEO scores can be plotted graphically to create a "personality profile."

If a person does the NEO-PI-R as a self-report, and another person fills out the rater-report version, a highly detailed and quite complicated profile emerges. An example is presented in Figure 9-2.

The publishers of the NEO-PI-R even provide a service whereby a person completes the inventory on a machine-scorable answer sheet, which is then interpreted by a computer program! These interpretations include a global description of the respondent's personality, as well as a detailed interpretation of the facets and possible implications (such as the way the individual would probably cope with daily stress).

Table 9-2
The Personality Domains and Facets Covered by the NEO-PI-R

NEUROTICISM	EXTRAVERSION	OPENNESS	AGREEABLENESS	CONSCIENTIOUSNESS
Anxiety	Warmth	Fantasy	Trust	Competence
Anger-Hostility	Gregariousness	Aesthetics	Straight-forwardness	Order
Depression	Assertiveness	Feelings	Altruism	Dutifulness
Self-consciousness	Activity	Actions	Compliance	Achievement Striving
Impulsiveness	Excitement-Seeking	Ideas	Modesty	Self-Discipline
Vulnerability	Positive Emotions	Values	Tender-Mindedness	Deliberation

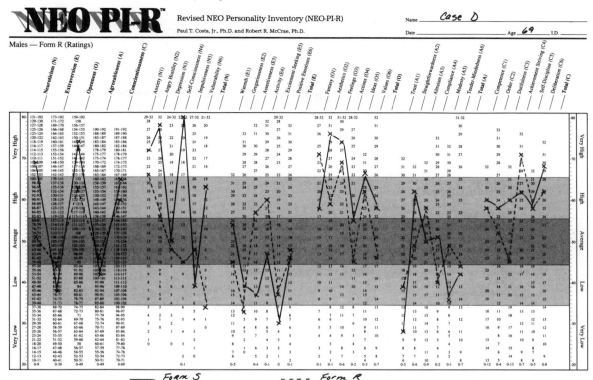

------- FORM S   - - - - FORM R

Figure 9-2
Sample NEO-PI-R profile.
Reproduced by special
permission of the publisher,
Psychological Assessment
Resources, Inc., 16204 North
Florida Avenue, Lutz, Flor-
ida 33549, from the NEO
Personality Inventory-Revised
Professional Manual, by Paul
Costa, and Robert McCrae.
Copyright 1978, 1985, 1989,
1992 by PAR, Inc. Further
reproduction is prohibited
without permission of PAR,
Inc.

The NEO-FFI

For purposes of detailed assessment, full-scale profiles are useful, but often
a simpler, more global assessment is all that is needed. The NEO-FFI was
developed for this purpose.

The NEO-FFI has 60 items, with 10 items representing each domain. It
does not provide separate facet scales, but has the advantage that most people
can complete it in less than 15 minutes. The NEO-FFI comes as a test booklet
and answer sheet in one, and can be scored in less than a minute. Note,
however, that *interpretation* of a NEO-FFI profile is not straightforward, and
may require considerable time and additional information about the person
being assessed.

**PERSONALITY
INVENTORIES
AND PERSONNEL
SELECTION**

No self-report personality inventory is, by itself, adequate for selecting ideal
candidates for important jobs. The accuracy of predictions made with these
tests simply is not high enough. But what about using personality inventories
to *exclude* individuals who may be unsuitable for critical occupations that
require a strong sense of responsibility and personality stability, such as
nuclear power plant operators? The likelihood of accidents in those jobs
might be reduced by screening out applicants who show any signs of
psychopathology (Butcher, 1979).

■ *Demonstration 9-1:*
FIRSTHAND EXPERIENCE WITH A SELF-REPORT PERSONALITY INVENTORY

We have been talking about self-report personality inventories, and you may want to try one. Most of the major inventories (e.g., the MMPI and the NEO-PI) would be inappropriate for this sort of trial because special training and a technical manual are required to interpret personality profiles meaningfully. But Willerman (1975) has published a short inventory that can yield some interesting insights.

Procedure

1. First, remove Work Sheet 9-1 (depicted in Table 9-3) from the Demonstration Materials section at the back of the book. Next, before reading further, consider *how true for you* each of the 15 items in Table 9-3 is. Use a scale that goes from 1 (hardly at all) to 5 (a lot). Circle the scale number on the work sheet.

2. Before you can score the inventory, items 2, 4, 5, and 10 (which have an *R* after them) need to be reversed. In other words, if you indicated "5," change it to "1." Similarly, change "4" to "2," "2" to "4," and "1" to "5" ("3" remains unchanged). Write the scale for each item (reversed if applicable) in the space provided.

3. To score the inventory, group your answers into three clusters: items 1–5, 6–10, and 11–15. Sum your answers to obtain a total score for each of the three clusters. Write the sums in the spaces provided.

4. You are now ready to evaluate the inventory. Items 1–5 pertain to *Sociability*, items 6–10 to *Activity Level*, and items 11–15 to *Emotionality*. (We will see in Chapter 10

Table 9-3
Sample work sheet for Demonstration 9-1

ITEM	HARDLY AT ALL				A LOT	SCALE SCORE	SUM
How true is this of you?							
1. I make friends easily.	1	2	3	4	5	_____	
2. I tend to be shy. (R)	1	2	3	4	5	_____	
3. I like to be with others.	1	2	3	4	5	_____	_____
4. I like to be independent of people. (R)	1	2	3	4	5	_____	
5. I usually prefer to do things alone. (R)	1	2	3	4	5	_____	
6. I am always on the go.	1	2	3	4	5	_____	
7. I like to be off and running as soon as I wake up in the morning.	1	2	3	4	5	_____	
8. I like to keep busy all of the time.	1	2	3	4	5	_____	_____
9. I am very energetic.	1	2	3	4	5	_____	
10. I prefer quiet, inactive pastimes to more active ones. (R)	1	2	3	4	5	_____	
11. I tend to cry easily.	1	2	3	4	5	_____	
12. I am easily frightened.	1	2	3	4	5	_____	
13. I tend to be somewhat emotional.	1	2	3	4	5	_____	_____
14. I get upset easily.	1	2	3	4	5	_____	
15. I tend to be easily irritated.	1	2	3	4	5	_____	

that some psychologists believe these three dispositions to be partly inherited.)

5. Most self-report personality inventories can be understood only with respect to group norms, and this one is no exception. Willerman (1975) reported that two-thirds of University of Texas at Austin students score within the ranges given below and added: "If your score falls below or above these ranges, you may regard yourself as high or low in that disposition" (p. 35).

	MALES' AVERAGE RANGE	FEMALES' AVERAGE RANGE
Sociability	13-19	15-20
Activity Level	13-19	13-20
Emotionality	9-16	11-18

6. Several other considerations regarding the Demonstration have to do with the utility of the measure. For example, did you think that you knew what the questions were "getting at" as you answered them? Do you think you purposely (or unwittingly) biased your answers in any way? Could someone else use a copy of your answers to actually predict your behavior from them? Somewhat more technically, were your responses influenced by the form of the question (reversed or not)? Were they affected by possible social judgments of its content (e.g., our culture does not admire those who are easily frightened)? We will look at these issues later in the chapter.

Use of the MMPI for screening out candidates who may be unsuitable for a particular job has generated a history of controversy and litigation (Dahlstrom, 1980). In the summer of 1977, five men sued two Jersey City, New Jersey, officials and the Laboratory of Psychological Studies, which had conducted psychological screening of the emotional fitness of aspiring fire fighters. This suit, which was later joined by several civil liberties organizations, was instigated by two fire fighters, two applicants for a position in the fire department, and one unsuccessful candidate.

The plaintiffs charged that the use of psychological tests such as the MMPI requires applicants to disclose highly personal information and is an invasion of privacy. (Some of the items from the MMPI allude to sexual practices and religious and political beliefs.) The suit further charged that the testing violated fundamental rights of freedom of belief protected by the First and Fourteenth Amendments to the U.S. Constitution.

After a lengthy trial, presiding Judge Coolahan issued his opinion (*McKenna v. Fargo*, 451 F. Supp. 1355 [1978]). He said that the heart of the case involved the "involuntary disclosure" that accompanied responding to psychological tests. The job applicants did not always know exactly what their responses to specific items were revealing about their personalities. Therefore, privacy was being invaded on some level.

Nevertheless, Judge Coolahan dismissed the allegation that the applicants' constitutional right of freedom of belief had been violated. It did not appear that the applicants were being tested for their beliefs or values. The fire department received only a testing summary; they never received the raw scores of the tests, which would be needed to find out how applicants responded to specific items. Further, the judge thought the job of fire fighter entailed life-threatening risks to the applicant and the public. He therefore recognized the need for the state to protect its interests by hiring only those individuals who were emotionally fit.

Judge Coolahan decided "that the constitutional protection afforded privacy interests is not absolute. State interests may become sufficiently compelling to sustain State regulations or activities which burden the right to privacy." He further determined that psychological evaluation is an acceptable selection procedure, largely because psychological factors play a major role in fire fighting. This decision was later upheld by a Circuit Court of Appeals.

The MMPI continues to be used as a screening test for many "sensitive" jobs. The biggest drawback of this practice is that it probably falsely excludes many appropriate candidates. A team of psychologists recently stressed that "organizations must ultimately decide upon the degree to which they are willing to sacrifice candidates who may have been successful in order to screen out those who are unsuitable" (Inwald & Brockwell, 1991, p. 522).

ALTERNATIVES TO TRADITIONAL PERSONALITY INVENTORIES

Self-report inventories are not the only way to assess dispositions. We will consider three alternatives: ratings, nominations, and composite profiles.

Ratings

Perhaps the most obvious alternative to self-reports is to observe the person directly in many situations. Whether he or she "gets mad often," "tires easily," and so on can be determined by direct observation. However, in most assessment efforts, it is impractical to observe the person over a range of situations and for enough time for a proper assessment. One practical alternative is to obtain observational data indirectly through the reports of individuals who know the person well. Assessment data obtained in this way are given the general name **ratings**.

Ratings of one kind or another enjoy extremely wide use. Almost everyone has been a rater and has been rated by others. Ratings are often used, for example, in letters of recommendation from former employers and teachers. Mental-health workers may use ratings in reports of a client's behavior or progress. Formal rating scales are used in personality assessment and research. Typically, the psychologist will ask a person who knows the subject well (such as a teacher, friend, or spouse) to indicate whether or not the subject has a particular characteristic. Or the rater may be asked to assign a number (say, from 0 to 10) that indicates how much of a given characteristic the subject has.

A strong word of caution needs to be introduced about ratings, however. Unless rating scales are designed very carefully, they are open to a number of serious biases and distortions. These biases come from the rater and distort the picture he or she gives about the subject of the assessment. Several major types of bias are shown in Table 9-4.

Table 9-4
Possible sources of bias in personality rating scales

SOURCE OF ERROR	EXPLANATION
Error of Leniency	When raters know a person well, as they must to offer an informed evaluation, they tend to rate the person higher (or sometimes lower) than they should.
Error of Central Tendency	Raters are often reluctant to use the extreme ends of a rating scale even when these are appropriate, preferring to stick closer to the middle range of descriptions. (We all do this when we describe a very ugly person as "not being that attractive.")
Halo Effect	Raters tend to permit their *general* impression of a person to influence their ratings for most of the person's specific characteristics, just as a halo casts a pleasant, diffuse light over an angel or cherub.
Contrast Error	Raters often describe others as being less like themselves than is actually the case. A relatively submissive rater, for example, may see others as being considerably more dominant than they really are.
"Logical" Error	Raters often assume that two characteristics should be related ("it seems logical") and bias their evaluations accordingly. For example, a rater who believes that *hostility* and *abrasiveness* go together may rate people who are abrasive as being more hostile than they really are.
Proximity Error	When a standard rating form is used, characteristics that are near one another on the list often receive similar ratings just because they are close together. This is a type of response set problem.

Source: Based on the analysis offered in *Psychometric Methods*, 2nd ed., by J. P. Guilford, 1954, New York: McGraw-Hill.

Nominations   In contrast to evaluations by one or two raters, nominations involve a variety of people and situations. Nominations are based on observations made over extended periods by a number of observers who see the subject from a variety of perspectives and with whom the subject has had different relationships. Neale and Weintraub (1977), for example, collected peer nominations for a large number of children of schizophrenic parents. The subjects were assessed in part using a 35-item peer nomination procedure (Pekarik, Prinz, Liebert, Weintraub, & Neale, 1976).

The procedure involves distributing the 35-item Pupil Evaluation Inventory to all the children in the subject's classroom. The inventory asks the children to name (nominate) other children in the class who have various characteristics (e.g., "those who can't sit still," "those who are liked by everyone," and "those who make fun of people"). A subject's score for any category is his or her percentage of the possible nominations in that category; thus, a child in a class of 50 who was nominated by 10 classmates as among "those who can't sit still" would receive a score of 20%; a child in a class of 25 who was nominated by 20 classmates would receive a score of 80%.

The procedure's usefulness has been clearly demonstrated (Pekarik et al., 1976), but the cost of using it is high because the inventory must be administered to an entire class to assess a single child. In fact, to assess a single individual, gathering data through an adequate nomination technique is often out of the question except in the case of schoolchildren.

The "Composite Profile" Approach to Assessment

Rather than rely on one method of personality measurement, some investigators have proposed a multimethod approach to ensure that the findings are valid (Campbell & Fiske, 1959; Harris, 1980). As many different measures of the same trait as possible are used. It is assumed that the measurement error associated with any one method will be less likely to distort the final measure when many methods of assessment are combined. An example is assessing an individual's generosity. People may want to present themselves in a favorable light, and therefore overestimate their generosity in a self-report questionnaire. However, peers could also be asked to rate these individuals for the trait in question. When the two different measures are combined, a more accurate picture will emerge.

Following this rationale, Harris (1980) proposed employing three methods of assessment to approximate an individual's "true" personality profile. He suggested (1) starting with a carefully constructed personality inventory that objectively assesses formally defined variables, (2) obtaining both peer ratings and self-report ratings on the variables assessed by the inventory, and (3) averaging the three separate assessments to produce a composite profile.

Harris demonstrated that such composite profiles are considerably more stable over time than single-method profiles. Further, composite profiles yield valid measures of personality. So long as one's time and budget are sufficient, Harris' three-method approach offers an alternative that is clearly better than the single-method approach to personality assessment.

PROBLEMS WITH SELF-REPORT AND RATING DATA

In 1934, Richard LaPiere, a sociologist, wrote letters to 250 hotels and restaurants across the United States asking, "Will you accept members of the Chinese race as guests in your establishment?" A majority of the proprietors answered LaPiere's letter. More than 90% of the respondents replied that they would *not* serve Chinese guests. This should not have been surprising because there was a good deal of anti-Chinese sentiment in the United States in the mid-1930s. What was surprising was that the proprietors did not mean

The attitudes that people express do not always correspond to or predict their behavior.
Photo by Christopher O'Keefe and Michael D. Spiegler

it, as LaPiere well knew. Six months earlier, he had toured the country with a Chinese couple. They had stopped at each of the 250 establishments to which LaPiere had written. And the Chinese couple had in fact been served in 249 of them, for the most part with very pleasant treatment!

More recent studies have repeatedly confirmed LaPiere's basic finding. People's stated attitudes or intentions may tell us little or nothing about how they will behave. A law-and-order political attitude does not necessarily go along with adherence to certain municipal laws (Wrightsman, 1969); church attendance cannot usually be predicted from expressed attitudes toward church (Wicker, 1971); it is almost impossible to predict how often individual students will cut classes from their attitudes toward their professors (Rokeach & Kliejunas, 1972); and attitudes toward tax evasion do not appear to predict who will actually cheat on taxes (Hessing, Elffers, & Weigel, 1988).

There is a general point underlying these findings. The answers received in personality assessment often depend on the method of inquiry or test used. Many innkeepers might have been labeled harsh bigots based on their written sentiments. But they would have been perceived as fair-minded and unbiased on the basis of their observed actions. This finding—a person's stated attitudes may reveal little about his or her behavior—is why many investigators have tried to identify the weaknesses in personality inventories.

Faking on Personality Inventories

People taking tests such as the MMPI have devised various schemes for faking their answers. They may want to make a good impression when applying for a job. Or they may want to give a bad impression when being tested for sanity in connection with a murder trial. How successful are these conscious efforts to achieve a desired impression?

Some fakers, particularly those who overdo it, will be detected by one or more of the validity scales included in most self-report personality inventories (Gillis, Rogers, & Dickens, 1990; Grossman, Haywood, Wasyliw, & Cavanaugh, 1990). Still, on the average, people seem to get "better" scores on self-report personality inventories when told to simulate a "nice personality" (Helmes & Holden, 1986; Krahe, 1989).

In general, faking can be detected only imperfectly. The detection rate is probably no higher than 80% with most inventories and there appear to be as many as 10% *false positives*, that is, individuals who did not fake but appear to have done so on the basis of validity scales (Schretlen, 1988; Schretlen & Arkowitz, 1990). Not surprisingly, faking is more likely on the most transparent or obvious items (Schretlen, 1990). Many personality psychologists therefore fear that undetected faking is quite common with self-report personality inventories (Cernovsky, 1988; Wetzler & Marlowe, 1990). Finally, other kinds of test-taking attitudes, known as *response sets*, may distort the personality picture presented by self-report inventories.

Response Sets

Psychologists often assume that a person's response to any item on a personality inventory is a reaction to the *content* of the item. For example, they assume that a person who responds "true" to the statement "I like parties" often attends social functions. Is this a valid assumption? Perhaps not.

People with particular test-taking attitudes may not be answering the items in terms of content. **Response sets** are characteristic and consistent ways of responding to a test regardless of what the items say. For instance, **response acquiescence** is the tendency to agree with items, no matter what their content. **Response deviation** is the tendency to answer items in an uncommon direction, such as answering "true" to the statement: "I always get along well with other people."

Social Desirability as a Response Set

The response set that has received the most attention is **social desirability,** which involves answering items in the most socially accepted direction, whether the answers are correct for the respondent or not. For example, an individual who prefers to be alone and dislikes social gatherings might answer "true" to the statement "I like parties." The response is given because he or she feels that it is socially desirable to enjoy parties, or that there is something wrong with anyone who doesn't like parties.

Several methods have been devised for controlling the influence of social desirability (O'Grady, 1988). One method is to measure the respondent's tendency to answer items on a self-report inventory in the socially desirable direction. The person's score on the inventory is then adjusted to take the degree of this tendency into account.

Another approach involves employing neutral items with respect to social desirability. These statements are rated in the middle of the social desirability/undesirability scale. An example is "I am easily awakened by noise." It is often difficult, however, to find or rewrite items that meet the requirement of neutrality and simultaneously convey the necessary content (Fristad, 1988). Imagine how hard it would be to rewrite the statement "Most of the time I wish I were dead" to make it more socially desirable without changing the meaning substantially. (This is an actual MMPI item that is rated as extremely undesirable.)

A third approach for controlling the effects of social desirability is to use a *forced-choice inventory,* in which respondents must choose which of two statements is more characteristic of them. All the statements in the inventory are first scaled for social desirability and then paired according to their scale values. The choices in each pair have approximately the same social desirability scale value but different content. Therefore, when respondents choose the statement in each pair that is more characteristic of them, the choices cannot be based on social desirability. Edwards (1953) constructed his Personal Preference Schedule in this way to control for social desirability. The Personal Preference Schedule is a self-report personality inventory developed for counseling and research with nonpsychiatric individuals. Examples of items appearing on it are given in Table 9-5.

Response Styles: An Alternative View of the Data   Some psychologists try to rid self-report inventories of the distorting influence of response sets. Other psychologists claim that these characteristic ways of responding might not be sources of error at all (e.g., Edwards &

Table 9-5
Examples of items from the Edwards Personal Preference Schedule

ALTERNATIVES	ITEMS
A B	A: I like to tell amusing stories and jokes at parties. B: I would like to write a great novel or play.
A B	A: I like to have my work organized and planned before beginning it. B: I like to travel and see the country.
A B	A: I feel like blaming others when things go wrong for me. B: I feel that I am inferior to others in most respects.
A B	A: I like to avoid responsibilities and obligations. B: I feel like making fun of people who do things that I regard as stupid.

Source: From *Manual for Edwards Personal Preference Schedule* by A. L. Edwards, 1953, San Antonio: Psychological Corporation.

Edwards, 1991). The latter group suggests looking at test-taking attitudes as personality traits rather than as situation-specific reactions. The salient measures of personality in self-report inventories might be *how* someone responds rather than what they respond to (i.e., the content of the items).

Response tendencies can be viewed either as a source of distortion (error) or as an indication of personality dispositions. Assigning different terms to describe each situation is useful. Response sets, as we have said, are sources of distortion. **Response styles** are personality dispositions (Jackson & Messick, 1958). We have already examined social desirability as a response set. Now, we will consider it as a response style — that is, a personality disposition.

Social Desirability as a Response Style   Edwards (1953) developed the best-known measure of social desirability. He chose 150 items from the MMPI and asked 10 judges to respond to each of them in the socially desirable direction. The judges agreed perfectly on 79 of the 150 items; these 79 items formed the first *Social Desirability (SD) Scale*. Later, Edwards reduced the SD scale to 39 items by selecting those items that showed the greatest differentiation between subjects who had high and low total scores. He hypothesized:

> If the SD scale does provide a measure of the tendency of subjects to give socially desirable responses to statements in self-description, then the correlations of scores on this scale with other personality scales, given under standard instructions, should indicate something of the extent to which the social desirability variable is operating at the time. (1957, pp. 31, 33)

Studies by Edwards and other investigators support this hypothesis (e.g., Edwards, 1953, 1957; Edwards & Edwards, 1991; Merrill & Heathers, 1956). Scales measuring socially desirable traits — such as dominance, responsibility, status, cooperativeness, agreeableness, and objectivity — correlate positively with the SD scale. In contrast, scales measuring socially undesirable traits — such as social introversion, neuroticism, hostility, dependency, insecurity, and anxiety — are negatively correlated with the SD scale (Edwards, 1970).

What are the implications of the correlations between Edwards' SD scale and other personality scales? One implication is that the traits these scales measure may be, despite their names (e.g., dominance and introversion), only different aspects of social desirability. It might be more fruitful from the standpoint of prediction and explanation, as well as parsimony, to view the traits that correlate strongly with the SD scale as measures of social desirability. For example, Edwards believed that the trait measured by the Taylor Manifest Anxiety (MA) scale (Taylor, 1953), a measure of the disposition to be anxious derived from the MMPI, should be interpreted as social desirability/undesirability.

The MA scale is negatively correlated with the SD scale. High anxiety tends to be associated with low social desirability; low anxiety tends to be associated with high social desirability. This finding is not surprising if one looks at the actual items involved. Statements like "I am a very nervous person," "I am certainly lacking in self-confidence," and "I cry easily" appear on the MA scale. These characteristics are unquestionably socially undesirable in our society. Thus, high scores on the MA scale can be viewed as endorsing socially undesirable statements. Low scores on the MA scale can be seen as denying socially undesirable characteristics. (It is interesting that for certain subgroups of our culture—such as residents of psychiatric hospitals or homes for the aged—these characteristics are less undesirable and may even be construed as socially desirable because they lead to attention and care.)

The MA scale has been used to select subjects with high and low anxiety. One finding is that, for certain kinds of verbal learning, low-anxiety subjects make fewer errors and learn faster than high-anxiety subjects (Montague, 1953; Ramond, 1953; Taylor & Spence, 1952). Edwards (1957) explained these results in terms of social desirability:

> I believe it possible . . . to describe the low group on the Taylor scale as those who desire to make a good impression on others and the high group as those who are less interested in what others may think of them. I would predict that the group desiring to make a good impression on the Taylor scale, that is to say, those with low scores, might also desire to make a good impression in terms of their performance on the learning task. They are, in other words, perhaps more highly motivated by the desire to "look good," not only in their responses to the Taylor scale, but also in their performance in the learning situation itself. Surely, to be able to learn fast is, in our society, a socially desirable characteristic. If a subject has a strong tendency to give socially desirable responses in self-description, is it unreasonable to believe that he may also reveal this tendency in his behavior in a learning situation where he is aware of what would be considered socially desirable, namely to learn fast, to do his best? The high group, on the other hand, being less interested in making a good impression, showing less of a tendency to give socially desirable responses in self-description, caring less about how others may value them, does not have equal motivation with the low group in the learning situation. (p. 89)

The arguments favoring a response-style or response-set interpretation of self-report inventories are interesting, but they have certainly not gone unchallenged. In fact, several psychologists argue that the tendency to respond to items on the basis of characteristics other than content may be minimal (Block, 1965; McCrae & Costa, 1983). Recently, Costa and McCrae reported that "socially desirable responding is not a threat to the validity of the NEO-PI-R scales in most cases" and add that "[using] social desirability scales to screen or correct NEO-PI-R or NEO-FFI scales is *not* [italics added] recommended" (1992, p. 42).

THE FACTOR-ANALYTIC APPROACH

Raymond Cattell, a prominent dispositional psychologist, quipped that "the trouble with measuring traits is that there are too many of them!" (1965, p. 55). To solve this problem, Cattell introduced the use of **factor analysis**, a statistical tool that takes a highly sophisticated approach to personality assessment. His intent was to use questionnaire and rating data to discover

Raymond Cattell
(1905-   )
introduced the use of
factor analysis in the
study of personality.
Courtesy of Raymond B.
Cattell

empirically the natural personality structures that exist in people. Cattell (1965) explained the rationale behind his approach using the following analogy:

> The problem which baffled psychologists for many years was to find a method which would tease out these functionally unitary influences in the chaotic jungle of human behavior. But let us ask how, in the literal tropical jungle, the hunter decides whether the dark blobs which he sees are two or three rotting logs or a single alligator? He watches for movement. *If they move together—come and disappear together—he infers a single structure* [italics added]. (p. 56)

In the "jungle" of human behavior, however, perfect covariation is rare. Psychological variables do not always go together. One may get a fleeting glimpse of some strong covariations but never the perfect data generated by Cattell's alligator. How can personality psychologists deal with this situation? Part of the answer lies in the correlation coefficient, which allows the evaluation of degrees of relationship that are less than perfect. The other part lies in factor analysis, which allows psychologists to analyze a large number of correlation coefficients at the same time.

Basically, factor analysis reduces a large number of relationships (correlations) to a smaller, more manageable and comprehensible number of relationships. The smaller group is essentially a summary of the entire array of intercorrelations.

Factor analysis was first developed in 1904 by Charles Spearman, a British statistician. Its popularity today results from the availability of high-speed computers; without them, much of the current work using the technique would be virtually impossible.

A Hypothetical Example of a Factor Analysis

Suppose that an investigator wants to analyze college students' patterns of academic performance in order to discover what underlying skills are involved. Factor analysis could be used in such research. If it were, the investigation would proceed through the five steps summarized in Figure 9-3: collecting data; producing a correlation matrix (i.e., determining the relationship of each variable to every other variable); extracting factors; determining factor loadings; and naming the factors.

Collecting Data

The first step in factor analysis is data collection. In our example, let us say the investigator gathered a large number of students (subjects) and gave them seven different tests (measures).

Producing a Correlation Matrix

The next step involves producing a **correlation matrix,** which is a table that shows the exact relationship between each measure and every other measure. Consider the correlation matrix in Table 9-6; it contains the correlations of each of the seven measures with every other measure. This matrix shows that there is a high positive relationship between *a* and *b* (+ .70), *a* and *c* (+ .80), *a* and *d* (+ .80), *b* and *c* (+ .90), *b* and *d* (+ .70), *c* and *d* (+ .80), *e* and *f*

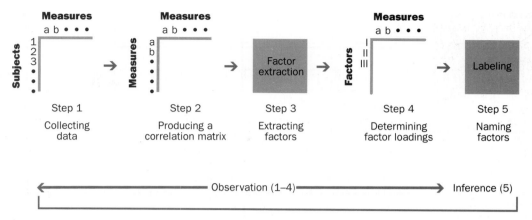

Figure 9-3
The five steps involved in factor analysis. The purpose of the procedure is to reduce the information available about a large number of measures (variables) to manageable size, and to interpret the pattern that emerges.

(+.80), *e* and *g* (+.70), and *f* and *g* (+.70). There is virtually no systematic relationship (i.e., correlation coefficients are in the vicinity of 0) between *a* and *e* (.10), *a* and *f* (.00), *a* and *g* (.00), *b* and *e* (+.10), *b* and *f* (+.10), *b* and *g* (.00), *c* and *e* (.10), *c* and *f* (.10), *c* and *g* (.10), *d* and *e* (.00), *d* and *f* (.10), and *d* and *g* (.00).

Extracting Factors
Our example yielded a correlation matrix (see Table 9-6) from a relatively small number of measures. However, it is not uncommon for 100 or more variables to be correlated in actual factor-analytic studies. Still, the complexities and sheer time needed to summarize and interpret the data should be apparent from the rather laborious enumeration of the results just presented. A major function of factor analysis is to reduce large sets of data to manageable units. By means of complex mathematical formulas, the data are reduced to small numbers of relatively homogeneous dimensions, called **factors**. The factors are said to be *extracted* from the data.

Determining Factor Loadings
Factors extracted in the previous step are the "common denominators" of all relationships between the variables. The factors are like the three primary colors from which all colors are composed. The next step is determining the relationship between each of the measures and each of the factors. The correlation of a measure with a particular factor is its **factor loading**. Thus, a variable is said to "load" on a factor to the extent that it is correlated with that factor.

Naming the Factors
Factor naming is the last step in a factor analysis. It is the point at which inference and subjective judgment enter the picture.

Let us return to the correlation matrix in Table 9-6. Suppose that the measures were aptitude tests in academic areas, where *a* = English, *b* = fine arts, *c* = history, *d* = French, *e* = mathematics, *f* = physics, and *g* =

Table 9-6
Hypothetical correlation matrix

MEASURE	a	b	c	d	e	f	g
a	+1.00	+.70	+.80	+.80	−.10	.00	.00
b		+1.00	+.90	+.70	+.10	+.10	.00
c			+1.00	+.80	−.10	−.10	−.10
d				+1.00	.00	−.10	.00
e					+1.00	+.80	+.70
f						+1.00	+.70
g							+1.00

engineering. The factor analysis reveals a distinct pattern among these seven measures (*a* through *g*). Specifically, *a*, *b*, *c*, and *d* seem to "go together." They are highly correlated with one another but show little or no relationship (i.e., near 0) to the other three measures.

Similarly, *e*, *f*, and *g* are highly related to one another but not to the other measures. Thus, two units or *factors* emerge from the seven measures. One factor consists of English, fine arts, history, and French; the other factor consists of mathematics, physics, and engineering. These factors might simply be labeled *X* and *Y*. We could also inspect the related measures for common qualities and give the two factors more meaningful names. However, the naming itself would be a subjective judgment; it is *not* a logical consequence of the mathematical factor analysis (Tracy, 1990).

Some people might insist that factor *X* represents a "literary" aptitude and factor *Y* a "scientific" aptitude; others might say that factor *Y* involves understanding inanimate forces, whereas factor *X* involves understanding people and their products. It is important to remember that "there is nothing in the factor-analytic methods themselves that can demonstrate that one factor solution is more scientifically useful than another" and "the correctness of interpretations based on factor-analytic results must be confirmed by evidence outside the factor analysis itself" (Comrey, 1973, p. 11).

A number of dispositional psychologists rely on factor analysis in their research, but they fashion the details of their technique by selecting certain measures and by making various technical decisions along the way. We will discuss three of the more prominent factor analytic research programs—those of Cattell, Eysenck, and McCrae and Costa—in Chapter 10.

SUMMARY   1. Self-report personality inventories are specialized questionnaires in which respondents answer a wide range of statements categorically. The responses are then scored according to the specific scales the inventory was designed to assess. The inventories are usually supported by norms, and by studies attesting to their reliability and validity.

2. The Minnesota Multiphasic Personality Inventory (MMPI), the most widely used self-report personality inventory, was developed by empirical keying. The latest version consists of 14 clinical scales and 4 validity scales. The scale scores of each individual are often graphed as a personality profile that can be matched with the personality descriptions of others with similar profiles appearing in MMPI atlases. The scores have been used to improve prediction of a variety of psychological and behavioral events that will occur in the future, ranging from criminal activities, to cancer, to business success.

3. The NEO inventories were developed to assess Neuroticism, Extraversion, Openness, Agreeableness, and Conscientiousness, the domains identified by the five-factor model of personality. The full scale NEO-PI-R assesses not only the major factors, but also the subscales or facets within each factor. The NEO-FFI only assesses the major factors, but it is quick to administer and easy to score.

4. There has been a long and heated controversy over the legitimacy of using personality inventories for personnel selection. Court decisions acknowledge that submitting to such tests involves an invasion of privacy at some level, but have found that the tests do not violate the fundamental constitutional right of freedom of belief. So, personality inventories are now held to be a legitimate selection procedure and will probably continue to enjoy wide use in personnel screening. This practice invariably leads to disqualifying some individuals unfairly.

5. Ratings, nominations, and composite profiles are the major alternatives to self-report inventories. Ratings involve asking people who know the subjects well to rate them on the degree to which they display the characteristics of interest. Such ratings are open to a number of biases, including a tendency for raters to be too lenient or to allow their general opinions to color their ratings of specific characteristics (halo effect).

6. Nominations, unlike ratings, are based on the impressions of many people rather than just a few. The information they yield tends to be highly reliable, but the cost is prohibitive in most cases.

7. The composite-profile approach involves combining information from several different assessment sources, such as self-report personality inventories, self-report ratings, and peer ratings.

8. The major limitation of self-report and rating data is that the written responses obtained may not correlate very well with the person's actual behavior. This discrepancy may result from deliberate faking or from a variety of unintentional factors that distort the way people describe and evaluate themselves and others.

9. Self-report inventories may be biased by response sets, which are characteristic ways of responding to inventory items regardless of what the

items say. Response sets include response acquiescence (agreeing with statements irrespective of their content), response deviation (answering many items in an uncommon direction), and social desirability (answering in the most socially approved direction).

10. Social desirability may be controlled to some extent by measuring it and then removing its influence statistically; by developing personality inventories in which all the items are socially neutral; or by using a forced-choice procedure in which the respondent must choose between items equivalent in social desirability.

11. Some psychologists believe that social desirability and other factors that have been shown to influence responses to self-report inventories should be considered personality dispositions in their own right. These researchers use the term "response styles" rather than response sets. Edwards considered social desirability to be an important and stable response style. He argued that various personality characteristics, such as the tendency to report or deny symptoms of anxiety, may be explained largely by individual differences in social desirability.

12. Factor analysis is a statistical procedure used to summarize large correlation matrices in terms of a small number of mathematical entities (factors).

Trait and Type Approaches

n this chapter, we will examine several different ways of thinking about traits and types. What these perspectives have in common is that they all consider traits and types to be real, psychologically meaningful entities. The founder of the modern dispositional strategy, Gordon Allport, described this approach as **heuristic realism**. Heuristic [your-IST-tick] has Greek and Latin roots and means "to find out or discover." Allport (1966) meant the term to convey that "the person who confronts us possesses inside his skin generalized action tendencies (or traits) and that it is our job scientifically to discover what they are" (p. 3). Allport did not believe that traits are physical entities, like glands or organs. He did, however, believe that psychological traits are real attributes of persons; they serve to *explain* behavior rather than merely to describe it.

Suppose, for example, a 5-year-old girl and a 25-year-old woman are given a 50-pound barbell to lift. Assuming that both subjects are motivated, it is a safe bet that the woman will succeed but the girl will fail. Most people would say this is because the woman is stronger than the girl. The difference in strength is a real characteristic of the people involved. Therefore, pointing out that the woman is much stronger than the girl explains why one succeeded and the other failed. In much the same way, trait and type theorists believe it is legitimate to say that a person behaves aggressively because she has an aggressive trait or because he is an aggressive type.

THE SEARCH FOR IMPORTANT DISPOSITIONS

Hundreds of words can be used to describe human personalities: aggressive, friendly, warm, pleasant, hostile, eager, bold, intense, irritable, callous, serious—the list goes on and on. Which are the important traits? How do they work together? A fundamental task of the dispositional strategy is to bring some order to the enormous number of possible human traits (Buss & Craik, 1985).

Dispositional psychologists have tried to identify the most basic or important traits and types using three broad approaches: the lexical approach, the theoretical approach, and the statistical approach.

The *lexical approach* is based on the assumption that the more important a disposition is, the more often it will be referred to in ordinary language. (Lexical derives from *lexicon*, which means "dictionary.") Following this approach, many researchers consider aggressiveness an important disposition. The word *aggressive* and its synonyms are common in everyday language when discussing and comparing people.

As the name suggests, the *theoretical approach* looks to theory to suggest which human dispositions are most central or important. For example, psychoanalytic theory suggests that ego strength is a dimension on which people differ.

Finally, there is the *statistical approach*. In this approach, very large amounts of data about many people are analyzed with statistical procedures designed to identify the basic factors that underlie the data. Factor analysis (see Chapter 9) has been a favorite tool of researchers using the statistical approach.

In the remainder of this chapter, each of these approaches will be discussed as we consider some of the most influential dispositional theories.

ALLPORT'S TRAIT APPROACH

Gordon Allport spent virtually his entire career trying to understand human personality. For more than 35 years, he adhered to the idea of *heuristic realism*. Allport insisted that the task of finding out "what the other person is really like" should not be abandoned even though it is difficult.

Traits as the Units for Studying Personality

Allport believed that traits are the basic units of personality. His eight theoretical assertions are as follows:

Gordon Allport
(1897-1967)
is considered the founder of the modern dispositional strategy. His philosophy, heuristic realism, is that traits should be considered real characteristics, residing within the person.
Harvard University Archives

1. *Traits have more than nominal existence.* They are not just summary labels of observed behavior. Rather, traits are part of the person.
2. *Traits are more generalized than habits.* Brushing one's teeth, Allport noted, may well be a habit, but it is not properly called a trait (although an underlying trait, such as cleanliness, might account for it).
3. *Traits are dynamic and determine behavior.* Traits direct action and are not mere structural artifacts. And unlike the intrapsychic structures posited by Freud, traits do not require energizing from somewhere else.
4. *Traits may be established empirically.* Allport was steeped in the tradition of experimental psychology and unequivocally acknowledged that psychologists must finally defer to their data.
5. *Traits are only relatively independent of other traits.*
6. *Traits are not synonymous with moral or social judgments.*
7. *Traits may be viewed either in the light of the personality that contains them (idiographically) or in the light of their distribution in the population (nomothetically).*
8. *Acts, and even habits, that are inconsistent with a trait are not proof of the nonexistence of the trait.* For example, if a person with a trait of assertiveness acts passively, this does not indicate that the person lacks the trait of assertiveness. It simply means that, in this instance, the person's trait is not being expressed.

Allport's eight assertions have been a guiding light for trait psychology ever since (Funder, 1991).

Pervasiveness of Specific Traits

Allport proposed that traits differ in the extent that they pervade any given individual's personality. He called the most pervasive traits **cardinal dispositions**. A cardinal disposition dominates the individual. It cannot stay hidden; it often makes its possessor famous. For example, Niccolo Machiavelli, the 16th century Italian political philosopher, is closely associated with the conviction that the ends justify the means. The adjective *Machiavellian* has come to be used to describe anyone who apparently holds this belief. According to Allport, very few people have cardinal dispositions.

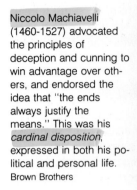

Niccolo Machiavelli (1460-1527) advocated the principles of deception and cunning to win advantage over others, and endorsed the idea that "the ends always justify the means." This was his *cardinal disposition*, expressed in both his political and personal life.
Brown Brothers

Central dispositions are the relatively small number of traits that tend to be highly characteristic of a person. They might be thought of as the characteristics one would mention when writing a detailed letter of recommendation. According to Allport, everyone has a few central dispositions that characterize them; the typical number is between 3 and 10.

Secondary dispositions are characteristics that operate only in limited settings. Preferences for particular kinds of food, specific attitudes, and other "peripheral" or situationally determined characteristics are included in this category.

Allport described two distinct perspectives from which to view human psychological traits. One view is to think of traits as characteristics that allow comparison of one person with another (much like comparing body weights). The other view is to think of traits as characteristics that are unique to a person and do not invite, or even permit, comparison with other people. In essence, this is the *nomothetic/idiographic* distinction (see Chapter 1).

Common Traits

Trait comparisons across people presume that there are **common traits**. Life situations continually make us compare people. Business executives must choose among candidates for a secretarial job; colleges must identify the best applicants for higher education. Whenever the job or role is fixed, someone must identify the personality or person who "fits" it. Most individuals make rough, approximate comparisons among people daily. The researcher committed to discovering common traits must formalize the criteria for identifying a common trait and also specify the procedures for measuring it.

According to Allport, when scaled for the population at large, common traits often have a *normal distribution*. That is, if the scores of a large sample are plotted on a graph, they produce a bell-shaped curve. The majority of cases pile up as average scores in the middle; the high and low scores taper off at the more extreme positions (Figure 10-1).

"Patterned Individuality"   Allport acknowledged the merits of comparing personalities along common dimensions (the nomothetic approach). Yet he insisted that others can really be understood only by coming to grips with the uniqueness of personality (the idiographic approach). Each person, Allport believed, has a unique inner organization of motives, traits, and personal style. The result is a "patterned individuality" that will never again be repeated exactly.

Some personality psychologists favor a nomothetic approach and seek general principles of behavior. These psychologists often argue that uniqueness merely reflects the combination of common traits in varying strengths. Allport disagreed, claiming that a person's traits always interact to form a unique pattern that cannot be fully explained by its separate parts. As an analogy, he compared a molecule of water with a molecule of hydrogen peroxide. They "have the same universals—hydrogen and oxygen; they differ only quantitatively (H_2O versus H_2O_2), but a small quantitative difference leads to totally unlike products. Try them on your hair and see" (1961, p. 10).

Allport used the term **individual traits** to refer to those important characteristics of the individual that do not lend themselves to comparison across persons. Most of Allport's research focused on common traits and was nomothetic. But he believed that such studies provided only an approximation of what people are really like: All of an individual's behavior and thought is unique to that person. "Even the acts and concepts that we apparently 'share' with others," he wrote, "are at bottom individual . . . It is true that some acts and concepts are more idiosyncratic than others, but none can be found that lacks the personal flavor" (1961, p. 29).

Figure 10-1
The distribution of scores from a test measuring dominance/submission.
Source: From *Pattern and Growth in Personality* by G. W. Allport, 1961, New York: Holt, Rinehart & Winston.

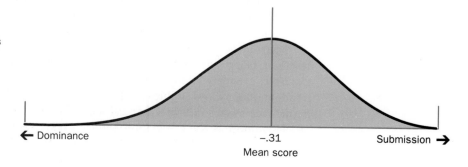

← Dominance   −.31   Submission →
                              Mean score

**20TH CENTURY
TYPOLOGIES**

The idea that people can be categorized by a small number of types has been popular since ancient times. To show how 20th-century personality psychology has employed this idea, we will look at two quite different typologies. The first typology originated from the fact that people have noticeably different physiques or body types. This typology tries to relate physical differences to differences in personality. The other typology began with the observation that people with a certain behavior pattern seem to be at high risk for heart attack. This typology has been used to examine differences between people who do and do not display the behavior pattern.

**Body Types and
Personality**

In 1921, German psychiatrist Ernst Kretschmer published *Physique and Character*, which contained the basics of the first modern type approach to personality. From observations made in his clinical practice, Kretschmer investigated the relationship between physique and mental disorders. He proposed three fundamental types of physique: (1) the *asthenic*, a fragile, narrowly built physique; (2) the *athletic*, a muscular type; and (3) the *pyknic*, a plump physique. More unusual types of physique were grouped together as *dysplastic* (Figure 10-2). After examining 400 psychiatric patients, Kretschmer concluded that pyknics are most likely to be diagnosed as manic depressive—that is, as experiencing alternating periods of elation and sadness. The remaining types were most likely to be diagnosed as schizophrenic—that is, as suffering from thought disorders.

Following Kretschmer's lead, American psychologist William Sheldon (1942) tried to relate physique to normal behavior. Sheldon first developed taxonomies of physique and temperament. As had Kretschmer, Sheldon identified three components of body structure: *endomorphy* (plump), *mesomorphy* (muscular), and *ectomorphy* (frail) (Figure 10-3). Unlike Kretschmer, however, Sheldon did not classify people as one type or the other; rather, he developed a system of **somatyping** using a seven-point scale. Each individual was rated for all three body types. In somatyping, the first number is endomorphy, the second, mesomorphy, and the last, ectomorphy. Thus, Superman is estimated to be a 1-7-2, whereas Jesus was a 2-3-5. The most common somatype is 4-4-3 for men and 5-3-3 for women (Brant, 1988).

Sheldon then correlated somatypes with personality. He somatyped 200 Caucasian males and followed their lives for 5 years. A clear picture seemed to emerge. Endomorphs tended to be relaxed, easygoing, and to love creature comforts. Ectomorphs were generally restrained, inhibited, and apprehensive. Finally, mesomorphs tended to be bold, assertive, and action-oriented.

Spurred by Sheldon's provocative findings, the search for relationships between body type and personality continued through the 1950s. For example, a widely cited study compared the somatypes of delinquent and nondelinquent boys (Glueck & Glueck, 1950, 1956). A much larger percentage of mesomorphs than ectomorphs were delinquent (Figure 10-4).

How close is the association between body type and personality? Rees (1961) summed up 15 years of research this way:

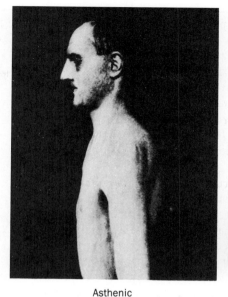

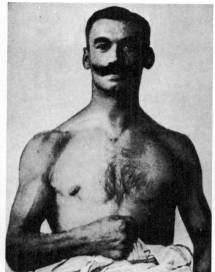

Asthenic

Athletic

Figure 10-2
The four body types
identified by Kretschmer.
Source: From *Physique and
Character: An Investigation
of the Nature of Constitution
and of the Theory of Tem-
perament* by E. Kretschmer
(W. J. H. Sprott, Trans.),
1926, New York: Harcourt.

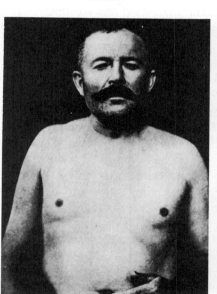

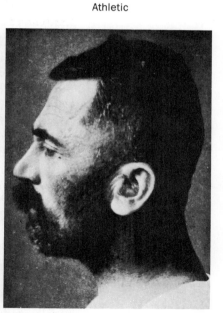

Pyknic

Dysplastic

One might say that the evidence suggests that there are tendencies for different
types of physique to be associated with certain psychological characteristics . . . but the majority of investigations do not report any correlations as
high as those reported by Sheldon . . . The available evidence suggests that the
correlations between physical characteristics and personality traits . . . are
nearly always too small to be trusted for the needs of individual prediction.
(p. 377)

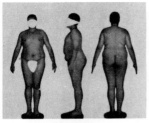

Endomorph

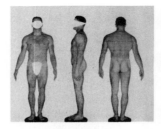

Mesomorph

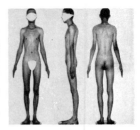

Ectomorph

Figure 10-3
Three views of the
extremes of Sheldon's
somatypes.
Source: From *Atlas of Men:
A Guide for Somatotyping
the Adult Male at All Ages* by
W. H. Sheldon, 1954, New
York: Harper & Row.

Thus, an individual cannot be psychologically "sized up" with any degree of accuracy by body type alone. Nonetheless, *on average*, people with certain body types do tend to show recognizable patterns of personality characteristics.

**The Type A
Behavior Pattern**

Physicians have long noted that the personalities of individuals with heart problems appear to differ from those without such problems. It wasn't until the late 1950s, however, that the contribution of psychological and behavioral variables to the development of coronary problems began to be examined systematically.

At that time, two cardiologists, Meyer Friedman and Ray Rosenman, sent a questionnaire to 150 businesspeople in San Francisco. The questionnaire asked for information about the behavior of friends who had had heart attacks. Over 70% of the respondents said "excessive competitive drive and meeting deadlines" were the most prominent characteristics of the heart disease victims they had known. Friedman and Rosenman called this combination of characteristics the **Type A behavior pattern**. They hypothesized that Type A behavior is a major cause of coronary artery and heart disease (Friedman & Rosenman, 1974).

Type A Behavior and Coronary Disease

Next, Friedman and Rosenman undertook an ambitious longitudinal investigation of the relationship between Type A behavior and heart disease. They identified over 3500 middle-aged men who had no heart problems initially, and obtained health reports for them over the next 8 years. Men displaying Type A behavior at the beginning of the study were several times more likely to have developed heart problems by the time the study was over than were those displaying a more easygoing and relaxed behavior pattern, called **Type B** (Rosenman, Jenkins, Brand, Friedman, Straus, & Wurm, 1975).

Subsequent research painted a picture of the Type A individual as constitutionally prone to biochemical and physiological overarousal. Biochemically, Type As were found to produce increased serum cholesterol and catecholamine when under pressure (Glass, 1977). Either substance may contribute, over time, to coronary problems. Type As were also found to

Figure 10-4

A portion of Glueck and Glueck's comparison of the somatypes of matched pairs of delinquent and nondelinquent boys. Among the delinquents there are more mesomorphs and fewer ectomorphs than would be expected by chance, a finding consistent with Sheldon's constitutional theory.

Source: From data published in *Unraveling Juvenile Deliquency* by S. Glueck and E. Glueck, 1950, New York: Commonwealth Fund.

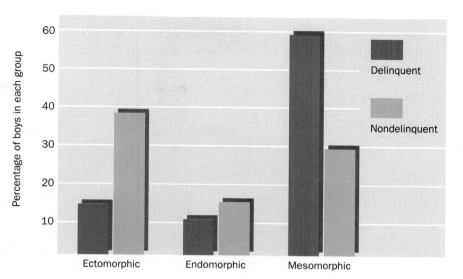

differ from Type Bs in certain glandular and metabolic responses that may result in increased risk of coronary difficulties (Williams, Friedman, Glass, Herd, & Schneiderman, 1978). Physiologically, Type As appeared to display more arousal (e.g., increased blood pressure) when working on challenging tasks than Type Bs (Holmes, McGilley, & Houston, 1984; Houston, 1983).

Finally, considerable evidence was accumulated to suggest that Type As tend to ignore signs of physical distress when working intensely on tasks (Matthews & Carra, 1982; Weidner & Matthews, 1978; Burke, 1988). This may mean that they ignore physical warnings from their bodies and literally drive themselves into heart attacks.

Once an individual has had a heart attack, the presence of Type A behavior is the best single predictor of whether he or she will have another. However, before a heart attack occurs, Type A individuals are notorious for denying their behavior patterns (Smith & Anderson, 1986; Wright, 1988).

Refining the Type A Construct: The Two Types of Type As

Initially, individuals who might be called *Type As* appeared to be a distinct but uniform group. One team of investigators painted the picture of a "tense, driven business executive who struggles for long hours at his desk, tapping his fingers and pencil, gulping down his lunch, and talking rapidly into two telephones at once while grimacing hostilely at his dallying assistant" (Friedman, Hall, & Harris, 1985, p. 1299). Another investigator simply described Type As as people with "hurry sickness" (Matthews, 1982). But research in the next decade was to show that Type As are a considerably more diverse lot than was initially assumed (Gray & Jackson, 1990).

Friedman, Hall, and Harris (1985) were among the first to suggest that the so-called *Type A personality* might encompass more than one type. They pointed out that not all highly vigorous individuals are impatient, hostile, and tense, and not all slow-paced individuals are calm, contented, and relaxed. A subsequent study compared various groups of middle-aged men (Friedman &

This executive is exhibiting one of the key characteristics of the Type A behavior pattern: a sense of time urgency that includes doing a number of tasks simultaneously.

Photo by Michael D. Spiegler

Booth-Kewley, 1987). The results indicated that the men with the poorest emotional adjustment were the ones most likely to have had heart attacks.

Another team of researchers analyzed college students' responses to a questionnaire measure of the Type A behavior pattern and found two relatively independent factors, which they labeled *Achievement Strivings* and *Impatience-Irritability*. Scores on the Achievement Strivings scale were related to students' grade point averages but *not* to their physical complaints (as measured by a health survey); on the other hand, scores on the Impatience-Irritability measure were related to physical complaints but *not* to grades. These and other results suggest that a tendency toward irritability and impatience is the active ingredient in the Type A pattern that leads to health risks (Spence, Helmreich, & Pred, 1987; Helmreich, Spence, & Pred, 1988).

What, then, is the central characteristic of individuals who are at higher risk for heart attacks and other health problems? Some investigators have called it "quality of adjustment"; others have called it "impatience-irritability." But a recent breakthrough in research suggests that the best descriptor of the illness-prone Type As is that they are plagued by *cynical hostility*.

Greenglass and Julkunen (1991) used the Cook-Medley hostility scale, derived from the MMPI (see Chapter 9), as a measure of cynical hostility. They, and other investigators, have come up with a remarkably consistent finding. It seems to be this one ingredient, cynical hostility, that predisposes an individual to heart attacks and other forms of physical illness (Greenglass & Julkunen, 1989, 1991; Keltikangas-Jarvinen & Raikkonen, 1990; Smith & Pope, 1990).

What does this kind of hostility encompass? Greenglass and Julkenen recently developed a special 17-item scale to measure it. Here are three of the beliefs endorsed by those who are cynically hostile:

No one cares much what happens to you.

Most people are honest chiefly through fear of being caught.

Most people make friends because friends are likely to be useful to them.

So, there seem to be two types of Type As. One type is engaged in healthy achievement striving, and "competitive" only in accepted ways. The other type is poorly adjusted, impatient, irritable, and hostile. In these people, competitiveness takes a destructive, antisocial form. And, back to the original point, it seems clear that it is only this latter type who run abnormally high health risks. Moreover, research is beginning to show that they run more psychological and social risks as well (Barling, Bluen, & Moss, 1990; Volkmer & Feather, 1991).

Type A Behavior in Children and Adolescents

Health psychologist Karen Matthews developed the Matthews Youth Test for Health, the MYTH, as a way to assess Type A behaviors in children. The MYTH, a rating scale used by teachers, consists of 17 statements describing children's behaviors (e.g., "gets irritated easily," "does things in a hurry"). Teachers rate the target child for each of the statements on a five-point scale from *extremely characteristic* to *extremely uncharacteristic*. Using the MYTH to identify Type A children, Matthews and her associates found that, independent of ability (IQ scores), Type A children show more early accomplishments than Type B children (Matthews, Stoney, Rakaczky, & Jamison, 1986). And, most significant, recent research with children from preschool through adolescence shows that, as in adults, youthful Type As come in two subtypes: those who are competitive and achievement-oriented in a prosocial way and those who are aggressive, hostile, and impatient (Blaney, 1990; Keltikangas-Jarvinen, 1990; Lundberg, Westermark, & Rasch, 1990).

HERITABLE ASPECTS OF PERSONALITY

The view that individual differences in personality are inherited (and therefore innate) is widely held. Is there support for such a belief? To answer this question, personality researchers have used both the twin study method and the adoptee/family method.

Twin and Adoptee/Family Research

One out of every 85 births produces twins. Approximately two-thirds of all twins are *fraternal*, or *dizygotic*; that is, they develop from separate ova and sperm. Fraternal twins share only a birthday with their "womb mates." Otherwise, they are no more alike genetically than siblings born separately. The remaining third are *identical*, or *monozygotic* twins, who develop from the same ovum and sperm. Consequently, they have the same genetic endowment. The **twin study method** capitalizes on these facts by attempting to identify and measure a disposition thought to be inherited. Then its degree of *concordance*—mutual occurrence among many pairs of identical and fraternal twins—is determined. Greater concordance among the identical twins is taken to be evidence that the disposition is heritable.

When parents rear their biological children, they may influence them through either the genes or the environment they provide. But when rearing adopted children, the only influence the adoptive parents can have is through the environment and the only influence the biological parents can have is through heredity. By comparing the personality dispositions of adopted children with those of both their adoptive and biological parents, one can get a sense of the relative importance of heredity and environment for each disposition. By noting the similarity among biological and adopted children brought up in the same home (that is, the same environment), one can get a further sense of the degree of environmental impact. Such comparisons form the basis of the **adoptee/family method**.

Heritability of Abnormality and Deviance

In the 1940s, Franz Kallman, a German psychiatrist, examined large samples of persons who were diagnosed schizophrenic and who had a twin. He then determined the percentage of the twins who were also schizophrenic (Jackson, 1960). Kallman found that *concordance*, or agreement, in diagnosis of schizophrenia was significantly higher for monozygotic twins than for dizygotic twins. Later twin research has replicated these findings (Fischer, 1973; Hoffer & Pollin, 1970; Nicol & Gottesman, 1983; Pardes, Kaufmann, Pincus, & West, 1989).

Adoptee/family research has shown that schizophrenia is more common among adopted children who had a schizophrenic biological parent than among those who had two psychiatrically normal biological parents (Kety, Rosenthal, Wender, & Shulsinger, 1968). Equally important, there is a definite association between being related to a schizophrenic and manifesting subclinical levels of schizoid thought disorder (Romney, 1990).

Both twin and adoptee/family research also suggest that, in addition to schizophrenia, there is a genetic component to bipolar affective disorder, unipolar depression, alcoholism, juvenile delinquency, eating disorders, and adult crime (Fichter & Noegel, 1990; Kutcher & Marton, 1991; McGuffin & Katz, 1989; Mirin & Weiss, 1989; Moldin, Reich, & Rice, 1991; Pihl & Peterson, 1990; Rosenhan & Seligman, 1984; Rushton, Russell, & Wells, 1985; Torgerson, 1990). However, none of these problems is caused solely by a person's genetic endowment. At worst, a person's genes can only predispose him or her to various psychological difficulties—which may or may not be activated depending on environmental factors.

Heritability of Personality Within the Normal Range

Are variations in normal personality inherited to any significant degree? A pair of impressive studies by John Loehlin and his associates persuasively answers, yes.

Loehlin's first study used the twin method. This study compared 514 pairs of monozygotic twins with 336 relatively comparable same-sexed dizygotic twins. The twin pairs were chosen from the almost 600,000 persons who, in high school, had taken the National Merit Scholarship test in 1962. Subjects included opposite-sexed and same-sexed pairs. Each subject was given a wide variety of personality, attitude, and interest tests and questionnaires. What is most impressive about the sample is that it was drawn from the entire United States, rather than from a single geographic region or ethnic group. The sample also included more than 5% of the entire United States twin population in the age group studied. The results showed that monozygotic twins were far more alike than dizygotic twins on a wide range of personality scales (Loehlin & Nichols, 1976).

In the second study, Loehlin and his colleagues used the adoptee/family method. They followed more than 400 children who were brought up in either biological or adoptive families. Adopted children resembled their biological parents in many personality characteristics, although they had never been in contact. In contrast, adopted children did not resemble their adoptive parents in personality, even though they had lived with them from birth (Loehlin, Willerman, & Horn, 1987).

We may ask, though: What exactly *are* the inborn personality characteristics? This leads to the concept of *temperament traits*.

Temperament Traits: Aspects of Personality Most Susceptible to Genetic Influence

Recently, several writers have distinguished between **temperament traits** that are observed in infancy and early childhood and **personality traits** as they are observed in adults (Strelau, 1987; Tarter, 1988). Similarly, Endler has argued that *"temperament refers to the raw material out of which personality evolves"* (1989, p. 151).

Evidence has been mounting that three broad aspects of personality—Sociability, Emotionality, and Activity Level—may qualify as temperament traits. They are all present at birth, stable across time, and pervasive in their influence (Buss & Plomin, 1984; Goldsmith, 1983; Plomin, Pedersen, McClearn, Nesselroade, & Bergeman, 1988; Royce & Powell, 1983). We will now consider these three temperament traits.

Sociability

Sociability encompasses opposite styles of dealing with the social environment. At one extreme, some infants attempt to withdraw from all social situations; they prefer to withdraw from people rather than approach them. In contrast, other infants show unusual ease among people, great friendliness, and a marked ability and willingness to interact with just about anybody.

What is the evidence that Sociability is innate? Friendly infants tend to become friendly adolescents, and unfriendly infants are likely to become unfriendly adolescents (Kagan & Snidman, 1991; Schaefer & Bayley, 1963). In one interesting study of extremely unsociable children, subjects were followed longitudinally for 30 years. The investigators concluded:

> Shy boys were more likely than peers to delay entry into marriage, parenthood, and stable careers [and] to attain less occupational achievement and stability . . . Shy girls were more likely than peers to follow a conventional pattern of marriage, childbearing, and homemaking. (Caspi, Elder, & Bem, 1988, p. 824).

In addition, monozygotic twins are considerably more alike on Sociability measures than dizygotic twins (Buss, Plomin, & Willerman, 1973;

Royce & Powell, 1983). One study dealt with almost 13,000 pairs of Swedish twins (Floderus-Myrhed, Pedersen, & Rasmuson, 1980). The Sociability measure was correlated .54 and .47, respectively, for monozygotic female and male twin pairs; the corresponding correlations for dizygotic twins were only .21 and .20.

Similarly, Daniels and Plomin (1984) found that adopted infants tend to be more similar in Sociability to their biological mothers, with whom they have had no contact, than to their adoptive mothers. This finding is taken as strong evidence that Sociability is largely a genetically determined trait (Plomin, 1986).

Emotionality

Considerable evidence suggests that the degree to which a person is emotionally reactive has an innate component and that children differ in Emotionality from birth (Birns, 1965; Goldsmith & Campos, 1990; Thomas & Chess, 1977; Thomas, Chess, & Birch, 1970; Worobey, 1986). For example, Thomas and his associates have been following the development of 141 individuals for more than 30 years, since the subjects were infants. The researchers interviewed each youngster's parents every 3 months during the first year, every 6 months until age 5, and every year thereafter. They obtained behavioral data from a variety of sources: teacher interviews; direct classroom observation; personality tests conducted when the children were 3, 6, and 9 years old; and direct interviews with each child between the ages of 16 and 17. These data and other observations reveal that human beings have well-established emotional patterns by the time they are 2 or 3 months old and that the tendency to be emotionally reactive or unreactive then follows them consistently into their adult lives (Birns, 1965; Fox, 1989; Loehlin, 1989; Schaffer & Emerson, 1964).

Activity Level

Buss and his associates (1973) referred to Activity Level as "the sheer amount of response output" of the individual. There seems little doubt that a person's activity level is a temperament trait having a substantial heritable component (Eaton & Enns, 1986). During the first 2 years of life, Activity Level for a given infant is highly stable (Goldsmith & Campos, 1990), but there are marked individual differences among infants (Riese, 1988). Torgersen (1985) found a correlation of .93 for the activity levels of monozygotic twins, but only .14 for dizygotic twins.

Numerous studies have also shown that hyperactive children may be as much as 10 times more likely than nonhyperactive children to have had hyperactive parents (Cantwell, 1972; Morrison & Stewart, 1971). In addition, there are significant correlations between the activity levels of normal children and the activity levels of both parents when they were children (Willerman & Plomin, 1973). All this evidence adds up to a strong case that there are innate individual differences in Activity Level and that Activity Level qualifies as a major temperament trait.

The Gene/Environment Interaction

Recent commentators have pointed out that genetic and environmental factors always *interact*; that is, they combine through a dynamic process whereby a person's environment is partly caused by their genetic makeup (Bergeman, Plomin, McClearn, Pederson, & Friberg, 1988; Gifford, 1990; Plomin & Bergeman, 1991; Scarr & McCartney, 1983).

Consider two infants, Michelle and Vicki. Suppose both are born into similar environments and that their parents begin by giving each of them a moderate amount of attention and playful interaction. Michelle, a baby who just seems to have been born friendly, responds to this attention with winning smiles and coos of joy. Vicki, on the other hand, has seemed rather shy since the day she arrived. Attempts to play with her must be very low key to succeed; she often seems not to want to play at all. Soon the parents will *react* to these differences; in time, Michelle's family environment will become more friendly and sociable than Vicki's. These differences in environment, in turn, will further reinforce the initial differences in temperament with which each child was born.

As they grow older, Michelle and Vicki will seek out different activities to pursue. Michelle will prefer activities that bring her into contact with people; Vicki will prefer activities in which she can work by herself. Their initial dispositions, strengthened by the reactions they have gotten from others early in life, now lead them to actually create different environments for themselves. Given this process, it should come as no surprise that genetic effects on personality do not diminish over time and, in fact, *increase* with age (Plomin & Nesselroade, 1990).

But what of adult personality traits? They are presumably products of innate and environmental factors. They may or may not overlap with the temperament traits. To identify adult personality traits, dispositional psychologists have primarily relied on factor analysis. We will consider examples of this work in the remainder of the chapter.

CATTELL'S TRAIT APPROACH

Raymond Cattell (1965; 1979; Cattell & Kline, 1977), introduced in Chapter 9, proposed that there should be three broad sources of data about personality. He believed that all three sources are required for any factor analysis that aims to uncover all the major dimensions of personality. He labeled the three sources of personality data: L-data, Q-data, and T-data.

L-data are gathered from a person's life records (e.g., school records and work history). **Q-data** are gathered from questionnaires and interviews; the common feature is that the individual answers direct questions about himself or herself, based on personal observations and introspection (e.g., "Do you have trouble making and keeping friends?"). **T-data** are obtained from objective testing situations. "The subject is placed in a miniature situation and simply acts . . . [and] *does not know on what aspect of his behavior he is really being evaluated*" (Cattell, 1965, p. 104). Several hundred tests meet these criteria of objectivity (Cattell & Warburton, 1967).

Table 10-1
The 16 major factors in Cattell's analysis of personality

LOW-SCORE DESCRIPTION	FACTOR		FACTOR	HIGH-SCORE DESCRIPTION
Reserved	$A-$	vs.	$A+$	Outgoing
Less intelligent	$B-$	vs.	$B+$	More intelligent
Emotional	$C-$	vs.	$C+$	Stable
Humble	$E-$	vs.	$E+$	Assertive
Sober	$F-$	vs.	$F+$	Happy-go-lucky
Expedient	$G-$	vs.	$G+$	Conscientious
Shy	$H-$	vs.	$H+$	Venturesome
Tough-minded	$I-$	vs.	$I+$	Tender-minded
Trusting	$L-$	vs.	$L+$	Suspicious
Practical	$M-$	vs.	$M+$	Imaginative
Forthright	$N-$	vs.	$N+$	Shrewd
Placid	$O-$	vs.	$O+$	Apprehensive
Conservative	Q_1-	vs.	Q_1+	Experimenting
Group-tied	Q_2-	vs.	Q_2+	Self-sufficient
Casual	Q_3-	vs.	Q_3+	Controlled
Relaxed	Q_4-	vs.	Q_4+	Tense

Source: The Scientific Analysis of Personality by R. B. Cattell, 1965, Baltimore: Penguin.

According to Cattell, the three sources of data must be integrated to capture the full complexity of human personality. Traditionally, psychologists have looked at only one slice at a time. Their research has been *univariate*—that is, the experimenters change one (independent) variable and examine its effects on one other (dependent) variable. In contrast, **multivariate approaches,** which examine many variables simultaneously, have the advantage that "with sufficient analytical subtlety we can tease out the connections from the behavior of the man in his actual life situation—without the false situation of controlling and manipulating" (Cattell, 1965, p. 20).

In *The Scientific Analysis of Personality,* Cattell (1965) reported that he had scientifically derived 16 personality traits using factor-analytic and related procedures. He believed that these factors represented the major dimensions of differences in human personality. The 16 traits are listed in Table 10-1. We will consider the three most important traits (i.e., A, B, and C).

Three Source Traits Derived from Factor Analysis
Cattell called his 16 personality traits **source traits**—the building blocks of personality. He maintained that source traits can be discovered only by factor analysis. We will take a closer look at Cattell's three most important factors, A, B, and C.

Consider factor A. If it is a source trait, we would expect the same pattern of results to emerge from L-data and Q-data. That is, if the trait is really an underlying dimension of personality, it should be reflected in all measures of personality. Sample L-data and Q-data that load high on factor A are shown in Table 10-2. Considering these Q-data, and referring back to the L-data, Cattell (1965) concluded: "The warm sociability at one pole, and the aloofness and unconcern with people at the other are as evident here as in the observers' ratings" (p. 71). Note the similarity between factor A and the dimension called Introversion/Extraversion.

Using both L-data and Q-data, Cattell concluded that the second largest source trait, factor B, "looks like nothing less than general intelligence, and correlates well with actual test results" (1965, p. 72).

Cattell labeled the third largest source trait, factor C, as Ego Strength. The L-data and Q-data in Table 10-3 illustrate the nature of this source trait. Cattell noted the following about factor C:

> The essence of factor C appears to be an inability to control one's emotions and impulses, especially by finding for them some satisfactory realistic expression.

Table 10-2
L-data and Q-data for factor A

BEHAVIOR RATINGS (*L*-DATA) THAT LOAD ON FACTOR A		
A+ (POSITIVELY LOADED)		*A*− (NEGATIVELY LOADED)
Good natured, easygoing	vs.	Critical, grasping
Cooperative	vs.	Obstructive
Attentive to people	vs.	Cool, aloof
Softhearted	vs.	Hard, precise
Trustful	vs.	Suspicious
Adaptable	vs.	Rigid

FACTOR *A* IN QUESTIONNAIRE RESPONSES (Q-DATA)

I would rather work as:	
(a) An engineer	(b) *A social science teacher*
I could stand being a hermit.	
(a) True	(b) *False*
I am careful to turn up when someone expects me.	
(a) *True*	(b) False
I would prefer to marry someone who:	
(a) Is a thoughtful companion	(b) *Is effective in a social group*
I would prefer to read a book on:	
(a) *National social service*	(b) New scientific weapons
I trust strangers:	
(a) Sometimes	(b) *Practically always*

Note: A person who selects all the bold italic answers has a highly outgoing personality.
Source: The Scientific Analysis of Personality by R. B. Cattell, 1965, Baltimore: Penguin.

Table 10-3
L-data and Q-data for factor C

BEHAVIOR RATINGS (*L*-DATA) THAT LOAD ON FACTOR *C*

C+ (POSITIVELY LOADED)		C− (NEGATIVELY LOADED)
Mature	vs.	Unable to tolerate frustration
Steady, persistent	vs	Changeable
Emotionally calm	vs.	Impulsively emotional
Realistic about problems	vs.	Evasive, avoids necessary decisions
Absence of neurotic fatigue	vs.	Neurotically fatigued (with no real effort)

FACTOR *C* IN QUESTIONNAIRE RESPONSES (*Q*-DATA)

Do you find it difficult to take no for an answer even when what you want to do is obviously impossible?
   (a) Yes   (b) *No*

If you had your life to live over again, would you
   (a) *Want it to be essentially the same?*   (b) Plan it very differently?

Do you often have really disturbing dreams?
   (a) Yes   (b) *No*

Do your moods sometimes make you seem unreasonable even to yourself?
   (a) Yes   (b) *No*

Do you feel tired when you've done nothing to justify it?
   (a) *Rarely*   (b) Often

Can you change old habits, without relapse, when you decide to?
   (a) *Yes*   (b) No

Note: A person who selects all the bold italic answers has high ego-strength, whereas selection of all the nonitalicized responses indicates low ego-strength.

Source: The Scientific Analysis of Personality by R. B. Cattell, 1965, Baltimore: Penguin.

> Looked at from the opposite or positive pole, it sharpens and gives scientific substance to the psychoanalytic concept of "ego strength," which it [factor C] has come to be called. (1965, pp. 73–74)

EYSENCK'S TYPE APPROACH   Almost from its original publication, Cattell's model was criticized for having too many traits (G. Matthews, 1989). Hans J. Eysenck has focused on a considerably smaller number of basic personality *types*.

In Eysenck's view, types are not categories that a few people fit; rather, types are dimensions on which all persons differ. Types, like traits, tend to be normally distributed; that is, they are continuous dimensions and most people fall around the average mark. This is in dramatic contrast to ancient theories that considered types to be dichotomous so that, for example, a person was either an extravert or an introvert (just as the person was assumed to be either good or bad).

Eysenck's model of personality is structural. Types are at the top of the personality structure and, therefore, exert the most commanding

Hans J. Eysenck
(1916-   )
identified two major
factors in personality:
extraversion and
neuroticism.
Mark Gerson, courtesy of
H.J. Eysenck

Figure 10-5
Eysenck's hierarchical
model of personality.
Source: Adapted from *The
Biological Basis of Personal-
ity* by H. J. Eysenck, 1967,
Springfield, Ill.: Charles C
Thomas.

influence. Types are composed of traits; traits are composed of habitual responses. At the most specific level, specific responses are the elements from which individuals form habits. This overall view is shown in Figure 10-5.

Using factor analysis, Eysenck and his colleagues have performed dozens of studies over more than 40 years. As far back as World War II, for example, Eysenck applied factor analysis to ratings and classifications of approximately 10,000 soldiers. He has concluded from all this research that personality can be understood in terms of three basic personality factors: Extraversion, Neuroticism, and Psychoticism. He also acknowledged the importance of the response style factor, Social Desirability (see Chapter 9). When measured by Eysenck's own personality inventory, the Eysenck Personality Questionnaire (or EPQ), these same factors show up in many different cultures and thus appear to be universal dimensions of personality (Eysenck & Eysenck, 1985; S. B. G. Eysenck & Haapasalo, 1989; S. B. G. Eysenck & Long, 1986; S. B. G. Eysenck & Tambs, 1990).

Extraversion and Neuroticism have received the greatest amount of attention by Eysenck and other investigators (Stelmack, 1991). Both factors represent a continuous, normally distributed range between polar opposites. In essence, each person can be positioned somewhere along the line between extreme introvert and extreme extravert and between perfect emotional stability and complete emotional chaos. Moreover, most people will be somewhere near the middle. Eysenck has repeatedly cautioned that "extremes in either direction are rare, and that most people are somewhere intermediate" (1975, p. 190).

Eysenck's position is that these major types are largely inherited. "However we look at the facts," argued Eysenck after summarizing 35 years of research, "heredity is responsible for a good proportion of the individual

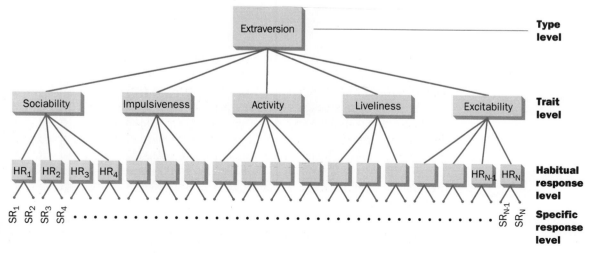

differences observed in our type of society" (1975, p. 201). A massive Finnish twin study (involving over 14,000 twin pairs) of the heritability of Extraversion and Neuroticism provides strong support for Eysenck's assertion (Rose, Koskenvuo, Kaprio, Sarna, & Langinvainio, 1988). As can be seen in Figure 10-6, for both males and females, Extraversion and Neuroticism were much more closely related among monozygotic twins than among dizygotic twins.

Eysenck's third underlying aspect of personality is **Psychoticism,** which plays a somewhat smaller role than Extraversion and Neuroticism. Psychoticism includes a disposition toward psychosis (a mental disorder characterized by poor contact with reality and inability to handle daily tasks) and a degree of psychopathy (characterized by an absence of real loyalties to any person, group, or code). Those high on Psychoticism also tend to be quite impulsive (Roger & Morris, 1991). As a general characterization, Psychoticism has been called the opposite of Freudian "superego strength" (McKenzie, 1988).

According to Eysenck, people who score high on Psychoticism are characterized by 11 dispositions:

1. Solitary, not caring for people.
2. Troublesome, not fitting in.
3. Cruel, inhumane.
4. Lacks feeling, insensitive.
5. Sensation seeking, underaroused.
6. Hostile to others, aggressive.
7. Likes odd, unusual things.

Figure 10-6
The most extensive recent study of the heritability of Extraversion and Neuroticism was done in Finland and involved more than 14,000 twin pairs. Note that for both males and females Extraversion and Neuroticism were much more closely related among monozygotic than dizygotic twin pairs.
Source: From data reported in "Shared Genes, Shared Experiences, and Similiarity of Personality; Data from 14,288 Adult Finnish Co-twins" by R. J. Rose, M. Koskenvuo, J. Kaprio, S. Sama, and H. Langinvainio, 1988, *Journal of Personality and Social Psychology, 54,* p. 164.

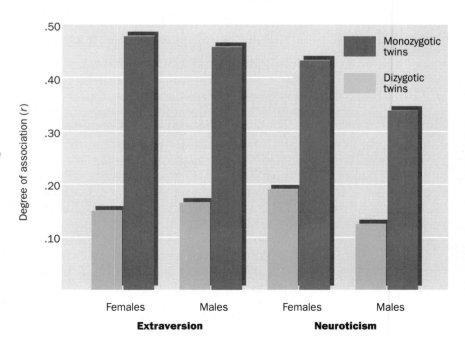

8. Disregards danger, foolhardy.
9. Likes to make fools of other people, upsetting them.
10. Opposes accepted social customs.
11. Engages in little personal interaction; prefers "impersonal" sex.

(1975, p. 197)

Psychoticism is higher in men than in women, heritable, higher in prisoners than in nonprisoners (and highest in individuals imprisoned for sexual or aggressive offenses), and lower in psychiatric patients who have improved than in those who have not improved. The higher an individual is in Psychoticism, the more negative are his or her attitudes and behavior toward authority (Rigby & Slee, 1987).

Biological Bases of Extraversion and Neuroticism

If Extraversion and Neuroticism are heritable, as Eysenck believed, then they must ultimately refer to individual differences in biological makeup from one person to another. In this vein, Eysenck has hypothesized that differences in Extraversion and Neuroticism result from individual differences in two identifiable brain systems.

Individuals high in Extraversion are presumed to have less-arousable cortexes and higher sensory thresholds. They must seek stimulation to maintain their brain activity levels and avoid boredom. "Extraverts," Eysenck wrote, "tend to have a level of arousal which is too low much of the time, unless their environment can provide excitement and stimulation; hence they tend to be stimulus hungry and sensation seeking" (1975, p. 194). In contrast, extreme introverts (very low in Extraversion) are so easily aroused that they shy away from stimulation. Evidence has been mounting recently to support this analysis (Bolger & Schilling, 1991; Davis & Cowles, 1988; Ljubin & Ljubin, 1990; Pearson & Freeman, 1991; Stelmack, 1990).

When exposed to the same levels of stimulation, introverts become more physiologically aroused than extraverts. Likewise, when given their choice of an optimal level of stimulation, introverts choose less intense levels (Dornic & Ekhammar, 1990; Geen, 1984). Introverts are also more likely to be inhibited by punishment than extraverts (Nichols & Newman, 1986; Pearce-McCall & Newman, 1986). This may be because, for a given level of painful stimulation, introverts actually seem to experience more pain (Howard, Cunningham, & Rechnitzer, 1987).

According to Eysenck, individuals high on Neuroticism have more arousable autonomic nervous systems than more emotionally stable individuals. People very high in Neuroticism can be said to have overreactive systems. This biological reactivity leads to the psychological state of instability. Likewise, people who are so stable that they seem "steady as a rock" are actually displaying the underreactivity of their emotional systems. Consistent with Eysenck's claim, research has shown that individual differences in Emotionality among young children are related to individual differences in nervous system functioning (Kagan, Reznick, & Snidman, 1987; Kagan & Snidman, 1991).

PERSONALITY TRAITS OF ADULTS: THE FIVE ROBUST FACTORS

Robert McCrae
(1949-   )
McCrae and Costa expanded the five-factor model of personality by showing that it applies across different methods of assessment.
Courtesy of Robert McCrae

More than 30 years ago, psychologist Warren Norman factor-analyzed a large number of adult peer nomination personality ratings. Norman (1963) then extracted five primary factors: Surgency (an exotic term for Extraversion), Agreeableness, Conscientiousness, Emotional Stability, and Culture. Later researchers have repeatedly confirmed that a five-factor model adequately accounts for the domain of dispositional terms adults use to rate the personalities of other adults (Digman & Inouye, 1986; Goldberg, 1990; McCrae & Costa, 1987; Noller, Law, & Comrey, 1987). Although the names are not the same, essentially the same five factors seem to emerge in almost every study. (Remember that, in factor analysis, naming of factors is always a subjective process.)

Robert McCrae and Paul Costa expanded the significance of the five-factor model for dispositional personality psychology by demonstrating that the same five-factor structure also applies to questionnaires, self-ratings, and observer reports of personality. The fact that the same set of five factors emerges from all these different sources provides strong support for the claim that they are the important, underlying dimensions by which individual differences in adult personality can be understood (McCrae & Costa, 1985, 1987). Costa and McCrae's own personality inventories, the NEO-PI, NEO-PI-R, and NEO-FFI (described in Chapter 9) have proved to be excellent tools in assessing these factors in individuals.

Table 10-4 shows the five robust factors identified by McCrae and Costa and some adjective pairs that define each factor. The most significant departure in factor naming from Norman's original scheme concerns the dimension he called "Culture." McCrae and Costa noted that this factor has only small factor loadings with items referring to being intelligent or cultured, but loads heavily on ratings of originality, creativity, independence, and daring. They therefore labeled this factor *Openness*.

Using the NEO-PI, Costa and McCrae (1988) undertook a major longitudinal study in which they followed hundreds of men and women longitudinally for 6 years, using both self-reports and spouse ratings of personality. The same five factors emerged again, and all five dispositions were remarkably stable over the six-year period.

Over the past few years, the five-factor model has become the dominant model in dispositional trait psychology (Goldberg, 1990). The model has held up in replications using other data sets (Peabody & Goldberg, 1989), in other languages and countries (Borkenau, 1988; Digman, 1990), using other methods of self-report (Brand & Egan, 1989), and in studies of children and youth (Digman, 1989). Moreover, the model has been shown to subsume earlier models that presented human trait structure in a different way (Costa & McCrae, 1988; McCrae & Costa, 1989).

Paul Costa
(1942-   )
Courtesy of Paul Costa

THE SUPERTRAITS: CONVERGING EVIDENCE

A major goal of the dispositional strategy is to identify and characterize the important dispositions that underlie personality. In the past decade, a true consensus has begun to emerge among dispositional psychologists that there are a small number of "supertraits" and that research is closing in on them

Table 10-4
McCrae and Costa's five robust factors

NEUROTICISM/STABILITY

Worrying/calm; nervous/at ease; high-strung/relaxed; insecure/secure; vulnerable/hardy

EXTRAVERSION/INTROVERSION

Sociable/retiring; fun-loving/sober; affectionate/reserved; talkative/quiet; joiner/loner

OPENNESS

Original/conventional; creative/uncreative; independent/conforming; untraditional/traditional; daring/unadventurous

AGREEABLENESS/ANTAGONISM

Good-natured/irritable; courteous/rude; lenient/critical; flexible/stubborn; sympathetic/callous

CONSCIENTIOUSNESS/UNDIRECTEDNESS

Reliable/undependable; careful/careless; hardworking/lazy; punctual/late; persevering/quitting

---

Source: From data reported in "Validation of the Five-Factor Model of Personality Across Instruments and Observers," by R. R. McCrae and P. T. Costa, Jr., 1987, *Journal of Personality and Social Psychology, 52,* pp. 81-90. Copyright by the American Psychological Association. Reprinted by permission of the authors.

rapidly (Goldberg, 1981; Digman & Inouye, 1986; Funder, 1991; McCrae & Costa, 1987; Noller, Law, & Comrey, 1987).

The number of supertraits acknowledged will depend in part on the definitions chosen and the kind of data relied on. For example, observations of infants in the nursery are more likely to reveal differences in Activity Level than in Conscientiousness; similarly, Intelligence can appear as a supertrait only if relevant measures have been included in the research on which the supertrait model is based.

In this final section, we will attempt to summarize and integrate the previous discussion. Our reading of the data, taken all together, is that six dispositions appear to be good candidates as supertraits: Extraversion, Neuroticism, Openness, Agreeableness, Conscientiousness, and Intelligence.

Extraversion   Cattell labeled his factor A "Reserved vs. Outgoing"; Eysenck concluded that Extraversion is one of the major dimensions of personality, and many other researchers have found Sociability to be one of the three stable, heritable personality dispositions. The tendency to be socially inhibited or uninhibited has been observed as a clear individual difference among infants and young children (Kagan & Reznick, 1986; Kagan & Snidman, 1991). Finally, Costa and McCrae (1988; McCrae & Costa, 1987), using ratings and self-report data, found a major factor that they called Extraversion. There seems to be little doubt, then, that Extraversion is a well-confirmed, major disposition (i.e., one of the supertraits). Table 10-5 shows some of the recent findings on the nature of Extraversion.

Table 10-5
Recently reported differences between extraverts and introverts

> Extraverts report finding more meaning in life.[1]
> Extraverts are happier.[2]
> Extraverts are better able to interpret facial expressions and "body language."[3]
> Extraverts tend to appraise stressful events as challenges.[4]
> Extraverts learn faster but less accurately on a maze.[5]
> Extraverts respond better to efforts to elevate their mood.[6]
> Extraverts are better able to handle time pressure.[7]
> Extraverts are better drivers.[8]

[1]Addad (1987)

[2]Argyle and Lu (1990); Furnham and Brewin (1990)

[3]Aker and Panter (1988)

[4]Gallagher (1990)

[5]Howard and McKillen (1990)

[6]Larsen and Ketelaar (1989, 1991)

[7]Rawlings and Carnie (1989)

[8]G. Matthews, Dorn, and Glendon (1991)

Neuroticism   McCrae and Costa (1987) considered Neuroticism and Extraversion to be the two supertraits about which there is most agreement. Like Extraversion, Neuroticism has shown up repeatedly in numerous factor-analytic studies. Cattell's factor C, which he called Ego Strength, appears to correspond closely with Neuroticism except that the emphasis is on the nonneurotic, stable end of the dimension. And, as we saw, Emotionality has consistently appeared as a major, heritable temperament trait.

Research over the past few years has filled in a more complete picture of the nature of Neuroticism. Negative emotions appear to be its hallmark. The individual high on Neuroticism is worrisome, insecure, self-conscious, and temperamental. Associated with a variety of adjustment and mental health problems, high Neuroticism puts an individual at risk for depression, one of the most common psychiatric problems (Jorm, 1987). Moreover, people high in Neuroticism tend to be anxious, to engage in self-blame, and to withdraw quickly from frustrating situations (Parkes, 1986). On the other hand, the lower people are in Neuroticism, the more meaning they find in life (Addad, 1987).

Openness   Individuals high on Openness (to experience) tend to be original, imaginative, and daring. Their interests tend to be quite broad. Openness may manifest itself in a wide range of fantasy experiences, in creative or unusual ideas or products, or in a high degree of tolerance for what others do, say, and think. Perhaps not surprisingly, open individuals are more susceptible to hypnosis than are closed minded ones (Roche & McConkey, 1990).

McCrae recently described Openness this way:

> We conceive of the open individual as being interested in experience for its own sake, eager for variety, tolerant of uncertainty, leading a richer, more complex, less conventional life. By contrast, the closed person is seen as being impoverished in fantasy, insensitive to art and beauty, restricted in affect, behaviorally rigid, bored by ideas, and ideologically dogmatic. (1990, p. 123)

Openness is a dimension of personality that can only be detected when personality measures are broad enough to ask the right questions. But if the right questions *are* asked, then Openness appears consistently as a personality trait and is quite stable across adulthood (Costa & McCrae, 1988; Digman & Inouye, 1986; McCrae & Costa, 1985, 1987). Interestingly, McCrae (1976) found that Cattell's 16 personality factors could be meaningfully grouped into three clusters, one of which was Openness. (The other two clusters were Neuroticism and Extraversion.)

Agreeableness

The agreeable person tends to be sympathetic, cooperative, trusting, and interpersonally supportive. In its extreme form, though, Agreeableness becomes unappealing and may be manifested in a dependent, self-effacing manner when dealing with others.

The opposite pole of Agreeableness is antagonism, or the tendency to set oneself against others. The antagonistic person tends to be mistrustful, skeptical, unsympathetic, uncooperative, stubborn, and rude. McCrae and Costa also noted the similarity between antagonism and Eysenck's dimension Psychoticism. The hostility associated with certain aspects of Type A behavior also bears a striking similarity to antagonism. Like Openness, Agreeableness is thought to be mainly a product of learning and socialization, rather than being biologically based (Costa & McCrae, 1988).

Conscientiousness

The conscientious individual is hardworking, ambitious, and energetic. He or she perseveres in the face of difficulty and tends to be careful and thorough. Conscientious students tend to get better grades and to do more extra credit assignments than those low in Conscientiousness (Digman, 1989; Dollinger & Orf, 1991). The opposite pole of conscientious is undirected. McCrae and Costa (1987) noted, "In our view, the individual low in Conscientiousness is not so much uncontrolled as undirected, not so much impulse ridden as simply lazy" (p. 88).

Conscientiousness was one of the source traits reported by Cattell (see p. 206). Conscientiousness also appears to bear a considerable similarity to what need theorists have called achievement motivation (which we will discuss in Chapter 11). Like Openness, Conscientiousness is probably a result of learning and socialization and has a definite evaluative component—in other words, it is considered "better" to be conscientious than to be undirected.

Intelligence   Cattell concluded that his factor B is "nothing less than general intelligence." This factor appears in Cattell's work and not in Eysenck's or McCrae and Costa's work simply because their research did not include measures that could pick up an intelligence factor (Brand & Egan, 1989). Dispositional psychologists are in virtually complete agreement that Intelligence is a supertrait in the sense that it is an important, stable dimension on which people differ. (See Liebert, Wicks-Nelson, & Kail, 1986, for an extensive review.) In addition, studies of twins reared apart show that IQ is largely (but not entirely) attributable to heredity (Bouchard, Lykken, McGue, Segal, & Tellegen, 1990). But there is disagreement on whether Intelligence should be thought of as a true *personality* trait.

SUMMARY   1. In their search for important dispositions, personality psychologists have used three different approaches. The lexical approach begins with the words that people use to describe others and themselves in everyday conversation. The theoretical approach relies on theory as a guide to identifying important dispositions. The statistical approach feeds large amounts of data about people into complex statistical procedures, especially factor analysis, to identify the most basic personality dimensions on which people differ.

2. Allport is generally acknowledged as the founder of the modern dispositional strategy. His basic philosophy is called heuristic realism, meaning that traits actually exist as part of the person.

3. Allport acknowledged three levels of dispositions that varied in their pervasiveness. The most pervasive traits are cardinal dispositions, which dominate the personalities of those who have them. Central dispositions are the small set of traits that are highly characteristic of the individual. Secondary dispositions operate only in limited settings.

4. Allport spoke of both common traits and patterned individuality. Common traits are the dispositions on which people can be compared; they are usually normally distributed. But each of us also displays a uniquely patterned individuality that does not lend itself to comparison with other persons.

5. Kretschmer pioneered the modern type approach by showing that among mental patients there is a link between body type and psychiatric diagnosis. Sheldon studied the relationship between physique and normal personality. He reported that those individuals with a plump body type (endomorphy) tend to be easygoing and to love comfort, those with a frail body type (ectomorphy) tend to be inhibited and apprehensive, and those with a muscular body type (mesomorphy) tend to be bold and action-oriented. Later studies have confirmed these relationships to some extent, but the correlations between physique and temperament are too small to allow individual personality predictions based merely on body type.

6. Friedman and Rosenman found that hard-driving, competitive people who are always hurrying to meet deadlines (Type A individuals) are at considerably greater risk for heart attack than more relaxed, easygoing individuals (Type B). Recently, investigators have been exploring the possibility that it is not achievement striving but poor emotional adjustment and an outlook of cynical hostility that predisposes an individual to heart attacks and other health and social risks. A similar pattern appears to hold for children.

7. Both the twin study and the adoptee/family methods are used to determine whether personality dispositions are heritable. Research using both of these methods has shown that several types of abnormality and deviance are partly heritable. Within the normal range of personality, Sociability, Emotionality, and Activity Level all seem to be observable from birth and to have a significant heritable component. They are the so-called temperament traits, which then interact with the environment in complex ways to produce an individual's adult personality.

8. Cattell pioneered the use of factor analysis to determine the underlying dispositions (source traits) on which people differ. Using a combination of questionnaires and interviews (Q-data), observations made in test situations (T-data), and information drawn from people's life records (L-data), Cattell concluded that the three most significant source traits of adults are Introversion/Extraversion, Intelligence, and Ego Strength.

9. Eysenck used factor analysis to search for underlying dimensions of personality. He also found Introversion/Extraversion and Emotional Stability/Instability (which he called Neuroticism) to be two major dimensions on which people differ. In addition, Eysenck identified a third dimension, Psychoticism, which does not consist of polar opposites but instead is present to a greater or lesser degree in all personalities. Psychoticism includes a tendency to be solitary, troublesome, insensitive, sensation-seeking, aggressive, and foolhardy. Over the years, Eysenck has come to share the geneticists' view that the major dispositions are to a considerable extent heritable.

10. McCrae and Costa have found that the same five "robust factors"— Neuroticism/Stability, Extraversion/Introversion, Openness, Agreeableness/ Antagonism, and Conscientiousness/Undirectedness—appear in self-report inventories and in trait ratings made by peers and spouses.

11. Taken together, research on traits and types suggest that six "supertraits" appear with great regularity. These supertraits are Neuroticism, Extraversion, Openness, Agreeableness, Conscientiousness, and Intelligence.

Needs And Motives

he idea that people vary in what "drives them"—that is, in their underlying motivations—has fascinated personality psychologists since Freud. Those who pursued this idea further were confronted with many specific questions: Is there a set of common human motives that can be measured? Do these motives have a general influence on behavior? Do things people say, such as their favorite verbal metaphors and the kinds of stories they tell, reflect their motivations?

All the dispositional psychologists we will discuss in this chapter would answer yes to each of these questions. In their view, people's needs differ in both kind and amount. In turn, these differences motivate people to think, feel, and act differently. Thus, needs supply motives that lead to thought and action. Put another way, a **need** is a requirement, whereas a **motive** is the desire to satisfy that need. The relationship between needs and motives is shown in Figure 11-1.

The motivational approach to dispositions differs from the trait and type approaches discussed in Chapter 10 in several basic ways. One difference is that motivational theorists are greatly influenced by two psychoanalytic ideas: (1) the importance of driving, impelling forces for explaining a person's behavior and (2) the use of projective responses and elicited fantasies to reveal something about an individual's personality. Thus, need and motive theories have ties with the psychoanalytic strategy.

McClelland, Koestner, and Weinberger (1989) recently suggested another difference. In their view, traits and types, as derived from self-report questionnaires, only get at conscious or *explicit motives*. Motivational personality psychologists are interested in **implicit motives**. McClelland feels that implicit motives are more primitive; that is, that they are more like animal drives than like conscious goals. As such, implicit motives are better able to explain the long-term trends in a person's behavior. We will see examples supporting this claim when we turn to McClelland's own work on achievement motivation later in this chapter.

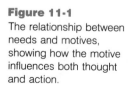

Figure 11-1

The relationship between needs and motives, showing how the motive influences both thought and action.

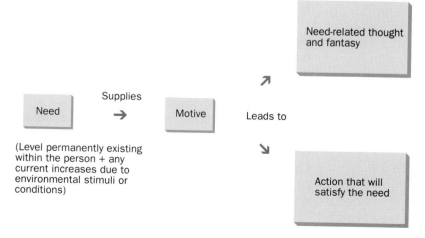

However, the theorists we will discuss in this chapter still remain within the dispositional framework. They assume that (1) there are measurable individual differences between people (in this case, in their needs and motives); (2) these individual differences manifest themselves in a wide range of actions and are relatively stable over time; and (3) motives and needs, as dispositions within the person, are the basis for predicting, explaining, and understanding behavior.

Whereas the psychoanalytic strategy emphasizes the *similarity* of motivations of all people, motive theories emphasize the dispositional strategy's basic approach: to identify and elaborate the *differences* between individuals in terms of the strength of their motives and the ways those motives are manifested.

THE CONCEPT OF MOTIVE

David Winter (1973), another prominent motivational theorist, says that the modern concept of motive involves six related points.

First, motive *is used to explain changes in behavior*. Motivational issues arise when we ask "why," such as "Why did John cross the street?" Some answers refer to external causes (e.g., a barricade blocked the sidewalk), but most answers refer to explanations that are *within the person*. For instance, the answer may be "John crossed the street because he wanted to get a newspaper." This is a motivational explanation of John's behavior, as is "John crossed the street to keep from slipping on the ice ahead." Thus, " 'motive' is a way of explaining those changes in behavior that cannot readily be explained by external forces alone" (Winter, 1973, p. 21).

Second, a motive-based explanation *typically connects a specific behavior to a more general disposition*. If John wants a newspaper today, he probably has wanted one in the past, and he probably will want one in the future as well. So we say that John "likes to," "tends to," or "often does" buy the newspaper.

Third, a motive explanation of behavior *usually implies a goal* and indicates knowledge about certain means-ends relationships. John must know that newspapers exist, what they are, and how and where to buy one.

Fourth, and very important, the motive explanation *gives rise to predictions of how the person will behave in other situations*. It also defines the limits of the behavior that has been observed. If John has already bought or read the newspaper today, we can predict that he probably will not cross the street again to buy another one. (Assuming, of course, that he usually reads only one newspaper.)

Fifth, under some circumstances, a motive explanation *may let us anticipate an entire sequence of behaviors*. John may find that the newsstand is out of papers. He may then "go out of his way" to find another newsstand. Or he may be more likely to tune in the news on his car radio that evening.

Sixth, a motive explanation *leaves out habit and stylistic factors*. "We do not know whether John will walk, run, jump, or perhaps even use a pogo stick to get across the road. We do not know whether he will cross the road at a right angle or take a diagonal course directly to the front of the newsstand. To answer those questions, we would ask about his *habits*" (Winter, 1973, p. 22).

Approach and Avoidance: The Two Faces of Motivation

One component of motivation is the positive or *approach tendencies* associated with a need or motive. For instance, one person may strive for achievement or power. Another person may seek the approval of others or affiliation with them. But *avoidance tendencies* may also dominate a person's motivation, as we will see later in this chapter. Some people are driven by success; others are motivated to avoid failure (Atkinson & Litwin, 1960). Some people hope for power; others fear it (Winter, 1973).

MURRAY'S NEED THEORY

The father of modern need theory is Henry A. Murray. When Murray began his career in psychology, the dynamic aspects of Freud's theory were already well known. Murray himself was psychoanalyzed, and the experience led him to conclude that Freud was correct in focusing on unconscious motivational forces (Anderson, 1988).

Murray wanted to do more than acknowledge the importance of motives, however. He wanted to identify and catalog the full range of human needs and to explain how motives lead people to think, feel, and act as they do. In short, he wanted to take the bold step of writing a comprehensive need theory of personality.

Primary Constructs

Murray believed that the individual and the environment must be considered together—a person/environment interaction—in analyzing personality. However, to analyze this interaction, he first had to separate forces within the individual, called *needs*, from environmental forces, called *press*. (*Note*: The plural of press is *press*, not presses.)

Needs

A **need** (*n*) is a theoretical construct, referring to "a readiness to respond in a certain way under given conditions. . . . It is a noun which stands for the fact that a certain trend is apt to recur" (Murray, 1962, p. 61). Thus, needs are identified with particular effects or temporary end states (e.g., satisfying the need for sex is identified with orgasm).

Murray identified 39 human needs, which could be divided into biological and psychological needs. *Biological needs* represent the organism's physical requirements. There are 12 such needs, including the need for air, water, food, sex, and physical safety. It is relatively easy to agree on the external or internal conditions that will arouse one of these needs (e.g., it is when we are thirsty that we are motivated to seek a drink). There is less agreement on Murray's 27 *psychological needs* (Table 11-1).

Press

Murray believed that needs constitute only half of the process that determines behavior. **Press** (*p*) are the complementary, and equally important, directional forces provided by objects, situations, or events in the environment. Some common examples of press appear in Table 11-2.

Murray identified two types of press. *Alpha press* are objective descriptions of environmental situations (e.g., a certain grade point average is required for admission to medical school). *Beta press* are ways of interpreting significant environmental influences (e.g., "If I don't make the required grade point average for medical school, I am a total failure"). To function adequately, a person's alpha press (objective experience) and beta press (subjective experience) in the same situation should be fairly similar. If alpha press and beta press sharply diverge, the result is called *delusion*.

Murray's Approach to Personality Assessment

Murray assumed that needs are sometimes *manifest* (observed in overt behavior) and sometimes *latent* (inhibited, covert, or imaginal). Manifest needs are readily apparent from a person's actions. A person who reports, "I was asleep as soon as my head touched the pillow" is displaying a manifest and immediate need for sleep. Assessing latent needs is more complicated.

The Assessment of Latent Needs: The TAT

According to Murray:

> The chief differences between an imaginal need and an overt need is that the former enjoys in reading, or represents in fantasy, in speech or in play what the latter objectifies in serious action. Thus, instead of pushing through a difficult enterprise, a subject will have visions of doing it or read books about others doing it; or instead of injuring an enemy, he will express his dislike of him to others or enjoy playing an aggressive role in a play. . . . The term "imaginal need" is convenient for the expression "the amount of need tension that exhibits itself in thought and make-believe action." (Murray, 1962, p. 257)

Assessment of latent needs follows from this description. A strong latent need "is apt to perceive . . . what it 'wants.' . . . A subject under the influence of a drive has a tendency to 'project' into surrounding objects some of the imagery associated with the drive that is operating" (Murray, 1962, p. 260). This reasoning led Murray to develop a widely used projective technique, the **Thematic Apperception Test (TAT)**.

The TAT consists of a set of 20 pictures. There are separate sets for men, women, and children. Most of the pictures show at least one person, thereby providing someone with whom the respondent can identify. Figure 11-2 is an example of a TAT picture.

The TAT is introduced with the following instructions:

> This is a test of your creative imagination. I shall show you a picture and I want you to make up a plot or story for which it might be used as an

Henry A. Murray
(1893-1988)
considered the father of modern need theory, insisted that both forces within the individual (needs) and environmental factors (press) combine to determine how a person will behave.
Harvard University News Office

Table 11-1
Murray's list of psychological needs

MAJOR CATEGORY	NEED	BEHAVIORAL EXAMPLE
Ambition	*n* Achievement	Overcoming obstacles
	n Recognition	Boasting
	n Exhibition	Making efforts to shock or thrill others
	n Acquisition	Acquiring things by working or stealing
	n Conservance	Repairing possessions
	n Order	Tidying up
	n Retention	Hoarding
	n Construction	Organizing or building something
Defense of status	*n* Inviolacy	Maintaining psychological "distance"
	n Infavoidance	Concealing a disfigurement
	n Defendance	Offering explanations or excuses
	n Counteraction	Engaging in acts of retaliation
Response to human power	*n* Dominance	Dictating to or directing others
	n Deference	Cooperating with others
	n Similance	Imitating others
	n Autonomy	Manifesting defiance of authority
	n Contrariance	Taking unconventional or oppositional views
	n Aggression	Assaulting or belittling others
	n Abasement	Apologizing, confessing, or surrendering
	n Blamavoidance	Inhibiting unconventional impulses
Affection between people	*n* Affiliation	Joining groups
	n Rejection	Discriminating against or snubbing others
	n Nurturance	"Mothering" a child
	n Succorance	Crying for help
	n Play	Seeking diversion by "having fun"
Exchange of information	*n* Cognizance	Asking questions
	n Exposition	Lecturing to, or interpreting for, others

Source: Information from *Explorations in Personality* by H. A. Murray, 1962, New York: Science Editions.

Table 11-2
Common examples of press

PRESS	EXAMPLE
p Achievement	Others getting good grades
p Order	A messy desk
p Counteraction	Being attacked (verbally or physically)
p Autonomy	Overprotective parents
p Abasement	Doing something wrong
p Affiliation	Friendly companions
p Play	Saturday night
p Cognizance	Not understanding a lecture

Figure 11-2
Example of a TAT
picture.

illustration. What is the relation of the individuals in the picture? What has happened to them? What are their present thoughts and feelings? What will be the outcome? Do your very best. Since I am asking you to indulge your literary imagination, you may make your story as long and detailed as you wish. (Murray, 1962, p. 532)

Stories are scored for various needs and press, based on the explicit or implicit themes in the stories. For example, a story that focuses on a character's concerns with a business failure might be scored as reflecting a need for achievement.

Of the extensive list of human needs suggested by Murray and others, Winter (1987a) argued that two seem to be especially important: achievement and power.

THE NEED   Murray's dispositional approach has stimulated a great deal of research. A
TO ACHIEVE   prime example is the work of David McClelland, who was introduced at the

beginning of this chapter. For more than 30 years, McClelland investigated the need to achieve (i.e., Murray's *n* Achievement). Murray and McClelland shared a common bias concerning the nature of human personality, but they differed in their basic approach. Murray chose to catalog and study a large number of needs, whereas McClelland focused his attention on a single need.

McClelland justified his approach in this way:

> Concentration on a limited research problem is not necessarily narrowing; it may lead ultimately into the whole of psychology. In personality theory there is inevitably a certain impatience—a desire to solve every problem at once so as to get the "whole" personality in focus. We have proceeded the other way. By concentrating on one problem, on *one* motive, we have found in the course of our study that we have learned not only a lot about the achievement motive but other areas of personality as well. (McClelland, Atkinson, Clark, & Lowell, 1953, p. vi.)

The McClelland-Atkinson Approach to Defining and Measuring Motives

The first step in studying achievement, or any personality construct, is finding a way to define and measure it. The approach devised by McClelland and his colleague John Atkinson is the basis for most of the research discussed in the rest of this chapter (Atkinson, 1958; Atkinson & McClelland, 1948; McClelland et al., 1953).

In brief, the McClelland-Atkinson approach involves the following steps. First, subjects are exposed to a motive-arousing experience. They might be told they are taking an important examination to arouse the achievement motive, or they might watch a stirring political film to arouse the power motive. Control subjects are exposed to a neutral experience that presumably does not arouse the motive in question. Subjects in both groups then write TAT-type stories about standard pictures. The differences in the imagery produced by the motive-aroused and motive-nonaroused group are taken as evidence of the motive.

To develop a scoring system for *n* Achievement, McClelland and his colleagues exposed college students to either achievement-arousing situations (e.g., they were given success or failure experiences) or to situations that did not arouse achievement (e.g., the experimental tasks were presented in a casual, relaxed way). The students were then asked to write stories about four TAT-type pictures that were especially pertinent to *n* Achievement. The instructions were similar to those Murray used with the TAT. Stories were scored for a number of different categories related to achievement. Categories that differentiated subjects exposed to varying degrees of achievement arousal were defined as measures of *n* Achievement.

The Nature of Achievement Motivation

As a first step, McClelland and his associates compared people with high and low achievement TAT imagery scores. They found:

> In general, people with a high achievement imagery index score complete more tasks under achievement orientation, solve more simple arithmetic problems on a timed test, improve faster in their ability to do anagrams, tend to get

David McClelland
(1917-   )
chose to focus on
individual motives
(particularly achievement
motivation), rather than
to examine a person's
entire motivational
structure.
Harvard University News
Office

better grades, use more future tenses and abstract nouns in talking about themselves ... and so on. (McClelland et al., 1953, p. 327)

The beauty of these imagery measures of latent motivation is that the scoring system for TAT stories can be used with any written material. McClelland could therefore study *n* Achievement by examining political documents, novels and stories, letters, and so on. For example, McClelland and his associates studied the relationship between independence training and achievement motivation in Native American tribes by scoring their folktales for *n* Achievement (McClelland et al., 1953; Winter & Carlson, 1988).

An even more ambitious task involved McClelland's (1967) attempt to "search for the broadest possible test of the hypothesis that a particular psychological factor—the need for Achievement—is responsible for economic growth and decline" (p. vii). Specifically, McClelland tried to "predict" the economic growth of 23 countries from 1929 to 1950 based on the amount of achievement imagery in children's stories in those countries in the preceding decade (1920–1929). He found an impressively high positive correlation (+.53) between achievement emphasis in children's stories and economic growth. This evidence suggests that a society's aspirations may well be found in the stories that it offers its children. And independent experiments suggest that such stories do seem to influence children who hear them (McArthur & Eisen, 1976).

Having found a dramatic link between achievement motivation and productivity, McClelland then undertook the boldest step of his career: He developed a theoretically-based course for teaching people to become more achievement-oriented, and actually offered it to local citizens in various countries around the world (McClelland, 1965; McClelland & Winter, 1969).

An Intensive Course in Achievement Motivation

The course was structured as a retreat for self-study, offered for anywhere between 10 and 25 people. Whenever possible, these retreats were held in isolated resort hotels. (Such locations increase concentration and minimize outside interference.) Participants lived and ate together, and were immersed in achievement-oriented thinking around the clock for a solid week or more. Here is an example of the flavor of the course, in McClelland's own words:

> Participants are asked to take the fantasy test of *n* Achievement at the beginning of the program and are taught to score it for themselves. We point out that if they think their score is too low, that can be easily remedied, since we teach them how to code and how to write stories saturated with *n* Achievement; in fact, that is one of the basic purposes of the course: to teach them to think constantly in *n* Achievement terms. (McClelland, 1965, p. 325)

McClelland's earlier work showed that individuals high in achievement motivation (1) like challenges in their work and prefer moderate risk, (2)

Achievement motivation
may be manifested in
different ways. Academic
excellence is one way,
but so too is being a
skilled aircraft mechanic
or winning road races.
Top left: Photo by
Christopher O'Keefe; top
right: Photo by Michael D.
Spiegler; bottom: Courtesy
of Bobby Doyle.

want concrete feedback on how well they are doing, and (3) like to take personal responsibility for meeting work goals.

To develop these characteristics, McClelland used lectures, discussion groups and specially designed "games." The games let participants learn achievement-oriented actions both by playing the game and by seeing others play.

The game is designed to mimic real life: they must order parts to make certain objects (e.g., a Tinker Toy model bridge) after having estimated how many they think they can construct in the time allotted. They have a real chance to take over, plan the whole game, learn from how well they are doing . . . and show a paper profit or loss at the end. . . . [T]hey usually get emotionally involved in observing how they behave under pressure of a more or less "real" work situation. (McClelland, 1965, p. 326)

At the end of the course, participants write an essay outlining their aspirations and plans for the next 2 years. Describing one's future realistically is emphasized, as is setting moderate (rather than high) goals. The essay helps participants use the practical implications of the course and serves as the basis for course evaluation.

Effects of the Course

How successful have McClelland's courses been? Based on a number of concrete, economic measures, course participants increased their achievement motivation substantially more than businesspeople who applied for the course but were not accepted (i.e., control subjects). As can be seen in Table 11-3, in one study course participants and controls were similar in the two-year period before the course. Following the course, however, significantly more participants than controls engaged in actions that directly improved business, worked longer hours, started new businesses, and employed more workers (McClelland & Winter, 1969).

Here is one case study that illustrates the potential impact of the course:

A short time after participating in one of our courses in India, a 47-year-old businessman rather suddenly and dramatically decided to quit his excellent job

Table 11-3
Examples of the economic effects of McClelland's achievement motivation courses

		BEFORE COURSE (1962–1964)	AFTER COURSE (1964–1966)
1. Rated at highest business activity level*	Participants	18%	51%
	Controls	22%	25%
2. Working longer hours	Participants	7%	20%
	Controls	11%	7%
3. Starting new business	Participants	4%	22%
	Controls	7%	8%
4. Employing more people at end of two-year period	Participants	35%	59%
	Controls	31%	33%

* Subjects' business activity was rated on a four-point scale, with the highest level being exemplified by an action that directly resulted in an improvement in a business venture (e.g., increased profit).

Source: Data from *Motivating Economic Achievement* by D. C. McClelland and D. G. Winter, 1969. New York: Free Press.

and go into the construction business on his own in a big way. A man with some means of his own, he had had a very successful career as employee-relations manager for a larger oil firm. His job involved adjusting management-employee difficulties, negotiating union contracts, etc. He was well-to-do, well thought of in his company, and admired in the community, but he was restless because he found his job increasingly boring. At the time of the course, his original *n* Achievement score was not very high and he was thinking of retiring and living in England where his son was studying. In an interview, 8 months later, he said the course had served not so much to "motivate" him but to "crystallize" a lot of ideas he had vaguely or half consciously picked up about work and achievement all through his life. It provided him with a new language (he still talked in terms of standards of excellence, . . . moderate risk, goal anticipation, etc.), a new construct which served to organize those ideas and explain to him why he was bored with his job, despite his obvious success. He decided he wanted to be an *n*-Achievement-oriented person, that he would be unhappy in retirement, and that he should take a risk, quit his job, and start in business on his own. He acted on his decision and in 6 months had drawn plans and raised over $1,000,000 to build the tallest building in his large city, to be called the "Everest Apartments." He is extremely happy in his new activity because it means selling, promoting, trying to wangle scarce materials, etc. His first building is part way up and he is planning two more. (McClelland, 1965, p. 332)

The benefits of high achievement motivation do not end when a person retires from the business or professional world. Individuals accustomed to achievement by their own efforts in midlife have the highest morale as senior citizens (Die, Seelbach, & Sherman, 1987):

> Persons with achieving styles approach tasks by means of individual effort and may acquire a sense of competence because of a lifetime of dealing directly with life's problems. This pattern of relying on one's own efforts or skills to achieve goals or conquer obstacles may facilitate the development of a variety of effective, competent coping strategies that may, in turn, equip one to deal directly and successfully with many problems associated with old age. Indeed, aging may become simply another obstacle for which an effective coping strategy is found and used. (p. 408)

Over the past 10 years research on *n* Achievement has shed further light on the work characteristics of individual who are high in need achievement. Some of these findings are shown in Table 11-4.

Achievement Motivation in Women

Historically, achievement has been a highly sex-stereotyped activity in Western culture. The stereotype has been so strong that many early studies (such as McClelland's) were restricted to men. With the advent of the feminist movement, however, researchers began looking at factors leading to or blocking high achievement in women. This research has made it clear that, from childhood, males and females have very different experiences regarding the cultivation and expression of achievement (Helgeson & Sharpsteen, 1987). The traditional belief has been: Males are the ones who are "supposed" to do the achieving. As a result, the backgrounds of women who did achieve in this milieu became a topic of considerable interest.

Table 11-4
Characteristics of high need achievers at work

Report pushing themselves to their fullest potential[1]
Prefer achievement-oriented supervisors to "supportive" supervisors[2]
Pass quickly over easy tasks to reach more difficult ones[3]
Show increased effort on tasks as time runs out[4]

[1] Emmons and McAdams (1991)

[2] Matheiu (1990)

[3] Slade and Rush (1990)

[4] Beh (1989)

Childhood and Family Lives of High Achieving Women

A consistent body of research points to the conclusion that a relatively difficult or stressful home life fosters achievement motivation in women. In contrast, men are most likely to become achievers when they come from supportive, unstressed family backgrounds.

For example, a classic study found that mothers of achieving girls were aggressive, competitive, and critical of their daughters (Kagan & Moss, 1962). Another study found that mothers of academically successful elementary school girls are *less* affectionate and *less* nurturant toward their daughters than are mothers of academically unsuccessful girls (Crandall, Dewey, Katkovsky, & Preston, 1964). Completing the picture with high school students, Pierce (1961) described the mothers of high achieving girls as more strict, authoritarian, and controlling than the mothers of low achieving girls.

Coming from a broken home also appears to have a stimulating effect on female achievement motivation. A nationwide study found that women whose parents were divorced or separated were more likely to have high *n* Achievement scores than women from intact homes or women whose parents had died (Veroff, Atkinson, Feld, & Gurin, 1960). The reverse is true for men (Figure 11-3). Veroff and his associates (1960) interpreted the pattern as follows:

> A boy, having lost his masculine model for achievement, may become highly involved in avoiding failure. In doing so, his achievement motivation, his positive motivations for success, become weakened. On the other hand, girls living with a divorced mother have a readily available model for achievement identification. Resentment of the father can reinforce the need for feminine independence and self-reliance in a masculine world. The fact that her mother is apparently self-sufficient further enhances an image of the achievement orientation of women. (p. 27)

Anxiety about Achievement: The Motive to Avoid Success

Other evidence suggested that women, more than men, experience conflict over the role of striving for achievement in their lives (French & Lesser,

1964; Lesser, 1973; Lesser, Krawitz, & Packard, 1963). Possible negative consequences of success for women—competition with men, loss of femininity, the threat of social rejection by peers—were even discussed in some of the classic writings of Freud (1965) and the noted anthropologist Margaret Mead (1949).

Against this backdrop, psychologist Matina Horner (1973) theorized that women experience great anxiety when they confront any achievement situation. Horner (1973) called anxiety about the negative consequences of success the **motive to avoid success.** She viewed it as "a stable personality predisposition within the person acquired early in life in conjunction with sex-role standards" (p. 224).

In an often-cited study, Horner (1973) asked women and men to write a story in response to a written lead. The lead was designed to elicit a motive to avoid success. The women in Horner's study were given the lead:

> After first-term finals, *Anne finds herself* at the top of her medical school class.

The lead for males was identical, except that the name of the story character was changed:

> After first-term finals, *John finds himself* at the top of his medical school class.

Scores for the motive to avoid success were based on negative imagery related to success, including concern about success or the consequences of success, denial of success, and bizarre responses to the situation. As Horner predicted, the women's responses were strikingly different from the men's. More than 65% of the women in the sample had high fear of success, versus less than 10% of the men.

Times have unquestionably changed since Horner's data were actually collected in the mid-1960s. There is a consensus that women today

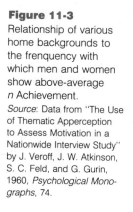

Figure 11-3

Relationship of various home backgrounds to the frenquency with which men and women show above-average *n* Achievement.

Source: Data from "The Use of Thematic Apperception to Assess Motivation in a Nationwide Interview Study" by J. Veroff, J. W. Atkinson, S. C. Feld, and G. Gurin, 1960, *Psychological Monographs*, 74.

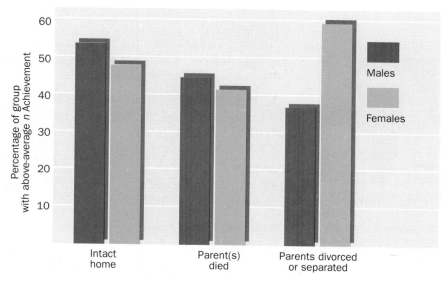

experience less anxiety about success than they did 30 years ago (Heatherington, Crown, Wagner, & Rigby, 1989; Hyland, Curtis, & Mason, 1985).
But recent research also suggests that women still perceive more danger than
men in TAT cards that are suggestive of achievement-related situations
(Helgeson & Sharpsteen, 1987). Moreover, high *n* Achievement women are
still less likely than high *n* Achievement men to pursue entrepreneurial
careers (Jenkins, 1987).

Women who do pursue careers stay in school longer, and marry and start
a family later (Elder & MacInnis, 1983). When they finally begin their
careers, they are motivated to dress and act in a highly professional manner
(Ericksen & Sirgy, 1989).

POWER: THE ANATOMY OF A MOTIVE

David Winter is the leading theorist and researcher on the need for power.
Winter (1973) viewed "the striving for power as one important motive or
disposition in individuals." He defined **power** as a person's ability or capacity
to produce intended effects on the behavior or emotions of someone else.
Winter's research tried "to determine whether there are differences in the
extent to which people want power, or strive to affect the behavior of others
according to their own intentions; to measure these differences; and to
determine their further consequences and associated characteristics" (p. 5).
In fact, Winter (1967, 1968, 1972, 1973; Winter & Carlson, 1988) and other
investigators have gathered an enormous amount of evidence indicating that
there are individual differences in power motivation (or *n* Power).

The Measurement and Meaning of Power Motivation

According to Winter (1973), the goal of the power motive is the status of
having power. He wrote:

> By the power motive, I mean a disposition to strive for certain kinds of goals,
> or to be affected by certain kinds of incentives. People who have the power
> motive, or who strive for power, are trying to bring about a certain state of
> affairs—they want to feel "power" or "more powerful than." Power is their
> goal. We would expect that they tend to construe the world in terms of power
> and to use the concept of "power" in categorizing human interaction, but they
> do more than that. Not only do they categorize the world in terms of power, but
> they also want to feel themselves as the most powerful. (p. 18)

As with *n* Achievement, *n* Power can be measured either by the use of
TAT-like pictures or by thematic analysis of almost any verbal material
(Winter, 1987b).

What themes in imagery and prose indicate a high power motive?
According to Winter, there are three: (1) strong, vigorous actions expressing
power; (2) actions that produce strong emotional reactions in others; and
(3) statements expressing concern about a person's reputation or position.

David G. Winter
(1939-   )
extensively studied the
various manifestations of
the power motive.
Courtesy Wesleyan
University

The Hope and Fear of Power

The use of power-related themes in projective stories does not always imply
a hope of power. Sometimes the reaction expressed in such themes seems
riddled with conflict or doubt.

Winter believed that there are two aspects to the power motive: Hope of Power and Fear of Power. **Hope of Power** and the overall power motive are positively correlated. Therefore, Hope of Power and *n* Power are treated as roughly equivalent in our discussion. On the other hand, Hope of Power and Fear of Power show a slight negative correlation; that is, people with high Hope of Power tend to have low Fear of Power, and vice versa.

Fear of Power: A Closer Look

Fear of Power is simultaneous interest in and worry about power, especially when the individual fears being the victim of power. For example, Winter (1973) investigated the relationship between Fear of Power and attitudes toward academic work among college students. He gave over 200 college freshmen an extensive questionnaire that included the following questions:

Would you prefer to have your academic work organized to allow:

A predominance of class work, class assignments, regular examinations, etc.

A predominance of independent reading, writing, and research.

In the average humanities or social sciences course, do you generally prefer:

Objective examinations (e.g., true/false, multiple choice).

Essay examinations.

If class size permitted, which type of instruction would you prefer?

All or mostly lectures.

All or mostly discussions.

(Winter, 1973, p. 150)

Most students showed some preference for the less-structured alternatives (printed in italics). But students high in Fear of Power showed a strong preference for the less-structured alternative.

One interpretation of these results is that the autonomy concerns of those high in Fear of Power derive from a fear of structure, especially structure that is imposed by someone else of high status or power (e.g., a professor or university administrator). Specified programs, assigned work, lectures, and "objective" examinations are all constraints on behavior that originate from the "outside." Fearing the structure that someone else imposes is thus one manifestation of a fear of the potential power of other people (Winter, 1973, p. 149).

This interpretation was supported by two further studies, which showed that students high in Fear of Power were more likely to be late with major term papers, even in the face of warnings (e.g., the papers would be graded down for lateness). They were also more likely to take "incompletes" in their courses.

A clear implication of these findings is that Fear of Power is often unadaptive. Winter has other evidence pointing in this direction. For example, college students high in Fear of Power tend to have more automobile accidents than other students. They are also relatively more inefficient when playing a competitive bidding game. When their power is threatened, those with high Fear of Power seem to become debilitated.

Action Correlates
of the Power
Motive

A major part of Winter's research has been looking for what he called the *action correlates* of individuals who are high in *n* Power. These correlates are the overt manifestations of the power motive.

Presentation of Self

The data show consistently that both men and women with high *n* Power tend to have more "prestige possessions" than those with low *n* Power (Winter, 1968, 1972; Winter & Barenbaum, 1985)—even when income or spending money is held constant. Students high in *n* Power are more likely to put their names on the doors of their dormitory rooms, and they tend to report their college grades in a "favorable" light. For example, Winter (1973) asked students to indicate the lowest final grade they had received thus far in college. Those students high in *n* Power tended to lie and report their lowest grade as higher than it really was.

There is a bit more to the picture, though. Winter (1973) asked middle-class business executives and college students which automobile they would most like. He found that individuals high in *n* Power did not want the most expensive cars; they chose cars that handled best. This finding was true for both the students and the executives as well as for those who chose American cars and for those who chose foreign cars.

Apparently, *control*—of people, possessions, and situations—is a central concern of people motivated by *n* Power. Such control may be gained through force, prestige possessions, or the embellishment of one's products. Here is an interesting example:

> At Wesleyan University as elsewhere, students submit term papers in a great variety of formats, bindings, and conditions of neatness. Some hand in a few ragged sheets of paper full of typing mistakes and bound precariously with a paper clip. Others submit neatly typed, carefully proofread papers which are impressively bound in colored plastic covers with plastic grips running along the left margin.
>
> To the extent that professors judge a paper by its cover—a misleading but human tendency—the paper that is neatly and impressively bound will fare a little better or at least get a favorable first reaction. In a small way, such bindings use prestige to enhance reputation—they are an "impressive show." In one introductory psychology course, those thirteen students who bound their term papers in colored plastic or colored paper binders were significantly higher in Hope of Power than those fifty students who turned in ordinary papers. (Winter, 1973, p. 133)

In a related study, Veroff (1957) found that college men high in *n* Power tended to be argumentative in class. They were also eager to convince their instructors or fellow students of their point of view. This may be why men high in *n* Power do well in college courses that require classroom participation (McKeachie, 1961).

Selection of Friends

Surprisingly, individuals high in *n* Power tend to prefer friends who are *not* popular or well known. Winter explained:

> To a power-motivated person, such friends are attractive because they are presumably not a threat, since they do not compete for power and prestige. Being less well known, such friends are also more disposed to form strong ties of friendship, regard, and support for the power-motivated "leader." (1973, p. 114)

One of the most remarkable characteristics of individuals high in *n* Power is that they gather a group of followers to whom they are both generous and understanding. At the same time, they display a competitive stance toward people outside the circle.

Winter (1973) asked students: "Do you generally like to do things in your own way and without regard for what other students around you may think?" Most students low in power motivation answered yes, whereas a majority of those high in power motivation answered no. To be powerful, you must have a following; to maintain a following, you must show consideration toward those who follow you. Or so it seems.

People high in *n* Power have a rough-and-ready attitude toward those who oppose them. For example, Winter (1973) asked students: "If you could say one sentence—any sentence—to *anyone*, anywhere in the world, in person and without fear of reprisal, what would you say?" Students high in *n* Power were significantly more likely to say something with a strong negative effect, usually something obscene, than were those low in *n* Power.

Relative Indifference to Time and Risk

Winter believed that people high in *n* Power are relatively indifferent to time and risk. In the autumn of 1967, during the Vietnam War, most United States college men faced the serious likelihood of being drafted into the army. At that time, Winter asked 145 men whether they would enlist after college. (This would ensure admission to the branch of their choice but would commit the students to some form of military service.) The other choice was waiting to be drafted and thus taking their chances. Men high in *n* Power were significantly more likely to take their chances. "Thus they are prepared to gamble about military conscription," observed Winter, "just as they also like to gamble when they play ordinary games" (1973, p. 181).

In another study, Winter examined the *n* Power scores of 35 undergraduates who kept calendars of some sort in their rooms. Their scores were significantly lower than the scores of an otherwise comparable group of 35 students who had no calendars. It is unclear whether the latter students felt that they did not need to know what day it was or that they did not need to be reminded by an "external" source. In either event, though, the message is clear. "I'm not worried," thinks the person with high power motivation. "I have it all under control."

Reactivity to Power Stresses

McClelland (1982) hypothesized that individuals high in *n* Power would react more to "power stresses" than those low in *n* Power. He predicted that in situations that arouse power motivation but do not allow power to be exercised, the power-motivated individual will experience a high degree of emotional arousal.

Fodor (1984) tested this hypothesis by creating an industrial simulation with college students (who were either high or low in power motivation) acting as "supervisors" of a work crew. During the experiment, members of the work crew either expressed no work concerns or expressed increasing concerns about their performance. (Crew members were, in fact, confederates and were told what to say by the experimenter.)

The concerns were expressed in comments made to the supervisor. "We're trying to outdo the other groups but we're getting all upset because we're not doing well." "What stress! I never realized money could mean so much to people." "I think we're not really making the grade. Bad scene." (Fodor, 1984, p. 855). The supervisors could do little to change the crew's attitudes or performance, thus creating considerable power stress. They were monitored for emotional arousal as they got feedback from their crews.

Supervisors high and low in power motivation had almost identical levels of arousal when their groups expressed no concern about performance. However, consistent with McClelland's prediction, when the crew did express performance concerns, supervisors high in power motivation became much more aroused. The pattern of results is shown in Figure 11-4.

Figure 11-4
Degree of arousal displayed by supervisors who were high and low in *n* Power in Fodor's experiment, as a function of the concern expressed by their work crews about how the work was going.
Source: From data presented in "The Power Motive and Reactivity to Power Stresses," by E. M. Fodor, 1984, *Journal of Personality and Social Psychology, 47*, pp. 853-859.

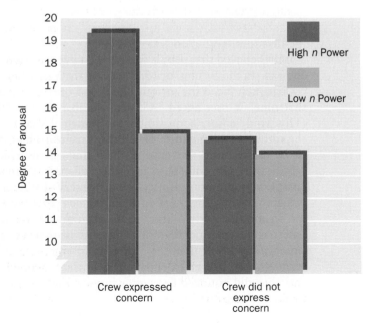

Sexual Behavior and Power

Sexual behavior and power have been closely related both in literature and in psychology. The suggested link has some basis in fact. Male students who report having had sexual intercourse before entering college have appreciably higher *n* Power scores than those who do not report having sex before entering college (Winter, 1973). Men high in *n* Power have also been found to be more likely to physically abuse their partners (Mason & Blankenship, 1987).

Winter also found that college men high in *n* Power were more likely to say that they considered a woman who was dependent an "ideal wife."

> While a dependent wife may interfere with her husband's power, she probably enhances his *feelings* of power; presumably he then thinks that *he* is not dependent on *her*. Thus this combination of qualities is attractive to high *n* Power men because it gives them . . . feelings of superiority. (1973, p. 178)

The Power Motive in Women   Women high in *n* Power are remarkably similar to high *n* Power men in the ways they seek social power and prestige (Winter & Barenbaum, 1985.) However, high *n* Power does not appear to produce "profligate impulsive behaviors" (drinking, aggression, sexual exploitation) in women as it does in men (Winter, 1988). Instead, women high in *n* Power are more likely to engage in helping behavior than are other women (Hirschowitz, 1987).

Alcoholism and Power   McClelland and his co-workers have proposed that the need for power plays a major role in problem drinking (McClelland, Davis, Kalin, & Wanner, 1972). In a 10-year research program, these investigators found that men's feelings of power increased after drinking alcohol. In addition, men with an intense need for power drank even more to satisfy that need. The investigators concluded that dependence on alcohol to satisfy the need for power is the basis of alcoholism. Other research suggests that men's hope of power is distinctly high at midlife, which may be when their real power starts to dwindle (Veroff, Reuman, & Feld, 1984). So, the high incidence of alcoholism in middle-age men can be understood in terms of a need for power.

Indirect support for this conclusion came from an investigation of the use of a power-motivation training program in combination with standard therapy for alcoholism (McClelland, 1977). The program gave participants feedback on their need for power and the way alcohol satisfied that need (Cutter, Boyatzis, & Clancy, 1977). They also received training in more appropriate ways of satisfying their need for power. Only 25% of the alcoholics given the standard treatment alone stayed rehabilitated one year after treatment. In contrast, nearly 50% of the alcoholics given standard therapy and power-motivation training remained rehabilitated at the one-year follow-up. These results support the idea that need for power plays a role in alcoholism.

MOTIVATIONAL TYPES

A new direction in need and motive research has been to look for motivational types; that is, patterns of behavior associated with clusters of motives instead of with a single motive. This research is still in its infancy, but we would like to note three interesting patterns that have been reported.

High n *Power/Low* n *Intimacy.* Individuals high in *n* Power but low in *n* Intimacy tend to be narcissistic (Carroll, 1987). Narcissus was the legendary Greek youth who fell in love with his own reflection in a pool. Narcissistic individuals are self-centered and lack empathy for others. Like their mythical namesake, they have fallen in love with themselves.

High n *Power/High* n *Intimacy.* Individuals who are high in both the need for power and the need for intimacy tend to be depressed, fatalistic, and self-doubting (Zeldow, Daugherty, & McAdams, 1988).

High n *Achievement/High* n *Affiliation.* Individuals who rise to high leadership positions appear to be high in both the need for achievement and the need for affiliation (Sorrentino & Field, 1986). Consistent with this pattern, a recent study by Winter and his associates found that George Bush and Mikhail Gorbachev were high in both *n* Achievement and *n* Affiliation (Winter, Hermann, Weintraub, & Walker, 1991).

SUMMARY

1. Psychologists interested in needs and motives as dispositions have been influenced by psychoanalytic theory in that they view behavior as determined by guiding, impelling forces within the individual. They also believe that information about personality can be extracted from projective responses and other elicited fantasies. The dispositional need and motive theorists share with other dispositional psychologists the view that stable and relatively generalized individual differences allow us to predict, control, and understand behavior.

2. Approach and avoidance tendencies are the two faces of motivation. A motive may be important to an individual because of what he or she wants to get (e.g., hope of success) or wants to avoid (e.g., fear of failure).

3. Murray is the father of modern need and motive theories. His theory states that behavior is determined both by needs within the individual and by environmental pressures ("press").

4. Murray argued that needs may be either manifest or latent. Manifest needs can be assessed by observing overt behavior, but latent needs must be assessed by probing the individual's fantasies. Murray assessed latent needs using the Thematic Apperception Test (TAT), in which subjects are shown pictures and asked to make up stories about them.

5. McClelland picked up on Murray's broad scheme but focused his attention on an in-depth analysis of one motive—the need to achieve. Using his own variation of the TAT, McClelland found that individuals scoring high in need achievement fantasy tend to perform better on a variety of measures, such as getting better grades, than those scoring low in need achievement.

6. McClelland developed a formal course to increase achievement motivation. The course, which runs from one to two weeks, 12 to 18 hours a day, has been found to increase the entrepreneurial efforts and accomplishments of participants.

7. Achievement motivation in women appears to develop under somewhat different conditions than it does in men. For example, maternal hostility and criticism are linked to achievement striving in girls, whereas having a supportive family is associated with high achievement striving in boys. Divorce seems to increase achievement striving in girls and decrease it in boys. Finally, whereas men fear achievement failure, women may fear achievement success, apparently because they think success makes them less attractive to men.

8. Winter has studied the need for power, which he measured using TAT-like pictures. People high in the need for power tend to cultivate a group of followers toward whom they are generous and understanding, while taking a competitive stance toward outsiders. Individuals with a high need for power become emotionally aroused when they feel powerless.

9. Alcohol appears to provide a temporary inner feeling of power. Thus a high need for power, especially when unsatisfied, is associated with alcoholism.

10. Recently researchers have begun to look for motivational types; that is, combinations of motive patterns.

Liabilities of the Dispositional Strategy

s we did with the psychoanalytic strategy, we now turn to the major problems facing the dispositional strategy.

Six major criticisms have been leveled repeatedly at the dispositional strategy. Namely, the strategy (1) lacks its own theoretical concepts, (2) fails to provide adequate explanations, (3) does not predict individual behaviors, (4) pays inadequate attention to personality development and change, (5) overlooks the many subjective decisions involved in factor analysis, and (6) has not adequately confronted the social desirability problem.

LACK OF ITS OWN THEORETICAL CONCEPTS

Theory plays a central role in all science. However, the dispositional strategy has operated without adequate theoretical guidelines. The only theoretical idea common among most dispositional psychologists seems to be Allport's heuristic realism principle—the idea that traits really exist and that the personality psychologist's job is to find them. This lack of theory has led to confusion and often leaves dispositional researchers talking past one another.

For example, when Cattell encountered a constellation of measures that referred to emotional stability, he provided a meaningless name ("factor C") and later borrowed a name from the psychoanalytic strategy ("Ego Strength"). Meanwhile, other dispositional researchers called the same constellation "Emotionality," and yet others applied a psychiatric label, "Neuroticism."

This same lack of agreement on theoretical concepts has left many dispositional phenomena hanging in space. For example, the Type A behavior pattern involves both a high level of activity and a high level of achievement striving. Yet almost no attention has been given to determining whether standard measures of activity level (such as those used by Willerman) or standard measures of achievement motivation (such as those used by McClelland) are related to the Type A pattern.

The nature/nurture issue is another area of confusion for the theoretical concepts used by the dispositional strategy. The term *trait* was borrowed from genetics. It is still unclear how much similarity there is between the biological and the psychological concepts. For example, what is the relationship between the temperament traits most often associated with observations of infants and children (and all said to be heritable) and the personality traits identified by McCrae and Costa? Because of the absence of a shared theoretical base, researchers are giving almost no attention to this question.

FAILURE TO PROVIDE ADEQUATE EXPLANATIONS

In discussing the liabilities of the psychoanalytic strategy, we noted that psychoanalysts have committed certain logical errors in interpreting their observations. The dispositional strategy is also prone to a logical error; namely, confusing description with explanation.

When consistencies or regularities occur in behavior, it is convenient to summarize them with a descriptive label. Thus, "Introversion" is a label for an observed pattern of behavior or set of relationships. This labeling process is perfectly legitimate if our purpose is description, but the label obviously does not explain our observations. Yet the logical error of confusing description with explanation is repeatedly made by dispositional personality psychologists.

Skinner (1953) developed a related argument many years ago. Notice how Skinner's argument can be applied to Introversion, achievement motivation, or any of the other labels that have been invented to describe behavior:

> When we say that a man eats because he is hungry, smokes a great deal because he has the tobacco habit, fights because he has the instinct of pugnacity, behaves brilliantly because of his intelligence, or plays the piano well because of his musical ability, we seem to be referring to causes. But on analysis, these phrases prove to be merely redundant descriptions. A single set of facts is described by the two statements: "He eats" and "He is hungry." A single set of facts is described by the statements "He smokes a great deal" and "He has the smoking habit." A single set of facts is described by the two statements: "He plays well" and "He has musical ability." The practice of explaining one statement in terms of the other is dangerous because it suggests that we have found the cause and therefore need search no further. (p. 31)

Finally, it should be noted that failing to provide adequate explanations cannot be escaped by dispositional psychologists who claim that dispositions are meant only as descriptions. In that case, the dispositional strategy, by its own admission, does not provide an explanation of behavior.

INABILITY TO PREDICT INDIVIDUAL BEHAVIORS

Advocates of the dispositional strategy have discovered many reliable and intriguing relationships, such as the link between physical appearance and personality. And no one doubts that there is some consistency in the way people behave. But almost no basis is provided for predicting the behavior of a single individual with a high degree of accuracy.

For example, many people with delicate builds love action and adventure, despite the general tendency for this group to be somewhat introverted. Many powerful leaders refrain from alcohol or sexual exploits and drive cars that would hardly be found at a grand prix, despite the statistical association between high power need and a taste for sex, alcohol, and action.

To compound the problem even further, recent analyses by Baumeister and his colleagues show that *only some people are consistent*, that is, behave as if they have some constant amount of a trait that follows them across time and situations. Thus, the dispositional strategy may be forced to deal with **metatraits**, the trait of having or not having a particular trait (Baumeister, 1991; Baumeister & Tice, 1988).

To illustrate the risks in predicting individual behavior from dispositional self-report measures, let us consider an exaggerated hypothetical example. Suppose that an investigator informally observes that some people seem to be more intrusive than others. To reflect this idea, he defines *intrusiveness* as "a tendency to provide unsolicited information or advice, to show up uninvited, and to examine and use the belongings of others without asking." Next, the investigator administers a wide array of assessment techniques to measure intrusiveness, including peer ratings, self-report measures, and fantasy measures. The procedure yields reliable intrusiveness scores that show considerable individual differences among people.

At this point, the investigator begins to compare the backgrounds of subjects who are high (above average) and low (below average) in intrusiveness. He finds high intrusives tend to report that their parents used to leave the doors to their rooms—and even their homes—unlocked. Apparently they worried little about privacy. In contrast, individuals low on intrusiveness report that their parents locked their doors and emphasized everyone's "right to privacy."

Suppose that, given this information, you meet a young woman who mentions that her parents always left their doors unlocked. You would certainly be tempted to think that your new acquaintance is likely to be intrusive. However, that would not be sound logic. There is a decent chance that your assumption would be wrong.

Part of the reason can be seen in Figure 12-1, which shows our hypothetical intrusiveness data. We have assumed that intrusiveness is normally distributed. (Recall that modern dispositional psychologists commonly assume normal distributions.) We also show a difference between the "locked-door" and the "unlocked-door" groups that is large enough to be reliable (statistically significant). Thus, Figure 12-1 represents the usual magnitude of difference between "trait-high" and "trait-low" people in typical dispositional research.

Three areas of the figure deserve comment. The dark colored portion indicates *overlap* and accounts for more than half of the area under the curves. This overlap shows that most people will tend to get an average intrusiveness score, regardless of whether the doors in their homes were locked or not.

The two light colored areas indicate *partial overlap*. Some members of both groups obtain scores in this range, but one group predominates in each area. Notice, for example, that some individuals from each background obtained an intrusiveness score of 4, but most were in the locked-door group.

Finally, the white areas indicate *nonoverlap*; only one group is represented. In the figure, the only people with scores as low as 2 came from homes where the doors were locked. The only people with scores as high as 9 came from homes where the doors were unlocked. *The most important thing to note about the areas of nonoverlap is how small they are*; only a small percentage of people fall in these extreme ranges.

With this analysis in mind, what conclusion can we draw about an individual's intrusiveness, knowing that she comes from a home where the doors were never locked? We certainly do not want to conclude that the person must be highly intrusive. (Even among people from unlocked-door homes, the majority are only about average in intrusiveness.) As a matter of

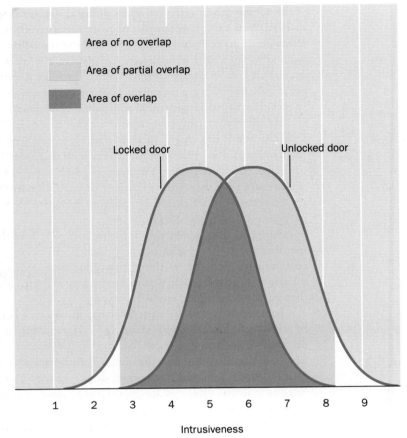

Figure 12-1
Hypothetical distributions
of scores for the dispo-
sition "intrusiveness,"
showing that a significant
difference between the
average trait scores of
two groups (here,
"locked-door" versus
"unlocked-door" back-
grounds) does not
ordinarily provide the
basis for predicting what
any specific individual
will be like.

fact, our new acquaintance could be less intrusive than average—maybe even very unintrusive—and still come from a home where the doors were left unlocked. In this case at least, to reach any other conclusion would be stereotyping the person.

This finding does not mean that dispositional assessment is worthless. Rather, it means that the dispositional strategy has provided assessment procedures that improve our guessing (above chance) about what other people will be like or what they will do, but it is still guessing.

Mischel (1968), in a now-classic critique of the dispositional strategy, made the point this way:

It is important to clearly distinguish between "statistically significant" associations and equivalence. A correlation of .30 easily reaches statistical significance when the sample of subjects is sufficiently large, and suggests an association that is highly unlikely on the basis of chance. However, the same coefficient accounts for less than 10 percent of the relevant variance [i.e., what the variables share in common]. Statistically significant relationships of this magnitude are sufficient to justify personality research on individual and group differences. It is equally plain that their value for making statements about an individual are severely limited. Even when statistically significant behavioral consistencies are found, and even when they replicate reliably, the relationships usually are not large enough to warrant individual assessment and treatment decisions except for certain screening and selection purposes. (p. 38)

Underestimation of the Importance of Situational Factors

A related liability is that the dispositional strategy underestimates—sometimes overlooks entirely—the influence of the situation and circumstances in determining behavior. For example, for years psychologists sought to determine what traits make a person a leader. Ultimately, however, it was recognized that, in most groups, a leader is selected based on how well he or she can facilitate attainment of the group's particular goals.

What was overlooked . . . in the view that leaders are uniquely endowed . . . was the actual fact of daily life, that is, that persons function as leaders in a particular time and place, and that these are both varying and delimiting conditions; that there are several pathways to leadership, sometimes from higher authority, other times from group consent. . . . Indeed, if any point stands forth in the modern day view of leadership it is that leaders are made by circumstances. . . . The leader's emergence or waning of status is . . . inextricably linked to the prevailing situation. (Hollander, 1964, pp. 4–5, 15)

Failure to Specify When Dispositions Will Be Manifested in Behavior

The last of Allport's eight assumptions about traits is: "Acts, and even habits, that are inconsistent with a trait are not proof of the nonexistence of the trait." The intent of this assumption is clear. People do not always act consistently, and Allport did not want that fact to invalidate a trait approach. At some point, though, the argument is stretched to absurdity. If *all* of a person's acts are inconsistent with a trait, surely that is proof that the person does not possess the trait. Otherwise, one can describe people in any dispositional way one likes, without regard to their behavior. An example would be to say that a minority group has the trait of dishonesty even though you have always known its members to behave honestly. How much inconsistency can a dispositional approach endure?

Critics have repeatedly challenged the assumption that human behavior is consistent enough across situations to justify a dispositional view of personality (e.g., Bandura & Walters, 1963; Mischel, 1968; Rotter, 1954). They have gathered empirical evidence from psychological investigations and compelling everyday examples to support their argument. For instance, an individual who is aggressive at the office may be timid at home, completely dominated by his or her family.

Overstated, the criticism becomes unfair. Allport's point was that a person with the trait of hostility will not be hostile in every situation. But if a person is not hostile in every situation, it is essential to know when the characteristic will appear. The dispositional strategy fails to provide useful ways of describing or predicting when a person's disposition will or will not show up—this is a fundamental deficit.

PAYS INADEQUATE ATTENTION TO PERSONALITY DEVELOPMENT AND CHANGE

As much as any other strategy, the dispositional view has examined longitudinal data. The characteristics of people have been measured at various times (e.g., in childhood and again in adulthood), and similarities and differences have been noted. These data certainly indicate some consistency in personality over time. But *changes* over time are also apparent for most people. The dispositional strategy has paid little attention to these changes and has hardly been concerned with the processes underlying development or with changing a person's traits, types, or needs over time. When and how do source traits develop? Why does one behavior pattern emerge and not another? Such questions are not simply unanswered from the dispositional perspective. The strategy does not even call on the investigator to ask them.

The dispositional strategy has also contributed almost nothing to personality-change techniques. Individual dispositional psychologists—such as Murray, Eysenck, and McClelland—have been involved in personality-change work. However, their approaches, like many of their basic theoretical concepts, are borrowed from other strategies. Murray's approach to personality is based on needs, yet he practiced as a therapist in the Harvard Psychological Clinic using procedures influenced primarily by psychoanalysis. Eysenck was a major advocate of the type approach based on factor analysis, but he was also one of the most ardent proponents of personality-change procedures associated with the behavioral strategy. McClelland's program to increase achievement motivation was based on principles derived from the psychoanalytic, phenomenological, and behavioral strategies, as well as from social psychology.

In sum, the dispositional strategy tries to capture and describe a *static person*. The strategy ignores the dynamics of development, growth, and change, although they are obviously important aspects of personality.

FACTOR ANALYSIS INVOLVES MANY SUBJECTIVE DECISIONS

Factor analysis, the unique research tool of the dispositional strategy, entails many subjective decisions. Since these decisions can greatly influence the apparent structure of personality, it is incorrect to say that "the structure of personality can be objectively discovered by factor analysis."

Because factor analysis involves sophisticated mathematical procedures, it has an aura of precision and objectivity. However, naming factors is invariably a subjective decision. Additionally, the number and kinds of factors extracted will depend on the mathematical procedure chosen—another subjective decision. Thus, Eysenck finds two factors and Cattell finds 16. In part, this is due to the statistical analysis each selected. Obviously, then, Eysenck did not *discover* a small number of types, and Cattell did not *discover* 16 personality traits. Both investigators made subjective decisions that forced their data into the patterns that emerged.

The preconceptions of raters, and of researchers, can influence factor analyses. There is evidence that Norman's original "discovery" of five supertraits was largely determined by the preconceptions and stereotypes regarding personality organization that his raters held. Norman (1963) used factor analysis to look at peer ratings across a number of diverse groups of people. He consistently found a stable set of the same five factors. Later, however, Passini and Norman (1966) showed that very similar factors emerged when students rated classmates with whom they were unacquainted. Passini and Norman concluded that ratings do not reflect the "true" organization of traits in the rated persons. Instead, they reflect the ideas raters have about personality (e.g., the belief that some behaviors ought to go together).

Dispositional psychologists, then, confuse subjective impression with objective discovery. This problem is by no means limited to factor analysts. There are endless arguments about the definition of achievement, power, aggression, and other traits in the dispositional literature. Consider, for example, the striking difference between Murray's and McClelland's ideas of *n* Achievement. They both use the same term (and it is a novel and technical-sounding term at that), but they are referring to very different concepts.

By *n* Achievement, Murray meant a permanent characteristic set down in childhood and operating almost unconsciously. In contrast, McClelland had in mind a conscious attitude and orientation that can be readily taught to adults. Both researchers used the same basic measuring instrument, the TAT, but for different ends. For Murray, a person writing achievement-saturated stories in response to a TAT picture displays the latent need for *n* Achievement. The person was probably not even aware of this need. The value of the TAT, Murray (1951) wrote, "is its capacity to reveal things that the subject is unwilling to tell or unable to tell because he is unconscious of them" (p. 577).

In contrast, McClelland used the TAT to teach people to become achievement-oriented by making them consciously aware of achievement strivings. McClelland did not do this because he discovered that Murray was wrong about the difference between latent and manifest needs. He changed the meaning of *n* Achievement because he decided subjectively that the new concept would be more "fruitful" than the old one.

DISPOSITIONAL ASSESSMENT HAS NOT ADEQUATELY CONFRONTED THE SOCIAL DESIRABILITY PROBLEM IN SELF-REPORTS

There is ample evidence that most people try to put their best foot forward and make a good impression whenever they can. We are speaking of the general phenomenon of social desirability, which has been extensively studied by dispositional psychologists. However, for the most part, the dispositional strategy has not adequately confronted the social desirability problem in personality assessment. This is especially unfortunate because social desirability is a major threat to the validity of self-report inventories.

The psychoanalytic strategy takes into account the fact that people will present themselves in a favorable light when asked about psychological or personal matters. The intense, in-depth nature of the psychoanalytic session and the subtlety of interpretation of the responses to projective techniques are intended to penetrate a person's superficial veneer.

In contrast, the dispositional strategy relies heavily on arm's-length assessment—that is, subjects or their friends and relatives fill out a questionnaire and hand it in or mail it. The absence of a professional observer makes the evaluation impersonal and distant. Respondents need not fear, for example, that facial expressions or other signs of nervousness will give them away. Instead, the inaccurate or misleading response is made by simply checking a category or circling a number.

Numerous studies have shown that faking can be quite successful under these conditions (e.g., Anastasi, 1988b). Often, self-reports do not correspond with objective ratings of the relevant behavior (Lowman & Williams, 1987; Hessing, Elffers, & Weigel, 1988). Thus, it appears that the problem of social desirability in dispositional assessment has not been adequately handled.

SUMMARY   1. The dispositional strategy lacks its own theoretical concepts; they must be borrowed from the other strategies.

2. The dispositional strategy fails to provide adequate explanations for the causes of behavior. To explain a behavior by saying that it is caused by a disposition and then claim that the presence of the disposition is proved by the occurrence of the behavior is a circular argument.

3. The dispositional strategy cannot accurately predict the behavior of individuals or specify when dispositions will or will not be manifested in behavior. One reason for this inability is that situational factors often exert considerable influence over people's behavior. Dispositional psychologists tend to minimize or completely ignore the influence of situational factors. They are also inattentive to the possibility that only some people behave in a traitlike way across time and situations.

4. The dispositional strategy fails to explain personality development and provides few hints as to how personality can be changed. Personality change procedures used by dispositional psychologists are borrowed from other strategies.

5. Dispositional psychologists make many subjective decisions using factor analysis, so factor analysis can hardly be described as a completely objective procedure.

6. The dispositional strategy has not been adequately concerned about the problem of social desirability in personality assessment. Self-report and rating data have been relied on excessively, even though such data can be faked or distorted by a variety of biases.

THE PHENOMENOLOGICAL STRATEGY

Chapter Thirteen

Introduction to the Phenomenological Strategy

I noticed her pen with the green cap the first time I sat next to Myrna in class. Over the course of the semester, I also became familiar with the copious notes she wrote in green ink. Myrna was constantly writing in her notebook, and I often glanced at her notes to see what she thought was so important.

On the last day of class, I had forgotten a pen, and I asked to borrow Myrna's for a moment. She handed me her pen, and as I began to write, I laughed out loud. "Cute," I said to Myrna, "You switched the ink cartridge." Her green pen was writing in blue ink.

"No, I didn't. It has always had blue ink," Myrna replied.

"But your notes are in green. I've seen them dozens of times," I retorted.

"No, they're in blue," responded Myrna as she reached for her notebook. *In fact*, the notes were written in blue, and, *in fact*, I clearly remembered seeing them in green dozens of times.

The two drivers undoubtedly have differing subjective realities about the single objective reality.
Photo Source Inc./St. Louis

It is easy to understand how the green cap on the pen would lead a person to believe that it contained green ink. However, the surprised student had *seen* Myrna's notes in green, many times. He did not think her notes were green; he *knew* they were green!

The story illustrates the difference between so-called objective and subjective reality. **Objective reality** refers to observations of an event about which a number of observers agree. **Subjective reality** is each individual's personal experience of an event. Subjective reality is the focus of the phenomenological strategy.

ALL IN THE EYE OF THE BEHOLDER

The idea that *reality of phenomena lies solely in the way they are perceived* is the essence of phenomenology and the basis for the phenomenological approach to personality. What is real to an individual is what is in the person's **internal frame of reference**—or subjective world—which includes everything the person is aware of at a particular point in time.

For centuries, the phenomenological view was in disrepute among philosophers of science because it seemed to deny the possibility of establishing "objective facts." But modern philosophers and contemporary scientists have recently begun to show a new respect for the idea that all experiences, and thus all knowledge, depend on subjective interpretation (Heelan, 1983; Manicas & Secord, 1983; Rock, 1983; Watzlawick, 1984). At the heart of this new acceptance is the growing recognition that *perception is an interpretive act.* To prove this for yourself, take 5 minutes to do Demonstration 13-1 right now, before reading further.

■ *Demonstration 13-1:*
PERCEPTION AS A CREATIVE PROCESS

PART I

Look at Figure 13-1. You probably see a star and a dot. In the Demonstration Materials section at the back of the book, you will find an enlarged copy of the star and the dot for use in the Demonstration. Remove this copy and proceed with the following directions.

1. Hold the copy of the dot and the star in your right hand at arm's length.

2. Close your left eye and fixate on the star.

3. Move the paper very slowly toward you.

What happens to the dot? When the paper is held between 12 and 14 inches from your eye, the dot will disappear. (If the dot does not disappear, hold the dot and the star about 6 inches from your eye and then move it very slowly away from you.)

4. Once you have found the critical distance at which the dot disappears, hold the paper at that distance and continue fixating on the star.

5. Maintaining the critical distance, move the paper in a circular motion.

What happens to the dot now? If the paper is held at the critical distance, the dot will remain invisible.

Why does the dot disappear? The explanation is actually quite simple. At the critical distance (between 12 and 14 inches), the image

Figure 13-1
Visual stimuli for Demonstration 13-1, Part I.

of the dot falls on the *blind spot* of the retina. This is the small area of the retina that contains no receptor cells because the optic nerve is attached there. An image falling on the blind spot is not perceived.

What is most intriguing about the blind spot is that we are not aware of it. Because any object whose image falls on the blind spot cannot be seen, some area of the visual field always falls on the blind spot. Consequently, we always experience gaps in our vision. Look around the room. Are there parts of your visual field that you are missing right now? Have you ever been aware of gaps in your visual field? Probably not. Phenomenologists explain this lack of awareness in terms of the prominent role that interpretation plays in perception. The reason is that we *fill in the gaps* in our visual fields. We know—or, more accurately, we *believe*—that there are no gaps. For example, you assumed that the dot was still there when its image was reflected on your blind spot. But was it? Most people believe that it was still there. And the dot was still there for them because of that belief—even though the image did not appear on the retina.

PART II

Let's examine another simple example of the role that interpretation plays in perception. Read and carry out each of the following directions before going on to the next direction.

1. Look at the wine goblet in Figure 13-2 on page 256; then return to this page and read the next direction.

2. Next look at the two faces in silhouette in Figure 13-2 on page 256; then return to this page and read the next direction.

3. Now try looking at the figure steadily for a minute or so. You may see it flip back and forth between a goblet and faces. (Some people report that they can make it look like a goblet or like two faces at will.)

Is the figure a wine goblet or two silhouettes? It is both and neither, depending on how you, the perceiver, interpret the figure. What you see is more than a simple mirroring of the "world out there." The figure does not change at all when your perception shifts from a goblet to faces. Rather, the change occurs in your mind!

The common phrase "*only* in your mind" does not mean that subjective reality is trivial. In fact, just the opposite is true. Subjective phenomena—such as the change between a goblet and faces—are as important as objective phenomena. And phenomenologically, subjective reality takes precedence over objective reality. How we interpret events—that is, our subjective reality—is what influences how we behave. This position has important practical implications. For instance, taking into account people's subjective realities has been applied to city planning.

> In a sense, social scientists find, the city does not exist. There is no such single entity, but rather many cities, as many as there are people to experience them. And researchers now believe that the subjective reality is every bit as important to understanding and fostering successful urban life as the concrete and asphalt of objective measurement.

> Although most earlier approaches to assessing the quality of city life led researchers to consider such factors as noise levels and density, the new work shows that how people actually perceive their environments is as important as the environments themselves. (Goleman, 1985, p. C1)

From the phenomenological perspective, reality is *reality as it is perceived.* Two people observing the "same" event may perceive two very different happenings. The reports of eyewitnesses to crimes, for example, often appear to refer to separate incidents (e.g., Kohnken & Maass, 1988).

The importance of how events are perceived and experienced subjectively is illustrated by an experiment on stress (Geer, Davison, & Gatchel, 1970). The investigators hypothesized that the stress people experience is influenced by whether they *believe* that they can control what is happening. In the experiment, all the subjects received a series of identical electric shocks. None of the subjects had any control over the shocks. However, some of the subjects *believed* that they could control the shocks, whereas others *believed* that they could not.

The experiment was presented to the subjects as a study of reaction time and was conducted in two phases. In Phase I, all of the subjects were treated alike. They were given painful electric shocks, each lasting 6 seconds. To measure their reaction time, the subjects were told to press a switch as soon as the shock began. During this period, the subjects' levels of physiological arousal were recorded as a measure of stress.

During Phase II, half the subjects were assigned to a *perceived control condition*; they were told that they could cut the duration of the next 10 shocks in half if they pressed the switch "quickly enough" (although the necessary speed was not specified). The remaining subjects were assigned to a *perceived noncontrol condition*; they were told that the next 10 shocks would be shorter. Actually, all of the subjects received shocks lasting 3 seconds, during which time their physiological arousal was again measured.

If stress was influenced by the belief that one can control the situation, perceived control subjects should have experienced less arousal during Phase II than perceived noncontrol subjects. This is what occurred, as you can see from Figure 13-3. The two groups had similar levels of arousal in Phase I, but the perceived control subjects had significantly lower levels of arousal than the perceived noncontrol subjects in Phase II. These results support the idea that humans create their

> own gods to fill in gaps in . . . knowledge about a sometimes terrifying environment, creating at least an illusion of control which is presumably

Figure 13-2
Reversible figure-ground pattern (see Demonstration 13-1, Part II).

comforting. Perhaps the next best thing to being master of one's fate is being deluded into thinking one is. (Geer et al., 1970, pp. 737–738)

Subjective experience may or may not coincide with objective reality. Consider the following somewhat whimsical example.

A man construes [views] his neighbor's behavior as hostile. By that he means that his neighbor, given the proper opportunity, will do him harm. He tries out his construction [view] of his neighbor's attitude by throwing rocks at his neighbor's dog. His neighbor responds with an angry rebuke. The man may then believe that he has validated his construction of his neighbor as a hostile person.

The man's [perception] of his neighbor as a hostile person may appear to be "validated" by another kind of fallacy. The man reasons, "If my neighbor is hostile, he will be eager to know when I get into trouble, when I am ill, or when I am in any way vulnerable. I will watch to see if this isn't so." The next morning the man meets his neighbor and is greeted with the conventional, "How are you?" Sure enough, the neighbor is doing just what was predicted of a hostile person. (Kelly, 1955, pp. 12-13)

In many instances, objective reality is not as clear as in the preceding example. Practically, what a person perceives—subjective experience—determines the ultimate reality of a situation for that person. Consider 8-year-old Beth. Her family has just moved to a new city. After her first day at the new school, Beth's parents ask, "How was school today?" Beth replies:

I hated it. The kids are really unfriendly. When I came into the class, all the kids stared at me. They were grinning and thought I was funny looking. Only two kids in the whole class talked to me at lunch.

Now consider how Beth might have *perceived* the same situation differently and reported a very different experience.

> I liked it. The kids are really friendly. When I came into the class, they were all interested in me. The kids were looking at me and smiling. And two kids, who I didn't even know, came over to talk to me at lunch!

The same situation could have led Beth to have either of these two very different subjective experiences, depending on how she interpreted it. (It is also likely that Beth's reactions would influence how her classmates reacted to her and change the nature of the objective situation in later interactions.)

Psychology is a scientific endeavor that seeks objective knowledge, which comes from observations on which others can agree. Subjective knowledge always involves a single individual's experiences; others cannot directly verify this knowledge. Phenomenological psychologists solve this problem by seeking what Rogers (1964) called **phenomenological knowledge, which** comes from understanding a person from the person's own internal frame of reference.

The importance of subjective experience is acknowledged in everyday psychology with expressions such as "Beauty is in the eye of the beholder," "One person's meat is another person's poison," and "Try stepping into the other person's shoes." In fact, we get into trouble when we *fail* to take other

Figure 13-3
The effects of perceived control on the amount of arousal subjects experienced while awaiting electric shocks in Geer et al.'s experiment. During Phase I, all subjects received shocks of six seconds' duration. During Phase II, all subjects received shocks of three seconds' duration. Subjects in the perceived control group believed that the shorter shocks were a result of their own quick reaction times, whereas subjects in the perceived noncontrol group believed that shock duration was unrelated to their responses and therefore not within their control.
Source: Adapted from "Reduction of Stress in Humans Through Nonveridical Perceived Control of Aversive Stimulation" by J. H. Geer, G. C. Davison, and R. I. Gatchel, 1970, *Journal of Personality and Social Psychology, 16*, pp. 731-738.

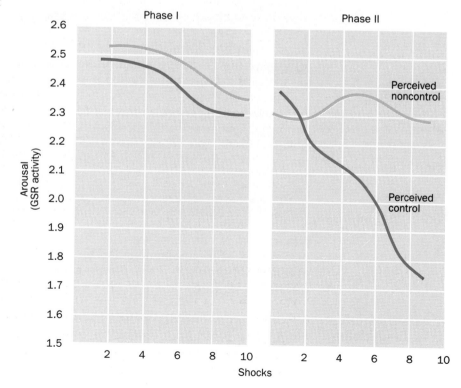

people's subjective experiences into account. For example, if David kids Ann when she is anxious about being 2 minutes late for a dinner at a friend's house, Ann gets angry. From Ann's perspective, being punctual is very important, whereas David considers being uptight about being 2 minutes late as humorous.

We will examine two somewhat different phenomenological approaches to personality. The *self-actualization approaches* of Carl Rogers and Abraham Maslow consider personality to be each person's unique inclinations to develop and change in particular directions. This perspective is part of *humanistic psychology*, which has also been called the "third force" in psychology because it was founded in the 1960s as a reaction to psychoanalysis and behaviorism, the two predominant orientations at the time (DeCarvalho, 1990b, 1991a, 1991b; Smith, 1990). George Kelly's *personal construct approach* deals with how people interpret and anticipate the events in their lives, and thereby develop unique personalities.

PHENOMENOLOGICAL PERSONALITY THEORY

The three phenomenological personality theories we will describe in Chapters 14 through 16 differ in two basic respects. First, there are differences in the breadth of their coverage. Rogers' and Kelly's theories of personality are comprehensive, attempting to account for the full range of human behaviors. In contrast, Maslow's theory is narrower, centering on several specific aspects of human behavior. Second, many of the specific concepts are unique to each individual theory.

Despite these differences, all three phenomenological personality theories share broad, underlying theoretical assumptions about the nature of personality. In turn, these common assumptions have important implications for how personality is to be studied.

Focus on Higher Human Functions

Phenomenological personality theories deal with "higher" human functions. Although phenomenological theories acknowledge the importance of basic biological needs, they are not the focus of attention. Rather, the theorizing concentrates on the nature of human personality *after* one's basic needs have been satisfied. Specifically, Rogers and Maslow were concerned with self-actualization (striving to reach one's potential), and Kelly focused on how people interpret their experiences and predict future outcomes.

Phenomenological theories assume that humans are *rational*. Each person's actions represent "sensible" responses to the world as that person perceives it. This assumption implies that people are aware of their psychological processes. Thus, the phenomenological strategy emphasizes *conscious* experience.

Active Nature of Human Beings

All personality theories deal with the basic issue of motivation: what "moves" people to act (the word *motivation* comes from the Latin *movere*, "to move"). Motivation involves factors that initiate behavior—what gets us "moving"—and factors that determine the direction, intensity, and persistence of behavior (Evans, 1989).

Phenomenological personality theories begin with the assumption that human beings are naturally *active*. Therefore, there is no reason to posit a special force from within the person (e.g., oral gratification or need to achieve) or outside the person (e.g., weaning or a college entrance exam) to account for what gets people "moving." Humans act because they are alive.

Phenomenological motivation theory, then, deals exclusively with factors that account for the direction in which people "move"—that is, what behaviors they perform—and the strength and endurance of these behaviors. (This is another illustration of the focus on "higher" human functions.) To explain the direction that an individual's behavior takes, each of the three phenomenological theories advances a general principle. Rogers posited that behavior is directed by each person's unique self-actualizing tendency. Maslow proposed that behavior is determined by a hierarchy of needs. Kelly theorized that people act to maximize their ability to accurately anticipate events in their lives.

Being active involves more than just "being in motion." People are assumed to be dynamic—in a more or less constantly changing state. As Rogers (1961) put it: "Life, at its best, is a flowing, changing process in which nothing is fixed" (p. 27). Accordingly, phenomenological theories pay little attention to stable and enduring personality characteristics (the focus of the dispositional strategy).

Present and Future as Salient Time Frames

The phenomenological strategy is most concerned with what is going on in the present (e.g., Bohart, 1991a). Moreover, the focus is often on the time frame that is considered most salient for people—namely, the momentary experience, which is called the here-and-now. In contrast to the *present*, which may mean this hour or day or even the current year, *here-and-now* refers to what is occurring at this very moment. For example, your here-and-now is reading these words (and perhaps some other experiences).

Although it is acknowledged that past experiences influence present behavior, the past is important only in terms of how it affects here-and-now perceptions. For example, there is little attention paid to a person's experiences in early childhood (the focus of the psychoanalytic strategy).

The future, too, has a role in phenomenological theories in that each person is considered to be constantly in a process of evolving. Further, Rogers' and Maslow's theories are concerned with individuals' striving to fulfill their potentials, which is a future-oriented process. Kelly's theory specifically deals with people anticipating future events.

Holistic Approach

Phenomenological theories are holistic: they view and explain specific acts in terms of an individual's entire personality. The holistic view implies that there is consistency within one's personality—the parts fit together in a coherent whole. The importance of personality consistency is a theme running through phenomenological theories. For instance, Rogers stressed the importance of agreement between how people see themselves and how they would like to be. Another example of holistic thinking is Kelly's refusal to differentiate among thoughts, feelings, and actions. He considered them all to be psychological processes governed by the same principles.

Idiographic Approach

The appreciation of individuality is central to the phenomenological strategy. Phenomenological theories employ a fundamentally *idiographic* approach to studying personality. They focus on the uniqueness of each person and minimizes comparisons among people. For instance, Rogers and Maslow held that all behavior is governed by a self-actualizing tendency, although the nature of the tendency is idiosyncratic for each individual. Kelly believed that all human behavior is determined by the ways in which persons view the world, but these world views are unique for each person.

Existential Psychology and the Phenomenological Strategy

The phenomenological strategy and existential psychology share some important elements (e.g., DeCarvalho, 1990a, 1990b, 1991a). Rollo May (1967) described *existential psychology* as

> an *attitude*, an approach to human beings, rather than a special school or group . . . it is not a system of therapy but an attitude toward therapy, not a set of new techniques but a concern with the understanding of the structure of the human being and his experience. (p. 245)

This existential attitude requires an intimate understanding of a person's experiences. Thus, psychologists should try to *know* people rather than merely *know about* them. Rogers (1965, 1973) is especially adamant on this point in his approach to both therapy and research.

Three themes in existential psychology are central to the phenomenological strategy: *free will, choice,* and *"being there."* We will repeatedly see the related themes of free will and choice in phenomenological personality theories. Both Rogers and Maslow assumed that individuals are capable of directing their own lives. Rogers' formula for personality change involves establishing conditions conducive to self-growth. Kelly's personality theory is based on the assumption that people can choose to view events in their lives in an almost limitless variety of ways.

Consistent with the existential notions of free will and choice, phenomenologists assume that people can freely choose how they will behave. People are not viewed as victims of their past, as in the psychoanalytic strategy; or of enduring personality characteristics, as in the dispositional strategy; or of the environment, as in the behavioral strategy. Thus, the phenomenological strategy would be considered *non*deterministic.

The third common theme in existential and phenomenological psychology is the emphasis on momentary experiences. Existentialists focus on *Dasein,* the German word for "being there," which emphasizes immediate experience. Phenomenologists focus on the here-and-now—a very similar concept.

**PHENOMENOLOGICAL
PERSONALITY
ASSESSMENT**

A basic dilemma for the phenomenological strategy arises in personality assessment. How can person *A* know how person *B* is perceiving the world when all that person *A* truly can know is what person *B* describes? Ignoring issues of trust and accuracy, how can one be sure that the experience another person describes is even remotely like the one that he or she has in mind? Think of all the possible meanings of a simple statement such as "I'm tired," "I'm scared," or "I love you."

Phenomenological personality assessment involves gaining knowledge of private mental events. Recall that this is also the essential task of psychoanalytic personality assessment. In both strategies, behavior is neither the basic unit of personality nor the exclusive means of understanding personality.

Consider the student who does not speak up in class. What can be inferred from this behavior? Is it that the student has not done the assigned reading and is not prepared to participate? Or is the student familiar with the reading but afraid of being considered a show-off? The student's behavior will not answer these questions because the same behavior can have vastly different *meanings*.

Within broad limits, behavior can yield information about an individual's personality, but for more specific information, one must find the meaning of the behavior for that person. Phenomenological personality assessment is aimed at discovering personal *meaning*. The meaning of experiences for people constitutes their personalities and determines their actions.

Often people confuse their own view of events with someone else's. Consider the case of Jim, a college sophomore, who told his parents that he wanted to drop out of school because he wasn't learning anything. Jim's parents told him, "We understand exactly how you feel. When we were in college there were times that we were tired and depressed and wanted to quit." What Jim's parents "understood" was how *they* had felt in a similar situation. They did not know how their son was feeling. Phenomenological knowledge is *what the experience means for the person*, not what the experience means for the assessor or for people in general.

Phenomenological personality assessment requires empathy—understanding a person's experiences in terms of what they mean for that person. To empathize with another, one must abandon one's connotations of the words and phrases the other person uses, one's interpretation of the experiences, and one's preconceived ideas about such experiences. Instead, one attempts to grasp the idiosyncratic meaning of the other person's verbal descriptions of the experience. (We will have more to say about empathy in Chapter 14.)

Phenomenological assessment focuses on the present, often on the here-and-now. An individual's past experiences are important only insofar as they clarify present perceptions. For example, in a Rogerian interview, if a person talked about past experiences, the interviewer would not consider them significant unless they specifically related to present experiences.

Phenomenological personality assessment is relatively straightforward, which contrasts with the largely inferential tack of the psychoanalytic and dispositional strategies. Most phenomenological personality-assessment techniques involve self-report measures. Descriptions of subjective experiences are accepted more or less at face value (Jankowicz, 1987). They are *not* considered signs or indications of some inferred psychological state, such as an intrapsychic conflict. Neither are they used to indicate some underlying personality disposition. The assessment remains on the level of phenomenological knowledge.

Conscious experiences are taken as direct evidence of important personality functions. They are not necessarily viewed as indicators of underlying unconscious processes. A basic assumption of the phenomenological strategy is that people are generally aware of their subjective experiences. In fact, this awareness is presumed to guide behavior. Although not denying the existence of experiences outside awareness, phenomenologists believe unconscious processes have little influence on normal behavior. However, unconscious processes are assumed to play a greater role in abnormal behavior.

■ *Demonstration 13-2:*
PERCEIVING FROM ANOTHER'S INTERNAL FRAME OF REFERENCE

In this Demonstration you will attempt to understand another person's subjective experiences. A series of statements made by a 30-year-old man at the beginning of a psychotherapy session follows. Your task is to assume the therapist's role by commenting on the man's statements so that *you let him know that you understand what he is saying from his perspective.* For each of the client's statements, write a sentence or two that meet this goal.

1. "I thought I'd have something to talk about—then it all goes around in circles. I was trying to think of what I was going to say. Then coming here, it doesn't work out. . . . I tell you, it seemed that it would be much easier before I came."

2. "I tell you, I just can't make a decision; I don't know what I want. I've tried to reason this thing out logically—tried to figure out which things are important to me."

3. "I thought that there are maybe two things a man might do; he might get married and raise a family. But if he was just a bachelor, just making a living—that isn't very good."

4. "I find myself and my thoughts getting back to the days when I was a kid, and I cry very easily. The dam would break through."

5. "I was in the army 4½ years. I had no problems then, no hopes, no wishes. My only thought was to get out when peace would come."

Now compare your responses to those in Table 13-1 to see how you did. If you responded from the client's internal frame of reference, your responses would be similar to those in the left-hand column. If you responded from your own external frame of reference, your responses would more closely

Table 13-1
Attitudes and thoughts representing internal and external frames of reference*

INTERNAL FRAME OF REFERENCE	EXTERNAL FRAME OF REFERENCE
1. It's really hard for you to get started.	1. Should I help you get started talking? Is your inability to get underway a type of dependence?
2. Decision making just seems impossible to you.	2. What is the cause of your indecisiveness?
3. You want marriage, but it doesn't seem to you to be much of a possibility.	3. Why are you focusing on marriage and family? You appear to be a bachelor. I didn't know that.
4. You feel yourself brimming over with childish feelings.	4. The crying, the "dam," sounds as though you were repressing a great deal.
5. To you the army represented stagnation.	5. You're a veteran. Were you a psychiatric patient? I feel sorry for anybody who spent 4½ years in the service.

* Statements quoted or paraphrased from *Client-Centered Therapy* by C. R. Rogers, 1965, Boston: Houghton Mifflin, pp. 33–34.

resemble the responses in the right-hand column. The responses in the right-hand column represent an external frame of reference because they "are all attitudes which are basically sympathetic. There is nothing 'wrong' with them. They are even attempts to 'understand,' in the sense of 'understanding about,' rather than 'understanding with.' The locus of perceiving is, however, outside of the client" (Rogers, 1965, p. 33).

PHENOMENOLOGICAL RESEARCH

A majority of research in the phenomenological strategy has employed correlational and case studies. These two methods are optimal for studying people as they are. Rogers' perspective on research is consistent with the existential approach, which is to gain knowledge *of* people rather than from them. Rogers (1973) advocated a research approach that did not view the person as an object (of study) and did not "push the individual into some contrived situation to investigate some hypothesis we have imposed" (p. 380). Instead, he suggested that psychologists study personality by learning from people and by being open to "hearing" what they are "saying."

Phenomenological research is often idiographic, using the case-study method. A prime example is Maslow's large-scale investigation of self-actualizing people, which we will discuss in Chapter 15. The data were detailed, qualitative descriptions of subjective, intensely personal experiences. They yielded rich, in-depth portraits of single personalities. By studying subjects with a particular characteristic, such as self-actualization, the researcher can combine data to produce a composite of that personality characteristic. Thus, what begins as a series of idiographic investigations can also yield nomothetic information applicable to many people.

Phenomenological research is often related to and conducted in conjunction with psychotherapy, much like psychoanalytic research. As clinical psychologists, Rogers and Kelly developed their theories and approaches to personality while actively practicing psychotherapy. Phenomenological approaches also emphasize application of theory to other practical human problems. For example, Rogers' and Kelly's theories have been applied to a vast array of human endeavors besides psychotherapy, including education, politics, health, and environmental planning.

PHENOMENOLOGICAL PERSONALITY CHANGE

Because personality is considered a product of perceptions and subjective evaluations, phenomenological personality change involves modifying these private experiences. Among other things, this means helping people become more aware of their subjective experiences and the influence of these experiences on their behaviors.

Self-determination is a major theme of phenomenological personality-change procedures. It is assumed that people can change their own personalities. Further, clients (as "patients" are called) know themselves and their own subjective experiences far better than anyone else can know them. Therefore, the client, rather than the therapist, must assume responsibility for the change process.

The therapist's major role is to facilitate the client's changing, which requires that the therapist understand the client's experiences from the client's perspective (e.g., Chambers, 1985). The therapist does not judge the client and his or her problems. Nonevaluative support is assumed to facilitate clients' abilities to develop new perspectives and bring about constructive changes in their lives.

In contrast to psychoanalysis, phenomenological personality change devotes little attention to the past. Instead, it is primarily present-oriented. Often the locus of time is here-and-now—in other words, what is going on in the therapy session is the topic worked on during the session. This includes all of a client's thoughts and feelings during the therapy hour, as well as the interactions between the client and the therapist.

SUMMARY

1. The phenomenological strategy is based on the idea that the reality of events rests solely on the way they are perceived. Thus, the same objective event may be perceived and/or interpreted in subjectively different ways. Individuals' subjective experiences (internal frames of reference) make up their personalities and determine their feelings and actions.

2. The phenomenological strategy's interest in subjective knowledge is problematic for a scientific study of personality that emphasizes objective knowledge. Phenomenologists deal with this problem by attempting to gain an understanding of a person's views of events (phenomenological knowledge).

3. The theories of Rogers, Maslow, and Kelly illustrate the phenomenological strategy and share a number of features. They deal with "higher" human functions; view people as active beings who are constantly changing; focus on the present, often on immediate experience (here-and-now), and the future; are holistic in that they view personality as consistent and as involving an interrelationship among its various aspects; and subscribe to an idiographic approach.

4. The phenomenological strategy is related to existential psychology in that it emphasizes free will, choice, and "being there."

5. Phenomenological personality assessment requires gaining access to private, subjective experiences, primarily through self-report measures. The assessor attempts to understand the individual's experiences from that person's perspective (empathy). The focus is on present, often here-and-now, conscious experiences.

6. Consistent with an interest in subjective experience, phenomenological research is often idiographic and primarily uses correlational and case studies. The research is frequently related to psychotherapy.

7. Phenomenological personality change involves modifying subjective experience. It is primarily present-oriented, and clients are given major responsibility for change.

Chapter Fourteen

Rogers' Self-Actualization Theory

Carl Rogers
(1902-1987)
believed that people have unique, innate self-actualizing tendencies that guide their behaviors in positive directions.
Courtesy of Carl Rogers

E ach of us has a unique potential to develop, grow, and change in healthy and positive directions. That potential will guide all of our behaviors if we are free of external influences or constraints. This central theme, known as the *principle of self-actualization,* guided Carl Rogers' theorizing, research, and therapy for more than 50 years (Gendlin, 1988; Rogers, 1974).

When Rogers began his work in 1927, personality psychology was essentially the psychoanalytic strategy. Rogers proposed the first theory that was a comprehensive alternative to psychoanalysis. In contrast to the deterministic and pessimistic perspective of psychoanalysis, Rogers' theory offered an optimistic outlook on humans' ability to develop and enhance themselves in positive and healthy ways.

Although many differences between the theories of Rogers and Freud exist, some interesting parallels also can be drawn. Like Freud, Rogers began as a psychotherapist. Rogers used his experiences in therapy both as a source of ideas about personality and as a setting for testing, refining, and revising them. Rogers developed a new form of personality change that became the first significant alternative to psychoanalytic psychotherapy. Rogers' theory was comprehensive and innovative, as was Freud's. Finally, Rogers' ideas, like Freud's, have been widely adopted and applied to diverse human problems, including interpersonal relations, education, and the development and survival of cultures.

NORMAL PERSONALITY DEVELOPMENT AND FUNCTIONING

Rogers' personality theory is based on two major assumptions: (1) behavior is guided by each person's unique self-actualizing tendency, and (2) all humans have a need for positive regard. First, we will examine these concepts in terms of normal personality development and functioning. Then we will look at how they can become distorted and result in abnormal behavior.

The Actualizing Tendency

Rogers believed that personality is governed by an inborn **actualizing tendency**: "the inherent tendency of the organism to develop all its capacities in ways which serve to maintain or enhance the organism" (Rogers, 1959, p. 196). The actualizing tendency affects both biological and psychological functions. It maintains an individual by meeting fundamental biological needs (e.g., for oxygen and food); it also governs physical maturation and regeneration. Psychologically, the actualizing tendency guides people toward increased autonomy and self-sufficiency, expands their experiences, and fosters personal growth. Thus, the actualizing tendency guides us toward positive or healthful behaviors rather than toward negative or unhealthful behaviors (e.g., Bozarth & Brodley, 1991). In Rogers' (1980) words,

the organism does not tend toward developing its capacity for nausea, . . . for self-destruction, nor . . . to bear pain. Only under unusual or perverse circumstances do these potentialities become actualized. It is clear that *the actualizing tendency is selective and directional — a constructive tendency* [italics added] (p. 121).

How does the actualizing tendency lead people to act in positive ways? According to Rogers, individuals evaluate each experience they have in terms of how well it maintains or enhances them—a process called the **organismic valuing process**. Experiences include all that is going on at a given moment that the person can potentially be aware of (Rogers, 1959). Experiences perceived as maintaining or enhancing the individual are evaluated positively; they result in feelings of satisfaction, and people actively seek them. In contrast, experiences perceived as opposing maintenance or enhancement are evaluated negatively; they result in dissatisfaction, and people actively avoid them.

The actualizing tendency can be thought of as having two aspects. One aspect consists of *shared* biological tendencies—inclinations that result in behaviors that keep us alive. The other aspect involves each individual's *unique* tendencies toward increased autonomy, self-sufficiency, and personal growth (cf. DeCarvalho, 1990a). The unique aspect is called **self-actualization** because it involves maintenance and enhancement of the self, a central concept in Rogers' theory (cf. Ford, 1991b).

The Self **Self** or **self-concept** (the terms are synonymous) is a theoretical construct that refers the ways in which people see themselves (Rogers, 1959). The self-perceptions that comprise the self (1) are *organized* in a unified, orderly fashion; (2) are *consistent* or compatible with one another; and (3) go together to make up a *whole* rather than merely being a set of unrelated aspects (e.g., Jensen, Huber, Cundick, & Carlson, 1991).

Rogers emphasized the importance of consistency of self-perceptions for normal personality functioning. When our self-perceptions conflict with one another, we must somehow reconcile them so the self can remain a consistent whole. One way to do this is to compartmentalize the conflicting self-perceptions, such as by making them relevant to different aspects of one's life. As an example, one of the authors of this book thinks of himself as being both organized and disorganized. He sees himself as organized in terms of ideas but disorganized with respect to belongings (you'd agree if you saw his office, and you have on p. 64).

Because the self is made up of many interrelated aspects of self-knowledge, it would be more accurate to refer to a person's *selves* or self-concepts, although the singular usage is more common (e.g., Neisser, 1988, 1991). Among the dimensions of the self that have been suggested are self-esteem, positive self-regard, moral self-concept, self-confidence, self-reliance, self-control, selfishness, self-disclosure, self-as-agent, self-critical, self-identity, and self-reflection (Jensen et al., 1991).

Rogers divided the self into two basic aspects. The **actual self** (sometimes called *real self*) refers to the way people actually see themselves. The **ideal self** refers to how people would like to see themselves.

Other theorists have made finer distinctions. For example, Wylie (1968) first divided the generic self-concept into actual and ideal (Figure 14-1). Next, each of these subdivisions are further divided into (1) private aspects—how one sees oneself (*private self-concept*) and would like to see

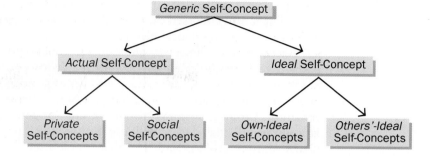

Figure 14-1
Wylie's division of the
self-concept.
Source: Adapted from
Wylie, 1968

oneself (*social self-concept*)—and (2) public aspects—how one presents oneself to others (*own-ideal self-concepts*) or thinks others would like one to be (*others'-ideal self-concepts*).

Life Satisfaction and the Self-Concept

Not surprisingly, people with psychological problems see themselves (actual self) differently from the way they would like to see themselves (ideal self), especially in terms of satisfaction with life or happiness (cf. Csikszentmihalyi, 1990). In Western societies, life satisfaction is evaluated in terms of the degree to which one achieves ideals. Traditionally, the similarity between a person's actual self-concept and ideal self-concept has been used as an index of life satisfaction. The more similar they are, the more satisfied people feel about themselves.

Another measure of personal satisfaction has recently been proposed. Ogilvie (1987, 1988) suggested looking at the discrepancy between one's actual self-concept—how one sees oneself—and one's *undesirable self-concept*—the personality characteristics and behaviors that one considers undesirable in oneself (see also Paprota, 1988). The greater the difference between the actual and undesirable self-concepts, the more satisfied people would feel about themselves.

In a study with college students, Ogilvie (1987) found that life satisfaction can be predicted better by the discrepancy between actual and undesired self-concepts than by the similarity between actual and ideal self-concepts. Ogilvie suggested that this finding may indicate that "the implicit standard individuals use to assess their well-being is how close (or how distant) they are from subjectively being like their most negative images of themselves" (p. 383). The reason that life satisfaction may not be predicted as well from comparing actual and ideal self-concepts (as has been thought) may be explained by reconceptualizing the actual self.

Actual Self-Concept: A Reconceptualization

The idea that healthy psychological adjustment depends on accurate perception of one's self has been around a long time. "Know thyself," which implies accurate knowledge, has been recommended for centuries by philosophers, theologians, and sages (Brown, 1991). More recently, personality theorists including Freud (1957; Sackeim, 1983), Erikson (1950),

Fromm (1955), and Allport (1943), as well as Rogers (1951) and Maslow (1950), have also endorsed the importance of undistorted self-knowledge as important for psychological health.

Recent studies, however, question the traditional wisdom about self-knowledge. It appears that most people have a pervasive tendency to evaluate the self and their world more favorably than is justified (e.g., Brown, 1991; Dunning, Meyerowitz, & Holzberg, 1989; Taylor & Brown, 1988). Generally, people's portraits of the self are "brighter, more colorful, and more beautiful" than they actually are (Brown, 1991, p. 173). The good news is that research evidence indicates that people's self-enhancing illusions are "associated with, and may contribute to, psychological adjustment and superior functioning" (Brown, 1991, p. 173). Self-enhancing illusions seem to be most effective when they are only slightly more positive than can be reasonably justified (Baumeister, 1989). Estimates of one's abilities or attributes that are either overly grandiose or excessively modest are likely to result in poor psychological adjustment and functioning.

The findings on self-evaluation call into question the usual distinction between one's actual self and ideal self. The actual self may, in fact, be closer to the ideal self than has been previously assumed. A better term for the actual self, then, would be the *perceived self*.

The high prevalence of self-enhancing illusions means that we engage in considerable self-deception—albeit with apparently healthy consequences. Yet, few people are aware of their self-deception, and they certainly would not want to admit it. How do we maintain our self-enhancing illusions and associated self-deception so easily? The answer lies in the host of strategies we use to avoid, cope with, and deal with negative feedback (Brown, 1991).

As a first line of defense, we engage in behavioral strategies to maximize our exposure to positive feedback and minimize our exposure to negative feedback. For instance, teenagers are more likely than adults to ask peers about the suitability of the clothes they wear.

When it is not possible to avoid negative feedback, we employ cognitive strategies to cope with the inevitable negative feedback we receive. These strategies involve selectively attending to, remembering, interpreting, and explaining the negative feedback. A student who gets back a term paper with mainly negative comments may (1) glance over the negative comments quickly but read the positive comments several times; (2) remember only the positive comments; (3) interpret any negative comments that are ambiguous as "backward compliments"; or (4) attribute the negative comments to the professor's critical nature.

Finally, when negative feedback is unavoidable and too blatant to be ignored, we resort to strategies that minimize the damage to our overall sense of worth. We may, for example, belittle the value of a skill that we know we are lacking (e.g., "I don't need to be good at math to be a musician"). Another "damage control" strategy involves downward social comparison. For example, women who have breast cancer often compare their condition to women who have more serious diseases (Wood, Taylor, & Lichtman, 1985).

The Q-sort: Assessing the Self

The **Q-sort** is standardized assessment procedure of the self-concept. It entails making comparative judgments of statements about one's self (e.g., "I am lazy"; "I don't like to be with other individuals"). The statements are printed on cards, and people place the cards in piles according to how characteristic each statement is for themselves—that is, based on the degree to which the statements fit their self-concepts. Usually, the number of statements per pile is specified (Figure 14-2). Both a person's actual self-concept and ideal self-concept can be assessed by the Q-sort. With an **actual-self sort** the instructions are to "sort the statements in terms of how you actually see yourself." For an **ideal-self sort** the instructions are to "sort the statements in terms of how you would like to see yourself."

A single Q-sort can be used to assess a person's self-concept at a given point in time. Multiple Q-sorts can assess how the self-concept changes over time, as well as the relationship between a person's actual self and ideal self. For example, to assess the effectiveness of psychotherapy, Rogers (1961; Rogers & Dymond, 1954) had clients do actual-self and ideal-self sorts before, during, and after therapy to measure changes.

Figure 14-3 shows changes that occurred for a 40-year-old female client whom Rogers (1961) described as being very unhappy in her marriage and as "deeply troubled." At the beginning of therapy, there was a low correlation (.21) between the client's ideal (*I1*) and actual (*A1*) self-sorts—simply put, she did not like herself very much. Her actual self-concept became more like her ideal self-concept over the course of therapy

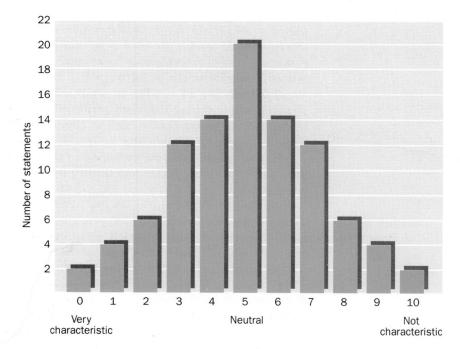

Figure 14-2
Example of the distribution of self-referent statements in a Q-sort. Subjects must sort the statements so that the specified number is put in each pile.

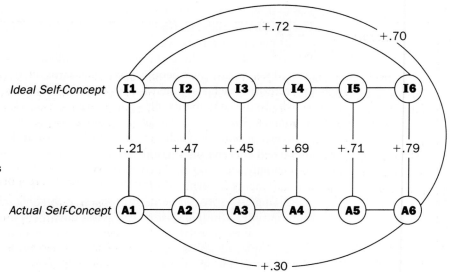

Figure 14-3
The changes in a client's actual and ideal self-concepts before, during, and after therapy.
Source: Adapted from Rogers, 1961.

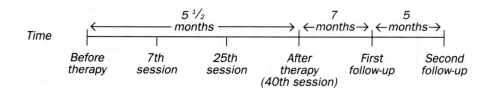

$(A2\text{-}I2 = .47; A3\text{-}I3 = .45; A4\text{-}I4 = .69)$, and this trend continued after therapy $(A5\text{-}I5 = .69; A6\text{-}I6 = .79)$. Further, the woman's actual self-concept changed considerably over time, which is evidenced in the relatively weak correlation between the first and last assessment of her actual self sort $(A1\text{-}A6 = .30)$. In contrast, her ideal self-concept remained relatively stable during that time period $(I1\text{-}I6 = .72)$. Finally, note that in the end the woman saw herself as close to the person she had wanted to be originally $(A6\text{-}I1 = .70)$.

Having talked about the usefulness of the Q-sort technique, you might like to try one yourself. Demonstration 14-1 will take 10 to 15 minutes to complete.

Positive Regard: A Basic Need

The second major assumption in Rogers' theory is that all people have a need for positive regard. **Positive regard** is a generic term for acceptance, respect, sympathy, warmth, and love. Rogers believed that positive regard is essential for the healthy development of the self (e.g., Raskin, Novacek, & Hogan, 1991), as well as for successful interpersonal relations (e.g., Lutfiyya, 1991). For example, children raised by parents with significant psychological problems, such as alcoholism, are likely to receive less positive regard from their parents (Jones & Houts, 1992). In turn, the lack of positive regard may contribute to adult children of parents with alcoholism having problems

■ *Demonstration 14-1*
SORTING YOUR VALUES

To see firsthand how the Q-sort works, this Demonstration provides instructions for performing two Q-sorts of some of your personal values at two points in your life. Each Q-sort will reveal the relative strength, for you, of the values sampled. Comparing the two Q-sorts will indicate differences in how you have prioritized the values at periods of your life.

PREPARATION

1. Go to the Demonstration Materials section at the back of the book and remove the three pages containing materials for Demonstration 14-1. On the first two pages, cut out: (1) the 16 statements about personal values (listed in Table 14-1); (2) the seven pile headings (listed in Table 14-2); and (3) the three broad agreement categories. You will use Recording Sheet 14-1 (Figure 14-4) later.

FIRST Q-SORT

2. First, divide the 16 statements into three broad categories according to how you feel about each statement at this point in your life: (1) definitely agree, (2) definitely disagree, and (3) ambivalent. On a flat surface, lay out the slips of paper with these category names. Place each of the 16 statement slips of paper in one of the three categories.

Table 14-1

List of values for Q-sort in Demonstration 14-1

1. I like to study.
2. I prefer socializing with people my own age.
3. I like to be successful.
4. I believe in God.
5. I dislike crude language.
6. I take good care of my body.
7. I am sensitive to other people's needs.
8. I think it is okay to get drunk occasionally.
9. I prefer to save money rather than spend it.
10. I am concerned with how I look.
11. My appearance is important to me.
12. I enjoy being alone.
13. I have high standards for my work.
14. I think it is important to obey the law.
15. My family is important to me.
16. I like meeting new people.

Table 14-2

Piles for Q-sort in Demonstration 14-1

PILE	DEGREE OF AGREEMENT	REQUIRED NUMBER IN EACH PILE	RANK
1	Strongly agree	1	1.0
2	Moderately agree	2	2.5
3	Slightly agree	3	5.0
4	Ambivalent (neutral)	4	8.5
5	Slightly disagree	3	12.0
6	Moderately disagree	2	14.5
7	Strongly disagree	1	16.0

Attitude number	First sort rank	Second sort rank	Difference	Difference squared
1				
2				
3				
4				
5				
6				
7				
8				
9				
10				
11				
12				
13				
14				
15				
16				
Sum of difference squared =				

Figure 14-4
Sample recording sheet for Q-sort in Demonstration 14-1.

3. The actual Q-sort involves sorting or categorizing the statements on the 7-point scale. Place the 7 pile headings in numerical order (from left to right), thereby forming a 7-point scale. Start with the "definitely agree" category. Place each statement in the appropriate pile. Be sure you do not exceed the number of statements required for each pile. Repeat the procedure with the "definitely disagree" category and then with the "ambivalent" category.

4. Check each pile to make sure that it contains the correct number of statements and that you have placed each statement in the pile you think is appropriate.

5. Next, assign a rank order to each of the statements (from agree most with to agree least with). All statements in the same pile receive the same ranking, which is written on the pile number slips of paper and also in the last column of Table 14-2. On the recording sheet, write the rank of each statement in the column designated "First Sort Rank."

By examining the Q-sort you have just produced, you can get a sense of some of your present values, just as a therapist can gain some understanding of a client's self-concept by looking at the client's Q-sort of self-referent statements.

SECOND Q-SORT
6. To have a comparison Q-sort, repeat steps 2 through 5, but now sort the value statements as you would have done *10 years ago*. Record the rank of each statement in the column designated "Second Sort Rank" on the recording sheet.

COMPARISON OF Q-SORTS
7. You are now ready to compare the two Q-sorts. Although this can be done by visual inspection alone, correlating the rankings of the value statements on the two sorts is a more precise and potentially more meaningful method of comparison. The correlation can be easily computed by using the rank-order correlation method, outlined in simple, step-by-step fashion as follows:

a. For each pair of ranks (i.e., for each statement), calculate the difference between the ranks. (The smaller number can be subtracted from the larger, disregarding the algebraic sign, because the difference will be squared.) Record the differences in the "Difference" column on your recording sheet.

b. Square each difference and record the squared differences in the last column of the recording sheet.

c. Add all the squared differences found in Step **b**.

d. Multiply the sum obtained in Step **c** by 6.

e. Divide the product obtained in Step **d** by 4080.

f. Subtract the quotient obtained in Step **e**

from 1.00. The resulting number is the rank-order correlation coefficient, designated by the Greek letter *rho*.*

If *rho* is positive, your values tapped in this Demonstration have tended to remain the same. The closer *rho* is to $+1.00$, the greater is the similarity between your values in the two sorts. If *rho* is negative, then your values tend to be different from those you had in the past. The closer *rho* is to -1.00, the more dissimilar your present values are from your past values.

---

*Lest the reader think that the steps in calculating the rank-order correlation coefficient (*rho*) have been magically rather than mathematically determined, the formula is:

$$rho = 1 - \frac{6\Sigma d^2}{N(N^2 - 1)}$$

where d = differences in ranks of each pair and N = number of pairs of ranks (in the present example $N = 16$).

---

with assertive behavior and intimacy–trust issues (Black, Bucky, & Wilder-Padilla, 1986).

For infants and young children, positive regard comes exclusively from parents, older children, and other adults—that is, **positive regard from others**.* As children develop more autonomy and a sense of self, they are able to provide positive regard for themselves. This **positive *self*-regard** is, in large part, modeled after the positive regard from others one has received (Figure 14-5). Thus, the more positive regard from others one receives, the more likely children and adults will experience positive self-regard. Rogers thought that the need for positive regard is probably learned, rather than being inborn. Whatever its origin, the need for positive regard is a powerful motivator.

Positive regard is reciprocal. When an individual gives another person positive regard, he or she automatically receives it as well (somewhat like the popular idea that to get love one must give love).

Most often, one receives and gives positive regard for specific behaviors, which is called **conditional positive regard**. It is based on what the person does—in other words, it is conditional. For example, you receive conditional positive regard whenever you are praised for doing something well.

Unconditional Positive Regard

Positive regard need not be conditional. **Unconditional positive regard** can also be given independently of the worth or value placed on anything the

---

*The term *positive regard* is ambiguously used by Rogers and others to refer to both the generic concept of positive regard and positive regard from others. For clarity, we will use the term *positive regard* (all forms of positive regard) and *positive regard from others*.

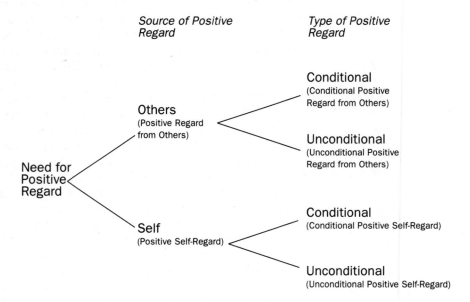

Figure 14-5
The need for positive re-
gard can be met by
others or by oneself.
Both sources of positive
regard can be condi-
tional or unconditional.

person does. The person is valued because he or she is entitled to positive regard as a human being and not for any specific behaviors.

Unconditional positive regard provides an optimal state for being guided by one's self-actualizing tendency. In the absence of judgments about one's actions, how one behaves can be governed solely by the self-actualizing tendency. One retrospective study in Sweden found that men and women's self-esteem in adulthood was positively related to perceiving unconditional positive regard as children, especially from their fathers (Forsman, 1989). In contrast, conditional positive regard, which involves value judgments, usually interferes with the self-actualizing tendency.

Unconditional positive regard can come from others or from oneself. **Unconditional positive regard from others** is the model for **unconditional positive *self*-regard.** Unconditional positive self-regard is most important because the individual relies on herself or himself rather than on others for overall feelings of worth and esteem.

The prototype of unconditional positive regard is the ideal of parents' love for a child, in which they accept their child "because it is . . . their child, not because the child has fulfilled any specific condition, or lived up to any specific expectation" (Fromm, 1963, p. 35). Fromm (1963), in *The Art of Loving,* speaks of *motherly love* as unconditional love and *fatherly love* as conditional love. These definitions are consistent with Western cultural stereotypes of the roles mothers and fathers play (e.g., Wagner, 1988). However, Fromm's concept of motherly love is not restricted to mothers; it refers to a type of love that can be given by anyone. Similarly, fatherly love is not restricted to fathers.

Unconditional positive regard involves valuing all of what a person does equally. To put it another way, a person's actions are not evaluated as positive or negative in any objective sense. All of a person's actions are part of the person, and unconditional positive regard involves *accepting a person as a whole, worthwhile individual* (cf. Jaison, 1991; Spiegler, 1991). To provide such unconditional positive regard, you need not approve of the person's actions—that is, they may be undesirable from *your* perspective (e.g., E. O'Leary, 1989). However, offering unconditional positive regard requires viewing another's actions from the *other person's* perspective. Thus, the parent who disapproves of a child's misbehavior can still give the child unconditional positive regard. In effect, the parent is saying, "I do not approve of what you did, but I approve of you."

How prevalent is unconditional positive regard? In your own life, how often are you regarded positively by others regardless of how you act? How often do you give other people unconditional positive regard? Unconditional positive regard is the exception rather than the rule (e.g., Culp, Culp, Osofsky, & Osofsky, 1991). It may be that we can receive unconditional positive regard only from our parents and from ourselves. Of course, most parents rarely, if ever, provide such a gift to their children (e.g., Gaylin, 1987), and most people probably are reluctant to provide it for themselves.

Child-Rearing Practices That Foster Creativity

Rogers (1954) theorized that parents can foster creativity in their children by establishing two basic conditions: psychological safety and psychological freedom. *Psychological safety* requires a social environment that provides (1) unconditional positive regard (Ford & Harris, 1990), (2) an absence of evaluation from others, and (3) empathy. *Psychological freedom* exists when permission is given to engage in unrestricted creative expression.

These theoretical ideas were tested as part of an ongoing longitudinal study of personality and intellectual development (Harrington, Block, & Block, 1987). The study involved 106 boys and girls who had been studied for 10 years, beginning between the ages of 3½ and 4½. When the children entered the study, their mothers and fathers were independently asked to describe their child-rearing attitudes and practices. The researchers translated Rogers' ideas about creativity-fostering environments into concrete child-rearing practices (Table 14-3). Judges rated the parents' preschool child-rearing descriptions to determine how well they fit with Rogers' proposed conditions for fostering creativity. The judges' ratings were positively correlated (+.38 to +.49) with measures of the children's creative potential when they were early adolescents. The results provide some support for Rogers' (1954) suggestion that children who are reared in an atmosphere of psychological safety and freedom will develop their creative potential more than children who are not provided with such an environment (Harrington et al., 1987; cf. Runco, Ebersole, & Mraz, 1991).

Conditions of Worth

In our everyday lives, the conditional positive regard we receive is usually based on *external* standards, rather than being guided by the individual's unique self-actualizing tendency. Such conditional positive regard is less

Table 14-3

Rogers' ideas about creativity-fostering environments translated into concrete child-rearing practices

CONCRETE CHILD-REARING PRACTICES JUDGED *MOST* TYPICAL OF ROGERS' CREATIVITY-FOSTERING ENVIRONMENT

I respect my child's opinions and encourage him or her to express them.

I feel a child should have time to think, daydream, and even loaf.

I let my child make many decisions for himself or herself.

My child and I have warm, intimate times together.

I encourage my child to be curious, to explore and question things.

I make sure my child knows I appreciate what he or she tries or accomplishes.

CONCRETE CHILD-REARING PRACTICES JUDGED *LEAST* TYPICAL OF ROGERS' CREATIVITY-FOSTERING ENVIRONMENT

I teach my child that in one way or another punishment will find him or her when he or she is bad.

I do not allow my child to get angry with me.

I try to keep my child away from children or families who have different ideas or values from our own.

I believe that a child should be seen and not heard.

I feel my child is a bit of a disappointment to me.

I do not allow my child to question my decisions.

Source: Adapted from Harrington, D. M., Block, J., & Block, J. H. (1987). Testing aspects of Carl Rogers' theory of creative environments: Child-rearing antecedents of creative potential in young adolescents. *Journal of Personality and Social Psychology, 52,* 851–856.

likely to maintain and enhance an individual than unconditional positive regard. Nonetheless, our need for positive regard is extremely powerful, and we will seek it in any form available. (Think about how important it is for you to feel that others consider you worthy and that you respect yourself.)

We are also influenced by the opposite of conditional positive regard — the criticism, scorn, and punishment (from other people and ourselves) for our behaviors that are judged to be undesirable according to external standards. Such evaluations might be called *conditional negative regard* (although Rogers never used that term). We tend to avoid acting in ways that result in "conditional negative regard," just as we engage in behaviors that result in conditional positive regard. The values placed on a person's specific behaviors, independent of whether they maintain or enhance the person, are called **conditions of worth**. Conditions of worth are made up of conditional positive regard and "conditional negative regard."

Conditions of worth are an inevitable part of living. It is difficult to conceive of others' regarding each of a person's behaviors equally, just as it is highly unlikely that anyone values all of his or her own behaviors equally—at least on a consistent basis.

Conditions of worth result in a person feeling prized in some respects and not prized in other respects (Rogers, 1959). Further, conditions of worth substitute for and interfere with the organismic valuing process (which is guided by one's unique self-actualizing tendency). Thus, conditions of worth, which are based on external standards, often prevent us from functioning freely and with maximum effectiveness. Nature is being tampered with, so to speak.

DISRUPTION OF NORMAL PERSONALITY DEVELOPMENT AND FUNCTIONING: IMPEDIMENTS TO SELF-ACTUALIZATION

Psychological adjustment depends on the extent to which the self-actualizing tendency, rather than conditions of worth, serves as a guide for a person's behaviors. Psychological disorders develop when conditions of worth predominate. Optimal personality functioning would occur if the self were governed exclusively by the organismic valuing process. This would mean that the person's experiences are being evaluated only in terms how well they maintain and enhance the individual. If these conditions prevailed, the self would remain consistent and whole because a single "set of rules"—based on one's self-actualizing tendency—is being applied to evaluate experiences. Unfortunately, such ideal circumstances exist in theory only.

Threat

In the normal course of personality development, conflict arises because experiences are evaluated by two sets of rules. One set of rules is based on the organismic valuing process. The other set comes from conditions of worth that have become part of the self because positive regard becomes important to the individual. Conflict inevitably arises between an individual's self-concept and experiences. For instance, failing an exam would be in conflict with the self-concept of being a competent student. Conflict occurs because externally imposed values from conditions of worth differ from internally imposed values from the organismic valuing process. This kind of conflict threatens to fragment the self.

Rogers (1959) defined **threat** as the perception—conscious or unconscious—that there is some incongruity between an experience and one's self-concept. The conflict is threatening because the individual's personality may not remain a consistent whole and continue to be regulated by a single standard (the organismic valuing process). Rogers (1959) described this as

the basic estrangement in man. He has not been true to himself, to his own natural organismic valuing of experience, but for the sake of preserving the positive regard of others has now come to falsify some of the values he experiences and to perceive them only in terms based upon their value to others. Yet this has not been a conscious choice, but a natural—and tragic—development.... [In contrast], the path of development toward psychological maturity, the path of therapy, is the undoing of this estrangement in man's functioning, the dissolving of conditions of worth, the achievement of a self which is congruent with experience, and the restoration of a unified organismic valuing process as the regulator of behavior. (pp. 226–227)

Threat is experienced as a vague uneasiness and tension — in other words, as anxiety. Anxiety serves as a warning that the unified self-concept is in danger of being disorganized. The anxiety, in turn, leads to defensive processes that reduce the incongruity between one's self and one's experiences.

Defensive Processes

Defensive processes maintain consistency within one's personality. Rogers (1959) divided defensive processes into two categories: perceptual distortion and denial. Through **perceptual distortion**, we change (distort) our perceptions of threatening experiences to make them compatible with our self-concepts. For example, 15-year-old Grace considered herself popular, but she complained that no one asked her to do things on weekends. Grace explained this apparent inconsistency by telling herself that her peers don't invite her because they think she must be busy on weekends (because she is so popular). This explanation became Grace's perception of the situation — that is, her reality. From the phenomenological perspective, an experience is the person's perception of it. Perceptual distortion changes the experience itself.

Denial, the second category of defensive process, prevents us from becoming aware of the experiences that are incongruent with our self-concepts. In one way or another, the self is "convinced" that the experience does not exist. Grace could have denied her threatening experiences — not being asked to do things by her friends — by believing that her friends invited her, but that she chose not to accept. Phenomenologically, if you deny the experience, it does not exist.

Examples of the defensive processes that result from perceptual distortion and denial, separately and in combination, are presented in Table 14-4. The table also indicates parallel psychoanalytic ego defense mechanisms. The two theoretical perspectives posit quite different sources of threat and anxiety: sexual and aggressive impulses in psychoanalysis versus experiences that are incompatible with one's self-concept in Rogers' theory. Still, the basic ways people defend themselves appear to be similar (cf. Zhurbin, 1991).

Breakdown and Disorganization

Psychologically well-adjusted people generally perceive themselves and their environment as other people do. This statement may seem paradoxical, given the phenomenological emphasis on subjective reality. However, psychological adjustment is a social phenomenon; it requires dealing successfully with an environment that involves other people. Thus, psychological adjustment requires correspondence between subjective experience and external reality.

Even the most psychologically well-adjusted individuals are occasionally threatened by experiences that are inconsistent with their self-concepts. When this happens, their defensive processes keep them from becoming totally aware of the inconsistency.

Table 14-4

Examples of defensive processes resulting from perceptual distortion and denial and their parallel with ego defense mechanisms as noted in parentheses

---

Situation: A wealthy man who spends 12 to 14 hours every day working at his job views himself as being a devoted husband and father.

PERCEPTUAL DISTORTION

"I have to work so hard to provide for my family's needs." (*Rationalization*)

"I am always doing things with my family." (*Fantasy*)

PERCEPTUAL DISTORTION AND DENIAL

"I spend so much time with my family that I am neglecting my work." (*Reaction formation*)

"I think it is horrible that some men work so hard that they have no time for their families." (*Projection*)

DENIAL

"I spend as much time with my family as I do at work." (*Denial*)

The man is totally unaware of how little time he spends with his family. (*Repression*)

However, when the inconsistency between self and experience becomes too great, the individual's defenses may be incapable of distorting or denying the experience. In this defenseless state, the person becomes fully aware of the threatening incongruent experience, and the self-concept becomes fragmented, instead of remaining whole.

The behaviors of a person whose self-concept is fragmented often seem strange to others because they are "not like the person." However, the seemingly out-of-character behaviors may actually be congruent with experiences the individual was never fully aware of because they had been distorted or denied. The behaviors are odd only insofar as they are incongruent with how the person is seen by others. Consider the example of Sonia, a woman who had denied her tendencies to express her independence and had always put her family's needs first during her 20 years of marriage. Recently Sonia began to do more things for herself and on her own. Sonia's family found this new behavior strange and thought that it was alien to her personality. From her family's perspective, the woman was a different person. In fact, Sonia's behavior was consistent with her personality, albeit an aspect of which she, and they, had been unaware.

Personality disorganization can occur because the person, behaving in "uncharacteristic" ways, feels that she or he is not understood. There is no consensual validation (affirmation from other people) for the person's view of the world. Rogers (1980) explains that when a person tries to share something that is very personal with another individual and it is not received and not understood, this is a very deflating and a very lonely experience. I have come to believe that such an experience makes some individuals psychotic. It causes them to give up hoping that anyone can understand them. Once they have lost that hope, then their own inner world, which becomes more and more bizarre, is the only place where they can live. They can no longer live in any shared human experience. I can sympathize with them because I know that when I try to share some feeling aspect of myself which is private, precious, and tentative, and when this communication is met by evaluation, by reassurance, by distortion of my meaning, my very strong reaction is, "Oh, what's the use!" At such a time, one knows what it is to be alone. (p. 14)

Reintegration   We all know people whom we would describe as "uptight" or "always on the defensive." Such colloquial descriptions usually refer to individuals who constantly appear to distort or deny their experiences. Their behaviors illustrate the potential negative consequences of defensive processes. For example, Joan questions the meaning and sincerity of even the most innocent comments made by others. She is quick to respond as if the comments were negative. From her internal frame of reference, the innocent remarks are negative because she perceives them in a distorted form.

Edvard Munch's "The Scream" (1895) depicts he utter despair that occurs when, according to Rogers, total personality disorganization occurs.
Art Resource/Archive Foto Marburg

People who inaccurately perceive experiences are not able to function fully. They are closed to (defended against) many experiences because they must avoid potentially threatening aspects of life. Consider the case of a college senior, Jeff, whose self-concept included only the perception of himself as successful. He was threatened by any situation in which he might fail. Jeff distorted his view of such situations from ones that could lead to failure to ones that were undesirable. He thereby successfully avoided potential failures. Rather than apply to graduate school, Jeff "decided" he could do just as well with a B.A. He "reasoned" that he might as well be making money while his friends in graduate school were taking out loans.

Discrepancies between one's self-concept and experiences, such as Jeff encountered, can be reduced by a process of reintegration within the personality. **Reintegration** restores consistency to the self-concept by reversing the process of defense. Reintegration involves the individual becoming aware of previously distorted or denied experiences. For example, reintegration for Jeff could mean realizing that he might not be admitted to graduate school. Jeff could make this possibility acceptable by integrating it into his self-concept. His self-concept would then include the idea: "It is not necessary for me to succeed at everything I try." This reintegration would make him less likely to be threatened by situations at which he could potentially fail.

Rogers believed that we can face minor, inconsistent experiences and restructure our self-concept to reintegrate them. All that is required is an *absence of threat*. For example,

> the child who feels that he is weak and powerless to do a certain task, to build a tower or repair a bicycle, may find, as he works rather hopelessly at the task, that he is successful. This experience is inconsistent with the concept he holds of himself, and may not be integrated at once; but if the child is left to himself he gradually assimilates, upon his own initiative, a revision of his concept of self, that while he is generally weak and powerless, in this respect he has ability. This is the normal way in which, free from threat, new perceptions are assimilated. But if this same child is repeatedly told by his parents that he is competent to do the task, he is likely to deny it, and to prove by his behavior that he is unable to do it. The more forceful intrusion of the notion of his competence constitutes more of a threat to self and is more forcefully resisted. (Rogers, 1965, p. 519)

Rogers (1965) maintained that reintegration on one's own (in the absence of threat) is possible only when the inconsistency between the self and experience is minor. When the inconsistency is great, reintegration requires a relationship with another person who provides acceptance in the form of unconditional positive regard. Such a relationship is the core of client-centered therapy.

CLIENT-CENTERED THERAPY Rogers' theory of personality was both a reaction to and a radical departure from psychoanalysis. The same is true for Rogers' (1942, 1965) innovative psychotherapy, **client-centered therapy**. It was the first major alternative to psychoanalytic psychotherapy, and it is the contribution for which Rogers is best known (e.g., Gendlin, 1988).

The name *client-centered therapy* is consistent with the phenomenological perspective. The therapy is focused (centered) on the person seeking help, the *client*. Therapy deals with the client's unique problems, feelings, perceptions, attitudes, and goals. In short, client-centered therapy proceeds from the client's internal frame of reference. Although one person can never *fully* understand another person's subjective experiences, the therapist tries to learn as much as possible about how the client views his or her particular experiences (Bozarth, 1990).

The essence of client-centered therapy can be seen in Rogers' (1965) choice of the term *client*, which "seems to come closest to conveying the picture of [someone] . . . who comes actively and voluntarily to gain help on a problem, but without any notion of surrendering . . . responsibility for the situation" (p. 7). Note that Rogers assumed that clients were responsible for their behaviors, including solving their own problems (albeit with the help of a therapist). Rogers (1942) originally called his psychotherapy *nondirective therapy* to emphasize that the therapist did not direct the course of therapy (see also Grant, 1990; Hayashi, Kuno, Osawa, Shimizu, & Suetake, 1992).

The Basic Ingredients of Client-Centered Therapy

In a nutshell, client-centered therapy establishes conditions in which the client is able to assume responsibility for making the changes required to deal with the problems that brought the client to therapy (e.g., Bozarth & Brodley, 1991; Bozarth & Shanks, 1989). Rogers believed that the therapist must provide three ingredients for such growth-enhancing conditions to exist.

1. *Empathic understanding.* The therapist attempts to see the client from the client's internal frame of reference, and the client experiences that he or she is being perceived accurately by the therapist.
2. *Unconditional positive regard.* The therapist provides the client with a nonpossessive acceptance and respect no matter what the client is doing or feeling at the time (e.g., Cain, 1990b).
3. *Genuineness or congruence.* The therapist is open or transparent, totally being who she or he is, with no holding back and no facades. Such a self-presentation serves as a model of openness for the client (e.g., Boy, 1990).

Empathic Understanding

Rogers (1975) considered empathy to be the single most potent factor in fostering personality change. Indeed, empathy is a prerequisite for unconditional positive regard. Rogers (1959) explained:

> If I know little or nothing of you, and experience an unconditional positive regard for you, this means little because further knowledge of you may reveal aspects which I cannot so regard. But if I know you thoroughly, knowing and empathically understanding a wide variety of your feelings and behaviors, and still experience an unconditional positive regard, this is very meaningful. It comes close to being fully known and fully accepted. (p. 231)

Empathy also is important in other types of psychotherapy, although its function is different (Bohart, 1991a). For example, psychoanalysts primarily use empathy to gain understanding of the client's unconscious dynamics. In contrast, client-centered therapists primarily use empathy to create a psychological climate that is conducive to reintegration and personal growth (e.g., Bohart, 1991a; Bozarth & Brodley, 1991).

The Process of Client-Centered Therapy

Client-centered therapy creates a nonthreatening situation in which clients feel understood (empathy) and accepted as a whole person (unconditional positive regard). Without conditions of worth, client's behaviors can be guided solely by their organismic valuing processes. Under these special circumstances, clients can safely become aware of and examine experiences that are inconsistent with their self-concepts. How does the therapist create these basic conditions for effective client-centered therapy?

Client-centered therapy involves a verbal interchange between the client and the therapist, focusing on the here-and-now (the client's experiences during the session). The therapist listens to the client and accepts equally and without evaluation all of the client's feelings and behaviors (unconditional positive regard). This is especially important for the host of "negative" feelings and behaviors that clients bring to therapy. Thus, the therapist models what the client should be doing—namely, removing the conditions of worth associated with undesirable aspects of the self and replacing them with unconditional positive self-regard.

The therapist conveys empathy and unconditional positive regard by *reflecting back* to the client what the therapist believes the client is feeling and thinking. To do this, client-centered therapists employ two basic responses (e.g., Essig & Russell, 1990; Mahrer, Nadler, Stalikas, Schachter, & Sterner, 1988). One is **clarification of feelings**, in which the therapist synthesizes or reorganizes the feelings the client has expressed, directly or indirectly. The other is **restatement of content**, in which the therapist rephrases the cognitive or intellectual aspects of what the client has expressed, explicitly or implicitly. The major difference between these two basic responses is whether the focus is on the client's emotions (clarification of feelings) or thoughts (restatement of content). Because the emphasis in client-centered therapy is on the client's feelings, clarification of feelings is considered more important than restatement of content. For either type of response to be empathic, the therapist must experience what the client is relating from the client's internal frame of reference.

Clarification of feelings and restatement of content serve three functions. First, the client learns how she or he is being viewed by the therapist; the client is then able to confirm or correct these views. Second, when the therapist's reflections are accurate, they indicate that therapist is empathizing with the client. Third, the reflections provide the client with a slightly different perspective on the problems at hand—a "stepping back from oneself" phenomenon. (In our daily lives, we often gain insight about our thoughts and feelings when people reflect back to us what we are telling them.)

In the following excerpt from a client-centered therapy session, each of the therapist's comments (numbered in parentheses) is either an example of clarification of feelings or of restatement of content. See whether you can identify the type of response in each case. The client is a 20-year-old college woman whose right hand is malformed.

Client: After I left here last time—that night during dinner the student dean in our house asked to speak to my roommate. My roommate told me about it afterwards—Miss Hansen asked if I would be embarrassed as hostess at the table. She said she didn't want to hurt me! These darn student deans who think that they must guard us! The other student dean I had before never raised the issue. It makes me so mad!

Therapist (1):   You feel that this incident helped to accentuate the difficulty.

Client: That was the first time with a student dean. Really though, it struck me very funny. She watches us like a hawk. We can't make a move but she knows it.

Therapist (2):   You resent her activity.

Client: I just don't like it on general principles. Oh, I suppose that she was trying to save me embarrassment.

Therapist (3):   You can see why she did that.

Client: I think that she is really afraid of us—she's queer. I don't know, but so far as I am concerned, I'm pretty indifferent to her.

Therapist (4):   You feel that she doesn't affect you one way or the other. (Snyder, 1947, p. 278)

The therapist's first, third, and fourth comments are restatement of content; the second is clarification of feelings.

As the brief excerpt from a client-centered therapy session illustrates, client-centered therapists do not interpret clients' statements, behaviors, or displays of emotion (Bohart, 1991b; cf. Weinrach, 1990). Interpretations are inappropriate because they always come from an external frame of reference. Client-centered therapists believe that the meaning of a client's behavior is only relevant from the client's internal frame of reference. Client-centered therapists also do not offer advice. The therapist assumes the client's organismic valuing process is the client's best source of guidance. The therapist offers an accepting and nonthreatening atmosphere that allows the client to be directed by his or her organismic valuing process.

Recent Developments in Client-Centered Therapy

In recent years, the practice of client-centered therapy has been expanding to include procedures from other therapy approaches (e.g., Bohart, 1990; Barrineau, 1992; Kahn, 1989; Levant & Shlien, 1987; Lietaer, 1981; Patterson, 1990a, 1990b; Purton, 1989; Sutton, 1991; Tobin, 1991). This process is consistent with the current trend toward eclecticism and integration of psychotherapies (e.g., Arkowitz, 1991, 1992; Garfield & Bergin, 1985; Mahoney, 1992).

Confronting clients is new to client-centered therapy (e.g., Lietaer, 1984). For instance, therapists may interject their own here-and-now experiences, as the following excerpt illustrates.

Client: I'm just devastated about my girlfriend's breaking up with me. It's really bad.

Therapist: You say that your girlfriend's ending your relationship is difficult to take. But as you said that, I must tell you that I did not feel that you were upset. Does my reading of your feelings fit with yours in any way?

Confrontation obviously diverges from the traditional practice of letting the client dictate the flow of therapy. The rationale for confrontation is that the therapist's impressions of the client and the feelings the client evokes in the therapist may be important for the client to hear. These impressions may stimulate further self-explorations in the client.

Confrontation differs from interpretation when therapists clearly state their reactions as their own and do not impose them on clients. To maintain unconditional positive regard, the therapist communicates that the reactions are toward specific, concrete behaviors rather than toward the client as a person. To remain *client*-centered, the therapist remains vigilant to the effects of the confrontation on the client and responds appropriately (Lietaer, 1984).

Another recent development in client-centered therapy involves the manner in which therapists show empathy (e.g., Bozarth, 1984). Traditionally, therapists have demonstrated their empathic understanding primarily by reflecting the client's feelings. Another way to communicate empathy involves entering the client's internal frame of reference and participating in it. Consider how the therapist responds to a client who expressed a grandiose scheme for making money.

Client: I won't have any trouble selling the idea. People will be so pleased with my service that they will tell others about it. Pretty soon I'll have so many customers that I'll have to open up other service centers.

Therapist: With all the money you'd be making, you could do all those things you've always wanted to do, such as buying a house in the country and traveling.

By making specific suggestions about how the money might be spent, the therapist becomes involved in the client's experience. The therapist's response demonstrates to the client that the therapist believes that the client could make the money, which would be showing empathic understanding of the client's internal frame of reference.

Traditionally, psychological tests have not been used in client-centered therapy. Such tests are based on nomothetic data, whereas client-centered therapy is definitively idiographic in its approach. However, testing may be consistent with the principles of client-centered therapy (1) if the need for testing emerges from the client–therapist dialogue and (2) when the test results are used to compare the client's decision with an external standard (Bozarth, 1991; Seeman, 1991). It is crucial, however, that clients remain the authority regarding the direction of change in their lives.

Other areas in which client-centered therapy is being expanded include its use with couples and families (Anderson, 1989; Bozarth & Shanks, 1989;

Cain, 1989, 1990a; Ellinwood, 1989; Gaylin, 1989; Sabbe, 1991) and its integration with other therapeutic approaches (e.g., C. J. O'Leary, 1989; Synder, 1989; Warner, 1989); in career counseling (Freeman, 1990); and in clinical case conferences and supervision of therapists (e.g., Baradell, 1990).

A Case Example of Personality Growth and Change

The following letter was written to Rogers (1980) by a young woman who was in therapy; Rogers did not know either the woman or her therapist. (The numbers in the margin refer to parts of the letter about which Rogers commented; his comments follow the letter.)

Dear Dr. Rogers,

... I have just read your book, *On Becoming a Person,* and it left a great impression on me ... It's kind of a coincidence because right now I need something to help me find *me*. I do not feel that I can do much for others until I find me.

... I began to lose me when I was in high school. I always wanted to go into work that would be of help to people but my family resisted, and I thought they must be right. Things went along smoothly for everyone else ... until about two years ago. I met a guy that I thought was ideal. Then nearly a year ago I took a good look at us, and realized that I was everything that *he* wanted me to be and nothing that *I* was. I have always been emotional and I have had many feelings. I could never sort them out and identify them. My fiancé would tell me that I was just mad or just happy and I would say okay and leave it at that. Then when I took this good look at us I realized that I was angry because I wasn't following my true emotions. 1 2 3 4 5

I backed out of the relationship gracefully and tried to find out where all the pieces were that I had lost. After a few months of searching had gone by, I found that there were many more than I knew what to do with and I couldn't seem to separate them. I began seeing a psychologist.... He has helped me to find parts of me that I was not aware of. Some parts are bad by our society's standards, but I have found them to be very good for me.... 6 7

I remember one night in particular. I had been in for my regular appointment with the psychologist that day and I had come home feeling angry ... because I wanted to talk about something but I couldn't identify what it was. By eight o'clock that night I was so upset I was frightened. I called him and he told me to come to his office.... I got there and cried for at least an hour and then the words came. I still don't know all of what I was saying. All I know is that *so much hurt* and *anger* came out of me that I *never really knew existed*. I went home and it seemed that an *alien* had taken over and I was hallucinating like some of the patients I have seen in a state hospital. I continued to feel this way until ... I realized that this alien was the *me* that I had been trying to find. 8 9 10 11

... since that night people no longer seem so strange to me.
Now it is beginning to seem that life is just starting for me. I am alone
right now, but I am not frightened and I don't have to be doing
something. I like meeting me and making friends with my thoughts and
feelings. Because of this I have learned to enjoy other people. One older   12
man in particular — who is very ill — makes me feel very much alive. He
accepts everyone. He told me the other day that I have changed very
much. According to him, I have begun to open up and love. I think that   13
I have always loved people and I told him so. He said, "Were they aware
of it?" I don't suppose I have expressed my love any more than I did
my anger and hurt.

Among other things, I am finding out that I never had too much
self-respect. And now that I am learning to really like me, I am finally
finding peace within myself. . . . (pp. 208–210)   14

Rogers (1980) commented on this letter by paraphrasing what he
considered to be the critical statements concerning the woman's feelings and
attitudes. His remarks provide a good summary of his view of personality
development, growth, and change.

1. *I was losing me.* Her own experiences and their meanings were being denied,
   and she was developing a self that was different from her real experienced
   self, which was becoming increasingly unknown to her.
2. *My experience told me the work I wanted to go into, but my family showed
   me that I couldn't trust my own feelings to be right.* This phrase shows how
   a false concept of self is built up. Because she accepted her parents' meanings
   as her own experience, she came to distrust her own organismic experience. . . . As she distrusted more and more of her own experience, her sense
   of self-worth steadily declined until she had very little use for her own
   experience or herself.
3. *Things went along smoothly for everyone else.* What a revealing statement!
   Of course things were fine for those whom she was trying to please. This
   pseudoself was just what they wanted. It was only within herself, at some
   deep and unknown level, that there was a vague uneasiness.
4. *I was everything he wanted me to be.* Here again she was denying to
   awareness all her own experiencing — to the point where she no longer really
   had a self and was trying to be a self wanted by someone else.
5. *Finally my organism rebelled and I tried to find me again but I couldn't,
   without help.* Why did she finally rebel and take a good look at her
   relationship with her fiancé? One can only attribute this rebellion to the
   actualizing tendency that had been suppressed for so long but that finally
   asserted itself.
6. . . . because she had distrusted her own experience for such a long period
   and because the self by which she was living was so sharply different from
   the experiences of her organism, she could not reconstruct her true self
   without help. The need for help often exists when there is such a great
   discrepancy.
7. *Now I am discovering my experiences — some bad according to society,
   parents, and boyfriend, but all good as far as I am concerned.* The locus of
   evaluation that formerly had resided in her parents, in her boyfriend, and

others, she is now reclaiming as her own. She is the one who decides the values of her experience. She is the center of the valuing process, and the evidence is provided by her own senses. Society may call a given experience bad, but when she trusts her own valuing of it, she finds that it is worthwhile and significant to her.

8. *An important turning point came when a flood of the experiences that I had been denying to awareness came close to the surface. I was frightened and upset.* When denied experience comes close to awareness, anxiety always results because these previously unadmitted experiences will have meanings that will change the structure of the self by which one has been living. Any drastic change in the self-concept is always a threatening and frightening experience. She was dimly aware of this threat even though she did not yet know what would emerge.

9. *When the denied experiences broke through the dam, they turned out to be hurts and angers that I had been completely unaware of.* It is impossible for most people to realize how completely an experience can be shut out of awareness until it does break through into awareness. Every individual is able to shut out and deny those experiences that would endanger his or her self-concept.

10. *I thought I was insane because some foreign person had taken over in me.* When the self-concept is so sharply changed that parts of it are completely shattered, it is a very frightening experience, and her description of the feeling that an alien had taken over is a very accurate one.

11. *Only gradually did I realize that this alien was the real me.* What she was discovering was that the submissive, malleable self by which she had been living, the self that had been guided by the statements, attitudes, and expectations of others, was no longer hers. This new self that had seemed so alien was a self that had experienced hurt and anger and feelings that society regards as bad, as well as wild hallucinatory thoughts—and love. . . .

12. *I like meeting me and making friends with my thoughts and feelings.* Here is the dawning of the self-respect and self-acceptance of which she has been deprived for so long. She is even feeling affection for herself. One of the curious but common side effects of this change is that now she will be able to give herself more freely to others, to enjoy others more, to be more genuinely interested in them.

13. *I have begun to open up and love.* She will find that as she is more expressive of her love, she can also be more expressive of her anger and hurt, her likes and dislikes, and her "wild" thoughts and feelings (which will turn out to be creative impulses). She is in the process of changing from psychological maladjustment to a much healthier relationship to others and to reality.

14. *I am finally finding peace within myself.* There is a peaceful harmony in being a whole person, but she will be mistaken if she thinks this reaction is permanent. Instead, if she is really open to her experience, she will find other hidden aspects of herself that she has denied to awareness, and each such discovery will give her uneasy and anxious moments or days until it is assimilated into a revised and changing picture of herself. She will discover that growing toward a congruence between her experiencing organism and her concept of herself is an exciting, sometimes disturbing, but never-ending adventure. (pp. 211–214, numbers added)

**THE PERSON-
CENTERED
APPROACH:
BEYOND CLIENT-
CENTERED
THERAPY**

Carl Rogers' career as a psychologist spanned more than half a century; he was still professionally active when he died suddenly at the age of 85 following surgery for a broken hip (Gendlin, 1988). In the last two decades of his life, Rogers broadened his interests and professional endeavors considerably. Still, his basic views about personality remained unchanged (e.g., Bozarth, 1990; Kirschenbaum, 1991).

Identifying the conditions that allow a person's unique resources to be freely expressed was one of Rogers' major contributions. Rogers found that empathic understanding, unconditional positive regard, and genuineness were essential for effective client-centered therapy. Moreover, he later came to realize that these factors are not restricted to therapy (e.g., Horton & Brown, 1990; Walsh, 1991). Rogers (1980) believed they

> apply whether we are speaking of the relationship between therapist and client, parent and child, leader and group, teacher and student, or administrator and staff. The conditions apply, in fact, in any situation in which the development of the person is a goal. (p. 115)

Rogers (1980) even boldly asserted that these conditions might

> be effective in situations now dominated by the exercise of raw power—in politics, for example, especially in our dealings with other nations. I challenge . . . the current American belief, evident in every phase of our foreign policy, and especially in our insane wars, that "might makes right." That, in my estimation, is the road to self-destruction. I go along with Martin Buber and the ancient Oriental sages: "He who imposes himself has the small, manifest might; he who does not impose himself has the great, secret might" (p. 45).

An example of Rogers' reliance on this "secret might" occurred when he worked for 5 days with a group of therapists and educators in what was then the Soviet Union. The group members spent the entire first day debating about who should be included in the group (which was to be limited to 40 people). An experienced professional told Rogers that the infighting would stop only when he explicitly gave some signal that the bitterness was to end. Rogers did not agree. Consistent with his faith in self-direction, Rogers predicted that change in the group interactions would be instigated from "within" the group. Sure enough, when the members realized they had only a limited time to be together and that how they spent that time was their choice, a dramatic shift in the group's interactions spontaneously occurred.

Rogers (1979) used the term **person-centered approach** when principles of client-centered therapy are extended beyond the boundaries of psychotherapy. A person-centered approach has been applied by Rogers and his followers to discover and create psychological climates that facilitate growth and enhancement in diverse human endeavors, including:

> fostering student-centered learning, whereby students are given freedom to learn in their own way (e.g., Bell & Schniedewind, 1989; DeCarvalho, 1991c; Rogers, 1983; Hayashi et al., 1992; Thomas, 1988; cf. Meuris, 1988)

humanizing medical treatment and education (Barnard, 1984; Rogers, 1980)

humanizing psychological research so that the people studied are not viewed as "objects" or "subjects" of investigation and experimentation (Mearns & McLeod, 1984; Patton, 1990)

promoting interracial and intercultural harmony, including an attempt to ease tensions between Catholics, Protestants, and the English in Northern Ireland (McGaw, Rice, & Rogers, 1973)

discovering alternatives to potential nuclear holocaust (Bakan, 1988; Blight, 1988; Mitroff, 1988; Rogers & Ryback, 1984; Smith, 1988; Solomon, 1988)

The Future of Humankind   Rogers' most far-reaching speculations dealt with the future of humankind. He believed that a variety of contemporary trends run counter to human beings' self-actualizing, including:

> advances in computer intelligence and decision making; "test-tube" babies . . . ; new species of . . . life being created through recombinant work with the genes; cities under domes, with the whole environment controlled . . . ; completely artificial environments permitting human beings to live in space: these are some of the new technologies that may affect our lives. They have in common the fact that each removes humankind further from nature, from the soil, the weather, the sun, the wind, and all natural processes. (Rogers, 1980, pp. 342–343)

Always optimistic, Rogers (1980) noted other trends that he thought boded well for the future of humankind. In particular, he noted that there are " . . . developments . . . that alter our whole conception of the potentialities of the individual; that change our perceptions of 'reality'; that change our ways of being and behaving; that alter our belief systems" (p. 343). He cited the increased interest in various forms of meditation that utilize inner resources and the growing appreciation and use of intuition (e.g., research on the functioning of the right side of the brain). He also pointed to holistic health practices, such as the increasing recognition that physical diseases, such as cancer, may be cured or alleviated through the "intentional use of our conscious and nonconscious minds" (e.g., Simonton, Mathews-Simonton, & Creighton, 1980).

Rogers believed that to survive in a world characterized by increasing technology and artificiality, human beings will have to become interpersonally oriented and natural—that is, more person-centered. Rogers (1980) enumerated qualities that he thought would be characteristic of the "survivors" in the future: (1) openness to experience; (2) desire for authenticity; (3) skepticism regarding science and technology; (4) desire for wholeness; (5) desire for intimacy; (6) being process persons (always changing); (7) caring for others; (8) feeling of closeness to nature; (9) being anti-institutional; (10) trust in inner authority and distrust of external authority; (11) indifference to materialism; and (12) yearning for spirituality. Obviously, no single individual will have all of these qualities. However,

Rogers' hypothesized optimal qualities for tomorrow's human beings parallel the characteristics that Abraham Maslow identified in self-actualizing individuals, as you will see in Chapter 15.

SUMMARY   1. Rogers' theory of personality was the first major alternative to psychoanalysis. The basis of the theory is the self-actualizing tendency, which holds that each person has a unique potential to develop, grow, and change in basically positive ways.

2. The self-actualizing tendency operates through the organismic valuing process, which evaluates experiences in terms of whether they maintain or enhance the person.

3. The self or self-concept embodies all of an individual's perceptions of himself or herself in an organized, consistent whole. Rogers divided the self into the actual and ideal self-concept.

4. Similarity between one's actual and ideal self-concept has been a standard measure of life satisfaction. However, the actual and ideal self-concepts may be less distinct then previously thought because of the tendency to evaluate one's self in a favorable light. An alternative measure of life satisfaction is the difference between one's actual and undesirable self-concept.

5. The Q-sort is a standard means of gaining information about a person's self-concept. People make comparative judgments of statements about themselves by sorting the statements in terms of how self-descriptive they are. Repeated Q-sorts are used to show changes in the self over time.

6. Rogers assumed that all people have a need for positive regard (acceptance, love, and respect). Conditional positive regard is given for specific behaviors, whereas unconditional positive regard is independent of the person's specific behaviors. Both forms of positive regard come first from others and later from the person (positive self-regard).

7. Rogers believed that creativity can be fostered in children if they experience psychological safety and psychological freedom.

8. Conditions of worth are positive or negative values placed on specific behaviors by others and by oneself. They often supersede the organismic valuing process in evaluating experiences and thus interfere with self-actualization.

9. The presence of conditions of worth inevitably leads to some conflict or incongruity between self and experience. This conflict is threatening to the wholeness of the personality and is experienced as anxiety. To prevent such incongruity and decrease anxiety, people use two defensive processes: perceptual distortion and denial.

10. Psychological adjustment results from congruence between self and experience. To effect personality reintegration, there must be a reduction in

conditions of worth and an increase in unconditional positive regard, which allows the self-actualizing tendency to predominate.

11. Client-centered therapy establishes conditions that make it possible for clients to assume responsibility for making needed personality changes. The therapist provides three key ingredients—empathy, unconditional positive regard, and genuineness. The therapist communicates these ingredients through restatement of content and clarification of feelings.

12. New developments in client-centered therapy have expanded its procedures to include confrontation, participation in the client's internal frame of reference, and the use of psychological tests. But the therapy still remains client-centered.

13. Rogers' person-centered approach has extended the principles of client-centered therapy to diverse human endeavors and problems. These applications follow the underlying principle of establishing conditions that will allow individuals to follow their self-actualizing tendencies.

Chapter Fifteen

Maslow's Theory of Human Motivation

braham Maslow was a leading spokesperson for the psychology of health and strength. He shared with Carl Rogers a
distinctly optimistic view of human nature. Maslow believed
that people are inherently good and that they are fully capable
of developing in healthy ways if circumstances allow their
innate potential to be expressed.

In contrast to Rogers, Maslow did not develop a comprehensive theory
of personality. Instead, his theory and research deal with the factors that
motivate behavior. In particular, Maslow explored in depth the role of
self-actualization motives, including how such motives are manifested at the
highest levels of human functioning.

Maslow conceptualized motivation in terms of levels of needs. You may
find it useful to examine briefly some of your own needs before learning
about Maslow's ideas. Before reading further, take a few minutes to
complete Demonstration 15-1.

Abraham Maslow
(1908-1970)
emphasized the healthy
side of personality,
proposed a hierarchy of
needs that motivate
human behavior, and
extensively studied the
hightest level of needs,
self-actualization.
Courtesy Abraham Maslow,
photo by William Carter

■ *Demonstration 15-1:*
WHAT DO YOU NEED?*

Psychologists have identified various basic
needs that motivate human behavior. Table
15-1 lists five categories of needs that Maslow
believed are essential for all individuals, along
with specific examples of each.

1. First, read through the examples in the
table.

2. Then, think of *three significant examples
of activities that you have engaged in over the
past month that fit into each category.* The
activities can be either overt actions or covert
behaviors, such as thoughts or fantasies.
Record your examples on the Work Sheet
15-1 (Figure 15-1), which you may remove
from the Demonstration Materials section at
the end of the book.

3. Next, consider *how satisfied you are
that your needs have been met by the activities
you have listed* in each category. Using the
scale that follows, rate the degree to which

you are satisfied that your needs have been met
in each category. Record the scale numbers on
the work sheet.

1 = totally unsatisfied
2 = generally unsatisfied
3 = slightly unsatisfied
4 = slightly satisfied
5 = generally satisfied
6 = totally satisfied

4. Now, think about *how important the
needs in each category are to you.* Using the
scale that follows, rate the degree of importance for each category of needs. Record the
scale numbers on the work sheet.

1 = very important
2 = moderately important
3 = slightly important
4 = slightly unimportant
5 = moderately unimportant
6 = totally unimportant

5. Finally, consider *how concerned you are
with meeting the needs* in each category. The

*Adapted from Grasha (1978)

Table 15-1
Maslow's categories of needs with examples (for Demonstration 15-1)

SELF-ACTUALIZATION NEEDS

Examples:

Living up to your potential
Accepting your strengths and limitations
Accepting other people for who and what they are
Being spontaneous
Acting creatively
Acting independently (of others' opinions)

ESTEEM NEEDS

Examples:

Self-esteem	*Esteem from others*
Achievement	Recognition
Confidence	Appreciation
Mastery	Attention
Strength	Status
	Reputation

BELONGINGNESS AND LOVE NEEDS

Examples:

Love
Affection
Belonging (to family, group)
Friendship
Spending time with other people

SAFETY NEEDS

Examples:

Physical security
Dependence
Stability, order, structure
Freedom from fear

PHYSIOLOGICAL NEEDS

Examples:

Food and water
Rest and sleep
Exercise
Health

Need category	Examples of recent behavior	Satisfaction rating	Importance rating	Salience rating
Self-actualization	1. 2. 3.			
Esteem	1. 2. 3.			
Belongingness and Love	1. 2. 3.			
Safety	1. 2. 3.			
Physiological	1. 2. 3.			

Figure 15-1
Sample work sheet for Demonstration 15-1.

salience of the need for you (how concerned you are about it) would be seen in the degree to which you think about the need and do things to satisfy the need. Using the scale that follows, rate the degree to which you are satisfied that your needs have been met in each category. Record the scale numbers on the work sheet.

1 = very concerned
2 = moderately concerned
3 = slightly concerned
4 = slightly unconcerned
5 = moderately unconcerned
6 = totally unconcerned

As you read about Maslow's hierarchy of needs, consider what you have learned from this brief assessment of your own needs, including how well they are satisfied, how important they are to you, and how preoccupied you are with them.

MASLOW'S HIERARCHICAL THEORY OF MOTIVATION

For Maslow, the source of human motivation resides in needs that are common to all human beings. First, we will discuss the specific nature of these needs, and then we will examine how needs are met in hierarchical order.

Instinctoid Needs

Maslow (1970) theorized that human needs are common to our species and thus have a biological basis, although they are modified by the environment (e.g., Neher, 1991). However, he believed that human needs do not motivate people automatically or instinctively, as biological needs motivate other species. Instinctual motivation decreases as animals proceed up the evolutionary scale. Humans are only minimally influenced by biological instincts.

For example, "if we examine the sexual life of the human being we find that sheer drive itself is given by heredity but that the choice of object and the choice of behavior must be acquired or learned in the course of the life history" (Maslow, 1970, p. 27).

To distinguish human and nonhuman biologically based needs, Maslow used the term **instinctoid** to refer to human needs having a biological basis. Everyone is born with identical instinctoid needs. However, the specific behaviors that are motivated by and that fulfill instinctoid needs are idiosyncratic for each person. The behaviors depend on the person's unique biological makeup and environmental experiences.

Content of the Need Hierarchy

Maslow postulated five levels of basic human needs. Listed from strongest to weakest, these needs are *basic physiological* (e.g., food); *safety* (e.g., shelter); *belongingness and love* (e.g., companionship); *esteem* (e.g., feeling competent); and *self-actualization* (e.g., creativity). The hierarchy is shown pictorially in Figure 15-2.

The lower a need is in the hierarchy, the more basic it is in terms of survival. Lower needs exert a more powerful influence on behavior. The higher a need is in the hierarchy, the less basic it is and thus the weaker is its potential influence. Also, the higher a need in the hierarchy, the more distinctly human it is. Humans definitely share physiological and safety needs with other animals; humans may share belongingness and love needs with

Figure 15-2
Schematic representation of Maslow's hierarchy of instinctoid needs. The higher the need in the hierarchy, the weaker is the need in terms of motivating human behavior.

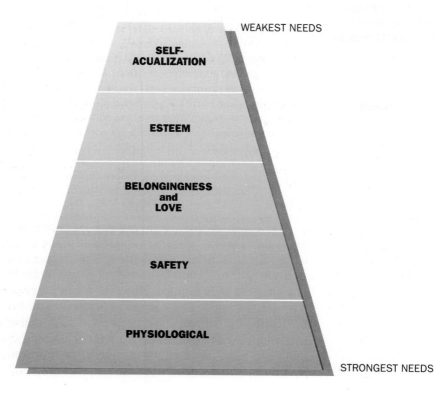

WEAKEST NEEDS

SELF-ACUALIZATION

ESTEEM

BELONGINGNESS and LOVE

SAFETY

PHYSIOLOGICAL

STRONGEST NEEDS

higher animal species; but it is assumed that humans alone have esteem and self-actualization needs.

Movement within the Need Hierarchy

As people satisfy their needs at one level in the hierarchy, they progress to the next level (cf. Neher, 1991). Needs at a particular level do not have to be totally satisfied before people can begin to fulfill needs at the next level. Usually we are not concerned with meeting higher needs until our lower needs have been at least partially satisfied, but there are exceptions to this rule.

An individual may forgo basic needs — such as for food and sleep — in order to persevere at some task. The stereotype of the "starving artist" is an example. People may ignore personal safety as well as physiological needs in order to engage in political protest. For instance, Irish militants have marched against armed soldiers and gone on hunger strikes to protest British policies in Northern Ireland. There may also be some individuals who are content meeting a higher need before fulfilling a lower need or even without ever meeting a lower need. People who devote a lifetime to achieving in a career (esteem needs) with little or no time spent with family or friends (belongingness needs) would be exceptions. Most people, however, would pay a price for ignoring lower needs.

Consider the case of a successful, unmarried, 35-year-old business executive. He described an experience he had one night.

> I was enjoying my work, going over the draft of a marketing report I had written. I felt content to be working at my desk late at night, a kind of "all's well with the world" sensation except . . . except something was missing to make it complete. What could be missing? I had a good, secure job that I enjoyed. I had been getting good exposure in the field. My boss openly expressed her pleasure about my performance, and I was admired and respected by my co-workers. I was making good money. I was healthy. I had interests to keep me occupied when I wasn't working. What more could I want? Finally it hit me that all this good life was solely mine and that I did not share it with anyone else, especially with a close loved one. I had not had much social life recently but did not miss it since I was very much into my work. But the more I thought about it, the more I realized that I would have felt more content — more full — if there were a woman in my life with whom I could have shared my otherwise very positive life.

How would this man's feelings be explained in terms of Maslow's hierarchy? He was primarily functioning at the esteem level, which involves needs that are satisfied when other people recognize our accomplishments as well as when we acknowledge our self-worth. From his own report, the man's esteem needs were fulfilled. However, his belongingness and love needs were not being satisfied. These lower needs must have been gratified at one time in his life for him to have progressed to a higher level. Apparently his single-minded devotion to his work (esteem needs) created a temporary void in his life. Thus, the man was compelled to return to a lower level to satisfy his unmet belongingness needs.

At various times in our lives, some of our basic needs will inevitably be frustrated. When this occurs, we must temporarily engage in behaviors that will satisfy those basic needs before higher needs can once again be attended to. A common example is when we are too physically ill to perform normal daily functions, including work and social obligations. Until we recover, our life revolves around physiological needs. Higher social and esteem needs, and even some safety needs, are, of necessity, placed "on a back burner."

Physiological Needs

Our most basic needs are physiological, including food, water, oxygen, elimination, and rest. Because physiological needs are directly related to survival, they are the most powerful human needs. When a basic need is not met, it consumes a person's life until it is satisfied. Food becomes the central focus of the hungry person's life; it pervades actions, thoughts, and fantasies. Such a person would be said to "live by bread alone" (Maslow, 1970).

You and people you know do not experience a deprivation of food or other physiological need on a regular basis. Thus, physiological needs play a small role in motivating you. Unfortunately, this is not the case for an alarming number of people in the world. Starving Somalians as well as homeless people in the United States rarely move beyond the physiological level.

Safety Needs

Safety needs include physical well-being as well as psychological security, including a need for stability, order, and structure in our lives. Most of your safety needs are largely satisfied, such as through laws and by police and fire departments, or can be met easily, such as by purchasing insurance and having a savings account. Thus, in Western cultures safety needs generally do not motivate adult behaviors.

In contrast, safety needs are dominant in children, especially infants who "will react in a total fashion and as if they were endangered, if they are disturbed or dropped suddenly, startled by loud noises . . . or . . . by rough handling, by general loss of support in the mother's arms" (Maslow, 1970, p. 39). The urgency of safety needs can be readily seen when a child suffers illness or injury.

> At such a moment of pain, it may be postulated that, for the child, the whole world suddenly changes from sunniness to darkness, so to speak, and becomes a place in which anything at all might happen, in which previously stable things have suddenly become unstable. Thus, a child who because of some bad food is taken ill may for a day or two develop fear, nightmares, and a need for protection and reassurance never seen . . . before. (Maslow, 1970, p. 40)

Another indication of children's heightened safety needs is their preference for predictable, undisrupted routines, such as having meals at a set time.

Adult abnormal behavior is similar to the child's desire for safety. The adult may see the world as hostile, threatening, and overwhelming. The person may behave "as if a great catastrophe were almost always impending . . . usually responding as if to an emergency" (Maslow, 1970, p. 42). For example, people with an obsessive-compulsive disorder will "try frantically to order and stabilize the world so that no unmanageable, unexpected, or unfamiliar dangers will ever appear" (Maslow, 1970, p. 42).

Belongingness and Love Needs

When physiological and safety needs are substantially gratified, needs related to affiliation, affection, and love emerge. Individuals experience deep feelings of loneliness when friends, family, and loved ones are absent. They long for affectionate relationships and a secure place in a primary group, such as a family. When belongingness and love needs predominate, people are keenly aware of and upset by feelings of rejection, friendlessness, and rootlessness.

Maslow and other personality psychologists (e.g., Fromm, 1963) believed that unsatisfied belongingness and love needs are a major problem in contemporary Western societies. The personal-growth movement (e.g., encounter groups) in the 1960s and the more recent proliferation of a myriad of support groups (e.g., for women, men, children of alcoholics, parents without partners) may be partly due to an

> unsatisfied hunger for contact, for intimacy, for belongingness and by the need to overcome . . . widespread feelings of alienation, aloneness, strangeness, and loneliness, which have been worsened by our mobility, by the breakdown of traditional groupings, the scattering of families, the generation gap. (Maslow, 1970, p. 44)

Esteem Needs

If needs in the first three levels of the hierarchy are adequately satisfied, the person becomes concerned with meeting esteem needs. Maslow (1970) distinguished two types of esteem needs.

Esteem from others includes the desire for recognition, appreciation, attention, prestige, reputation, status, and fame. In short, individuals need to feel respected by other people for what they can do, and they want others to recognize their worth.

Self-esteem involves a desire for competency, mastery, achievement, strength, adequacy, confidence, independence, and freedom. When these needs are met, people feel worthwhile, confident, capable, useful, and necessary. If these needs are frustrated, they feel inferior, weak, and helpless. Enduring and healthy self-esteem is based on the *deserved* respect of others—recognition earned through a person's efforts—rather than on status or fame.

Self-Actualization Needs

Most people spend their lives trying to fulfill physiological, safety, belongingness and love, and esteem needs. And they never completely accomplish the task. A small number of individuals, however, substantially gratify their needs in the first four levels of the hierarchy and are motivated by self-actualization needs. Maslow (1970) defined **self-actualization** as "the desire to become more and more what one idiosyncratically is, to become everything that one is capable of becoming" (p. 46). (This definition is essentially the same as Rogers'.)

Self-actualization is a goal that is never fully attained by any person. A few people — Maslow estimated a fraction of a percent of the population — come close to reaching it (Hoffman, 1992). Movement toward self-actualization is neither automatic nor easy, even for people successfully meeting their lower needs. First, self-actualization needs are the weakest of the instinctoid needs. Second, Maslow believed that people are often afraid of the self-knowledge necessary for self-actualization. Accurate self-knowledge can be threatening; it may change one's self-concept. Third, self-actualization requires freedom to express oneself and to explore, to act without restriction (within the normal bounds of not harming others) and to pursue such values as truth, justice, and honesty. There are few environments in which this is possible. For instance, Western cultures, through established social customs about the "proper" expression of feelings, inhibit the genuine spontaneity that tends to characterize self-actualizing individuals.

The specific nature of self-actualization needs varies considerably from person to person. This contrasts with lower needs that are relatively uniform. Self-actualization, however, does not necessarily involve special talent or creative and artistic endeavors. Self-actualization may be manifested in any human activity.

Assessing One's Position in the Hierarchy

Although we have discussed separately how each of the levels of needs motivates our behaviors, usually our actions are motivated by needs at more than one level. For instance, making love generally fulfills both physiological and belongingness needs. Moreover, the same behavior may be motivated by different needs in different individuals. Thus, some people engage in sex to fulfill esteem needs (e.g., sex as a conquest) and some to fulfill safety needs (e.g., to feel secure in a relationship or in one's sexuality).

Recently, a multidimensional measure of one's position on three levels of Maslow's hierarchy — safety, belonging, and esteem — has been developed. The Maslowian Assessment Survey is a self-report inventory consisting of 195 statements to which respondents indicate their level of agreement on a 6-point scale (Williams & Page, 1989). Four dimensions of each need level are assessed: (1) need *gratification* (e.g., "The neighborhood I live in is unsafe"); (2) need *importance* (e.g., "It is important to me to live in a safe neighborhood"); (3) need *salience* (e.g., "I worry often about being safe where I live"); and (4) need *self-concept* (e.g., "I consider myself to be a rather nervous person"). The self-concept dimension measures the degree to which a person is like a prototypic individual motivated primarily by each need level.

The advantage of measuring multiple dimensions is that the dimensions may be independent. For example, it matters little if a need is met (need gratification) if the need does not motivate the person (need importance). The Maslowian Assessment Survey appears to be both reliable and valid in samples of traditional college-age students, for whom the scale was designed (Williams & Page, 1989).

GROWTH   Maslow placed self-actualization needs at the top of the hierarchy of human
MOTIVATION   motives. But, in a sense, these needs do not fit within the hierarchy; they are
fundamentally different from the basic needs in the first four levels. Maslow
(1955) theorized that the first four levels of needs motivate people by *deficit*,
whereas self-actualization needs are motivated by *growth* (cf. Neher, 1991).

Deficit motivation involves reducing tension or filling a temporary lack.
We drink because we are thirsty. We seek company when we are lonely.
Deficit motivation is *goal-oriented*, where the goal is decreasing or eliminating the need. Being hypervigilant while driving home on icy roads is motivated by safety needs. Once safely home, what we do is likely to be determined by other needs, such as checking on the welfare of family members.

Growth motivation is *process-oriented,* where the process is continued
enhancement or growth consistent with the person's unique self-actualizing
tendency. Growth motives are self-actualization motives, which often involve
"intrinsic values" such as beauty, truth, and self-sufficiency. Other examples
of typical growth motives are listed in Table 15-2.

Satisfying growth motives often results in an increase in tension, whereas
satisfying deficit motives often leads to a decrease in tension. For example,
satisfying the growth motive for beauty by hiking through the mountains is
likely to lead to increased wonder and awe as vistas open up along the trail.
In contrast, the deficit motive for safety can be satisfied by staying in the
valley, protected from the dangers of traversing narrow, precipitous trails.

Fulfilling growth needs involves the common goal of personal enhancement or growth. Growth needs are of equal value in this sense: They are
interchangeable and can be readily substituted for one another depending on
the circumstances in a person's life.

When people are motivated by growth needs, even routine work takes
on a "higher" meaning. It becomes broader and more universal and less
narrow and self-centered. For example, "The law is apt to be more a way of
seeking justice, truth, goodness . . . than financial security, admiration, status,
prestige, dominance, masculinity." (Maslow, 1971, p. 310).

Table 15-2
Examples of growth motives identified by Maslow

TRUTH	JUSTICE
GOODNESS	ORDER
BEAUTY	SIMPLICITY
UNITY, WHOLENESS	RICHNESS, TOTALITY,
ALIVENESS, PROCESS	COMPREHENSIVENESS
UNIQUENESS	EFFORTLESSNESS
PERFECTION	PLAYFULNESS
COMPLETION	SELF-SUFFICIENCY
	MEANINGFULNESS

Table 15-3
Contrast between growth love and deficit love

GROWTH LOVE	DEFICIT LOVE
Other-centered	Self-centered
Giving	Taking
Nonpossessive	Possessive
Independence	Dependence
Wanting	Needing
Absence of anxiety/hostility	Presence of anxiety/hostility
Increases over time	Decreases over time
Never satisfied	Sometimes satisfied

Growth motivation generally is associated with self-actualization needs (such as those in Table 15-2). However, many lower needs that usually motivate through deficit can also motivate through growth. The differences between deficit love and growth love are presented in Table 15-3.

MASLOW'S STUDY OF SELF-ACTUALIZING PEOPLE

Theories of normal personality have been based primarily on observation of abnormal behaviors, which inevitably leads to a pessimistic and distorted image of human nature (e.g., DeCarvalho, 1991a). Relatively little theorizing and research have been done on optimal functioning and the healthy personality (cf. Seeman, 1984). Rogers (1963) did speculate that *fully functioning people* are guided by their organismic valuing processes; they are open to all experiences (cf. Mittelman, 1991); their self-concepts are whole and consistent with their experiences; they are free of threat and anxiety and therefore have no defenses. In short, the fully functioning person epitomizes psychological health or adjustment. Actually, the type of person Rogers described is an ideal—such a (living) specimen has yet to be found (cf. Coan, 1991; Landsman & Landsman, 1991; Miller, 1991). However, some individuals come close to the goal of being fully functioning or self-actualizing.

Maslow (1954) launched the study of self-actualizing individuals. He described the impetus for this work as follows.

> My investigations on self-actualization . . . did not start out as research. They started out as the effort of a young intellectual to try to understand two of his teachers whom he loved, adored, and admired and who were very, very wonderful people. It was a kind of high-IQ devotion. I could not be content simply to adore, but sought to understand why these two people were so different from the run-of-the-mill people in the world. These two people were Ruth Benedict and Max Wertheimer.* They were my teachers . . . and they were most

---

*Ruth Benedict, an anthropologist at Columbia University, studied Native Americans. Max Wertheimer, a pscyhologist at the New School for Social Research, was one of the founders of Gestalt psychology.

remarkable human beings. My training in psychology equipped me not at all for understanding them. It was as if they were not quite people but something more than people. My own investigation began as a prescientific or nonscientific activity . . . When I tried to understand them . . . I realized in one wonderful moment that their two patterns could be generalized. I was talking about a kind of person, not about two noncomparable individuals. There was wonderful excitement in that. I tried to see whether this pattern could be found elsewhere, and I did find it elsewhere. (Maslow, 1971, pp. 41–42)

Selection of Subjects and Methods

Maslow selected his subjects using a negative criterion and a positive criterion. The negative criterion was absence of psychological disorders. The positive criterion was evidence of self-actualization, which Maslow (1970) defined as *"the full use and exploitation of talents, capacities, potentialities* [italics added]" (p. 150). He elaborated by saying that self-actualizing people

> seem to be fulfilling themselves and to be doing the best that they are capable of doing, reminding us of Nietzche's exhortation, "Become what thou art!" They . . . have developed or are developing to the full stature of which they are capable . . . These potentialities may be either idiosyncratic or species-wide. (p. 150)

People meeting this criterion generally have fulfilled lower needs. They "felt safe and unanxious, accepted, loved and loving, . . . respected, and . . . they had worked out their philosophical [and] religious . . . bearings" (Maslow, 1970, pp. 150–151).

Using the case-study method, Maslow gathered data from interviews with a relatively small, select group of subjects and from the written accounts of historical figures. He selected 60 subjects in all. Ethical considerations prevented giving the names of his living subjects. The historical persons are known and include those shown in Figure 15-3.

Maslow (1963) was aware that his research on the self-actualizing person was outside the bounds of traditional psychological research, which places a premium on objectivity and repeatability. Thus, he felt compelled to justify his work.

> I consider the problem of psychological health to be so pressing, that any suggestions, any bits of data, however moot, are endowed with great heuristic value. This kind of research is in principle so difficult . . . that if we were to wait for conventionally reliable data, we should have to wait forever. (p. 527)

Characteristics of Self-Actualizing People

Through extensive interviewing and analysis of biographical material, Maslow compiled detailed impressions of his subjects. With such qualitative data, the ability of the investigator to accurately and graphically summarize the impressions is paramount. Fortunately, Maslow had a distinct talent in this regard, and we will rely heavily on direct quotations of Maslow's (1963) highly expressive and communicative impressions.

Maslow identified 15 key characteristics of self-actualizing people. Three important points should be kept in mind as you read about them. First, self-actualization is a *process,* not an end state. No one is ever self-actuliz*ed* (i.e., finished with the process). But people can be in the process of self-actualiz*ing*. Second, the characteristics overlap, but each characteristic contributes to an understanding of the self-actualizing person. Third, none of Maslow's subjects exhibits every characteristic. However, self-actualizing individuals have a large number of them.

Efficient Perception of Reality

Self-actualizers are able to easily and accurately judge themselves and others. Their judgments are not distorted by personal needs, fears, or beliefs.

> The first form in which this capacity was noticed was an unusual ability to detect the spurious, the fake, and the dishonest in personality, and in general to judge people correctly and efficiently. . . . As the study progressed, it slowly became apparent that this efficiency extended to many other areas of life—indeed all areas that were tested. In art and music, in things of the intellect, in scientific matters, in politics and public affairs, they seemed as a group to be able to see concealed or confused realities more swiftly and more correctly than others. . . .an informal experiment indicated that their predictions of the future from whatever facts were in hand at the time seemed to be more often correct, because [they were] less [likely to be] based upon wish, desire, anxiety, fear, or upon generalized, character-determined optimism or pessimism. (Maslow, 1963, p. 531)

Acceptance (of Self, Others, and Nature)

Self-actualizers accept themselves, others, and nature without complaint and without thinking much about it (e.g., Flett, Hewitt, Blankstein, & Mosher, 1991).

> They can accept their own human nature in stoic style, with all its short-comings, with all its discrepancies from the ideal image without feeling real concern. . . . they are [not] self-satisfied . . . rather . . . they can take the frailties and sins, weaknesses, and evils of human nature in the same unquestioning spirit with which one accepts the characteristics of nature. One does not complain about water because it is wet, or about rocks because they are hard, or about trees because they are green. As the child looks out upon the world with wide, uncritical innocent eyes, simply noting and observing what is the case, without either arguing the matter or demanding that it be other-wise, so does the self-actualizing person look upon human nature. (Maslow, 1963, p. 533)

Continued Freshness of Appreciation

Beyond acceptance, self-actualizing persons continually appreciate even the most ordinary events in their lives (cf. Csikszentmihalyi, 1990). They have

> the wonderful capacity to appreciate again and again, freshly and naively, the basic goods of life, with awe, pleasure, wonder, and even ecstasy, however stale these experiences may have become to others . . . Any sunset may be as beautiful as the first one, any flower may be breathtaking, even after . . . seeing a million

Figure 15-3
Some of the historical figures whom Maslow identified as self-actualizing. **A:** Martin Buber (1878-1965), theologian; **B:** William James (1842-1910), psychologist; **C:** Harriet Tubman (1821-1913), abolitionist; **D:** Thomas Jefferson (1743-1826), political philosopher; **E:** George Washington Carver (1864-1943), agricultural chemist; **F:** Abraham Lincoln (1809-1865), politician; **G:** Albert Einstein (1879-1955), physicist; **H:** Jane Addams (1860-1935), peace activist; **I:** Sholom Aleichem (1858-1916), author; **J:** Ralph Waldo Emerson (1803-1882), writer; **K:** Albert Schweitzer (1875-1965), medical missionary; **L:** Benjamin Franklin (1706-1790), inventor.

All photos from The Bettmann Archive except **A:** UPI/Bettmann Newsphotos; **C:** Library of Congress; **I:** Sperus College of Judaica, Chicago.

G

H

I

J

K

L

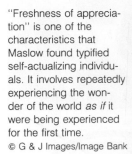

"Freshness of appreciation" is one of the characteristics that Maslow found typified self-actualizing individuals. It involves repeatedly experiencing the wonder of the world *as if* it were being experienced for the first time.
© G & J Images/Image Bank

flowers . . . For such people, even the casual workaday, moment-to-moment business of living can be thrilling, exciting, and ecstatic. These intense feelings do not come all the time; they come occasionally rather than usually, but at the most unexpected moments. (Maslow, 1963, pp. 539–540)

Continued fresh appreciation can be considered "counting one's blessings," but with one proviso. Most people realize the worth of others, their health, their economic well-being, and the like only after losing them. Self-actualizers value these aspects of life as they are experienced, in the here-and-now.

Spontaneity, Simplicity, and Naturalness

Self-actualizers tend to act spontaneously. But they are not the stereotyped unconventional people in society.

Their behavior is marked by simplicity and naturalness, and by lack of artificiality or straining for effect. This does not necessarily mean consistently unconventional behavior . . . It is his impulses, thought, consciousness that are so unusually unconventional, spontaneous, and natural. Apparently recognizing that the world of people in which he lives could not understand or accept this, and since he has no wish to hurt them or fight with them over every triviality, he will go through the ceremonies and rituals of convention with a good-humored shrug and with the best possible grace. Thus I have seen a man accept an honor he laughed at and even despised in private, rather than make an issue of it and hurt the people who thought they were pleasing him. (Maslow, 1963, p. 535)

Problem-Centered

Self-actualizers have a sense of mission or purpose in life (e.g., Ebersole & Humphreys, 1991), and they efficiently go about fulfilling it. Their problems tend to be broad and outside the narrow sphere of themselves. They are

> ordinarily concerned with basic issues and eternal questions of the type that we . . . call philosophical or ethical. Such people live customarily in the widest possible frame of reference. They seem never to get so close to the trees that they fail to see the forest. They work within a framework of values that is broad and not petty, universal and not local, and in terms of a century rather than the moment. In a word, these people are all in one sense or another philosophers, however homely. (Maslow, 1963, p. 537)

Discrimination Between Means and Ends, Right and Wrong

Self-actualizers clearly discriminate between means and ends. They usually focus on ends rather than means. However, their ends are what most people consider means. Self-actualizers are more interested in the *process* of meeting a goal than in obtaining the goal; they focus on "getting there" rather than "arriving." "It is occasionally possible for them to make out of the most trivial and routine activity an intrinsically enjoyable game or dance or play" (Maslow, 1963, p. 545; cf. Csikszentmihalyi, 1990).

A characteristic related to distinguishing between means and ends is the clear set of ethical standards that self-actualizing people also have. They tend to do the "right" thing. At one time they would have been described as "walking in the path of God." Very few of Maslow's subjects were traditionally religious, however (cf. Watson, Morris, & Hood, 1990).

Detachment

Self-actualizers enjoy solitude and privacy more than the average person. They are often able to remain undisturbed by events that create turmoil in others. Their detachment allows them to concentrate to an extraordinary degree. A by-product is "absentmindedness, the ability to forget and to be oblivious to outer surroundings. Examples are the ability to sleep soundly, to have undisturbed appetite, to be able to smile and laugh through a period of problems, worry, and responsibility" (Maslow, 1970, p. 161). Self-actualizers make decisions based on their own inclinations, and they are self-starters.

Independence from Culture and Environment

Self-actualizing people do not depend on other people or the external environment for meeting their needs (e.g., Bordages, 1989; Hjelle, 1991). They

> may actually be *hampered* by others. The determinants of satisfaction and of the good life are for them . . . inner-individual and *not* social. They have become

strong enough to be independent of the good opinion of other people, or even of their affection. The honors, the status, the rewards, the popularity, the prestige, and the love . . . [others] can bestow must have become less important than self-development and inner growth. (Maslow, 1970, p. 162)

Resistance to Enculturation

Self-actualizers fit in with their culture in many ways, but they maintain an inner detachment as well. Outwardly — in dress, speech, and behavior — they are within the limits of convention. They are not among those in the forefront of social action, but they are likely to challenge authority when necessary, especially in the face of injustice. And they are committed to social change. One of Maslow's (1963) subjects

who was a hot rebel in his younger days, a union organizer in the days when this was a highly dangerous occupation, had given up in disgust and hopelessness. As he became resigned to the slowness of social change . . . he turned finally to education of the young. (p. 548)

Maslow (1963) observed that self-actualizers exhibit "a calm, long-time concern with cultural improvement that seems . . . to imply an acceptance of slowness of change along with the unquestioned desirability and necessity of such change" (p. 548).

Deep Desire to Help Humankind

Awareness of the importance of social change is a part of self-actualizers' "deep feeling of identification, sympathy, and affection" for human beings in general (although they occasionally may be angry, disgusted, or impatient with a particular person). Self-actualizers have a genuine desire to help people (e.g., Hjelle, 1991). Furthermore, they tend to treat all individuals as most people treat a family member.

Democratic

It is no wonder, then, that Maslow described self-actualizers as being deeply democratic. They are free of prejudice regarding characteristics such as race or ethnic background. They respect all persons. For example, they are willing to learn from anyone who can teach them something.

At the same time, self-actualizers do not indiscriminately equalize all human beings. Rather, self-actualizers, "themselves elite, select for their friends elite, but this is an elite of character, capacity, and talent, rather than of birth, race, blood, name, family, age, youth, fame, or power" (Maslow, 1963, p. 544).

Deep Interpersonal Relations

Self-actualizers have deeper, more profound interpersonal relations than do most people. Becoming close to another person takes considerable time. As a consequence, self-actualizers tend to have deep ties with only a few individuals. Their circles of friends are small. As one of Maslow's (1963) subjects noted: "I haven't got time for many friends. Nobody has, that is, if they are to be real friends" (p. 542).

Although self-actualizers have few close relationships, they tend to attract admirers. Such relationships are apt to be one-sided; the admirer expects more from the self-actualizing person than she or he wants to give. But self-actualizers are likely to act kindly toward their unwanted admirers while trying to avoid such relationships gracefully.

Philosophical Sense of Humor

Self-actualizers tend to have a philosophical sense of humor that is free of hostility. Many people enjoy humor that pokes fun at someone's inferiority, that hurts someone, or that is "off-color." Self-actualizing people find humor in the foolishness of humans in general. Such thoughtful, philosophical humor typically elicits a smile rather than a laugh. Their humor is pervasive in their lives. They use it to put a serious endeavor in perspective so that, without minimizing its importance, they are able to see its absurdities and make light of it.

Creativeness

Without exception, Maslow found that self-actualizers are original and inventive (see also Runco, Ebersole, & Mraz, 1991). They perceive the environment in a fresh way. This creativeness is different from unusual talent or genius. It is more like the

> naive and universal creativeness of unspoiled children . . . a potentiality given to all human beings at birth. Most human beings lose this as they become enculturated, but . . . [self-actualizers] seem either to retain this fresh and naive, direct way of looking at life, or if they have lost it . . . they later in life recover it. (Maslow, 1963, p. 546)

This special creativeness need not manifest itself in art, music, writing, and other endeavors typically associated with *creativity*. It can show up in the mundane. A delicious homemade pizza would indicate more creativeness than an average painting!

Peak Experiences

A **peak experience** refers to a brief, intense feeling that may include a sense of limitless horizons opening up; of being simultaneously more powerful and more helpless than ever before; of ecstasy, wonder, and awe. Conventional dimensions of time and space may be absent. And the peak experience may lead people to believe that something very significant and valuable has occurred (Thomas & Cooper, 1980). The experience sometimes results in one changing in some way and being strengthened in one's daily life.

Peak experiences may occur in conjunction with any activity or event. The experience itself consists of feelings that are more or less independent of the circumstances. Peak experiences transcend immediate, concrete occurrences. However, many people cite particular events as triggers for peak experiences, including nature, music, quiet reflection, and prayer (Keutzer, 1978).

Peak experiences are brief, lasting a few seconds to a few minutes. But the effects of the peak experience can be long lasting.

Maslow believed that peak experiences are always growth producing; they have some effect on the individual beyond the peak experience itself. However, for a peak experience to enhance the person, the experience must be recognized as significant and accepted by the person. Maslow (1966) conjectured that people may reject peak experiences or their significance in order to defend themselves "against being flooded by emotion, especially the emotions of humility, reverence, mystery, wonder, and awe" (p. 139).

Peak experiences are spontaneous; they cannot be created or anticipated. An individual may expect an event to be special, but that is no guarantee that it will result in a peak experience. In fact, expecting a peak experience will almost guarantee that it will not occur, at least not in the form anticipated.

Maslow (1962) believed—and subsequent empirical studies seem to indicate—that most people probably have occasional peak experiences (Davis, Lockwood, & Wright, 1991; Greeley, 1974; Thomas & Cooper, 1980). Definitive assessment of peak experiences, as with dreams, depends on self-reports, and people may be reluctant to report peak experiences. A recent survey of 246 college students found that the major reasons given for not telling others about one's peak experiences are: (1) the peak experience is too intimate to share, (2) fear that the experience will be devalued by others, and (3) inability to adequately describe the experience (Davis et al., 1991).

Having peak experiences is a characteristic of self-actualizing people because Maslow (1963) found they tend to have more peak experiences than most people (see also Thomas & Cooper, 1980; cf. Daniels, 1988). Additionally, self-actualizers' openness to and acceptance of all their experiences make it more likely that they will (1) recognize peak experiences and (2) be able to use them to enhance themselves.

Examples of peak experiences   The variety of events that stimulate peak experiences is almost limitless. Let's look at two different personal accounts of peak experiences. The first involves a successful struggle to overcome a difficult situation.

It was to be the last and most difficult climb of our brief climbing trip. Because I was the novice of the group, Richard and Christopher briefed me on what lay above, giving special attention to the overhang in the third and last pitch [segment of a climb]. Some 50 feet below the summit there was a five-foot horizontal outcropping (at a right angle to the face of the cliff and parallel to the ground). Quite simply, to proceed to the summit, a climber would, for a brief time, be in a position where his or her back was parallel to the ground as the overhang was negotiated. I had never done anything like that before, but my more experienced team members assured me that it was within my capabilities.

The first two pitches were relatively uneventful, as was most of the third. Then there was a short traverse to the left along a narrow ledge, and I found myself directly below the overhang. I was being belayed [protected from a fall by a rope] from above by Christopher who, because of the overhang, was out of sight and sound. Fortunately, Richard was below me and gave me detailed instructions as to how to negotiate the overhang. It would involve jamming [wedging] both feet in a large crack in the vertical wall while my right hand gripped the underside of the overhang at about the position of my right knee and my left hand made a small but secure finger jam in a crack on the underside of the overhang at about the level of my shoulder. In fact, it was easier to get into this position than the description might sound, and because it was a secure position, I felt relatively safe to rest in it for the moment. However, the next and critical move would require me to let go of my secure right grip, straighten my legs, and reach up and around the overhang to blindly feel for a large handhold on the top side of the overhang.

That was easier explained than done. My right hand must have started its assigned journey a dozen times in the next five minutes, only to quickly retreat to its secure hold each time. Finally, it was time to take a risk. My right hand quickly found the crack on the top, and it was not difficult to then move my left hand into the same crack, release my legs from their supports, and mantle [raise oneself by pressing downward with the arms] to the top of the overhang.

I was exhilarated, triumphant, almost giddy with joy. As I climbed the last bit to the top, I had to keep reminding myself that I'd better pay attention lest I fall on this relatively easy final ascent.

Safely on top, I told Christopher, "Off belay," and we proceeded to embrace each other. I asked him if he wanted me to belay Richard to the top; he said no, that he was fine and that I should rest. So I walked along the summit and shortly came to a magnificent overlook, displaying the entire lush green valley to the southeast. As I stood there, glowing in the warmth of the afternoon sun and my own energy, I had the following thoughts, which I will never forget.

I was surely not ready to die. I may never have felt more alive—that life was so full and worth living—than at that moment. But, if I had to die, I was more ready to—because I had lived.

The events that result in peak experiences are usually pleasant, but they also can be unpleasant. The peak experience itself, however, is always enriching and growth producing if the person recognizes it as such.

A woman related a peak experience that was initially stimulated by intense flulike symptoms (Liebert & Spiegler, 1990). She was delusional from high fever, and her whole body ached, which kept her from sleeping. After about 12 hours, she finally dozed off for three-quarters of an hour. She described the peak experience she had when she awoke as follows.

I was immediately aware that the fever had broken. I was cool, without having chills; I was thinking straight; my body was still sore but it no longer ached as it had. I could not get over the sudden, drastic change. I may never have been more aware of my physical self than at that moment. (cited in Liebert & Spiegler, 1990, p. 336)

The two people whose peak experiences we just described were not self-actualizers. Fortunately, all people have occasional peak experiences, although they tend to have them less often than self-actualizers. Maslow considered peak experiences to be "transient moments of self-actualization of ordinary people" (Chiang & Maslow, 1977).

■ *Demonstration 15-2:*
BECOMING AWARE OF YOUR PEAK EXPERIENCES

Becoming aware of peak experiences is necessary for our being able to use them to enhance ourselves. This Demonstration will help you recognize peak experiences.

To identify your peak experiences, think of the most wonderful experiences of your life. They may be the happiest moments, the most ecstatic moments, moments of rapture. They may have come from being in love, from listening to music, from "being struck" by a book or painting, from some creative moment, from having a profound insight. They may have arisen from doing something—even a minor task—extremely well. These special moments will be unique to you; it does not matter whether anyone else would consider them special.

To qualify as a peak experience, the experience must have been *brief,* ranging from a few seconds to several minutes. It must also be an *actual experience* that fulfills the definition of a peak experience. Do *not* include experiences that are "supposed" to be "peak experiences" because "everyone knows" they are special (e.g., winning a contest, graduating from high school, becoming engaged, and making love).

This Demonstration involves four simple steps. Write the information for each step on Work Sheet 15-2, which you can remove from the Demonstration Materials section at the back of the book.

1. Write a brief account of three peak experiences in your life. Record your description in the first column of the work sheet.

2. In the second column, write, in a few words, the *general* nature of each peak experience (e.g., "finally getting something to work," "being in love," "getting an 'A'"). In other words, label each experience.

3. In the third column, list words or phrases that describe how you felt during each peak experience. In particular, note *how you felt* differently *from the way you generally feel*—how you were at the moment a different person in some way.

4. Circle those feelings you listed in step 3 that are relevant to more than one of your peak experiences.

Exploring your peak experiences and how you felt during them can be enlightening. For example, you may find that some of your happiest, most special moments have come at times that you would not have predicted—perhaps in the midst of rather ordinary activities or events. By discovering the circumstances in your life that are most likely to result in peak experiences, you may choose to repeat the circumstances more often merely because they have, at times, led to peak experiences.

You may wish to compare your peak experiences with the peak experiences of other students who have done this Demonstration. You do not have to reveal the intimate details of your peak experiences. You can share what you have written in the second and third columns of the work sheet.

Imperfections of Self-Actualizing People

Despite the idealistic nature of the characteristics of self-actualizing people, Maslow (1963) made it clear that these individuals are not perfect.

They too are equipped with silly, wasteful, or thoughtless habits. They can be boring, stubborn, irritating. They are by no means free from a rather superficial vanity, pride, partiality to their own productions, family, friends, and children. Temper outbursts are not rare. Our subjects are occasionally capable of an extraordinary and unexpected ruthlessness. It must be remembered that they are very strong people. This makes it possible for them to display a surgical coldness when this is called for, beyond the power of the average man. The man who found that a long-trusted acquaintance was dishonest cut himself off from this friendship sharply and abruptly and without any pangs whatsoever . . . [A] woman who was married to someone she did not love, when she decided on divorce, did it with a decisiveness that looked almost like ruthlessness. Some of them recover so quickly from the death of people close to them as to seem heartless. (pp. 550–551)

Besides having their share of human frailties, self-actualizers need not be highly intelligent or educated, at least in the traditional sense. They also do not have to be famous and need not make noteworthy contributions. Self-actualizers may be quietly and privately living to their full potential—undistinguished in the public eye, but distinctive in being as fully human as they are capable of being.

Self-Actualizing by Chance?   The main character in the movie *Being There* (based on Jerzy Kosinski's 1970 novel by the same name) might be considered a self-actualizing person. Chance (played by the late Peter Sellers) would be labeled a "simpleton." He is illiterate and uneducated. His life consists of watching television and gardening (he is fairly skilled at the latter). His basic needs are provided for by virtue of his being a permanent "guest" of a rich old man.

When his benefactor dies, Chance, by a quirk of fate, becomes the temporary guest of another rich and influential man, Ben Rand. Ben is quickly impressed by Chance's fresh appreciation of life, his complete candor and spontaneity, his genuineness and total lack of pretense, and his acceptance of his life for what it is. Chance has undoubtedly become everything that he is capable of becoming (and, in some sense, even more). The irony, and the source of the story's humor, is that although Chance's intellectual potential appears very limited, most people believe he is deep and profound. Even the President of the United States, whom Chance meets through Ben, is impressed with him. When the President asks for Chance's opinion on the faultering national economy, he replies: " 'In a garden . . . growth has its season. There are spring and summer, but there are also fall and winter. And then spring and summer again. As long as the roots are not severed, all is well and all will be well' " (Kosinski, 1970, p. 54). The President takes Chance's comments to indicate that the economy, like nature, has its inevitable ups and downs. The President is impressed with how "refreshing and optimistic" Chance's remarks are and praises his "good solid sense." In fact, given Chance's minimal intellectual capacity, his ideas about seasonal changes might well be considered extremely insightful from a phenomenological perspective.

Thus, Chance has a number of the characteristics of self-actualizers, and he is clearly living up to his potential. But is Chance a self-actualizer (albeit an atypical example)? Many people find it hard to answer a clear "yes." Their hesitancy focuses on Chance's intellectual capacities. What do you think?*

ASSESSING SELF-ACTUALIZATION

A major criticism of Maslow's research is that the criteria for identifying self-actualizers are highly subjective; they are based almost entirely on the clinical impressions of Maslow and his co-workers. Partially in response to this criticism, some objective tests of values and behaviors related to self-actualization have been developed. These self-report inventories provide a means of efficiently assessing self-actualization.

The Personal Orientation Inventory

The *Personal Orientation Inventory* (POI) consists of 150 forced-choice items to which respondents merely indicate which of two statements more consistently applies to them (Knapp, 1976; Shostrom, 1963, 1964, 1974; Shostrom, Knapp, & Knapp, 1976). Table 15-4 contains examples of the type of items found on the POI. The POI has become a standard measure in research examining factors related to self-actualization (e.g., Alexander, Rainforth, & Gelderloos, 1991; Burwick & Knapp, 1991; Duncan, Konefal, & Spechler, 1990; Faulkender, 1991; Sherrill et al., 1990). The POI has also been used for personnel and clinical screening, evaluation, and classification purposes, but its validity for such individual applications is questionable (Whitson & Olczak, 1991).

The POI provides information about a person's fundamental personal orientations on two scales. *Time ratio* indicates the degree that a person is present-oriented versus past-oriented and future-oriented. Self-actualization

*If you'd like more information on which to base your opinion, *Being There* is readily available for rental on videotape.

Table 15-4

Items and instructions similar to those appearing on the Personal Orientation Inventory (POI)

---

1. *a* I enjoy listening to dirty stories.
   b. I rarely enjoy listening to dirty stories.
2. *a*. I am afraid of expressing my emotions.
   b. I am not afraid of expressing my emotions.
3. *a*. Daydreaming about the future is harmful.
   b. Daydreaming about the future is good.
4. *a*. I have a lot of bad memories.
   b. I have very few bad memories.
5. *a*. People are naturally friendly.
   b. People are naturally hostile.

Note: Choices that are consistent with self-actualizing would be *b* for all items except item 5.

Figure 15-4
Schematic representation
of the difference between
time competence (living
in the present), which
is characteristic of
self-actualizers, and *time
incompetence* (living in
the past and future),
which is characteristic of
non-self-actualizers.
Source: Adapted from *Manual for the Personal Orientation Inventory* by E. L.
Shostrom, 1974, San Diego,
EdiTS.

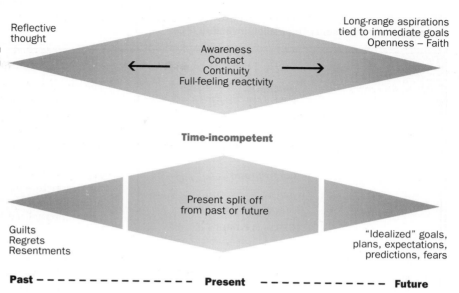

is associated with greater emphasis on the present (*time competence*) than the past or future (*time incompetence*). The difference between time competence and time incompetence is summarized in Figure 15-4.

The other major scale of the POI is the *support ratio,* which assesses the degree to which an individual is self-oriented versus other-oriented. Self-actualizers tend to be more self-directed than other-directed, in a ratio of about 3:1. Non–self-actualizers tend to have approximately a 1:1 ratio (an even balance between self-orientation and other-orientation).

The POI also measures key components of self-actualization on 10 subscales. Brief descriptions of the scales and subscales appear in Table 15-5.

Interpreting the POI involves examining the pattern of scores obtained on the 2 scales and 10 subscales. A profile is plotted on a psychogram; this method is used in many self-report inventories (see Figure 9-1, p. 171). To interpret the POI, a psychologist must understand the inventory and its rationale and be conversant with the theoretical concept of self-actualization.

**The Short
Index of
Self-Actualization**
The POI is the most frequently used paper-and-pencil measure of self-actualization, despite some criticism of its original validation studies (e.g., Weiss, 1987, 1991). However, one practical limitation of the 150-item POI for research is its length. Accordingly, a Short Index of Self-Actualization made up of 15 items from the POI has been developed (Crandall & Jones, 1991; Jones & Crandall, 1986; Richard & Jex, 1991; Tucker & Dyson, 1991; cf. Flett, Blankstein, & Hewitt, 1991; cf. Weiss, 1991). Table 15-6 presents the items on the Short Index.

Table 15-5
The scales of the Personal Orientation Inventory (POI)

	SCALE NAME	DESCRIPTION
I. Ratio scores	*Time ratio*	The ratio of time incompetence to time competence indicates the degree to which a person lives in (is oriented toward) the past and future versus the present, respectively.
	Support ratio	The ratio of other to inner indicates the degree to which a person relies primarily on social or external factors versus internalized factors, respectively, to guide behavior.
II. Subscales* Valuing	*Self-actualizing value*	Measures extent to which person holds values of self-actualizing people.
	Existentiality	Measures degree of flexibility in applying principles to one's life.
Feeling	*Feeling reactivity*	Measures sensitivity to one's own feelings and needs.
	Spontaneity	Measures one's ability to express feelings behaviorally, to be onself, to be uninhibited.
Self-perception	*Self-regard*	Measures ability to like oneself because of one's strengths and worth.
	Self-acceptance	Measures ability to like oneself in spite of one's strengths and weaknesses.
Awareness	*Nature of man*	Measures the extent to which a person views people as essentially good.
	Synergy	Measures the ability to view opposites in life as meaningfully related (e.g., viewing work and play as not really different).
Interpersonal sensitivity	*Acceptance of aggression*	Measures ability to accept one's anger or aggression as natural and to not deny such feelings.
	Capacity for intimate contact	Measures the ability to make meaningful, close relations with other people.

*The subscales can be grouped into complementary pairs—valuing, feeling, self-perception, awareness, and interpersonal sensitivity—representing the balancing that is important for self-actualization.

Table 15-6
Items on a short index of self-actualization

1. I do not feel ashamed of any of my emotions.
2. I feel I must do what others expect me to do.
3. I believe that people are essentially good and can be trusted.
4. I feel free to be angry at those I love.
5. It is always necessary that others approve of what I do.
6. I don't accept my own weaknesses.
7. I can like people without having to approve of them.
8. I fear failure.
9. I avoid attempts to analyze and simplify complex domains.
10. It is better to be yourself than to be popular.
11. I have no mission in life to which I feel especially dedicated.
12. I can express my feelings even when they may result in undesirable consequences.
13. I do not feel responsible to help anybody.
14. I am bothered by fears of being inadequate.
15. I am loved because I give love.

Note: Agreeing with items 1, 3, 4, 7, 10, 12, and 15 and disagreeing with items 2, 5, 6, 8, 9, 11, 13, and 14 are scored as self-actualizing.

Source: Jones & Crandall, 1986.

CROSS-VALIDATION OF MASLOW'S CONCEPT OF SELF-ACTUALIZATION

Researchers have attempted to validate the findings of Maslow's classic investigation of self-actualizers. Most of this research has used the POI or the Short Index of Self-Actualization. Table 15-7 presents some of the variables that have been found to be positively and negatively correlated with self-actualization and that are consistent with Maslow's findings and theorizing.

One limitation of these findings is that they are all based on the concept of self-actualization embodied in the POI, which is not entirely consistent with Maslow's theory (e.g., Weiss, 1991). For example, one study has found that self-actualization scores on the POI are positively related to masculinity and negatively related to femininity (Faulkender, 1991). Given the independence from their culture that Maslow observed in self-actualizers, it would be expected that self-actualization scores would be independent of cultural stereotypes (cf. Coan, 1991).

CHARACTERISTICS OF SELF-ACTUALIZERS AS GUIDES FOR LIVING

The characteristics of self-actualizers are attractive to many people. Self-actualizers represent something of ideal human beings. You may, in fact, have wondered whether you could develop some of the characteristics of self-actualizers and thus become more self-actualizing yourself. The answer is not entirely clear.

Maslow believed that self-actualizing individuals comprise a fraction of 1% of the population (Hoffman, 1992). Further, his writings imply that

Table 15-7
Variables found to be correlated with self-actualization that are consistent with Maslow's conceptualizations

POSITIVE CORRELATION

personal autonomy[1]
social interest[2]
having a life purpose[3]
optimism[4]
self-esteem[4]
creativeness[5]
assertiveness[6]
religiosity[7]
acceptance of failure[8]

NEGATIVE CORRELATION

perfectionism[8]
boredom proneness[9]
trait anxiety[4]
depression[10]
life stress[10]

[1]Bordages, 1989; Hjelle, 1991

[2]Hjelle, 1991

[3]Ebersole & Humphreys, 1991

[4]Richard & Jex, 1991

[5]Runco et al., 1991

[6]Crandall, McCown, & Robb, 1988

[7]Watson et al., 1990 (when no antireligious items appear on the scale)

[8]Flett, Hewitt, et al., 1991

[9]McLeod & Vodanovich, 1991

[10]Ford & Procidano, 1990

they are an elite group (cf. Rule, 1991). These assumptions can "easily foster the belief that self-actualization is an all-or-none affair and that the achievement of this exalted state is the prerogative of 'Great Men' (Maslow's sample is predominantly male)" (Daniels, 1988, p. 22).

Maslow did not clarify whether self-actualization is a goal that can be sought or whether it must "come about" as a result of life experiences (Daniels, 1988). Researchers have attempted to identify factors that might increase a person's self-actualizing. Studies have shown, for example, that practicing transcendental meditation (Alexander, Rainforth, & Gelderloos, 1991), training in neurolinguistic programming (Duncan, Konefal, & Spechler, 1990), and participating in a growth group (Barnette, 1989) were associated with increased self-actualization scores on the POI.

It is doubtful, however, that meditating or attending training or growth groups will result in a person becoming a self-actualizer—at least not becoming the type of person whom Maslow identified as such. One does not enroll in courses to learn to become a self-actualizer. There is no prescribed curriculum that, once mastered, allows one to graduate with an M.S.A. (Master of Self-Actualization!).

The process of becoming self-actualizing appears to be complex, involving exposure to experiences that are more pervasive and long-term than specific training could provide. For instance, an investigation of case studies of people who were functioning at the level of self-actualization indicated that they had had emotionally difficult and disruptive life experiences as well as intense, life-affirming experiences (Brennan & Piechowski, 1991).

Thus, it is highly unlikely that a person can become a self-actualizer by setting out to achieve that goal. More realistically, however, it seems quite possible for most people to use the characteristics of self-actualizers as goals or guides for living and to develop specific attitudes and behaviors that are consistent with those characteristics.

SUMMARY

1. Maslow developed a general theory of motivation. He is especially noted for his investigations of the role of self-actualization motives.

2. Maslow believed that people are motivated by a common set of instinctoid needs that have a biological basis. They are arranged in a hierarchy of levels that are, in order of decreasing strength: physiological, safety, belongingness and love, esteem, and self-actualization.

3. People progress up the hierarchy, beginning with the strongest needs. Generally, when needs at a particular level are met, the individual works on meeting needs in the next level. Exceptions to this upward movement occur when previously met needs are temporarily not being met.

4. In most Western cultures, physiological and safety needs are generally met as a matter of course, and thus they are not strong motivators. Love and belongingness and esteem needs motivate most adult behaviors.

5. Self-actualization needs are concerned with a person's fulfilling his or her unique potential. They are the weakest needs and are only goals toward which people strive. Most people's behaviors are minimally motivated by self-actualization needs. Self-actualization needs motivate by growth, and they are qualitatively different from the other four levels of needs, which motivate by deficit.

6. Maslow identified individuals who are primarily motivated by self-actualization needs and studied them intensively to discover their common characteristics. The 15 characteristics are as follows: efficient perception; acceptance; continued freshness of appreciation; spontaneity; problem-

centered; discrimination between means and ends, right and wrong; detachment; independence from culture and environment; resistance to enculturation; desire to help others; democratic; deep interpersonal relations; philosophical sense of humor; creativeness; and peak experiences. Self-actualizers are not perfect human beings, nor are they always highly intelligent or famous.

7. Although self-actualizers tend to have more peak experiences than most people, almost everyone has them occasionally. They are characterized by a brief, spontaneous, and intense feeling that is recognized as significant. Peak experiences are always growth producing.

8. The Personal Orientation Inventory (POI) is a forced-choice self-report inventory that assesses values and behaviors related to self-actualization. Two important scales derived from the POI concern time orientation (present versus past and future) and support orientation (self versus other).

Chapter Sixteen

Kelly's Personal Construct Theory

I n the classic movie, *Lawrence of Arabia,* T. E. Lawrence is leading an Arab military expedition across the Nefud Desert to attack the port city of Akaba. When one of the men, Gasim, is discovered missing, Lawrence wants to go back to rescue him. An older Arab tells Lawrence that it is no use. "Gasim's time is come, Lawrence. It is written." Lawrence vehemently disagrees, declaring, "Nothing is *written!*" Another Arab warns that if he goes back after the man, Lawrence will never reach their goal, Akaba. To this Lawrence replies, "I shall be in Akaba. That is written—in here [pointing to his head]."

T. E. Lawrence's words are the essence of **constructive alternativism**, the philosophical position that *there are always alternative ways of viewing the world.* Thus, "nothing is written." At the same time, each person can choose to view events as he or she desires. In other words, "what is written" is a construction of one's mind. One implication of this position is that no one need be completely the victim of present circumstances or history. Constructive alternativism is the basis for George A. Kelly's theory of personal constructs (Stewart & Barry, 1991).

Early in his career, Kelly, like Rogers and many other personality theorists, was a clinician doing psychotherapy, which, in 1931, meant psychoanalysis. The more he interpreted his clients' behaviors, the more he began to realize that the accuracy of his interpretations was not critical. What was important in helping clients change was that the interpretations allowed clients to see themselves and their problems in new ways. Kelly (1969) tried an informal experiment, which he described as follows:

> I began fabricating "insights." I deliberately offered "preposterous interpretations" to my clients. Some of them were about as unFreudian as I could make them . . . My only criteria were that the explanation account for the crucial facts as the client saw them, and that it carry implications for approaching the future in a different way. (p. 52)

Eventually Kelly concluded that clients had their own interpretations of happenings in their lives, which were ultimately responsible for their problems. He came to believe that clients would change their abnormal behaviors if he could help them reinterpret themselves and events in their lives differently. Kelly used the term *event* to refer to anything going on in a person's life, including people, things, and happenings (Horley, 1988).

In 1955, Kelly published *The Psychology of Personal Constructs,* a two-volume, 1,200-page *magnum opus.* In it, Kelly laid out what may be the most organized presentation of a comprehensive theory of personality ever written (e.g., Barris, 1990; John & Soyland, 1990). However, his theory received little recognition at the time. One reason was that Kelly's theory was viewed as a *cognitive* theory, which was counter to the alternative approaches in the 1950s (i.e., psychoanalytic, behavioristic, and humanistic). Today we can see that Kelly's ideas were ahead of their time, antedating the prominence of cognitive psychology and cognitive-behavioral therapy by almost 20 years (Adams-Webber, 1990; Anastasi, 1988a; Jankowicz, 1987; Mischel, 1980).

George Kelly
(1905-1967)
theorized that personality consists of a unique, organized set of personal constructs—ways of viewing experiences that people create to anticipate events in their lives.
Courtesy of National Library of Medicine

Kelly (1966) himself did not think of personal construct theory as a "cognitive" theory (Mascolo & Mancuso, 1990; Rychlak, 1990; Warren, 1990, 1991). He treated cognitions, actions, and feelings in the same psychological terms, rather than as separate processes—which is consistent with the holistic emphasis in the phenomenological strategy.

PEOPLE AS SCIENTISTS

Kelly (1955) noted a paradox in the way personality psychologists studied people.

> It is customary to say that the scientist's ultimate aim is to predict and control . . . .Yet curiously enough, psychologists rarely credit the human subjects in their experiments with having similar aspirations. It is as though the psychologist were saying . . . "I, being . . . a scientist, am performing this experiment in order to improve the prediction and control of certain human phenomena; but my subject, being merely a human organism, is obviously propelled by inexorable drives welling up within . . . or else is in gluttonous pursuit of sustenance and shelter." (p. 5)

This elitist position erroneously assumes that scientists are the only beings interested in prediction and control.

Many times every day, we make predictions about events in order to exert some control over them. Specifically, our behaviors are guided by implicit hypothesis testing (Berzonsky, 1989, 1990). For instance, you are reading these words right now because you predict that the information they convey is important in some way. If your hypothesis is confirmed (as by doing well when you are tested on this material), you are likely to employ the theory (construct) again in similar circumstances. If your hypothesis is disconfirmed, you will revise or discard the theory (construct).

Most of the time, we are unaware of this implicit predictive process in which we are continually engaged (Berzonsky, 1990). We may become more aware of it when our predictions fail. For example, rushing to brush his teeth before going to work, Pedro grabs the tube on the sink, predicting that it is toothpaste. When he is rudely surprised to find that he is brushing his teeth with hair gel, he realizes that his assumption (prediction) that the tube held toothpaste was incorrect.

Human beings are constantly predicting and controlling events in their lives. This observation led Kelly to view all people as "scientists" who have implicit theories that they test to guide their actions in dealing with people and events.

PERSONAL CONSTRUCTS: THE BASIC UNITS OF PERSONALITY

Kelly (1955) suggested that each of us views the world through *transparent patterns* or *templates*. We create these templates and then attempt to fit them over the realities that constitute the world (see Figure 16-1). **Constructs,** as Kelly called the templates, are representations or interpretations of events—

Figure 16-1
Kelly likened constructs to templates that people fit over events in order to make sense of them. In this representation, a template of a house is being placed over a nonconventional dwelling place. In other words, the construct of house is being used to interpret the unusual dwelling.

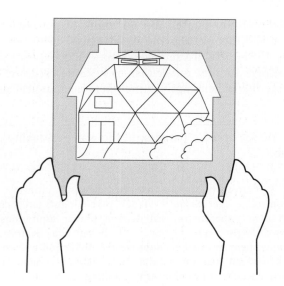

ways of viewing something. In other words, constructs are *imposed* on events; constructs are *not* abstracted from the events they are being used to interpret (Kirkland & Anderson, 1990).

No event is inextricably associated with any particular construct — an event can *always* be viewed from a variety of different perspectives. As people change the constructs they use to construe an event, their behaviors change. Consider the case of a psychiatric patient we will call Kay (Neale, 1968). Kay's behavior was among the most deviant on the ward. Her speech was unintelligible. She had extremely poor personal habits. She babbled and made strange gestures in the presence of other patients and visitors. One day, a nurse took her to the beauty parlor to have her hair done and then dressed her in an attractive outfit, including stockings, high heels, and lipstick. When Kay returned to the ward several hours later, she no longer behaved in the bizarre ways that had been her trademark. Yet, she was still a patient in a psychiatric hospital. In every other respect, her *circumstances* were the same. It seemed, however, that she had changed the *way she construed herself*. And her new constructs resulted in new behaviors.

Kellian constructs always take the form of one characteristic *versus* another (often opposite) characteristic. (We will discuss the bipolar nature of constructs later.) Examples of Kellian constructs would be:

> *just vs. unjust*
>
> *stable vs. changing*
>
> *flexible vs. dogmatic*
>
> *warm vs. aloof*
>
> *friend vs. lover.*

Personal constructs are always unique. Thus, Kelly called them *personal*. But the *labels* we use to describe our constructs are not unique. For instance, virtually everyone makes occasional use of the labels *smart* and *dumb*, but each person's *meaning* for them is different. Verbal labels are *not* constructs; they are merely symbols of the constructs. Two constructs with the same label do not necessarily have the same meaning. Consider the varied meanings that constructs labeled *success vs. failure* and *difficult vs. easy* have for different people. "Language falsifies reality by artificially structuring and simplifying our raw experience of it" (Delmonte, 1989, p. 87). Thus, to understand an individual's personal constructs, one must explore how they are used to construe experiences.

Constructs are used to **construe**, or place an interpretation on, events. In construing an event, a person generates a hypothesis based on a construct to *predict* something about the event. Then the person tests the hypothesis by acting as the construct dictates. Pedro, who hurriedly brushed his teeth, used a construct *toothpaste vs. not toothpaste* and tested the hypothesis that the tube on the sink contained toothpaste.

The validity of a construct depends on its success in anticipating events, which is called its **predictive efficiency**. People hold on to constructs that predict events and discard or revise those that fail to predict events.

Properties of Constructs

Constructs differ on three important dimensions: (1) their range of convenience; (2) their focus of convenience; and (3) their degree of permeability.

Range of Convenience

Each construct is useful for construing only a limited set of events. The set of events to which a construct is applicable is its **range of convenience**. A construct's range of convenience defines its usefulness. For example, the construct *religious vs. not religious* can be used to construe a variety of human endeavors, but it is hardly applicable for predicting the behavior of a pet. The construct *religious vs. not religious* will not predict whether Spotty will sit on command. Spotty's actions are simply outside the construct's range of convenience.

Constructs differ in how wide their ranges of convenience are. *Good vs. bad* has a much wider range of convenience than *brave vs. cowardly* because the former can be used to construe many more events.

Focus of Convenience

Within its range of convenience, each construct is especially successful at predicting a restricted set of events, called its **focus of convenience**. For example, the focus of convenience of *religious vs. not religious* might be the customs and ceremonies of a church. Cheating on an exam *could* be construed by *religious vs. not religious,* but it would be more efficiently construed by *honest vs. dishonest*. Cheating falls within the range of convenience of both constructs, but it is only the focus of convenience of *honest vs. dishonest*.

Permeability

The degree to which a given construct can be used to construe new events is called its **permeability**. The more open a construct is to construing new events, the more permeable it is. A relatively permeable construct is "open" and can be used to construe many new events. A relatively impermeable construct is "closed" to construing most new events.

Bernie's construct of *good symphonic music vs. bad symphonic music* was sufficiently permeable to account for just about any new piece of music the Chicago Symphony Orchestra played. The first time he heard computer-synthesized music, he was able to construe it as either *good* or *bad*. In contrast, Barbara's construct of *good symphonic music vs. bad symphonic music* was impermeable to any sounds other than those made by traditional orchestral instruments. Thus, Barbara could not use the construct to construe computer-synthesized music. Instead, she used the construct *pleasant sound vs. unpleasant sound.*

A construct is permeable only to events in its range of convenience. For instance, animals, ideas, and computers fit in the range of convenience of *intelligent vs. stupid.* Thus, the construct is permeable to construing those events. Rocks and trees, however, are not in the construct's range of convenience. The construct is impermeable to rocks and trees.

THE FUNDAMENTAL POSTULATE AND ITS COROLLARIES

Kelly's theory of personal constructs is organized around a fundamental postulate and 11 corollaries (see Table 16-1). Kelly's words are sometimes difficult to understand, perhaps because his "language reaches toward alternative ways of saying things that have become lost in too much familiarity" (Mair, 1990, p. 129). Once "translated," his words are rich in meaning, as you will see.

Predicting Events

The Fundamental Postulate and the Construction and Choice corollaries deal with how people predict events, which is the role of personal constructs.

Fundamental Postulate

Kelly's Fundamental Postulate indicates that *the purpose of personality* (and other psychological processes) *is to predict events,* which is why Kelly referred to people as "scientists" (Walker, 1992). Kelly, like Rogers, saw humans as active organisms who do not need to be pushed by needs or drives or pulled by incentives (Castorina & Mancini, 1992; Walker, 1990). Instead, people are motivated to actively anticipate events simply because that is their "reason for being." Kelly's theory is concerned with *active processes* rather than static personality structures (Delmonte, 1990).

Construction Corollary

People make predictions about events by viewing them in terms of *recurrent themes.* In other words, we search for characteristics of events that are relatively stable over time and in different circumstances. This is necessary

Table 16-1
Kelly's fundamental postulate and corollaries

FUNDAMENTAL POSTULATE	A person's processes are psychologically channelized by the ways in which the person anticipates events.
Construction Corollary	A person anticipates events by construing their replications.
Choice Corollary	A person chooses that alternative in a dichotomized construct through which he or she anticipates the greater possibility for extension and definition of his or her system.
Dichotomy Corollary	A person's construct system is composed of a finite number of dichotomous constructs.
Range Corollary	A construct is convenient for the anticipation of a finite range of events only.
Organization Corollary	Each person characteristically evolves, for convenience in anticipating events, a construct system embracing ordinal relationships between constructs.
Experience Corollary	A person's construct system varies as the person successively construes the replications of events.
Modulation Corollary	The variation in a person's construction system is limited by the permeability of the constructs within whose range of convenience the variants lie.
Fragmentation Corollary	A person may successively employ a variety of construction subsystems which are inferentially incompatible with each other.
Individuality Corollary	Persons differ from each other in their construction of events.
Commonality Corollary	To the extent that one person employs a construction of experience which is similar to that employed by another, his or her processes are psychologically similar to those of the other person.
Sociality Corollary	To the extent that one person construes the construction processes of another, he or she may play a role in a social process involving the other person.

Adapted from *The Psychology of Personal Constructs* (Vols. 1 and 2) by G. A. Kelly, 1955, W. W. Norton & Company.

because no two events are ever exactly the same. Fortunately, we can identify characteristics of events that remain relatively stable. If we could not, daily life would be chaotic. There would be no basis for predicting even the most minor events. Each day, one would have to "start from scratch" in dealing with hundreds of events. For example, each class a student attends is different. Yet there are enough similarities (recurrent themes), such as the general roles played by students and teachers, that students can predict what will happen in each new class and thus know how to act.

Construing Similarities and Differences   To construe events, we must identify themes that are both similar and different. Differences provide *contrasts* that are necessary to comprehend any concept. Without knowledge of a contrast or opposite, concepts have no meaning. "Delicious meal," "dry wine," and "stimulating companion" mean something to us only because we can refer to their contrasts: "tasteless meal," "sweet wine," and "boring companion." Without the contrasts, we might enjoy the meal, wine, and companion, but we would not be able to refer to them as "delicious," "dry," or "stimulating." As another illustration of the importance of contrasts, the next time you are sick, consider how your temporary pain and discomfort is made worse by knowing how it feels to be well (cf. Jackson, Markley, Zelhart, & Guydish, 1988).

Nonverbal constructs   Many constructs cannot be put into words. Infants use **preverbal constructs** involving physiological, kinesthetic, and emotional patterns. As adults, when our verbal constructs fails us, our "last line of 'defense' is often the preverbal constructions of infancy; for example, extreme dependency" (Kenny & Delmonte, 1986, p. 12). "Resorting to childhood preverbal constructs" would be a Kellian definition of the Freudian concept of regression (Delmonte, 1990).

    Adults also use **nonverbal constructs**, which, unlike preverbal constructs, are *potentially* verbalizable. For instance, most constructs dealing with sexuality are physical rather than verbal, but we can attempt to "put them into words" (Cummins, 1992). "Riding a bicycle" is another example of a complex, nonverbal construct (Polanyi, 1959). Even after years of no practice, we are able to ride a bike—although we cannot say how we do it (at least not without a great deal of thought).

    Adult nonverbal constructs may be those that developed as a young child, to which verbal labels were never attached. They also may develop later in life, but the person still may be unable to verbalize them. Sexual abuse is an experience that people typically construe nonverbally because of its threatening, "unthinkable" nature. People who have been sexually abused may be repulsed by any sexual or even nonsexual touch but have no (verbal) explanation for their reaction. As one woman put it: "When my husband touches me, I feel a chill go through me. I don't know why, as he is a really caring man and I know he would not hurt me" (Cummins, 1992, p. 360). On an everyday basis, we've all had the experience of understanding an event but not being able to put the understanding into words. Kelly (1955) likened the experience to "handling a live fish in the dark; not only does it wiggle but it is slippery and hard to see" (p. 1082).

Choice Corollary

In the course of a day, we encounter hundreds of events about which we must make predictions. In each instance, we choose (1) one of our personal constructs and (2) one of the two poles of that construct to interpret the event. The criterion we use to make these choices is predictive efficiency. We enhance the predictive efficiency of a construct either by *defining* it more precisely or by *extending* its range of convenience to new events.

Definition involves using a construct in the same way as we have used it on past occasions. If the present prediction is accurate, the construct becomes more precise (defined) because it has successfully predicted another event.

Extension involves choices that are most likely to expand the usefulness of the construct by increasing its range of convenience. One way to extend a construct is to use it to anticipate a familiar event in a new way. For example, Dave had always used the pole *plain* of the construct *attractive vs. plain* to characterize women with short hair. When he fell in love with Kristina, who had short hair, he was "forced" to use the *attractive* pole, which extended his construct.

The other way to extend a construct is to use it to anticipate a new class of events. For instance, Charles was, by his own admission, a "couch potato." He used his construct *active vs. passive* to construe the pace of TV shows. When his friends convinced Charles to join a health club with them, Charles began to use *active vs. passive* to anticipate a whole new set of events.

Definition can be thought of as a relatively safe wager with a modest payoff; if the prediction is correct, the construct becomes slightly more precise. Extension is a riskier bet with a larger payoff; if the prediction is correct, the construct becomes substantially more comprehensive. Kelly (1955) spoke of the difference between definition and extension as being between security and adventure. "One may anticipate events by trying to become more and more certain about fewer and fewer things [definition] or by trying to become vaguely aware of more and more things on the misty horizon [extension]" (p. 67).

The Nature of Constructs

The Dichotomy and Range corollaries are concerned with the specific nature of personal constructs.

Dichotomy Corollary

Kelly conceived of constructs as having two dichotomous poles. A construct must have two poles so that both similarity and difference can be recognized. But to construe an event, a person needs *three* events: (1) the event being construed; (2) a second event that is similar to it; and (3) a third event that is different from the first two.

Consider the example of Elmer who dives into a swimming pool and screams, "It's freezing." To construe the water as *freezing*, Elmer must *compare* it to water he previously construed as *freezing*. He also must *contrast* it to water that is some other temperature, such as *hot*. His concept of *freezing* has no meaning without both the comparison and the contrast. If he had only been in water that he considered *freezing*, then he could not make any comparison with *hot* water. In that case, Elmer could only use a construct such as *water vs. not water*.

One pole of a construct specifies similarity, the other pole specifies difference. The **emergent pole,** which designates similarity, is used directly or explicitly to construe an event. The **implicit pole,** which designates difference, is used indirectly as a contrast. In the previous example of *freezing vs. hot*, *freezing* was the emergent pole and *hot* was the implicit pole. Which pole is emergent and which is implicit depend on the situation. If Elmer were a penguin, he might consider the water *hot*. Then the poles would be reversed: *Hot* would be the emergent pole and *freezing* the implicit pole.

The implicit pole of a construct consists only of contrasting events. It does *not* include irrelevant events as well (Kelly, 1955; Millis & Neimeyer, 1990; Slife, Stoneman, & Rychlak, 1991). In other words, events that are placed at the implicit pole must be in the construct's range of convenience. For example, suppose *friendly* was the emergent pole of the construct *friendly vs. unfriendly*. The implicit pole *unfriendly* could be used to construe people, pets, and some places (e.g., a friendly atmosphere). But it would not make sense to use it to construe luggage, linen, or lollipops because they fall outside the construct's range of convenience.

The two poles of a construct are *discrete and mutually exclusive*. They are not the ends of a continuum. Thus, in interpreting an event, a person places it at either one pole or the other—not somewhere in between. How, then, can events be construed in degrees? Kelly's (1955) solution is that a series of dichotomous constructs can form a scale. For instance, constructs such as *cold vs. warm* and *chilly vs. lukewarm* in addition to *freezing vs. hot* would allow a person to construe various levels of temperature.

Evidence concerning the basic idea of bipolar constructs is mixed (e.g., Castorina & Mancini, 1992). Some studies support the view that constructs are bipolar (e.g., Millis & Neimeyer, 1990; Rychlak, 1991; Rychlak, Barnard, Williams, & Wollman, 1989; Slife, Stoneman, & Rychlak, 1991). Other investigations indicate that bipolarity may not be an essential aspect of personal constructs (e.g., Bonarius, 1984; Riemann, 1990). What is clear, however, is that the meaning of a personal construct requires contrast, as Kelly asserted. But the contrast may be with more than two concepts (Riemann, 1990).

Range Corollary

A construct's range of convenience is limited. Thus, we sometimes encounter events that we cannot construe. Either we have no applicable construct to interpret the new event, or our existing constructs that are relevant to the event are too impermeable to deal with it. Consider what happens when we visit a foreign culture very different from our own. We are likely to encounter "strange" customs that we cannot comprehend—in other words, that we cannot construe because of the limitations of our existing constructs.

Even in our everyday lives, we encounter events we cannot make sense of because we do not have adequate constructs to interpret them. When this happens, we experience **anxiety**.

Construct System: The Structure of Personality

A **construct system** consists of all of an individual's constructs, arranged in hierarchical order. Whereas constructs are the units of personality, the relation of constructs to one another—the construct system—makes up the *structure* of personality. The Organization, Experience, Modulation, and Fragmentation corollaries explain the nature of a construct system.

Organization Corollary

Constructs are arranged in a hierarchical order that facilitates anticipating events. People differ not only because they use different constructs but also because their constructs are organized in different ways. Two people can have similar personal constructs yet have vastly different personalities because their constructs are ordered differently (e.g., Chiari, Mancini, Nicolo, & Nuzzo, 1990).

Even the organization of just two constructs can have important implications. Take the two possible orders of the constructs *like vs. dislike* and *acceptable behavior vs. unacceptable behavior.* There is a substantial difference between viewing acceptable behavior in terms of its likability and viewing what is liked in terms of the acceptability of behavior.

Most constructs are subordinate to some constructs and superordinate to others. This organization allows a person to move from one construct to another in an orderly fashion and to resolve conflicts and inconsistencies among constructs. Consider the relationships among three of David's constructs depicted in Figure 16-2. *Loving vs. unloving* is superordinate to *giving vs. selfish* and *pleasant vs. unpleasant,* which are on the same level.

David has planned to spend the day at the beach with his friends. He is faced with the dilemma of deciding whether to let his younger brother, Miles, come along. If he takes Miles, David would construe himself as *giving* but the day at the beach as *unpleasant.* If he chooses not to take Miles, David would construe himself as *selfish* but the day as *pleasant.* Thus, using the two subordinate constructs, David is in a no-win situation. To resolve this conflict, David uses the superordinate construct *loving vs. unloving* to construe taking Miles to the beach. Now David can view his generous act as *giving* and *pleasant* because both of these poles are subsumed under *loving.*

Experience Corollary: How a Construct System Changes

A person's construct system changes as the person continuously construes the similar features of events. As we construe and reconstrue events, inevitable failures in predicting them occur; that is, our assumptions of similarity between previous events and new events do not always hold. When this

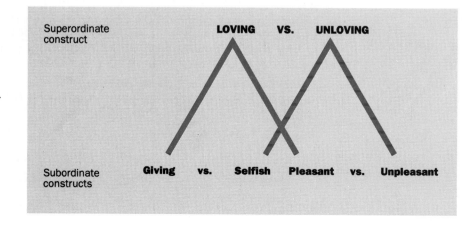

Figure 16-2
An example of a hierarchical structure among three personal constructs.

happens, the construct used must be modified or discarded. Modifying individual constructs results in changes in the construct system. *Minor* changes in our personal construct systems occur constantly (e.g., Castorina & Mancini, 1992).

In order to gain experience, our construct systems must change. Kelly (1955) defined **experience** as successively construing events. Thus, experience involves more than being a passive observer. To gain experience, people must interpret events differently than they have before—in short, they must *reconstrue* events. Kelly (1980) believed that events do not change people; rather, people change themselves by reconstruing events—that is, through experience.

Kelly's view of experience has intriguing implications. For example, it calls into question some people's alleged "experience," as in doing a particular job. A professor who gives the same lectures for 20 years can legitimately claim only 1 year of teaching experience. Another implication is that learning is an active process rather than a static outcome (Spiegler, 1989). Learning requires reconstruing events—seeing things differently. When students complete courses and still hold the same views of the subject matter that they had before they took the course, the students have not learned.

Modulation Corollary

For change in a construct system to occur, two basic conditions must be met. First, one's constructs must be permeable. When one's constructs are permeable, one's construct system can change.

Second, a person must be able to construe the change itself. Changing a construct or a group of constructs is an event. Thus, for the change to influence behavior, one must have a construct that can make sense of *a change occurring.*

Kelly (1955) provided the example of a man who shifts from using a construct of *fear vs. domination* to a construct of *respect vs. contempt.* Formerly, the man divided people in terms of those he was afraid of and those he could dominate. Now, he divides people between those whom he respects and those for whom he has contempt. To make this change in his construct system, the man needs a superordinate construct that can construe the change. Specifically, he needs a construct "within whose range of convenience . . . *fear vs. domination* . . . lies and which is sufficiently permeable to admit new ideas of *respect vs. contempt*" (Kelly, 1955, p. 82). *Childishness vs. maturity* would be such a construct (see Figure 16-3).

Emotion: Awareness of Construct Change

In personal construct theory, **emotions** are defined as the awareness of change or the need for change in one's construct system. The degree and nature of the change varies with different emotions (McCoy, 1981). The change can be:

1. *major* or *minor*—involving many constructs or a few;
2. *validating* or *invalidating*—involving successful or unsuccessful prediction of events; and

Figure 16-3
A person replaces an old construct, *fear vs. domination,* with a new construct, *respect vs. contempt.* To do this, the person must have a superordinate construct that can construe the change. *Childishness vs. maturity* qualifies because it can construe both constructs.

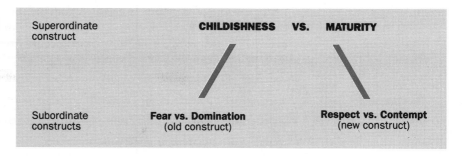

Superordinate construct	**CHILDISHNESS VS. MATURITY**	
Subordinate constructs	**Fear vs. Domination** (old construct)	**Respect vs. Contempt** (new construct)

3. *core* or *peripheral*—involving constructs that are comprehensive, relatively impermeable, and essential to one's identity or constructs that are narrower, more permeable, and not critical to one's identity.

Table 16-2 contains examples of common emotions defined according to personal construct theory.

Emotions may be viewed as primitive constructs; they may be present even before birth (Fisher, 1990a, 1990b). Emotions begin with sensorimotor experiences and are preverbal (Fisher, 1990a). Infants express their primitive emotional constructs in their preferences. Some respond positively to being cuddled; others do not. Some smile; others remain passive.

Individual Differences and Similarities

One's personality is what makes one both different from and similar to others. The Individuality, Commonality, and Sociality corollaries explain the basis of the unique and shared aspects of personality.

Individuality Corollary

Each person has a unique set of personal constructs, which means that people differ from one another in the way they construe events. No two people ever have exactly the same interpretation of an event (see Figure 16-4). All qualities, not just beauty, are in the eyes of the beholder. One interesting source of support for the Individuality Corollary comes from research on preference for television programs, which appears to be based on individual differences in people's construing television (Clair & Preston, 1990).

Construing events differently from other people can lead to disagreements about "the way things are." For instance, the "generation gap" that children and parents often experience may be more accurately a "personal construct gap" (Hjelle & Ziegler, 1981).

Commonality Corollary

The Commonality Corollary, the flip side of the Individuality Corollary, states that similarities between people are due to similarities in construing events. Two people are likely to behave similarly if they construe events in similar ways.

People can act alike even if they are exposed to different events, as long as they construe the different events by using similar constructs. Take the

Table 16-2
Emotions as defined by personal construct theory

Threat*	Awareness of imminent major change in one's core constructs
Fear*	Awareness of imminent minor change in one's core constructs
Bewilderment	Awareness of imminent major change in one's peripheral constructs
Doubt	Awareness of imminent minor change in one's peripheral constructs
Love	Awareness of validation of one's core constructs
Happiness	Awareness of validation of part of one's core constructs
Satisfaction	Awareness of validation of part of one's peripheral constructs
Complacency	Awareness of validation of a small part of one's peripheral constructs
Anger	Awarenss of invalidation of one's constructs, which leads to hostility
Sadness	Awareness of the invalidation of implications of a part or all of one's core constructs
Guilt*	Awareness of deviating from one's core role constructs
Self-confidence	Awareness of one's self-concept fitting with one's core role constructs
Shame	Awareness of one's self-concept deviating from another person's construing of one's role
Contempt (Disgust)	Awareness that core constructs of another person is different in a major way from one's own and/or do not meet norms of social expectation
Surprise	Sudden awareness of a need to construe an event
Anxiety*	Awareness that events lie outside the range of convenience of one's constructs
Contentment	Awareness that events lie within the range of convenience of one's constructs

*These definitions are Kelly's (1955); the others are derived from his theory (McCoy, 1977).

Source: Adapted from "A Reconstruction of Emotion" by M. M. McCoy, 1977, in D. Bannister (Ed.), *New Perspectives in Personal Construct Theory*, London: Academic Press.

example of Mary and Steve, who are standing outside a Mexican restaurant. Mary notices the pleasant atmosphere. Steve sees on the menu in the window that they have some of his favorite dishes. Independently, each decides to have dinner at the restaurant. Their decisions are made by construing two separate events: atmosphere and food. However, they construe the different events similarly—namely, as an acceptable restaurant. Therefore, they engage in the same behavior—namely, eating at the restaurant.

A *culture* generally refers to a group of people who exhibit similar behaviors because they have had similar experiences. From the perspective of personal construct theory, it is not the similar experiences themselves that define a cultural group but the similarities in how people construe their experiences.

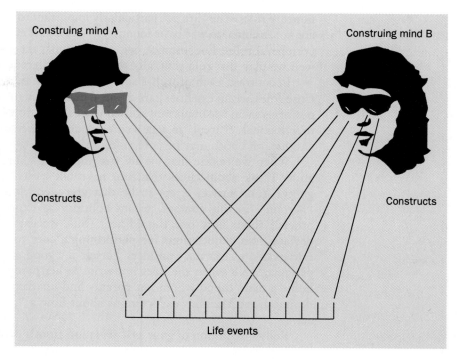

Figure 16-4
The same life events are viewed somewhat differently by different people because they are perceived through unique individual constructs, which are analogous to different colored glasses.
Source: Adapted from "The Psychology of Personal Constructs" by George A. Kelly, 1973, in J. Rychlak (Ed.), *Introduction to Personality and Psychotherapy,* Boston: Houghton Mifflin.

Sociality Corollary

The basic requirement for an interpersonal relationship is that *one person is playing a role in relation to another person.* To do this, the role player must construe how the other person views the role being played. Suppose Maria wants to play the role of "student" in relation to Professor Smart. Maria must predict how Professor Smart construes "student" and then act accordingly. For example, if Maria believes Professor Smart thinks that asking a lot of questions is essential to the student role, then she will ask questions.

Accurately construing another person's constructs is important in interpersonal interactions. Moreover, the ability of person *A* to play a role with respect to person *B* increases as *A* construes constructs that are more personally meaningful to *B* (Benesch & Page, 1989). The most personally meaningful constructs are **core constructs**; they define us, form the basis of our identity, and have value for us (Horley, 1991).

An interpersonal relationship requires that at least one person construes the other's perspective; that is, one person must play a role with respect to the other person. The role playing need not be reciprocal. However, an optimal relationship involves mutual understanding. This understanding may be limited in scope, as with a student and a teacher, or it may be extremely broad, covering most of each person's construct system, as in a good marriage (e.g., Neimeyer & Hudson, 1985).

Guilt

We play many roles in the course of our daily lives: student, child, friend, team member, listener, helper, joker, and so on. Most of the roles we play are

noncore roles. They are not particularly important to us in the long run; they are not essential to our basic identity. We can shift easily in and out of these peripheral roles. For instance, we often assume the role of customer; how well we play that role generally makes little difference.

In contrast, each of us has some **core roles** that are critical in our lives. Core roles are an essential part of one's personal identity, and how well one performs them has important consequences. Core roles vary from individual to individual. "Parent" may be a core role for one person, "breadwinner" for another, and both may be core roles for a third.

When we realize that we are straying from a core role, we experience **guilt**. Think about times that you have felt guilty. What made you feel guilty? Your answer is apt to be that you were doing something wrong. "Wrong," in this context, means contrary to expectations (our own or others') about how one should act. Thus, we experience guilt when we deviate from expectations for performing a core role (e.g., Green, 1988). For example, Martha considers herself a "good daughter." Martha experiences guilt when she does not write to her parents or when she brings home a male friend whom her parents find unacceptable. These behaviors deviate from Martha's expectations about how a "good daughter" should act.

Kelly's definition of guilt as a deviation from a core role is value-free. It is different than traditional definitions that are value-laden with moralistic judgments about evil (cf. Mascolo & Mancuso, 1990). In fact, many of Kelly's unique definitions of key personality concepts, such as anxiety, are marked by an absence of evaluation. Moreover, Kelly's definitions often implicitly suggest how personality constructs can be modified, as Demonstration 16-1 illustrates.

■ *Demonstration 16-1*:
GUILT IS ALL IN THE ROLE OF THE BEHAVER

This Demonstration has two purposes. First, it should help you understand and appreciate the usefulness of Kelly's definition of *guilt*. Second, it should help you reconstrue the traditional view of guilt; in turn, you might change how you react to feeling guilty (Spiegler, 1985).

1. Think about instances in the recent past when you have felt guilty and about which you still feel guilty. Write a brief description of three of these instances in the first column of the Work Sheet 16-1 (which you can remove

from the Demonstration Materials section in the back of the book).

2. Consider the first description and answer the question: *"What important role that I was expected to play in the situation did I fail to play (or did I play poorly)?"* (Examples of roles would be "loyal friend," "competent worker," and "patient listener.") The expectations may have come from others or from yourself. Write the role in the second column of the work sheet.

3. Ask yourself, *"Was it important for me to be playing that role at the time?"* You should answer this question independently of

*Based on Spiegler, 1985.

the expectations you or others had regarding the appropriateness of the role. Write "yes" or "no" in the third column of the work sheet.

If your answer is "yes," continue to step 4.

If your answer is "no," consider the possibility that your guilt is unwarranted, according to Kelly's definition. *Guilt* is the awareness that you are not performing a role you consider important. Thus, if the role is not important to you, perhaps you have no reason to feel guilty. (For example, Arthur believes that "voter" is an expected role, but it is not an important role for him. In this case, there is no reason for Arthur to feel guilty if he fails to vote in an election.)

4. Ask yourself, *"Approximately what percentage of the time do I play the role satisfactorily,* when it is appropriate to be playing the role?" (For instance, you might conclude that about 80% of the time you are in class,

you play the role of "attentive student.") Write the percentage in the fourth column of the work sheet.

5. Ask yourself, *"Is this a reasonably* high *or low percentage?"* If you think it is reasonably high, consider the following implication: If you often play the role satisfactorily, then you may be doing as well as you can (or want to) and still remain a fallible human being. No one plays any expected role 100% of the time. It may be perfectly acceptable to play your expected roles much, but not all, of the time.

If you believe that the percentage is relatively low, use this information as feedback. You may want to play the role more often, or you may choose to reconstrue the importance of the role for you.

6. Repeat steps 2 through 5 for the remaining situation(s) you described in step 1.

THE ASSESSMENT OF PERSONAL CONSTRUCTS

Identifying an individual's personal constructs is not an easy task because personal constructs are not directly observable. An individual's overt behaviors are, at best, suggestive of how a person construes events. Two people may behave quite similarly although they construe events in very different ways.

Consider a group of men who play golf together on Saturday mornings. If we only wanted to predict what each golfer would be doing next Saturday morning, merely observing the men's behaviors might work. However, to predict how each man would behave in other situations, we must know the construct each uses to construe golf. For instance, construing golf as an opportunity for competing or socializing or exercising would lead to different predictions about how each man would act in various situations.

Another tactic for assessing personal constructs would be to ask people about their constructs directly. However, people are not accustomed to communicating their personal constructs. Further, constructs cannot always be communicated in words. Even when they can be, the meanings of the words are often too general to yield much predictive information. Thus, direct questions are not likely to elicit personal constructs.

The Role Construct Repertory Test (Rep Test)

Kelly devised a procedure for assessing personal constructs that eliminates some of the problems associated with behavioral observations and direct questioning. The **Role Construct Repertory Test (Rep Test)** elicits constructs used to construe other people. A **role construct** is a construct an individual uses to understand another's views (constructs). In the Rep Test, the subject compares and contrasts important people in his or her life. The process is called *sorting*.

The Rep Test uses a *grid*. Significant people in the subject's life, called *figures,* are listed across the top of the grid. The constructs used to construe the figures are recorded on the side. Referring to the abbreviated Rep Test grid in Figure 16-5, we will outline the steps that are involved in completing the grid.

1. First, the subject writes the name of a person to fit each of the role descriptions at the top of the grid.
2. Next, the subject considers the three people designated by the circles in the boxes under the names in the first sort (Terry, Stephen, and Harry in Figure 16-5). The subject decides in what important way *two of the people are alike and different from the third.* The subject places an *X* under the names of the two people who are alike (Stephen and Harry), and the characteristic that makes them alike becomes the emergent pole of the construct (*organized*). The characteristic that makes the third person (Terry) different becomes the implicit pole of the construct (*spontaneous*).
3. Next, the subject considers the figures not compared and contrasted in the sort (Al, Anne, Martin, and Barbara) and places an *X* under the

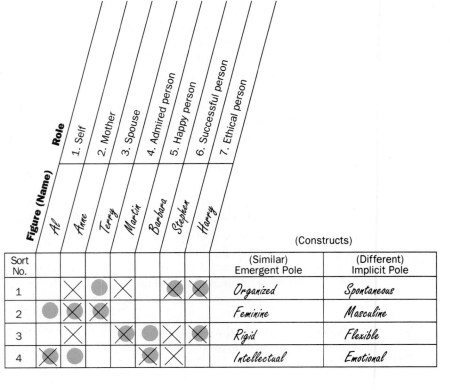

Figure 16-5
Example of part of a completed grid form of the Rep Test.

names of those people who also would be described by the emergent pole (Anne and Martin).

4. The subject repeats steps 2 and 3 for each of the sorts.

The pattern of Xs in the Rep Test grid indicates the similarity of the constructs. Constructs with identical patterns of Xs are assumed to be equivalent, even if the verbal labels assigned to the constructs are different. In Figure 16-5, for example, *organized vs. spontaneous* is equivalent to *rigid vs. flexible.*

We have just described how the Rep Test is used to elicit constructs about other people. The basic idea of sorting figures in terms of their similarities and differences to yield constructs can be employed to identify a person's constructs about any type of event (e.g., Adams-Webber, 1989; Metzler & Neimeyer, 1988; Watson, Doster, & Michaelsen, 1990). In market research, for example, the Rep Test has been used to identify the basis of consumers' judgments in evaluating products (Stewart & Stewart, 1982). Products are substituted for people as the "figures." A sample of consumers compare and contrast various combinations of products and label the constructs they used to construe them. Another illustration of the versatility of the Rep Test is in assessing changes in cognitive conflicts as a measure of success of psychoanalytic therapy (Bassler, Krauthauser, & Hoffmann, 1992).

The Rep Test has proved to be a highly useful and versatile means of assessing personal constructs (e.g., Beail, 1985; Landfield & Epting, 1987). The analysis of complex grids has been made possible by computer technology (e.g., Mancuso & Shaw, 1988; Sewell, Adams-Webber, Mitterer, & Cromwell, 1992). The Rep Test is, by far, the most frequently used assessment procedure in research related to personal construct theory (Neimeyer, Baker, & Neimeyer, 1990).

A significant limitation of the Rep Test is that it does not provide direct information about how constructs are organized. One way to assess the hierarchical order of constructs is through *implications grids* that are created by asking subjects such questions as: "If construct Y changed, what other constructs would also change?" (Caputi, Breiger, & Pattison, 1990).

■ *Demonstration 16-2:*
EXPLORING YOUR INTERPERSONAL CONSTRUCTS

This Demonstration allows you to explore your personal constructs by completing a Rep Test.

DESIGNATING FIGURES

1. Begin by removing Work Sheet 16-2 (the copy of the Repertory Grid in Figure 16-6) from the Demonstration Materials section at the end of the book.

2. Next, read each of the role definitions in Table 16-3.

3. Next, you will write, in the appropriate diagonal space at the top of the grid, the first name of the person who best fits that role in your life, using the definitions in Table 16-3.

Start by writing your name next to the role *Self.* Then write your brother's name (or the

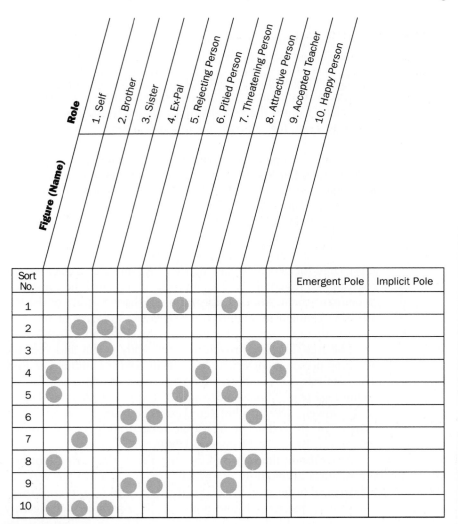

Figure 16-6
Repertory Grid for Demonstration 16-2.

name of the person who has played the role of a brother in your life) next to the name *Brother*. Continue until you have selected individuals for all 10 roles. If you cannot remember the person's name, put down a word or brief phrase that will bring the person to mind. Do *not* repeat any people as figures; if someone has already been listed, make a second choice.

SORTING FIGURES

Starting with Sort 1 (the first row of the grid) and then proceeding to each of the other nine sorts, complete the following steps.

4. Consider the three people who are designated by circles under their names. Decide how *two of them are alike in an important way and different from the third*.

Table 16-3
Definition of roles for Demonstration 16-2

1. *Self*: Yourself.
2. *Brother*: Your brother who is nearest your own age or, if you do not have a brother, a male near your own age who has been most like a brother to you.
3. *Sister*: Your sister who is nearest your own age or, if you do not have a sister, a female near your own age who has been most like a sister to you.
4. *Ex-Pal*: A person of the same sex as yourself whom you once thought was a close friend but in whom you were badly disappointed later.
5. *Rejecting person:* A person with whom you have been associated who, for some unexplained reason, appeared to dislike you.
6. *Pitied person:* The person whom you would most like to help or for whom you feel most sorry.
7. *Threatening person:* The person who threatens you the most or the person who makes you feel the most uncomfortable.
8. *Attractive person:* A person whom you have recently met whom you would like to know better.
9. *Accepted teacher:* The teacher who influenced you most.
10. *Happy person:* The happiest person whom you know personally.

From *The Psychology of Personal Constructs* (vols. 1 and 2) by G. A. Kelly, 1955, W.W. Norton & Company.

5. Put an X in the circles corresponding to the names of the two people who are alike and leave the remaining circle blank.

6. In the Emergent Pole column, write a word or brief phrase describing the way in which the two people are *alike*.

7. In the Implicit Pole column, write a word or brief phrase describing the way in which the third person is *different* from the two who are alike.

8. Consider the remaining seven people. Place an X in the squares corresponding to those people who can also be characterized by the description in the Emergent Pole column.

DISCUSSION

Think about how the Rep Test has elicited your constructs. What is the range of convenience of the constructs? Which of your constructs are relatively permeable? Which are relatively impermeable? What relation do the constructs have with one another? Do the sorts compare people randomly, or is there a rationale behind each sort? Finally, consider what you have learned about the way you construe important people in your life.

PERSONALITY CHANGE   Personal construct theory has been applied to a wide variety of topics in psychology and other fields. Table 16-4 contains examples. Psychotherapy is the major application of personal construct theory (e.g., Neimeyer & Neimeyer, 1990; Winter, 1990a, 1990b). Personality change is a natural

Table 16-4
Examples of areas of applications of personal construct theory

ABNORMAL PSYCHOLOGY

Mental health[1]
Recidivism in psychiatric patients[2]
Childhood sexual abuse[3]
Juvenile delinquency[4]
Psychology of death[5]
Suicide[6]
Therapist supervision[7]
Psychotherapy research[8]

EDUCATION

Experiential learning[9]
Children's science learning[10]
Mentally handicapped children[11]
Writing[12]
Psychoeducational groups for older adults[13]
Teacher education[14]
Educational research[15]
Artificial intelligence[16]

PERCEPTION

Effects of television[17]
Hypnosis[18]
Aesthetic judgment[19]

INTERPERSONAL RELATIONS

Love styles[20]
Marital relationships and marital therapy[21]

GROUP BEHAVIOR

Industrial/organizational psychology[22]
Architecture and urban design[23]
Political events[24]

[1]Warren (1992).
[2]Smith, Stefan, Kovaleski, and Johnson (1991).
[3]Cummins (1992).
[4]Kelly and Taylor (1981); Miller and Treacher (1981).
[5]Warren and Parry (1981).
[6]Kelly (1961); Stephan and Linder (1985).
[7]Feixas (1992).
[8]Herman and Heesacker (1991).
[9]Harri-Augstein (1985).
[10]Shapiro (1991).
[11]McConachie (1983, 1985).
[12]Boscolo and de Bernardi (1992).
[13]Botella (1991).
[14]Burke, Noller, and Caird (1992); Diamond (1983, 1990); Pope, Denicolo, and de Bernardi (1990); Salmon (1988); Thomaz and Gilbert (1989).
[15]Postlethwaite and Jaspars (1986).
[16]Boose (1985); Rychlak (1991).
[17]Clair and Preston (1990).
[18]Burr and Butt (1989).
[19]O'Hare and Gordon (1976); Rosenberg (1977).
[20]Hall, Hendrick, Hendrick (1991).
[21]Green and Kirby-Turner (1990); Kremsdorf (1985); Loos (1991); Neimeyer and Hudson (1985); Waring (1990).
[22]Gray (1992); Jankowicz (1987, 1990); Stewart and Stewart (1982).
[23]Honikman (1976); Hudson (1974).
[24]DuPreez (1977).

consequence of personal construct theory because the theory is based on constructive alternativism. If people can view events in different ways, then they have the option of changing their personalities (construct systems) (Viney, 1990). Kelly (1955) considered psychotherapy to be a reconstruing process in which clients change their outlooks on aspects of their lives.

Clients' Problems Construed by Personal Construct Theory

According to personal construct theory, abnormal behaviors, like all behaviors, are caused by how people construe events. Individuals engage in abnormal behaviors because they anticipate events in ways that result in maladaptive functioning. Anxiety disorders may be caused by (1) a deficit in appropriate constructs; (2) constructs that are too impermeable; and (3) constructs that are too permeable (Winter, 1990b). For example, individuals with social anxiety may have few or no constructs that allow them to view interacting with other people as safe. Their existing constructs that are appropriate for construing interpersonal relations may be severely limited, such as only in relation to immediate family. Or their constructs regarding threatening events may be so overinclusive that they view just about any event, including social interactions, as scary.

Other psychological disorders may be associated with the organization of constructs (Winter, Baker, & Goggins, 1992). There is some evidence that the constructs of people with schizophrenia are relatively unconnected to one another (Landfield, 1980). This low degree of relationship among constructs results in the individual being "faced with a world that appears . . . chaotic, fragmented, and meaningless" (Klion, 1988, p. 440).

The Process of Personal Construct Therapy

The overall goal of personal construct psychotherapy is for clients to develop construct systems that allow them to follow their own natural development. This goal is the same as that for client-centered therapy. Another similarity between the two therapies is that personality change is conceived of as a continuing *process*. After successful therapy, clients are open to experiencing events, which means continually reconstruing events and revising their construct systems in minor ways. Toward this end, personal construct therapists demonstrate the role of a scientist for their clients. They formulate theory-based hypotheses (predictions based on a personal construct) about future events, test them, and then revise their theories (constructs) in order to increase predictive efficiency.

The process of changing one's personal constructs is indirect. Specifically, the therapist encourages clients to change how they act with regard to specific events. This is done in order to change how they construe the events. In other words, the client *first* behaves differently and *then*, as a result, begins to construe events differently. This process is the basis for *fixed-role therapy*, one example of Kelly's innovative therapy procedures (Dunnett, 1988; Epting & Nazario, 1987).

Fixed-Role Therapy

In **fixed-role therapy**, the client plays the role of a fictitious person whose behavior is consistent with a construct system that would be beneficial for the client. By playing this **fixed role**, the client behaves in ways that will modify his or her existing construct system.

Based on extensive personality assessment and evaluation of the client's problem, the therapist writes a **fixed-role sketch**. The sketch describes the fixed role the client will play. The fixed-role character is assigned a name to make the role more credible. This also helps to distinguish the fixed role from the client's customary role. The following fixed-role sketch was written for a male client who was having difficulties with his sex-role identity. He characterized himself as passive, self-conscious, shy, and occasionally boring.

> Dick Benton is probably the only one of his kind in the world. People are always just a little puzzled as to how to take him. About the time they decide that he is a conventional person with the usual lines of thinking in religion, politics, school . . . they discover that there is a new side to his personality that they have overlooked. At times, they think that he has a brand-new way of looking at life, a really fresh point of view. Some people go through an hour of conversation with him without being particularly impressed; while others find that afterwards they cannot get some of his unusual ideas out of their minds. Every once in a while he throws an idea into a discussion like a bomb with a very slow fuse attached. People don't get it until later.
>
> At times he deliberately makes himself socially inconspicuous. Those are the times when he wishes to listen and learn, rather than to stimulate other people's thinking. He is kindly and gentle with people, even on those occasions when he is challenging their thoughts with utterly new ideas. Because of this, people do not feel hurt by his ideas, even when they seem outrageous.
>
> He is devoted to his wife and she is the only person who always seems to understand what is going on in his mind.
>
> His work in college is somewhat spotted and the courses are interesting to him only to the extent that they give him a new outlook.
>
> All in all, Dick Benton is a combination of gentleness and intellectual unpredictability. He likes to take people as they are but he likes to surprise them with new ideas. (Kelly, 1955, p. 421)

Clients are not asked to *be* the person described in the fixed-role sketch or even to adopt the role as their own. They are told merely to play the role for a week or two. However, clients often stop thinking of their new behaviors as a prescribed role. They begin to consider the role as their own "natural" way of behaving. They adjust the fixed role so that it is more consistent with their other behaviors and styles. Clients who can "get into" the fixed role begin to adopt the constructs that underlie the fixed-role behaviors.

Fixed-role therapy is aimed at creating minor personality changes. Thus, the fixed role deals with only a few of the client's constructs. It often includes some of the client's positive attributes or strengths, which bolsters the client's most efficient constructs and makes the role easier to enact. Although originally designed as an individual therapy (Kelly, 1955), fixed-role therapy has been adapted to marital therapy (Kremsdorf, 1985) and group therapy (Beail & Parker, 1991).

By doing Demonstration 16-3, you will experience the essence of fixed-role therapy through an analogous process.

■ *Demonstration 16-3:*
PLAYING DEVIL'S ADVOCATE: AN ANALOGY TO FIXED-ROLE THERAPY

Formal debating involves supporting arguments that are either for or against a particular statement. Debaters must be able to defend a point of view whether they agree with it or not. Frequently they must advocate for a position that is alien to their own views. This situation is analogous to what a client does in fixed-role therapy — namely, behave in a manner consistent with a new set of constructs. In this Demonstration you will "debate" familiar issues to help you appreciate what fixed-role therapy is like for a client.

1. First, *write on index cards five statements about five social issues with which you strongly agree.* Choose statements in which you have a strong, personal investment. Write the statements so that your position on the issue is clear. For example, if you believe that 18-year-olds should be allowed to drink legally, you should write "The drinking age should be 18" and not "drinking age" (which does not specify your position on the issue).

2. Next, *shuffle the cards and "blindly" pick one.*

3. Now, *write as many arguments as you can think of* against *the statement you picked.* This may not be easy, given that you strongly agree with the statement. But keep thinking of negative arguments, and resist countering the negative arguments you generate. Assume a "devil's advocate" position and argue as strongly *against* the idea as you would argue for it.

4. Finally, repeat the steps for at least one more of the remaining issues.

An alternative way of doing this Demonstration is to actually debate the issue with a friend who strongly agrees with the position (as you actually do).

In evaluating what you learned about being a client in fixed-role therapy from this Demonstration, you should bear in mind two things. First, in contrast to a client in fixed-role therapy, you are only verbalizing, not acting in accord with new constructs. Second, you are doing this for only a brief time, rather than consistently over the course of a week or more.

SUMMARY

1. Kelly's theory of personal constructs is based on constructive alternativism, the position that there are always different ways of viewing the world.

2. Kelly believed that all people behave as scientists; that is, they predict events by advancing theories about the nature of the events and then testing the theories.

3. Constructs are the "theories" through which people view the world. Constructs are interpretations of events; they are not properties of the events.

The validity of a construct is its predictive efficiency. Each person has a unique set of personal constructs. The verbal labels we give to constructs are not the constructs themselves.

4. Each construct has a range of convenience that specifies the events to which it is applicable and a focus of convenience that indicates the events it predicts best. Constructs differ in their permeability, which refers to how open they are to construing new experiences.

5. Kelly's theory is presented in the form of a fundamental postulate and 11 corollaries.

6. Kelly believed that human behavior is directed toward predicting events. Personality consists of active processes rather than static structures.

7. People predict events by looking for the recurrent themes in them (how the events are similar to other events they have encountered) and by considering how the event is both similar to and different from other events.

8. Children use preverbal constructs before they acquire language. Adults may also use nonverbal constructs. Such constructs involve physiological, kinesthetic, and emotional patterns.

9. The predictive efficiency of a construct can be enhanced by either defining the construct (making it more precise) or extending the construct (expanding the events it can construe).

10. Kellian constructs are bipolar (a similarity versus a difference) and dichotomous (not a continuum).

11. The range of convenience of constructs is limited. Anxiety results from not having a construct to construe an event.

12. Constructs are arranged in a hierarchical construct system that facilitates prediction of events.

13. A construct system changes as events are reconstrued. Experience involves reconstruing events, not just being exposed to events.

14. Emotions involve becoming aware of change or the need for change in one's construct system.

15. Change in a construct system is possible only if constructs exist that can construe the change.

16. Each person has a unique construct system that distinguishes that person from others. At the same time, individuals behave similarly if they have similar constructs.

17. Relating to another person involves playing roles with respect to the other person. This is done by construing the other's constructs. Guilt is experienced when one deviates from a core role—a role that is central to one's identity.

18. The Role Construct Repertory Test (Rep Test) is a major means of assessing constructs. Role constructs are elicited by having a person compare and contrast important people in his or her life.

19. Personality change ultimately involves changing one's constructs. However, the process involves directly changing overt behaviors, which results in viewing events differently. In fixed-role therapy, the client temporarily plays the role of a fictitious person who uses constructs that the client might benefit from using.

Chapter Seventeen

Liabilities of the Phenomenological Strategy

I n Chapters 13 through 16, we presented the strengths of the phenomenological strategy, of which there are many. Now it is time to cast a critical eye on the strategy. Most of the criticisms are germane to the strategy as a whole.

The phenomenological strategy has been subject to seven major criticisms. The strategy (1) is limited in scope; (2) presents a simplistic view of personality; (3) pays inadequate attention to nomothetic concerns; (4) employs circular reasoning; (5) provides inadequate coverage of personality development; (6) places excessive reliance on self-report measures; and (7) presents a romantic, nonscientific vision of personality.

LIMITED IN SCOPE

Psychoanalytic personality theory has been called a "rubber sheet theory" because it can be stretched to fit (explain) any observations. The dispositional strategy has been accused of a different, but equally serious, theoretical problem: The strategy has no theoretical concepts of its own and uses those concepts that it has borrowed inconsistently or sloppily. And, not surprisingly, phenomenological personality theories also have their problems. Specifically, the theories are restricted by assuming that everything we need to know about a person can be gleaned from the person's *conscious, momentary* experiences. Further, there are some glaring gaps in coverage.

Unconscious Experience Is Ignored

By focusing on conscious experience, the phenomenological strategy comes close to dealing with aspects of behavior that laypersons most often think should be the focus of psychological investigations—namely, their conscious thoughts and feelings about themselves, others, and events in their lives. Thus, the phenomenological strategy "makes sense intuitively." It is consistent with commonsense notions of personality.

This focus excludes from study events of which a person is not immediately or fully aware. Can behavior be predicted accurately if one knows only what is in the person's immediate awareness? Many personality psychologists would say "no." Psychoanalysts, for example, argue that events that are unconscious, even permanently, form the core of personality and play a crucial role in determining behavior.

The Past Is Ignored

Can present actions be explained without reference to past experiences? Again, many personality psychologists would say "no." They believe that knowledge of past experiences is essential for predicting and understanding present behaviors and personality. The phenomenological strategy is limited by almost totally ignoring the influence of the past and focusing instead on immediate, subjective experiences. This extreme point of view disregards important variables in other time frames.

Phenomenological psychologists do acknowledge that the past can affect a person's immediate experiences, but they do not account for its influence. Neither do they explain the nature and extent of the influence. Further, phenomenologists do not attempt to examine an individual's past experiences, even when the past experiences might directly relate to present experiences. The strategy assumes that if a past experience is important in the present, it will be manifested in the person's present experiences. This assumption implies that there is no need to look at the past.

Moreover, phenomenological psychologists believe that the form the past experience assumes in the present is all that is relevant to an understanding of current personality functioning. All these assumptions are largely unsubstantiated.

Gaps in Coverage   Phenomenological approaches have large gaps in coverage that result from the particular emphasis of the theories. For instance, Rogers' approach focuses on the emotional aspects of human functioning and largely ignores the intellectual, thinking aspects. Kelly's bias is exactly opposite; the theory of personal constructs emphasizes cognitive processes but pays relatively little attention to emotions. Bruner (1956) remarked that Kelly was so perturbed by psychoanalytic, dispositional, and radical behavioral psychologists who regard humans as irrational (emotional) animals that he overreacted and turned *Homo sapiens* into a species of superrational college professors.

As another example of theory-generated tunnel vision, consider Maslow's assertion that most adult behaviors are motivated by needs beyond the physiological and safety level. No doubt this is true for the college students Maslow taught, his acquaintances, and even the majority of people in the United States. But what of the millions of people in the world for whom hunger is a primary source of motivation? In fairness to Maslow, all Western personality psychologists have theorized about and studied an unrepresentative sample of the world's population and then have overgeneralized to all humankind.

The source of Maslow's tunnel vision seems to be his focus on healthy and optimal personality functioning. That bias also may have accounted for Maslow's belief that safety needs are largely met in adults. Even if we remain within the restricted sample of humans to which his theory is most applicable, Maslow may have underestimated the extent to which people's safety needs are unmet.

Consider psychological safety or security. Uncertainties — such as about one's grades, job, relationship, and future — are a pervasive part of most people's lives. Many people suffer from personal insecurities, such as about their abilities and attractiveness. It is estimated that one-third of people in the United States suffer from a serious psychological disorder during their lifetimes (Holmes, 1991; Wilson, O'Leary, & Nathan, 1992). Indeed, safety needs appear to play more of a role in adult motivation than Maslow assumed. And it is arguable that some substantial minority of people in the United States, such as those who live in our large inner cities, are concerned about their physical safety on a daily basis.

Vacuous Nature of Phenomenological Theory   Phenomenological personality theories, especially Kelly's and Rogers', provide the structure of personality with little attention paid to the content. It is analogous to learning about human anatomy only from a skeleton.

Kelly presented an elaborate description of the nature of personality or, in his terms, a personal construct system. The system is composed of a finite number of personal constructs that are bipolar and dichotomous, and they are arranged in a hierarchical order. As sturdy as this "skeleton" is, it contains no "flesh."

The theories of Rogers and Maslow do put more "meat" on the "bones" of their basic structures. A variety of substantive personality processes are theorized to be operative in all people. For example, Rogers proposed that all people have a basic need for positive regard, and he spelled out the nature and functions of this universal need. The same is true for Maslow's hierarchy of needs, the content of which is described in detail.

Still, self-actualization, which is at the heart of Rogers' and Maslow's theoretical approaches, remains a unique process in each person. The nature of self-actualization—the inherent potentialities of each individual—remains almost completely unspecified (Ford, 1991a; Maddi, 1989). As one critic noted:

> Having appreciated the view that the inherent potentialities function to maintain and enhance life, we are in a position to inquire further as to their precise content. Extraordinary though it is, Rogers is almost completely mute on this matter! About the most insight one can gain through careful reading of Rogers is that he is thinking in terms of some sort of genetic blueprint to which substance is added as life progresses. But the precise outlines of the blueprint are a mystery. (Maddi, 1989, p. 102)

SIMPLISTIC VIEW OF PERSONALITY

Phenomenological theorists often criticize other personality theories as being oversimplified. Yet in many ways, phenomenologists themselves have been simplistic.

As an alternative to the positions they consider limited, phenomenologists offer various inborn tendencies—to actualize one's potentialities or to construe events—as "explanations" of the causes of behavior. However, phenomenological psychologists do not specify the origins of these tendencies; they are simply said to exist. For example, Rogers (1965) categorically stated: "The organism has one basic tendency and striving—to actualize, maintain, and enhance the experiencing organism" (p. 487). And Kelly (1955) said in his Fundamental Postulate that a person's processes are psychologically channelized by the ways in which he or she anticipates events. Having stated that these natural, inborn tendencies exist, Rogers and Kelly then used them as all-purpose "explanations" of behavior. The problem with this tack, according to one critic, is that it "provides too few parameters to account for complex behaviors. Some *ad hoc* way must be found to stuff many diverse observations into one or two pigeonholes, yielding serious distortions and omissions" (Wylie, 1968, pp. 731–732).

The fundamental premises of the three phenomenological approaches that we have examined can be easily stated in a sentence or two. Each approach has a single core idea about the nature of personality and builds an entire comprehensive theory of personality on it. This simplicity may make understanding the positions easier and may give the theories internal consistency. But such a simplification may be inappropriate for the study of a topic as complex as human personality. As Albert Einstein put it, "Everything should be made as simple as possible, but no simpler."

Another facet of this oversimplification is that the phenomenological strategy expresses a naive vision of human social life (e.g., Neher, 1991). For example, Millon (1967) criticized phenomenological psychologists' simplistic conception of human nature as follows:

> The notion that man would be a constructive, rational, and socially conscious being, were he free of the malevolent distortions of society, seems not only sentimental but invalid. There is something grossly naive in exhorting man to live life to the fullest and then expecting socially beneficial consequences to follow. What evidence is there that one's inherent self-interest would not clash with the self-interests of others? There is something as banal as the proverbs of a fortune cookie in the suggestion "be thyself." Conceiving man's emotional disorders as a failure to "be thyself" seems equally naive and banal. (p. 307)

INADEQUATE ATTENTION TO NOMOTHETIC CONCERNS

The major criticism of phenomenological personality research is that it is highly idiographic, and therefore its findings cannot be generalized to form scientific laws.

A hallmark of the phenomenological strategy is its appreciation of the uniqueness of human personality. The idiographic approach to studying personality — with its interest solely on the single individual — is more evident in the phenomenological strategy than in any of the other three strategies.

One basic assumption is that each person is directed by psychological processes whose content is unique to the individual. The nature of the self-actualizing tendency varies from individual to individual, and each person has a different set of personal constructs. Thus, to understand a given individual's personality, it is necessary to have knowledge of the unique processes as they occur in that person.

The idiographic approach is most applicable when a single individual is the focus of interest, such as in personality change procedures. However, a heavy emphasis on an idiographic approach to personality creates a dilemma. Personality psychology is predominantly a basic science. Its goals are to develop theories and collect data that will allow prediction, control, and understanding of the behaviors of *people in general* rather than individuals. The phenomenological strategy is severely limited in its ability to generalize its theory and findings to people in general.

USE OF CIRCULAR REASONING

Phenomenological explanations involve circular reasoning and thereby confuse description and explanation. Consider the following line of reasoning.

1. You observe that Vivian reads a great deal. She always has a book or magazine with her. The first thing she does each morning is read the newspaper, and she reads each night before going to sleep.

2. Curious about her extensive reading, you inquire: "Why does Vivian read so much?"
3. Her husband, Roger, a phenomenological psychologist, answers: "Vivian reads because reading is consistent with her self-actualizing tendency."
4. You might inquire further: "How do you know that reading is consistent with her self-actualizing tendency?"
5. Roger replies: "Just look at how much time Vivian spends reading."

This reasoning is tautological: $A = A$, Vivian *is* who she is. It provides only pseudoexplanations because it concludes exactly where it began. Such a journey is not enlightening, as travel is supposed to be. The danger is that pseudoexplanations of this sort may appear convincing and pass as genuine explanations. In fact, they provide no more information than we had originally and do not help us to predict other behaviors.

Circular reasoning is standard in the phenomenological strategy. Kelly uses personal constructs and the hierarchical order in construct systems to "explain" a person's behaviors (e.g., Vivian is a prolific reader because she construes reading as worthwhile or enjoyable). In studying self-actualizing individuals, Maslow ran headlong into this problem (Coan, 1991). A priori, he defined certain individuals as self-actualizing; then he studied such people; finally, from what he learned about them, he further described the characteristics of self-actualizers. This approach is completely circular.

Phenomenological psychologists are not the only ones to fall into the alluring trap of circular reasoning. Psychoanalysts confuse observation and inference (see Chapter 7), and dispositionalists mistake description for explanation (see Chapter 12). This raises the question of whether circular reasoning is endemic to personality psychology. The answer will emerge in our discussion of the behavioral strategy.

INADEQUATE COVERAGE OF PERSONALITY DEVELOPMENT

All three phenomenological positions we have covered provide inadequate coverage of personality development.

Kelly certainly did not believe that people are born with personal constructs. In fact, he stated that constructs develop in order to predict events in one's life. Kelly also asserted that preverbal constructs begin to develop shortly after birth. But little in Kelly's theory specifically outlines how constructs develop (Jankowicz, 1987; Katz, 1984; Solas, 1992; Warren, 1989). The psychology of personal constructs describes the nature of constructs, how they operate, and how they change. But this information is applicable only to an already construing person—someone who has (magically?) developed a set of constructs through which experiences are viewed.

The needs in Maslow's hierarchy are inborn. However, they develop and change as the individual attempts to meet them. Maslow's theory does not specify what factors result in changes in either the needs themselves or how a person satisfies them. Presumably, how people satisfy their needs becomes more sophisticated and complex as they grow older and have more experience with them. However, Maslow's theory says little about such developmental issues.

Maslow's theorizing about self-actualizing individuals fails to address how a person develops into a self-actualizer. Does every person have the potential to become self-actualizing? What is different in the biological endowment or life experiences of the small number of people who are self-actualizers? These obvious and tantalizing questions remain unanswered in Maslow's theory.

Rogers' theory *does* include discussion of the development of personality, particularly in relation to the self-concept and conditions of worth. However, he does not make the developmental *process* explicit. For instance, Rogers indicates that the self-concept develops as part of the actualizing tendency's process of differentiation — that is, as one learns what is "me" and "not me." But how does 2-month-old Laura distinguish between herself and her mother, with whom she is so close? Rogers provides few details of how the process operates. A more serious problem with Rogers' concepts of personality development is that little empirical support for them exists, which is related to the criticism of ignoring nomothetic concerns discussed earlier (cf. Cartwright, DeBruin, & Berg, 1991; Cartwright & Mori, 1988).

EXCESSIVE RELIANCE ON SELF-REPORT MEASURES

The major liability of phenomenological personality assessment is its excessive reliance on self-report measures.

The goal of phenomenological personality assessment is to learn about a person's subjective experiences in order to understand the world from that person's internal frame of reference. Only the individual has direct knowledge of subjective experiences. Thus, phenomenological personality assessment relies almost entirely on self-reports.

Two basic assumptions are made in phenomenological personality assessment: (1) people are *willing* to describe their private experiences, and (2) they are *able* to do so accurately. How valid are these assumptions?

People are not always willing to share their personal experiences. This often occurs when private experiences are intimate or reveal unfavorable aspects of personality. People may disclose highly personal information only after they trust the examiner, which develops over time. However, personality assessment is often a "one-shot deal" (in both research and clinical practice).

Both psychological research and everyday observations suggest that self-reports are often intentionally distorted. People tend to report what they want others to know about them. Usually, they will distort their personality picture in a favorable light (e.g., Brown, 1991). Occasionally individuals distort their responses so they are seen unfavorably, as when one wants to be dismissed from a job. People may also distort their self-reports in ways they are not fully aware of, such as answering questions with a response set (see Chapter 9).

Both psychoanalytic and dispositional assessment involve self-reports and thus share all of the problems we just have outlined. Psychoanalysts and dispositionalists deal with the problems by using indirect methods of assessment, such as projective techniques and empirically keyed personality inventories, so that the respondent is not fully aware of what is being assessed. Indirect methods are not an option for phenomenologists because indirect methods involve deception, which is contrary to the basic theme of straightforwardness or openness that permeates the phenomenological strategy.

Even if a person were willing to report his or her experiences honestly, there is still the problem of whether the person *can* report them accurately. Phenomenological personality assessment assumes that people are aware of all the private experiences that directly influence their behavior. Psychoanalysts argue that people are often unaware of the determinants of their behavior.

Memory is another factor that determines the accuracy of self-reports. When memories are vague or lacking, people construct the memories they report (e.g., Ross, 1989; Shapiro, 1991). Moreover, in this process "must be" becomes "is so." This is similar to the phenomenon of making up a story and then later believing it yourself. For example, when David failed to make his high school swimming team, he told his friends that he had injured himself. Years later, when asked about his high school activities, he reports what he believes to be true—namely, that injury kept him from being on the swim team.

Finally, can people describe their subjective experiences in a way that is both meaningful and useful to others? We have all experienced frustration in trying to tell someone else how we feel. Our inability to describe feelings to others, or even specify them for ourselves, is partly due to the limitations of language. It may also occur because Western societies place a higher value on thought and rationality than on emotion and irrationality.

Moreover, for language to convey information to another person, the meanings of words and phrases must be commonly agreed on and understood. However, it is often difficult to translate private experiences into words that fully describe them and, at the same time, communicate them to others. When language is imprecise, observers can only base their understanding of the words on their own experiences and perspectives, which is not phenomenological knowledge. Thus, although the words were understood, the meaning was lost.

In sum, there are numerous factors that raise doubts about the general assumptions that people are able and willing to accurately relate their subjective experiences. Thus, phenomenologists may rely too heavily on self-report measures.

ROMANTIC VISION   Both Rogers and Maslow, and to some extent Kelly, presented an extremely optimistic and life-affirming view of human personality. Their theories emphasize positive, creative aspects of human nature. On the one hand, this is to their credit because many other views of personality are overly pessimistic. The psychoanalytic strategy, to which phenomenological approaches were at least partly a reaction, is a prime example (DeCarvalho, 1990b, 1991b). Freud's theory, for instance, focused on the "seedy side" of human nature, such as our being victims of unconscious urges that offend society's sensibilities and are difficult to change. The dispositional strategy also relegates us to the fate of largely immutable traits. In such company, the rosy picture of human nature painted by phenomenological psychologists is refreshing.

On the other hand, in their zeal to emphasize the positive, Rogers and Maslow presented an idealistic view of human beings. They assume that people are, by nature, good and that they have the potential to enhance themselves and grow independently. Some of their writings about personality sound more like fairy tales than scientific description. Landsman and Landsman (1991), for example, have referred to Maslow's self-actualizer as a "beautiful and noble person" (cf. Rule, 1991)! Phenomenological theories may say more about how humans *should be* than about how they actually are (e.g., Walker, 1992).

It has been suggested that the concept of self-actualization functions as a "*myth* of human development,"

> a symbolic language that enables people to make sense of their existence, to plan their route through life, to conjure elusive experiences. . . . It is a mistake, therefore, to consider research on self-actualization only as a . . . scientific enterprise. More fundamentally, it is a personal . . . quest. (Daniels, 1988, p. 13)

Furthermore, the concept of self-actualization sometimes seems more philosophical, moral, religious, and poetic than psychological. It is "concerned with assumptions about a person's ultimate good or essential purpose and with the right ways in which to live" (Daniels, 1988, p. 9). According to some critics, this concern is not the legitimate subject matter of the scientific study of personality (e.g., Gladstone, 1990).

The phenomenological strategy fails to meet the requirements of scientific psychology in yet another way. The subject matter of the strategy is subjective experience, which, by definition, can be fully known only by one person—the subject. Scientific psychology requires agreement among observers and the repeatability of findings. Obviously, it is not possible to reach objective agreement about subjective experience. Indeed, objectivity, the basis of science, is antithetical to the phenomenological approach. Requiring agreement about observations and repeatability distinguishes the psychological approach to studying human behavior from philosophical, religious, historical, and literary approaches. One has left the realm of science when one abandons scientific criteria in favor of plausibility, common sense, or a romanticized vision of what human beings potentially can become. In this regard, the phenomenological strategy, like the psychoanalytic strategy, appears to violate the basic tenets of scientific psychology.

SUMMARY   1. The phenomenological strategy is limited in its scope. In assuming that conscious and momentary experiences are sufficient for understanding personality, the influence of unconscious and past experiences on personality is ignored. Each of the theoretical positions is limited by its specific focus, which results in large gaps in coverage.

2. Phenomenological personality theories provide the structure of personality with little attention paid to the content.

3. The strategy also tends to be rather simplistic, positing a single principle to account for all aspects of personality.

4. Phenomenological personality research is highly idiographic, and therefore its findings cannot be generalized to form scientific laws.

5. Phenomenological explanations are often circular in nature. Various inborn tendencies are simply invoked as "explanations."

6. Phenomenological theories do not adequately explain personality development. They are most useful in explaining already developed individuals.

7. Phenomenologists rely too heavily on self-reports. Self-report measures are problematic because people may be unwilling or unable to reveal private information, and they may choose to distort their reports.

8. Phenomenological theories express naive and romantic views of personality that are more ideals of how humans should be than how they are. This style is more philosophical than scientific. Dealing with subjective experience also is not consistent with a science based on agreement among observers and repeatability of findings.

THE BEHAVIORAL STRATEGY

Introduction to the Behavioral Strategy

ll personality psychologists begin studying personality by examining behavior. In most strategies, however, psychologists are not interested in behaviors themselves. Instead, they consider behaviors to be *signs* or indications of underlying personality. For example, psychoanalysts listen to people *reporting* their dreams, which is a behavior, but analysts are not concerned with the dream reports themselves. Instead, they want to know what the reports reveal about unconscious processes. Dispositional psychologists study the *responses* people make (also behaviors) on the MMPI, but not for their own sake. Instead, the responses are taken as signs of various traits. Phenomenological psychologists examine how a person *sorts* (again, behavior) self-referent statements in a Q-sort—not because they are interested in sorting behaviors but because they want to learn about the person's self-concept.

THE PREEMINENCE OF BEHAVIOR

In contrast to the other three strategies, the behavioral strategy is concerned with *behavior for its own sake*. Behavioral psychologists use observations of behaviors as *samples*—rather than signs—of a general class of behaviors. For example, volunteering time in a homeless shelter is a sample of altruistic behavior and would be used to predict future helping behaviors.

We engage in two types of behavior. **Overt behavior** is anything we do that others can observe directly. **Covert behavior** is private and not observable directly by others. Consider what you are doing right now. Your overt behavior may include sitting at a desk, underlining the words in this book, and turning the pages; your covert behavior may include reading, thinking, memorizing, and daydreaming. Covert behaviors must always be inferred from overt behaviors. A friend may observe you holding your personality text, looking at the pages, and turning a page every few minutes. But your friend can only *infer* that you are reading.

Given that behavior is of ultimate concern in the behavioral strategy, what is personality? In the behavioral strategy, *personality* is the sum and organization of an individual's behaviors. Personality and behavior are closer to being synonymous in the behavioral strategy than in any of the other strategies.

BEHAVIORISM: THE ROOTS OF THE BEHAVIORAL STRATEGY

Historically, the behavioral strategy grew out of *behaviorism*, an approach to psychology founded by John Broadus Watson in the early years of the 20th century. Watson (1914) wrote:

> Psychology as the behaviorist views it is a purely objective experimental branch of natural science. Its theoretical goal is the prediction and control of behavior. . . . The behaviorist attempts to get a unitary scheme of animal response. He recognizes no dividing line between man and brute. The behavior of man, with all of its refinements and complexity, forms only a part of his total field of investigation. . . . It is possible to write a psychology, to define it as. . . . the "science of behavior" . . . and never go back upon the definition:

John Watson
(1878-1958)
the father of
behaviorism, believed
that psychology should
deal only with
observable stimuli and
responses.
The Ferdinand Hamburger, Jr.,
Archives, The Johns Hopkins
University.

never to use the terms consciousness, mental states, mind, content, will, imagery, and the like.... Certain stimuli lead ... organisms to make ... responses. In a system of psychology completely worked out, given the responses the stimuli can be predicted; given the stimuli the responses can be predicted. (pp. 1, 9, 10)

Watson (1914, 1919) believed that psychology should be a natural science, in the tradition of physics and biology. He made no distinction between human and nonhuman behavior. He believed that there was no need to study subjective phenomena, such as thoughts and feelings. Instead, Watson's "stimulus-response" psychology was concerned only with predicting overt behaviors by knowing the external stimuli that influence them and vice versa.

The approach Watson favored is known as **radical behaviorism**. It takes the extreme position that only *overt* behaviors and external stimuli should be studied. Besides dictating the subject matter of psychology, radical behaviorism specifies the methods used to study them—namely, direct observation of behavior, objectivity, precise definitions, and controlled experimentation. In contrast, **methodological behaviorism** prescribes that the same scientific methods be used but does not specify what can be studied.

Paradigmatic Behaviorism

In founding behaviorism, Watson hoped to provide a model for studying all of psychology. Although behaviorism has provided a framework for the study of a variety of aspects of behavior, it has never realized Watson's ultimate goal (Lee, 1988; Staats, 1989b, 1991, 1993b).

Arthur Staats has developed an alternative form of behaviorism (cf. Plaud, 1992; Staats, 1993b). **Paradigmatic** (pronounced *PAR-a-dig-MAT-ic*) **behaviorism** is intended to provide a broad model or paradigm of psychology (cf. Kuhn, 1970) and has more recently been called **psychological behaviorism** (e.g., Staats, 1993a; Staats & Burns, 1992; Tryon, 1990). Paradigmatic behaviorism basically follows the tradition of methodological behaviorism. It employs rigorous scientific methods to study a broader range of psychological phenomena than external events that are the sole subject matter of radical behaviorism (e.g., Eifert & Evans, 1990; Rosenfarb, 1992).

We will briefly examine the paradigmatic behavioral model of personality (Staats, 1993a, 1993b; Staats & Burns, 1992). The components of the model are (1) learned repertoires of behaviors; (2) environmental eliciting stimuli; and (3) biological conditions.

Basic Behavioral Repertoires

In paradigmatic behaviorism, *personality* consists of a person's **basic behavioral repertoires** (BBRs), which are complex sets of skills that we learn, beginning at birth (Staats, 1993a). The three BBRs that make up personality are *language-cognitive*, *emotional-motivational*, and *sensory-motor* (Staats, 1989a, 1990; Staats & Eifert, 1990). Each of the BBRs consist of many *subrepertoires*; for example, the language-cognitive BBR includes verbal imitation, speech, reading, and writing.

BBRs overlap with one another because most human behaviors require skills from more than one BBR. Consider what is required for one to learn to swim. Obviously sensory-motor skills are required. Language-cognitive skills also are important for understanding instructions and processing what is being learned. And emotional-motivational skills may play a role in overcoming fear of the water.

Staats (1993a) argues that BBRs explain personality phenomena better than traditional personality constructs because BBRs are more fundamental. For example, separate personality constructs such as attitudes, anxiety, and hostility are part of one's emotional-motivation BBR.

Paradigmatic behavioral personality assessment involves identifying elements of a person's BBRs (Fernández-Ballesteros & Staats, 1992; Staats, 1986). Indeed, Staats contends that traditional personality tests, such as self-report inventories, measure individual differences in BBRs (e.g., Staats & Burns, 1981, 1982).

Environmental Factors

Environmental factors play two interdependent roles in determining behavior (Fernández-Ballesteros & Staats, 1992). First, BBRs are made up of skills that are learned through experience. Thus, the environmental conditions one is exposed to determine the skills one acquires. The learning is a *cumulative-hierarchical process*. This means that increasingly more sophisticated BBRs can be acquired only after more basic BBRs have been learned.

Second, environmental stimuli, such as the situations one finds oneself in, elicit various behaviors. However, the behaviors called for in a given situation can be performed only if they part of the person's previously learned BBRs.

Biological Factors

Organic or biological factors influence behavior at three points (cf. Moore, 1990). First, our biological endowment may affect learning the skills that make up our BBRs. For example, brain damage at birth may limit an individual's ability to acquire skills.

Second, organic conditions can affect the ability of a person to use skills in a variety of ways. These include remembering how to perform the skills, which depends on one's memory, and being physically capable of performing the skill, which is influenced by one's physical condition. For instance, a man may have learned to drive an automobile. However, under the influence of alcohol, he may not remember how to start the car and he may not be able to steer it around a corner.

Third, organic conditions can influence how we perceive and process environmental conditions that elicit behaviors. For example, visual and auditory acuity will affect our ability to respond appropriately to environmental cues.

The Model: Putting the Pieces Together

Figure 18-1 shows the paradigmatic behavioral model. Note how behavior is determined by three factors: personality (BBRs), environmental influences,

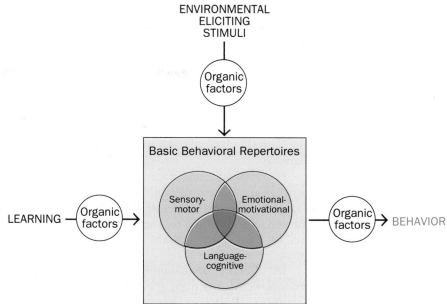

Figure 18-1
In the paradigmatic behavioral model, behavior is determined by learned, overlapping basic behavioral repertoires of skills and environmental eliciting stimuli. Organic (biological) factors influence the original learning, the processing of external eliciting stimuli, and the enactment of the skills.

and biological factors. Present environmental stimuli call for a particular class of behaviors to be performed. The specific behaviors the person can engage in depend on those that are in the person's BBRs, due to past environmental conditions that resulted in learning. Organic factors influence (1) learning the skills that make up one's BBRs; (2) sensory responses to eliciting environmental stimuli; and (3) the ability to perform skills in one's BBRs.

None of the major behavioral approaches to personality specifically follows the model presented by paradigmatic behaviorism. However, there are a number of parallels, such as Bandura's principle of triadic reciprocal determinism (Chapter 20) and Mischel's person variables (Chapter 21).

THREE BASIC BEHAVIORAL APPROACHES

The behavioral strategy consists of three major approaches to personality: *radical-behavioral*, *social learning*, and *cognitive-behavioral*. The radical-behavioral approach, as its name implies, follows the dictates of radical behaviorism and studies only overt behaviors and external stimuli.

Social learning and cognitive-behavioral approaches are consistent with principles of methodological behaviorism. Both approaches deal with covert events. However, covert events are studied differently in the behavioral strategy than in other personality strategies (Spiegler & Guevremont, 1993). First, covert events are defined in explicit measurable terms. Second, the covert events often are linked to observable behaviors. For example, learning is a covert behavior. It is frequently defined as *performance on a test,* an overt, directly observable behavior.

Despite some basic differences, the three behavioral approaches overlap. We turn next to two fundamental issues that all three approaches emphasize.

These issues distinguish the behavioral strategy from the other strategies: (1) an emphasis on learning and experience and (2) the situational specificity of behavior.

THE KEY ROLE OF LEARNING AND EXPERIENCE

Behavior develops and is modified primarily through learning and experience rather than as a result of hereditary and biological factors. This is a basic assumption of the behavioral strategy. Three different learning processes are emphasized: classical conditioning, operant conditioning, and observational learning.

In **classical conditioning**, behavior is learned through *association* between stimuli and responses. For example, Professor Sharp wears jeans to a faculty party at which most of his male colleagues wear suits. He may have learned to dress in this manner because he has come to associate the look and feel of jeans with pleasant experiences in the past, such as being with attractive women.

In **operant conditioning**, behavior is learned primarily from the *consequences* of actions (i.e., reinforcement and punishment). From this perspective, Professor Sharp might wear jeans to parties because he receives compliments on how he looks.

In **observational learning**, one learns behaviors by observing what others (models) do and the consequences of their actions. Professor Sharp may have learned to wear jeans to parties by seeing his students in jeans. He probably observed that the students appeared to be more comfortable than men in business suits.

These three processes reflect different but not necessarily incompatible accounts of learning. Most human behavior is acquired and sustained by a combination of learning processes. For example, Professor Sharp may wear jeans because he saw his students wearing them, because he felt good while wearing them, *and* because people complimented him on his casual attire.

BEHAVIOR IS SITUATION SPECIFIC

Accounting for the apparent consistency of people's behaviors is a fundamental task for all personality theories. Psychoanalytic theories posit that lifelong patterns of behavior are developed early in life. Dispositional approaches speak of relatively stable and enduring personality characteristics that result in consistent behaviors. Phenomenological theories attribute behavioral consistency to how people view themselves, others, and events in their lives.

Behavioral personality theories hold that the consistency of behavior depends on the *situation* in which the behavior is performed. Situational cues indicate which behaviors are expected, are likely to meet with approval, and will be adaptive in that particular circumstance. Thus, behavioral personality theories hold that people's behaviors are consistent in the *same or similar* situations but vary in *different* situations. In other words, behavior is *situation-specific*.

For example, Greg sits quietly in classes, is mildly animated in casual conversation at the cafeteria, and vigorously expresses his support for his college athletic teams. In each case, Greg's behaviors are influenced by the requirements and restrictions of the situation. This means that how Greg acts will be consistent within similar situations. He will tend to say little in each of his classes, for example. But Greg's behaviors will vary in different situations. For instance, he cheers loudly at basketball games and says nothing in his classes. This situation-specific viewpoint contrasts with the generality-consistency assumptions of the dispositional strategy, which would categorize Greg as a passive or active type.

What constitutes the situation differs among the behavioral approaches. Within radical-behavioral approaches, the situation consists of stimuli in the external environment, including other people. In social learning and cognitive-behavioral approaches, the individual's perceptions and interpretations also are part of the situation and are considered important determinants of behavior.

BEHAVIORAL PERSONALITY THEORY	Behavioral approaches vary in the amount and kind of theorizing they spawn. Considerably more theorizing occurs in the social learning and cognitive-behavioral approaches than in radical-behavioral approaches (e.g., Schlinger, 1992). However, three characteristics are common to all behavioral theories. They (1) are relatively parsimonious, (2) minimize the use of theoretical constructs, and (3) minimize inferences.
Parsimonious Explanations	Behavioral personality theories tend to be parsimonious, or simple, in the sense of being based on few assumptions. Often a single set of principles is used to explain a variety of different phenomena. Take the common experience of forgetting the name of a person you know well. This is an example of *unexpressed behavior*, which refers to an act that a person can perform but is not performing at the moment. The explanation is simple and straightforward: You don't remember the person's name because the stimuli that elicit it are absent. At a later time, some cue immediately brings the name to mind. Remembering and forgetting are thus explained by the same principle: the presence of appropriate stimuli.

In contrast, the psychoanalytic explanation of the same phenomenon makes two assumptions. First, levels of consciousness exist. Second, conscious responses are made unconscious by a defensive process, such as repression. This implies that something personally threatening caused the person to forget. Clearly, this psychoanalytic explanation is considerably more complicated and makes more assumptions than the behavioral explanation.

Minimal Use of Theoretical Constructs	Compared with the other three personality strategies, the behavioral theories employ relatively few theoretical constructs. Behavioral theories are not free of theoretical constructs, but they typically avoid explanations that involve special processes within the person. For example, behavioral theories do not

posit any kind of unifying force or structure for personality. There are no behavioral equivalents of ego or self (because aspects of personality are viewed semi-independently).

Theoretical constructs often serve as shorthand summaries of personality phenomena. Because behavioral psychologists use theoretical constructs sparingly, behavioral descriptions of personality phenomena tend to be lengthy but *precise and specific* (e.g., Addis, 1993). Compare the behavioral description "avoids talking about painful past experiences" with the psychoanalytic theoretical construct "repressed."

Minimal Inferences	Personality psychologists make inferences whenever they assume something about one event based on information from another event. Inferences always provide indirect information, but how indirect an inference is depends on how far removed the two events are. Consider two very different kinds of inferences. A psychoanalyst posits the existence of an Oedipus complex from observing 5-year-old Calvin's affection toward his mother and avoidance of his father. A high degree of inference is involved because the analyst must make a series of inferential steps, beginning with overt behavior and ending with a theoretical construct. In contrast, suppose a behavioral psychologist predicted that Calvin would go to his mother when he had a problem based on Calvin's recently spending more time with his mother. In this case, there is little inference because a single level of inference is involved, from one behavior to another.

BEHAVIORAL PERSONALITY ASSESSMENT	Behavioral personality assessment can be characterized as (1) direct, (2) present-oriented, and (3) highly-focused.
Direct	The difference between indirect and direct approaches to personality is illustrated by a tongue-in-cheek contrast. A psychoanalyst and a behavioral psychologist are trying to determine whether a man hates his mother. The analyst interprets the man's dreams and slips of the tongue about women. The behavioral psychologist simply asks the man: "Do you hate your mother?"

It is not the methods of assessment themselves that distinguish behavioral personality assessment. Rather, it is the way the methods are employed. Consider the use of self-report inventories to assess personality directly. The Fear Survey Schedule is a behavioral self-report inventory used to assess fear (Wolpe & Lazarus, 1966). Subjects rate the degree of fear they have for a number of different situations and objects (see Table 18-1). The Fear Survey Schedule directly *samples* the subject's fears. The examiner takes the subject's answers at face value and does not use them as signs indicating a fear of something else. For instance, if Monroe reports being afraid of climbing ladders, the behavioral psychologist assumes he is afraid of climbing ladders. In contrast, a psychoanalyst might conclude that Monroe was actually afraid of sex (because climbing ladders is considered a symbol of sexual intercourse).

The clearest example of direct assessment is observing a person engaging

Table 18-1
A portion of a Fear Survey Schedule

Instructions: The items in this questionnaire are objects, experiences, or ideas that may cause fear, anxiety, or other unpleasant feelings. Using the scale below, write the appropriate number after each item to describe the degree to which the item causes you to feel fear, anxiety, or other unpleasant feelings.

1 = Not at all
2 = A little
3 = A moderate amount
4 = Much
5 = Very much

1. Open wounds	25. Blood
2. Being alone	26. Enclosed places
3. Speaking in public	27. Flying in airplanes
4. Falling	28. Darkness
5. Automobiles	29. Lightning
6. Being teased	30. Doctors
7. Dentists	31. Losing control
8. Thunder	32. Making mistakes
9. Failure	33. Older people
10. High places	34. Going blind
11. Receiving injections	35. Drowning
12. Strangers	36. Examinations
13. Feeling angry	37. Cancer
14. Insects	38. Fog
15. Sudden noises	39. Being lost
16. Crowds	40. Police
17. Large open spaces	41. Talking on the telephone
18. Cats	42. Death of a loved one
19. Being watched while working	43. Pain
20. Dirt	44. Suicide
21. Dogs	45. War
22. Sick people	46. Going insane
23. Fire	47. Violence
24. Mice	48. Psychologists

Source: Developed in "Some Correlates of Self-Reported Fear," by M. D. Spiegler and R. M. Liebert, 1970, *Psychological Reports*, 26, pp. 691-695.

in the behaviors to be assessed. For example, to learn how an individual is likely to act under stressful conditions, the behavioral psychologist might observe the person in one or more stressful situations (such as at work). When this is not possible, the psychologist asks the subject how he or she has behaved in stressful circumstances in the recent past.

Present-Oriented   To predict future behaviors, behavioral psychologists look to the individual's present and recent past behaviors. This is consistent with the concept of

Direct observation of overt behavior provides an important source of data about personality for behavioral psychologists. It is often carried out in naturalistic settings where subjects are engaged in their normal activities.

Photo Source, Inc./St. Louis

situational specificity. There is little reason to explore adults' childhood experiences to assess their present personality. This emphasis on the present has two rational justifications.

First, it acknowledges that past events may have been responsible for a person's originally developing the behavior. However, these past events cannot directly influence the person's continuing to engage in the behavior; quite simply, the factors that existed in the past do not exist in the present. A behavior can be influenced only by present events. For instance, crying as a reaction to frustrating events may have been learned by observing scenes such as your mother's reacting this way in the past, and your father's comforting her. But the habit will persist in adulthood only if it continues to be reinforced in the present, such as by sympathy from friends.

Second, trustworthy information about the past is not likely to be available. Accurately assessing what occurred in a person's early childhood, for example, is not possible (without a time machine!). At best, correlations between past and present personality variables can be obtained, but such relationships rarely yield clear-cut information about causation. For example, a man who is compulsively neat in his daily life may also have been severely toilet trained. This correlation does not necessarily imply that the man's early toilet training history contributed to his current compulsive habits.

Highly-Focused   Behavioral personality assessment examines aspects of an individual's total personality rather than the whole personality. Aspects of personality are assumed to be semi-autonomous. The situation specificity of behavior holds even for different types of the same class of behaviors. Take the example of Pam, who regularly refuses unreasonable requests. Can we infer from this behavior pattern that she also will make her personal desires known to others? Both are assertive behaviors, but they must be assessed independently. The specific focus of behavioral personality assessment contrasts with the holistic approach of the phenomenological strategy, which maintains that each component of personality must be viewed in relation to the total personality.

The assumption that a person's behaviors are semi-autonomous also has implications for behavioral research and personality change. In research, specific personality phenomena are studied in depth. In psychotherapy, particular behaviors rather than the client's total personality are the targets of change.

■ *Demonstration 18-1:*
OBSERVING AND RECORDING YOUR OWN BEHAVIORS

Direct observation and recording of behaviors are important behavioral assessment procedures. In this Demonstration, you will observe and record one of your own behaviors. (The instructions can easily be adapted to observing and recording another person's behaviors.)

1. First, *choose a response* to observe and record. Table 18-2 contains examples of

behaviors you might select, but you can pick any response that meets the following two requirements:

A. You should be able to define the response precisely so that there will be no doubt whether you have engaged in it.
B. The response should occur at a frequency that makes recording possible. If the response occurs at a very high rate (e.g., eye

Table 18-2

Example of target behaviors to observe and record (Demonstration 18-1)

BEHAVIOR	UNIT OF BEHAVIOR	UNIT OF TIME
Reading	Pages	Day or hour
Writing	Lines	Day or hour
Jogging	¼ mile	Day
Swimming	Laps in a pool	Day
Being late	Times late for an appointment	Day
Daydreaming	Minutes spent	Day or hour
Talking on the telephone	Minutes spent on phone calls	Day or hour
Swearing	Curse words	Day or hour
Learning a foreign language	Words learned	Day
Studying	Minutes spent	Day
Engaging in bull sessions	Minutes spent	Day
Drinking		
(a) Coffee	(a) Cups	
(b) Beer	(b) Ounces	
Smoking	Cigarettes	Day or hour

blinks), it will be difficult to record. If the response occurs only occasionally, you will have nothing to record. (Getting married does not occur often enough to be used in this Demonstration—at least for most people!)

2. Next, *select a unit of behavior and observation time period* that are appropriate for the response. Table 18-2 contains examples. No matter what the response, you will be counting the number of behavioral units that occur in a specified time period.

3. Now *decide on a unit of time* that is appropriate for the response and also practical for recording. A behavior that you engage in many times a day would most likely be recorded in hours or minutes, whereas a less frequent behavior would probably be recorded per day.

4. The final preparatory step is to *devise a convenient means of recording* how often the response occurs. For example, mark off a 3 × 5 index card in time intervals and then simply make a tally mark each time you perform the behavior, as shown in Figure 18-2. At the end of each day (or other unit of time

you are using), total the tally marks. This number becomes your rate for the day (e.g., "26 pages read per day"). Other ways of recording responses include making tally marks on a piece of masking tape on your watchband, wallet, or purse, or using an inexpensive golf or knitting counter.

The recording procedure should be available whenever you are observing the behavior and should be easy to use. You should also make brief notes about special events that may have influenced the frequency of the response (see Figure 18-2).

5. Now you are ready to *record the behavior* whenever it occurs. You should record for a minimum of six time units (e.g., days or hours).

6. To help you inspect and interpret the data you've collected, *graph your observations.* The horizontal axis should be marked off in time intervals, such as days or hours. The vertical axis should represent the number of responses per unit of time.

As an example, the data recorded in Figure 18-2 have been graphed in Figure 18-3. Notice

		Total Per Day
Mon.	ʈʰʈ ʈʰʈ ʈʰʈ ʈʰʈ ʈʰʈ ɪ	26
Tues.	ʈʰʈ ʈʰʈ ʈʰʈ ʈʰʈ ʈʰʈ ɪɪɪ	28
Wed.	ʈʰʈ ʈʰʈ ʈʰʈ ʈʰʈ ʈʰʈ ɪɪɪ	28
Thurs.	ʈʰʈ ʈʰʈ ʈʰʈ ʈʰʈ ʈʰʈ ʈʰʈ ʈʰʈ ʈʰʈ ʈʰʈ ʈʰʈ ʈʰʈ ɪ	56
Fri.	ʈʰʈ ʈʰʈ ʈʰʈ ʈʰʈ ʈʰʈ ʈʰʈ ʈʰʈ ʈʰʈ ʈʰʈ ʈʰʈ ʈʰʈ ɪɪ	57
Sat.	ʈʰʈ ʈʰʈ ʈʰʈ ʈʰʈ ʈʰʈ ʈʰʈ	30
Sun.		0
Sat. night big date		
Sunday slept till 1:30 p.m.		

Figure 18-2
Example of an index-card record of pages read in a week (Demonstration 18-1).

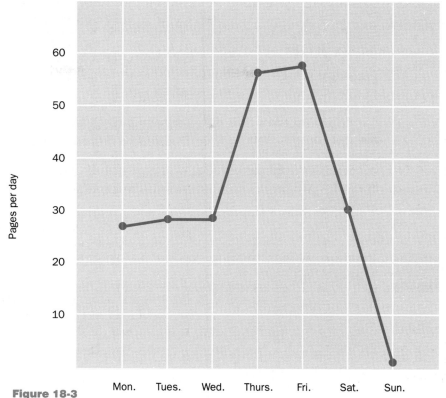

Figure 18-3
Graph of a week's reading behavior (Demonstration 18-1).

that the person read approximately the same number of pages for the first 3 days. On Thursday, the number of pages nearly doubled and continued at this same high rate on Friday. On Saturday, the number of pages dropped-back to approximately the Monday-through-Wednesday rate, perhaps because the Saturday night date was more compelling than reading. And on the seventh day, no pages were read (perhaps the person rested).

In doing this Demonstration, you may have encountered some of the common problems associated with self-recording behaviors. First, you may have been unsure at times whether you performed the behavior. This was probably a consequence of your not having defined the behavior specifically enough. Second, you may have forgotten to record the behavior

and/or found recording a burden. Such problems can be minimized by making the recording procedures as simple as possible.

Third, you may have noticed that the frequency of your behavior changed simply because you were observing and recording it. This problem, known as *reactivity,* is more likely to occur if you specifically want to increase or decrease how often you engaged in the behavior.

You may also have learned something about the particular behavior you were observing. The data may provide information about how often and when (time of day or day of the week) you perform the behavior and may suggest ways to modify the behavior, if you are interested in doing so.

BEHAVIORAL RESEARCH	In the tradition of methodological behaviorism, behavioral research emphasizes studying personality phenomena through systematic, controlled research, especially experiments. The research frequently is carried out in psychology laboratories where strict control of conditions is possible. The dependent variables are samples of the behavior being studied. For example, in studying aggression, the measures are direct samples of aggressive responses, such as giving an electric shock to another person.

Behavioral research is predominantly nomothetic—samples of subjects are studied with the aim of making generalizations to a larger population. Idiographic, single-subject studies may be used to evaluate the effectiveness of personality-change techniques. The focus of behavioral personality research is on specific behaviors rather than on total personality or global dispositions.

BEHAVIORAL PERSONALITY CHANGE	Behavioral personality-change procedures are known as **behavior therapy** or *behavior modification*. Behavior therapy is not a single method of personality change, like client-centered therapy or fixed-role therapy. *Behavior therapy* refers to a class of therapies of which there are many. Particular behavior therapies are associated with each of the three basic approaches in the behavioral strategy. The commonality of behavior therapies lies in their (1) dealing with target behaviors, (2) treating maintaining conditions, and (3) being action-oriented.

Target Behaviors

Clients typically enter therapy with multiple problems that are described vaguely (e.g., "I'm uptight most of the time, and I am lonely"). Behavior therapy begins by narrowing the client's complaints to one or two problems. Then a specifically defined, measurable aspect of the problem, known as a **target behavior,** is specified as the focus of change. "Spending time with other people" is an example of a target behavior for the problem of being lonely.

One or two target behaviors are treated at a time. When the initial target behaviors have been successfully treated, therapy turns to other target behaviors. Thus, multiple problems are treated sequentially rather than simultaneously.

Maintaining Conditions

Behavior therapy involves two major tasks. First, the factors that are *currently* maintaining (causing) the target behavior—known as **maintaining conditions**—must be assessed. Second, the maintaining conditions are modified in order to change the target behavior. Behavior therapists look for the maintaining conditions of a target behavior in the current antecedents and consequences of the behavior.

Antecedents are the stimuli present *before* the target behavior occurs. They include *situational cues* (where the target behavior occurs), *temporal cues* (time of day), and *interpersonal cues* (who is present). These cues indicate that it is appropriate to perform the behavior. Antecedents also include the personal and material prerequisites for performing the target

Table 18-3

Antecedents and consequences of a client's "binge eating junk food"

ANTECEDENTS	CONSEQUENCES
At home	Provides an activity
Alone	Lowers anxiety
Evening, weekend	Enjoy the junk food
Nothing to do	Get a stomachache
Feel anxious	Gain weight
Have bought junk food	Clothes don't fit
Junk food in house	Get tired when exercising

behavior, such as knowing how to write and having a pen and pad. Antecedents maintain behaviors by setting the conditions under which they are performed.

Consequences are events that occur *after* and as a result of performing the target behavior. Consequences include immediate and long-range outcomes—for the client, for other people, and for the physical environment. Consequences maintain behaviors by determining whether the person will engage in the behavior again. Typically, favorable consequences make it more likely and unfavorable consequences make it less likely that the person will perform the behavior in the future.

Table 18-3 lists the antecedents and consequences of one client's target behavior, "binge eating junk food." This target behavior was defined as eating more than one item of junk food per hour.

Action-Oriented Techniques

In behavior therapy, personality change does not come about through a verbal dialogue between client and therapist, as in so-called verbal psychotherapies (e.g., psychoanalysis and client-centered therapy). Clients in behavior therapy are expected to actively do things to alleviate their problems, rather than merely being asked to talk with the therapist about their problems and feelings. For example, clients often are given "homework assignments." They may be asked to observe and record their target behaviors; practice adaptive behaviors they have learned in the therapy sessions; and set up conditions (antecedents and consequences) in their lives to elicit and reinforce adaptive behaviors. Behavior therapy often takes place directly in the client's natural environment—that is, where the client's problem is occurring (Spiegler & Guevremont, 1993).

THE LEARNING/ COGNITIVE PROCESSES CONTINUUM

The relative emphasis placed on experience (learning) and thought (cognitive processes) differs in the three basic behavioral approaches. Although learning is a common theme in the behavioral strategy, specific approaches within the strategy vary both (1) in terms of the kind of learning emphasized and (2) in the overall focus on learning in their theoretical accounts of personality.

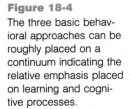

Figure 18-4

The three basic behavioral approaches can be roughly placed on a continuum indicating the relative emphasis placed on learning and cognitive processes.

Radical-behavioral approaches deal with classical and operant conditioning. These forms of learning involve environmental stimuli and observable responses, which is consistent with radical behaviorism. In social learning approaches the importance of classical and operant conditioning is acknowledged but observational learning is added. Moreover, explanations of observational learning refer to internal cognitive processes, such as the acquisition and recall of modeling cues. Although cognitive-behavioral psychologists acknowledge the importance of learning, they do not focus on it. Rather, they deal with thoughts and images that are both the antecedents and consequences of overt behaviors.

The three behavioral approaches can be roughly aligned on a continuum from *learning to cognitive processes,* as seen in Figure 18-4. Radical-behavioral approaches that emphasize learning are at one end of the continuum and cognitive-behavioral approaches that stress cognitive processes are at the other end. Social learning approaches that deal with both learning and cognitive processes lie in the middle.

SUMMARY

1. The behavioral strategy is concerned with behavior itself, which distinguishes the strategy from the other three strategies. Overt behavior is public and can be observed by others. Covert behavior is internal, private, and not directly observable by others.

2. Radical behaviorism deals only with environmental stimuli and overt behaviors, studying them through objectively verifiable observations and controlled research methods. Methodological behaviorism uses the same methods of investigation but studies covert events as well.

3. Paradigmatic behaviorism presents a model in which environmental stimuli elicit learned skills that are part of one's basic behavioral repertoires (personality). Biological factors mediate the environmental effects as well as the performance of the behavior.

4. Three basic behavioral approaches to personality can be identified. The radical-behavioral approach deals only with overt behaviors and environmental stimuli. The social learning approach acknowledges the importance of covert as well as overt behaviors. The cognitive-behavioral approach focuses on covert events.

5. A central assumption of all three behavioral approaches is that behavior develops and changes primarily through learning and experience.

6. Three different learning processes can be distinguished. Classical conditioning involves learning to associate stimuli and responses. Operant conditioning is learning from the consequences of behaviors. Observational learning refers to learning by observing others and noting the consequences that they receive for their actions.

7. Behavioral psychologists agree that behavior is situation specific: What people do primarily depends on the immediate situation in which they find themselves. For the radical-behavioral approach, the situation consists only of environmental stimuli. The social learning and cognitive-behavioral approaches also include the individual's perception and interpretation of these stimuli as part of the situation.

8. Behavioral personality theories are parsimonious, use few theoretical constructs, and minimize inferences.

9. Behavioral assessment is direct, present-oriented, and highly-focused.

10. Behavioral research involves systematic, controlled research, especially experiments. It often is carried out in laboratory settings. The dependent variables are samples of behaviors.

11. Behavior therapy procedures focus on specific target behaviors; identify and change the current maintaining conditions of these target behaviors; and are action-oriented.

12. The three behavioral approaches can be placed on a continuum with the focus on learning at one end (radical-behavioral) and the focus on cognition at the other end (cognitive-behavioral), with attention to both learning and cognition in the middle (social learning).

The Radical-Behavioral Approach

he radical-behavioral approach emphasizes the study of overt behaviors and the environmental conditions that influence them. In studying how behaviors are learned and maintained, radical-behavioral psychologists focus on either classical conditioning or operant conditioning.

CLASSICAL CONDITIONING

In the late 19th century, Russian physiologist Ivan Pavlov (1849–1936) was studying the digestive processes of dogs (see Figure 19-1). To induce salivation, meat powder was placed on the dogs' tongues. One day, Pavlov noticed that dogs that had been in the study for some time salivated even before food was put on their tongues. Pavlov recognized the potential importance of his accidental discovery. He spent much of the rest of his career studying this phenomenon, which came to be called *classical conditioning.*

Pavlov's first approach was introspective — trying to imagine the situation from the dog's point of view — and led up blind alleys. His assistants could not agree on what the dog ought to think or feel! Pavlov subsequently banned introspection from his laboratory and turned to a more objective, verifiable approach (Hyman, 1964). He reasoned that the animal's natural, or reflexive, tendency to respond to the food in its mouth with salivation had somehow also come to be evoked by the mere sight of food. The latter reaction was not innate. It had to be *conditioned* (learned) by environmental events, which meant that it could be studied experimentally.

The order of events in a traditional classical conditioning experiment is illustrated in Figure 19-2. First, a **conditioned stimulus (CS)**, such as a light, is presented; the CS does not initially produce the relevant response (salivation in Pavlov's work). Very shortly thereafter (a fraction of a second to no more than a few seconds), a stimulus that reflexively produces the desired response is introduced; this is the **unconditioned stimulus (UCS)**. The response that it produces is the **unconditioned response (UCR)**. In Pavlov's studies, the food was the UCS and salivary flow was the UCR. After the CS

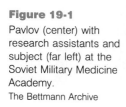

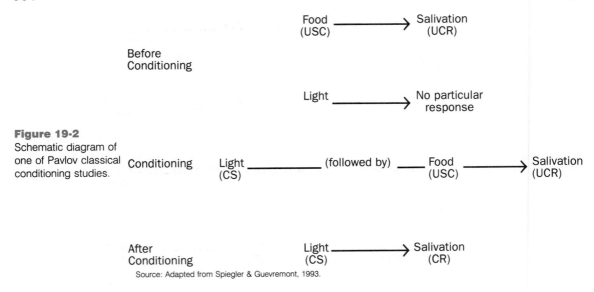

Figure 19-2
Schematic diagram of one of Pavlov classical conditioning studies.

Source: Adapted from Spiegler & Guevremont, 1993.

and UCS were presented together a number of times, the CS (light) came to produce salivary flow even before the UCS (food) was presented. The behavior elicited by the CS is known as the **conditioned response (CR)**, which was salivation in Pavlov's experiments.

Classical Conditioning of Emotional Reactions

John Watson was inspired by Pavlov's conditioning experiments. Watson believed that classical conditioning had vast implications for understanding and managing human behavior. In his classic case study of "little Albert," he and Rosalie Rayner demonstrated that fear could be conditioned (Watson & Rayner, 1920).

Albert, an 11-month-old apathetic child, appeared to be afraid of nothing except the loud sound made by striking a gong with a steel bar. Watson and Rayner attempted to classically condition another fear in Albert. They placed a white rat (CS) in front of him and simultaneously made the loud sound he feared (UCS). Albert had experienced no fear of white rats previously. After seven presentations of the rat and the loud sound, the rat aroused a definite fear reaction (CR), including Albert's crying and trying to escape from the situation (see Figure 19-3).

Watson and some of his followers considered the case of little Albert clear evidence that emotional reactions could be conditioned in humans. Later, critics found methodological flaws in the study (Harris, 1979; Marks, 1981; Paul & Blumenthal, 1989). But Watson's basic idea inspired many psychologists to study the role of classical conditioning in developing emotional reactions (cf. Eysenck, 1985).

Geer (1968), for example, showed color photographs of victims of violent and sudden death (UCS) to college students. The photos elicited a strong emotional reactions, as measured by *galvanic skin responses* (changes in skin conductivity). The students saw the photos 5 seconds after the

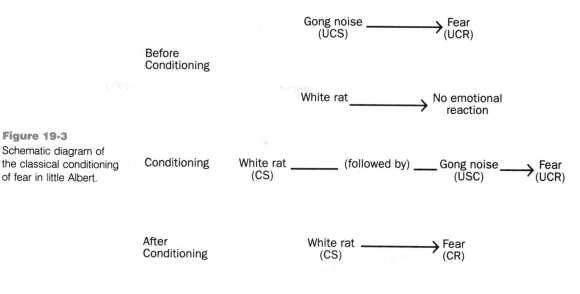

Figure 19-3
Schematic diagram of
the classical conditioning
of fear in little Albert.

Source: Adapted from Spiegler & Guevremont, 1993.

presentation of a tone (CS) that initially elicited no emotional response. After 20 such pairings, the previously neutral tone produced galvanic skin responses.

Positive emotional reactions can also be classically conditioned. In the latter years of his career, Watson applied classical conditioning to marketing techniques. A new product (CS) was associated with a positive UCS (such as a sexy model using the product) to make it more appealing. Today's marketing and advertising firms continue to use classical conditioning in this way with great success (e.g., Shimp, Stuart, & Engle, 1991; Stuart, Shimp, & Engle, 1987).

Neo-Classical Conditioning

Pavlov's basic model can be summarized as follows: One stimulus (CS) comes to evoke the original response (UCR) to a different stimulus (UCS) as a result of the two stimuli being paired. Since the time of Pavlov's initial discovery, the study and understanding of the classical conditioning process have been expanded greatly (Kimmel, 1989; Turkkan, 1989a, 1989b).

Today, it is recognized that classical conditioning is more accurately described as "the learning of relations among events so as to allow the organism to represent its environment" (Rescorla, 1988, p. 151). Classical conditioning is no longer viewed as a mechanical association of any two stimuli that happen to occur together (e.g., Gardner & Gardner, 1989; Huertas-Rodriguez, 1991). The information that the CS provides about the UCS is critical, not the simple CS-UCS pairing.

What is learned in classical conditioning is that *the CS will predict the occurrence of the UCS* (e.g., Power, 1991; Van den Hout & Merckelbach, 1991). Thus, the contemporary perspective on classical conditioning holds that the organism is "an information seeker using logical and perceptual relations among events, along with its own preconceptions, to form a sophisticated representation of its world" (Rescorla, 1988, p. 154). Figure 19-4 presents a model of human classical conditioning that is consistent with an information processing or cognitive perspective (e.g., Davey, 1989b; Feinberg, 1990; Levey & Martin, 1991).

Anxiety as a Classically Conditioned Response

Anxiety may be learned through classical conditioning (e.g., Levis, 1985; Öst & Hugdahl, 1985; Sandin, Chorot, & Fernández-Trespalacios, 1989; Wolpe & Rowan, 1988, 1989). Take fear of going to the dentist as an example. A person's initial visit to the dentist, often as a child, usually elicits no anxiety (unless the person has heard that dental work is painful). However, if the person experiences pain or discomfort while at the dentist's, the previously neutral cues in the dentist's office may come to elicit discomfort.

Pavlov's traditional model of classical conditioning—based on CS-UCS pairing—presents problems in explaining how anxiety develops. For instance, how is it that all people who are exposed to painful experiences during dental treatment do not develop dental phobias? This important question can be handled by contemporary models of classical conditioning that stress evaluation of the UCS (Davey, 1989b).

First, people should be less likely to develop dental anxiety following a painful experience at the dentist if they had experienced a number of previously painless dental visits. This phenomenon—in which the CS is less likely to predict the UCS if the CS has been previously presented without the

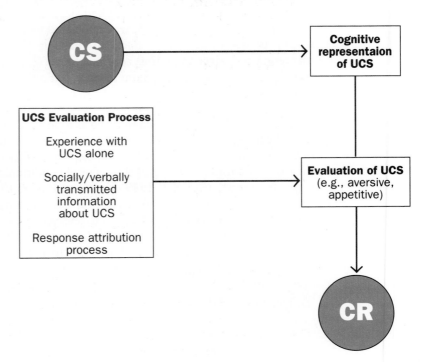

Figure 19-4
Schematic diagram of the neo-classical conditioning model in humans. The nature and strength of the CR is dependent directly on the person's evaluation of the UCS.

UCS—is known as *latent inhibition*. In fact, people who have had painful dental visits and do not develop dental anxiety tend to have had their first painful experience after a number of dental visits. In contrast, people who develop dental anxiety tend to have their initial painful experience after fewer visits (Davey, 1989a).

Second, people may fail to develop dental anxiety because factors other than the pain are more important in evaluating the dental situation (UCS). Some may focus on the beneficial effects of regular dental treatment (cf. Davey, 1989a). Others may believe that pain is a necessary evil of dental treatment. Still other individuals may have a higher tolerance for pain. Each of these factors result in evaluations that render the UCS less aversive and therefore less likely to lead to the development of dental anxiety.

Wider Applications of Classical Conditioning

Traditional classical conditioning theory primarily has been used to explain the learning of simple reflexive (e.g., salivation, eye blink) and emotional (e.g., galvanic skin) responses. Consistent with the broadening of theoretical explanations of classical conditioning, the areas to which classical conditioning is being applied also has been expanded (e.g., Turkkan, 1989a, 1989b). We will consider two areas of application: placebo effects and the effects of psychoactive drugs.

Placebo Effects

A *placebo effect* occurs when a patient is given an inert substance or treatment—a *placebo*—that results in a healing or therapeutic effect (White, Tursky, & Schwartz, 1985). Placebo effects have been demonstrated for a wide array of physical disorders ranging from the common cold, cough, and headache to insomnia, rheumatoid arthritis, hypertension, and angina (Evans, 1985).

Classical conditioning provides a parsimonious explanation of placebo effects (Turkkan & Brady, 1985). The placebo is a neutral (inert) event (CS), such as a "sugar pill." It is administered in a medical context (UCS)—such as a physician prescribing a pill—that has a history of resulting in a patient's feeling better or getting well (CR). The patient easily associates the placebo (CS) with stimuli (UCS) that typically lead to therapeutic benefits (UCR). Thus, the placebo comes to elicit therapeutic benefits (CR).

Interestingly, voodoo may be explained as the opposite of the placebo effect, or what has been called a "nocebo effect" (Wickramasekera, 1985). Voodoo rituals (CS) become associated with common stimuli related to illness and death (UCS) and hence result in the demise of the victim.

Effects of Psychoactive Drugs

Consider the following scenario. College students are recruited for a study of the effects of alcohol. In groups, they are provided with pitchers of beer and left alone to drink as much as they wish and to socialize with each other. The researcher returns about 15 minutes later and asks how they are doing. One student volunteers that she has become giddy. Another observes that the group now is more talkative. A third student reports tingling sensations in his arms, which, he explains, he typically experiences after a few beers. What accounts for the students' behaviors?

The effects of psychoactive drugs — substances that act on the brain to create psychological changes — are determined by two factors: the biochemical action of the drugs and learned responses to the drugs. The study we just described illustrates the powerful effects of learned responses, because the students were drinking *non*alcoholic beer (unbeknown to them)!

As with the placebo effect, cues (CS) associated with drinking (UCS) — pitchers of beer, liquid that smells and tastes like beer, socializing — predict the psychological and physiological effects of alcohol (e.g., Lang, Goeckner, Adesso, & Marlatt, 1975; Marlatt & Rohsenow, 1980; Rohsenow & Marlatt, 1981). In fact, people addicted to heroin have been known to inject themselves with water when they do not have access to heroin in order to produce heroin-like effects (McKim, 1986).

The finding that stimuli associated with drug use can create druglike effects provides an explanation for the development of *tolerance,* which is one indication of physical dependence on a drug. *Tolerance* refers to a person's needing larger and larger doses of a drug to experience the same effect. Tolerance, like other drug effects, has both biochemical and learned components.

The learned aspects could arise from associating stimuli related to taking the drug — such as the syringe and needle — with the physiological response to the drug. Such an association results in the contextual stimuli (CSs) alone coming to elicit one of two types of responses (CRs): drug-mimicking or drug-mirroring effects (Siegel, 1985). Drug-mirroring is a response that is opposite to that produced by the drug. With morphine, for example, the contextual stimuli would make the person *more* sensitive to pain. To deal with the heightened sensitivity to pain, the person would require a higher dose of the morphine to experience the same numbing effect, which is what tolerance is (Siegel & Ellsworth, 1986).

CLASSICAL CONDITIONING BEHAVIOR THERAPIES	A variety of behavior therapies use classical conditioning techniques. The goal of these techniques is to substitute an adaptive behavior for a maladaptive one. This is done by changing the CS-UCS pairings that have led to the problem. We will look at three examples: the urine alarm method for treating nocturnal enuresis; systematic desensitization for treating anxiety; and aversion therapy for treating maladaptive behaviors.
The Urine Alarm Method	*Nocturnal enuresis* refers to the inability of persons older than 3 to control urination while sleeping. The normal sequence is for bladder tension (UCS) to awaken the person before urination (UCR) begins. More than 50 years ago, Mowrer and Mowrer (1938) developed a simple classical conditioning procedure that teaches the person to wake up in response to bladder tension. It became the prototype of the **urine alarm method** that pairs bladder tension (a CS for people who bedwet) with an alarm (UCS). The alarm wakes (UCR) the person so that he or she can reach the toilet in time.

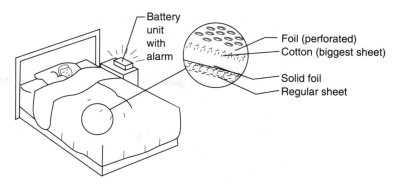

Figure 19-5
The essential elements of the bell-and-pad apparatus used to treat nocturnal enuresis.

Mowrer and Mowrer's original procedure was called the **bell-and-pad method.** The child sleeps on a specially prepared pad, consisting of two pieces of screening separated by heavy cotton (see Figure 19-5). When urination begins, (1) the urine seeps through the cloth, (2) closes an electric circuit, and (3) sounds an alarm. After a number of such sequences, bladder tension (CS) alone comes to wake (CR) the child before urination occurs. Another type of urine alarm attaches directly to the pants that the child sleeps in. Treatment involves using the alarm on a nightly basis for 6 to 12 weeks.

The urine alarm method has been used for more than 50 years and is effective in 70% to 80% of cases (e.g., Abramson, Houts, & Berman, 1990; Doleys, 1977; Houts, 1991; Johnson, 1980; Walker, Milling, & Bonner, 1988). Although quicker procedures have been developed (and will be discussed later in this chapter), none are as simple to implement as the urine alarm method (e.g., Azrin, Sneed, & Foxx, 1973; Houts & Liebert, 1984; Houts, Peterson, & Whelan, 1986; Liebert & Fischel, 1990).

Systematic Desensitization

Systematic desensitization, developed by Joseph Wolpe (1958), is a behavior therapy for alleviating anxiety. The client is gradually exposed to increasingly more anxiety-evoking stimuli while engaging in a behavior that competes with anxiety, such as muscle relaxation.

In classical conditioning terms, the goal is to substitute an adaptive response (CR) for the anxiety (UCR) elicited by particular stimuli (CSs). Before therapy, the stimuli that lead to anxiety are UCSs; after therapy, the same stimuli become CSs that lead to the adaptive response (CR).

Competing Response: Deep-Muscle Relaxation

Deep-muscle relaxation is most often used as the competing response to anxiety. Other competing responses include thinking pleasant thoughts, laughing, and eating.

Deep-muscle relaxation training proceeds systematically, covering major skeletal muscle groups (e.g., arms, head, neck, shoulders, and so on). Clients first learn to differentiate between relaxation and tension by tensing and relaxing each set of muscles. Then, clients practice just relaxing their muscles, both in the therapy sessions and at home. The following excerpt from a

Joseph Wolpe
(1915-   )
developed systematic
desensitization, a widely
used behavior therapy
for treating anxiety, fear,
and other negative
emotions.
Courtesy of Joseph Wolpe

therapist's relaxation instructions illustrates the beginning phases of relaxation training.

> Close your eyes. Settle back comfortably. We'll begin with your right hand. Clench your right hand into a fist. Clench it tightly and study the tensions you feel. Hold that tension . . . (5-second pause) and now relax. Relax your hand and let it rest comfortably. Just let it relax, let the muscles smooth out (15-second pause). Now, once again, clench your right hand . . . clench it tightly and study those tensions . . . (5-second pause) and now relax. Relax your hand and note the very pleasant contrast between tension and relaxation.

Anxiety Hierarchies

A careful assessment of the specific stimuli that make a client anxious is undertaken. Using this information, the client and therapist construct one or more lists of the anxiety-evoking stimuli, which the client rank-orders in terms of the amount of anxiety they evoke. The resulting list is called an **anxiety hierarchy**. Often there is a common theme among the stimuli in an anxiety hierarchy, as the examples in Table 19-1 illustrate.

Desensitization: Exposure to Anxiety-Evoking Stimuli

The final step in systematic desensitization involves gradually exposing the client to anxiety-evoking stimuli—that is, the actual desensitization process. The aim is to associate the stimuli that provoked anxiety with relaxation, which will "break" the maladaptive association between the stimuli and anxiety.

Deep muscle relaxation
is the most frequently
used response to
counter anxiety in
systematic desensitiza-
tion. Clients learn deep
muscle relaxation by first
tensing and then
relaxing various muscle
groups. The aim is to
learn to discriminate
between tension and
relaxation, which helps
the client achieve the
latter.
Photo Source Inc./St. Louis

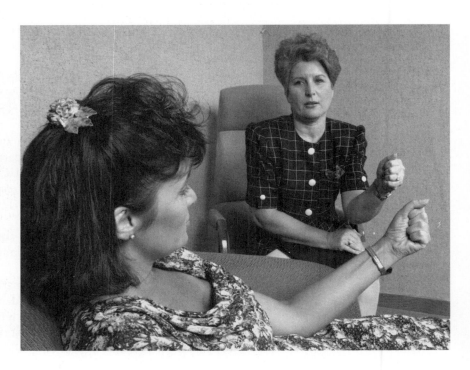

Table 19-1
Examples of anxiety hierarchies. The higher an item is on the list, the more anxiety it produces.

EXAMINATION SERIES

1. On the way to the university on the day of an examination.
2. In the process of answering an examination paper.
3. Before the unopened doors of the examination room.
4. Awaiting the distribution of examination papers.
5. The examination paper lies face down before her.
6. The night before an examination.
7. One day before an examination.
8. Two days before an examination.
9. Three days before an examination.
10. Four days before an examination.
11. Five days before an examination.
12. A week before an examination.
13. Two weeks before an examination.
14. A month before an examination.

DISCORD BETWEEN OTHER PEOPLE

1. Her mother shouts at a servant.
2. Her young sister whines to her mother.
3. Her sister engages in a dispute with her father.
4. Her mother shouts at her sister.
5. She sees two strangers quarrel.

Source: Behavior Therapy Techniques: A Guide to the Treatment of Neurosis by J. Wolpe and A. A. Lazarus, 1966, New York: Pergamon Press.

A desensitization session begins with the client becoming deeply relaxed, using the relaxation skills previously learned. Then, the client is asked to *imagine* the scenes or items in the anxiety hierarchy, beginning with the least anxiety-evoking scene and working toward the most anxiety-evoking item. Each scene is repeated, before going on to the next highest, until the client reports virtually no disturbance while visualizing it.

Variations of Systematic Desensitization
A number of variations on Wolpe's basic technique have been developed. It can be used with groups of clients (Deffenbacher & Suinn, 1988) and to treat problems other than anxiety, such as anger (e.g., Schloss, Smith, Santora, & Bryant, 1989; Smith, 1973) and insomnia (e.g., Steinmark & Borkovec, 1974).

Clients can also be exposed to the actual anxiety-evoking stimuli, a procedure known as **in vivo desensitization** or **in vivo exposure** (e.g., G.J. Hill, 1989; Marks, 1987). In vivo exposure can be more effective than systematic desensitization, and it allows clients to carry out the exposure on their own (e.g., Marks, 1978).

Aversion Therapy   Systematic desensitization substitutes positive responses, such as muscle relaxation, for negative responses, such as anxiety. In other instances, just the opposite effect is called for. **Aversion therapy** creates a negative emotional reaction to a maladaptive behavior (that is usually pleasurable). The target behaviors are most often addictive or sexually deviant behaviors. A UCS that normally produces an unpleasant, distasteful, or otherwise negative reaction (UCR) is paired with a CS associated with the pleasurable, maladaptive behavior. This classical conditioning continues until the CS elicits a similar negative reaction as a CR.

As an example, aversion therapy was used to treat a man who wished to stop his crossdressing (Lavin, Thorpe, Barker, Blakemore, & Conway, 1961). The 22-year-old married truck driver reported a desire to dress as a woman since the age of 8. From age 15 and through his military service and marriage, he derived erotic pleasure from wearing women's clothes and then looking at himself in a mirror. At the same time, he had a good sexual relationship with his wife.

The therapist photographed the client in various stages of female dress, and the client made an audiotape describing the activities in the pictures. As expected, he became sexually aroused while looking at the pictures and listening to the tape.

The treatment involved pairing wearing women's clothes with nausea, produced by injection of a drug. As soon as the injection took effect, the pictures and tape were presented. These stimuli were removed only after the client began to vomit. After six sessions of aversion therapy, the client no longer wanted to wear women's clothes. Follow-up over a 6-month period, involving interviews with both the client and his wife, suggested that the man's recovery was complete.

OPERANT CONDITIONING   Classical conditioning focuses on the antecedents of behaviors. In contrast, *operant conditioning* deals primarily with the *consequences* of behaviors. In operant conditioning, one learns to *operate* on the environment by engaging in behaviors that produce certain consequences. When the consequences are pleasant, the behavior is likely to be repeated; when they are aversive, the behavior is not likely to be repeated. Many of our everyday behaviors are learned and maintained by operant conditioning. Operant conditioning is also known as **instrumental conditioning**, because the person is *instrumental* in producing the effects.

The Skinnerian Tradition   B. F. Skinner's name is synonymous with the operant approach. He set the ground rules for the approach, which he considered the "scientific study of behavior." Skinner believed that behavior is primarily determined by *external environmental influences,* particularly by the consequences of one's actions (e.g., Skinner, 1989). He challenged the notion that humans are autonomous beings whose behaviors are influenced by internal factors, such as unconscious impulses, traits, or self-actualizing tendencies.

B. F. Skinner
(1904-1990)
believed that behavior is
primarily determined by
external environmental
influences, particularly
the consequences of
one's actions.
Courtesy of B. F. Skinner

Skinner (1953) rejected explanations of behavior in terms of theoretical constructs, which he viewed as *convenient but redundant fictions.*

> The practice of looking inside the organism for an explanation of behavior has tended to obscure the variables which are immediately available for a scientific analysis. These variables lie outside the organism, in its immediate environment and in its environmental history . . . .The objection to inner states is not that they do not exist, but that they are not relevant . . . (pp. 31, 35)

In place of creating theoretical constructs, Skinner advocated discovering empirical relationships between behaviors and the conditions that influence them. As a radical behaviorist, he was concerned only with observable characteristics of the environment (stimuli) that influence overt behaviors (responses) (Delprato & Midgley, 1992; Hineline, 1992). In a sense, Skinnerian psychology deals with an "empty organism." Variables that come between, or mediate, stimulus and response and that cannot be explained in terms of stimulus or response are outside the domain of the operant approach. Skinner's (1956) maxim was: "Control your conditions and you will see order." Like Watson, Skinner believed that there were only two goals of psychology: prediction and control (Biglan, 1993; Delprato & Midgley, 1992).

Skinner (1974) did not deny the existence of private events, such as thoughts and emotions. Instead, he was interested in identifying and studying the environmental conditions that influence private events (Delprato & Midgley, 1992; Hayes & Brownstein, 1986; Holland, 1992; Throne, 1992).

Reinforcement

At the heart of operant conditioning is the concept of **reinforcement**—the process by which the consequences of a behavior increase the chances that the behavior will be performed again. This is an *empirical* definition because the occurrence of reinforcement depends on an observed effect—namely, an increased likelihood of the behavior occurring—and not on subjective desirability. In most cases, however, **reinforcers**—the consequences that increase behaviors—are pleasurable or desirable events.

Two broad categories of reinforcement have been distinguished: positive and negative. With **positive reinforcement**, a stimulus is *presented* (added) following a behavior. For example, a father praises his son for cleaning his room. With **negative reinforcement**, a stimulus is *removed* (subtracted) following a behavior. For instance, a father stops yelling at his son after the boy has cleaned his room. In both cases, if the consequence increases the likelihood of repeating the behavior, reinforcement has occurred. Reinforcement always refers to *increasing* (strengthening) a behavior. The designation *positive* indicates the presentation (addition) of a stimulus and *negative* the removal (subtraction) of a stimulus.

Negative reinforcement should not be confused with *punishment.* **Punishment** is defined empirically as the process by which the consequence of a behavior *decreases* the chances of its recurrence. Thus, punishment has the opposite effect of negative reinforcement.

The role of reinforcement in operant conditioning is illustrated in the therapy procedures used to increase a young boy's studying. The treatment was evaluated with a **single-subject reversal design.** This research design compares a subject's behavior in periods in which a treatment is presented with periods in which it is withdrawn (reversed).

The Case of Robbie

Robbie, an elementary school boy, frequently disrupted class activities and spent little time studying (Hall, Lund, & Jackson, 1968). Initially, Robbie was observed during seven 30-minute *baseline* periods in his classroom. The naturalistic observations were carried out when pupils were supposed to be working in their seats.

Figure 19-6 shows a record of Robbie's study behavior, defined as "having his pencil on paper for at least half of a 10-second observation period." As you can see from the graph, during the baseline period, Robbie engaged in study behavior an average of 25% of the time. He spent the remaining time in such behaviors as "snapping rubber bands, playing with toys from his pocket, talking and laughing with peers, slowly drinking the half pint of milk served earlier in the morning, and subsequently playing with the empty carton" (Hall et al., 1968, p. 3). In the course of the naturalistic observation, it was noted that Robbie's teacher frequently paid attention to Robbie's nonstudy behaviors, such as by urging him to work or reminding him to put away his toys.

Following the baseline period, the *conditioning phase* of the study was begun. Now, every time Robbie engaged in 1 minute of continuous studying, an observer signaled the teacher, who promptly reinforced the behavior with

Figure 19-6
A record of Robbie's study behavior.
Note: Postcheck observations were made during the 4th, 6th, 7th, 12th, and 14th weeks after the completion of reinforcement conditioning.
Source: Adapted from "Effects of Teacher Attention on Study Behavior," by R. V. Hall, D. Lund, and D. Jackson, 1968, *Journal of Applied Behavior Analysis, 1, pp. 1-12.*

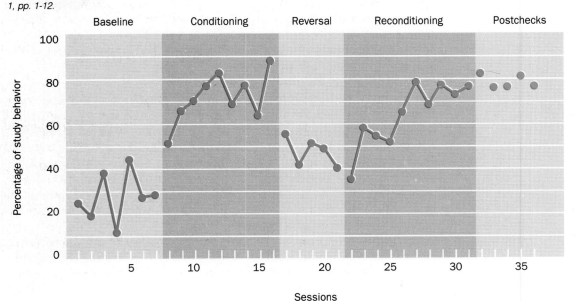

attention. The teacher ignored Robbie at all other times. The results were striking. When Robbie received attention only when he studied, his studying increased markedly in the first session and continued to rise in subsequent sessions (see Figure 19-6). Robbie spent an average of 71% of his time studying during the conditioning phase, compared to 25% during baseline.

Reinforcement appeared to be responsible for Robbie's increased rate of studying. This conclusion is based on the fact that studying increased from the baseline period in which reinforcement for studying had not been given. Still, some other factor, which occurred in the conditioning phase but not in the baseline period, could have led to Robbie's increased studying. For example, Robbie's parents might have begun to reward him when he said he studied at school. To provide additional evidence that the reinforcement rather than some other factor had increased Robbie's study behavior, a *reversal phase* was instituted. The teacher stopped reinforcing Robbie's studying, which reinstated (reversed) the circumstances before the conditioning phase. This period was an *extinction phase*. **Extinction** refers to the withdrawal of reinforcement. If Robbie's studying were controlled by reinforcement, his study behavior should decrease when the reinforcement was withdrawn. Robbie's studying declined to a mean of 50% during the reversal period (see Figure 19-6).

The researchers could have ended the procedures at this point if the only goal had been to demonstrate that reinforcement was maintaining Robbie's study behavior. However, the major objective of the investigation was to increase Robbie's studying. Therefore, a *reconditioning phase* was included. Specifically, teacher attention was reinstated as a reinforcer for studying. Robbie's study rate increased, stabilizing at between 70% and 80% (see Figure 19-6).

Periodic checks made during the remainder of the school year showed that Robbie's studying was maintained at an average rate of 79% (see Figure 19-6). Further, Robbie's teacher reported that the quality of his studying had also improved. He was now completing written assignments and missing fewer words on spelling tests.

Eliciting Behaviors: Prompting and Shaping

For a behavior to be reinforced, it first must occur. When the behavior occurs at least occasionally, like Robbie's studying, it can be reinforced — although one may have to wait some time for the behavior. But suppose the baseline level for a particular behavior is at or near zero. In such cases, prompting and shaping are used to elicit an infrequently occurring behavior so it can be reinforced.

Prompting involves telling or reminding someone to perform the behavior. Prompting cues may be *verbal* (as when a parent tells a child, "Say thank you") or *physical* (as when a coach moves a student's arms to prompt a swimming stroke). Once the behavior occurs often enough to be reinforced, the prompts are gradually withdrawn — a procedure called **fading**.

Prompting and subsequent fading often are used to teach language to children with severe mental handicaps. For instance, to teach the name of an object, the teacher points to it and says, "What is this? Cup." As the child begins to say "cup," the teacher fades the prompt by saying "cup" at successively lower volumes, then silently mouthing the word, and finally withdrawing all prompts (so the teacher says only, "What is this?").

Another way to elicit behavior is to shape it. **Shaping** involves reinforcing progressively closer approximations of the behavior. First, the desired behavior is broken down into its component parts. Then each component is reinforced until the entire behavior occurs. The logic of shaping is illustrated schematically in Figure 19-7.

The children's game of "hot and cold" is similar to shaping. One child has to find an object in a room. A playmate directs the child by saying "hot" when the child gets closer to the object and "cold" when the child moves farther away.

Prompting and Shaping Speech

Prompting and shaping are often used together to elicit behavior. Consider the case of a 40-year-old man with schizophrenia who had been completely mute during 19 years of hospitalization. To elicit the word *gum*, the experimenter first reinforced eye movement indicating attention, then lip movements, next vocalizations, and finally successive approximations of the word *gum*.

> The subject [S] was brought to a group therapy session with other . . . [patients] (who were verbal), but he sat in the position in which he was placed and continued with withdrawal behaviors that characterized him. He remained impassive and stared ahead even when cigarettes, which other members accepted, were offered to him and were waved before his face. At one session, when the experimenter [E] removed cigarettes from his pocket, a package of chewing gum accidentally fell out. S's eyes moved toward the gum and then returned to their usual position. This response was chosen by E as one with which he would start.
>
> S met individually with E three times a week. The following sequence of procedures was introduced in the private sessions.
>
> *Weeks 1, 2.* A stick of gum was held before S's face, and E waited until S's eyes moved toward it. When this response occurred, E as a consequence gave him the gum. By the end of the second week, response probability in the presence of the gum was increased to such an extent that S's eyes moved toward the gum as soon as it was held up.
>
> *Weeks 3, 4.* The E now held the gum before S, waiting until he noticed movement in S's lips before giving it to him. Toward the end of the first session of the third week, a lip movement spontaneously occurred, which E promptly reinforced. By the end of this week, both lip movement and eye movement occurred when the gum was held up. The E then withheld giving S the gum until S spontaneously made a vocalization, at which time E gave S the gum. By the end

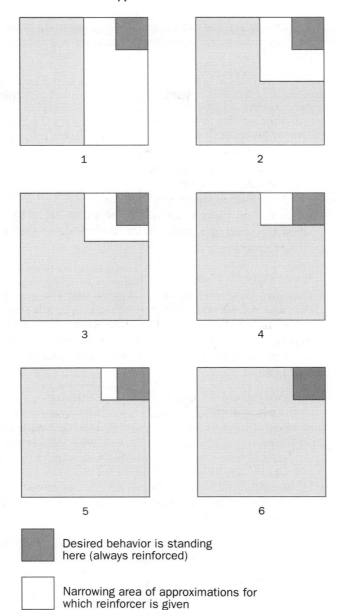

Figure 19-7
A diagram representing
the principle of shaping.

Desired behavior is standing
here (always reinforced)

Narrowing area of approximations for
which reinforcer is given

of this week, holding up the gum readily occasioned eye movement toward it,
lip movement, and a vocalization resembling a croak.

Weeks 5, 6. The E held up the gum, and said, "Say gum, gum," repeating
these words each time S vocalized. Giving S the gum was made contingent upon
vocalizations increasingly approximating gum. At the sixth session (at the end of
Week 6), when E said, "Say gum, gum," S suddenly said, "Gum, please." (Isaacs,
Thomas, & Goldiamond, 1960, pp. 9–10)

■ *Demonstration 19-1:*
SHAPING*

To do this Demonstration, you will need the help of a friend for about 20 minutes.

1. First, *select a behavior to shape.* Choose a relatively simple behavior, such as the suggestions in Table 19-2. The behavior should be brief (requiring less than a minute to complete) and should have easily definable components.

2. *Write down the major components of the behavior,* such as the examples in Table 19-3.

*Based on Spiegler & Guevremont, 1993.

Keep these in mind as *possible* components to reinforce. However, your friend may not perform each of the specific components you have identified. You may have to break down the components you have identified into finer components. Remember, reinforce only closer approximations to the final behavior.

3. Now you are ready for your friend's help. *Read the following instructions* to your friend.

I am going to try to get you to perform a simple behavior by saying "good" each time you get closer to doing it. I can't tell you anything about

Table 19-2
Examples of responses suitable for operant conditioning in Demonstration 19-1

MOTOR RESPONSES	VERBAL RESPONSES
Opening and closing a book	Criticizing
Taking top off a pen and replacing it	Talking about the future
Standing up and sitting down	Talking about schoolwork
Nodding head	Using plural nouns

Table 19-3
Major components of two simple responses

OPENING AND CLOSING A BOOK

1. Movement of either hand
2. Movement of either hand in the direction of the book
3. Touch the book with the hand
4. Opening the book partially
5. Opening the book fully
6. Closing the book partially
7. Closing the book fully

CRITICIZING

1. Any verbal utterance
2. Any statement
3. Any negative statement
4. Any negative statement that is a criticism

Source: Spiegler & Guevremont, 1993.

the behavior I want you to perform, but it is something simple that you will have no trouble doing. I'll let you know that you are getting closer to the final behavior by saying "good" each time you do something that is closer to the final behavior.

If your friend asks, "What do you want me to do?" answer, "Just get me to say "good.""

4. To get started, *reinforce*—by saying "good"—*the first movement* (or utterance, for a verbal behavior) your friend makes (as the experimenter did with the man who had been mute for 19 years).

5. Once your friend is active, *reinforce behaviors that are closer and closer to the final behavior.* Be sure you reinforce each component *immediately* after your friend performs it. Otherwise, your friend may associate the reinforcer with some extraneous response that he or she made at about the same time.

6. *Continue* to reinforce successively closer approximations *until your friend has performed the final behavior.* At that point, explain the shaping procedure you have been using, and ask your friend for any comments.

Schedules of Reinforcement

A **schedule of reinforcement** refers to the sequence or pattern in which reinforcement is received. In a **continuous reinforcement schedule**, the individual is reinforced every time he or she performs the behavior to be increased. Continuous reinforcement is used initially to establish a response, as in the examples of Robbie and the mute psychiatric patient.

Once the behavior has been established, intermittent reinforcement generally is used. With **intermittent** or **partial schedules**, only some instances of the desired behavior are reinforced. Behaviors that have been reinforced intermittently will be maintained longer, even without reinforcement, than behaviors that have been reinforced continuously (Pittenger & Pavlik, 1988; Pittenger & Pavlik, 1989; Pittenger, Pavlik, Flora, & Kontos, 1988). Most of our habitual everyday behaviors are reinforced on intermittent schedules.

Four basic schedules of intermittent reinforcement are produced by the combination of two dimensions: (1) the number of responses versus the period of time since the last reinforcement and (2) fixed versus variable quantity (see Figure 19-8). With **ratio schedules**, reinforcement occurs after a certain *number of responses* have been made. That number can be *fixed* (e.g., after every fifth response) or *variable* (e.g., after the third response, then after the seventh response, and so on). With **interval schedules**, reinforcement occurs if the person performs the behavior (at least once) after a specified *period of time* since the last reinforcement. The time interval can be *fixed* (e.g., after 5 minutes) or *variable* (e.g., 3 minutes, then 7 minutes, and so on). The four schedules of intermittent reinforcement are compared in Figure 19-9.

Fixed-Interval Schedules

In a **fixed-interval schedule**, a reinforcer is given for the first response made after a set time period has elapsed, such as every 2 minutes (see Figure 19-9). Studying for college examinations and working for a salary are common examples of behaviors maintained by fixed-interval schedules. Fixed-interval

	Interval (time since last reinforcement)	**Ratio** (number of responses)
Fixed (set time period or number)	FIXED-INTERVAL	FIXED-RATIO
Variable (changing time period or number)	VARIABLE-INTERVAL	VARIABLE-RATIO

Figure 19-8
The four basic schedules of intermittent reinforcement.

schedules produce a reliable pattern of responding that looks "scalloped" when graphed cumulatively (see Figure 19-10, p. 403).* The person makes few responses immediately after reinforcement, and then the rate of responding accelerates as the time for the next reinforcer nears.

Think about your own study habits. You are not likely to study much right after a test in a class, and your studying increases dramatically as the time of the next test approaches. You are in distinguished company. Even members of the U.S. Congress behave on a fixed-interval schedule (Weisberg & Waldrop, 1972). They pass bills at a very low rate in the first few months of each session. As adjournment draws closer, the number of bills passed increases sharply, which produces the "scalloped" cumulative record in Figure 19-11.

*In a cumulative record, the steeper the curve, the gretaer the rate of responding. Near-vertical curves indicate very high rates of responding, and near-horizontal curves indicate very low rates. A totally horizontal (flat) curve means no responding.

Figure 19-9
Comparison of fixed- versus variable- interval and ratio schedules of reinforcement (arrows indicate reinforcement).

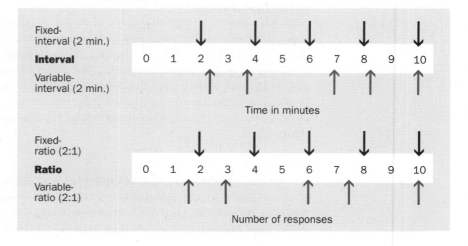

Many workers are paid on an hourly basis. This is an example of a fixed-interval schedule of reinforcement.
Photo Source Inc./St. Louis

Fixed-Ratio Schedules

With **fixed-ratio schedules**, reinforcers are administered after a set number of responses. For example, a 4:1 fixed ratio means that every fourth response is reinforced. A salesperson who is earning a commission and a student who gets a grade for solving a specified number of problems are being reinforced on fixed-ratio schedules.

Fixed-ratio schedules generally produce considerably higher rates of responding than either continuous reinforcement or fixed-interval schedules. As Figure 19-10 shows, the cumulative curve for a fixed-ratio schedule is steeper than for a fixed-interval schedule, indicating a higher response rate. If the number of responses required for reinforcement is gradually increased, people will continue to respond on extremely "lean" schedules, where the ratio of nonreinforced to reinforced responses is very high (e.g., 1,000:1).

Variable-Interval Schedules

In everyday life there is often variability in the way we receive reinforcers. With **variable-interval schedules**, the interval between reinforcers is randomly varied around a specified time. For instance, *on average*, an individual might be reinforced every 2 minutes (see Figure 19-9).

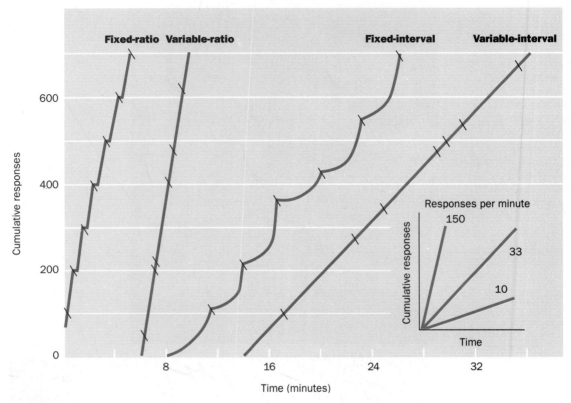

Dialing a telephone number that has been busy is an example of a common behavior that is reinforced on a variable-interval schedule (Shaver & Tarpy, 1993). The amount of time for a connection to occur (reinforcement) varies from one phone call to another. Hunting and fishing provide another example of behaviors reinforced on variable-interval schedules. Even though both endeavors involve skill, the availability of reinforcers—that is, the presence of game or fish—is based on an undetermined time schedule (Lundin, 1961). Variable-interval schedules produce steady but relatively low response rates (see Figure 19-10).

Variable-Ratio Schedules

With a **variable-ratio schedule**, the number of responses required for reinforcement is varied randomly around a ratio that is the average of the number of required responses (see Figure 19-9 on p. 400). Variable-ratio schedules are among the most potent for inducing very high, steady rates of responding (see Figure 19-10). Compulsive gambling illustrates the potentially powerful effect of variable-ratio schedules.

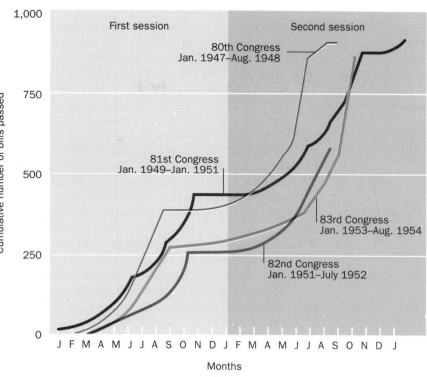

Figure 19-11
Cumulative number of
bills passed during the
legislative sessions of
Congress from January
1947 to August 1954.
Source: "Fixed-Interval Work
Habits of Congress" by P.
Weisberg and P. B. Waldrop,
1972, *Journal of Applied
Behavior Analysis,* 5,
pp. 93-97.

Piecework is an example
of reinforcement based
on a fixed-ratio schedule.
© 1989 Michael Melford/
Image Bank

> Even though the returns are very slim, . . . [the gambler] never gives up. Families are ruined and fortunes lost; still the high rates of behavior are maintained, often to the exclusion of all alternate forms of activity. Witness the "all night" crap games in which a single person will remain until all . . . funds and resources are gone. . . . (Lundin, 1961, p. 91)

Matching Theory   How often a behavior is performed depends on more than the schedule on which it is being reinforced. Response rate also is influenced by the amount of reinforcement available to all other possible responses (Herrnstein, 1970). Specifically, Herrnstein's **matching theory** predicts that if there are a number of alternative behaviors you can perform, your frequency of engaging in each will be directly proportional to the amount of reinforcement you receive for each.

One of the practical implications of matching theory is that the response rate of a given behavior can be affected by the amount of reinforcement provided for other behaviors (e.g., Martens, 1990, 1992; Martens & Houk, 1989; Martens, Lochner, & Kelly, 1992; McDowell, 1988). As an example, matching theory was used to design a treatment to reduce a mildly retarded 22-year-old man's "oppositional behaviors," which included failure to comply with requests, arguing, and displaying temper tantrums (McDowell, 1982).

The treatment involved increasing the reinforcement available for behaviors unrelated to the man's oppositional behaviors, such as shaving, helping prepare dinner, and reading. By the eighth week of treatment, the frequency of oppositional behaviors decreased by about 80%. Note that nothing was done to decrease the reinforcement for the oppositional

Fishing is reinforced on a variable-interval schedule. The time between catches is variable and often the person will continue fishing even though a long time has passed since catching the last fish.
© Jim Grace/Photo Researchers

Gambling pays off on a variable-ratio schedule. The number of bets between winning is quite variable, and gamblers continue to bet even though many preceding bets have not paid off. This is one explanation of the lure of and even the addiction to gambling.
Photo by Dave Bellak/ Jeroboam

behaviors; the treatment merely involved increasing the reinforcement for other behaviors.

STIMULUS CONTROL

Learning involves knowing (1) how to perform a behavior and (2) *when* and *where* the behavior is likely to be reinforced. **Discriminative stimuli** are environmental cues that indicate when a response is likely to be reinforced. They "set the stage" for the behavior to occur, which allows it to be reinforced. Behaviors that are cued by discriminative stimuli are said to be under **stimulus control**.

Many of our everyday behaviors are under stimulus control. The ringing telephone signals you to pick up the receiver and say hello. You are more likely to smile at someone who smiles rather than frowns at you. A police car up ahead may be a discriminative stimulus for slowing down.

Different discriminative stimuli may control the same response for different people. For example, in countries where food is scarce, people eat when their stomachs "tell" them they are hungry. In more affluent societies, people tend to eat when the clock "tells" them they are hungry.

The right amount of stimulus control is necessary for functioning efficiently. Too much or inappropriate stimulus control leads to rigidity. For example, parents of young children sometimes discover that bedtime is likely to be observed only when they are home and not when the children are left with babysitters. The parents have become the discriminative stimuli for observing bedtime; the children have not learned to *generalize* the behavior to other discriminative stimuli.

More often, problems arise from insufficient appropriate stimulus control. Insomnia, for instance, may occur because sleeping is not under

Table 19-4
Rules clients follow in stimulus-control treatment of insomnia

RULE	RATIONALE
1. *Go to sleep only when sleepy.*	Establish feeling sleepy as a discriminative stimulus for sleeping.
2. *Use bed only for sleeping.*	Establish bed as a discriminative stimulus for sleeping and not for any other behavior (e.g., reading, eating). Sexual activity is the one exception.
3. *If unable to fall asleep (within 10 minutes) get out of bed.*	Establish bed as a discriminative stimulus for falling asleep quickly.
4. *If unable to fall asleep after returning to bed, repeat rule 3.*	Same as above.
5. *Get up at same time every morning.*	Helps establish consistent sleep rhythm.
6. *Do not nap.*	Disrupts sleep rhythm and decreases chances of being sleepy at bed time.

Source: Based on "Behavioral Treatments for Insomnia" by R. R. Bootzin and P. M. Nicassio, 1978, in M. Hersen, R. M. Eisler, and P. M. Miller (Eds.), *Progress in Behavior Modification,* Vol. 6. New York: Academic Press.

appropriate stimulus control. One behavior therapy treatment for insomnia involves establishing appropriate stimulus control (e.g., Bootzin, 1985; Spielman, Saskin, & Thorpy, 1987). The client is asked to follow a basic set of rules, like those in Table 19-4. The rules help to make being in bed a discriminative stimulus for sleeping and no other activities, such as reading, talking on the phone, and, especially, staying awake at night.

BEHAVIOR MODIFICATION: OPERANT CONDITIONING THERAPIES

The principles of operant conditioning have been applied extensively to personality change. **Behavior modification,** as operant therapy procedures often are called, primarily involves changing the *consequences* of behaviors to modify them. You have already read about two specific applications: to increase Robbie's study behaviors and to reinstate speech in man who had been mute for 19 years. Stimulus control procedures, such as in the treatment of insomnia, are also part of behavior modification.

Behavior modification procedures have three goals: (1) to increase desirable or adaptive target behaviors; (2) to decrease undesirable or maladaptive target behaviors; or (3) to simultaneously decrease undesirable target behaviors and increase desirable target behaviors.

Increasing Adaptive Behaviors

Reinforcement therapies are used to increase adaptive behaviors that clients are not performing frequently enough. Examples are social interaction in clients suffering from schizophrenia and assertive behaviors for clients who do not stand up for their rights. Unlike many verbal, insight-oriented psychotherapies (e.g., psychoanalysis and client-centered therapy), reinforcement therapies can be used with almost any client, including those who have minimal intellectual functioning or are mute (Spiegler & Guevremont, 1993). We will look at two specific applications of reinforcement therapy to illustrate its versatility.

The Premack Principle

Activities people frequently engage in can serve as powerful reinforcers. Some 30 years ago, David Premack (1965) discovered that high-probability behaviors can serve as reinforcers for low-probability behaviors. This finding has come to be called the **Premack principle**. Any lower-frequency behavior will increase if it is made contingent on the higher-frequency behavior—even if the higher-frequency behavior is not considered pleasurable.

For example, suppose you decided that you wanted to make your bed each morning, which you almost never do. You notice that you brush your teeth without fail the first thing each morning. If you allow yourself to brush your teeth only after you make your bed, you will make your bed more often. Note that although you regularly brush your teeth, it is not something you would say you particularly enjoyed. But it is a high-probability behavior.

The Premack principle is especially useful with clients for whom it is difficult to identify reinforcers. Consider the case of B. H., a 44-year-old woman in a psychiatric hospital who rarely interacted with other people (Spiegler & Guevremont, 1993). She spent virtually all her waking hours sitting in one particular chair. The hospital staff were able to shape the time B. H. spent in social interactions by permitting her to sit in her chair only after spending a specified time with others.

Token Economies

A **token economy** is a reinforcement system designed to motivate clients to perform adaptive behaviors. Clients are reinforced with *tokens,* such as poker chips or points, for adaptive behaviors. The tokens can be exchanged for various **backup reinforcers**, such as desirable items (e.g., candy) and activities (e.g., watching TV).

Token economies often are used with groups of clients, such as children in a classroom. A list of desirable behaviors and the number of tokens earned for performing each as well as a list of backup reinforcers and their costs are posted (see Table 19-5). Thus, clients know ahead of time exactly what they have to do to earn tokens and how they can spend them (Spiegler & Agigian, 1977).

Token economies have been successfully used in a variety of group settings, including treatment programs for psychiatric patients, intellectually handicapped individuals, predelinquent adolescents, and "normal" children

Table 19-5
Example of a list posted in a foster home token economy of (1) desirable behaviors and the number of tokens earned for performing each and (2) backup reinforcers and their costs

HOW YOU CAN EARN TOKENS	
BEHAVIOR	TOKENS EARNED
Reading the newspaper for 15 minutes.............................	15
Watching TV news program.................................	15
Pleasure reading for 20 minutes.........................	15
Washing dishes...	10
Making bed...	5
Washing hands before meals...........................	5
Having room considered neat at daily inspection..............	10
Finishing homework before dinner.................................	10
Being on time for school.................................	5
Doing chores...	10-30

HOW YOU CAN SPEND TOKENS	
REWARD	TOKEN COST
Riding bike for 1 hour..	10
Watching TV for ½ hour.................................	20
Listening to music per ½ hour...........................	10
Playing games per ½ hour.................................	10
Snack...	15
Dinner out at favorite restaurant.........................	35
Going to movies...	25
All-day excursion...	60

in classrooms (Glynn, 1990; Spiegler & Guevremont, 1993). Token economies for individual clients have also been developed, especially for children, but occasionally for adults. An example of the latter is a token program for an 82-year-old man who had suffered a massive heart attack (Dapcich-Miura & Hovell, 1979). The token program was aimed at motivating the man to engage in critical aftercare behaviors such as walking and taking medication.

Decreasing Maladaptive Behaviors

Strengthening adaptive behaviors to substitute for maladaptive behaviors is the optimal way of weakening maladaptive behaviors (Spiegler & Guevremont, 1993). For example, when Robbie's studying behaviors were increased, his disruptive behaviors decreased. Sometimes it is necessary to decrease undesirable behaviors directly. The basic process involves changing the consequences of the undesirable behavior by (1) eliminating reinforcement or (2) making the consequences aversive. Both procedures make it less likely that the client will engage in the maladaptive behavior in the future.

Eliminating Reinforcement

Extinction, as a therapy procedure, involves withdrawing or withholding the reinforcers that have been maintaining a behavior. Extinction often is used when the reinforcer is social attention. For example, it appeared that 4-year-old Cindy's severe temper tantrums were maintained by her mother's attention (Piacentini, Schaughency, & Lahey, 1985). Accordingly, the therapist instructed Cindy's mother to ignore the tantrums.

To deal with Cindy's verbal and physical aggression, **time-out from positive reinforcement (time-out,** for short) was instituted. Time-out involves withdrawing a client's access to positive reinforcers for a brief, preset period immediately after the client engages in the maladaptive behavior. Whenever Cindy behaved aggressively, she was put in her room for 5 minutes, thereby removing her access to the many potential reinforcers outside her room. Extinction and time-out were supplemented with positive reinforcement of appropriate behaviors. The combined treatments successfully eliminated Cindy's temper tantrums.

Establishing Aversive Consequences

Response cost decreases maladaptive behaviors by removing a valued item or privilege whenever the maladaptive behavior is performed. For example, Ellen, a college senior, used a response cost procedure to decrease her habit of failing to put her clothes away after she wore them (Spiegler, 1989). Each morning Ellen collected all articles of clothing not in their proper places (e.g., a drawer, closet, or hamper) and put them in a large box. She did not allow herself to remove any of the clothes until the end of the week, which meant that she frequently had to do without favorite articles of clothing. This relatively simple procedure substantially reduced her longstanding habit of failing to put away her clothes.

Often the threat of response cost is a powerful incentive that prevents the client from engaging in the undesirable behavior. In one case, a client addicted to amphetamines gave her therapist ten $50 checks (Boudin, 1972). The therapist was to forward the checks as a donation to the Ku Klux Klan if the client (who was African-American) used amphetamines. During 3 months of treatment, the response-cost contingency had to be used only once. The client was drug-free at a 15-month follow-up.

Overcorrection reduces undesirable behaviors by first having the client correct the negative effects of the maladaptive behavior and then having the client intensively practice an alternative, adaptive behavior. Thus, overcorrection simultaneously (1) decreases the undesirable behavior by introducing aversive consequences and (2) increases an alternative, desirable behavior. Overcorrection is the major component of *dry bed training* for bed wetting (Azrin, Sneed, & Foxx, 1973, 1974). Whenever the child wets the bed, the child is awakened to change wet sheets and nightclothes and then practice going to the toilet several times before going back to sleep. Dry bed training ordinarily takes less than a week (Azrin, Thienes-Hontos, & Besalel-Azrin, 1979).

SUMMARY   1. The radical-behavioral approach emphasizes the study of overt behaviors and the environmental conditions that influence them. One way that behaviors are learned is through classical conditioning, which was first described by Pavlov. Emotional responses, including anxiety, can develop through classical conditioning.

2. Contemporary theories of classical conditioning emphasize learning of relations among events that serve to organize one's environment; these theories de-emphasize mechanical association of stimuli. Applications of classical conditioning have been expanded to include such phenomena as placebo effects and the psychological effects of psychoactive drugs.

3. The urine alarm method uses principles of classical conditioning to treat bedwetting by teaching the person to awaken to bladder tension.

4. Systematic desensitization treats anxiety by gradually exposing clients to anxiety-evoking stimuli while they engage in an incompatible response (such as deep-muscle relaxation).

5. Aversion therapy involves associating an unpleasant stimulus with a response to be eliminated. This method is primarily used to treat addictive and sexually deviant behaviors.

6. Operant conditioning focuses on the consequences of behaviors influencing their future occurrence. Skinner, the leading proponent of operant conditioning, advocated looking to the external environment to find the causes of behaviors.

7. Positive reinforcement, the central concept in operant conditioning, involves the consequences of a behavior increasing the likelihood that the behavior will be performed again. Negative reinforcement occurs when the removal of a stimulus increases the future likelihood of the response.

8. Prompts are used to elicit infrequently occurring behaviors so they can be reinforced. Prompting involves reminding someone to perform a behavior. Shaping is the process of reinforcing successively closer approximations of the desired behavior.

9. A schedule of reinforcement describes the pattern or sequence in which reinforcers are administered. The four basic schedules of intermittent reinforcement are fixed interval, fixed ratio, variable interval, and variable ratio.

10. According to matching theory, the frequency of a behavior is influenced by the amount of reinforcement available from other responses.

11. Discriminative stimuli are environmental cues that tell people when or where a particular response will be reinforced. Behavior that is cued by discriminative stimuli is said to be under stimulus control. Problems develop when a behavior is under too much or too little stimulus control.

12. Behavior modification procedures apply the principles of operant conditioning to changing problem behaviors. The Premack principle reinforces low-probability behaviors with high-probability behaviors. A token economy is a reinforcement system for motivating adaptive behaviors.

13. Extinction removes the reinforcers that are maintaining a maladaptive behavior. Time-out from positive reinforcement removes the client from access to all positive reinforcers for a brief, preset time as a consequence of performing an undesirable behavior.

14. Response cost reduces an undesirable behavior by removing a valued item or privilege when the client engages in the behavior. Overcorrection decreases an undesirable behavior by having the client correct the negative effects of the behavior and then practicing an alternative, desirable behavior.

Chapter Twenty

Social Learning Theories

he social learning approach to personality begins where radical-behavioral approaches left off. Radical-behavioral approaches stress the importance of learning—classical and operant conditioning—and situational factors in the genesis and evolution of personality. Social learning theories go several steps further. They emphasize the *social* aspects of the situation that influence personality, including the important influence of learning and changing one's behaviors by observing how other people behave. Social learning theories also are concerned with personality processes, such as cognitions that influence how we act.

The first social learning theory was developed more than 50 years ago by Neal Miller (1909–) and John Dollard (1900–1980). Miller and Dollard (1941; Dollard & Miller, 1950) applied the learning theory of Clark Hull to personality phenomena. Hull theorized that behavior is learned through a sequence of four events: (1) a *drive* motivates the behavior; (2) *cues* determine when, where, and how people respond to a drive; (3) a *response* is made that will satisfy the drive; and (4) *reinforcement* occurs in the form of drive reduction.

Miller and Dollard's theory has had little impact on contemporary social learning theorizing; it has only historical significance as the first social learning theory. The concept of social models as factors that affect how people act and think is the only remnant of Miller and Dollard's theory in contemporary social learning theories.

We will examine the two major contemporary social learning theories developed by Rotter and Bandura.

ROTTER'S SOCIAL LEARNING THEORY

Shortly after Miller and Dollard had completed their theorizing, Julian Rotter (1954) formulated a comprehensive social learning theory. Rotter's theory emphasizes the importance of situational factors and reinforcement as determinants of behavior, as did radical-behavioral theories. However, Rotter believed the situation and reinforcers have only an indirect influence on behavior. Much of Rotter's theory deals with the cognitive factors that mediate the effects of the situation and reinforcers. Specifically, one's personal values and expectancies directly determine how one behaves.

Rotter's theory is based on four basic constructs: the psychological situation, reinforcement value, expectancy, and behavior potential. These four factors operate as follows. *Within a given psychological situation, the likelihood that a person will engage in a particular behavior (behavior potential) is determined by two factors: (1) the value the person places on the reinforcer for the behavior (reinforcement value) and (2) the person's expectancy that the reinforcer will be obtained.* Let's look at each of these factors in more detail.

Reinforcement Value

Generally, people act to bring about their most preferred outcomes. **Reinforcement value** refers to a person's individual preference for a particular outcome or reinforcer relative to other possible outcomes or reinforcers.* Assuming that you could spend an evening (1) going to a movie, (2) attending a concert, or (3) having dinner at a local restaurant, which would you prefer? Obviously, people differ in the value they place on these activities.

Now suppose you had a fourth choice: flying to Paris on the Concorde for dinner. Which of the four would you choose? Unless you are afraid of flying or don't like plush Parisian restaurants, you are likely to choose the evening in Paris. Thus, reinforcement value not only is an individual matter, but it is relative to the reinforcers available as well.

Expectancy

Besides preferences for various reinforcers, each person has an **expectancy** about the chances that a particular behavior will result in a given reinforcer. In a sense, we assign a probability level to each potential reinforcer.

Expectancy is independent of reinforcement value. You may value a free evening in Paris highly, but you may believe that there is little chance that you'll be offered it. In contrast, going to the movies may be your last choice, but it may be the activity that you feel is most likely to be available to you.

Expectancy, like reinforcement value, is subjective. What matters is how the person sees the chances of getting a particular reinforcer rather than the objective probabilities themselves. Margie may believe that she is more likely to be invited to spend an evening in Paris than an evening at a local movie theater. Even though most people would say the opposite, it is *her* expectancy that will influence her actions.

Rotter (1982) distinguished between two types of expectancies: specific and generalized. A **specific expectancy** is a person's subjective estimate of the chances of obtaining a particular outcome by performing a particular behavior. An example is the probability that asking a friend for a loan will get you the money you need.

Through learning, some expectancies come to be applied to a variety of related experiences. A **generalized expectancy** is a person's subjective prediction of the chances of obtaining a particular *class* (category) of outcomes by engaging in a particular *class* of behaviors. Your overall estimate of the probability that asking for favors will get you what you want is an example. We use generalized expectancies when we perceive an important psychological similarity in a range of situations. Thus, people come to respond to the similar situations in similar ways. Later we will discuss *locus of control,* a generalized expectancy that has been studied extensively. For now, our discussion concerns only specific expectancies.

Julian Rotter
(1916-   )
developed a social learning theory that emphasizes cognitive factors, such as values and expectations, that mediate the effects of environmental factors on behavior.
Courtesy University of Connecticut

The Psychological Situation

All behavior occurs in a context of external and internal stimuli. Rotter (1981) recognized that people perceive and respond to stimuli differently. Thus, the context of behavior is the **psychological situation**—the existing circumstances *from each individual's perspective.*

---

*Rotter's (1954) use of *reinforcement* in this context actually refers to all *outcomes,* whether or not they increase the likelihood that the behavior will recur (which is the definition of *reinforcement;* see Chapter 19).

Reinforcement values and expectancies always depend on the psychological situation. Earning $20 is likely to be more reinforcing if you have been laid off from work than if you have just gotten a paycheck. Similarly, the chances of getting a date with someone you have known for a while may be greater than the chances of getting a date with someone you have just met.

Behavior Potential

In most situations, a person can behave in any number of ways. **Behavior potential** is the likelihood that a person will engage in a particular behavior to obtain a particular outcome. Behavior potential depends on two factors: reinforcement value and expectancy. Because reinforcement value and expectancy are independent factors, behavior potential must be predicted by taking both factors into account simultaneously. It is convenient to state the relationship as a formula:

Behavior Potential = Reinforcement Value × Expectancy

The presence of a multiplication sign has important implications.* When either reinforcement value or expectancy is low, the likelihood that the individual will engage in the behavior will be low. Moreover, when either reinforcement value or expectancy is zero, the behavior will not be performed because the behavior potential is zero. Thus, the most valued reinforcer will not motivate us to perform a behavior when we believe it is unobtainable. Likewise, an easily obtainable reinforcer will not motivate us when it has no value for us.

The usefulness of Rotter's basic formula can be seen in a hypothetical example. Kathie wants to go to medical school. She must choose between Math 101, a basic course, and Math 199, an advanced course, to fulfill the mathematics requirements for a B.A. The perceived value of an "A" in Math 199 is higher than the value of an "A" in Math 101. So, if reinforcement value were the only relevant factor, Kathie would choose Math 199.

Clearly, reinforcement value is not the only consideration. Kathie's expectancy of getting an "A" would almost certainly be greater for Math 101. Suppose Kathie believes that she has an 80% chance of earning an "A" in Math 101 and only a 20% chance of getting an "A" in Math 199. She might then choose to take the basic course, even though an "A" in the advanced course, if obtained, would be worth considerably more to her.

Kathie's *subjective perceptions*—not objective reality—determine her behavior. If, for instance, Kathie actually had a high math aptitude, she might actually have a 90% chance of getting an "A" in Math 199. Nonetheless, her perceived (subjective) expectancy—20%—and not the "real" (objective) chance—90%—influences her behavior. Similarly, medical schools might consider a "B" in the advanced course to be worth even more than an "A" in the basic course. But if Kathie is unaware of this fact or chooses to ignore it, it will play no part in her choice of courses.

*Rotter's (1954) original formula used "and" instead of the multiplication sign. However, Rotter later concluded that the relationship is most probably multiplicative.

Locus of Control   When you receive an outcome you want, such as a high grade on a test or a bonus at work, to what do you attribute the outcome? When you receive an undesirable outcome, such as a low grade on a test or a layoff notice at work, what do you consider the source of the outcome? One answer to these questions is that the outcome resulted from your own effort, ability, or skill. Another answer is that the outcome was due to external factors beyond your personal control, including chance or fate.

Some outcomes are clearly due to one's own efforts, such as getting straight "A"s three semesters in a row; other outcomes are clearly due to chance, such as holding a royal flush in three consecutive poker hands. However, in many situations, whether an outcome is due to one's abilities or to external sources is ambiguous. The concept of *locus of control* is primarily applicable to ambiguous or novel situations in which the individual has no prior experience on which to base expectations about potential of outcomes (Strickland, 1989).

Locus of control refers to each person's view of the source of his or her outcomes (Rotter, 1966). **Internal locus of control** is the belief that outcomes are the result of our own efforts and resources. **External locus of control** is the belief that outcomes are the due to outside forces over which we have no control. **Powerful others control** and **chance control** are two components of external locus of control (e.g., Rosolack & Hampson, 1991).

Locus of control is always from the individual's perspective. Even when the source of an outcome may be "objectively" internal or external, the way the person perceives the source is what determines the individual's locus of control.

Locus of control is both *general* and *specific*. *General locus of control* is a person's average perception, in many different situations, of the degree to which he or she believes outcomes are a consequence of internal versus external factors. *Specific locus of control* is an individual's expectation about the locus of control in particular situations. For example, Anita's general locus of control and her specific locus of control related to work are both internal; but her specific locus of control in social situations is external.

Our perceptions of locus of control develop as a result of life experiences, such as the childrearing practices to which we have been exposed. For example, parental approval and attention to positive behaviors is associated with a child's developing *internal control;* parental reinforcement based on social comparisons of the child's behaviors is associated with *powerful others control;* and devaluing the child, without attention to the child's specific behaviors, is associated with *chance control* (Krampen, 1989).

On a broader scale, demographic variables such as social class and the society we live in are likely to influence our locus of control (e.g., Tyler, Dhawan, & Sinha, 1989). For instance, a comparison of large samples of residents of nine European countries found that degree of internal control was positively correlated with social class (see Figure 20-1). Further, as Figure 20-2 shows, there were wide differences in locus of control according to country of residence (Jensen, Olsen, & Hughes, 1990).

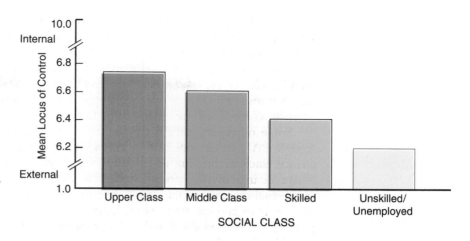

Figure 20-1
Mean differences in locus of control (higher score is more internal) by social class among residents of nine European countries.
Source: Adapted from Jensen, Olsen, and Hughes, 1990.

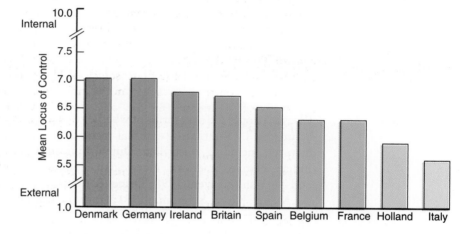

Figure 20-2
Mean differences in locus of control (higher score is more internal) of residents in nine European countries.
Source: Adapted from Jensen, Olsen, and Hughes, 1990.

Assessing Locus of Control

Locus of control typically is assessed by brief self-report inventories. For example, Rotter's (1966) **I-E Scale** consists of 29 forced-choice items: 23 items that tap locus of control and 6 filler items that partially disguise the purpose of the test. Respondents are asked to choose the alternative that better describes them in each case. See if you can identify the alternative in the following two items that suggests an *internal* locus of control.

> a. In the long run people get the respect they deserve in this world.
> b. Unfortunately, an individual's worth often passes unrecognized no matter how hard one tries.

> a. Many times I feel that I have little influence over the things that happen to me.
> b. It is impossible for me to believe that chance or luck plays an important role in my life.*

*The internal response was *a* in the first item and *b* in the second item.

Individuals who choose a majority of internal alternatives are called *internals,* and those who choose a majority of external alternatives are called *externals*.

Rotter's I-E Scale is the most widely used measure of *general* locus of control in adults. Other scales have been developed for children (e.g., Nowicki & Strickland, 1973; Richaud de Minzi, 1991), including a cartoon version for preschool children (Nowicki & Duke, 1974). A series of life-span I-E scales that allow comparison of locus of control from preschool through elderly populations also exists (Nowicki & Duke, 1983).

Many scales for tapping situation-specific locus of control also have been developed. Examples include assessing locus of control related to work (Orpen, 1991; Spector, 1988), academics (Mooney, Sherman, & lo Presto, 1991; Trice & Hackburt, 1989), economics (Heaven, 1989), health in general (e.g., Lefcourt, 1981, 1982; Strickland, 1977), smoking (Bunch & Schneider, 1991; Georgiou & Bradley, 1992), drinking (Johnson, Nora, Tan, & Bustos, 1991), conflict (Canary, Cunningham, & Cody, 1988), and affiliation (Lefcourt, Martin, Fick, & Saleh, 1985).

Sometimes locus of control is measured by a single question about the source of one's outcomes (e.g., Jensen et al., 1990). Locus of control can also be assessed by a structured interview (Boone, De Brabander, Gerits, & Willeme, 1990).

Correlates of Locus of Control

Clearly, people differ in terms of whether they generally believe outcomes are controlled by internal or external factors. This has been shown in diverse cultures, including Australian, Dutch, Finnish, Greek, Hispanic American, Indian, Native American, Norwegian, Philippino, South African, Swedish, and Turkish (Heaven, 1990; Ormel & Schaufeli, 1991; Härkäpää, Järviko-ski, Mellin, Hurri, & Luoma, 1991; Doganis, Theodorakis, & Bagiatis, 1991; Strassburger, Rosen, Miller, & Chavez, 1990; Singh & Verma, 1990; Thurman, Jones-Saumty, & Parsons, 1990; Hoffart & Martinsen, 1991; Lester, Castromayor, & Icli, 1991; Maqsud & Rouhani, 1991; Engstrom, 1991; and Lester et al., 1991, respectively).

Individual differences in locus of control appear to be related to a variety of behaviors including information seeking, achievement, and dealing with others. Differences are also found in physical health and psychological adjustment.

Information seeking Internals are more likely to seek information than externals (e.g., Ingold, 1989; Phares, 1984). Because internals consider themselves responsible for their outcomes, they want information that improves their chances of obtaining desirable outcomes and helps them avoid undesirable ones. In one study, internal students consulted with their instructor before a classroom examination more than external students (Prociuk & Breen, 1977). Another study showed that internals were more likely to seek information about the negative side of the careers they were considering (Friedrich, 1988).

Achievement   Generally, internals are higher achievers, especially on intellectual and performance tasks (e.g., Ashkanasy & Gallois, 1987; Bigoness, Keef, & Du Bose, 1988; Wildstein & Thompson, 1989). For instance, from elementary school to college, internal students tend to do better academically than their external peers (e.g., Boss & Taylor, 1989; Pani, 1991; cf. Wilhite, 1990). Internal locus of control also is associated with higher achievement motivation (Volkmer & Feather, 1991), as well as more daydreaming about achievement and less daydreaming about fear of failure (Brannigan, Hauk, & Guay, 1991).

Dealings with others   Internals tend to be independent but cooperative in their dealings with others. They resist undue social pressure more than externals (Phares, 1978), but generally they are less hostile and have more favorable attitudes toward authority figures (Heaven, 1988). Internals' coping skills in social situations tend to be highly adaptive (Parkes, 1984). For instance, their methods of achieving marital happiness are direct and active and tend to be successful (Miller, Lefcourt, Holmes, Ware, & Saleh, 1986).

Physical health   Internals also seem to have the advantage over externals when it comes to physical health (e.g., Marshall, 1991; Rosolack & Hampson, 1991). They seek more general information about health maintenance, have more knowledge of healthful behaviors, engage in more precautionary health practices, have more positive attitudes about exercise, and are less likely to have cardiac problems (e.g., Quadrel & Lau, 1989; Strickland, 1978, 1979; Tinsley & Holtgrave, 1989; Waller & Bates, 1992). An internal locus of control is associated with less severe physical illness (e.g., Brandon & Loftin, 1991; Engstrom, 1991). Internals tend to be more responsive to treatment (e.g., Härkäpää et al., 1991; Johnson, Magnani, Chan, & Ferrante, 1989), such as being more successful in quitting smoking (Segall & Wynd, 1990). Internals also are less likely to be substance abusers (Haynes & Ayliffe, 1991).

Psychological adjustment   Internals tend to have better psychological adjustment than externals. Internals have been found to be less anxious and less likely to be diagnosed as having psychiatric illnesses (e.g., Hoffart & Martinsen, 1990, 1991; Katerndahl, 1991; Lester et al., 1991; Ormel & Schaufeli, 1991). Moreover, internals are more likely to benefit from psychotherapy (e.g., Trice, 1990) and less likely to relapse after therapy (e.g., Hoffart & Martinsen, 1991).

In general, internals cope with stress better than externals (e.g., Cummins, 1988; Jennings, 1990; Lefcourt, Martin, & Saleh, 1984; Lunenburg & Cadavid, 1992). For example, internals in the process of divorce experience less stress after the divorce than externals (Brown, Perry, & Harburg, 1977; Pais, 1979). However, internals experience more stress before the divorce; the reason may be that internals, consistent with their accepting control of their lives, try to solve problems sooner than externals (Barnet, 1990). Finally, in an investigation of seventh-grade children who were faced with frustration, internals were more likely to react with positive assertive responses and externals with negative aggressive responses (Romi & Itskowitz, 1990).

Internal locus of control is positively correlated with such healthy characteristics as self-esteem and self-efficacy (e.g., Doganis et al., 1991; Ormel & Schaufeli, 1991; Rokke, al-Absi, Lall, & Oswald, 1991). Internals also report more job satisfaction than externals (e.g., Achamamba & Kumar, 1989; Bein, Anderson, & Maes, 1990).

Internal or External Locus of Control: Which Is Better?

From our discussion so far, it would seem that it is better to have an internal locus of control. Generally, this is true. But there is one major exception. When little opportunity to exercise personal control exists, external locus of control can be more adaptive. One study dealt with elderly people who were institutionalized and therefore had little control over their circumstances. External locus of control was associated with better adjustment and feelings of satisfaction in the institutional setting (Felton & Kahana, 1974). The reverse was found in a group of noninstitutionalized elderly individuals (Wolk & Kurtz, 1975).

When other people are necessary for meeting goals, an external orientation may be more adaptive. One study looked at the effects of health locus of control on factors that influence treatment of alcohol abuse (Dean & Edwards, 1990). Clients who had a *powerful other* locus of control behaved very differently than clients who had either an internal orientation or a chance orientation. Those with a powerful other orientation sought help earlier, attempted treatment more often, and stayed in Alcoholics Anonymous longer.

Congruent versus Defensive Externals

Externals are by no means a uniform group, despite their striking contrast with internals. There seem to be two different subtypes (Evans, 1982; Phares, 1979). **Congruent externals** are individuals whose beliefs that most outcomes are simply out of their control are consistent with their own life and experiences. Often, congruent externals have grown up in deprived socioeconomic conditions, or their childhoods have been chaotic and unpredictable.

Defensive externals, in contrast, are individuals whose reported beliefs sometimes contradict their experiences and behaviors. Defensive externals claim that the world is beyond their control *only when it is to their advantage*. They take credit for their successes without accepting responsibility for their failures (Lloyd & Chang, 1979).

Changes in Locus of Control

An individual's locus of control is relatively stable. However, locus of control (as well as other generalized expectancies) may change as life circumstances change. For example, one study found that shortly after divorce many women became less internal; they tended to return to predivorce levels of internal locus of control as they learned to deal with their new circumstances (Doherty, 1983). Similarly, beginning college students who were externals became more internal at the end of a semester-long course that emphasized taking personal responsibility for success in college (Cone & Owens, 1991).

BANDURA'S SOCIAL COGNITIVE THEORY

About a decade after Rotter first outlined his theory, Albert Bandura introduced another social learning theory (Bandura & Walters, 1963). Like Rotter's theory, Bandura's *social cognitive theory* expanded the radical-behavioral view that explained human behavior exclusively in terms of situational factors.

Triadic Reciprocal Determinism

According to Bandura's (1986a, 1986b) social cognitive theory, our *behavior* is influenced by both *environmental factors* and *personal variables*, including our thoughts and feelings. Moreover, each of the three factors—behavior, environment, and personal variables—can influence and be influenced by the other two factors (see Figure 20-3). Bandura calls the process **triadic reciprocal determinism**.

The potential of three-way bidirectional influences of behavior (*B*), environment (*E*), and personal variables (*P*) can be seen in a simple example. Heather is learning to ski (*B*) because her school offers weekly skiing lessons at a nominal cost (*E*) and she believes that she can become a decent skier (*P*). The reinforcement Heather gets from her ski instructor (*E*) and the better she skis (*B*), the more confidence she has in her skiing ability (*P*). When Heather is skiing poorly on a particular day (*B*) and her confidence begins to wane (*P*), she finds easier ski trails (*E*) so that she can practice her basic skills and restore her confidence (*P*).

Observational Learning

Bandura believed that a comprehensive account of personality required more than classical and operant conditioning as explanations of how human behavior develops and is maintained. Like Miller and Dollard, Bandura noted that we often learn merely by observing what others do and what happens to them.

Observational learning is the process through which the behavior of one person, an *observer*, changes as a result of being exposed to the behavior of another, a *model*. Specific components of a model's behavior are called **modeling cues**, which can be live or symbolic. **Live modeling** refers to observing models "in the flesh"—that is, models who are physically present.

Figure 20-3
Schematic diagram of Bandura's principle of triadic reciprocal determinism. Each of the three factors influences and is influenced by the other two factors.

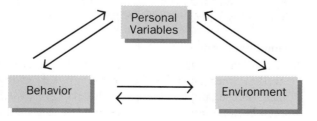

Albert Bandura
(1925-)
developed a social
cognitive theory that
views personality as an
interaction of behavior,
environment, and
personal variables and
stresses the role of
observational learning
and self-efficacy.
Photo by Chuck Painter,
News and Publications
Service, Sanford University

Symbolic modeling involves being exposed to models indirectly, such as in movies, by reading, and through oral descriptions of a person's behavior.

Three Stages of Observational Learning

Observational learning can be viewed as a three-stage process: (1) being exposed to modeling cues, (2) acquiring the information contained in the cues, and (3) subsequently accepting the cues as a guide for behavior (Liebert, 1973). This process is depicted schematically in Figure 20-4.

Exposure to (observation of) modeling cues is the obvious first stage. **Acquisition** (learning and remembering) of modeling cues is the second stage. Acquisition does not follow automatically from adequate exposure; it requires that a person pay attention to the modeling cues and store them in memory. Acquisition is a cognitive process, a covert behavior. However, it is defined operationally as an overt behavior: the observer's *recall* of the model's behavior. Such a definition makes acquisition publicly verifiable.

When both exposure and acquisition have occurred, the third and final stage in observational learning becomes relevant. **Acceptance** refers to whether the observer uses (accepts) the modeling cues as a *guide* for her or his own actions. To measure acceptance, the person is observed in a situation in which he or she is free to use the model's behavior as a guide.

Acceptance can take one of four forms: imitation or counterimitation, either of which can be direct or indirect. **Imitation** is acting as the model did. **Counterimitation** is acting in the opposite way. When modeling has a direct influence and the observer engages in the same behavior as the model, this is *direct imitation*. When the observer does exactly the opposite of what the model did, this is *direct counterimitation*. Modeling cues also may indirectly influence observers by suggesting acceptance of a *general class* of behaviors. *Indirect imitation* involves behaving similarly to the model. *Indirect counterimitation* involves behaving differently than the model. Table 20-1 provides examples of each of the four possible types of acceptance of modeling cues.

The three-stage process of observational learning makes it clear that exposure and acquisition are necessary but not sufficient conditions for acceptance (imitation or counterimitation). Simply stated, there is a distinction between (1) what a person "sees" and remembers and (2) what the person eventually does. The importance of this distinction was first demonstrated in Bandura's (1965) classic "Bobo doll study."

Bandura's "Bobo Doll Study"

In this experiment, nursery school children were the observers. The modeling cues were provided symbolically in a 5-minute film. In the film, an adult female model walked up to an adult-size plastic Bobo doll that looked like a clown and ordered it out of the way. When the doll did not comply, the model performed a series of four aggressive responses (Bandura, 1965, pp. 590–591).

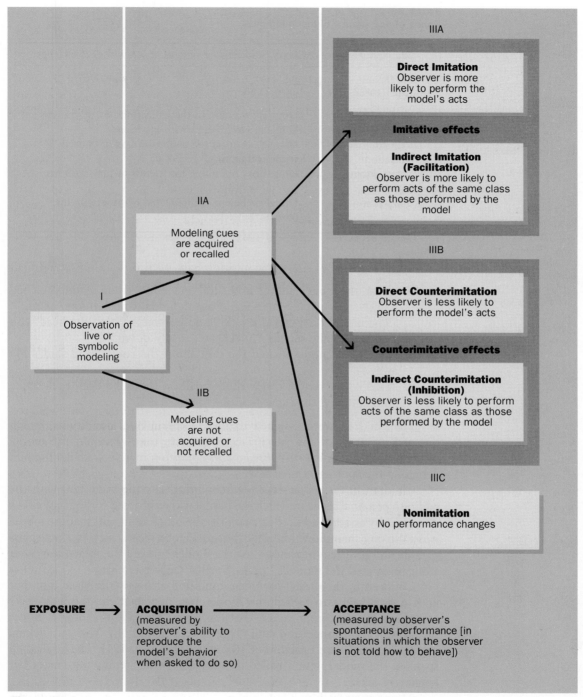

Figure 20-4
The three stages of
observational learning.

Table 20-1
Forms of acceptance of modeling cues

Situation: *Five-year-old Doug often sees his parents donate money to charities*	
TYPE OF ACCEPTANCE	EXAMPLES
Direct imitation	Doug puts a coin in the collection box at church
Indirect imitation	Doug shares his toys with his friends
Direct counter-imitation	Doug walks past the collection box at church without donating
Indirect counter-imitation	Doug does not allow his friends to play with his toys
Nonimitation	Doug's behavior is unaffected by observing his parents' behavior

1. "First, the model laid the Bobo doll on its side, sat on it, and punched it in the nose while remarking, 'Pow, right in the nose, boom, boom.'"
2. "The model then raised the doll and pommeled it on the head with a mallet" while saying, "Sockeroo . . . stay down."
3. Next, "the model kicked the doll about the room" and said, "Fly away."
4. "Finally, the model threw rubber balls at the Bobo doll, each strike punctuated with 'Bang.'"

The children were assigned to three experimental conditions, which differed in terms of the specific consequences they observed the model receive. Children in the *no consequences* condition merely watched the film depicting the four aggressive acts.

Children in the *model-rewarded* condition saw the same film with the addition of a final scene in which the model was reinforced for the aggressive responses by another adult. For example, the other adult said that the model was a "strong champion" and gave the model food treats, such as a large glass of soda and a variety of candies. As the model enjoyed the treats, the other adult recounted the model's "praiseworthy" aggressive acts.

Children in the *model-punished* condition also saw the basic film, but with a final scene in which the model was punished for the aggressive responses by the other adult. For example, the adult shook a finger menacingly at the model and said, "Hey there, you big bully. You quit picking on that clown. I won't tolerate it" (Bandura, 1965, p. 591). The adult then spanked the model with a rolled-up magazine while reminding her of her aggressive acts.

After seeing the film, each child was taken to a room containing a plastic Bobo doll, balls, a mallet, a pegboard, plastic farm animals, and other toys. Each child was left alone with the toys for 10 minutes. From behind a

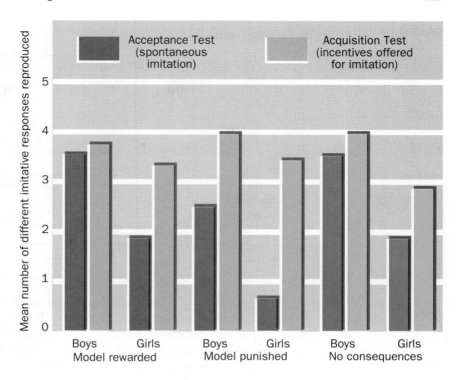

Figure 20-5

Results of Bandura's Bobo doll study demonstrating the importance of the acquisition-acceptance distinction in observational learning. Children acquired more of the model's responses than they accepted (spontaneously performed).

Source: Adapted from *Social Learning* and *Personality Development* by A. Bandura and R.H. Walters, 1963, New York: Holt, Rinehart & Winston.

one-way mirror, judges observed the children to assess their *acceptance* of the model's behaviors.

Then, the children's *acquisition* was assessed by determining the degree to which they could reproduce the modeled behaviors. The experimenter gave the child a small treat of fruit juice and then told the child that he or she would get more juice and a sticker for each of the model's behaviors that he or she could reproduce. Incentives for reproducing the model's behavior were provided to minimize possible reluctance to demonstrate the model's aggressive acts. Such reluctance was especially expected among children in the model-punished condition.

The results clearly support the view that acquisition and acceptance must be distinguished. As you can see in Figure 20-5, the children acquired more aggressive behaviors through observational learning than they accepted (spontaneously performed); this was especially true of children in the model-punished condition.

One of the most remarkable findings of this study was how precisely children imitated the model's aggressive acts when they were given incentives for reproducing them in the acquisition test. This can be seen in the comparison of the model's acts and the children's acts in Figure 20-6. This finding demonstrates the power of modeling in teaching behaviors.

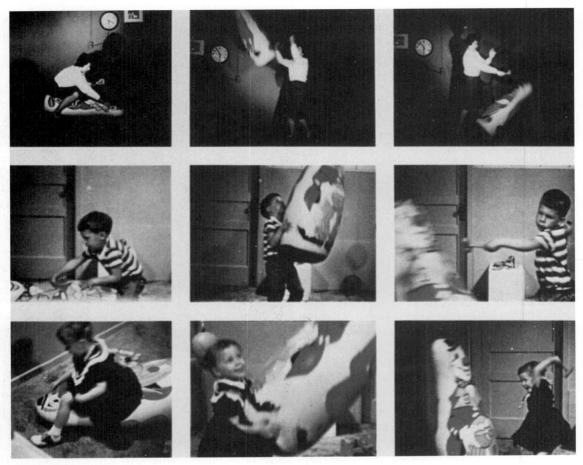

Figure 20-6

Examples of the model's aggressive acts (top row) and children's imitation of the model's acts (middle and bottom rows) in Bandura's Bobo doll study.

Source: From "Imitation of Film-Mediated Aggressive Models" by A. Bandura, D. Ross, and S. A. Ross, 1963. *Journal of Abnormal and Social Psychology,* pp. 3–11. Copyright 1963 by the American Psychological Association. Reprinted by permission.

Vicarious Consequences

Observing a model usually provides information about (1) what the model did and (2) what the effects of the model's action were. **Vicarious consequences** are the outcomes of a model's behavior. From vicarious consequences, observers infer the outcomes they will likely receive for similar actions. Thus, vicarious consequences are indirect (vicarious) consequences for the observer.

Vicarious reward refers to a consequence for the model that an observer views as desirable; vicarious reward increases the chances that the observer will imitate the model. **Vicarious punishment** is a consequence that the observer considers undesirable; vicarious punishment decreases the chances that the observer will imitate the model (e.g., Schnake & Dumler, 1990).

Vicarious consequences influence an observer's *acceptance* of a model's behavior. This occurred in Bandura's Bobo doll study: children in the model-punished condition imitated fewer of the model's actions than children in the model-rewarded or no-consequences conditions (see Figure 20-5, page 425).

(No consequences for socially prohibited behaviors, such as aggression, are likely to indicate that the modeled behavior is acceptable.)

In everyday life, we benefit from vicarious consequences. We frequently "check out" what happens to other people when they engage in a behavior we might engage in ourselves. For example, students learn how a professor will respond to questions in class by observing the professor's reaction to other students' questions.

Vicarious consequences serve another function besides telling the observer the *type* of reaction a particular behavior will probably elicit. They also indicate that the model's behavior is important enough to warrant a reaction, either positive or negative. This *attention-focusing* function of vicarious consequences increases the likelihood that the observer will attend to and remember what the model did. Thus, children who see a model *either* rewarded *or* punished for some behavior show better acquisition of the behavior than those who see the same behavior performed without consequences (e.g., Cheyne, 1971; Liebert & Fernandez, 1969; Spiegler & Weiland, 1976).

Modeling Therapies

Modeling therapies capitalize on the efficiency by which people learn from the experiences of others. Modeling usually is combined with other behavior therapy procedures, including prompting, shaping, reinforcement, in vivo exposure, and behavior rehearsal. In **behavior rehearsal,** the client practices adaptive behaviors learned in therapy. Modeling therapies have been used to treat two broad classes of psychological problems: skills deficits and fear.

Skills Deficits Treated by Modeling

Clients' problems are often maintained by *skills deficits* — in other words, the clients do not know how to perform certain appropriate or adaptive behaviors. Modeling is an important component in skills training; direct instruction may not convey adequately the subtleties involved in performing complex skills, and prompting and shaping alone may not be sufficient (e.g., Charlop & Milstein, 1989). Live modeling typically is used with severe skills deficits, such as in teaching language to clients suffering from autism (e.g., Celiberti, Alessandri, Fong, & Weiss, 1993; Lovaas, 1977, 1987), mental retardation (e.g., Goldstein & Mousetis, 1989), learning disabilities (e.g., Rivera & Smith, 1988), and head injuries (e.g., Foxx, Martella, & Marchand-Martella, 1989). The therapist models the response, then prompts the client to imitate, and finally reinforces imitation. An example would be:

> Therapist: This is a table.
> Therapist: What is this?
>   Client: Table.
> Therapist: That's right! Table.

Symbolic modeling is more efficient than live modeling and can be used to treat less severe social skills deficits. For instance, modeling films have been effective in increasing social interaction among children who are socially withdrawn (e.g., O'Connor, 1969; Rao, Moely, & Lockman, 1987). These films portray children interacting with other children and receiving reinforcing consequences for their actions (an example of vicarious reward).

Self-modeling is another form of symbolic modeling in which clients serve as their own models (e.g., Dowrick, 1991; Kahn, Kehle, Jenson, & Clark, 1990; Kehle, Owen, & Cressy, 1990; Pigott & Gonzales, 1987). A videotape is made of the client performing the target behavior, and the client watches the self-modeling tape. Various cinematic techniques are employed so that in the final self-modeling tape the client appears to be performing the target behavior competently (Dowrick, 1991). For example, Jamal was an 8-year-old who was unable to focus his attention on school work for more than 30 seconds. Jamal was videotaped doing math problems for a number of 20-second segments. The segments were edited so that the final self-modeling videotape that Jamal watched showed him working on the math problems for 5 minutes straight.

Fear Treated by Modeling

Clients who experience fear or anxiety usually do not have a skills deficit. Rather, they are afraid of performing the target behavior, such as speaking in public or being in crowded places. Vicarious consequences are essential components of modeling therapies that deal with fear or anxiety. Clients are exposed to live or symbolic models who deal with fear-evoking situations without experiencing negative consequences. Thus, clients *vicariously* learn that it is "safe" to perform the dreaded behavior. This process is known as **vicarious extinction**.

Participant modeling is an especially potent treatment for fear (e.g., Downs, Rosenthal, & Lichstein, 1988; Ritter, 1969; Williams & Zane, 1989). It combines the therapist's live modeling of the feared behavior with closely supervised practice of the behavior by the client. (Live modeling generally is more effective, although less efficient, than symbolic modeling in treating fears.) Participant modeling involves three basic steps.

1. The therapist models the fear-evoking behavior.
2. The client performs the same behavior with the therapist's verbal and, if necessary, physical prompts. For example, the therapist holds the client's arm and accompanies the client up an escalator (the feared behavior).
3. Gradually, the therapist fades the prompts, so that eventually the client is performing the feared behavior alone.

The behaviors that are modeled and practiced are arranged in an anxiety hierarchy. Therapy proceeds from the least to the most fear-evoking behavior, as in systematic desensitization (see Chapter 19).

Reducing fear of medical procedures is important for two reasons. First, it lessens patients' emotional upset both before and after the procedures (e.g., Peterson, Schultheis, Ridley-Johnson, Miller, & Tracy, 1984; Pinto & Hollandsworth, 1989). Second, it increases the chances that people will seek regular checkups and obtain necessary treatment. Many pediatric hospitals

Participant modeling is a potent behavior therapy for fears. A model demonstrates the feared behavior and then physically prompts the fearful person to imitate the nonfearful behavior.
Photo Source Inc./St. Louis

now use filmed modeling to prepare children for hospitalization and surgery on a regular basis (Peterson & Ridley-Johnson, 1980).

The first and most widely used of these films is *Ethan Has an Operation* (Melamed & Siegel, 1975; Peterson et al., 1984). The 16-minute modeling film shows the experiences of a 7-year-old boy who has been hospitalized for a hernia operation. The scenes depict various events that most children encounter when they are hospitalized for elective surgery, such as meeting hospital staff, having blood tests, separating from mother, and being in the recovery room. In the film, Ethan describes his feelings and concerns about the events.

Ethan is a **coping model** in that he initially is somewhat anxious and gradually overcomes his fears. Coping models, who enhance client-model similarity, usually are more effective for treating fears. In contrast, a **mastery model** is an exemplar who is fearless and competent from the beginning. Mastery models are more effective for teaching skills (e.g., Ozer & Bandura, 1990).

Modeling films similar to *Ethan* have been made to reduce fear of receiving injections (Vernon, 1974), having painful cancer treatments (Jay,

INSTRUCTIONS: For each question, please use the following scale to indicate your level of certainty.

10	20	30	40	50	60	70	80	90	100
very uncertain				moderately uncertain					very certain

Figure 20-7
Examples of the type of questions asked on self-efficacy scales. This particular scale would be used to assess self-efficacy for school achievement.

1. How certain are you that you can learn new material?

2. How certain are you that you can do well on tests?

3. How certain are you that you can write good papers?

4. How certain are you that you can get good grades?

Elliot, Ozolins, Olson, & Pruitt, 1985), and dental work (e.g., Kleinknecht & Bernstein, 1979; Melamed, 1979).

Perceived Self-Efficacy

In the children's book *The Little Engine That Could,* the Little Engine successfully pulls the stranded train over the mountain while chanting, "I think I can." The Little Engine succeeds, the story tell us, because she believes that she can. Like the Little Engine, our daily functioning is enhanced by beliefs in our ability to solve problems and overcome difficulties.

An individual's estimate of his or her ability to perform a specific behavior is called **self-efficacy.** Self-efficacy is more than telling ourselves that we can succeed. Self-efficacy involves a strong conviction of competence that is based on our evaluation of various sources of information about our efficacy (Bandura, 1989a, 1989b).

Assessing Self-Efficacy

Perceived self-efficacy is measured in terms of **efficacy expectations** — one's personal prediction of the odds of being able to perform a particular behavior. Efficacy expectations typically are assessed by self-report scales. Figure 20-7 shows examples of the type of questions asked on self-efficacy scales. A majority of self-efficacy scales are for adults, but a number of scales also have been developed for children and adolescents (e.g., Cowen et al., 1991; Holden, Moncher, Schinke, & Barker, 1990; St. Mary & Russo, 1991).

Efficacy expectations are good predictors of one's actual behaviors. For example, one study examined factors that predicted the performance of people with agoraphobia (fear of leaving home and being in public) in actual feared situations, such as being in enclosed places and walking on a busy street (Kinney & Williams, 1988). The subjects' self-efficacy ratings were highly predictive of their performance in the feared situations. In contrast, self-report inventories that measured the degree to which subjects said they would avoid the situations were poor predictors of their actual avoidance behavior.

Self-Efficacy Theory

According to Bandura's (1992a) *theory of perceived self-efficacy,* whether a person undertakes a task depends, in part, on his or her *perceived* level of efficacy regarding that task. Perceived self-efficacy is independent of one's actual abilities. People who are highly competent at a particular task but have little faith in their ability are unlikely to attempt the task. Research supports the independence of actual ability and self-efficacy (e.g., Bouffard-Bouchard, Parent, & Larivée, 1991).

Efficacy expectations can be distinguished from *outcome* expectations (e.g., Bandura, 1986a; Shell, Murphy, & Bruning, 1989; Skinner, 1992). **Outcome expectations** refer to one's estimate that a given action will result in a particular outcome; they are beliefs about the responsiveness of one's environment (Gecas, 1989). In contrast, efficacy expectations are beliefs about one's own competence. Optimal performance usually requires both efficacy and outcome expectations to be high (e.g., Lent, Lopez, & Bieschke, 1991).

Bandura's (1986a) theory also predicts that once a task is undertaken, the amount of energy we expend and how long we persist in the face of difficulties are influenced by our perceived self-efficacy. The stronger our self-efficacy, the more vigorous and persistent are our efforts in the face of obstacles and setbacks (e.g., Cervone, 1989; Schwarzer, 1992b).

Although high self-efficacy is desirable in most circumstances, there may be times when self-efficacy is too high and results in unrealistic complacency about one's abilities. For example, the chances of ex-smokers who have smoked again resuming abstinence may be higher when self-efficacy for *recovery* of abstinence is *moderate,* rather than high or low (Haaga & Stewart, 1992, 1993). The explanation is simple (Bandura, 1986a). Recovery of abstinence requires high enough self-efficacy so that ex-smokers do not feel hopeless. But the ex-smokers' self-efficacy should not be so high that they are tempted to experiment with smoking.

The Reciprocal Determinism of Self-Efficacy

Our self-efficacy influences how we think and feel as well as how we act. Cognitive processes, such as analytic thinking and academic performance, are enhanced by a strong sense of competence (e.g., Bandura, 1992a, 1992b; Bandura & Wood, 1989; Bouffard-Bouchard et al., 1991; Multon, Brown, & Lent, 1991; Wood & Bandura, 1989). Low self-efficacy is associated with anxiety, depression, helplessness, and feeling shy (e.g., Brandstädter, 1992; G.J. Hill, 1989; Jerusalem & Schwarzer, 1992; Kavanagh, 1992; Williams, 1992).

Consistent with Bandura's principle of reciprocal determinism, there is an interaction between self-efficacy and actions, emotions, and cognitive processes. This interaction is bidirectional and multiply determined (Bandura, 1992a), as Figure 20-8 depicts. Consider just two of many possible paths of influence. A happy mood can heighten self-efficacy, which, in turn, may lead people to accept more challenges and perform more competently (e.g., McAuley & Courneya, 1992). Thinking about factors that would enhance

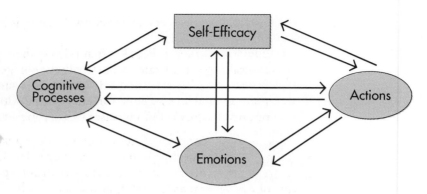

Figure 20-8
The relationship between self-efficacy and actions, cognitive processes, and emotions is reciprocal and multiply determined, involving two or more of the components.

one's performance may increase self-efficacy, which, in turn, may result in greater persistence at a task (e.g., Cervone, 1989).

Self-Efficacy as a Mediating Variable

The preceding two examples illustrate how self-efficacy serves as a *mediator* (an intermediary) between two variables. In those examples, emotion and thinking did not directly influence behavior. Their effects on behavior were mediated by their influence on self-efficacy, which, in turn, affected behavior.

For instance, numerous studies have found a positive relationship between perceived social support (the degree to which people believe they can count on the support of others) and psychological adjustment to stressful life events (e.g., Cohen & Syme, 1985; Cohen & Willis, 1985). However, the factors that account for the beneficial effects of social support are unclear. A recent study of women who underwent abortions sheds some light on this issue (Major et al., 1990). Social support from the women's partners, friends, and family was not directly related to psychological adjustment to the stress of the abortion. However, each form of social support was related to self-efficacy for coping with the stressful event. In turn, the coping self-efficacy was related to psychological adjustment.

Sources of Efficacy Expectations

Our efficacy expectations stem from four major sources of information.

1. *Performance accomplishments.* When we perform competently at a task, our efficacy expectations are strengthened. Also, the threat of occasional failure is likely to be reduced, which may increase our persistence. Performance accomplishments are a powerful source of efficacy information because they provide direct experiences of personal mastery.
2. *Vicarious experience.* By observing others succeed at a task, we develop expectations we can "do it" as well.
3. *Verbal persuasion.* Being told by others that we can succeed increases our efficacy expectations. Verbal persuasion is the most common

source of self-efficacy expectations because it is easy to provide and generally available.

4. *Emotional arousal.* People often rely on their state of physiological arousal (e.g., heart rate and breathing) to judge their level of fear or anxiety. Feeling calm and relaxed (or even moderately aroused, if some arousal is necessary for effective performance) may serve as positive feedback that increases efficacy expectations.

Information from each of these sources will increase self-efficacy only if we interpret it as indicative of one's own efforts. For instance, when people attribute their successes to external factors, such as help from others, then the effects of the performance accomplishments on self-efficacy are likely to be reduced (Toshima, Kaplan, & Ries, 1992).

The Situational Specificity of Self-Efficacy

No one feels equally competent to succeed at all tasks. For instance, one study of high school students found that males had higher self-efficacy in athletics and females had higher self-efficacy in leadership (Peters & Brown, 1991). Thus, perceived self-efficacy usually is considered to be *situation specific* — rather than a global personality trait that influences diverse behaviors. To appreciate just how situation specific the measurement of self-efficacy can be, consider a sample of the behaviors for which self-efficacy has been assessed: maternal behavior (Teti & Gelfand, 1991), infant care (Froman & Owen, 1989), sexual behavior (Rosenthal, Moore, & Flynn, 1991), condom use (Brafford & Beck, 1991), diabetes (Padgett, 1991), breast self-examination (Gonzalez & Gonzalez, 1990), dieting (Stotland, Zuroff, & Roy, 1991), and resistance to drug use (Hays & Ellickson, 1990).

A few researchers have examined self-efficacy as a global concept, the composite of importance successes and failures that people attribute to themselves (e.g., Eden & Kinnar, 1991; Jerusalem & Schwarzer, 1992; Shelton, 1990; Waller & Bates, 1992). However, task-specific self-efficacy scales are better predictors of actual behavior (e.g., Wang & Richarde, 1988). For example, efficacy expectations are related to specific health-relevant behaviors, such as stopping smoking and tolerating pain. A person's efficacy expectations concerning the ability to quit smoking would not predict that individual's ability to tolerate pain.

The Generality of Self-Efficacy Theory

The generality of self-efficacy theory has been demonstrated across many domains. Consider just two: career development and health-related behavior. Occupational preferences and success are related to an individual's perceived self-efficacy (e.g., Landino & Owen, 1988; Lent & Hackett, 1987; Lent et al., 1991; Poidevant, Loesch, & Wittmer, 1991; Post, Stewart, & Smith, 1991). Specifically,

> the stronger people's belief in their efficacy, the more career options they consider possible, the greater the interest they show in them, the better they prepare

themselves educationally for different occupations and the greater their staying power and success in different occupational pursuits. (Bandura, 1992b, p. 11)

Self-efficacy influences a variety of health-related behaviors (e.g., Ewart, 1991; Holden, 1991; Kok, De Vries, Mudde, & Strecher, 1991). For example, higher self-efficacy is associated with losing weight (e.g., Clark, Abrams, Niaura, Eaton, & Rossi, 1991; Slater, 1989; Stotland & Zuroff, 1991; Stotland et al., 1991); decreasing alcohol abuse (e.g., Sitharthan & Kavanagh, 1991; Solomon & Annis, 1990); stopping smoking (e.g., DiClemente et al., 1991; Garcia, Schmitz, & Doerfler, 1990; Kok et al., 1992; Pederson, Strickland, & DesLauriers, 1991); adaptation to serious and chronic illness (e.g., Cunningham, Lockwood, & Cunningham, 1991; Holman & Lorig, 1992; Schiaffino, Revenson, & Gibofsky, 1991); coping with medical procedures (e.g., Gattuso, Litt, & Fitzgerald, 1992); complying with medical regimens, such as aftercare procedures and rehabilitative exercise (e.g., Heller & Krauss, 1991; Schwarzer, 1992a); and changing risk behaviors, such as the use of condoms and clean needles to prevent AIDS (e.g., Bandura, 1990, 1991; Kok et al., 1991; McKusick, Coates, Morin, Pollack, & Hoff, 1990).

High self-efficacy can promote health in diverse ways (O'Leary, 1992). One primary path of influence is to increase the adoption of healthful behaviors, such as regular exercise and good diet (e.g., Ewart, 1992; Kok et al., 1992; Schwarzer, 1992a). Another path is to affect directly components of the physiological stress response, including the immune system (e.g., Bandura, 1992c; Dienstbier, 1989; Wiedenfeld et al., 1990).

Perceived self-efficacy has become one of the most extensively studied theoretical constructs in personality. To illustrate the nature of the research efforts, we will examine in detail two experimental investigations dealing with the control of pain and personality change.

Self-Efficacy and Pain Tolerance

Pain is the most common complaint that patients report to physicians and the most frequently cited cause of disability. Our beliefs about pain and its treatment can affect how we experience pain. For example, patients who are given a placebo drug, which they believe is an actual painkiller, report less pain than patients who receive nothing. Placebo subjects, in fact, sometimes seem to experience as much pain relief as those who take real painkillers (Evans, 1974).

Self-efficacy regarding the ability to tolerate pain is one type of belief that can influence pain tolerance (e.g., Bandura, 1991, 1992c; Holman & Lorig, 1992; Kores, Murphy, Rosenthal, Elias, & North, 1990; Williams & Kinney, 1991). This was demonstrated in an experiment in which subjects were exposed to intense pain stimulation (holding their hands in ice water) to assess their tolerance for pain (Bandura, O'Leary, Taylor, Gauthier, & Gossard, 1987).

Subjects were assigned to one of three conditions. Those in the *cognitive coping skills* condition received training in such techniques as diverting attention away from pain and imagining pain sensations as if they were other, nonpainful sensations. These cognitive coping skills were chosen to produce changes in subjects' self-efficacy regarding both their ability to withstand pain and their ability to reduce it. A second group of subjects were given a *placebo*. A third group served as *no-treatment controls.*

Overall, self-efficacy for pain tolerance and actual pain tolerance were strongly related (average correlation of +.75). Relative to the no-treatment control group, both the coping skills and placebo groups showed an increase in their self-efficacy for withstanding pain. However, only the coping skills group showed an increase in their self-efficacy for actually reducing pain once it was experienced. Thus, the coping skills had a broader effect on self-efficacy for pain tolerance than did the placebo.

These findings regarding self-efficacy were parallel to those for increasing pain tolerance. The coping skills subjects showed the greatest gains in actual pain tolerance. The placebo group showed a small gain, while the control group showed almost no gain.

To identify the mechanisms that led to increased pain tolerance, the researchers used a clever procedure. Half the subjects in each pain treatment group were given an injection of weak saltwater; the remaining subjects received an injection of *naloxone*. Weak saltwater has virtually no physiological effect. Naloxone blocks the action of *endorphins,* which are naturally occurring opioids that reduce pain. Thus, subjects given naloxone could not benefit from the body's "natural painkillers." By comparing the naloxone and saltwater subjects in each treatment group, the influence of endorphins in reducing pain could be determined.

Subjects in the cognitive coping skills and placebo groups given naloxone showed less improvement in pain tolerance than those who had received saltwater. This finding was expected because the naloxone subjects could not have benefited from endorphins.

However, even with endorphin action blocked, subjects using cognitive coping skills that created high self-efficacy exhibited the most tolerance for pain. In the critical pain tests (20 and 60 minutes after their injections), the coping skills group showed greater improvement in pain tolerance than the placebo group, who, in turn, did better than the no-treatment controls (see Figure 20-9). Thus, procedures that heighten self-efficacy lead to changes in pain tolerance beyond those produced by the action of endorphins.

Self-Efficacy as a Mechanism in Personality Change

Why do people benefit from psychotherapy? Bandura (1984) has hypothesized that *all forms of personality change are effective because they create and strengthen a client's perceived self-efficacy*. Figure 20-10 provides examples of the primary source of efficacy expectations postulated to occur in various therapeutic procedures. Much of the research examining the role of self-efficacy in psychotherapy has examined behavior therapy treatments of anxiety and fear (e.g., Williams, 1992).

If perceived self-efficacy accounts for changes in therapy, then the more effective a treatment is, the more it will enhance clients' efficacy expectations.

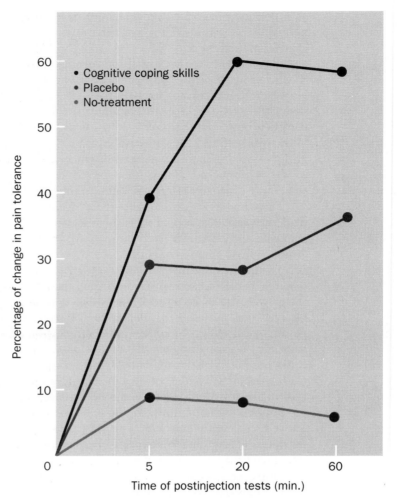

Figure 20-9
Average percentage change in pain tolerance achieved by cognitive coping skills, placebo, and no-treatment control subjects when the opioid action of endorphins was blocked by naloxone. In the critical pain tests (20 and 60 minutes postinjection), the coping skills group showed greater improvement in pain tolerance than the placebo group who, in turn, did better than the no-treatment controls.

To test this hypothesis, Bandura, Adams, and Beyer (1977) recruited adults whose fear of snakes restricted their lives in some significant way. Before and after treatment, these subjects were given a behavioral avoidance test.

In a *behavioral avoidance test,* people are asked to perform a series of tasks requiring increasingly more threatening interactions with a feared object or situation. In this experiment, there were 29 tasks. The first was looking at a boa constrictor in a glass cage; the last was allowing the snake to crawl freely in their laps. To assess changes in self-efficacy, subjects rated their expectations for performing each of the steps in the behavioral avoidance test on a 100-point probability scale.

The subjects were assigned to one of three conditions. Subjects in the *modeling* condition observed a female therapist perform a series of tasks that involved increasingly more threatening interactions with the snake. After observing the model, subjects in the *participant modeling* group practiced the

Self-Efficacy Source	Therapy Procedure
	Fixed-role therapy (16)
	Reinforcement therapy (19)
	In vivo exposure (19)
PERFORMANCE ACCOMPLISHMENTS	Participant modeling (20)
	Problem-solving therapy (21)
	Behavior rehearsal (20)
VICARIOUS EXPERIENCE	Modeling therapies (20)
	Interpretations (6)
VERBAL PERSUASION	Rational-emotive therapy (21)
	Cognitive therapy (21)
	Self-instructional training (21)
	Systematic desensitization (19)
EMOTIONAL AROUSAL	Relaxation training (19)
	Biofeedback

Figure 20-10

Examples of therapy procedures that are postulated to provide clients with each of the four primary sources of self-efficacy (numbers in parentheses refer to chapters in which the therapy procedures are discussed in this text).

same behaviors with the therapist's assistance. A third group of subjects, who served as *untreated controls,* were just given the assessment procedures.

Participant modeling provides two sources of efficacy information—namely, vicarious experience and performance accomplishments. Modeling provides only one source of efficacy information—vicarious experience. Thus, participant modeling should lead to higher efficacy expectations and consequently to more effective treatment than modeling alone.

The results are consistent with these predictions. Subjects' efficacy expectations were markedly enhanced by participant modeling, were moderately increased by modeling, and were unaltered in the control condition. The changes in self-efficacy were paralleled in the subjects' overt behaviors. Participant modeling produced slightly more approach behavior in the behavioral avoidance test than did modeling.

SUMMARY

1. Social learning theories focus on social aspects of the situation, including learning from observing the behaviors of others. They also emphasize the role of cognitions in personality.

2. Miller and Dollard developed the first social learning theory, which emphasized the importance of imitation.

3. Rotter's social learning theory employs four basic constructs. Reinforcement value is a person's subjective preference for various reinforcers. Expectancy is an individual's subjective likelihood that a given behavior will result in reinforcement. The psychological situation is the immediate environmental context, from the person's viewpoint. Behavior potential is the likelihood that a given behavior will occur in a particular situation. Behavior potential is determined by an interaction of expectancy and reinforcement value.

4. Locus of control is a generalized expectancy regarding the degree to which people believe that the outcomes they receive result from their own efforts (internal locus of control) or from outside forces over which they have no influence (external locus of control).

5. Locus of control is measured by self-report inventories, including scales that tap situation-specific locus of control.

6. Individual differences in locus of control are found in information seeking, achievement, dealing with others, physical health, and psychological adjustment. In general, internals are better off; the exception is in situations where there is little opportunity to exercise personal control.

7. Congruent externals' beliefs that outcomes are uncontrollable are consistent with their behavior and experience. Defensive externals' beliefs that outcomes are uncontrollable are contradictory with their behavior and experience; they subscribe to their external beliefs when it is to their advantage.

8. Bandura's social cognitive theory advances the principle of triadic reciprocal determinism: behavior, environment, and personal variables influence one another bidirectionally.

9. Observational learning can be viewed as a three-stage process, involving exposure to modeling cues, acquisition of the information contained in them, and subsequent acceptance of the cues as a guide for action. Acceptance involves either imitation or counterimitation, which can be either direct or indirect.

10. Observational learning is influenced by vicarious consequences, the rewards and punishments that models are observed to receive as a result of their behaviors. Vicarious reward tells us that modeled behaviors are appropriate and increases acceptance; vicarious punishment informs us that modeled behaviors are inappropriate and decreases acceptance. Both vicarious reward and vicarious punishment indicate that modeled behaviors are important, which serves an attention-focusing function that enhances acquisition.

11. Modeling therapies, combined with other behavior therapies, are used to treat two broad classes of problem behaviors: skills deficits and fear.

12. Live modeling with prompting and reinforcement is employed to alleviate severe social skills deficits. Symbolic modeling, such as modeling films and self-modeling videotapes, can be used to alleviate less severe social skills deficits.

13. Modeling is used to treat fear by exposing clients to live or symbolic models who successfully deal with fear-evoking situations without experiencing negative consequences; this process is known as vicarious extinction. Participant modeling combines the therapist's live modeling with prompting

and behavior rehearsal. Modeling films are used to reduce fear of medical procedures.

14. Self-efficacy refers to an individual's estimate of his or her ability to perform a specific task. Bandura's theory of perceived self-efficacy states that a person's decision to undertake a task depends on his or her self-efficacy regarding the task. Self-efficacy also influences energy expenditure and persistence in performing a task. Efficacy expectations — personal estimates of the odds of succeeding at a task — are independent of actual ability and outcome expectations, which are personal predictions of a given behavior resulting in a particular outcome.

15. Self-efficacy, actions, emotions, and cognitive processes influence one another bidirectionally. Self-efficacy serves as a mediator between variables.

16. Self-efficacy expectations stem from performance accomplishments, vicarious experience, verbal persuasion, and emotional arousal.

17. Self-efficacy usually is considered to be situation specific.

18. Bandura suggested that perceived self-efficacy is the cognitive process that underlies all psychotherapeutic change.

Chapter Twenty-One

The Cognitive-Behavioral Approach

he cognitive-behavioral approach is an outgrowth of the social learning theories we discussed in the previous chapter and the cognitive Zeitgeist (spirit of the time) in psychology (Gardner, 1985). In this chapter we will first look at the theory and research of Walter Mischel, the most prominent cognitive-behavioral theorist. Then we will describe the application of the cognitive-behavioral approach to personality change.

MISCHEL'S COGNITIVE-BEHAVIORAL THEORY AND RESEARCH

Mischel's cognitive-behavioral theory owes a debt to several personality psychologists. While earning his Ph.D. at Ohio State University, Mischel studied with both George Kelly and Julian Rotter, whose cognitive emphases clearly influenced him. Later, Henry Murray, one of his colleagues at Harvard, made Mischel aware of the importance of taking both personal and environmental variables into account when predicting behavior. You also will see parallels between Mischel's and Bandura's conceptualizations; they were colleagues at Stanford University for more than 20 years and collaborated on a number of studies.

We will examine four of Mischel's contributions: (1) his critique of traditional dispositional and psychoanalytic personality assessment, (2) the identification and investigation of critical *person variables* that affect personality, (3) an explanation of the *consistency paradox*, and (4) the investigation of the interaction of emotion and cognition.

Critique of Traditional Personality Assessment

In his 1968 book, *Personality and Assessment,* Mischel identified and challenged the assumptions underlying dispositional and psychodynamic personality assessment. Both approaches, according to Mischel, assume that a subject's responses on a personality test are a *sign* of his or her true underlying personality. For example, a person's score on the MMPI Social Introversion scale is assumed to show how introverted or extraverted the person "really is." Someone who scores high on this scale would be expected to be modest, shy, and self-effacing in a wide range of situations. However, the average correlation between Social Introversion scale scores and actual behavior in various situations is quite modest—typically about +.30. Correlations between test scores and actual behavior are no higher for most dispositional dimensions.

Mischel (1968) coined the phrase **personality coefficient** to refer to correlations between +.20 and +.30, the range typically found when a self-report inventory measure of a personality dimension is correlated with another type of measure of the same dimension. The size of personality coefficients does not allow much prediction of one variable from another. This is because two variables whose correlation is between .20 and .30 have between 4% and 9% in common.*

*Technically, squaring the correlation coefficient provides an estimate of the amount of variance that two variables have in common; for example, $.30^2 = .09$ or 9%.

Walter Mischel
(1930-   )
has advanced our
understanding of person
variables, delay of
gratification, the use
of plans, and the
intereaction of emotion
and cognition.
Courtesy of Walter Mischel

Nonetheless, in the 1960s personality test scores were commonly used to make important decisions about a person's life and future. Attacking such practices, Mischel (1968) argued that personality assessment should be based on *samples* of behavior (rather than signs). The samples should be taken in situations as similar as possible to actual performance circumstances. For example, suppose an employer wanted the best candidates to do telephone interviews. Observing the candidates doing mock telephone interviews would be a better assessment procedure than using their MMPI Social Introversion scores.

Mischel believed that situational variables were more important than personality dispositions in determining how one acts. However, he, like a growing number of behavioral psychologists, acknowledged that behavior is not completely situation specific (e.g., Carson, 1989; Haynes & Uchigaki-uchi, 1993; Kendrick & Funder, 1988; Russo, 1990).

> . . . we do not have to relearn everything in every new situation. We have memories, and our past predisposes our present behavior in critically important and complex ways. Obviously people have characteristics, and overall "average" differences in behavior between individuals can be abstracted on many dimensions and used to discriminate among persons for many purposes. Obviously knowing how a person behaved before can help predict how . . . [the person] will behave again in similar contexts. Obviously the impact of any stimulus depends on the organism that experiences it. No one suggests that the organism approaches every new situation with an empty head. (Mischel, 1973, pp. 261–262)

Thus, Mischel acknowledged the importance of **person variables**, the relatively enduring cognitive and behavioral attributes of each individual.

Person Variables   Five broad person variables are central to personality (Mischel, 1973).

1. *Competencies.* Each person has a set of behavioral and cognitive skills—overt and covert behaviors that the person is capable of engaging in when the circumstances call for them.
2. *Encoding strategies and personal constructs.* People have specific ways of sorting and categorizing the interpersonal and physical events they encounter, such as the personal constructs that Kelly considered the basis of personality (Chapter 16).
3. *Expectancies.* Each person makes individual probability estimates about the outcomes of particular courses of action in specific situations. For instance, the amount of studying a student will do for a test partially depends on the student's estimate of the chances that increased studying will result in a higher grade.
4. *Values.* People place a specific value or worth on each possible outcome of various courses of action. Two people with identical expectancies about the outcome of a particular behavior will behave differently if they value the outcome differently. Consider two men

who both expect a hangover the morning after a night of drinking. One man may consider a hangover a "price" worth paying for the "pleasures of the night," whereas the other man may think that the "price" is too high. (Note the parallel between Mischel's expectancies and values and Rotter's behavior potential formula involving expectancies and reinforcement values [Chapter 20].)

5. *Self-regulatory systems and plans.* People are not only influenced by extrinsically imposed conditions. Their behaviors also are influenced by self-imposed goals and self-reward for reaching their goals (e.g., Zimmerman, 1990).

Person Variables versus Dispositions

What is the difference between Mischel's person variables and traditional personality dispositions? Person variables vary with the specific situation. For instance, one's competencies are likely to vary in different circumstances. The professor who is highly articulate when she lectures or talks with students in her office may have difficulty speaking to people over the phone. In contrast, traditional personality dispositions are constant across situations. They are characteristic inclinations to behave in particular ways that are independent of the situation and determine one's actions. Thus, we would expect an "articulate" professor to converse well during her lectures, while talking with students, *and* in telephone conversations.

The Interaction of Person Variables and Situational Variables

According to Mischel's theory, behavior is determined by three factors, which are depicted in Figure 21-1: (1) the demands and restrictions of the situation, (2) the individual's person variables, and (3) the interaction of situational and person variables (e.g., Shoda, Mischel, & Wright, 1989).

The situation provides the cues as to appropriate or adaptive behavior. The cues are mediated by person variables. For example, how you view a situation will influence the course of action you take. Suppose you are walking down a road, and a passing motorist stops to offer you a ride. Whether you perceive the driver's question as a friendly gesture or a threat will influence your response. You also must have the relevant skills to respond—either being able to accept the driver's offer graciously or being able to run fast.

Figure 21-1
Mischel's theory holds that behavior is determined by the demands and restrictions of the situation, which are mediated by person variables.

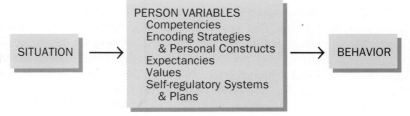

Delay of Gratification as a Basic Competency

Mischel has studied one particular person variable extensively — the ability to postpone gratification. **Delay of gratification** refers to forgoing small immediate rewards for larger rewards that will only become available later. Mischel devised a simple test of delay of gratification for children. Children are asked to choose either a small, immediately available reward or a larger reward for which they would have to wait. Using this test, Mischel (1966) found that the ability to delay gratification increases with age and that it is associated with higher intelligence, greater social responsibility, and higher achievement strivings.

Delay of gratification is influenced by a variety of conditions, including exposure to social models. In a now-classic study, Bandura and Mischel (1965) demonstrated that fourth-grade and fifth-grade children's delay-of-gratification preferences could be changed through modeling. The design of their experiment is shown in Figure 21-2.

To assess their initial preferences, the children made a series of 14 choices between a small, immediate reward and a larger, postponed reward. For example, children could have a small candy bar immediately or a larger one a week later. On the basis of this test, the children were classified as preferring *high delay of reward* or *low delay of reward.*

Next, Bandura and Mischel tried to change the children's delay preferences, from high to low and from low to high. The children observed an adult model make choices between immediate and postponed rewards. The model chose between items that were appropriate rewards for adults (e.g., a chess set or magazine) and that were different from the items offered to the children. Thus, the children could not merely copy the model's choices. They had to imitate the *principle* behind the model's behavior — that is, choosing either immediate or postponed rewards.

Children who preferred high delay of reward saw a model who consistently chose the immediate-reward item; children who preferred low delay of reward saw a model who selected the postponed-reward item. The model also expressed attitudes about delay of reward that were consistent with the modeled preference. For instance, one of the choices was between having a plastic chess set right then and waiting 2 weeks for a more expensive wooden set. The model in the low-delay-of-reward condition commented, "Chess figures are chess figures. I can get as much use out of the plastic ones right away" (Bandura & Mischel, 1965, p. 701).

The children were assigned to one of three conditions. In the *live modeling* condition, the model was actually present. In the *symbolic modeling* condition, the children read about the model's choices. In the *no-model-present* condition, children were shown only the series of paired items. This group served as a control for the possible effects of simple exposure to rewards on subsequent delay of gratification.

Delay preference was assessed immediately after observing the model and 1 month later. As Figure 21-3 shows, modeling produced marked and moderately stable changes in preference.

Stumphauzer (1972) reported similar findings among prison inmates (ages 18 to 20) who had shown low delay of gratification. The prisoners

PROCEDURES	Pretest to Classify Children	Division of Children into Two Groups	Experimental Conditions to Which Children were Assigned	Postexposure to Modeling	. . .	Generalization Test One Month After Modeling
DETAILS	4th & 5th Graders	High-Delay Preference	Live Low-Delay Model Symbolic Low-Delay Model No-model			
		Low-Delay Preference	Live High-Delay Model Symbolic High-Delay Model No-model			

Figure 21-2
Schematic diagram of the experimental design of Bandura and Mischel's study of the influence of modeling on delay-of-gratification preference.

observed two older inmates who modeled high-delay behavior. The prisoners' delay behavior markedly increased, which was still evident 4 weeks later. In addition, the effect generalized to saving money.

Strategies for Delaying Gratification

Theoretically it was important to demonstrate that delay of gratification could be modified in either direction, as Bandura and Mischel (1965) did. In practice, one is generally interested in increasing delay of gratification. In Western cultures, high delay of gratification is considered desirable and a sign of maturity.

Mischel and his colleagues have studied the strategies that children use to postpone gratification. This research reveals the operation of several person variables, including the way children set goals and use plans and strategies to increase the likelihood that their goals will be met (Mischel, Shoda, & Rodriguez, 1989).

Self-Distraction Freud theorized that people could increase delay of gratification by creating mental images of the desired object, which produced temporary substitute gratification. Freud's idea led Mischel and Ebbesen (1970) to predict that looking at the actual reward children are waiting for will increase their delay of gratification.

To test this hypothesis, preschool children were first asked whether they preferred cookies or pretzels. Each youngster was then told to wait alone in a room until the experimenter returned, at which time the child would be given the preferred food. The children were told that they could call the experimenter back at any time. However, if they called the experimenter, they would be given their *non*preferred food. The experimenter then left, returning in 15 minutes or earlier if the child called. Depending on the experimental condition, the child waited in full view of (1) both foods, (2) the preferred food only, (3) the nonpreferred food only, or (4) neither food.

Contrary to Mischel and Ebbesen's expectation, children who waited without either food showed significantly longer delay of gratification than those exposed to both foods or either food alone (see Figure 21-4).

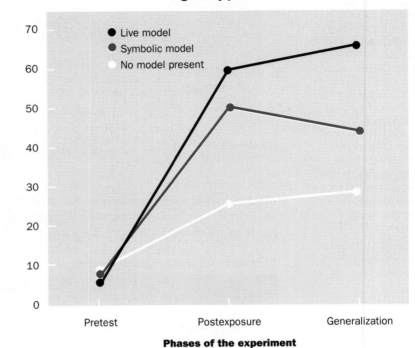

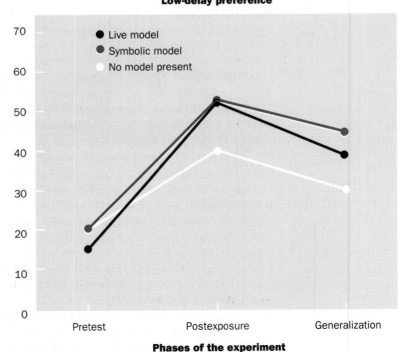

Figure 21-3
Mean percentage of
immediate-reward
choices by children who
initially preferred high
delay and mean
percentage of delayed-
reward choices by
children who initially preferred low delay in
Bandura and Mischel's
(1965) experiment.
Source: From "Modification
of Self-Imposed Delay of
Reward Through Exposure to
Live and Symbolic Models"
by A. Bandura and W. Mischel,
1965, *Journal of Personality
and Social Psychology,* 2,
pp. 698-705.

Figure 21-4

Average amount of time children were able to wait for the delayed but preferred reward in Mischel and Ebbesen's (1970) study. Children were able to wait longest when no foods were present in the room and were least able to control themselves when both foods were present. Which of the foods (delayed or immediate) was present did not seem to matter.

Source: Adapted from "Attention in Delay of Gratification" by W. Mischel and E. Ebbesen, 1970, *Journal of Personality and Social Psychology, 16,* pp. 329-337.

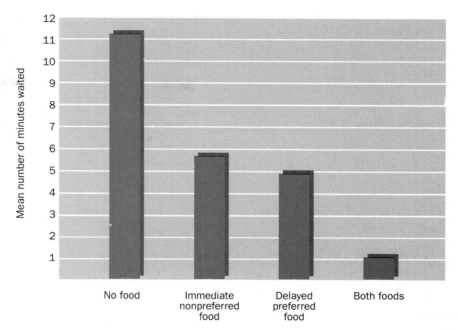

What strategies did the children use to delay gratification? Observations through a one-way mirror provided a clue. A number of children spontaneously used distraction techniques. They sang, talked to themselves, and invented games. Moreover, many of the children who successfully waited when the rewards were present avoided looking at the rewards; they covered their eyes or purposely focused on something else.

These observations suggested that children might be taught to distract themselves to increase their delay of gratification. Thus, in a subsequent experiment, some children were told to think about "fun things" or "sad things" while waiting for the larger reward; other children were given no instructions (Mischel, Ebbesen, & Raskoff, 1971). Children who thought about "fun things" waited the longest; those who thought about "sad things" were least able to wait.

But what happens if children think about the rewards themselves? Do such thoughts increase delay of gratification, as Freud suggested? Or do the thoughts arouse appetites and decrease the ability to wait, as the presence of the "real thing" did in the original study? The answers to these questions suggest that complex and subtle mental processes are involved in delay of gratification.

"Hot" versus "cool" thinking   Mischel and Baker (1975) gave nursery school children brief instructions that induced them to think about the reward they were waiting for in two different ways. One way of thinking focused on the *"hot"* or *consummatory qualities* of the reward, such as how marshmallows are sweet and chewy. The other way focused on *"cool"* or *nonconsummatory qualities*, such as how marshmallows look like white, puffy clouds.

When the children thought about the reward they were waiting for in "hot" ways, delay was very difficult, presumably because consummatory thoughts increase arousal and frustration (Mischel, 1979). Conversely, thinking about the "cool" qualities of the reward made waiting relatively easy. In fact, it made waiting easier than total distraction from the reward by not thinking about it at all.

Although the presence of the real rewards decreases delay time in preschoolers, pictures of the rewards *increase* delay time (Mischel & Moore, 1973). The actual versus symbolic presence seems to lead children to think about the rewards in fundamentally different ways. Specifically, the actual rewards may be arousing enough to trigger the motivation to have a reward; this is frustrating and makes delay more difficult. Symbolic presentations are not nearly as arousing simply because "one cannot consume a picture" (Mischel & Moore, 1980, p. 212). Nonetheless, symbolic presentations can be arousing if they are thought about in a "hot" way. Symbolic representation helps children delay gratification only if they think about the rewards in "cool" ways (Mischel & Moore, 1980).

Later Correlates of Childhood Delay-of-Gratification Competency

Delay-of-gratification competency in childhood appears to have implications for cognitive and social competence later in life. Mischel performed a series of long-term follow-up studies of the preschoolers in his original delay of gratification research (Mischel, 1984; Mischel, Shoda, & Peake, 1988; Shoda, Mischel, & Peake, 1990). The subjects' parents were asked to complete questionnaires about their now-teenage children's current cognitive and social functioning. Some of the correlations between childhood delay of gratification and adolescent behavior are shown in Table 21-1.

Subjects who had tolerated relatively long delays became adolescents whom their parents rated as verbally fluent, rational, attentive, planners, self-reliant and self-confident, dependable, curious, and concerned about moral issues, such as fairness (Mischel et al., 1988). In contrast, subjects who had had difficulty tolerating long delays as children were characterized as handling stress poorly, having poor self-images, experiencing difficulties in peer social relations, stubborn, concerned with getting their fair share, distrustful and jealous of others, and (as adolescents) showing low delay of gratification. These findings held for both sexes.

Next, the experimental conditions in which delay of gratification would best predict later behaviors were isolated (Shoda et al., 1990). Recall that Mischel's early research showed that children could delay gratification longer if the rewards they were anticipating were not visible than if they were visible. However, they could overcome the "temptation" of the visible rewards by employing cognitive strategies that took their minds off the rewards or made the rewards less attractive (i.e., with "cold" thoughts). Some of the children were given suggestions about how to think about the rewards in order to increase their delay of gratification while others were not. Children who were not given suggestions would have to generate them spontaneously, which would be indicative of a general delay-of-gratification competence. Such a

Table 21-1

Parents' ratings of adolescents' behaviors that correlated with the adolescents' preschool delay-of-gratification time in Mischel's original studies

POSITIVE		NEGATIVE	
Verbally fluent	+.48	Goes to pieces under stress	−.47
Uses and responds to reason	+.47	Feels unworthy	−.43
Attentive, able to concentrate	+.46	Is shy and reserved, makes social contacts slowly	−.39
Planful	+.42	Stubborn	−.36
Competent, skillful	+.38	Teases other children	−.32
Resourceful in initiating activities	+.35	Reverts to immature behavior under stress	−.31
Self-reliant, confident	+.32	Afraid of being deprived	−.27
Strongly involved with task at hand	+.29	Suspicious, distrustful of others	−.27
Trustworthy, dependable	+.29	Poor delay of gratification	−.26
Self-assertive	+.27	Jealous, envious of others	−.26
Curious, open to new experiences	+.25	Rigidly repetitive or immobilized under stress	−.26
Shows concern for moral issues (e.g., fairness)	+.25	Withdraws under stress	−.25

Note: All correlations are two-tailed, $p < .05$.

Source: Based on Mischel et al., 1988.

general competence should predict later competence. In fact, those children who spontaneously generated cognitive strategies to help themselves wait longer were the most likely to become adolescents who were rated as most competent academically and socially (Shoda et al., 1990).

Delay of Gratification in Older Children

The investigation of delay of gratification has concentrated on preschool children with no known self-control problems (cf. Funder & Block, 1989). A recent study has examined delay of gratification in children ages 6 to 12 (mean age of 10) who had problems with impulse control and social adjustment (Rodriguez, Mischel, & Shoda, 1989). The findings were generally consistent with those for preschool children. Older children who distracted themselves from focusing on the tempting reward delayed longer than children who did not use distraction. Children with higher verbal-intellectual ability used distraction more effectively and waited longer. Knowing about the use of "cold" rather than "hot" thoughts about the reward also was related to longer delay.

Mischel's research clearly supports his contention that the ability to delay gratification is an important person variable—a basic social competence that is correlated with a host of academic and social behaviors in later life. Moreover, this line of research illustrates the interaction between situational and person variables. For example, situational variables such as the presence of the actual reward or a picture of the reward can influence delay gratification. Person variables also are important because people can improve their delay of gratification by the way they think about the reward.

The Importance of Plans

Plans of action are another important person variable. Mischel (1979) used structured interviews to study the development of personal plans in children to discover what plans mean to children and how children define and use them.

Children as young as 8 years of age can discuss plans explicitly and provide concrete examples of how they use plans to structure and organize their actions. One 8-year-old spontaneously told an interviewer: "Tomorrow I'll clean up my room . . . Next week I'm gonna have a birthday party—if Mommy helps me" (Mischel, 1979, p. 749).

By age 11, children have a surprisingly good grasp of the nature, organization, and function of plans in their lives. They appreciate that plans have an intention or purpose. For example, "I'm going to clean up my room tomorrow because I'm planning to have a friend over." They also explicitly know the purpose a plan serves. For instance, "A plan tells you what to do and when and where and how to do it."

Further, most grade school children realize that having a plan is useless if it is not carried out. A 10-year-old explained: "You have to make yourself do it when the time comes; planning is the part you do beforehand, but then doing it is the actual right-there part" (p. 749). Some children are so good at planning that they seem to do it automatically. One 11-year-old saw himself as an expert planner. He explained:

> If I had to teach a plan to someone who grew up in the jungle—like a plan to work on a project at 10 a.m. tomorrow—I'd tell him what to say to himself to make it easier at the start for him. Like "if I do this plan on time I'll get a reward and the teacher will like me and I'll be proud." But for myself, I know all that already, so I don't have to say it to myself—Besides, it would take too long to say, and my mind doesn't have the time for that, so I just remember that stuff about why I should do it real quick without saying it—It's like a method that I know already in math; once you have the method you don't have to say every little step. (p. 749)

Children use plans and strategies more and more as they grow older. Consider what children say about how to delay gratification (Yates & Mischel, 1979). Young children incorrectly believe that seeing and thinking about the rewards will help them endure the delay. As they grow older, children realize that they must avoid thinking about the rewards, or they must think about them in ways that make the rewards less tempting. One child explained that someone could more easily wait for two pretzels by imagining they had gum stuck all over them!

The Consistency Paradox

Ask yourself the following question: Do you characterize people you know by placing them in broad dispositional categories, such as honest, outgoing, or confident? In other words, do you believe that people are generally consistent in their behavior across various situations? Most people would answer yes. For example, they might cite as "evidence" the "fact" that some people seem to be generally more honest than others. This widely held belief is contrary to research data showing that how a person behaves is often quite variable from situation to situation. A person who is honest in one situation is *not* necessarily honest in another, for example (e.g., Hartshorne & May, 1928).

This marked difference between our impressions of individual consistency and the research findings is called the **consistency paradox**. How can the paradox be explained? Mischel's answer draws on two main ideas: (1) the distinction between cross-situational and temporal consistency and (2) the concept of cognitive prototypes.

Cross-Situational Consistency versus Temporal Consistency

Cross-situational consistency refers to the extent that a person behaves the same way in different circumstances; it is consistency *across situations* and *across time* (see Figure 21-5). Consider 9-year-old Herbie. If we found him to be aggressive with virtually every child he meets, we would say that he shows substantial cross-situational consistency. In contrast, **temporal consistency** refers to an individual's behaving the same way in the same basic situation at different times; it is consistency *within situations across time* (see Figure 21-5). Herbie's aggressiveness would be considered temporally consistent if he were aggressive exclusively with younger children on the playground — today, tomorrow, next week, and next month.

Mischel (1984) argued that there is little reason to expect broad cross-situational consistency, but temporal consistency is likely. Both claims are based on real life contingencies. Herbie's aggression with younger children on the playground probably pays off. Younger children are likely to be intimidated by a playground bully. In turn, his aggression is reinforced because it gets him what he wants, such as first choice of games to be played. If Herbie's aggression is successful today, it will likely be successful tomorrow and the following week as well. Thus, aggression becomes a stable mode of responding *in this situation*.

Now suppose Herbie meets a group of older boys on the street. Here the contingencies are quite different. Older children may respond to aggression with counteraggression. Aggression in the first situation (with smaller children in the playground) would not predict aggression in the second situation (with older children in the street) — at least not if our bully could distinguish one situation from the other. Thus, Herbie's behavior would have temporal consistency but not cross-situational consistency.

Cognitive Prototypes

Research on how people categorize everyday objects shows that whether they place an object in a particular category depends on how "typical" it is of that category. Most people readily classify cows or rabbits as mammals. They are less likely to place whales and dolphins in the mammal category; these aquatic animals are viewed as less typical of mammals than familiar land animals such as cows and rabbits. People seem to categorize objects using *cognitive prototypes*—that is, the "best" examples of the concept (e.g., Tversky, 1977).

People also may use cognitive prototypes to categorize some behaviors as more typical of a dispositional category than others (Mischel, 1984). For example, college students believe that attending class regularly is more typical of a "conscientious student" than taking neat notes or coming to study sessions on time, even though the latter two behaviors have some relevance for conscientiousness.

The fact that we tend to see behaviors as more or less typical of a disposition helps explain the consistency paradox. Our general impression of consistency of behavior is likely to be temporal rather than cross-situational. This impression may be because people see the consistency in *prototypic behaviors* rather than in all behaviors that are indicative of a disposition. In other words, to see someone as having a particular disposition, say a trait of courage, the person must consistently exhibit at various times prototypic examples, such as rescuing someone from a burning building or sailing solo across the ocean. However, the person may not exhibit behaviors that are nonprototypic examples of that trait, such as admitting a lie to a friend. Nonprototypic examples are likely to be overlooked in forming the general impression that the individual is courageous.

Mischel's view is that people form their impressions from the *temporal consistency of the most prototypic behaviors*—without being aware that this is the basis for their impressions. This idea has received support in a study of one particular trait—conscientiousness—in 63 undergraduate students (Mischel, 1984). Parents and one close friend rated each student on conscientiousness. Students also rated themselves on how consistent or

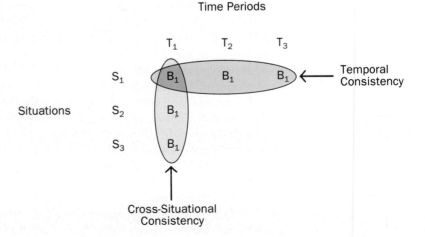

Figure 21-5
Temporal consistency refers to a person's engaging in the same behavior (B) across time (T) and within a given situation (S). Cross-situational consistency refers to a person's engaging in the same behavior in different situations.

Time Periods

T_1 T_2 T_3

S_1 B_1 B_1 B_1 ← Temporal Consistency

Situations S_2 B_1

S_3 B_1

↑
Cross-Situational
Consistency

variable they were in conscientiousness. Finally, the students were observed in a variety of actual situations related to the trait. These observations yielded measures of class attendance, assignment neatness, assignment punctuality, room neatness, and personal appearance. (Students considered all of these measures to be indicative of conscientiousness.)

Raters agreed much more on the overall conscientiousness of students who rated themselves consistently conscientious than on those who rated themselves as inconsistently conscientious. However, students who rated themselves as consistent on the trait were *not* actually more consistent than those who rated themselves as inconsistent on the trait.

Mischel and Peake (1982) hypothesized that this discrepancy could be explained with reference to cognitive prototypes. They divided the behavioral measures of conscientiousness into those judged by the students as more prototypic or less prototypic of the trait. As expected, students who saw themselves as highly conscientious were much more temporally consistent on the most prototypic conscientious behaviors than students who considered themselves as inconsistently conscientious.

Next, Mischel and Peake examined *all* behaviors related to conscientiousness—not just prototypic behaviors. In this case, students who rated themselves as highly consistent were *not* in fact any more cross-situationally consistent in their actual behaviors than those who saw themselves as inconsistent in conscientiousness (see Table 21-2). These data strongly support the idea that our perceptions about a person's consistency on a disposition come from *temporal consistency of prototypic behaviors*. They are not based on cross-situational consistency for all relevant behaviors.

When Are People Consistent?

Mischel concluded that people are generally consistent in their behavior in the same situation; that is, they show temporal consistency. Under normal circumstances, behavior does not show cross-situational consistency because people note that different behaviors are called for in different situations, and they change their behaviors accordingly.

However, there may be times when cross-situational consistency occurs. Specifically, it may be expected in abnormal circumstances, characterized by high stress and the need to behave beyond one's competency (Cantor, 1990; Wright & Mischel, 1987). In such extreme situations, it appears that people tend to act in a rigid fashion. They use "tried-and-true" means of coping, even though the coping strategies may not work in a given situation.

Evidence for this idea comes from a study of the behavior of emotionally disturbed children at a summer camp (Wright & Mischel, 1986). The camp staff observed the children in 21 distinct activities (e.g., music, athletics, and group cabin meetings) over a 40-day period. The staff rated each child's aggressive and withdrawing behaviors.

The cognitive and self-regulatory requirements of each situation were categorized according to the demand they placed on the child. *Low-demand situations* were within the children's capacities; *high-demand situations* were beyond their capacities. The cross-situational consistency of the children's

Table 21-2
The link between self-perceived consistency and actual behavior. Students who view themselves as highly consistent on conscientiousness are *not* more cross-situationally consistent than those who rate themselves as low in consistency; but they are more temporally consistent (stable) in their display of the behaviors most prototypical for conscientiousness. The data are correlation coefficients.

	SELF-PERCEIVED CONSISTENCY	
BEHAVIORAL DATA	HIGH	LOW
CROSS-SITUATIONAL CONSISTENCY		
More prototypical	.15	.13
Less prototypical	.09	.14
TEMPORAL STABILITY		
More prototypical	.71	.47
Less prototypical	.65	.64

Source: Adapted from "Beyond *Déjà Vu* in the Search for Cross-Situational Consistency" by W. Mischel and P. K. Peake, 1982, *Psychological Review, 89,* pp. 730–755.

behavior in low-demand and high-demand situations was compared. Some of the results are shown in Table 21-3. As predicted, the children showed much more cross-situational consistency in situations requiring a high degree of competency.

Thus, cross-situational consistency does occur under certain predictable conditions — namely, high-demand situations that elicit rigid functioning that is often incompetent because it is not relevant to the situation. In contrast, good adjustment and competence require that the person choose the specific responses that are likely to produce desirable results in the situation at hand. When people are sensitive to the context, their behaviors vary considerably from situation to situation.

To summarize, most often the consistency in a person's behavior that we observe is temporal. People have learned particular ways of behaving successfully in specific situations, and they tend to respond in the same situation-specific ways time after time. Thus, consistency in human behavior is not paradoxical. *Consistency occurs over time but, under normal circumstances, not across situations.*

A Conditional Approach to Dispositional Constructs
The traditional view of dispositions is that people have generalized tendencies to behave in certain ways. Mischel proposed a more integrative view based on the **conditional dispositional construct** (Mischel, 1988; Wright & Mischel, 1987). It is a rule that provides a meaningful "if-then" link between clusters of situations and clusters of behaviors.

Table 21-3
Mean cross-situational consistency coefficients as a function of a situation's cognitive and self-regulatory requirements. When the situation's requirements were high (and thus exceed the children's competencies), consistency was high; but when the situations were less demanding, there was considerably less cross-situational consistency.

	SITUATION COMPETENCY REQUIREMENTS	
BEHAVIOR CATEGORY	LOW	HIGH
1981		
Aggression	.37	.73
Withdrawal	.27	.69
1982		
Aggression	.32	.61
Withdrawal	.06	.37

Source: From data reported in "Convergences and Challenges in the Search for Consistency" by W. Mischel, 1984, *American Psychologist, 39,* pp. 351–364.

Consider the example of aggressiveness. From the traditional viewpoint, aggressiveness is a general disposition to behave aggressively across situations. In contrast, the conditional approach holds that aggressiveness refers to a tendency to respond to a *certain class of situations* (such as being threatened or frustrated) with a *certain class of behaviors* (such as striking out physically or yelling). In the absence of the relevant situations, the so-called aggressive person will be no more likely to engage in aggressive behaviors than the so-called nonaggressive person (e.g., Wright & Mischel, 1987).

The Interaction of Emotion and Cognition

The role that cognitions play in determining our emotional reactions has been an important area of cognitive-behavioral theorizing and research. For example, debilitating negative thoughts about one's performance are linked to anxiety (e.g., Beck & Emery, 1985; Ellis, 1989; Luccock & Salkovskis, 1988; Sarason, Sarason, & Pierce, 1990). Similarly, cognitive distortions, such as overgeneralizations and arbitrary inferences, are associated with depression (e.g., Beck & Weishaar, 1989; Dykman & Abramson, 1990; Stiles & Götestam, 1989; Stiles, Schröder, & Johansen, 1993).

The influence of emotions on cognitions has received less attention in the behavioral strategy. Mischel's research and theorizing about how our mood affects the way we evaluate situations and ourselves have begun to fill this deficit.

In one experiment, Wright and Mischel (1982) had college students imagine scenes that induced a positive (happy) or negative (sad) mood. Then the students performed a perception task that was set up so that they either succeeded or failed. To assess the effects of mood and success experience, the subjects were asked a series of questions about their performance on the perception task.

A positive mood resulted in higher estimates of past performance, higher expectations about future success, and higher overall self-evaluation of ability on the task. These results held both for subjects who had succeeded and those who had failed.

A negative mood had little effect on the self-evaluations of the success group. But subjects in the failure group were much less satisfied with their performance if they were in a negative mood. When subjects were asked to set minimal goals for future trials on the task, the combination of failure and a negative mood was particularly devastating. Subjects in this group were the only ones to set minimal goals that they did not expect to meet.

What is the process by which mood influences thought? Wright and Mischel (1982) suggested that people have a **mood-congruent bias**. We process information about past experience selectively, in a way that is consistent with our mood. In broad terms, people in a positive mood attend selectively to and recall success and other positive experiences. Conversely, people in a negative mood attend to and recall failure and other negative experiences.

Mood-congruent bias would explain Wright and Mischel's (1982) finding that subjects in a positive mood tended to recall their performance as more successful than it actually was. Specifically, the positive mood led to selective attention to and recall of success. Similarly, subjects in a negative mood who had had a failure experience focused on the failure, which resulted in a pessimistic outlook.

The same mechanism appears to operate in depression. In one study, the social competence of depressed and nondepressed individuals was rated by observers and by the individuals themselves (Lewinsohn, Mischel, Chaplin, & Barton, 1980). Contrary to expectations, depressed subjects rated themselves as they were seen by others, so that they were quite accurate. The nondepressed subjects rated themselves more positively than they were seen by others. As the depressed subjects' mood became more positive, their self-perceptions changed.

> In the course of treatment, the depressed not only rated themselves more positively [but] began to increase the discrepancy between how they rated themselves and how they were rated . . . their self-perceptions became more unrealistic in the sense that they began to see themselves more positively than the observers rated them. It is tempting to conjecture that a key to avoiding depression is to see oneself less stringently and more favorably than others see one. If so, the beliefs that unrealistic appraisals are a basic ingredient of depression and that realism is the crux of appropriate affect may have to be seriously questioned. To feel good about ourselves we may have to judge ourselves more kindly than we are judged. (Lewinsohn et al., 1980, pp. 211–212)

Cognitive behavior therapists have been dealing with the relationship of cognitions and emotions for some time. We turn next to this important practical application of the cognitive-behavioral approach.

COGNITIVE-BEHAVIOR THERAPY

According to the cognitive approach, maladaptive cognitions play a central role in the development and maintenance of psychological disorders. These cognitions may take the form of self-deprecating thoughts, illogical ideas, or irrational beliefs. **Cognitive-behavior therapies** modify the maladaptive cognitions (1) by directly changing the cognitions or (2) by changing overt behaviors to indirectly modify the cognitions. Most cognitive-behavioral therapies involve a combination of both tactics. Cognitive-behavioral interventions are the most frequently used behavioral treatments and are applicable to a wide array of disorders (Cottraux, 1990; Craighead 1990b; Goldfried, Greenberg, & Marmar, 1990; Mahoney, 1993b).

Cognitive Restructuring

Cognitive restructuring is the basic procedure used in many cognitive-behavior therapies. It involves modifying the thoughts, ideas, and beliefs that maintain the client's abnormal behaviors. Specifically, cognitive restructuring modifies **self-statements** or **self-talk,** what clients say to themselves (e.g., Dush, Hirt, & Schroeder, 1989). *Self-talk* involves the "soundless, mental speech, arising at the instant that we think about something, plan or solve problems in our mind . . .. We think and remember with the aid of words which we articulate to ourselves" (Sokolov, 1972, p. 1).

The client learns to recognize maladaptive cognitions and replace them with adaptive ones. For example, a client who lost her job believed that she would never get another job. This belief is maladaptive because it would not motivate the client to do anything about the situation. The client learned to restructure her beliefs by thinking such thoughts as "Many people lose jobs and find another" or "Maybe my next job will be better than the last one."

Rational-Emotive Therapy

Rational-emotive therapy (RET), developed by Albert Ellis, uses cognitive restructuring to change faulty or irrational thoughts that are associated with negative emotions, such as anxiety, depression, anger, and guilt (Ellis, 1962, 1993; Ellis & Dryden, 1987).

As Figure 21-6 shows, RET is based on the idea that negative emotions and accompanying maladaptive behaviors result *directly* from irrational thoughts and evaluative processes and only indirectly from precipitating external events (DeSilvestri, 1989; Ellis, 1985; Muran, 1991). This is contrary to the widely accepted notion that emotional upsets are a direct consequence of an external event (e.g., "*He* made me sad" or "*Taking tests* makes me anxious"). Ellis has identified five common forms of irrational thinking: (1) *absolute thinking* (all or none, no in-between), (2) *catastrophizing* (blowing things out of proportion), (3) *low frustration tolerance*, (4) *overgeneralization*, and (5) *personal worthlessness* (Bernard & DiGiuseppe, 1989; Ellis & Bernard, 1985). A *sense of duty* is a pervasive theme in irrational thinking; clients believe they "must" or "should" behave in certain ways (Ellis & Dryden, 1987).

In RET, the therapist helps the client identify the specific maladaptive self-statements about the external precipitating event. Then the therapist points out the irrational or illogical beliefs on which the self-statements are

Albert Ellis
(1913-   )
developed rational-emotive therapy, in which clients learn to change their irrational thoughts.
Courtesy of Albert Ellis

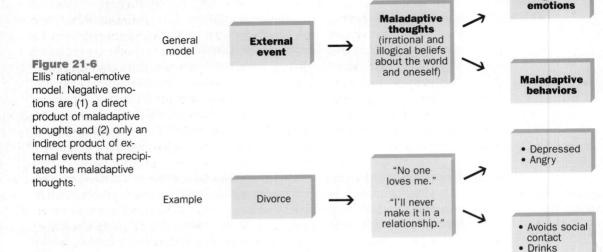

Figure 21-6
Ellis' rational-emotive model. Negative emotions are (1) a direct product of maladaptive thoughts and (2) only an indirect product of external events that precipitated the maladaptive thoughts.

based. For instance, Joe V., a 40-year-old businessman, felt guilty and depressed whenever he went off his diet. The therapist asked Joe to monitor what he was saying to himself whenever he overate. His self-statements included "I'll never be able to lose weight" and "I am going to be fat the rest of my life."

The therapist showed Joe that his self-statements were based on the irrational belief that he must be perfect and the illogical idea that he could never stay on his diet just because he occasionally went off it. After several therapy sessions, Joe began to see the connection between his thoughts and his feelings. Finally, Joe learned to substitute rational thoughts for irrational thoughts, such as replacing "I went off my diet again; I just can't stay on it" with "Just because I went off my diet today doesn't mean I can't stay on it tomorrow."

Cognitive Therapy   **Cognitive therapy**, developed by Aaron Beck, is similar to RET. The therapist and client collaborate to (1) identify the client's dysfunctional beliefs, (2) challenge their validity, and (3) provide the client with the skills and experiences that will result in more adaptive thinking (Beck & Weishaar, 1989). Specifically, the irrational beliefs are posed as hypotheses that the client then gathers evidence to refute. For example, clients who believe that they are worthless might be asked to make a list of their accomplishments, both small and large.

Cognitive therapy originally was designed to treat depression, and today it is considered one of the most effective treatments for that disorder (e.g., Beckham & Watkins, 1989; Dobson, 1989; Hollon, Shelton, & Davis, 1993; Thase, Bowler, & Harden, 1991; Thase, Simons, Cahalane, & McGeary,

Aaron Beck
(1921-   )
developed cognitive
therapy, in which clients
gather empirical
evidence to refute the
validity of the illogical
beliefs that are
maintaining their
abnormal behaviors.
Courtesy of Aaron Beck

1991). Recently, cognitive therapy has been expanded to treat other disorders (Beck, 1993), including anxiety (e.g., Beck & Emery, 1985; Butler, Fennell, Robson, & Gelder, 1991; Chambless & Gillis, 1993), personality disorders (Beck & Freeman, 1989), and marital discord (e.g., Baucom & Epstein, 1990; Dattilio & Padesky, 1990).

In analyzing the thoughts of depressed patients, Beck (1976, 1984) identified three common themes: (1) negative interpretation of external events, (2) pessimistic view of the future, and (3) self-dislike. Beck argued that these distorted views are all due to a common set of logical errors, which overlap with Ellis's list (see Table 21-4).

Cognitive therapy has both behavioral and cognitive components (DeRubeis & Beck, 1988). Variations of cognitive restructuring comprise the cognitive component. An example of a behavioral intervention is graded task assignments. Clients engage in a series of brief, simple behaviors that gradually become lengthier and more complex. The aim is to counter patients' views that they cannot competently perform various behaviors. The shaping procedure allows patients to succeed and thus prove to themselves that they can perform behaviors competently. For instance, a hospitalized patient who was depressed believed that he could not walk. First, Beck (1976) persuaded the man to walk 5 yards, then 10 yards, and so on. Each time the man protested that he could not walk the requested distance. However, when he succeeded each time, he was forced to revise his beliefs. Research suggests that the combination of cognitive restructuring and behavior rehearsal, as practiced in Beck's therapy, is more effective than either component alone (Zettle & Hayes, 1987).

Table 21-4
The six "cognitive errors" associated with depression

> **Arbitrary inference:** Drawing negative conclusions not warranted by evidence.
>
> **Selective abstraction:** Focusing on one negative aspect of a situation, while ignoring other (positive) aspects.
>
> **Overgeneralization:** Drawing an across-the-board negative conclusion from one or a few negative instances.
>
> **Magnification and minimization:** Greatly overestimating or underestimating the importance of an event, to make it seem grossly out of proportion.
>
> **Personalization:** Relating negative events to oneself without a reasonable basis.
>
> **Dichotomous thinking:** Thinking only in terms of black or white, "wonderful or terrible," instead of in gradations.

Source: Based on "Cognitive Therapy" by R. J. DeRubeis and A. T. Beck, 1988, in K. S. Dobson (Ed.), *Issues and Approaches in Personal Construct Theory*, Orlando, Fla.: Academic Press.

■ *Demonstration 21-1:*
COGNITIVE RESTRUCTURING*

Cognitive restructuring is a broadly useful skill for dealing with stressful events in your life. This Demonstration gives you practice in replacing negative self-statements with positive self-statements.

You will read brief descriptions of some common stress-evoking situations and one possible negative self-statement that a person might make when encountering the situation. The self-statements are maladaptive because they interpret the situation so that nothing can be done to cope with it. Each situation is undesirable, but it is not as disastrous as the negative self-statement implies.

For each negative self-statement below, write two alternative self-statements that are optimistic and adaptive. Your positive self-statements should be directly related to the situation and point to some constructive course of action that is realistic. For instance, if your brand-new car were stolen, it would be unrealistic to respond with "I don't need the car."

SITUATION

1. Having a long, difficult assignment due the next day

*Adapted from Spiegler (1983).

2. Having an accident with the family car

3. Moving away from friends and family

4. Breaking up with a person you love

5. Not getting into graduate school

6. Having to participate in a class discussion

NEGATIVE SELF-STATEMENT

1. "I'll never get this work done by tomorrow."

2. "Oh no, my father will 'kill' me."

3. "My whole life is left behind."

4. "I have nothing to live for; he/she was all I had."

5. "I guess I'm really dumb. I don't know what I'll do."

6. "Everyone else knows more than I do, so what's the use of saying anything."

After you have thought of alternative positive self-statements for each negative self-statement, compare them with the examples of positive self-statements listed in Table 21-5.

Table 21-5
Examples of positive self-statements that could be substituted for negative self-statements

SITUATION	NEGATIVE SELF-STATEMENT	ALTERNATIVE POSITIVE SELF-STATEMENTS
1. Having a long, difficult assignment due the next day	1. "I'll never get this work done by tomorrow."	1. "If I work real hard I may be able to get it all done for tomorrow." "This is going to be tough but it is still possible to do it." "It will be a real challenge finishing this assignment for tomorrow." "If I don't get it finished, I'll just have to ask the teacher for an extension."

Table 21-5
Examples of positive self-statements that could be substituted for negative self-statements (continued)

2. Having an accident with the family car	2. "Oh, no, my father will 'kill' me."	2. "What's done is done; I'll just have to make the best of it." "I'll just have to figure out a way that I can pay for this." "This is going to cost me, but thank God no one was injured." "Maybe my father will understand if I explain it to him calmly."
3. Moving away from friends and family	3. "My whole life is left behind."	3. "I'll miss everyone, but it doesn't mean we can't stay in touch." "Just think of all the new people I'm going to meet." "I guess it will be kind of exciting moving to a new home." "Now I'll have two places to call home."
4. Breaking up with a person you love	4. "I have nothing to live for. He/she was all I had."	4. "I really thought our relationship would work, but it's not the end of the world." "Maybe we can try again in the future." "I'll just have to try to keep myself busy and not let it bother me." "If I met him (her), there is no reason why I won't meet someone else someday."
5. Not getting into graduate school	5. "I guess I'm really dumb. I don't know what I'll do."	5. "I'll just have to reapply next year." "There are things I can do with my life other than going to grad school." "I guess a lot of good students get turned down. It's just so unbelievably competitive." "Perhaps there are a few other programs that I could apply to."
6. Having to participate in a class discussion	6. "Everyone else knows more than I do, so what's the use of saying anything."	6. "I have as much to say as anyone else in the class." "My ideas may be different, but they're still valid." "It's OK to be a bit nervous; I'll relax as I start talking." "I might as well say something; how bad could it sound?"

Source: From *Contemporary Behavioral Therapy* by M. D. Spiegler, 1983, Palo Alto, Calif.: Mayfield, pp. 403–404.

Self-Instructional Training

Donald Meichenbaum
(1940-)
is a leading spokesperson for cognitive-behavioral therapy and has developed a number of cognitive-behavioral interventions, including self-instructional training.
Courtesy of Donald Meichenbaum

Donald Meichenbaum (1986, 1991) is one of the architects of cognitive-behavioral therapy. He developed a procedure to capitalize on our inclination to "coach" ourselves when we are in difficult situations. For instance, when we lose our car keys, we may say to ourselves: "Don't panic. Just stop and think. Where did I put them when I came in?" Self-instructional training teaches clients to instruct themselves about how to act, feel, and think (Meichenbaum, 1985). We will illustrate self-instructional training by describing its initial use to decrease children's impulsive behaviors (Meichenbaum & Goodman, 1971).

Children who act impulsively do not think before they act, which often has undesirable consequences for themselves and others. The general goal of self-instructional training for impulsive behavior is to teach children to think and plan before they act—to "stop, look, and listen" (see Figure 21-7). Five steps are involved.

1. *Cognitive modeling*. An adult model performs a task while verbalizing an adaptive, counterimpulsive strategy. For example, while copying line patterns an adult model might say, "Okay, what is it I have to do? You want me to copy the picture with the different lines. I have to go slowly and carefully. Okay, draw the line down, down, good . . . " (Meichenbaum & Goodman, 1971, p. 117).
2. *Cognitive participant modeling*. The child performs the task as the model verbalizes the instructions.
3. *Overt self-instruction*. The child performs the task while verbalizing the instructions out loud.
4. *Fading the overt self-instruction*. The child performs the task while whispering the instructions.
5. *Covert self-instruction*. The child performs the task while saying the instructions silently.

The child first practices with brief and simple perceptual motor tasks, such as coloring figures within boundaries. Gradually the length and complexity of the tasks are increased.

Self-instructional training has been used to treat a variety of problems in a number of different populations, including anxiety (Meichenbaum,

Figure 21-7
Cue cards used to prompt children to use self-instructions in solving problems.
Source: From Think Aloud: Increasing Social and Cognitive Skills–A Problem-Solving Program for Children (Primary Level) by B. W. Camp and M. A. S. Bash, 1981, Champaign, Ill.: Research Press. Reprinted by permission.

What is my problem?   How can I do it?   Am I using my plan?   How did I do?

Figure 21-8
As in the children's story *The Little Engine That Could*, clients in self-instructional training tell themselves what they must do and repeatedly tell themselves that they can succeed.
Illustration by George and Doris Hauman reprinted by permission from *The Little Engine That Could*, retold by Watty Piper, copyright 1930, 1954, 1958 by Platt & Munk, Publishers. "I think I can, I think I can" is a trademark of Platt & Munk, Publishers.

"I think I can—I think I can—I think I can—I think I can."

Gilmore, & Fedoravicius, 1971) and lack of creativity in college students (Meichenbaum, 1975), deficits in problem solving among children (e.g., Camp & Bash, 1981) and the elderly (Labouvie-Vief & Gonda, 1976); academic skills in children (e.g., Guevremont, Osnes, & Stokes, 1988); pain in adults (Turk, Meichenbaum, & Genest, 1983); and schizophrenic speech (e.g., Meyers, Mercatoris, & Sirota, 1976).

Problem-Solving Therapy

The ability to solve problems is related to competence and adjustment. For example, the more consistently children generate effective solutions to social problems, the more socially competent they appear to be (Hopper & Kirschenbaum, 1985). Conversely, difficulty in problem solving is associated with interpersonal problems and psychological disorders such as depression (e.g., Asarnow & Callan, 1985; Lochman & Curry, 1986b; Nezu & D'Zurilla, 1989).

Problem-solving therapy teaches general problem-solving skills to clients with two aims: (1) to alleviate the particular personal problems for which clients have sought therapy (e.g., D'Zurilla & Nezu, 1982; Wasik, 1984) and (2) to provide clients with a general coping strategy for personal problems (e.g., Heppner, Neal, & Larsen, 1984). In problem-solving therapy, clients learn and practice a series of basic steps for solving problems: (1) *defining the problem*, (2) *selecting a goal*, (3) *generating alternative solutions*, (4) *choosing one of the alternative solutions*, (5) *implementing the chosen solution*, and (6) *evaluating the success of the solution*.

Problem-solving therapies have been used to treat a variety of personal and interpersonal difficulties (D'Zurilla, 1986). Examples include depression (e.g., Nezu, Nezu, & Perri, 1989), aggressive behaviors (e.g., Guevremont & Foster, 1993; Lochman, 1992), anger (e.g., Lochman & Curry, 1986a), marital conflicts (e.g., Jacobson, 1989, 1991, 1992), harmony among family members (e.g., Robin & Foster, 1989), and child abuse (e.g., MacMillan, Guevremont, & Hansen, 1989).

■ *Demonstration 21-2:*
BRAINSTORMING*

Successful problem solving often requires generating a large number of solutions from which to choose the most viable one. A form of *brainstorming* is used to do this. You list any and all potential solutions to the problem, *without regard to practicality*. Even if you know that a solution cannot be implemented, you should include it.

Your "wild" ideas may lead to more realistic solutions that you might not have considered otherwise. For instance, suppose you are having difficulty with one of your professors. While brainstorming you might come up with "Stop going to class." Although the solution itself has its problems, its outcome—no longer having to deal with the professor—may elicit other ways to achieve the same goal, such as switching to another section of the course.

To practice generating solutions to problems by brainstorming, write at least 20 different solutions for each of the problems described below. You might want to compete with a friend to see who comes up with the most solutions. Remember, the solution must solve the problem, but it need not be a feasible solution.

Situation 1. You are visiting a large city. While you are taking a shower in your hotel room, someone steals all of your clothes. The room has no phone. *What could you do?*

Situation 2. You have somehow made a date for a romantic dinner with two different people on the same evening. You have told both of them to meet you in front of a restaurant at 7:00 p.m. *What could you do?*

Situation 3. Telephone service to the city in which your parents live (200 miles from your home) will be out of order for the next 24 hours. It is imperative that you get a message to your parents in the next 2 hours. *What could you do?*

*Based on Spiegler & Guevremont (1993).

**Cognitive-
Behavioral
Marital Therapy**

Marital problems tend to be complex, and consequently treatment typically involves multiple interventions. Cognitive-behavioral marital therapies involve (1) communication and problem-solving training, (2) increasing positive behavior exchanges, and (3) cognitive restructuring (Spiegler & Guevremont, 1993).

Distressed couples generally have difficulties communicating and solving problems in the relationship (e.g., Geiss & O'Leary, 1981). Couples learn such communications skills as listening, restating what the other person has said, and giving constructive feedback. The skills are taught by modeling, prompting, shaping, role playing, and feedback.

Couples experiencing marital discord usually do not act positively or lovingly toward one another. The **caring-days technique** increases the number of positive behavior exchanges the couple has (Stuart, 1980). First, the partners individually make a list of specific positive behaviors that the other partner could do to show that he or she loves the other. Then, each partner is asked to do a set number of behaviors from the list each day.

Marital problems are often maintained by distorted views partners have of each other (Baucom & Epstein, 1990; Beck, 1989). For example, one spouse may erroneously attribute the other's silence to anger when in fact it is due to fatigue. Couples are encouraged to check out the validity of their beliefs and to change those that are faulty through cognitive restructuring.

Cognitive-behavioral marital interventions have been shown to be effective not only in alleviating marital distress but also in preventing it through premarital training (Hahlweg & Markman, 1988; Jacobson, 1989).

SUMMARY   1. Mischel was highly critical of traditional dispositional and psychoanalytic personality assessment. He coined the term "personality coefficient" to refer to the generally low correlations typically found between personality test scores and actual behavior.

2. Mischel identified five broad person variables: competencies, encoding strategies and personal constructs, expectancies, values, and self-regulating systems and plans. Unlike personality dispositions, person variables are not assumed to be constant across situations.

3. Delay of gratification is an important person variable. It is increased by exposure to delay-oriented models, by the ability to distract oneself from immediate temptations, and by thinking about immediate rewards in "cool" ways.

4. Delay of gratification competency in childhood is related to cognitive competency and social adjustment in adolescence.

5. The same factors that influence delay of gratification in children influence it in adolescents.

6. Plans are another important person variable. Children as young as 8 can discuss their use of plans explicitly.

7. The consistency paradox refers to our thinking of people as being quite consistent in their behavior in different situations, even though most people's behavior actually tends to vary a good deal from situation to situation. Mischel's research reveals that generally people's behaviors are consistent over time but not across situations. This is because people are sensitive to the behavioral demands in different situations. However, in stressful situations when the demands of the situation exceed their personal competencies, people may show cross-situational consistency.

8. Mischel's solution to the consistency paradox invokes the concept of cognitive prototypes. The impression of consistency is due to the fact that people are temporally consistent on a few behaviors that are most typical of a dispositional category, which gives the (false) impression of general consistency.

9. In studying the interaction of emotion and cognition, Mischel found that people have a mood-congruent bias; they selectively recall and interpret experiences in the direction of their current mood.

10. Cognitive-behavior therapy changes clients' maladaptive cognitions that are associated with psychological disorders. Cognitive restructuring, a basic procedure used in many cognitive-behavior therapies, involves substituting adaptive cognitions for maladaptive cognitions.

11. Rational-emotive therapy teaches clients to use cognitive restructuring to change irrational cognitions associated with negative emotions.

12. Cognitive therapy is similar to rational-emotive therapy except that it emphasizes refuting illogical beliefs with evidence. Both overt behavioral and cognitive interventions are used.

13. Self-instructional training teaches clients to tell themselves explicitly how to think, feel, and act.

14. Problem-solving therapy trains clients to solve their own problems through six steps: defining the problem, selecting a goal, generating alternative solutions, choosing a solution, implementing it, and evaluating its effectiveness.

15. Cognitive-behavioral marital therapy consists of communication and problem-solving training, increasing positive behavior exchanges, and cognitive restructuring.

Chapter Twenty-Two

Liabilities of the Behavioral Strategy

e conclude our presentation of the behavioral strategy, as we have concluded our discussions of the other three strategies, by looking at its liabilities. Four criticisms have been leveled at the strategy in general: (1) lack of comprehensive theory; (2) commitment of logical errors; (3) overdependence on laboratory experiments; and (4) excessive reliance on situational tests. Moreover, the radical-behavioral approach has problems with its acceptability to both psychologists and laypersons. Finally, there is the issue of the behavioral strategy's losing its identity.

LACK OF COMPREHENSIVE THEORY

Critics have faulted the psychoanalytic, dispositional, and phenomenological strategies on their theoretical adequacy. The behavioral strategy, too, has a major theoretical liability; namely, it does not even attempt a comprehensive account of personality. In fact, some critics have said that the strategy does not try to explain personality at all.

Behavioral approaches range from Skinner's essentially nontheoretical stance to relatively comprehensive social learning theories. Between these extremes are narrower theoretical positions like Mischel's cognitive-behavioral theorizing. The social learning theories of Rotter and Bandura are broader than most behavioral approaches. But neither of these conceptualizations is truly a comprehensive account of personality, such as exists in the psychoanalytic and phenomenological strategies. Contemporary behavioral and cognitive-behavioral theorizing alludes to general principles but actually deals with only narrow, selected areas of personality functioning, such as locus of control and perceived self-efficacy.

By its very nature, each strategy emphasizes some aspects of personality and devotes little or no attention to other aspects. Like each of the other three strategies, the behavioral strategy has "blind spots." Radical-behavioral approaches have the most glaring limitation because they focus on public, overt behaviors and ignore private, covert behaviors. Social learning and cognitive perspectives study broader phenomena, including covert events, most notably cognitions. Still, for the most part, the covert behaviors are measured by reference to overt behaviors. For example, thoughts are often assessed by asking subjects to report what they are saying to themselves (i.e., self-talk). These overt behavioral referents allow objective verification by more than one observer, yet they are not the same as the covert behaviors themselves. Thus, the behavioral psychologist is not studying the covert events directly, which means that information is lost along the way.

Finally, behavioral personality theories largely ignore the effects of biological and hereditary factors on personality (cf. Staats, 1993a, 1993b). Behavioral psychologists do not deny these influences. Even radical behaviorists like Skinner (1974) acknowledge their role. But behavioral psychologists choose to focus on other factors. In doing so, they can present only a partial conceptualization of personality.

The Relation of Theory to Behavior Therapy	Regarding personality change, critics have argued that no specific theory or theories underlie behavior therapies (Spiegler, 1983). Rather, behavior therapists may employ only a "nontheoretical amalgamation of pragmatic principles" from which their procedures derive strength (Weitzman, 1967, p. 303). For example, the effectiveness of systematic desensitization can be explained in terms of a variety of behavioral as well as nonbehavioral theories, including psychoanalysis (Spiegler & Guevremont, 1993; Weitzman, 1967). Moreover, most behavioral change techniques were in use long before behavioral personality theories were formulated (Breger & McGaugh, 1966; Wilson, 1986). Thus, behavioral theories have not generated the change techniques with which they are associated.

Bandura's theory of perceived self-efficacy does present a theoretical explanation of behavioral personality change procedures (although no behavior therapies based on the theory have been developed). However, Bandura argued that self-efficacy theory can explain the psychological changes achieved by all modes of psychotherapy. This claim is too broad. Critics argue that the application of self-efficacy theory may be limited to a particular class of problems—notably fear and anxiety—and to a particular class of treatment procedures—such as performance-based therapies like participant modeling (Eastman & Marzillier, 1984).

LOGICAL ERRORS	We have seen that the psychoanalytic, dispositional, and phenomenological psychologists commit logical errors in their reasoning. The behavioral psychologists also have been guilty of thinking illogically in certain respects. They have been accused of making two logical errors in particular: (1) mistakenly casting thoughts as causes of behavior and (2) committing the error of affirming the consequent.
Casting Thoughts as Causes of Behavior	Not surprisingly, proponents of the radical-behavioral approach have expressed serious reservations about the inclusion of cognitive processes in the scientific study of behavior (e.g., Eysenck, 1982; Rachlin, 1977; Skinner, 1974; Wolpe, 1978, 1989). They have especially objected to assigning these processes a causal role.

Radical-behavioral psychologists do not deny that people think. But they also do not consider thoughts to operate as independent causes of behavior. Rather, they hold that thoughts are the effect of people's reinforcement histories and biological conditions. Take, for example, a claim that Bandura would make: Observing a competent model leads people to feel that they have personal efficacy and therefore to perform better. Radical-behavioral psychologists would counter by claiming that feelings of self-efficacy are not the cause of improved performance but *merely one of its effects*. The issue, then, is one of directionality. For cognitive behaviorists, cognitions are causes; to radical behaviorists, they are effects.

In the practice of behavior therapy, radical behaviorists argue that cognitive-behavioral therapists do not act as if thoughts alone determine what people do or how they feel.

Cognitive-behavior therapy does not stop after the irrational idea is uncovered and the rational idea presented. If ideas themselves could control behavior . . . . then one would expect the change of ideas to result simply in a change of behavior, as when a general orders his army to advance or retreat. But far from ending after the client's ideas are changed, therapy barely begins at that point. The therapy consists of homework assignments that to all intents and purposes are identical with the sorts of things noncognitive behavior therapists do as a matter of course. [The use of graded task assignments in Beck's cognitive therapy (Chapter 21) is a good example.] (Rachlin, 1977, pp. 372–373)

The Error of Affirming the Consequent

Behavioral psychologists take great pride in the success of their therapy techniques. They often claim or imply that these successes demonstrate the validity of behavioral personality theory. The logic of such an assertion is faulty.

As an example, behavioral psychologists theorize that many fears are acquired through classical conditioning. One source of evidence they cite for this assertion is that fears can be eliminated by counterconditioning procedures, such as systematic desensitization. However, this does not prove that the fear was acquired through conditioning in the first place.

The logical fallacy at issue here is the *error of affirming the consequent*. It involves assuming that "because behavior is generated under one set of circumstances, every time this or similar behavior occurs in nature, it had developed because of the same set of controlling conditions" (Davison & Neale, 1974, p. 28). A common analogous experience further illustrates the erroneous reasoning. You take aspirin for a headache. Often, the medicine relieves your pain and "cures" your ailment. Still, the fact that taking aspirin eliminated the pain hardly means that your headache was caused initially by a lack of aspirin in your bloodstream. In general, when a behavior therapy procedure eliminates a psychological problem through a particular process, this does not indicate that the same process accounted for its development and maintenance. In fact, the success of the treatment reveals almost nothing about the processes that accounted for the problem.

OVERDEPENDENCE ON LABORATORY EXPERIMENTS

Controlled laboratory experiments are the favored method of research in the behavioral strategy. The advantage of controlled experiments is that conclusions regarding cause-and-effect relationships can be drawn with confidence. The strength of the experimental method notwithstanding, experiments in the field of personality have limitations.

Failure to Study Multivariate Phenomena

To achieve precision, experimental situations often are narrow and simplified. Experiments generally involve the effect of one or two independent variables on several dependent variables. However, real-life experiences tend to be much more complex. Behavior almost always is multiply determined.

Further, the many factors that influence our behaviors generally involve different response modalities: overt behavior, cognitions, emotions, and physiological reactions. The experimental method is not well suited to studying such complex interactions, at least not simultaneously.

Inadequacy of Experimental Analogs

Experiments are limited by the conditions that can be arranged in the laboratory. Many factors that influence human behavior and personality cannot be studied, due to both practical and ethical limitations. For instance, it would not possible to set up a real emergency, such as a fire, to investigate stress. Instead, psychologists are restricted to experimental analogs, such as creating mild stress by having subjects fail at solving puzzles.

The dependent variables that can be researched also are restricted by conducting experiments in the artificial confines of the psychological laboratory. In studying interpersonal aggression, for example, psychologists ethically cannot measure a subject's infliction of actual physical pain on another person. Instead, an experimental analog must be employed, such as having subjects ostensibly administer shock to another subject.

Laboratory situations often restrict the form and content of the subjects' responses, which differ from the free-responding characteristic of natural situations. For instance, angry experimental subjects are provided with only one option for expressing aggression, such as "administering shocks" to another person.

The motivation of subjects in laboratory experiments and of people in actual situations also is different. Often experimental subjects are asked to perform tasks in which they have no personal interest or investment.

Consider a consistent finding of laboratory studies of delay of gratification: Most children and adolescents are able to tolerate long delays while waiting for a promised reward (e.g., Funder & Block, 1989; Mischel et al., 1988; Mischel et al., 1989; Rodriguez et al., 1989). Do these findings mean that most children and adolescents have an easy time delaying gratification in their everyday lives? Probably not. More likely, the experimental conditions in delay-of-gratification studies have not duplicated real-life conditions.

> . . . the ordinary situations in life in which adaptive delay is so important typically involve both immediate and delayed rewards that are vastly larger, more powerfully motivating, and more conflicting than anything that can be ethically administered in a brief, experimental situation. (Funder & Block, 1989, p. 1049)

For example, it is difficult to equate forgoing a small, immediately available snack and forgoing the temptation of powerful and immediately available real-life gratifications such as sex or recreational drugs.

Because the conditions under which delay of gratification occurs in the psychology laboratory and in everyday life are so different, it would be risky to use the findings from the former to predict the latter. For instance, the laboratory findings that distraction and thinking "cool" thoughts help subjects delay longer do not necessarily mean that these strategies will be effective in real-life situations.

Thus, despite the rigor of controlled analog experiments, the results may have low external validity (e.g., LeShan, 1991; Wilson, 1982, 1984). The bottom line is that the experiments may reveal little about the phenomena as they occur in everyday life.

Behavioral psychologists often use situational tests to assess personality. For instance, to learn how people respond to frustration, subjects might be placed in a situation in which they are kept from reaching a goal and their reactions are observed and recorded.

Situational tests make sense "intuitively." Measuring a person's overt behaviors today is an "obvious" way of determining what the person will do tomorrow. Situational tests typically have high **face validity** — they look like they measure what is being tested. This high face validity is, in part, the reason that there has been little systematic evaluation of such personality assessment techniques.

A classic application of situational tests occurred during World War II. American and British armed forces had to rapidly select suitable officer candidates and individuals for military intelligence assignments (Morris, 1949; OSS Assessment Staff, 1948). Extensive situational tests were developed for this purpose. One test, for example, required subjects to assemble a small wooden building. They were "helped" by two other people who, unknown to the subjects, were instructed to impede progress. Observers rated candidates' performance and emotional reactions to the situation.

In general, the reliability of these tests was not high. Predictive validity — the ability to identify candidates who subsequently performed well on assignments — was quite low (Anastasi, 1976). This disappointing performance of situational tests is, no doubt, partially attributable to factors that were independent of the assessment methods. Wartime conditions necessitated the rapid development of mass assessment procedures, which provided less-than-ideal circumstances. Still, some of the failure appears to be due to the general problems of situational tests.

Merely being observed alters subjects' behaviors to an unknown degree. As a consequence of having to "perform," people may behave differently than they normally do. Some people become anxious, which causes them to "flub" their performance, even when they are normally competent in the behavior being assessed. Others rise to the occasion and perform better than they usually do, perhaps because they have an "audience" to perform for.

A related problem occurs with situational tests involving role playing ("make-believe") in simulated situations. The tests may tap somewhat different abilities than those called for in real life. For example, a soldier may be able to pretend to be a strong leader under test conditions but may not be an effective leader in the field when faced with real enemies.

Finally, situational tests may not be "lifelike" enough for adequate predictive validity. A person who can pick up a harmless snake in the laboratory may still show considerable fear when unexpectedly encountering a small snake while walking in the woods. Indeed, assuming that behavior always is situation specific, as behavioral psychologists do, it would be expected that people would act differently in the laboratory and in the woods.

Recently, the reliance on situational tests has decreased in the behavioral strategy (e.g., Jacobson, 1985), although they remain an important source of data (e.g., Foster & Cone, 1986). This is partly in response to the problems with situational test that we have just described. It is also due to the increased emphasis in the strategy on cognitive variables, which cannot be assessed through traditional situational tests. The *articulated thoughts during simulated situations method* is an example of a situational test that is intended to directly assess cognitions (e.g., Davison, Robins, & Johnson, 1983; Haaga, 1990; White, Davison, Haaga, & White, 1992). Subjects are presented with tape recorded descriptions of hypothetical situations. Periodically, the tape is interrupted, and the subjects are asked to report what they are thinking.

LIMITED ACCEPTABILITY OF THE RADICAL-BEHAVIORAL APPROACH

Acceptability is one criterion by which theories are judged (see Chapter 1). To the extent that both psychologists and laypersons have difficulty accepting the radical-behavioral approach, the approach has an added burden to "prove" itself. The acceptability of the radical-behavioral approach is limited by (1) its seemingly simplistic view of personality and (2) its deterministic stance.

Simplistic View of Personality

The radical-behavioral view of personality can be seen as simplistic. Stimulus and response are the two essential variables. People are reluctant to view their own behaviors and those of others in such simple terms. We like to think of ourselves as highly complex organisms.

Moreover, there is nothing ennobling about being governed by the same psychological principles as Skinner's pigeons and rats. We are *Homo sapiens,* thinking beings. Yet, since Watson's (1914) insistence that there is "no dividing line between man and brute," some radical-behaviorists such as Skinner have derived behavioral principles almost exclusively from the study of laboratory animals (e.g., LeShan, 1991).

Deterministic Stance

Free will and self-determination are considered essential human values. However, the radical-behavioral approach is highly deterministic. How we act, feel, and think is determined primarily by environmental factors.

Humans may not have free will, as radical-behavioral psychologists argue. But people seem to have a need to think they do, which appears to be beneficial. For example, research on locus of control indicates that internals (individuals who believe they control their own fate) generally are healthier and more successful than externals (people who believe they are the pawns of external circumstances).

Social learning and cognitive-behavioral approaches present a more balanced and appealing view of personality than radical-behavioral approaches. For instance, Bandura's principle of triadic reciprocal determinism clearly provides people with a role in influencing their behaviors.

There is a way in which the highly deterministic stances of the psychoanalytic and dispositional strategies may be more palatable than the determinism of the radical-behavioral approach. With psychoanalytic and dispositional determinism, the factors affecting our behavior are located within us rather than being external to us. Our unconscious desires and traits are our own, are part of us.

Thus, the seemingly simplistic view of human personality and the emphasis on environmental determinism make the radical-behavioral approach a hard "product" to sell. Indeed, experience has shown that it is one that many people will not buy.

LOSS OF IDENTITY

The behavioral strategy has changed significantly in the past 25 years (cf. Liebert & Spiegler, 1970). The prominent role once played by the radical-behavioral approach has diminished with the growth of social learning and cognitive-behavioral approaches.

The trend toward admitting phenomenological experience (i.e., thoughts and feelings) and disposition-like concepts into the behavioral strategy has been welcomed by many behavioral psychologists. For example, it is consistent with the increasing recognition within the strategy that behavior is not completely situation specific (e.g., Carson, 1989; Haynes & Uchigakiuchi, 1993; Russo, 1990). At the same time, the trend toward integrating nonbehavioral concepts has diluted the essence of the strategy.

This trend is not just restricted to theory. Behavioral personality assessment has been looking less behavioral in recent years. The use of self-report inventories, such as those used to measure perceived self-efficacy, has increased (Guevremont & Spiegler, 1990). Self-report measures are needed to assess cognitions like efficacy expectancies because only the subject has direct access to the cognitions.

Behavior therapy also is becoming less distinct from the change procedures used by other strategies (Goldfried, 1992; Spiegler & Guevremont, 1993). This is consistent with a general trend toward psychotherapy integration (e.g., Mahoney, 1993a; Norcross & Goldfried, 1992; Striker & Gold, 1993). An early example is Beck's cognitive therapy approach to changing cognitions by having people behave in ways that are consistent with new cognitions. This strategy is similar to Kelly's fixed-role therapy. More recently, cognitive therapy has included procedures that are even further removed from the behavioral perspective, such as psychoanalytic techniques (e.g., Safran, 1990; Turner, 1990).

The integration of nonbehavioral and behavioral concepts and procedures is viewed by some as progress (e.g., Craighead, 1990a, 1990b). The process can be said to broaden understanding and application by overcoming some of the limitations of the behavioral strategy (e.g., Craigie & Houde, 1992; Hickey, 1993; Houts & Follette, 1992).

On the one hand, if the trend toward integration continues, the behavioral approach may lose its unique identity and thus cease to be a personality strategy (cf. Spiegler & Guevremont, 1993). On the other hand, the behavioral approach may succeed in turning itself into a unified personality strategy by absorbing the useful essence of each of the other strategies.

SUMMARY   1. The behavioral strategy has no comprehensive theory of personality, although it does include a number of theoretical concepts. The radical-behavioral approach ignores covert behaviors, and all behavioral approaches minimize the role of biological and hereditary factors.

2. Behavior therapy was not derived from theory. Bandura's theory of perceived self-efficacy is an attempt to account for change that occurs in behavior therapy, but its applicability may be limited to certain disorders and treatment procedures.

3. The behavioral strategy commits two logical errors: (1) casting thoughts as causes of behavior and (2) the error of affirming the consequent (in claiming that the success of behavior therapy validates behavioral personality theory).

4. The behavioral strategy relies too heavily on laboratory experiments. Research often is conducted in artificial environments in which subjects' responses are constrained. The motivation of subjects in the laboratory and of people in everyday life is likely to differ. Thus, the results of laboratory experiments may not generalizable to real-life settings.

5. Situational tests used in behavioral assessment are often contrived. Knowing that they are being observed, subjects may not act as they typically do in everyday situations. Thus, situational tests, especially when conducted in a laboratory setting, may not predict behavior in the natural environment very well.

6. People have difficulty accepting the radical-behavioral approach because of (1) its simplistic view of personality and (2) its deterministic stance.

7. Behavioral psychologists are increasingly blending their theory, assessment, and change procedures with concepts from other strategies. The result of this integration may be that the behavioral strategy will either lose its identity or become a unified personality strategy incorporating the essence of each of the other strategies.

Glossary

Note: Italics in the definitions indicate terms that are defined elsewhere in the Glossary.

acceptability The degree to which a theory is palatable to the scientific and general community.

acceptance In *observational learning*, the stage at which the model's behavior is accepted as a guide for one's own actions.

acquisition In *observational learning*, the stage at which the model's behavior is cognitively organized and stored in memory.

actual self The way people actually see themselves.

actual-self sort *Q-sort* in which subjects sort self-referent statements in terms of how they actually see themselves.

actualizing tendency (Maslow and Rogers) Inborn tendency of people to develop all of their capacities in a particular direction that maintains or enhances them.

adoptee/family method A procedure used to assess the degree to which a disposition is heritable by contrasting biological and adopted children brought up in the same home.

aggressive drive (Freud) The motivational force that accounts for destructive aspects of human behavior.

anal character (psychoanalysis) Adult behavior pattern that results from *fixation* at the *anal stage*.

anal erotic phase Portion of the *anal stage* during which pleasure is obtained by retaining feces.

anal eroticism (anal retentive) In the *anal stage*, pleasure from retaining feces; in later life, pleasure from being orderly and stingy.

anal expulsive character Individual fixated at the *anal sadistic phase*.

anal retentive character Individual fixated at the *anal erotic phase*.

anal sadism (anal expulsive) In the *anal stage*, pleasure from expelling feces; in later life, pleasure from being messy and disorderly.

anal sadistic phase Portion of the *anal stage* during which pleasure is obtained from expelling feces.

anal stage Freud's second *psychosexual stage* of development (age two to three) when the *libido* is centered in the anal area.

antecedents In *operant conditioning*, the stimuli present before the target behavior occurs (including situational, temporal, and interpersonal cues).

anxiety Generally, the emotional experience of threat or danger; the precise definition varies with the personality theory.

anxiety hierarchy List of situations that make a person anxious, ordered in terms of the amount of *anxiety* engendered; used in *systematic desensitization*.

archetypal dreams (Jung) Unusual dreams with mythical symbolism.

archetype (Jung) Predisposition to form a common idea that may direct behavior; part of the *collective unconscious*.

attributive projection (psychoanalysis) Projecting a characteristic that one is aware of (see *projection*).

aversion therapy Classical conditioning therapy that creates a negative emotional reaction to a maladaptive behavior.

backup reinforcers Tangible rewards, such as food, gum, or cigarettes that clients get by trading tokens they have earned for adaptive behaviors.

basic behavioral repertoires In *paradigmatic behaviorism*, complex sets of learned skills: language-cognitive, emotional-motivational, and sensory-motor.

behavior potential (Rotter) The likelihood that a given behavior will occur in a given situation.

behavior modification *Behavior therapy* that uses the principles of *operant conditioning*.

477

behavior rehearsal   Therapy procedure in which the client practices adaptive behaviors.

behavioral avoidance test   A series of tasks requiring increasingly more threatening interactions with a feared object or situation (e.g., from looking at a snake in a container to letting it crawl on one's lap).

behavior therapy   Any psychotherapy technique or combination of techniques derived from the behavioral approach.

bell-and-pad method   *Urine alarm method* of treating enuresis in which a child sleeps on a special pad that sounds an alarm to awaken the child when the pad becomes wet from urine.

birth trauma (Rank)   The initial biological separation of child and mother, which is the prototype for all separation, loss, and *anxiety* in later life.

cardinal disposition (Allport)   A trait that dominates a person's entire existence; very few people have cardinal dispositions.

caring-days technique   Cognitive-behavioral marital therapy technique used to increase the number of positive behavior exchanges a couple has.

case study   Research method involving detailed qualitative descriptions of the behavior of a single individual.

castration anxiety (Freud)   Male's fear of loss of his penis, usually considered the probable retaliation for unacceptable sexual desires (such as incest with mother). It is the impetus for resolving the *Oedipus complex.*

cathect (psychoanalysis)   To invest *psychic energy* in the mental representation of a person, behavior, or idea.

cathexis   The investment of *psychic energy* in the mental image of an activity or person. *Cathect* is the verb form.

central disposition (Allport)   A trait that manifests itself in many aspects of personality; most individuals have between 3 and 10 central dispositions.

chance control   Belief that personal outcomes are due to chance factors.

character type (psychoanalysis)   Adult personality characteristics resulting from *fixation* at a childhood *psychosexual stage.*

clarification of feelings (Rogers)   *Client-centered therapy* technique in which the therapist reflects the emotions that the client is expressing (cf. *restatement of content*).

classical projection (psychoanalysis)   Projecting a characteristic that one is unaware of (see *projection*).

classical conditioning   Learning process in which a stimulus comes to elicit a response because the stimulus is associated with another stimulus that already elicits the response.

client-centered therapy (Rogers)   Therapy in which the client assumes responsibility for working out the solutions to problems, and the therapist primarily restates the content of what the client has said and clarifies the client's feelings.

cognitive-behavior therapies   Therapy procedures that modify maladaptive cognitions.

cognitive behavior therapy   *Behavior therapy* that focuses on changing people's thoughts and perceptions in order to change their behavior.

cognitive prototypes (Mischel)   The "best examples" of a trait concept, from which people draw inferences about the degree to which a trait is generally present in themselves or another person.

cognitive restructuring   In *cognitive behavior therapy*, teaching clients to think about themselves in positive and adaptive ways, rather than in negative and maladaptive ways.

cognitive therapy (Beck)   Techniques for helping depressed patients think about themselves in more positive ways.

collective unconscious (Jung)   Level of awareness or division of the mind that is the product of the combined experiences of humans through their evolution.

common traits (Allport)   *Dispositions* that allow direct trait comparisons across people.

competence (White)   A person's fitness or ability to carry out those transactions with the environment that will result in maintaining, growing, and flourishing as an individual.

comprehensiveness   The breadth of the phenomena that a theory can encompass.

condensation   The *dream work* process in which separate thoughts are combined or compressed.

conditional dispositional construct (Mischel)   A rule that provides a meaningful "if-then" link between clusters of situations and clusters of behaviors.

conditional positive regard (Rogers)   Esteem (*positive regard*) from others based on how the person behaves (cf. *unconditional positive regard*).

conditioned response (CR)   A response acquired through pairing an initially neutral stimulus with a stimulus that already elicits the response in question.

conditioned stimulus (CS)   An initially neutral stimulus that acquires the ability to elicit a response after it has been paired with an *unconditioned stimulus.*

conditions of worth (Rogers)   Differential values that other people place on particular behaviors. Counterforce to the *self-actualization tendency.*

confrontation   In *object relations* therapy, the third stage of therapy, during which time the therapist confronts the patient's pathology directly.

congruent externals Persons whose life experiences are consistent with their belief that most outcomes are out of their hands (cf. *defensive externals*).

conscience (Freud) The sphere of the *superego* concerned with morally right behavior.

conscious (Freud) Part of the mind containing all that human beings are immediately aware of.

consequences In *operant conditioning*, the events or outcomes that occur as a result of target behaviors being performed.

consistency paradox (Mischel) The fact that people tend to see others' behavior as quite consistent across situations when, in fact, there is a good deal of cross-situational inconsistency.

construct (Kelly) A concept used to interpret events.

construct system (Kelly) The hierarchical order of an individual's *constructs*.

constructive alternativism (Kelly) Philosophical position that any event can be viewed in a variety of ways.

construe (Kelly) To place an interpretation on an event.

content validity The adequacy with which a test samples the domain it is intended to measure.

continuous reinforcement schedule A *schedule of reinforcement* in which the individual is reinforced every time the behavior to be strengthened is emitted.

control In psychological research, systematically varying, randomizing, or holding constant the conditions under which observations are made.

control group In an *experiment*, the group that does not receive the treatment being examined but is like the treated group in every other respect (cf. *experimental group*).

convergent validity The degree to which measures of presumably the same disposition in different forms (e.g., paper-and-pencil versus projective measures) correlate or agree with one another.

coping model Model who is initially somewhat fearful and incompetent, and then gradually overcomes the fear and becomes more competent.

core constructs (Kelly) Constructs that define us and form the basis of our identity.

core role (Kelly) A role a person plays that is central to his or her life.

correlation The co- or joint relationship between variables. Variables that are correlated "go together."

correlation coefficient A statistical index of the strength of a relationship, most often expressed as the Pearson product-moment correlation (r).

correlation matrix The array of correlations between each variable and every other variable in a set of variables of interest.

correlational study Research method that examines quantitative relationships between two or more variables for a group of people observed under the same conditions.

counterimitation Behaving in a way opposite to the way a model has behaved.

countertransference Feelings a psychoanalyst has for a patient that are inappropriate *displacements* from the analyst's past.

covert behavior Behavior that occurs inside the person and thus is not directly observable by others (cf. *overt behavior*).

cross-situational consistency The degree to which a person behaves in a consistent fashion from one situation to another.

day residues Elements of actual external events in waking life that appear in dreams.

debriefing The systematic explanation of the purpose of research, given to a subject after his or her participation is completed.

defense mechanisms *Unconscious* ego processes for reducing *anxiety*; primarily a psychoanalytic term.

defensive externals Persons who claim that most outcomes are out of their hands only when it suits them to make this claim (cf. *congruent externals*).

defensive identification A defensive process that involves becoming like a threatening person; follows the *unconscious* "reasoning": "If I cannot beat the person, I'll join the person."

defensive projection The *defense mechanism* whereby the individual unconsciously attributes his/her own unacceptable impulses or wishes to someone or something else.

deficit motivation (Maslow) Energizing and directing behavior to satisfy an unmet *need* (cf. *growth motivation*).

definition (Kelly) Choosing the pole of a *construct* that previously has been more successful at predicting events (cf. *extension*).

delay of gratification The ability to forego a small immediate reward for a large reward that requires waiting.

denial Defensive process in which the person does not acknowledge a threatening experience.

dependent variable In an *experiment*, the subject's behavior that is measured; it is expected to be influenced by (depend on) the *independent variable*.

differentiation (Mahler) Process whereby the child breaks away from the mother.

direct counterimitation Avoiding the specific behavior that one has seen a model perform.

direct imitation Copying the specific behavior that one has seen a model perform.

directionality problem In correlational research, the fact that a *correlation* does not, by itself, indicate which variable is causing the other (cf. *third-variable problem*).

discriminant validity The degree to which measures of presumably different *dispositions* assessed by the same form of assessment diverge (i.e., are not highly correlated).

discriminative stimulus A stimulus that sets the occasion for a response.

displacement As a *defense mechanism*, shifting an impulse from a threatening or unacceptable event or person to something less threatening or unacceptable. In a *dream*, shifting the emphasis from an important element to a seemingly trivial element.

disposition A tendency to behave in a particular way over time and across situations (e.g., a trait).

dream A mental experience during sleep that involves mainly vivid visual images.

dream work (Freud) Process of transforming *latent content* into *manifest content*.

drive (psychoanalysis) An inborn, intrapsychic force that, when operative, produces a state of excitation or tension.

dual theory of drives (Freud) Theory that human motivation is based on the operation of two independent drives—the sexual drive and the *aggressive drive*.

efficacy expectations (Bandura) The belief that one can perform the behaviors necessary to achieve a desired outcome.

ego (Freud) The reality-oriented aspect of personality; also mediates the demands of the other aspects of personality (*id* and *superego*).

ego ideal (Freud) The sphere of the *superego* concerned with urging the individual toward idealistic and perfectionistic goals.

ego psychologists Those who practice or subscribe to *ego psychology*.

ego psychology *Post-Freudian psychoanalysis* emphasizing *ego* and conscious aspects of personality.

Electra complex The female *Oedipus complex*.

electroencephalograph Device to measure brain waves.

electroencephalogram Tracings of brain waves made by an *electroencephalograph*.

emergent pole (Kelly) Pole of a *construct* used to directly interpret an event by noting its similarity to other events (cf. *implicit pole*).

emotions (Kelly) Feelings that result from an awareness of change or a need for change in one's *construct system*.

empathy Experiencing how another person is feeling from the other person's viewpoint.

empirical Relating to or obtained by objective methods so that observations and results can be independently confirmed.

empirical keying A method of test construction in which items are selected on the basis of their predictive power rather than their content.

empirical research Systematic attempts to gather evidence through observations and procedures that can be repeated and verified by others.

empirical validity The degree to which a theory is supported by evidence derived from observations.

engagement In *object relations* therapy, the first stage of therapy, during which time the therapist must become a significant person for the patient.

erogenous zone Area of the body especially sensitive to erotic stimulation (e.g., mouth, anus, genitals).

esteem from others (Maslow) Desire for recognition and appreciation from other people and the accompanying feelings of worthwhileness and competence (cf. *self-esteem*).

expectancy (Rotter) The subjective probability that a given behavior will result in a given reinforcer.

experience (Kelly) Interpreting an event in new ways (not just repeated exposure to the event).

experiment (experimental method) Research method that examines the quantitative cause-and-effect relationship between one or more *independent variables* and one or more *dependent variables*.

experimental group In an *experiment*, subjects who are exposed to the *independent variable* (cf. *control group*).

experimental hypothesis A prediction, which is operationally defined, about the effect of the *independent variable* on the *dependent variable*.

explicit pole (Kelly) Pole of a *construct* used to directly interpret an event (cf. *implicit pole*).

exploitative character (Fromm) Adult behavior pattern that develops from being raised in an environment that fostered the attitude of having to take in order to receive (cf. *receptive character*).

exposure Observation of modeling cues—the first stage in *observational learning*.

extension (Kelly) Choosing the pole of a *construct* that is more likely to expand the construct's ability to view new events (cf. *definition*).

extensiveness The breadth of the phenomena that a theory can deal with.

external locus of control (Rotter) The belief that the reinforcements one gets in life are due to chance factors or factors that are out of one's control.

extinction Cessation of responding when a learned response is no longer reinforced; also, cessation of *reinforcement* for a previously reinforced response.

extravert A person who tends to be outgoing with people (cf. *introvert*).

face validity The superficial appearance of actually testing for a personality characteristic (cf. *content validity*).

factor analysis A family of mathematical procedures for sorting personality measures and other variables into groupings such as factors or clusters.

factor loading In *factor analysis*, the *correlation* of a particular measure with a particular factor.

fading In operant *behavior therapy*, the gradual removal of prompts so that the person finally performs the response without cues.

Fear of Power (Winter) That portion of the power motive that seeks to avoid giving others *power* over oneself (cf. *hope of power*).

fixation Leaving a portion of *libido* permanently invested in an early *psychosexual stage*. The more difficult it is for a person to resolve the conflict, the more *libido* will remain fixated at the stage.

fixed-interval schedule A *schedule of reinforcement* in which the individual is reinforced for the first response made after a set time has elapsed.

fixed-ratio schedule A *schedule of reinforcement* in which the individual is reinforced after a set number of responses has occurred.

fixed role (Kelly) A role of a fictitious person whose behavior is consistent with a *construct system* that would be beneficial for a client to adopt (in *fixed-role therapy*).

fixed-role sketch (Kelly) A detailed description of a *fixed role*.

fixed-role therapy (Kelly) Therapy in which a client temporarily adopts the behavior of someone whose behavior is consistent with *constructs* that would be helpful for the client to adopt.

focus of convenience (Kelly) The events that a particular *construct* is best able to predict.

free association In psychoanalytic psychotherapy, the patient saying whatever comes to mind without any censoring.

Freudian Theories and practices that follow Freud's theory and practices (cf. *post-Freudian*).

Freudian slips Generic, lay term for mistakes that Freud believed had definite *unconscious* causes and meanings.

fully functioning person (Rogers) Person who is guided by his or her *organismic valuing processes*, is free of *threat*, and, in short, epitomizes psychological health.

generalized expectancies (Rotter) Expectations that apply across a range of situations.

generativity (Erikson) Involvement in guiding the next generation.

genital stage Freud's fourth and final *psychosexual stage* of development (puberty through adulthood) in which *libido* is centered in the genital region.

graded task assignments In *cognitive therapy*, a shaping exercise in which clients engage in a series of brief, simple behaviors that gradually become lengthier and more complex.

growth motivation (Maslow) Energizing and directing behavior by following one's *self-actualization tendency*.

guilt (Kelly) Awareness of not adequately playing an important role in one's life.

here-and-now Immediate experience—what is going on for the person at the moment.

heuristic realism (Allport) The belief that people really have traits.

holistic Approach in which all aspects of personality are related and must be viewed together as a whole; important position of the phenomenological strategy.

Hope of Power (Winter) That portion of the power motive that seeks to gain *power* (cf. *Fear of Power*).

hypotheses Plural of *hypothesis*.

hypothesis Any specific prediction derived from a theory.

id (Freud) Biological, instinctual, pleasure-oriented aspect of personality (cf. *ego*, *superego*).

ideal self (Rogers) How people would like to see themselves.

ideal-self sort *Q-sort* in which subjects sort self-referent statements in terms of how they would like to see themselves.

identification (psychoanalysis) Taking on other people's characteristics in order to reduce *anxiety*, envy, or other negative emotions.

identity As used by Erikson, the confidence that others see a person as the person sees himself or herself.

idiographic Pertaining only to a specific individual (cf. *nomothetic*).

I-E Scale (Rotter) A paper-and-pencil measure of the degree to which an individual has an *internal* or *external locus of control* (as a *generalized expectancy*).

imitation Making one's own behavior similar in some way to that of a model.

implicit motives (McClelland) Primitive, unconscious motives, said to be more like animal drives than like conscious goals.

implicit pole (Kelly) Pole of a *construct* used to indirectly interpret an event by acting as a contrast (cf. *explicit pole*).

implicit theory of personality A set of informal ideas that an individual has about the nature of personality.

incorporation (psychoanalysis) The "taking in" of others' values in a manner analogous to the way one takes in food.

independent variable In an *experiment*, the variable that is systematically varied by the experimenter and is expected to influence the *dependent variable*.

indirect counterimitation Avoiding the general type or class of behavior that one has seen a model perform.

indirect imitation Performing the general type or class of behavior that one has seen a model perform.

individual traits (Allport) Those important characteristics of the individual that do not lend themselves to comparison across persons.

individuality and emotional object constancy In Mahler's *object relations* theory, the last subphase of development in which the person achieves a defined lifelong individuality and a sense of permanence regarding the people in one's life.

individuation (Mahler) The earliest stage of identity, in which the individual discovers "that I am." Only later is there recognition of "who I am."

inferiority complex (Adler) Exaggerated, neurotic reaction to one's weaknesses.

insight (psychoanalysis) Emotional experiencing and accepting of parts of one's *unconscious*; necessary for cure in *psychoanalysis* (therapy).

instinctoid needs (Maslow) Biologically based human *needs*.

instrumental conditioning A term used interchangeably with *operant conditioning*.

intermittent (partial) schedule of reinforcement A pattern of *reinforcement* in which only some instances of the desired response are reinforced.

internal consistency The degree to which the propositions and assumptions of a theory are consistent and fit together into a coherent, larger explanation.

internal frame of reference A person's subjective view of the world.

internal locus of control (Rotter) The belief that the *reinforcements* one gets in life are due to one's own effort and ability.

internal reliability The degree to which the items on a test measure the same thing.

interpersonal trust (Rotter) A *generalized expectancy* that the words or promises of others can be relied on.

interpretation (psychoanalysis) Psychoanalyst pointing out *unconscious* meanings to a patient.

interrater reliability Agreement among raters or judges.

interval schedule of reinforcement A pattern of *reinforcement* in which a reinforcer is received if the desired response occurs (at least once) after a specified length of time has elapsed since the last *reinforcement*.

intimacy (Erikson) The capacity to commit to a relationship without losing one's own identity.

intrapsychic conflict (psychoanalysis) Discord within the personality occurring when the aims of *id*, *ego*, and *superego* are at odds.

intrapsychic events Processes occurring in the mind (usually in the *unconscious*), such as thoughts, images, and wishes.

introvert A person who tends to be shy and anxious in social situations (cf. *extravert*).

in vivo exposure Another term for *in vivo desensitization*.

in vivo desensitization The process of exposing a client to the actual stimuli in an *anxiety hierarchy*, instead of imagining them.

L-data (Cattell) Information that can be gathered from the life records of the individual.

latency In Freud's developmental sequence, the period between the *phallic* and *genital stages*.

latent content Underlying meaning of a dream (cf. *manifest content*).

libido (Freud) *Psychic energy* of the sexual drive.

line of perfect correlation In the case of a perfect *correlation*, the hypothetical line on a graph on which all points would fall.

live modeling The observation of the behavior of models "in the flesh"—that is, models who are physically present.

locus of control (Rotter) The generalized way that the person perceives the source of his or her outcomes (see *external* and *internal locus of control*).

maintaining conditions In *behavior therapy*, the factors that are currently (maintaining) the *target behavior*.

manifest content What a person remembers and reports of a dream (cf. *latent content*).

mastery model A model who is fearless and competent from the beginning.

matching theory Theory predicting that the frequency of engaging in each of a number of alternative behaviors will be directly proportional to the amount of *reinforcement* received for each.

metatraits (Baumeister) The trait of having or not having a particular trait.

methodological behaviorism The approach that emphasizes objectivity, direct observation of phenomena, precise definitions, and controlled experimentation (cf. *radical behaviorism*).

midlife crisis (Jung) The crisis people in their late 30s through the middle 40s experience when they come to realize that many of their goals have been set by others.

modeling cues Specific components of another's (the model's) behavior that may bring about changes in the behavior of the observer.

mood-congruent bias The tendency to process information about past experiences selectively, in a way that is congruent with present mood.

moral anxiety (Freud) Experience of guilt or shame resulting from an *id-superego* conflict (cf. *neurotic anxiety, objective anxiety*).

motivational types Patterns of behavior associated with clusters of motives instead of with a single motive.

motive A desire to satisfy a particular *need* (cf. *need*).

motive to avoid success (Horner) *Anxiety* about the negative consequences of success.

multivariate approaches Ways of studying personality that examine many variables simultaneously.

need (Murray) A tendency to seek or produce particular effects or temporary end states.

negative correlation A relationship between two variables in which high scores on one variable occur with low scores on the other and vice versa (cf. *positive correlation*).

negative reinforcement Removal of an aversive stimulus contingent on the performance of a desired response, which results in an increase in the response (cf. *positive reinforcement*).

neuroses A generic term for mental disorders that generally affect people in a limited sphere of their lives; symptoms include *anxiety*, depression, and physical complaints.

neurotic anxiety (Freud) Unrealistic fear or vague apprehension resulting from an *id-ego* conflict (cf. *moral anxiety, objective anxiety*).

nomothetic Pertaining to people in general (cf. *idiographic*).

noncore role (Kelly) A role a person plays that is peripheral or unimportant in his or her life (cf. *core role*).

nonrapid eye movement See *NREM*.

nonverbal constructs (Kelly) *Constructs* for which people do not have verbal labels but which are potentially verbalizable.

normal autism In Mahler's *object relations* theory, the first phase of development in which the infant is completely within itself, oblivious to an external world.

normal distribution The pattern of scores formed when a large sample, plotted as a graph, produces a bell-shaped curve.

normal symbiosis In Mahler's *object relations* theory, the second phase of development in which the infant is fused with the mother and does not distinguish between self and nonself.

NREM (nonrapid eye movement) period Period of Stage 1 sleep not associated with dreaming (cf. *REM period*).

object Psychoanalytic term for person (see *object relations*).

object relations Psychoanalytic term for interpersonal relations.

object-relations theorists Those who emphasize interpersonal issues and the concept of self, especially as they develop during the first two years of life.

object representations In *object relations* theories, the cognitive representations one has of oneself and others.

objective anxiety (Freud) Fear from a realistic, external threat (cf. *moral anxiety, neurotic anxiety*).

objective reality An event about which a number of observers agree.

observational learning The process by which the behavior of one person is changed through observing the behavior of another (rather than through direct experience, as in *classical* and *operant conditioning*).

Oedipus complex (Freud) The conflict in the *phallic stage* involving the child's *unconscious* wish to have sexual relations with the opposite-sexed parent and at the same time to do away with the same-sexed parent.

operant conditioning Learning process in which a behavior is strengthened or weakened because of its consequences.

oral character (psychoanalysis) Adult behavior pattern that results from *fixation* at the *oral stage*.

oral eroticism Pleasure from sucking and taking things in through the mouth during the early part of the *oral stage*.

oral sadism Pleasure from biting and chewing in the later part of the *oral stage*; begins with the eruption of teeth.

oral stage Freud's first *psychosexual stage* of development (first year of life) in which *libido* is centered in the mouth area.

organismic valuing process (Rogers) Process by which the *self-actualization tendency* evaluates experiences as maintaining or enhancing the person.

overcorrection *Behavior therapy* for reducing undesirable behaviors in which the client first corrects the negative effects of a maladaptive behavior and then intensively practices an alternative, adaptive behavior.

overt behavior Behavior that can be observed directly by others (cf. *covert behavior*).

paradigmatic behaviorism Broad model of psychology in the tradition of methodological behaviorism developed by Staats.

paradoxical sleep Phase of Stage 1 sleep in which the person is both alert and relaxed; associated with dreaming; same as *REM period*.

parsimonious The characteristic of being able to explain a phenomenon with the fewest possible assumptions or principles.

partial schedule of reinforcement Another term for *intermittent schedule of reinforcement*.

participant modeling The combination of a therapist's *live modeling* and *prompting* with closely supervised practice by the client.

peak experience (Maslow) Intensely fulfilling and meaningful experience.

penis envy (Freud) Woman's desiring to be like a man; part of the *Electra complex*.

perceptual defense *Unconscious* mechanism that keeps a person from experiencing threatening ideas.

perceptual distortion (Rogers) Changing how one perceives an experience to make it consistent with one's *self-concept*.

permeability (Kelly) Degree to which a *construct* is able to interpret new experiences.

person-centered approach (Rogers) Extension of the principles of *client-centered therapy* to other endeavors, such as education and international relations.

person variables (Mischel) The relatively enduring cognitive and behavioral attributes of an individual.

personal unconscious (Jung) Part of the mind containing images that one is not immediately aware of, but that one can easily become aware of; parallel concept to Freud's *preconscious*.

personality coefficient (Mischel) Term coined to describe the small *correlation* (between .20 and .30) that is the most that is usually found when any personality dimension inferred from a questionnaire is related to another type of response.

personality psychology The branch of psychology concerned with developing theories and conducting empirical research on the functioning of the individual as a totality.

personality traits Dispositions as they appear in older children, adolescents, and adults that probably have a learned component (cf. *temperament traits*).

phallic character type (psychoanalysis) Adult behavior pattern that results from *fixation* at the *phallic stage*.

phallic stage Freud's third *psychosexual stage* of development (ages four to five) where *libido* is centered in the genital area; *Oedipus complex* occurs in this stage.

phenomenological knowledge (Rogers) Understanding another person from that person's perspective.

phobia Strong, irrational fear of a particular situation or object.

pleasure principle (Freud) Immediate discharge of intrapsychic tension; the principle by which the *id* operates (cf. *reality principle*).

population In research, the complete set of people who are being investigated from which a smaller set (a *sample*) is selected for the research study.

positive correlation A relationship between two variables in which high scores on one variable occur with high scores on the other, and low scores on one occur with low scores on the other (cf. *negative correlation*).

positive regard (Rogers) Esteem from others in the form of acceptance, respect, sympathy, warmth, or love.

positive regard from others (Rogers) *Positive regard* that comes exclusively from other people (i.e., not oneself).

positive reinforcement Presentation of a stimulus contingent on the performance of a desired response, which results in an increase in the response (cf. *negative reinforcement*).

positive self-regard (Rogers) *Positive regard* that has been internalized and thus comes directly from the person and not from others.

post-Freudian Psychoanalytic theories and practices that are somewhat based on Freud's but deviate from them in varying degrees (cf. *Freudian*).

power (Winter) A person's ability or capacity to produce intended effects on the behavior or emotions of someone else.

powerful others control Belief that personal outcomes are caused by other people.

practicing (Mahler) The subphase going between 9 and 18 months of age, when infants explore their environments by crawling, climbing, and walking.

preconscious (Freud) Part of the mind that contains information that one is not immediately aware of but that one can easily become aware of.

prediction The ability to accurately anticipate a person's future behavior.

predictive efficiency (Kelly) How well a *construct* anticipates events; the measure of the *validity* of a *construct*.

Premack principle Principle stating that a lower-frequency behavior will increase if it is made contingent on a higher-frequency behavior.

press (Murray) An environmental circumstance that influences behavior.

preverbal constructs (Kelly) *Constructs* that consist of physiological, kinesthetic, and emotional patterns rather than verbal labels.

primary anxiety (Freud) Intense, negative experience in infants resulting from a *need* not being immediately satisfied.

primary drives (Miller and Dollard) Motivation coming from the biological *needs* of the individual.

primary needs (Murray) *Needs* of biological origin, representing the physiological requirements of the organism.

primary process (Freud) *Id* process that reduces intrapsychic tension by producing a mental image of an object that will satisfy the *need* (cf. *secondary process*).

projection *Defense mechanism* in which a person attributes threatening impulses to another person (e.g., "I don't want to kill you; you want to kill me").

projective hypothesis Assumption that when people are forced to impose meaning on an ambiguous stimulus, the response will reflect significant parts of their personalities; basis for *projective techniques*.

projective identification In *object relations* theories, the three-stage process whereby a person actually causes another to play out the role of his or her own "bad self."

projective techniques Indirect personality assessment procedures that present subjects with ambiguous stimuli (e.g., an inkblot) on which they must impose meaning.

prompting Reminding or instructing a person to perform a behavior so that it can be reinforced.

psychic energy (Freud) Unitary energy source for all psychological functions.

psychoanalysis Three common meanings: theory of personality, approach to research, and procedures for changing personality. All three were originally developed by Freud and subsequently extended and modified by other psychoanalysts.

psychological behaviorism Another term for *paradigmatic behaviorism*.

psychological situation (Rotter) The existing circumstances from each individual's perspective.

psychosexual (Freud) Description of the stages of personality development; referring to the belief that each stage is a new manifestation of the sexual drive.

psychosexual stages (Freud) Periods in one's life representing the development of the *libido* (sexual drive); specifically, the *oral, anal, phallic*, and *genital stages*.

psychosocial stages Periods proposed by *post-Freudians* (e.g., Erikson, Sullivan) that represent the development of social behaviors (cf. *psychosexual stages*).

psychoticism (Eysenck) The dimension of personality that includes a disposition toward psychosis and psychopathy.

punishment A consequence that reduces the likelihood of future occurrence of the behavior that preceded it; usually an aversive consequence.

Q-data (Cattell) Information about a person gathered from questionnaires and interviews.

Q-sort Assessment procedure in which people make comparative judgments of statements about themselves.

radical behaviorism The position that psychology should be concerned only with objective environmental events (stimuli) and *overt behaviors* (responses) (cf. *methodological behaviorism*).

range of convenience (Kelly) Events that a *construct* is able to predict.

rapid eye movement See *REM*.

rapprochement (Mahler) A balance between dependence and independence from one's mother that is necessary for normal development.

ratings A method of personality assessment in which observational data are gathered indirectly through the reports of individuals who know the person well.

ratio schedule of reinforcement A pattern of *reinforcement* in which the reinforcer is received after a certain number of responses have been made.

rational-emotive therapy (RET) Ellis's version of *cognitive restructuring* therapy.

rationalization *Defense mechanism* in which a person unconsciously finds a sensible reason or "excuse" for performing or thinking about an unacceptable behavior.

reaction formation *Defense mechanism* involving overemphasis on acting or thinking in ways opposite to a threatening impulse.

reactivity The tendency for the frequency of a response to change merely because it is being observed and recorded.

reality principle (Freud) Process of postponing tension reduction until an appropriate situation or object in the external world is found; the principle by which *ego* operates (cf. *pleasure principle*).

receptive character (Fromm) Adult behavior pattern that develops from being raised in an environment that fostered the attitude of expecting to receive (cf. *exploitative character*).

regression (psychoanalysis) *Defense mechanism* in which the person repeats a behavior that led to satisfaction in an early stage of development.

reinforcement The process that occurs whenever an event that follows a behavior (i.e., a consequence) increases the likelihood that the behavior will be repeated.

reinforcement value (Rotter) A person's subjective preference for a given reinforcer relative to other possible reinforcers in a given situation.

reinforcers Consequences of a behavior that increase its frequency.

reintegration (Rogers) A reverse of the process of defense in which consistency between experience and *self-concept* is restored.

relational propositions The formal statements that describe the relationship among theoretical constructs.

reliability Measure of the "repeatability" or stability of a test or measure; prerequisite for *validity*.

REM (rapid eye movement) period Phase of Stage 1 sleep associated with dreaming; also called *paradoxical sleep*.

repression The most basic *defense mechanism*, it involves completely putting out of consciousness a threatening experience.

resistance Any behavior that interferes with the progress of psychotherapy.

response acquiescence The tendency to agree with personality test items, regardless of their content.

response cost Removal of a valued item or privilege, contingent on the performance of an unwanted behavior.

response deviation The tendency to answer personality test items in an uncommon direction.

response sets Characteristic and consistent ways of responding to personality test items, regardless of what they say, taken to reflect distortion (cf. *response styles*).

response styles Characteristic and consistent ways of responding to personality test items, regardless of what they say, taken to reflect an underlying disposition (cf. *response sets*).

restatement of content (Rogers) *Client-centered therapy* technique in which the therapist rephrases what the client says (cf. *clarification of feelings*).

retest reliability Degree to which the same test (or an equivalent form) administered more than once yields the same basic results.

role construct (Kelly) A *construct* that one uses to understand another person's views.

Role Construct Repertory Test (Rep Test) Assessment device developed by Kelly for finding the *constructs* a person uses to construe other people.

Rorschach inkblots The most popular *projective technique*; subjects describe what they see in ambiguous, nearly symmetrical figures.

sample Relatively small group of people that is drawn from a much larger group (*population*) to study phenomena occurring in the *population*.

scatter diagram A graphic representation of the *correlation* between two variables; the stronger the relationship, the more the points look like a straight line.

schedule of reinforcement The rate or time interval at which desired responses are reinforced.

secondary disposition (Allport) A trait that manifests itself in only a few areas of personality.

secondary drives (Miller and Dollard) Motivation that has developed through association with *primary drives*.

secondary needs (Murray) *Needs* that have been learned.

secondary process (Freud) *Ego* process that reduces intrapsychic tension by problem solving and dealing directly with external reality (cf. *primary process*).

self-actualization tendency (Maslow, Rogers) Unique, inborn inclination to behave in ways that result in maintaining and enhancing the person; leads people to become all that they can be.

self-concept (self) How one views oneself, including how one actually views oneself (real self) and one's *ideal self*.

self-efficacy (Bandura) People's convictions that they can successfully execute the behavior required to produce a desired outcome in a particular situation.

self-esteem (Maslow) Desire for doing well by oneself and the accompanying feelings of worthwhileness and competence (cf. *esteem from others*).

self-instructional training (Meichenbaum) A *cognitive-behavior therapy* procedure that teaches clients *cognitive restructuring* through modeling and cognitive behavior rehearsal.

self-modeling Form of *symbolic modeling* in which clients serve as their own models.

self-report personality inventory A questionnaire containing a large number of questions about people, to which respondents answer true or false for themselves.

self-statements The soundless, mental speech that arises at the instant that people think, plan, or solve problems in their minds.

self-talk Another term for *self-statements*.

separation (Mahler) The process whereby the child achieves intrapsychic distinctiveness from the mother.

separation-individuation phase In Mahler's *object relations* theory, the third phase of development in which the person achieves independence from the mother and has a clear sense of self and nonself.

shaping Reinforcing progressively closer approximations to the desired behavior.

signal anxiety (Freud) Discomfort that warns the *ego* to institute *defense mechanism*s to prevent the intense experience of *primary anxiety*.

single-subject reversal Research design that compares a subject's behavior in periods in which a treatment is presented with periods in which it is withdrawn (reversed).

sociability A term used by some writers to refer to the Introversion/Extraversion continuum.

social desirability The tendency to answer personality test items in the most socially accepted direction, irrespective of whether such answers are correct for the respondent.

somatyping (Sheldon) A procedure for assessing physique by assigning scores on three dimensions of physical characteristics (endomorphy, mesomorphy, and ectomorphy).

source trait (Cattell) The underlying *dispositions* that determine behavior, often identified by *factor analysis*.

specific expectancy (Rotter) A person's subjective estimate of the chances of obtaining a particular outcome by performing a particular behavior.

splitting In *object relations* theories, the mental separation of objects into their "good" and "bad" aspects.

statistical significance An estimate of the likelihood that a particular research finding (e.g., a difference between two groups or a *correlation* between two variables) occurred by chance; by convention, a result must have a chance likelihood of less than 5 in 100 to be called statistically significant.

statistical test Mathematical test used to determine *statistical significance*.

stimulus control Behavior that occurs only when certain environmental circumstances (*discriminative stimuli*) are present.

strategy Any of the four broad approaches (psychoanalytic, dispositional, phenomenological, or behavioral) to the study of personality.

stress inoculation training (Meichenbaum) A *cognitive behavior therapy* that prepares clients to deal with stress-inducing events by teaching them self-control coping skills and then having them rehearse these skills while gradually being exposed to stressors.

striving for superiority (Adler) The fundamental human motive, it arises as the inevitable response to initial feelings of inferiority.

subjective reality Each individual's personal experience of an event.

sublimation *Defense mechanism* in which unacceptable desires are unconsciously channeled into socially acceptable outlets.

superego (Freud) Aspect of the personality incorporating ideals and the moral standards of one's parents and culture (cf. *ego*, *id*).

suppression *Conscious* forgetting of threatening thoughts; not a Freudian *defense mechanism* because it operates consciously.

surface traits (Cattell) Clusters of *overt behavior* that seem to go together, but do not necessarily have a common cause (cf. *source traits*).

symbolic modeling The indirect observation of the behavior of models, such as in movies, by reading, or through oral descriptions of another person's behaviors.

symbolization The process through which threatening objects or ideas are represented by nonthreatening ones.

systematic desensitization (Wolpe) A *behavior therapy* technique based on counterconditioning; the client is gradually exposed to increasingly anxiety-evoking stimuli while making a response that is essentially incompatible with *anxiety* (e.g., relaxation).

T-data (Cattell) Information gained from putting subjects in objective test situations without telling them which aspects of their behavior are being observed or evaluated.

target behaviors In *behavior therapy*, the specific behaviors that the client and therapist are trying to encourage, eliminate, or modify.

temperament traits *Dispositions* that are present at birth, stable across time, and pervasive in their influence (cf. *personality traits*).

temporal consistency (Mischel) Behavior that remains consistent and stable over time in the same or similar situations.

termination The final stage of therapy, in which progress is reviewed and the therapist and the patient or client separate from one another.

testability How well and how easily a theory can be subjected to empirical validation.

Thematic Apperception Test (TAT) A *projective technique* consisting of pictures about which respondents must make up stories.

theoretical constructs The basic terms and building blocks of a theory; they do not actually exist but are invented to describe or explain phenomena.

therapeutic alliance In *post-Freudian psychoanalysis*, a cooperative relationship between patient and analyst.

third-variable problem When two variables are correlated, neither may cause the other, but rather another (third) variable may account for both variables (cf. *directionality problem*).

threat (Rogers) Feelings that result from becoming aware of incongruity between one's experience and *self-concept*.

time out (from positive reinforcement) Withdrawing a client's access to positive reinforcers for a brief, preset period immediately after an unwanted behavior occurs.

token economy A systematically controlled environment in which clients earn tokens for performing various behaviors; the tokens can later be exchanged for tangible reinforcers and privileges.

trait elements Elements from which traits (factors) are derived using *factor analysis*.

transference Feelings a patient has for a psychoanalyst that are inappropriate *displacements* from the patient's past. Working through transference is critical in *Freudian* psychoanalytic psychotherapy.

triadic reciprocal determinism (Bandura) The theoretical assumption that personality develops through a continuing interaction among personal, behavioral, and environmental factors.

twin study method A procedure used to assess the degree to which a disposition is heritable by contrasting identical and fraternal twins.

Type A behavior pattern A pattern of responding characterized by a high competitive drive coupled with a continuous rush to meet deadlines ("hurry sickness"); it is predictive of later heart attacks (cf. *Type B behavior*).

Type B behavior pattern A pattern of responding characterized by an easy-going and relaxed manner (cf. *Type A behavior pattern*).

unconditional positive regard (Rogers) Esteem (*positive regard*) from others that does not depend on the person's behaviors and is thus nonevaluative.

unconditional positive regard from others (Rogers) *Unconditional positive regard* that comes exclusively from other people.

unconditional positive self-regard (Rogers) *Unconditional positive regard* that has been internalized and thus comes directly from the person and not from others.

unconditioned response (UCR) In *classical conditioning*, the response elicited by an *unconditioned stimulus* (cf. *conditioned response*).

unconditioned stimulus (UCS) In *classical conditioning*, a stimulus that naturally or automatically elicits a particular response.

unconscious Part of the mind containing information of which the person has no knowledge. For Freud, most personality is *unconscious*.

understanding Comprehension of, or the ability to explain, a process.

undesired self-concept Personality characteristics that one considers undesirable.

undoing *Defense mechanism* involving restitution for an unacceptable act.

urine alarm method Behavior therapy for treating enuresis that awakens the child when he or she begins to urinate.

validity The extent to which a test or measure taps what it is intended to measure.

variable-interval schedule A *schedule of reinforcement* in which the individual is reinforced for the first response made after a period of time that varies randomly around a specified time value.

variable-ratio schedule A *schedule of reinforcement* in which the number of responses required for *reinforcement* varies randomly around a particular number of responses.

vicarious consequences Rewards and punishments administered to a model that influence the observer's subsequent likelihood of performing the modeled behavior.

vicarious extinction The elimination of fear and *anxiety* in clients by the process of observing models who successfully deal with anxiety-evoking situations without incurring negative consequences.

vicarious punishment An observed consequence received by a model that is perceived by the observer as negative or undesirable.

vicarious reward An observed consequence received by a model that is perceived by the observer as positive or desirable.

visual representation The *dream work* process whereby abstract wishes, urges, and ideas are translated into concrete pictures or images.

wish fulfillment (Freud) Satisfying a desire through a mental image rather than in reality; part of *primary process*.

References

Abraham, K. (1927). The influence of oral eroticism on character formation. In K. Abraham (Ed.), *Selected papers on psychoanalysis.* London: Hogarth.

Abramson, H., Houts, A. C., & Berman, J. S. (1990, June). *The effectiveness of medical and psychological treatments for childhood enuresis.* Paper presented at the meeting of the Society for Psychotherapy Research, Wintergreen, VA.

Achamamba, B., & Kumar, K. G. (1989). I-E locus of control and job satisfaction among the workers of public and private sector undertaking. *Journal of the Indian Academy of Applied Psychology, 15,* 83–86.

Adams-Webber, J. (1989). Some reflections on the "meaning" of repertory grid responses. *International Journal of Personal Construct Psychology, 2,* 77–92.

Adams-Webber, J. (1990). Personal construct theory and cognitive science. *International Journal of Personal Construct Psychology, 3,* 415–421.

Addad, M. (1987). Neuroticism, extraversion and meaning of life: A comparative study of criminals and non-criminals. *Personality and Individual Differences, 8,* 879–883.

Addis, M. E. (1993). Learning in the trenches: A student's perspective on the cognitive versus radical debate. *the Behavior Therapist, 16,* 55–56.

Adler, A. (1964). *Social interest: A challenge to mankind.* New York: Putnam (Capricorn Books).

Adler, A. (1973). *Superiority and social interest: A collection of later writings.* (H. L. Ansbacher & R. R. Ansbacher, Eds.). New York: Viking Press.

Ainslie, R. C. (1989). Masters of the universe: Children's toys as reflections of contemporary psychoanalytic theory. *Journal of the American Academy of Psychoanalysis, 17,* 579–595.

Aker, R. M., & Panter, A. T. (1988). Extraversion and the ability to decode nonverbal communication. *Personality and Individual Differences, 9,* 965–972.

Alexander, C. N., Rainforth, M. V., & Gelderloos, P. (1991). Transcendental meditation, self-actualization, and psychological health: A conceptual overview and statistical meta-analysis [Special Issue: Handbook of self-actualization]. *Journal of Social Behavior and Personality, 6,* 189–248.

Allport, G. W. (1937). *Personality: A psychological interpretation.* New York: Holt, Rinehart & Winston.

Allport, G. W. (1943). *Becoming: Basic considerations for a psychology of personality.* New Haven, CT: Yale University Press.

Allport, G. W. (1961). *Pattern and growth in personality.* New York: Holt, Rinehart & Winston.

Allport, G. W. (1966). Traits revisited. *American Psychologist, 21,* 1–10.

Anastasi, A. (1976). *Psychological testing* (4th ed.). New York: Macmillan.

Anastasi, A. (1988a). *Psychological testing* (6th ed.). New York: Macmillan.

Anastasi, A. (1988b). Self-report inventories. In *Psychological Testing* (pp. 523–782). New York: Macmillan.

Anderson, J. W. (1988). Henry A. Murray's early career: A psychobiographical exploration. *Journal of Personality, 56,* 139–171.

Anderson, W. J. (1989). Family therapy in the client-centered tradition: A legacy in the narrative mode [Special Issue: Person-centered approaches with families]. *Person-Centered Review, 4,* 295–307.

Ansbacher, H. L., & Ansbacher, R. R. (1956). *The individual psychology of Alfred Adler: A systematic presentation in selections from his writings.* New York: Harper & Row.

Anzieu, D. (1986). *Freud's self-analysis.* Madison, CT: International Universities Press.

Arcaya, J. M., & Gerber, G. L. (1990). An object relations approach to the treatment of child abuse. *Psychotherapy, 27,* 619–626.

Argyle, M., & Lu, L. (1990). The happiness of extraverts. *Personality and Individual Differences, 11,* 1011–1017.

Arkowitz, H. (1991). Introductory statement: Psychotherapy integration comes of age. *Journal of Psychotherapy Integration, 1,* 1–3.

Arkowitz, H. (1992). Integrative theories of therapy. In D. K. Freedheim (Ed.), *The history of psychotherapy: A century of change* (pp. 261–303). Washington, DC: American Psychological Association.

Arlow, J. A., & Brenner, C. (1988). The future of psychoanalysis. *Psychoanalytic Quarterly, 57,* 1–14.

Asarnow, J. R., & Callan, J. W. (1985). Boys with peer adjustment problems: Social cognitive processes. *Journal of Consulting and Clinical Psychology, 53,* 80–87.

Aserinsky, E., & Kleitman, N. (1953). Regularly occurring periods of eye motility, and concomitant phenomena, during sleep. *Science, 118,* 273–274.

Ashkanasy, N. M., & Gallois, C. (1987). Locus of control and attributions of academic performance of self and others. *Australian Journal of Psychology, 39,* 293–305.

Atkinson, J. W. (Ed.). (1958). *Motives in fantasy, action, and society.* Princeton, NJ: Van Nostrand.

Atkinson, J. W., & Litwin, G. H. (1960). Achievement motive and test anxiety conceived as motive to approach success and motive to avoid failure. *Journal of Abnormal and Social Psychology, 60,* 52–63.

Atkinson, J. W., & McClelland, D. C. (1948). The projective expression of needs, II. The effect of different intensities of the hunger drive on thematic apperception. *Journal of Experimental Psychology, 38,* 643–658.

Azrin, N. H., Sneed, T. J., & Foxx, R. M. (1973). Dry bed: A rapid method of eliminating bedwetting (enuresis) of the retarded. *Behaviour Research and Therapy, 11,* 427–434.

Azrin, N. H., Sneed, T. J., & Foxx, R. M. (1974). Dry-bedtraining: Rapid elimination of childhood enuresis. *Behaviour Research and Therapy, 12,* 147–156.

Azrin, N. H., Thienes-Hontos, P., & Besalel-Azrin, V. (1979). Elimination of enuresis without a conditioning apparatus: An extension by office instruction of the child and parents. *Behavior Therapy, 10,* 14–19.

Bacciagaluppi, M. (1989). Erich Fromm's views on psychoanalytic "technique." *Contemporary Psychoanalysis, 25,* 226–243.

Badalamenti, A. F. (1988). Freud and the fall of man. *Journal of Religion and Health, 27,* 23–61.

Bagby, R. M., Parker, J. D. A., & Taylor, G. J. (1991). Reassessing the validity and reliability of the MMPI alexithymia scale. *Journal of Personality Assessment, 56,* 238–253.

Bakan, D. (1988). Some thoughts on reading Blight's article: "Can psychology reduce the risk of nuclear war?" *Journal of Humanistic Psychology, 28,* 59–61.

Bandura, A. (1965). Influence of models' reinforcement contingencies on the acquisition of imitative responses. *Journal of Personality and Social Psychology, 1,* 589–595.

Bandura, A. (1984). Recycling misconceptions of perceived self-efficacy. *Cognitive Therapy and Research, 8,* 231–255.

Bandura, A. (1986a). From thought to action: Mechanisms of personal agency. *New Zealand Journal of Psychology, 15,* 1–17.

Bandura, A. (1986b). *Social foundations of thought and action: A social cognitive theory.* Englewood Cliffs, NJ: Prentice–Hall.

Bandura, A. (1989a). Human agency in social cognitive theory. *American Psychologist, 44,* 1175–1184.

Bandura, A. (1989b). Perceived self-efficacy in the exercise of personal agency. *The Psychologist: Bulletin of the British Psychological Society, 10,* 411–424.

Bandura, A. (1990). Perceived self-efficacy in the exercise of control over AIDS infection. *Evaluation and Program Planning, 13,* 9–17.

Bandura, A. (1991). Self-efficacy mechanism in physiological activation and health-promoting behavior. In J. Madden (Ed.), *Neurobiology of learning, emotion and affect* (pp. 229–270). New York: Raven Press.

Bandura, A. (1992a). Exercise of personal agency through the self-efficacy mechanism. In R. Schwarzer (Ed.), *Self-efficacy: Thought control of action* (pp. 3–38). Washington, DC: Hemisphere.

Bandura, A. (1992b, April). *Perceived self-efficacy in cognitive development and functioning.* Paper presented at the annual meeting of the American Education Research Association, San Francisco.

Bandura, A. (1992c). Self-efficacy mechanisms in psychobiologic functioning. In R. Schwarzer (Ed.), *Self-efficacy: Thought control of action* (pp. 355–394). Washington, DC: Hemisphere.

Bandura, A., Adams, N. E., & Beyer, J. (1977). Cognitive processes mediating behavioral change. *Journal of Personality and Social Psychology, 35,* 125–139.

Bandura, A., & Mischel, W. (1965). Modification of self-imposed delay of reward through exposure to live and symbolic models. *Journal of Personality and Social Psychology, 2,* 698–705.

Bandura, A., O'Leary, A., Taylor, C. B., Gauthier, J., & Gossard, D. (1987). Perceived self-efficacy and pain control: Opioid and nonopioid mechanisms. *Journal of Personality and Social Psychology, 53,* 563–571.

Bandura, A., & Walters, R. H. (1963). *Social learning and personality development.* New York: Holt, Rinehart & Winston.

Bandura, A., & Wood, R. (1989). Effect of perceived controllability and performance standards on self-regulation of complex decision making. *Journal of Personality and Social Psychology, 56,* 805–814.

Baradell, J. G. (1990). Client-centered case consultation and single-case research design: Application to case management. *Archives of Psychiatric Nursing, 4,* 12–17.

Barling, J., Bluen, S., & Moss, V. (1991). Type A behavior and marital dissatisfaction: Disentangling the effects of achievement striving and impatience-irritability. *Journal of Psychology, 124,* 311–319.

Barnard, D. (1984). The personal meaning of illness: Client-centered dimensions of medicine and health care. In R. F. Levant & J. M. Shlien (Eds.), *Client-centered therapy and the person-centered approach: New directions in theory, research, and practice* (pp. 337–351). New York: Praeger.

Barnet, H. S. (1990). Divorce stress and adjustment model: Locus of control and demographic predictors. *Journal of Divorce, 13,* 93–109.

Barnette, E. L. (1989). Effects of a growth group on counseling students' self-actualization. *Journal for Specialists in Group Work, 14,* 202–210.

Barrineau, P. (1992). Person-centered dream work. *Journal of Humanistic Psychology, 32,* 90–105.

Barris, B. P. (1990). Affirming the "personal" in PCT [Review of *Working with people: Clinical uses of personal construct psychology*]. *International Journal of Personal Construct Psychology, 3,* 249–256.

Bass, E., & Davis, L. (1988). *The courage to heal: A guide for women survivors of child sexual abuse.* New York: Harper & Row.

Bassler, M., Krauthauser, H., & Hoffmann, S. O. (1992). A new approach to the identification of cognitive conflicts in the repertory grid: An illustrustive case study. *International Journal of Personal Construct Psychology, 5,* 95–111.

Baucom, D. H., & Epstein, N. (1990). *Cognitive-behavioral marital therapy.* New York: Brunner/Mazel.

Baudry, F. (1988). Character, character type, and character organization. *Journal of the American Psychoanalytic Association, 37,* 655–686.

Baumeister, R. E. (1991). On the stability of variability: Retest reliability of metatraits. *Personality and Social Psychology Bulletin, 17,* 633–639.

Baumeister, R. F. (1989). The optimal margin of illusion. *Journal of Social and Clinical Psychology, 8,* 176–189.

Baumeister, R. F., & Tice, D. M. (1988). Metatraits. *Journal of Personality, 56,* 571–598.

Beail, N. (Ed.). (1985). *Repertory grid technique and personal constructs: Applications in clinical and educational settings.* London: Croom Helm.

Beail, N., & Parker, S. (1991). Group fixed-role therapy: A clinical application. *International Journal of Personal Construct Psychology, 4,* 85–95.

Beck, A. T. (1976). *Cognitive therapy and the emotional disorders.* New York: International Universities Press.

Beck, A. T. (1984). Cognitive approaches to stress. In R. Woolfold & P. Lehrer (Eds.), *Principles and practice of stress management.* New York: Guilford Press.

Beck, A. T. (1989). *Love is never enough.* New York: Harper & Row (Perennial Library).

Beck, A. T. (1993). Cognitive therapy: Past, present, and future. *Journal of Consulting and Clinical Psychology, 61,* 194–198.

Beck, A. T., & Emery, G. (1985). *Anxiety disorders and phobias: A cognitive perspective.* New York: Basic Books.

Beck, A. T., & Freeman, A. (1989). *Cognitive therapy of personality disorders.* New York: Guilford.

Beck, A. T., & Weishaar, M. (1989). Cognitive therapy. In A. Freeman, K. M. Simon, L. E. Beutler, & H. Arkowitz (Eds.), *Comprehensive handbook of cognitive therapy* (pp. 21–36). New York: Plenum.

Beckham, E. E., & Watkins, J. T. (1989). Process and outcome in cognitive therapy. In A. Freeman, K. M. Simon, L. E. Beutler, & H. Arkowitz (Eds.), *Comprehensive handbook of cognitive therapy* (pp. 583–596). New York: Plenum.

Beh, H. C. (1989). Achievement motivation and the end-effect. *Perceptual and Motor Skills, 68,* 799–805.

Bein, J., Anderson, D. E., & Maes, W. R. (1990). Teacher locus of control and job satisfaction. *Educational Research Quarterly, 14,* 7–10.

Bell, L., & Schniedewind, N. (1989). Realizing the promise of humanistic education: A reconstructed pedagogy for personal and social change. *Journal of Humanistic Psychology, 29,* 200–223.

Bemporad, J. R. (1988). Psychodynamic treatment of depressed adolescents. *Journal of Clinical Psychiatry, 49,* 26–31.

Benesch, K. F., & Page, M. M. (1989). Self-construct systems and interpersonal congruence. *Journal of Personality, 57,* 139–173.

Bergeman, C. S., Plomin, R., McClearn, G. E., Pederson, N. L., & Friberg, L. T. (1988). Genotype-environment interaction in personality development: Identical twins reared apart. *Psychology and Aging, 3,* 399–406.

Berger, R. J., & Oswald, I. (1962). Eye movements during active and passive dreams. *Science, 137,* 601.

Bergman, A., & Ellman, S. (1985). Margaret S. Mahler: Symbiosis and separation-individuation. In J. Reppen (Ed.), *Beyond Freud: A study of modern psychoanalytic theorists.* Hillsdale, NJ: Analytic Press.

Bernard, M. E., & DiGiuseppe, R. (1989). Rational-emotive therapy today. In M. E. Bernard & R. DiGiuseppe (Eds.), *Inside rational-emotive therapy: A critical appraisal of the theory and therapy of Albert Ellis* (pp. 1–7). San Diego: Academic Press.

Bertrand, S., & Masling, J. M. (1969). Oral imagery and alcoholism. *Journal of Abnormal Psychology, 74,* 50–53.

Berzonsky, M. D. (1989). The self as a theorist: Individual differences in identity formation. *International Journal of Personal Construct Psychology, 2,* 363–376.

Berzonsky, M. D. (1990). Self-construction over the life span: A process perspective on identity formation. In G. J. Neimeyer & R. A. Neimeyer (Eds.), *Advances in personal construct psychology* (Vol. 1, pp. 155–186). Greewich, CT: JAI Press.

Bettelheim, B. (1976). *The uses of enchantment.* New York: Knopf.

Biglan, A. (1993). Recapturing Skinner's legacy to behavior therapy. *the Behavior Therapist, 16,* 3–5.

Bigoness, W. J., Keef, K. M., & Du Bose, P. B. (1988). Perceived goal-difficulty, locus of control, and performance ratings. *Psychological Reports, 63,* 475–482.

Birns, B. (1965). Individual differences in human neonates' responses to stimulation. *Child Development, 36,* 249–256.

Black, C., Bucky, S. & Wilder-Padilla, F. (1986). Interpersonal and emotional consequences of being an adult child of an alcoholic. *International Journal of the Addictions, 21,* 213–231.

Blanck, G., & Blanck, R. (1974). *Ego psychology: Theory and practice.* New York: Columbia University Press.

Blaney, N. T. (1990). Type A, effort to excel, and attentional style in children: The validity of the MYTH. *Journal of Social Behavior and Personality, 5,* 159–182.

Blatt, S. J., & Lerner, H. (1983). Investigations in the psychoanalytic theory of object relations and object representations. In J. Masling (Ed.), *Empirical studies of psychoanalytic theories.* Hillsdale, NJ: Erlbaum.

Blight, J. G. (1988). Can psychology help reduce the risk of nuclear war? Reflections of a "Little Drummer Boy" of nuclear psychology. *Journal of Humanistic Psychology, 28,* 7–58.

Bloch, D. (1989). Freud's retraction of his seduction theory and the Schreber case. *The Psychoanalytic Review, 76,* 185–201.

Block, J. (1965). *The challenge of response sets.* New York: Appleton-Century-Crofts.

Bloom, H. (Ed.). (1987). *The interpretation of dreams.* New York: Chelsea House.

Bly, R. (with W. Booth, Ed.). (1988). *A little book on the human shadow.* New York: Harper & Row.

Bohart, A. C. (1990). Psychotherapy integration from a client-centered perspective. In G. Lietaer, J. Rombauts, & R. Van Balen (Eds.), *Client-centered and experiential psychotherapy in the nineties* (pp. 481–500). Leuven, Belgium: Leuven University Press.

Bohart, A. C. (1991a). Empathy in client-centered therapy: A contrast with psychoanalysis and self psychology. *Journal of Humanistic Psychology, 31,* 34–48.

Bohart, A. C. (1991b). The missing 249 words: In search of objectivity. *Psychotherapy, 28,* 497–503.

Bolger, N., & Schilling, E. A. (1991). Personality and the problems of everyday life: The role of neuroticism in exposure and reactivity to daily stressors. *Journal of Personality, 59,* 355–386.

Bonarius, H. (1984). Personal construct psychology: Reappraisal of basic theory and its application. In H. Bonarius, G. Van Heck, & N. Smid (Eds.), *Personality psychology in Europe: Theoretical and empirical developments.* Lisse: Swets & Zeitlinger.

Boone, C., De Brabander, B., Gerits, P. & Willeme, P. (1990). Relation of scores on Rotter's I-E scale to short-term and long-term control expectancies and fatalism. *Psychological Reports, 66,* 1107–1111.

Boose, J. H. (1985). A knowledge acquisition program for expert systems based on personal construct psychology. *International Journal of Man-Machine Studies, 23,* 495–525.

Bootzin, R. R. (1985). Insomnia. In M. Hersen & C. G. Last (Eds.), *Behavior therapy casebook* (pp. 132–143). New York: Springer.

Bordages, J. W. (1989). Self-actualization and personal autonomy. *Psychological Reports, 64,* 1263–1266.

Borkenau, P. (1988). The multiple classification of acts and the big five factors of personality. *Journal of Research in Personality, 22,* 337–352.

Bornstein, R. F., & Masling, J. (1985). Orality and latency of volunteering to serve as experimental subjects: A replication. *Journal of Personality Assessment, 49,* 306–310.

Boscolo, P., & de Bernardi, B. (1992). Writing as a meaningful activity. *International Journal of Personal Construct Psychology, 5,* 341–353.

Boss, M. W., & Taylor, M. C. (1989). The relationship between locus of control and academic level and sex of secondary school students. *Contemporary Educational Psychology, 14,* 315–322.

Botella, L. (1991). Psychoeducational groups with older adults: An integrative personal construct rationale and some guidelines. *International Journal of Personal Construct Psychology, 4,* 397–408.

Bottome, P. (1957). *Alfred Adler: A portrait from life.* New York: Vanguard.

Bouchard, T. J., Lykken, D. T., McGue, M., Segal, N. L., & Tellegen, A. (1990). Sources of human psychological differences: The Minnesota study of twins reared apart. *Science, 250,* 223–228.

Boudin, H. M. (1972). Contingency contracting as a therapeutic tool in decelerating amphetamine use. *Behavior Therapy, 3,* 602–608.

Bouffard-Bouchard, T., Parent, S., & Larivée, S. (1991). Influence of self-efficacy on self-regulation and performance among junior and senior high-school age students. *International Journal of Behavioral Development, 14,* 153–164.

Boy, A. V. (1990). The therapist in person-centered groups. *Person-Centered Review, 5,* 308–315.

Bozarth, J. D. (1984). Beyond reflection: Emergent modes of empathy. In R. F. Levant & J. M. Shlien (Eds.), *Client-centered therapy and the person-centered approach: New directions in theory, research, and practice* (pp. 59–75). New York: Praeger.

Bozarth, J. D. (1990). The evolution of Carl Rogers as a therapist [Special Issue: Fiftieth anniversary of the person-centered approach]. *Person Centered Review, 5,* 387–393.

Bozarth, J. D. (1991). Person-centered assessment. *Journal of Counseling and Development, 69,* 458–461.

Bozarth, J. D., & Brodley, B. T. (1991). Actualization: A functional concept in client-centered therapy [Special Issue: Handbook of self-actualization]. *Journal of Social Behavior and Personality, 6,* 45–59.

Bozarth, J. D., & Shanks, A. (1989). Person-centered family therapy with couples [Special Issue: Person-centered approaches with families]. *Person Centered Review, 4,* 280–294.

Brafford, L. J., & Beck, K. H. (1991). Development and validation of a condom self-efficacy scale for college students. *Journal of American College Health, 39,* 219–225.

Bramel, D. (1963). Selection of a target for defensive projection. *Journal of Abnormal and Social Psychology, 66,* 318–324.

Brand, C. R., & Egan, V. (1989). The 'Big Five' dimensions of personality? Evidence from ipsative, adjectival self-attributions. *Personality and Individual Differences, 10,* 1165–1171.

Brandon, J. E., & Loftin, J. M. (1991). Relationship of fitness to depression, state and trait anxiety, internal health locus of control, and self-control. *Perceptual and Motor Skills, 73,* 563–568.

Brandstädter, J. (1992). Personal control over development: Implications of self-efficacy. In R. Schwarzer (Ed.), *Self-efficacy: Thought control of action* (pp. 127–145). Washington, DC: Hemisphere.

Brannigan, G. G., Hauk, P. A., & Guay, J. A. (1991). Locus of control and daydreaming. *Journal of Genetic Psychology, 152,* 29–33.

Brant, J. (1988, March). Typecasting. *Outside,* pp. 33–35.

Breger, L., & McGaugh, J. L. (1966). Learning theory and behavior therapy: A reply to Rachman and Eysenck. *Psychological Bulletin, 65,* 170–173.

Brennan, T. P., & Piechowski, M. M. (1991). A developmental framework for self-actualization: Evidence from case studies. *Journal of Humanistic Psychology, 31,* 43–64.

Breuer, J., & Freud, S. (1955). Studies in hysteria. In J. Strachey (Ed.), *The standard edition of the complete psychological works of Sigmund Freud* (Vol. 2). London: Hogarth. (Originally published, 1893–1895)

Brickman, B. (1988). Psychoanalysis and substance abuse: Toward a more effective approach. *Journal of the American Academy of Psychoanalysis, 16,* 359–379.

Brown, J. D. (1991). Accuracy and bias in self-knowledge. In C. R. Snyder & D. F. Forsyth (Eds.), *Handbook of social and clinical psychology: The health perspective* (pp. 158–178). New York: Pergamon Press.

Brown, N. O. (1959). *Life against death.* New York: Random House.

Brown, P., Perry, L., & Harburg, E. (1977). Sex role attitudes and psychological outcomes for black and white women experiencing marital dissolution. *Journal of Marriage and the Family, 39,* 549–561.

Brown, R. (1965). *Social psychology.* New York: Free Press.

Bruner, J. S. (1956). A cognitive theory of personality. *Contemporary Psychology, 1,* 355–356.

Buie, J. (1988, November). Psychoanalysis barriers tumble: Settlement opens door to non-MDs. *APA Monitor,* pp. 1, 15.

Buie, J. (1989a, January). Questions linger in analysis settlement. *APA Monitor,* p. 18.

Buie, J. (1989b, January). Traditional analysis may be changing. *APA Monitor,* p. 19.

Bunch, J. M., & Schneider, H. G. (1991). Smoking-specific locus of control. *Psychological Reports, 69,* 1075–1081.

Burke, M., Noller, P., & Caird, D. (1992). Transition from practioner to educator: A repertory grid analysis. *International Journal of Personal Construct Psychology, 5,* 159–182.

Burke, R. J. (1988). Type A behavior, occupational and life demands, satisfaction, and well-being. *Psychological Reports, 63,* 451–458.

Burnham, J. C. (1968). Historical background for the study of personality. In E. F. Borgatta & W. W. Lambert (Eds.), *Handbook of personality theory and research* (pp. 3–81). Chicago: Rand McNally.

Buros, O. K. (Ed.). (1965). *The sixth mental measurements yearbook.* Highland Park, NJ: Gryphon Press.

Buros, O. K. (Ed.). (1972). *The seventh mental measurements yearbook.* Highland Park, NJ: Gryphon Press.

Burr, V., & Butt, T. (1989). A personal construct view of hypnosis. *British Journal of Experimental and Clinical Hypnosis, 6,* 85–90.

Burwick, S., & Knapp, R. R. (1991). Advances in research using the Personal Orientation Inventory [Special Issue: Handbook of self-actualization]. *Journal of Social Behavior and Personality, 6,* 311–320.

Buss, A. H. (1989). Personality as traits. *American Psychologist, 44,* 1378–1388.

Buss, A. H., & Plomin, R. (1984). *Temperament: Early developing personality traits.* Hillsdale, NJ: Erlbaum.

Buss, A. H., Plomin, R., & Willerman, L. (1973). The inheritance of temperaments. *Journal of Personality, 41,* 513–524.

Buss, D. M., & Craik, K. H. (1985). Why not measure that trait? Alternative criteria for identifying important dispositions. *Journal of Personality and Social Psychology, 48,* 934–946.

Butcher, J. N. (1979). Use of the MMPI in personnel selection. In J. N. Butcher (Ed.), *New developments in the use of the MMPI.* Minneapolis: University of Minnesota Press.

Butcher, J. N., Graham, J. R., Dahlstrom, W. G., & Bowman, E. (1990). The MMPI-2 with college students. *Journal of Personality Assessment, 54,* 1–15.

Butler, G., Fennell, M., Robson, P., & Gelder, M. (1991). Comparison of behavior therapy and cognitive behavior therapy in the treatment of generalized anxiety disorder. *Journal of Consulting and Clinical Psychology, 59,* 167–175.

Cain, D. J. (1989). From the individual to the family [Special Issue: Person-centered approaches with families]. *Person-Centered Review, 4,* 248–255.

Cain, D. J. (1990a). Celebration, reflection and renewal: 50 years of client-centered therapy and beyond [Special Issue: Fiftieth anniversary of the person-centered approach]. *Person-Centered Review, 5,* 357–363.

Cain, D. J. (1990b). Further thoughts about nondirectiveness and client-centered therapy. *Person-Centered Review, 5,* 89–99.

Camp, B. W., & Bash, M. A. S. (1981). *Think aloud: Increasing social and cognitive skills—A problem-solving program for children (primary level).* Champaign, IL: Research Press.

Campbell, D. T., & Fiske, D. W. (1959). Convergent and discriminant validation by the multitrait-multimethod matrix. *Psychological Bulletin, 56,* 81–105.

Campbell, J. (1988). *The power of myth.* New York: Doubleday.

Canary, D. J., Cunningham, E. M., & Cody, M. J. (1988). Goal types, gender, and locus of control in managing interpersonal conflict. *Communication Research, 15,* 426–446.

Cantor, D. W., & Bernay, T. (1988). *Psychology of today's women: New psychoanalytic visions.* Hillsdale, NJ: Analytic Press.

Cantor, N. (1990). From thought to behavior: "Having" and "doing" in the study of personality and cognition. *American Psychologist, 45,* 735–750.

Cantwell, D. P. (1972). Psychiatric illness in the families of hyperactive children. *Archives of General Psychiatry, 27,* 414–417.

Caputi, P., Breiger, R., & Pattison, P. (1990). Analyzing implications grids using hierarchical models. *International Journal of Personal Construct Psychology, 3,* 77–90.

Carroll, L. (1987). A study of narcissism, affiliation, intimacy, and power motives among students in business administration. *Psychological Reports, 61,* 355–358.

Carson, R. C. (1989). Personality. *Annual Review of Psychology, 40,* 227–248.

Cartwright, D., DeBruin, J., & Berg, S. (1991). Some scales for assessing personality based on Carl Rogers' theory: Further evidence of validity. *Personality and Individual Differences, 12,* 151–156.

Cartwright, D., & Mori, C. (1988). Scales for assessing aspects of the person. *Person-Centered Review, 3,* 176–194.

Cartwright, R. D., & Ratzel, R. (1972). Effects of dream loss on waking behaviors. *Archives of General Psychiatry, 27,* 277–280.

Cashdan, S. (1973). *Interactional psychotherapy: Stages and strategies in behavioral change.* New York: Grune & Stratton.

Cashdan, S. (1988). *Object relations therapy: Using the relationship.* New York: Norton.

Caspi, A., Elder, G. H., & Bem, D. J. (1988). Moving away from the world: Life-course patterns of shy children. *Developmental Psychology, 24,* 824–831.

Castorina, M., & Mancini, F. (1992). Construct system as a knowing system. *International Journal of Personal Construct Psychology, 5,* 271–293.

Cattell, R. B. (1965). *The scientific analysis of personality.* Baltimore: Penguin.

Cattell, R. B. (1979). *Personality and learning theory.* (Vol. 1). New York: Springer.

Cattell, R. B., & Kline, P. (1977). *The scientific analysis of personality and motivation.* New York: Academic Press.

Cattell, R. B., & Warburton, F. W. (1967). *Objective personality and motivation tests: A theoretical introduction and practical compendium.* Urbana: University of Illinois Press.

Celiberti, D. A., Alessandri, M., Fong, P. L., & Weiss, M. J. (1993). A history of the behavioral treatment of autism. *the Behavior Therapist, 16,* 127–132.

Centerwell, B. S. (1989). Exposure to television as a cause of violence. In G. Comstock (Ed.), *Public communication and behavior* (Vol. 2). San Diego: Academic Press.

Cernovsky, Z. Z. (1988). A failure of the MMPI validity scale to detect random responding. *Psychological Reports, 62,* 930.

Cervone, D. (1989). Effects of envisioning future activities on self-efficacy judgments and motivation: An availability heuristic interpretation. *Cognitive Therapy and Research, 13,* 247–261.

Chambers, W. V. (1985). Personal construct integrative complexity and the credulous approach. *Psychological Reports, 57,* 1202.

Chambless, D. L., & Gillis, M. M. (1993). Cognitive therapy of anxiety disorders. *Journal of Consulting and Clinical Psychology, 61,* 248–260.

Charlop, M. H., & Milstein, J. P. (1989). Teaching autistic children conversational speech using video modeling. *Journal of Applied Behavior Analysis, 22,* 275–285.

Chase, M. H., & Morales, F. R. (1990). The atonia and myoclonia of active (REM) sleep. *Annual Review of Psychology, 41,* 557–584.

Cheyne, J. A. (1971). Effects of imitation of different reinforcement combinations to a model. *Journal of Experimental Child Psychology, 12,* 258–269.

Chiang, H., & Maslow, A. H. (Eds.). (1977). *The healthy personality: Readings* (2nd ed.). New York: Van Nostrand.

Chiari, G., Mancini, F., Nicolo, F., & Nuzzo, M. L. (1990). Hierarchical organization of personal construct systems in terms of the range of convenience. *International Journal of Personal Construct Psychology, 3,* 281–311.

Chodorow, N. J. (1990). *Feminism and psychoanalytic theory.* New Haven, CT: Yale University Press.

Clair, S., & Preston, J. M. (1990). Integration in personal constructs of television. *International Journal of Personal Construct Psychology, 3,* 377–391.

Clark, M. M., Abrams, D. B., Niaura, R. S., Eaton, C. A., & Rossi, J. S. (1991). Self-efficacy in weight management. *Journal of Consulting and Clinical Psychology, 59,* 739–744.

Coan, R. W. (1991). Self-actualization and the quest for the ideal human. [Special Issue: Handbook of self-actualization]. *Journal of Social Behavior and Personality, 6,* 127–136.

Cohen, D. (1987). *The development of play.* New York: New York University Press.

Cohen, S., & Syme, S. L. (Eds.). (1985). *Social support and health.* San Diego, CA: Academic Press.

Cohen, S., & Willis, T. A. (1985). Stress, social support, and the buffering hypothesis. *Psychological Bulletin, 98,* 310–357.

Colarusso, C. A., & Nemiroff, R. A. (1979). Some observations and hypotheses about the psychoanalytic theory of adult development. *International Journal of Psycho-Analysis, 60,* 59–71.

Colligan, R. C., & Offord, K. P. (1987). The MacAndrew alcoholism scale applied to a contemporary normative sample. *Journal of Clinical Psychology, 43,* 291–293.

Colligan, R. C., & Offord, K. P. (1988). The risky use of the MMPI hostility scale in assessing risk for coronary heart disease. *Psychosomatics, 29,* 188–196.

Colligan, R. C., Osborne, D., Swenson, W. M., & Offord, K. P. (1984). The aging MMPI: Development of contemporary norms. *Mayo Clinic Proceedings, 59,* 377–390.

Comer, R. J. (1992). *Abnormal psychology.* New York: Freeman.

Comrey, A. L. (1973). *A first course in factor analysis.* New York: Academic Press.

Cone, A. L., & Owens, S. K. (1991). Academic and locus of control enhancement in a freshman study skills and college adjustment course. *Psychological Reports, 68,* 1211–1217.

Conley, J. J. (1984). Longitudinal consistency of adult personality: Self-reported psychological characteristics across 45 years. *Journal of Personality and Social Psychology, 47,* 1325–1333.

Cooper, A. M. (1985). Will neurobiology influence psychoanalysis? *American Journal of Psychiatry, 142,* 1395–1402.

Cooper, A. M. (1990). The future of psychoanalysis: Challenges and opportunities. *Psychoanalytic Quarterly, 54,* 177–196.

Cooper, S. H. (1988). Recent contributions to the theory of defense mechanisms: A comparative view. *Journal of the American Psychoanalytic Association, 37,* 865–891.

Costa, P. T., Jr., & McCrae, R. R. (1988). From catalog to classification: Murray's needs and the five-factor model. *Journal of Personality and Social Psychology*, 55, 258–265.

Costa, P. T., Jr., & McCrae, R. R. (1988). Personality in adulthood: A six-year longitudinal study of self-reports and spouse ratings on the NEO personality inventory. *Journal of Personality and Social Psychology*, 54, 853–863.

Costa, P. T., & McCrae, R. R. (1992). *NEO-PI-R professional manual*. Odessa, FL: Psychological Assesssment Resources.

Cote, J. E., & Levine, C. G. (1989). An empirical test of Erikson's theory of ego identity formation. *Youth & Society*, 20, 388–415.

Cottraux, J. (1990). "Cogito ergo sum": Cognitive-behavior therapy in France. *the Behavior Therapist*, 13, 189–190.

Cowen, E. L., Work, W. C., Hightower, A. D., Wyman, P. A., Parker, G. R., & Lotyczewski, B. S. (1991). Toward the development of a measure of perceived self-efficacy in children. *Journal of Clinical Child Psychology*, 20, 169–178.

Craighead, W. E. (1990a). The changing nature of behavior therapy. *Behavior Therapy*, 21, 1–2.

Craighead, W. E. (1990b). There's a place for us: All of us. *Behavior Therapy*, 21, 3–23.

Craigie, F. C., Jr., & Houde, K. A. (1992). Religious involvement in behavior therapy training. *the Behavior Therapist*, 15, 59, 81.

Crain, W. C. (1980). *Theories of development*. Englewood Cliffs, NJ: Prentice-Hall.

Cramer, P. (1987). The development of defense mechanisms. *Journal of Personality*, 55, 597–614.

Cramer, P., & Gaul, R. (1988). The effects of success and failure on children's use of defense mechanisms. *Journal of Personality*, 56, 729–742.

Crandall, R., & Jones, A. (1991). Issues in self-actualization measurement. [Special Issue: Handbook of self-actualization]. *Journal of Social Behavior and Personality*, 6, 339–344.

Crandall, V. J., Dewey, R., Katkovsky, W., & Preston, A. (1964). Parents' attitudes and behaviors and grade-school children's academic achievement. *Journal of Genetic Psychology*, 104, 53–66.

Cronbach, L. J. (1949). Statistical methods applied to Rorschach scores: A review. *Psychological Bulletin*, 46, 393–429.

Csikszentmihalyi, M. (1990). *Flow: The psychology of optimal experience*. New York: Harper & Row.

Culp, R. E., Culp, A. M., Osofsky, J. D., & Osofsky, H. J. (1991). Adolescent and older mothers' interaction patterns with their six month old infants. *Journal of Adolescence*, 14, 195–200.

Cummins, P. (1992). Reconstruing the experience of sexual abuse. *International Journal of Personal Construct Psychology*, 5, 355–365.

Cummins, R. C. (1988). Perceptions of social support, receipt of supportive behaviors, and locus of control as moderators of the effects of chronic stress. *American Journal of Community Psychology*, 16, 685–700.

Cunningham, A. J., Lockwood, G. A., & Cunningham, J. A. (1991). A relationship between perceived self-efficacy and quality of life in cancer patients. *Patient Education and Counseling*, 17, 71–78.

Cutter, H. S. G., Boyatzis, R. E., & Clancy, D. D. (1977). The effectiveness of power motivation training in rehabilitating alcoholics. *Journal of Studies on Alcohol*, 38, 131–141.

Dahlstrom, W. G. (1980). Screening for emotional fitness: The Jersey City case. In W. G. Dahlstrom & L. Dahlstrom (Eds.), *Basic readings on the MMPI: A new selection on personality measurement*. Minneapolis: University of Minnesota Press.

Daniels, D., & Plomin, R. (1984). Origins of individual differences in infant shyness. *Developmental Psychology*, 21, 118–121.

Daniels, M. (1988). The myth of self-actualization. *Journal of Humanistic Psychology*, 28, 7–38.

Dapcich-Miura, E., & Hovell, M. F. (1979). Contingency management of adherence to a complex medical regimen in an elderly heart patient. *Behavior Therapy*, 10, 193–201.

Dattilio, F. M., & Padesky, C. A. (1990). *Cognitive therapy with couples*. Sarasota, FL: Professional Resource Exchange.

Davey, G. C. L. (1989a). Dental phobias and anxieties: Evidence for conditioning processes in the acquisition and modulation of a learned fear. *Behaviour Research and Therapy*, 27, 51–58.

Davey, G. C. L. (1989b). UCS revaluation and conditioning models of acquired fears. *Behaviour Research and Therapy*, 27, 521–528.

Davis, C., & Cowles, M. (1988). A laboratory study of temperament and arousal: A test of Gale's hypothesis. *Journal of Research in Personality*, 22, 101–116.

Davis, J., Lockwood, L., & Wright, C. (1991). Reasons for not reporting peak experiences. *Journal of Humanistic Psychology*, 31, 86–94.

Davis, L. J., Colligan, R. C., Morse, R. M., & Offord, K. P. (1987). Validity of the MacAndrew scale in a general medical population. *Journal of Studies on Alcohol*, 48, 202–206.

Davis, P. J., & Schwartz, G. E. (1987). Repression and the inaccessibility of affective memories. *Journal of Personality and Social Psychology*, 52, 155–166.

Davison, G. C., & Neale, J. M. (1974). *Abnormal psychology: An experimental-clinical approach*. New York: Wiley.

Davison, G. C., Robins, C., & Johnson, M. K. (1983). Articulated thoughts during simulated situations: A paradigm for studying cognition in emotion and behavior. *Cognitive Therapy and Research*, 7, 17–40.

Dean, P. R., & Edwards, T. A. (1990). Health locus of control beliefs and alcohol-related factors that may influence treatment outcomes. *Journal of Substance Abuse Treatment*, 7, 167–172.

DeCarvalho, R. J. (1990a). The growth hypothesis and self-actualization: An existential alternative. *Humanistic Psychologist*, 18, 252–258.

DeCarvalho, R. J. (1990b). A history of the "Third Force" in psychology. *Journal of Humanistic Psychology*, 30, 22–44.

DeCarvalho, R. J. (1991a). Abraham H. Maslow (1908–1970): An intellectual biography. *Thought*, 66, 32–50.

DeCarvalho, R. J. (1991b). *The founders of humanistic psychology*. New York: Praeger.

DeCarvalho, R. J. (1991c). The humanistic paradigm in education. *Humanistic Psychologist*, 19, 88–104.

Deffenbacher, J. L., & Suinn, R. M. (1988). Systematic desensitization and the reduction of anxiety. *The Counseling Psychologist*, 16, 9–30.

Delmonte, M. M. (1989). Existentialism and psychotherapy: A constructivist perspective. *Psychologia—An International Journal of Psychology in the Orient*, 32, 81–90.

Delmonte, M. M. (1990). George Kelly's personal construct theory: Some comparisons with Freudian theory. *Psychologia–An International Journal of Psychology in the Orient*, 33, 73–83.

Delprato, D. J., & Midgley, B. D. (1992). Some fundamentals of B. F. Skinner's behaviorism. *American Psychologist*, 47, 1507–1520.

Dement, W. C. (1964). Experimental dream studies. In J. H. Masserman (Ed.), *Science and psychoanalysis: Scientific proceedings of the Academy of Psychoanalysis*. New York: Grune & Stratton.

Dement, W. C. (1965). An essay on dreams: The role of physiology in understanding their nature. In *New directions in psychology* (Vol. 2). New York: Holt, Rinehart & Winston.

Dement, W. C., & Kleitman, N. (1957). The relation of the eye movements during sleep to dream activity: An objective method for the study of dreaming. *Journal of Experimental Psychology*, 53, 339–346.

Dement, W. C., & Wolpert, E. (1958). The relation of eye movements, body motility, and external stimuli to dream content. *Journal of Experimental Psychology*, 55, 543–553.

DeRubeis, R. J., & Beck, A. T. (1988). Cognitive therapy. In K. S. Dobson (Ed.), *Handbook of cognitive-behavioral therapies* (pp. 273–306). New York: Guilford Press.

DeSilvestri, C. (1989). Clinical models in RET: An advanced model of the organization of emotional and behavioral disorders. *Journal of Rational-Emotive and Cognitive-Behavior Therapy*, 7, 51–58.

Diamond, C. T. P. (1983). The use of fixed role treatment in teaching. *Psychology in the Schools*, 20, 74–82.

Diamond, C. T. P. (1990). Recovering and reconstruing teachers' stories. *International Journal of Personal Construct Psychology*, 3, 63–76.

DiClemente, C. C., Fairhurst, S. K., Velasquez, M. M., Prochaska, J. O., Velicer, W. F., & Rossi, J. S. (1991). The process of smoking cessation: An analysis of precontemplation, contemplation and preparation stages of change. *Journal of Consulting and Clinical Psychology*, 59, 295–304.

Die, A. H., Seelbach, W. C., & Sherman, G. D. (1987). Achievement motivation, achieving styles, and morale in the elderly. *Psychology and Aging*, 2, 407–408.

Diener, E., & Larsen, R. J. (1984). Temporal stability and cross-situational consistency of affective, behavioral, and cognitive responses. *Journal of Personality and Social Psychology*, 47, 871–883.

Dienstbier, R. A. (1989). Arousal and physiological toughness: Implications for mental and physical health. *Psychological Review*, 96, 84–100.

Digman, J. M. (1989). Five robust trait dimensions: Development, stability, and utility. *Journal of Personality*, 57, 195–214.

Digman, J. M. (1990). Personality structure: Emergence of the five-factor model. *Annual Review of Psychology*, 41, 417–440.

Digman, J. M., & Inouye, J. (1986). Further specification of the five robust factors of personality. *Journal of Personality and Social Psychology*, 50, 116–123.

Dobson, K. S. (1989). A meta-analysis of the efficacy of cognitive therapy for depression. *Journal of Consulting and Clinical Psychology*, 57, 414–419.

Doganis, G., Theodorakis, Y., & Bagiatis, K. (1991). Self-esteem and locus of control in adult female fitness program participants. *International Journal of Sport Psychology*, 22, 154–164.

Doherty, W. J. (1983). Impact of divorce on locus of control orientation in adult women: A longitudinal study. *Journal of Personality and Social Psychology*, 44, 834–840.

Doherty, W. J., & Baldwin, C. (1985). Shifts and stability in locus of control during the 1970s: Divergence of the sexes. *Journal of Personality and Social Psychology*, 48, 1048–1053.

Doleys, D. M. (1977). Behavioral treatment of nocturnal enuresis in children: A review of the recent literature. *Psychological Bulletin*, 84, 30–54.

Dollard, J., & Miller, N. E. (1950). *Personality and psychotherapy*. New York: McGraw-Hill.

Dollinger, S. J., & Orf, L. A. (1991). Personality and performance in "personality": Conscientiousness and Openness. *Journal of Research in Personality*, 25, 276–284.

Domino, G., & Affonso, D. D. (1990). A personality measure of Erikson's life stages: The Inventory of Social Balance. *Journal of Personality Assessment*, 54, 576–588.

Dornic, S., & Ekhammar, B. (1990). Extraversion, neuroticism, and noise sensitivity. *Personality and Individual Differences*, 11, 989–992.

Downs, A. F. D., Rosenthal, T. L., & Lichstein, K. L. (1988). Modeling therapies reduce avoidance of bath-time by the institutionalized elderly. *Behavior Therapy*, 19, 359–368.

Dowrick, P. W. (1991). *Practical guide to using video in the behavioral sciences*. New York: Wiley.

Drell, W. K. (1988). Countertransference and the obese patient. *American Journal of Psychotherapy*, 62, 77–85.

Duckworth, J. C. (1991). The Minnesota Multiphasic Personality Inventory-2: A review. *Journal of Counseling and Development*, 69, 564–567.

Duncan, R. C., Konefal, J., & Spechler, M. M. (1990). Effect of neurolinguistic programming training on self-actualization as measured by the Personal Orientation Inventory. *Psychological Reports*, 66, 1323–1330.

Dunnett, G. (Ed.). (1988). *Working with people: Clinical uses of personal construct psychology*. New York: Routledge.

Dunning, D., Meyerowitz, J. A., & Holzberg, A. (1989). Ambiguity and self-evaluation: The role of idiosyncratic definitions in self-serving assessments of ability. *Journal of Personality and Social Psychology, 57,* 1082–1090.

DuPreez, P. D. (1977). *Kelly's "matrix of decision" and the politics of identity.* Paper presented at the Second International Conference on Personal Construct Psychology, Oxford University. Cited in Adams-Webber, J. R. (1979). *Personal construct theory: Concepts and applications.* Chichester, England: Wiley.

Dush, D. M., Hirt, M. L., & Schroeder, H. E. (1989). Self-statement modification in the treatment of child behavior disorders: A meta-analysis. *Psychological Bulletin, 106,* 97–106.

Dyk, P. H., & Adams, G. R. (1990). Identity and intimacy: An initial investigation of three theoretical models using cross-lagged panel correlations. *Journal of Youth and Adolescence, 19,* 91–110.

Dykman, B. M., & Abramson, L. Y. (1990). Contributions of basic research to the cognitive theories of depression. *Personality and Social Psychology Bulletin, 16,* 42–57.

D'Zurilla, T. (1965). Recall efficiency and mediating cognitive events in "experimental repression." *Journal of Personality and Social Psychology, 37,* 253–256.

D'Zurilla, T. J. (1986). *Problem-solving therapy.* New York: Springer.

D'Zurilla, T., & Nezu, A. (1982). Social problem-solving in adults. In D. Kendall (Ed.), *Advances in cognitive-behavioral research and therapy* (Vol. 1, pp. 285–315). New York: Academic Press.

Eagle, M. N. (1984). *Recent developments in psychoanalysis: A critical evaluation.* New York: McGraw-Hill.

Eagle, M. N., & Wolitzky, D. L. (1985). The current status of psychoanalysis. *Clinical Psychology Review, 5,* 259–269.

Eastman, C., & Marzillier, J. S. (1984). Theoretical and methodological difficulties in Bandura's self-efficacy theory. *Cognitive Therapy and Research, 8,* 213–229.

Eaton, W. O., & Enns, L. R. (1986). Sex differences in human motor activity level. *Psychological Bulletin, 100,* 19–28.

Ebersole, P., & Humphreys, P. (1991). The short index of self-actualization and purpose in life. *Psychological Reports, 69,* 550.

Eden, D., & Kinnar, J. (1991). Modeling Galatea: Boosting self-efficacy to increase volunteering. *Journal of Applied Psychology, 76,* 770–780.

Edwards, A. L. (1953). *Manual for Edwards Personal Preference Schedule.* New York: Psychological Corporation.

Edwards, A. L. (1957). *The social desirability variable in personality research.* New York: Dryden.

Edwards, A. L. (1970). *The measurement of personality traits by scales and inventories.* New York: Holt, Rinehart & Winston.

Edwards, A. L., & Edwards, L. K. (1991). The first-factor loadings of the MMPI factor scales. *Bulletin of the Psychonomic Society, 29,* 229–232.

Edwards, N. (1987). The unconscious ego-ideal and analytic group psychotherapy. *Group, 2,* 165–176.

Eifert, G. H., & Evans, I. M. (Eds.). (1990). *Unifying behavior therapy: Contributions of paradigmatic behaviorism.* New York: Springer.

Elder, G. H., & MacInnis, D. J. (1983). Achievement imagery in woman's lives from adolescence to adulthood. *Journal of Personality and Social Psychology, 45,* 394–404.

Ellenberger, H. F. (1970). *The discovery of the unconscious: The history and evolution of dynamic psychiatry.* New York: Basic Books.

Ellinwood, C. (1989). The young child in person-centered family therapy [Special Issue: Person-centered approaches with families]. *Person-Centered Review, 4,* 256–262.

Ellis, A. (1962). *Reason and emotion in psychotherapy.* New York: Lyle Stuart.

Ellis, A. (1985). Expanding the ABCs of RET. In M. J. Mahoney & A. Freeman (Eds.), *Cognition and psychotherapy* (pp. 313–323). New York: Plenum.

Ellis, A. (1989). Comments on my critics. In M. E. Bernard & R. DiGiuseppe (Eds.), *Inside rational-emotive therapy: A critical appraisal of the theory and therapy of Albert Ellis* (pp. 199–233). San Diego: Academic Press.

Ellis, A. (1993). Reflections on rational-emotive therapy. *Journal of Consulting and Clinical Psychology, 61,* 199–201.

Ellis, A., & Bernard, M. E. (1985). What is rational-emotive therapy (RET)? In A. Ellis & R. M. Grieger (Eds.), *Handbook of rational-emotive therapy* (pp. 1–30). New York: Springer.

Ellis, A., & Dryden, W. (1987). *The practice of rational-emotive therapy.* New York: Springer.

Elms, A. C. (1988). Freud as Leonardo: Why the first psychobiography went wrong. *Journal of Personality, 56,* 19–40.

Emmons, R. A., & Diener, E. (1986). Situation selection as a moderator variable of response consistency and stability. *Journal of Personality and Social Psychology, 51,* 1013–1019.

Emmons, R. A., & McAdams, D. P. (1991). Personal strivings and motive dispositions: Exploring the links. *Personality and Social Psychology Bulletin, 17,* 648–654.

Endler, N. S. (1989). The temperamental nature of personality. *European Journal of Personality, 3,* 151–165.

Engstrom, I. (1991). Family interaction and locus of control in children and adolescents with inflammatory bowel disease. *Journal of the American Academy of Child and Adolescent Psychiatry, 30,* 913–920.

Epstein, S. (1966). Some theoretical considerations on the nature of ambiguity and the use of stimulus dimensions in projective techniques. *Journal of Consulting Psychology, 30,* 183–192.

Epting, F. R., & Nazario, A. (1987). Designing a fixed role therapy: Issues, techniques, and modifications. In R. A. Neimeyer & G. J. Neimeyer (Eds.), *Personal construct therapy casebook.* New York: Springer.

Erdelyi, M. H. (1974). A new look at the new look: Perceptual defense and vigilance. *Psychological Review, 81,* 1–25.

Erdelyi, M. H. (1985). *Psychoanalysis: Freud's cognitive psychology*. New York: W. H. Freeman.

Ericksen, M. K., & Sirgy, M. J. (1989). Achievement motivation and clothing behavior: A self-image congruence analysis. *Journal of Social Behavior and Personality, 4*, 307–326.

Erikson, E. H. (1950). *Childhood and society*. New York: W. W. Norton.

Erikson, E. H. (1954). The dream specimen of psychoanalysis. *Journal of the American Psychoanalytic Association, 2*, 5–56.

Erikson, E. H. (1963). *Childhood and society* (2nd ed.). New York: Norton.

Erikson, E. H. (1968). *Identity, youth, and crisis*. New York: Norton.

Essig, T. S., & Russell, R. L. (1990). Analyzing subjectivity in therapeutic discourse: Rogers, Perls, Ellis and Gloria revisited. *Psychotherapy, 27*, 271–281.

Evans, F. J. (1974). The placebo response in pain reduction. In J. J. Bonica (Ed.), *Advances in neurology* (Vol. 4, pp. 289–296). New York: Raven Press.

Evans, F. J. (1985). Expectancy, therapeutic instructions, and the placebo response. In L. White, B. Tursky, & G. E. Schwartz (Eds.), *Placebo: Theory, research, and mechanisms* (pp. 215–228). New York: Guilford Press.

Evans, P. (1989). *Motivation and emotion*. New York: Routledge.

Evans, R. G. (1982). Skill versus chance tasks: Comparison of locus of control, defensive externality, and persistence. *Personality and Social Psychology Bulletin, 8*, 129–133.

Ewart, C. K. (1991). Social action theory for a public health psychology. *American Psychologist, 46*, 931–946.

Ewart, C. K. (1992). The role of physical self-efficacy in recovery from heart attack. In R. Schwarzer (Ed.), *Self-efficacy: Thought control of action* (pp. 287–304). Washington, DC: Hemisphere.

Eysenck, H. J. (1963). *Uses and abuses of psychology*. Baltimore: Penguin.

Eysenck, H. J. (1975). *The inequality of man*. San Diego: EdITS/Educational & Industrial Testing Service.

Eysenck, H. J. (1982). *Personality genetics and behavior*. New York: Praeger.

Eysenck, H. J. (1985). Incubation theory of fear/anxiety. In S. Reiss & R. R. Bootzin (Eds.), *Theoretical issues in behavior therapy* (pp. 83–105). Orlando, FL: Academic Press.

Eysenck, H. J., & Eysenck, M. W. (1985). *Personality and individual differences: A natural science approach*. New York: Plenum Press.

Eysenck, S. B. G., & Long, F. Y. (1986). A cross-cultural comparison of personality in adults and children: Singapore and England. *Journal of Personality and Social Psychology, 50*, 124–130.

Eysenck, S. B. G., & Haapasalo, J. (1989). Cross-cultural comparisons of personality: Finland and England. *Personality and Individual Differences, 10*, 121–125.

Eysenck, S. B. G., & Tambs, K. (1990). Cross-cultural comparison of personality: Norway and England. *Scandinavian Journal of Psychology, 31*, 191–197.

Fairbairn, W. R. D. (1952). *Psychoanalytic studies of the personality*. London: Tavistock Publications and Routledge & Kegan Paul.

Faulkender, P. J. (1991). Does gender schema mediate between sex-role identity and self-actualization? *Psychological Reports, 68*, 1019–1029.

Feinberg, R. A. (1990). The social nature of the classical conditioning phenomena in people: A comment on Hunt, Florsheim, Chatterjee, & Kernan. *Psychological Reports, 67*, 331–334.

Feixas, G. (1992). A constructivist approach to supervision: Some preliminary thoughts. *International Journal of Personal Construct Psychology, 5*, 183–200.

Felton, B., & Kahana, E. (1974). Adjustment and situationally bound locus of control among institutionalized aged. *Journal of Gerontology, 29*, 295–301.

Fenichel, O. (1945). *The psychoanalytic theory of neurosis*. New York: Norton.

Fernández-Ballesteros, R., & Staats, A. W. (1992). Paradigmatic behavioral assessment, treatment and evaluation: Answering the crisis in behavioral assessment. *Advances in Behaviour Research and Therapy, 14*, 1–28.

Festinger, L. (1957). *A theory of cognitive dissonance*. Stanford, CA: Stanford University Press.

Fichter, M. M., & Noegel, R. (1990). Concordance for bulimia nervosa in twins. *International Journal of Eating Disorders, 9*, 255–263.

Finell, J. S. (1987). A challenge to psychoanalysis: A review of the negative therapeutic reaction. *Psychoanalytic Review, 74*, 487–515.

Fischer, M. (1973). Genetic and environmental factors in schizophrenia. *Acta Psychiatrica Scandinavica*. (Suppl. 238).

Fisher, D. D. V. (1990a). Emotional construing: A psychobiological model. *International Journal of Personal Construct Psychology, 3*, 183–203.

Fisher, D. D. V. (1990b). Emotions: Adaptive standards and/or primitive constructs: A reply to Mascolo and Mancuso. *International Journal of Personal Construct Psychology, 3*, 223–230.

Fisher, S. (1973). *The female orgasm*. New York: Basic Books.

Fisher, S., & Greenberg, R. P. (1977). *The scientific credibility of Freud's theories and therapy*. New York: Basic Books.

Flett, G. L., Blankstein, K. R., & Hewitt, P. L. (1991). Factor structure of the short index of self-actualization. [Special Issue: Handbook of self-actualization]. *Journal of Social Behavior and Personality, 6*, 321–329.

Flett, G. L., Hewitt, P. L., Blankstein, K. R., & Mosher, S. W. (1991). Perfectionism, self-actualization, and personal adjustment [Special Issue: Handbook of self-actualization]. *Journal of Social Behavior and Personality, 6*, 147–160.

Floderus-Myrhed, B., Pedersen, N., & Rasmuson, S. (1980). Assessment of heritability for personality based on a short form of the Eysenck Personality Inventory. *Behavior Genetics, 10*, 153–162.

Fodor, E. M. (1984). The power motive and reactivity to power stresses. *Journal of Personality and Social Psychology*, 47, 853–859.

Fonagy, P., & Moran, G. S. (1990). Studies in the efficacy of child psychoanalysis. *Journal of Consulting and Clinical Psychology*, 58, 684–695.

Ford, D. Y., & Harris, J. J. (1990). On discovering the hidden treasure of gifted and talented Black children. *Roeper Review*, 13, 27–32.

Ford, J. G. (1991a). Inherent potentialities of actualization: An initial exploration. *Journal of Humanistic Psychology*, 31, 65–88.

Ford, J. G. (1991b). Rogerian self-actualization: A clarification of meaning. *Journal of Humanistic Psychology*, 31, 101–111.

Forsman, L. (1989). Parent-child gender interaction in the relation between retrospective self-reports on parental love and current self esteem. *Scandinavian Journal of Psychology*, 30, 275–283.

Fosshage, J. L. (1987). New vistas on dream interpretation. In M. L. Glucksman & S. L. Warner (Eds.), *Dreams in new perspective: The royal road revisited*. New York: Human Sciences.

Foster, S. L., & Cone, J. D. (1986). Design and use of direct observation. In A. R. Ciminero, K. S. Calhoun, & H. A. Adams (Eds.), *Handbook of behavioral assessment* (2nd ed., pp. 253–324). New York: Wiley.

Fox, N. A. (1989). Psychophysiological correlates of emotional reactivity during the first year of life. *Developmental Psychology*, 25, 364–372.

Foxx, R. M., Martella, R. C., & Marchand-Martella, N. E. (1989). The acquisition, maintenance, and generalization of problem-solving skills by closed head-injured adults. *Behavior Therapy*, 20, 61–76.

Freeman, S. C. (1990). C. H. Patterson on client-centered career counseling: An interview. *Career Development Quarterly*, 38, 291–301.

French, E. G., & Lesser, G. S. (1964). Some characteristics of the achievement motive in women. *Journal of Abnormal and Social Psychology*, 68, 119–128.

French, T., & Fromm, E. (1964). *Dream interpretation*. New York: Basic Books.

Freud, A. (1958). Adolescence. *Psychoanalytic Study of the Child*, 13, 255–278.

Freud, A. (1966). *The ego and the mechanisms of defense* (rev. ed.). New York: International Universities Press.

Freud, S. (1953). The interpretation of dreams. In J. Strachey (Ed. and Trans.), *The standard edition of the complete psychological works of Sigmund Freud* (Vols. 4 and 5). London: Hogarth. (Original work published 1900)

Freud, S. (1955). Analysis of a phobia in a five-year-old boy. In J. Strachey (Ed. and Trans.), *The standard edition of the complete psychological works of Sigmund Freud* (Vol. 10). London: Hogarth. (Original work published 1909)

Freud, S. (1957a). On the history of the psycho-analytic movement. In J. Strachey (Ed. and Trans.), *The standard edition of the complete psychological works of Sigmund Freud* (Vol. 14). London: Hogarth. (Original work published 1914)

Freud, S. (1957b). Repression. In J. Strachey (Ed. and Trans.), *The standard edition of the complete psychological works of Sigmund Freud*, 14, pp. 143–158. London: Hogarth Press. (Original work published 1915)

Freud, S. (1959). Character and anal eroticism. In J. Strachey (Ed. and Trans.), *The standard edition of the complete psychological works of Sigmund Freud* (Vol. 9). London: Hogarth. (Original work published 1908)

Freud, S. (1961a). *The interpretation of dreams* (J. Strachey, Ed. and Trans.). New York: Science Editions. (Original work published 1900)

Freud, S. (1961b). Two encyclopedia articles. In J. Strachey (Ed. and Trans.), *The standard edition of the complete psychological works of Sigmund Freud* (Vol. 18). London: Hogarth. (Original work published 1923)

Freud, S. (1963). Introductory lectures on psychoanalysis. In J. Strachey (Ed. and Trans.), *The standard edition of the complete psychological works of Sigmund Freud* (Vol. 16). London: Hogarth. (Original work published 1916–1917)

Freud, S. (1964a). An outline of psychoanalysis. In J. Strachey (Ed. and Trans.), *The standard edition of the complete psychological works of Sigmund Freud* (Vol. 23). London: Hogarth. (Original work published 1940)

Freud, S. (1964b). Femininity. In J. Strachey (Ed. and Trans.), *The standard edition of the complete psychological works of Sigmund Freud* (Vol. 22). London: Hogarth. (Original work published 1933)

Freud, S. (1965). *New introductory lectures on psychoanalysis*. New York: Norton. (Original work published 1933)

Freud, S., & Jung, C. G. (1974). *The Freud/Jung letters* (W. McGuire, Ed.). Princeton, NJ: Princeton University Press.

Friedman, H. S., & Booth-Kewley, S. (1987). Personality, Type A behavior, and coronary heart disease: The role of emotional expression. *Journal of Personality and Social Psychology*, 53, 783–792.

Friedman, H. S., Hall, H. S., & Harris, M. J. (1985). Type A behavior, nonverbal expressive style, and health. *Journal of Personality and Social Psychology*, 48, 1299–1315.

Friedman, L. (1989). Hartmann's "ego psychology and the problem of adaptation." *Psychoanalytic Quarterly*, 58, 526–550.

Friedman, M., & Rosenman, R. H. (1974). *Type A behavior and your heart*. London: Wildwood House.

Friedrich, J. (1988). The influence of locus of control on students' aspirations, expectations, and information preferences for summer work. *Journal of College Student Development*, 29, 335–339.

Fristad, M. A. (1988). Assessing social desirability in family self-report. *Perceptual and Motor Skills*, 66, 131–137.

Froman, R. D., & Owen, S. V. (1989). Infant care self-efficacy. *Scholarly Inquiry for Nursing Practice*, 3, 199–211.

Fromm, E. (1947). *Man for himself: An inquiry into the psychology of ethics*. New York: Holt, Rinehart & Winston.

Fromm, E. (1955). *The sane society*. New York: Holt, Rinehart & Winston.

Fromm, E. (1963). *The art of loving*. New York: Bantam.

Frosh, S. (1987). *The politics of psychoanalysis: An introduction to Freudian and post-Freudian theory.* New Haven, CT: Yale University Press.

Funder, D. C. (1991). Global traits: A Neo-Allportian approach to personality. *Psychological Science, 2,* 31–39.

Funder, D. C., & Block, J. (1989). The role of ego-control, ego-resiliency, and IQ in delay of gratification in adolescence. *Journal of Personality and Social Psychology, 56,* 1041–1050.

Furnham, A. (1988). *Lay theories of behaviour: Everyday understanding of problems in the social sciences.* New York: Pergamon Press.

Furnham, A., & Brewin, C. R. (1990). Personality and happiness. *Personality and Individual Differences, 11,* 1093–1096.

Gackenbach, J. (Ed.). (1987). *Sleep and dreams: A sourcebook.* New York: Garland.

Gallagher, D. J. (1990). Extraversion, neuroticism and appraisal of stressful academic events. *Personality and Individual Differences, 11,* 1053–1057.

Gallego-Mere, A. (1989). The manifest content of dreams. *The American Journal of Psychoanalysis, 49,* 95–103.

Galton, F. (1884). Measurement of character. *Fortnightly Review, 42,* 179–185.

Garcia, M. E., Schmitz, J. M., & Doerfler, L. A. (1990). A fine-grained analysis of the role of self-efficacy in self-initiated attempts to quit smoking. *Journal of Consulting and Clinical Psychology, 58,* 317–322.

Garden, A. (1991). The purpose of burnout: A Jungian interpretation. *Journal of Social Behavior and Personality, 6,* 73–93.

Gardner, B. T., & Gardner, R. A. (1989). Beyond Pavlovian classical conditioning. *Behavioral and Brain Sciences, 12,* 143–144.

Gardner, H. (1985). *The mind's new science: A history of the cognitive revolution.* New York: Basic Books.

Garfield, S. L., & Bergin, A. E. (Eds.). (1985). *Handbook of psychotherapy and behavior change* (3rd ed.). New York: Wiley.

Gattuso, S. M., Litt, M. D., & Fitzgerald, T. E. (1992). Coping with gastrointestinal endoscopy: Self-efficacy enhancement and coping style. *Journal of Consulting and Clinical Psychology, 60,* 133–139.

Gay, P. (1988). *Freud: A life for our time.* New York: Norton.

Gaylin, N. L. (1989). The necessary and sufficient conditions for change: Individual versus family therapy. [Special Issue: Person-centered approaches with families]. *Person-Centered Review, 4,* 263–279.

Gaylin, W. (1987). *Rediscovering love.* New York: Penguin.

Gecas, V. (1989). The social psychology of self-efficacy. *Annual Review of Sociology, 15,* 291–316.

Gedo, J. E. (1979). *Beyond interpretation.* New York: International Universities Press.

Geen, R. G. (1984). Preferred stimulation levels in introverts and extraverts: Effects on arousal and performance. *Journal of Personality and Social Psychology, 46,* 1303–1312.

Geer, J. H. (1968). A test of the classical conditioning model of emotion: The use of nonpainful aversive stimuli as unconditioned stimuli in a conditioning procedure. *Journal of Personality and Social Psychology, 10,* 148–156.

Geer, J. H., Davison, G. C., & Gatchel, R. I. (1970). Reduction of stress in humans through nonveridical perceived control of aversive stimulation. *Journal of Personality and Social Psychology, 16,* 731–738.

Geisler, C. (1986). The use of subliminal psychodynamic activation in the study of repression. *Journal of Personality and Social Psychology, 51,* 844–851.

Geiss, S. K., & O'Leary, K. D. (1981). Therapist ratings of frequency and severity of marital problems: Implications for research. *Journal of Marital and Family Therapy, 7,* 515–520.

Gendlin, E. T. (1988). Carl Rogers (1902–1987). *American Psychologist, 43,* 127–128.

Georgiou, A., & Bradley, C. (1992). The development of a smoking-specific locus of control scale. *Psychology and Health, 6,* 227–246.

Gifford, F. (1990). Genetic traits. *Biology and Philosophy, 5,* 327–347.

Gilligan, C. (1982). *In a different voice: Psychological theory and women's development.* Cambridge, MA: Harvard University Press.

Gillis, J. R., Rogers, R., & Dickens, S. E. (1990). The detection of faking bad response styles on the MMPI. *Canadian Journal of Behavioral Science, 22,* 408–416.

Gladstone, R. (1990). Psychology versus philosophy. *American Psychologist, 45,* 782.

Glass, D. C. (1977). Stress, behavior patterns and coronary disease. *American Scientist, 65,* 177–187.

Glenn, J. (1987). Freud, Virgil, and Aeneas: An unnoticed classical influence on Freud. *American Journal of Psychoanalysis, 47,* 279–281.

Glueck, S., & Glueck, E. (1950). *Unraveling juvenile delinquency.* New York: Commonwealth Fund.

Glueck, S., & Glueck, E. (1956). *Physique and delinquency.* New York: Harper & Row.

Glynn, S. M. (1990). Token economy approaches for psychiatric patients: Progress and pitfalls over 25 years. *Behavior Modification, 14,* 383–407.

Goffman, E. (1959). *The presentation of self in everyday life.* Garden City, NY: Doubleday.

Goldberg, L. R. (1981). Language and individual differences: The search for universals in personality lexicons. In L. Wheeler (Ed.), *Review of personality and social psychology* (Vol. 2, pp. 141–165). Beverly Hills, CA: Sage.

Goldberg, L. R. (1990). An alternative "description of personality": The big-five factor structure. *Journal of Personality and Social Psychology, 59,* 1216–1229.

Golden, G. K. (1987). Creativity: An object relations perspective. *Clinical Social Work Journal, 15,* 214–222.

Goldfried, M. R. (1992). Psychotherapy integration: A mid-life crisis for behavior therapy. *the Behavior Therapist, 15,* 38–42.

Goldfried, M. R., Greenberg, L. S., & Marmar, C. (1990). Individual psychotherapy: Process and outcome. *Annual Review of Psychology, 41,* 659–688.

Goldsmith, H. H. (1983). Genetic influences on personality from infancy to adulthood. *Child Development, 54,* 331–355.

Goldsmith, H. H., & Campos, J. J. (1990). The structure of temperamental fear and pleasure in infants: A psychometric perspective. *Child Development, 61,* 1944–1964.

Goldstein, H., & Mousetis, L. (1989). Generalized language learning by children with severe mental retardation: Effects of peers' expressive modeling. *Journal of Applied Behavior Analysis, 22,* 245–259.

Goldwater, L., & Duffy, J. F. (1990). Use of the MMPI to uncover histories of childhood abuse in adult female psychiatric patients. *Journal of Clinical Psychology, 46,* 392–398.

Goleman, D. (1985, December 31). Scientists find city is a series of varying perceptions. *The New York Times,* pp. C1, C6.

Goleman, D. (1988, November 1). Narcissism looming larger as root of personality woes. *The New York Times,* pp. C1, C16.

Gonzalez, J. T., & Gonzalez, V. M. (1990). Initial validation of a scale measuring self-efficacy of breast self-examination among low-income Mexican American women. *Hispanic Journal of Behavioral Sciences, 12,* 277–291.

Gorkin, M. (1987). *The uses of countertransference.* Northvale, NJ: Aronson.

Gottesman, I. L., & Prescott, C. A. (1989). Abuses of the MacAndrew alcoholism scale: A critical review. *Clinical Psychology Reviews, 9,* 223–242.

Grant, B. (1990). Principled and instrumental nondirectiveness in person-centered and client-centered therapy. *Person-Centered Review, 5,* 77–88.

Grasha, A. F. (1978). *Practical applications of psychology.* Cambridge, MA: Winthrop.

Gray, A., & Jackson, D. N. (1990). Individual differences in Type A behavior and cardiovascular responses to stress. *Personality and Individual Differences, 11,* 1213–1219.

Gray, C. (1992). Enterprise trainees' self-construals as entrepreneurs. *International Journal of Personal Construct Psychology, 5,* 307–322.

Greeley, A. (1974). *Ecstasy: A way of knowing.* Englewood Cliffs, NJ: Prentice-Hall.

Green, D. (1988). Resisting the stigma of incest: An experiment in personal construct psychotherapy. *Journal of Adolescence, 11,* 299–308.

Green, D., & Kirby-Turner, N. (1990). First steps in family therapy: A personal construct analysis. *Journal of Family Therapy, 12,* 139–154.

Greenglass, E. R., & Julkunen, J. (1989). Construct validity and sex differences in Cook-Medley hostility. *Personality and Individual Differences, 10,* 209–218.

Greenglass, E. R., & Julkunen, J. (1991). Cook-Medley hostility, anger, and the Type A behavior pattern in Finland. *Psychological Reports, 68,* 1059–1066.

Greenson, R. R. (1965). The working alliance and the transference neurosis. *Psychoanalytic Quarterly, 34,* 155–181.

Greenson, R. R. (1967). *The technique and practice of psychoanalysis.* New York: International Universities Press.

Greenson, R. R. (1974). Loving, hating, and indifference toward the patient. *International Review of Psychoanalysis, 1,* 259–266.

Grieser, C., Greenberg, R., & Harrison, R. H. (1972). The adaptive function of sleep: The differential effects of sleep and dreaming on recall. *Journal of Abnormal Psychology, 80,* 280–286.

Grossman, L. S., Haywood, T. W., Wasyliw, O., & Cavanaugh, J. L. (1990). Sensitivity of MMPI validity scales to motivational factors in psychological evaluations of police officers. *Journal of Personality Assessment, 55,* 549–561.

Grubrich–Simitis, I. (Ed.). (1987). *A phylogenetic fantasy: Overview of the transference neurosis.* Cambridge, MA: Harvard University Press.

Grünbaum, A. (1984). *The foundations of psychoanalysis: A philosophical critique.* Berkeley: University of California Press.

Guevremont, D. C., & Foster, S. L. (1993). Impact of social problem-solving training on aggressive boys: Skill acquisition, behavior change, and generalization. *Journal of Abnormal Child Psychology, 21,* 13–27.

Guevremont, D. C., Osnes, P. G., & Stokes, T. F. (1988). The functional role of verbalizations in the generalization of self-instructional training with children. *Journal of Applied Behavior Analysis, 21,* 45–55.

Guevremont, D. C., & Spiegler, M. D. (1990, November). *What do behavior therapists really do?: A survey of the clinical practice of AABT members.* Paper presented at the meeting of the Association for Advancement of Behavior Therapy, San Francisco.

Haaga, D. A. F. (1990). Gender schematic parapraxes in the articulated thoughts of ex-smokers. *Social Behavior and Personality, 18,* 261–266.

Haaga, D. A. F., & Stewart, B. L. (1992). Self-efficacy for recovery from a lapse after smoking cessation. *Journal of Consulting and Clinical Psychology, 60,* 24–28.

Haaga, D. A. F., & Stewart, B. L. (1993). Self-efficacy for recovery from a lapse after smoking cessation. *the Behavior Therapist, 16,* 77.

Hahlweg, K., & Markman, H. J. (1988). Effectiveness of behavioral marital therapy: Empirical status of behavioral techniques in preventing and alleviating marital distress. *Journal of Consulting and Clinical Psychology, 56,* 440–447.

Hall, A. G., Hendrick, S. S., & Hendrick, C. (1991). Personal construct systems and love styles. *International Journal of Personal Construct Psychology, 4,* 137–155.

Hall, C. S., & Van de Castle, R. L. (1963). An empirical investigation of the castration complex in dreams. *Journal of Personality, 33,* 20–29.

Hall, R. V., Lund, D., & Jackson, D. (1968). Effects of teacher attention on study behavior. *Journal of Applied Behavior Analysis, 1,* 1–12.

Halpern, J. (1977). Projection: A test of the psychoanalytic hypothesis. *Journal of Abnormal Psychology, 86,* 536–542.

Hamilton, N. G. (1989). A critical review of object relations theory. *American Journal of Psychiatry*, 146, 1552–1560.

Hardin, H. T. (1987). On the vicissitudes of Freud's early mothering: I. Early environment and loss. *Psychoanalytic Quarterly*, 56, 628–644.

Hardin, H. T. (1988a). On the vicissitudes of Freud's early mothering: II. Alienation from his biological mother. *Psychoanalytic Quarterly*, 57, 72–86.

Hardin, H. T. (1988b). On the vicissitudes of Freud's early mothering: III. Freiberg, screen memories, and loss. *Psychoanalytic Quarterly*, 57, 209–223.

Härkäpää, K., Järvikoski, A., Mellin, G., Hurri, H., & Luoma, J. (1991). Health locus of control beliefs and psychological distress as predictors for treatment outcome in low-back pain patients: Results of a 3–month follow-up of a controlled intervention study. *Pain*, 46, 35–41.

Harrell, T. W. (1972). High earning MBAs. *Personnel Psychology*, 25, 523–530.

Harri-Augstein, S. (1985). Learning-to-learn languages: New perspectives for the personal observer. In D. Bannister (Ed.), *Issues and approaches in personal construct theory*. Orlando, FL: Academic Press.

Harrington, D. M., Block, J., & Block, J. H. (1987). Testing aspects of Carl Rogers's theory of creative environments: Child-rearing antecedents of creative potential in young adolescents. *Journal of Personality and Social Psychology*, 52, 851–856.

Harris, B. (1979). Whatever happened to little Albert? *American Psychologist*, 34, 151–160.

Harris, J. G., Jr. (1980). Nomovalidation and idiovalidation: A quest for the true personality profile. *American Psychologist*, 35, 729–744.

Hartley, D. E., & Strupp, H. H. (1983). The therapeutic alliance: Its relationship to outcome in brief psychotherapy. In J. Masling (Ed.), *Empirical studies of psychoanalytical theories* (Vol. 1). Hillsdale, NJ: Analytic Press.

Hartmann, H. (1951). Ego psychology and the problem of adaptation. In D. Rapaport (Ed. and Trans.), *Organization and pathology of thought: Selected sources*. New York: Columbia University Press.

Hartmann, H. (1958). *Ego psychology and the problem of adaptation*. New York: International Universities Press.

Hartmann, H. (1964). *Essays in ego psychology*. New York: International Universities Press.

Hartshorne, H., & May, M. A. (1928). *Studies in the nature of character* (Vol. 1). New York: Macmillan.

Hathaway, S. R., & Monachesi, E. D. (1952). The Minnesota Multiphasic Personality Inventory in the study of juvenile delinquents. *American Sociological Review*, 17, 704–710.

Hayashi, S., Kuno, T., Osawa, M., Shimizu, M., & Suetake, Y. (1992). The client-centered therapy and person–centered approach in Japan: Historical development, current status and perspectives. *Journal of Humanistic Psychology*, 32, 115–136.

Hayes, S. C., & Brownstein, A. J. (1986). Mentalism, behavior-behavior relations and a behavior analytic view of the purposes of science. *The Behavior Analyst*, 9, 175–190.

Haynes, P., & Ayliffe, G. (1991). Locus of control of behaviour: Is high externality associated with substance misuse? *British Journal of Addiction*, 86, 1111–1117.

Haynes, S. N., & Uchigakiuchi, P. (1993). Incorporating personality trait measures in behavioral assessment: Nuts in a fruitcake or raisins in a mai tai? *Behavior Modification*, 17, 72–92.

Hays, R. D., & Ellickson, P. L. (1990). How generalizable are adolescents' beliefs about pro-drug pressures and resistance self-efficacy? *Journal of Applied Social Psychology*, 20, 321–340.

Heatherington, L., Crown, J., Wagner, H., & Rigby, S. (1989). Toward an understanding of social consequences of "feminine immodesty" about personal achievements. *Sex Roles*, 20, 371–380.

Heaven, P. C. (1989). Economic locus of control beliefs and lay attributions of poverty. *Australian Journal of Psychology*, 41, 315–325.

Heaven, P. C. (1990). Suggestions for reducing unemployment: A study of Protestant work ethic and economic locus of control beliefs. *British Journal of Social Psychology*, 29, 55–65.

Heaven, P. C. L. (1988). Locus of control and attitudes toward authority among adolescents. *Personality and Individual Differences*, 9, 181–183.

Heelan, P. A. (1983). *Space-perception and the philosophy of science*. Berkeley: University of California Press.

Helgeson, V. S., & Sharpsteen, D. J. (1987). Perceptions of danger and affiliation situations: An extension of the Pollak and Gilligan versus Benton et al. debate. *Journal of Personality and Social Psychology*, 54, 727–733.

Heller, M. C., & Krauss, H. H. (1991). Perceived self-efficacy as a predictor of aftercare treatment entry by the detoxification patient. *Psychological Reports*, 68, 1047–1052.

Helmes, E., & Holden, R. R. (1986). Response styles and faking on the Basic Personality Inventory. *Journal of Consulting and Clinical Psychology*, 54, 853–859.

Helmreich, R. L., Spence, J. T., & Pred, R. S. (1988). Making it without losing it: Type A, achievement motivation, and scientific attainment revisited. *Personality and Social Psychology Bulletin*, 14, 495–504.

Heppner, P., Neal, G., & Larsen, L. (1984). Problem-solving training as prevention with college students. *Personnel and Guidance Journal*, 62, 514–519.

Herman, A., & Heesacker, M. (1991). A developing model of exploratory psychotherapeutic research: The process within the process. *International Journal of Personal Construct Psychology*, 4, 409–425.

Hermans, H. J. M. (1988). On the integration of nomothetic and idiographic research methods in the study of personal meaning. *Journal of Personality*, 56, 785–812.

Herrnstein, R. J. (1970). On the law of effect. *Journal of the Experimental Analysis of Behavior*, 13, 243–266.

Hesse, M. B. (1963). *Models and analogies in science*. Sheed & Ward: London.

Hessing, D. J., Elffers, H., & Weigel, R. H. (1988). Exploring the limits of self-reports and reasoned action: An investigation of the psychology of tax evasion behavior. *Journal of Personality and Social Psychology, 54,* 405–413.

Hickey, P. (1993). Behavior therapy—Have we compromised too much? *the Behavior Therapist, 16,* 117–119.

Hill, G. J. (1989). An unwillingness to act: Behavioral appropriateness, situational constraint, and self-efficacy in shyness. *Journal of Personality, 57,* 871–890.

Hill, P. (1989). Behavioural psychotherapy with children. *International Review of Psychiatry, 1,* 257–266.

Hineline, P. N. (1992). A self-interpretive behavior analysis. *American Psychologist, 47,* 1274–1286.

Hirschowitz, R. (1987). Behavioral and personality correlates of a need for power in a group of English-speaking South African women. *Journal of Psychology, 121,* 575–590.

Hjelle, L. A. (1991). Relationship of social interest to internal-external control and self-actualization in young women [Special Issue: Social interest]. *Individual Psychology Journal of Adlerian Theory, Research and Practice, 47,* 101–105.

Hjelle, L. A., & Ziegler, D. J. (1981). *Personality theories: Basic assumptions, research, and applications* (2nd ed.). New York: McGraw-Hill.

Hobson, J. A., & McCarley, R. W. (1977). The brain as a dream state generator: An activation-synthesis hypothesis of the dream process. *American Journal of Psychiatry, 134,* 1335–1438.

Hoffart, A., & Martinsen, E. W. (1990). Agoraphobia, depression, mental health locus of control, and attributional styles. *Cognitive Therapy and Research, 14,* 343–351.

Hoffart, A., & Martinsen, E. W. (1991). Mental health locus of control in agoraphobia and depression: A longitudinal study of inpatients. *Psychological Reports, 68,* 1011–1018.

Hoffer, A. (1985). Toward a definition of psychoanalytic neutrality. *Journal of the American Psychoanalytic Association, 33,* 771–795.

Hoffer, A., & Pollin, W. (1970). Schizophrenia in the NAS-NPC panel of 15,909 veteran twin pairs. *Archives of General Psychiatry, 23,* 469–477.

Hoffman, E. (1992, January/February). The last interview of Abraham Maslow. *Psychology Today,* 68–73, 89.

Holden, G. (1991). The relationship of self-efficacy appraisals to subsequent health related outcomes: A meta-analysis. *Social Work in Health Care, 16,* 53–93.

Holden, G. W., Moncher, M. S., Schinke, S. P., & Barker, K. M. (1990). Self-efficacy of children and adolescents: A meta-analysis. *Psychological Reports, 66,* 1044–1046.

Holland, J. G. (1992). B. F. Skinner (1904–1990). *American Psychologist, 47,* 665–667.

Hollander, E. P. (1964). *Leaders, groups, and influence.* New York: Oxford University Press.

Hollon, S. D., Shelton, R. C., & Davis, D. D. (1993). Cognitive therapy for depression: Conceptual issues and clinical efficacy. *Journal of Consulting and Clinical Psychology, 61,* 270–275.

Holman, H. R., & Lorig, K. (1992). Perceived self-efficacy in the management of chronic disease. In R. Schwarzer (Ed.), *Self-efficacy: Thought control of action* (pp. 305–323). Washington, DC: Hemisphere.

Holmes, D. S. (1972). Repression or interference? A further investigation. *Journal of Personality and Social Psychology, 22,* 163–170.

Holmes, D. S. (1978). Projection as a defense mechanism. *Psychological Bulletin, 85,* 677–688.

Holmes, D. S. (1991). *Abnormal psychology.* New York: HarperCollins.

Holmes, D. S., McGilley, B. M., & Houston, B. K. (1984). Task-related arousal of Type A and Type B persons: Level of challenge and response specificity. *Journal of Personality and Social Psychology, 46,* 1322–1327.

Holtzman, W. H. (1988). Beyond the Rorschach. *Journal of Personality Assessment, 52,* 578–609.

Holtzman, W. H., Thorpe, J. S., Swartz, J. D., & Herron, E. W. (1961). *Inkblot perception and personality: Holtzman Inkblot Technique.* Austin: University of Texas Press.

Honikman, B. (1976). Construct theory as an approach to architectural and environmental design. In P. Slater (Ed.), *Explorations of intrapersonal space* (Vol. 1). London: Wiley.

Hopper, R. B., & Kirschenbaum, D. S. (1985). Social problem solving and social competence in preadolescents: Is inconsistency the hobgoblin of little minds? *Cognitive Therapy and Research, 9,* 685–701.

Horley, J. (1988). Construal of events: Personal constructs versus projects. In F. Fransella & L. Thomas (Eds.), *Experimenting with personal construct psychology.* London: Routledge & Kegan Paul.

Horley, J. (1991). Values and beliefs as personal constructs. *International Journal of Personal Construct Psychology, 4,* 1–14.

Horne, J. (1988). *Why we sleep: The functions of sleep in humans and other mammals.* New York: Oxford University Press.

Horner, M. S. (1973). A psychological barrier to achievement in women: The motive to avoid success. In D. C. McClelland & R. S. Steele (Eds.), *Human motivation: A book of readings.* Morristown, NJ: General Learning Press.

Horney, K. (1939). *New ways in psychoanalysis.* New York: Norton.

Horton, G. E., & Brown, D. (1990). The importance of interpersonal skills in consultee-centered consultation: A review. *Journal of Counseling and Development, 68,* 423–426.

Houston, B. K. (1983). Psychophysiological responsivity and the Type A behavior pattern. *Journal of Research in Personality, 17,* 22–39.

Houts, A. C. (1991). Nocturnal enuresis as a biobehavioral problem. *Behavior Therapy, 22,* 133–151.

Houts, A. C., & Follette, W. C. (1992). Philosophical and theoretical issues in behavior therapy. *Behavior Therapy, 23,* 145–149.

Houts, A. C., & Liebert, R. M. (1984). *Bedwetting: A guide for parents and children.* Springfield, IL: Charles C Thomas.

Houts, A. C., Peterson, J. K., & Whelan, J. P. (1986). Prevention of relapse in Full-Spectrum Home Training for primary enuresis: A components analysis. *Behavior Therapy, 17,* 462–469.

Howard, J. H., Cunningham, D. A., & Rechnitzer, P. A. (1987). Personality and fitness decline in middle-aged men. *International Journal of Sport Psychology, 18,* 100–111.

Howard, R., & McKillen, M. (1990). Extraversion and performance in the perceptual maze test. *Personality and Individual Differences, 11,* 391–396.

Hudson, R. (1974). Images of the retailing environment: An example of the use of the repertory grid methodology. *Environment and Behavior, 6,* 470–495.

Huertas-Rodriguez, E. (1991). Cognitive techniques in human classical conditioning. *Journal of Psychophysiology, 5,* 5–10.

Hyland, M. E., Curtis, C., & Mason, D. (1985). Fear of success: Motive and cognition. *Journal of Personality and Social Psychology, 49,* 1669–1677.

Hyman, R. (1964). *The nature of psychological inquiry.* Englewood Cliffs, NJ: Prentice-Hall.

Ihilevich, D., & Gleser, G. C. (1986). *Defense mechanisms: Their classification, correlates and measurement with the Defense Mechanisms Inventory.* Owoso, MI: DMI Associates.

Ingold, C. H. (1989). Locus of control and use of public information. *Psychological Reports, 64,* 603–607.

Inwald, R. E., & Brockwell, A. L. (1991). Predicting the performance of government security personnel with the IPI and MMPI. *Journal of Personality Assessment, 56,* 522–535.

Isaacs, W., Thomas, J., & Goldiamond, I. (1960). Application of operant conditioning to reinstate verbal behavior in psychotics. *Journal of Speech and Hearing Disorders, 25,* 8–12.

Jackson, D. D. (Ed.). (1960). *The etiology of schizophrenia.* New York: Basic Books.

Jackson, D. N., & Messick, S. (1958). Content and style in personality assessment. *Psychological Bulletin, 55,* 243–252.

Jackson, T. T., Markley, R. P., Zelhart, P. F., & Guydish, J. (1988). Contributions to the history of psychology: XLV. Attitude research: George A. Kelly's use of polar adjectives. *Psychological Reports, 62,* 47–52.

Jacobson, N. S. (1985). The role of observational measures in behavior therapy outcome research. *Behavioral Assessment 7,* 297–308.

Jacobson, N. S. (1989). The maintenance of treatment gains following social learning-based marital therapy. *Behavior Therapy, 20,* 325–336.

Jacobson, N. S. (1991, September). *Marital therapy: Theory and treatment considerations.* Workshop sponsored by the Rhode Island Psychological Association. Warwick, RI.

Jacobson, N. S. (1992). Behavioral couple therapy: A new beginning. *Behavior Therapy, 23,* 493–506.

Jaffe, L. S. (1990). The empirical foundations of psychoanalytic approaches to psychological testing. *Journal of Personality Assessment, 55,* 746–755.

Jaison, B. (1991). Experiential learning: Reflections on Virginia Satir and Eugene Gendlin. *Journal of Couples Therapy, 2,* 155–163.

Jankowicz, A. D. (1987). Whatever became of George Kelly? Applications and implications. *American Psychologist, 42,* 481–487.

Jankowicz, A. D. (1990). Applications of personal construct psychology in business practice. In G. J. Neimeyer & R. A. Neimeyer (Eds.), *Advances in personal construct psychology* (Vol. 1, pp. 257–287). Greewich, CT: JAI Press.

Jay, S. M., Elliot, C. H., Ozolins, M., Olson, R. A., & Pruitt, S. D. (1985). Behavioral management of children's distress during painful medical procedures. *Behaviour Research and Therapy, 23,* 513–520.

Jenkins, S. R. (1987). Need for achievement and women's careers over 14 years: Evidence for occupational structure effects. *Journal of Personality and Social Psychology, 53,* 922–932.

Jennings, B. M. (1990). Stress, locus of control, social support, and psychological symptoms among head nurses. *Research in Nursing & Health, 13,* 393–401.

Jensen, L., Olsen, J., & Hughes, C. (1990). Association of country, sex, social class, and life cycle to locus of control in Western European countries. *Psychological Reports, 67,* 199–205.

Jensen, L. C., Huber, C. , Cundick, B., & Carlson, J. (1991). Development of a self theory and measurement scale. *Journal of Personality Assessment, 57,* 521–530.

Jerusalem, M., & Schwarzer, R. (1992). Self-efficacy as a resource factor in stress appraisal processes. In R. Schwarzer (Ed.), *Self-efficacy: Thought control of action* (pp. 195–213). Washington, DC: Hemisphere.

John, I. D., & Soyland, A. J. (1990). What is the epistemic status of the theory of personal constructs? *International Journal of Personal Construct Psychology, 3,* 51–62.

Johnson, E. E., Nora, R. M., Tan, B., & Bustos, N. (1991). Comparison of two locus of control scales in predicting relapse in an alcoholic population. *Perceptual and Motor Skills, 72,* 43–50.

Johnson, G. B. (1966). Penis envy or pencil needing? *Psychological Reports, 19,* 758.

Johnson, L. R., Magnani, B., Chan, V., & Ferrante, F. M. (1989). Modifiers of patient-controlled analgesia efficacy: I. Locus of control. *Pain, 39,* 17–22.

Johnson, S. B. (1980). Enuresis. In R. Daitzman (Ed.), *Clinical behavior therapy and behavior modification* (pp. 81–142). New York: Garland.

Jones, A., & Crandall, R. (1986). Validation of a short index of self-actualization. *Personality and Social Psychology Bulletin, 12,* 63–73.

Jones, D. C., & Houts, R. (1992). Parental drinking, parent-child communication, and social skills in young adults. *Journal of Studies on Alcohol, 53,* 48–56.

Jones, E. (1927). The early development of female sexuality. *International Journal of Psycho-Analysis, 8,* 459–472.

Jones, E. (1953). *The life and works of Sigmund Freud* (Vol. 1). New York: Basic Books.

Jorm, A. F. (1987). Sex differences in neuroticism: A quantitative synthesis of published research. *Australian and New Zealand Journal of Psychiatry, 21,* 501–506.

Josephs, L. (1988). A comparison of archaeological and empathic modes of listening. *Contemporary Psychoanalysis, 24*, 282–300.

Jung, C. G. (1933). *Modern man in search of a soul* (W. S. Dell & C. F. Baynes, Trans.). New York: Harcourt Brace.

Jung, C. G. (1969). General aspects of dream psychology. In *The collected works of C. G. Jung* (Vol. 8). Princeton: Princeton University Press.

Kagan, J., & Moss, H. A. (1960). *Birth to maturity*. New York: Wiley.

Kagan, J., & Reznick, J. S. (1986). Shyness and temperament. In W. H. Jones, J. M. Cheek, & S. R. Briggs (Eds.), *Shyness* (pp. 81–90). New York: Plenum.

Kagan, J., Reznick, J. S., & Snidman, N. (1987). The physiology and psychology of behavioral inhibition in children. *Child Development, 58*, 1459–1473.

Kagan, J., & Snidman, N. (1991). Temperamental factors in human development. *American Psychologist, 46*, 856–862.

Kahn, E. (1989). Heinz Kohut and Carl Rogers: Toward a constructive collaboration. *Psychotherapy, 26*, 555–563.

Kahn, J. S., Kehle, T. J., Jenson, W. R., & Clark, E. (1990). Comparison of cognitive-behavioral, relaxation, and self-modeling interventions for depression among middle-school students. *School Psychology Review, 19*, 196–211.

Katerndahl, D. A. (1991). Relationship between panic attacks and health locus of control. *Journal of Family Practice, 32*, 391–396.

Katz, J. O. (1984). Personal construct theory and the emotions: An interpretation in terms of primitive constructs. *British Journal of Psychology, 75*, 315–327.

Kavanagh, D. (1992). Self-efficacy and depression. In R. Schwarzer (Ed.), *Self-efficacy: Thought control of action* (pp. 177–193). Washington, DC: Hemisphere.

Kehle, T. J., Owen, S. V., & Cressy, E. T. (1990). The use of self-modeling as an intervention in school psychology: A case study of an elective mute. *School Psychology Review, 19*, 115–121.

Kelly, D., & Taylor, H. (1981). Take and escape: A personal construct study of car "theft." In H. Bonarius, R. Holland, & S. Rosenberg (Eds.), *Personal construct psychology: Recent advances in theory and practice*. New York: St. Martin's Press.

Kelly, G. A. (1955). *The psychology of personal constructs* (Vols. 1 and 2). New York: Norton.

Kelly, G. A. (1961). Suicide: The personal construct point of view. In N. L. Farberow & E. S. Schneidman (Eds.), *The cry for help*. New York: McGraw-Hill.

Kelly, G. A. (1966). A brief introduction to personal construct theory. In D. Bannister (Ed.), *Perspectives in personal construct theory* (pp 1–29). London: Academic Press.

Kelly, G. A. (1969). Sin and psychotherapy. In B. Maher (Ed.), *Clinical psychology and personality: The selected papers of George Kelly* (pp. 165–188). New York: Wiley.

Kelly, G. A. (1980). A psychology of the optimal man. In A. W. Landfield & L. M. Leitner (Eds.), *Personal construct psychology: Psychotherapy and personality* (pp. 18–35). New York: Wiley.

Keltikangas-Jarvinen, L. (1990). Continuity of Type A behavior during childhood, preadolescence, and adolescence. *Journal of Youth and Adolescence, 19*, 221–232.

Keltikangas-Jarvinen, L., & Raikkonen, K. (1990). Type A factors as predictors of somatic risk factors of coronary heart disease in young Finns–A six year followup study. *Journal of Psychosomatic Research, 34*, 89–97.

Kemp, S. (1988). Personality in ancient astrology. *New Ideas in Psychology, 6*, 267–272.

Kendrick, D. T., & Funder, D. C. (1988). Profiting from controversy: Lessons from the person-situation debate. *American Psychologist, 43*, 23–34.

Kenny, V., & Delmonte, M. (1986). Meditation as viewed through personal construct theory. *Journal of Contemporary Psychotherapy, 16*, 4–22.

Kern, S. (1973). Freud and the discovery of child sexuality. *History of Childhood Quarterly, 1*, 117–141.

Kernberg, O. (1975). *Borderline conditions and pathological narcissism*. New York: Aronson.

Kernberg, O. (1976). *Object-relations theory and clinical psychoanalysis*. New York: Aronson.

Kernberg, O. (1987). Projection and projective identification: Developmental and clinical aspects. *Journal of the American Psychoanalytic Association, 35*, 795–819.

Kety, S., Rosenthal, D., Wender, P. H., & Shulsinger, F. (1968). The types and prevalence of mental illness in the biological and adoptive families of adopted schizophrenics. In D. Rosenthal and S. Kety (Eds.), *The transmission of schizophrenia*. New York: Pergamon Press.

Keutzer, C. (1978). Whatever turns you on: Triggers to transcendent experiences. *Journal of Humanistic Psychology, 18*, 77–80.

Kimmel, H. D. (1989). The importance of classical conditioning. *Behavioral and Brain Sciences, 12*, 148–149.

Kinney, P. J., & Williams, S. L. (1988). Accuracy of fear inventories and self-efficacy scales in predicting agoraphobic behavior. *Behaviour Research and Therapy, 26*, 513–518.

Kirkland, J., & Anderson, R. (1990). Invariants, constructs, affordances, analogies. *International Journal of Personal Construct Psychology, 3*, 31–39.

Kirschenbaum, H. (1991). Denigrating Carl Rogers: William Coulson's last crusade. *Journal of Counseling and Development, 69*, 411–413.

Klein, G. S. (1976). *Psychoanalytic theory: An exploration of essentials*. New York: International Universities Press.

Kleinknecht, R. A., & Bernstein, D. A. (1979). Short term treatment of dental avoidance. *Journal of Behavior Therapy and Experimental Psychiatry, 10*, 311–315.

Kline, P. (1972). *Fact and fantasy in Freudian theory*. London: Methuen.

Kline, P. (1987). The experimental study of the psychoanalytic unconscious. *Personality and Social Psychology Bulletin, 13*, 363–378.

Klinger, E. (1966). Fantasy need achievement as a motivational construct. *Psychological Bulletin, 66*, 291–308.

Klion, R. E. (1988). Construct system organization and schizophrenia: The role of construct integration. *Journal of Social and Clinical Psychology, 6*, 439–447.

Klopfer, B., & Davidson, H. H. (1962). *The Rorschach technique: An introductory manual.* New York: Harcourt, Brace & World.

Kluckhohn, V., & Murray, H. A. (1953). Personality formation: The determinants. In C. Kluckhohn, H. Murray, & D. Schneider (Eds.), *Personality in nature, society, and culture* (pp. 53–67). New York: Knopf.

Kluft, R. P. (1991). Multiple personality disorder. In A. Tasman & S. M. Goldfinger (Eds.), *Review of Psychiatry* (Vol. 10). Washington, DC: American Psychiatric Press.

Knapp, P. H., Levin, S., McCarter, R. H., Wermer, H., & Zetzel, E. (1960). Suitability for psychoanalysis: A review of 100 supervised analytic cases. *Psychoanalytic Quarterly, 29,* 459–477.

Knapp, R. R. (1976). *Handbook for the Personal Orientation Inventory.* San Diego: EdITS Publishers.

Kohnken, G., & Maass, A. (1988). Eyewitness testimony: False alarms on biased instructions? *Journal of Applied Psychology, 73,* 363–370.

Kohut, H. (1977). *The restoration of self.* New York: International Universities Press.

Kohut, H. (1984). *How does analysis cure?* Chicago: University of Chicago Press.

Kok, G., de Vries, H., Mudde, A. N., & Strecher, V. J. (1991). Planned health education and the role of self-efficacy: Dutch research. *Health Education Research, 6,* 231–238.

Kok, G., Den Boer, D. J., De Vries, H., Gerards, F., Hospers, H. J., & Mudde, A. N. (1992). Self-efficacy and attribution theory in health education. In R. Schwarzer (Ed.), *Self-efficacy: Thought control of action* (pp. 245–262). Washington, DC: Hemisphere.

Kolotkin, R. L., Revis, E. S., Kirkley, B. G., & Janick, L. (1987). Binge eating and obesity: Associated with MMPI characteristics. *Journal of Consulting and Clinical Psychology, 55,* 872–876.

Kores, R. C., Murphy, W. D., Rosenthal, T. L., Elias, D. B., & North, W. C. (1990). Predicting outcome of chronic pain treatment via a modified self-efficacy scale. *Behaviour Research and Therapy, 28,* 165–169.

Kosinski, J. N. (1970). *Being there.* New York: Harcourt Brace Jovanovich.

Krahe, B. (1989). Faking personality profiles on a standard personality inventory. *Personality and Individual Differences, 10,* 437–443.

Krampen, G. (1989). Perceived childrearing practices and the development of locus of control in early adolescence. *International Journal of Behavioral Development, 12,* 177–193.

Kremsdorf, R. B. (1985). An extension of fixed role therapy with a couple. In F. R. Epting & A. W. Landfield (Eds.), *Anticipating personal construct theory.* Lincoln: University of Nebraska Press.

Kretschmer, E. (1926). *Physique and character: An investigation of the nature of constitution and of the theory of temperament* (W. J. H. Sprott, Trans.). New York: Harcourt.

Kris, E. (1950). On preconscious mental processes. *Psychoanalytic Quarterly, 19,* 540–560.

Kuhn, T. S. (1970). *The structure of scientific revolutions* (2nd ed.). Chicago: University of Chicago Press.

Kutcher, S., & Marton, P. (1991). Affective disorders in first-degree relatives of adolescent onset bipolars, unipolars, and normal controls. *Journal of the American Academy of Child and Adolescent Psychiatry, 30,* 75–78.

Kvavilashvili, L. (1987). Remembering intention as a distinct form of memory. *British Journal of Psychology, 78,* 507–518.

Labouvie-Vief, G., & Gonda, J. (1976). Cognitive strategy training and intellectual performance in the elderly. *Journal of Gerontology, 31,* 327–332.

Landfield, A. W. (1980). The person as a perspectivist, literalist, and chaotic fragmentalist. In A. W. Landfield & L. M. Leitner (Eds.), *Personal construct psychology: Psychotherapy and personality* (pp. 289–320). New York: Wiley.

Landfield, A. W., & Epting, F. R. (1987). *Personal construct psychology: Clinical and personality assessment.* New York: Human Sciences Press.

Landino, R. A., & Owen, S. V. (1988). Self-efficacy in university faculty. *Journal of Vocational Behavior, 33,* 1–14.

Landsman, T., & Landsman, M. S. (1991). The beautiful and noble person: An existentialist phenomenological view of optimal human functioning [Special Issue: Handbook of self-actualization]. *Journal of Social Behavior and Personality, 6,* 61–74.

Lang, A. R., Goeckner, D. J., Adesso, V. J., & Marlatt, G. A. (1975). Effects of alcohol on aggression in males. *Journal of Abnormal Psychology, 84,* 508–516.

Langer, E. J., & Abelson, R. P. (1974). A patient by any other name . . . "Clinician group difference in labeling bias." *Journal of Consulting and Clinical Psychology, 42,* 4–9.

Langs, R. (1987). Psychoanalysis as an Aristotelian science: Pathways to Copernicus and a modern-day approach. *Contemporary Psychoanalysis, 24,* 555–576.

Langs, R. (1988). Perspectives of psychoanalysis as a late arrival to the family of sciences. *Contemporary Psychoanalysis, 24,* 397–419.

LaPiere, R. T. (1934). Attitudes vs. actions. *Social Forces, 13,* 230–237.

Larsen, R. J., & Ketelaar, T. (1989). Extraversion, neuroticism and susceptibility to positive and negative mood induction procedures. *Personality and Individual Differences, 10,* 1221–1228.

Larsen, R. J., & Ketelaar, T. (1991). Personality and susceptibility to positive and negative emotional states. *Journal of Personality and Social Psychology, 61,* 132–140.

Lauer, C., Reimann, D., Lund, R., & Berger, M. (1987). Shortened REM latency: A consequence of psychological strain? *Psychophysiology, 24,* 263–271.

Lavie, P., & Hobson, J. A. (1986). Origin of dreams: Anticipation of modern theories in the philosophy and physiology of the eighteenth and nineteenth centuries. *Psychological Bulletin, 100,* 229–240.

Lavin, N. I., Thorpe, J. G., Barker, J. C., Blakemore, C. B., & Conway, C. G. (1961). Behavior therapy in a case of transvestism. *Journal of Nervous and Mental Disease, 33,* 346–353.

Lee, V. L. (1988). *Beyond behaviorism*. Hillsdale, NJ: Erlbaum.

Lefcourt, H. M. (Ed.). (1981). *Research with the locus of control construct: Assessment methods* (Vol. 1). New York: Academic Press.

Lefcourt, H. M. (1982). *Locus of control: Current theory and research* (2nd ed.). Hillsdale, NJ: Erlbaum.

Lefcourt, H. M., Martin, R. A., Fick, C. M., & Saleh, W. E. (1985). Locus of control for affiliation and behavior in social interactions. *Journal of Personality and Social Psychology, 48*, 755–759.

Lefcourt, H. M., Martin, R. A., & Saleh, W. E. (1984). Locus of control and social support: Interactive moderators of stress. *Journal of Personality and Social Psychology, 47*, 378–389.

Leichtman, M. (1990). Developmental psychology and psychoanalysis: I. The context for a revolution in psychoanalysis. *Journal of the American Psychoanalytic Association, 38*, 915–950.

Lent, R. W., & Hackett, G. (1987). Career self-efficacy: Empirical status and future directions. *Journal of Vocational Behavior, 30*, 347–382.

Lent, R. W., Lopez, F. G., & Bieschke, K. J. (1991). Mathematics self-efficacy: Sources and relation to science-based career choice. *Journal of Counseling Psychology, 38*, 424–430.

LeShan, L. (1991, January/February). Ratting on psychologists. *Hippocrates*, pp. 71–75.

Lesser, G. S. (1973). Achievement motivation in woman. In D. C. McClelland & R. S. Steele (Eds.), *Human motivation: A book of readings*. Morristown, NJ: General Learning Press.

Lesser, G. S., Krawitz, R., & Packard, R. (1963). Experimental arousal of achievement motivation in adolescent girls. *Journal of Abnormal and Social Psychology, 66*, 59–66.

Lessler, K. (1964). Cultural and Freudian dimensions of sexual symbols. *Journal of Consulting Psychology, 28*, 46–53.

Lester, D., Castromayor, I. J., & Icli, T. (1991). Locus of control, depression, and suicidal ideation among American, Philippine, and Turkish students. *Journal of Social Psychology, 131*, 447–449.

Levant, R. F., & Shlien, J. M. (1987). *Client-centered therapy and the person-centered approach: New directions in theory, research, and practice*. New York: Praeger.

Levenson, E. A. (1988). The pursuit of the particular: On the psychoanalytic inquiry. *Contemporary Psychoanalysis, 24*, 1–16.

Levey, A. B., & Martin, I. (1991). Human classical conditioning: The status of the CS. *Integrative Physiology and Behavioral Science, 26*, 26–31.

Levine, F. J., & Slap, J. W. (1985). George S. Klein: Psychoanalytic empiricist. In J. Reppen (Ed.), *Beyond Freud: A study of modern psychoanalytic theorists*. Hillsdale, NJ: Analytic Press.

Levinson, D. J., Darrow, C. N., Klein, E. B., Levinson, M. H., & McKee, B. (1978). *The seasons of a man's life*. New York: Knopf.

Levis, D. J. (1985). Implosive theory: A comprehensive extension of conditioning theory of fear/anxiety to psychopathology. In S. Reiss & R. R. Bootzin (Eds.), *Theoretical issues in behavior therapy* (pp. 49–82). Orlando, FL: Academic Press.

Levy, L. H. (1970). *Conceptions of personality: Theories and research*. New York: Random House.

Lewinsohn, P. M., Mischel, W., Chaplin, W., & Barton, R. (1980). Social competence and depression: The role of illusory self-perceptions. *Journal of Abnormal Psychology, 89*, 203–212.

Lewis, M. (1967). The meaning of a response, or why researchers in infant behavior should be Oriental metaphysicians. *Merrill-Palmer Quarterly, 13*, 7–18.

Lewis, O. (1961). *The children of Sanchez: Autobiography of a Mexican family*. New York: Random House.

Liebert, R. M. (1973). Observational learning: Some social applications. In P. J. Elich (Ed.), *The Fourth Western Symposium on Learning*. Bellingham: Western Washington State College.

Liebert, R. M., & Baron, R. A. (1972). Some immediate effects of televised violence on children's behavior. *Developmental Psychology, 6*, 469–475.

Liebert, R. M., & Fernandez, L. E. (1969). Vicarious reward and task complexity as determinants of imitative learning. *Psychological Reports, 25*, 531–534.

Liebert, R. M., & Fischel, J. E. (1990). The elimination disorders: Enuresis and encopresis. In M. Lewis & S. Miller (Eds.), *Handbook of developmental psychopathology* (pp. 421–429). New York: Plenum.

Liebert, R. M., Kail, R., & Wicks-Nelson, R. (1986). *Developmental psychology* (4th ed.). Englewood Cliffs, NJ: Prentice-Hall.

Liebert, R. M., & Spiegler, M. D. (1970). *Personality: An introduction to theory and research*. Homewood, IL: Dorsey Press.

Liebert, R. M., & Spiegler, M. D. (1990). *Personality: Strategies and Issues* (6th ed.). Pacific Grove, CA: Brooks/Cole.

Liebert, R. M., & Sprafkin, J. (1988). *The early window* (3rd ed.). Elmsford, NY: Pergamon Press.

Lietaer, G. (1981). The client-centered approach in the seventies. Part I: A structured review of the literature. *Tijdschrift voor Psychotherapie, 7*, 81–102.

Lietaer, G. (1984). Unconditional positive regard: A controversial basic attitude in client-centered therapy. In R. F. Levant & J. M. Shlien (Eds.), *Client-centered therapy and the person-centered approach: New directions in theory, research, and practice* (pp. 41–58). New York: Praeger.

Lindzey, G., & Herman, P. S. (1955). Thematic Apperception Test: A note on reliability and situational validity. *Journal of Projective Techniques, 19*, 36–42.

Ljubin, T., & Ljubin, C. (1990). Extraversion and audio-motor reflex. *Personality and Individual Differences, 11*, 977–984.

Lloyd, C., & Chang, A. F. (1979). The usefulness of distinguishing between a defensive and a nondefensive external locus of control. *Journal of Research in Personality, 13*, 316–325.

Lochman, J. E. (1992). Cognitive-behavioral intervention with aggressive boys: Three-year follow-up and preventive effects. *Journal of Consulting and Clinical Psychology*, 60, 426–432.

Lochman, J. E., & Curry, J. F. (1986a). Effects of social problem-solving training and self-instruction training with aggressive boys. *Journal of Clinical Child Psychology*, 15, 159–164.

Lochman, J. E., & Curry, J. F. (1986b). Situational social problem-solving skills and self-esteem of aggressive and nonaggressive boys. *Journal of Abnormal Child Psychology*, 14, 605–617.

Loehlin, J. C. (1989). Partitioning environmental and genetic contributions to behavioral development. *American Psychologist*, 44, 1285–1292.

Loehlin, J. C., & Nichols, R. C. (1976). *Heredity, environment, and personality*. Austin: University of Texas Press.

Loehlin, J. C., Willerman, L., & Horn, J. M. (1987). Personality resemblance in adoptive families: A ten-year follow-up. *Journal of Personality and Social Psychology*, 53, 961–969.

Loewenstein, R., Newmann, L. M., Schur, M., & Solnit, A. J. (Eds.). (1966). *Psychoanalysis—a general psychology: Essays in honor of Heinz Hartmann*. New York: International Universities Press.

Loos, V. E. (1991). Construing couples: The challenges of marital therapy. *International Journal of Personal Construct Psychology*, 4, 293–312.

Lorand, S. (1946). *Technique of psychoanalytic therapy*. New York: International Universities Press.

Lovaas, O. I. (1977). *The autistic child: Language development through behavior modification*. New York: Irvington.

Lovaas, O. I. (1987). Behavioral treatment and normal educational and intellectual functioning in young autistic children. *Journal of Consulting and Clinical Psychology*, 55, 3–9.

Lowman, R. L., & Williams, R. E. (1987). Validity of self-ratings of abilities and competencies. *Journal of Vocational Behavior*, 31, 1–13.

Lubetsky, M. J. (1989). The magic of fairy tales: Psychodynamic and developmental perspectives. *Child Psychiatry and Human Development*, 19, 245–255.

Lubin, B., Wallis, R. R., & Paine, C. (1971). Patterns of psychological test usage in the United States: 1935–1969. *Professional Psychology*, 2, 70–74.

Luccock, M. P., & Salkovskis, P. M. (1988). Cognitive factors in social anxiety and its treatment. *Behaviour Research and Therapy*, 26, 297–302.

Lundberg, U., Westermark, O., & Rasch, B. (1990). Type A behaviour in pre-school children: Interrater reliability, stability over six months and subcomponents. *Scandinavian Journal of Psychology*, 31, 121–127.

Lundin, R. W. (1961). *Personality*. New York: Macmillan.

Lunenburg, F. C., & Cadavid, V. (1992). Locus of control, pupil control ideology, and dimensions of teacher burnout. *Journal of Instructional Psychology*, 19, 13–22.

Lutfiyya, Z. M. (1991). "A feeling of being connected": Friendships between people with and without learning difficulties. *Disability, Handicap and Society*, 6, 233–245.

MacAndrew, C. (1965). The differentiation of male alcoholic outpatients from nonalcoholic psychiatric outpa-

tients by means of the MMPI. *Quarterly Journal of Studies on Alcohol*, 26, 238–246.

MacKinnon, D. W., & Dukes, W. F. (1962). Repression. In L. Postman (Ed.), *Psychology in the making*. New York: Knopf.

MacMillan, V., Guevremont, D.C., & Hansen, D.J. (1989). Problem-solving training with a multi-distressed abusive mother. *Journal of Family Violence*, 3, 69–81.

Maddi, S. (1989). *Personality theories: A comparative analysis* (6th ed.). Pacific Grove, CA: Brooks/Cole.

Magnusson, D. (1989). Personality research—challenges for the future. *European Journal of Psychology*, 4, 1–17.

Mahler, M. (1968). *On human symbiosis and the vicissitudes of individuation: Infantile psychosis* (Vol. 1). New York: International Universities Press.

Mahler, M., Bergman, A., & Pine, F. (1975). *The psychological birth of the infant: Symbiosis and individuation*. New York: Basic Books.

Mahoney, M. J. (1992, April). *Psychotherapy integration: Diversity, dynamics, and development*. Paper presented at the meeting of the Society for Exploration of Psychotherapy Integration, San Diego.

Mahoney, M. J. (1993a). Diversity and the dynamics of development in psychotherapy integration. *Journal of Psychotherapy Integration*, 3, 1–13.

Mahoney, M. J. (1993b). Introduction to special section: Theoretical developments in the cognitive psychotherapies. *Journal of Consulting and Clinical Psychology*, 61, 187–193.

Mahrer, A. R., Nadler, W. P., Stalikas, A., Schachter, H. M., & Sterner, I. (1988). Common and distinctive therapeutic change processes in client-centered, rational-emotive, and experimental psychotherapies. *Psychological Reports*, 62, 972–974.

Mair, M. (1990). Telling psychological tales. *International Journal of Personal Construct Psychology*, 3, 121–135.

Major, B., Cozzarelli, C., Sciacchitano, A. M., Cooper, M. L., Testa, M., & Mueller, P. (1990). Perceived social support, self-efficacy, and adjustment to abortion. *Journal of Personality and Social Psychology*, 59, 452–463.

Malinowski, B. (1927). *Sex and repression in savage society*. London: Routledge & Kegan Paul.

Mancuso, J. C., & Shaw, M. L. G. (1988). *Cognition and personal structure: Computer access and analysis*. New York: Praeger.

Manicas, P. T., & Secord, P. F. (1983). Implications for psychology of the new philosophy of science. *American Psychologist*, 38, 399–413.

Maqsud, M., & Rouhani, S. (1991). Relationships between socioeconomic status, locus of control, self-concept, and academic achievement of Batswana adolescents. *Journal of Youth and Adolescence*, 20, 107–114.

Marcus, D. M. (1988). Aspects of psychoanalytic cure. *Psychoanalytic Review*, 75, 231–243.

Marks, I. (1978). Behavioral psychotherapy of adult neurosis. In S. L. Garfield & A. E. Bergin (Eds.), *Handbook of psychotherapy and behavior change: An empirical analysis* (2nd ed., pp. 493–547). New York: Wiley.

Marks, I. (1981). *Cure and care of neuroses: Theory and practice of behavioral psychotherapy*. New York: Wiley.

Marks, I. M. (1987). *Fears, phobias, and rituals: Panic, anxiety and their disorders*. New York: Oxford University Press.

Marks, P. A., & Seeman, W. (1963). *An atlas for use with the MMPI: Actuarial description of abnormal personality*. Baltimore: Williams & Wilkins.

Marlatt, G. A., & Rohsenow, D. J. (1980). Cognitive processes in alcohol use: Expectancy and the balanced placebo design. In N. K. Mellow (Ed.), *Advances in substance abuse: Behavioral and biological research*. Greenwich, CT: JAI Press.

Marshall, G. N. (1991). A multidimensional analysis of internal health locus of control beliefs: Separating the wheat from the chaff? *Journal of Personality and Social Psychology, 61*, 483–491.

Martens, B. K. (1990). A context analysis of contingent teacher attention. *Behavior Modification, 14*, 138–156.

Martens, B. K. (1992). Contingency and choice: The implications of matching theory for classroom instruction. *Journal of Behavioral Education, 2*, 121–137.

Martens, B. K., & Houk, J. L. (1989). The application of Herrnstein's law of effect to disruptive and on-task behavior of a retarded adolescent girl. *Journal of the Experimental Analysis of Behavior, 51*, 17–27.

Martens, B. K., Lochner, D. G., & Kelly, S. Q. (1992). The effects of variable-interval reinforcement on academic engagement: A demonstration of matching theory. *Journal of Applied Behavior Analysis, 25*, 143–151.

Mascolo, M. F., & Mancuso, J. C. (1990). Functioning of epigenetically evolved emotions systems: A constructive analysis. *International Journal of Personal Construct Psychology, 3*, 205–222.

Masling, J. (Ed.). (1983). *Empirical studies of psychoanalytic theories* (Vol. 1). Hillsdale, NJ: Analytic Press.

Masling, J. (Ed.). (1985). *Empirical studies of psychoanalytic theories* (Vol. 2). Hillsdale, NJ: Analytic Press.

Masling, J., O'Neill, R., & Katkin, E. S. (1981). Orality and latency of volunteering to serve as experimental subjects. *Journal of Personality Assessment, 45*, 20–22.

Masling, J. M. (1960). The influence of situational and interpersonal variables in projective testing. *Psychological Bulletin, 56*, 65–85.

Masling, J. M., & Cohen, I. S. (1987). Psychotherapy, clinical evidence, and the self-fulfilling prophecy. *Psychoanalytic Psychology, 4*, 65–79.

Masling, J. M., Johnson, C., & Saturansky, C. (1974). Oral imagery, accuracy of perceiving others, and performance in Peace Corps training. *Journal of Personality and Social Psychology, 30*, 414–419.

Masling, J. M., Rabie, L., & Blondheim, S. H. (1967). Obesity, level of aspiration, and Rorschach and TAT measures of oral dependence. *Journal of Consulting Psychology, 31*, 233–239.

Masling, J. M., Weiss, L., & Rothschild, B. (1968). Relationships of oral imagery to yielding behavior and birth order. *Journal of Consulting and Clinical Psychology, 32*, 89–91.

Maslow, A. (1962). Lessons from the peak-experiences. *Journal of Humanistic Psychology, 2*, 9–18.

Maslow, A. (1966). *The psychology of science*. Chicago: Regnery.

Maslow, A. H. (1950). Self-actualizing people: A study of psychological health. *Personality, Symposium No. 1*, 11–34.

Maslow, A. H. (1954). *Motivation and personality*. New York: Harper & Row.

Maslow, A. H. (1955). Deficiency motivation and growth motivation. In M. R. Jones (Ed.), *Nebraska symposium on motivation* (Vol. 3). Lincoln: University of Nebraska Press.

Maslow, A. H. (1963). Self-actualizing people. In G. B. Levitas (Ed.), *The world of psychology* (Vol. 2, pp. 527–556). New York: Braziller.

Maslow, A. H. (1970). *Motivation and personality* (rev. ed.). New York: Harper & Row.

Maslow, A. H. (1971). *The farther reaches of human nature*. New York: Viking Press.

Mason, A., & Blankenship, V. (1987). Power and affiliation motivation, stress, and abuse in intimate relationships. *Journal of Personality and Social Psychology, 52*, 203–210.

Mathieu, J. E. (1990). A test of subordinates' achievement and affiliation needs as moderators of leader path-goal relationships. *Basic and Applied Social Psychology, 11*, 179–189.

Matthews, G. (1989). The factor structure of the 16PF: Twelve primary and three secondary factors. *Personality and Individual Differences, 9*, 931–940.

Matthews, G., Dorn, L., & Glenson, A. I. (1991). Personality correlates of driver stress. *Personality and Individual Differences, 12*, 535–549.

Matthews, K. A. (1982). Psychological perspectives on the Type A behavior pattern. *Psychological Bulletin, 91*, 293–323.

Matthews, K. A., & Carra, J. (1982). Suppression of menstrual distress symptoms: A study of Type A behavior. *Personality and Social Psychology Bulletin, 8*, 146–151.

Matthews, K. A., Stoney, C. M., Rakaczky, C. J., & Jamison, W. (1986). Family characteristics and school achievements of Type A children. *Health Psychology, 5*, 453–467.

May, R. (1967). Existential psychology. In T. Millon (Ed.), *Theories of psychopathology* (pp. 244–254). Philadelphia: Saunders.

Mayman, M. (1967). Object-representations and object relationships in Rorschach responses. *Journal of Projective Techniques and Personality Assessment, 31*, 17–24.

McArthur, L. Z., & Eisen, S. V. (1976). Achievements of male and female storybook characters as determinants of achievement behavior by boys and girls. *Journal of Personality and Social Psychology, 33*, 467–473.

McAuley, E., & Courneya, K. S. (1992). Self-efficacy relationships with affective and exertion responses to exercise. *Journal of Applied Social Psychology, 22*, 312–326.

McCallum, M., & Piper, W. E. (1988). Psychoanalytically oriented short-term groups for outpatients: Unsettled issues. *Group, 12*, 21–32.

McCann, S. J. H., Stewin, L. L., & Short, R. H. (1990). Frightening dream frequency and birth order. *Individual Psychology, 46,* 304–310.

McClelland, D. C. (1965). Toward a theory of motive acquisition. *American Psychologist, 20,* 321–333.

McClelland, D. C. (1967). *The achieving society.* New York: Free Press.

McClelland, D. C. (1977). The impact of power motivation training on alcoholics. *Journal of Studies on Alcohol, 38,* 142–144.

McClelland, D. C. (1982). The need for power, sympathetic activation, and illness. *Motivation and Emotion, 6,* 31–61.

McClelland, D. C., Atkinson, J. W., Clark, R. A., & Lowell, E. I. (1953). *The achievement motive.* New York: Appleton-Century-Crofts. (Reprinted 1976 by Irvington Publishers.)

McClelland, D. C., Davis, W. N., Kalin, R., & Wanner, E. (1972). *The drinking man.* New York: Free Press.

McClelland, D. C., Koestner, R., & Weinberger, J. (1989). How do self-attributed and implicit motives differ? *Psychological Review, 96,* 690–702.

McClelland, D. C., & Winter, D. G. (1969). *Motivating economic achievement.* New York: Free Press.

McConachie, H. (1983). Fathers, mothers, siblings: How do they see themselves? In P. Mittler & H. McConachie (Eds.), *Parents, professionals and mentally handicapped people.* London: Croom Helm.

McConachie, H. (1985). How parents of young mentally handicapped children construe their role. In D. Bannister (Ed.), *Issues and approaches in personal construct theory.* Orlando, FL: Academic Press.

McCoy, M. M. (1977). A reconstruction of emotion. In D. Bannister (Ed.), *New perspectives in personal construct theory.* London: Academic Press.

McCoy, M. M. (1981). Positive and negative emotion: A personal construct theory interpretation. In H. Bonarius, R. Holland, & S. Rosenberg (Eds.), *Personal construct psychology: Recent advances in theory and practice.* New York: St. Martin's Press.

McCrae, R. R. (1987). Creativity, divergent thinking, and openness to experience. *Journal of Personality and Social Psychology, 52,* 1258–1265.

McCrae, R. R. (1990). Traits and trait names: How well is Openness represented in natural languages? *European Journal of Personality, 4,* 119–129.

McCrae, R. R., & Costa, P. T. (1983). Social desirability scales: More substance than style. *Journal of Consulting and Clinical Psychology, 51,* 882–888.

McCrae, R. R., & Costa, P. T., Jr. (1985). Updating Norman's "adequate taxonomy": Intelligence and personality dimensions in natural language and questionnaires. *Journal of Personality and Social Psychology, 49,* 710–721.

McCrae, R. R., & Costa, P. T., Jr. (1987). Validation of the five-factor model of personality across instruments and observers. *Journal of Personality and Social Psychology, 52,* 81–90.

McCrae, R. R., & Costa, P. T. (1989). Reinterpreting the Myers-Briggs Type Indicator from the perspective of the five-factor model of personality. *Journal of Personality, 57,* 17–40.

McDowell, J. J. (1982). The importance of Herrnstein's mathematical statement of the law of effect for behavior therapy. *American Psychologist, 37,* 771–779.

McDowell, J. J. (1988). Matching theory in natural human environments. *The Behavior Analyst, 11,* 95–109.

McFarland, S. G., & Sparks, C. M. (1985). Age, education, and the internal consistency of personality scales. *Journal of Personality and Social Psychology, 49,* 1692–1702.

McGaw, W. H., Rice, C. P., & Rogers, C. R. (1973). *The steel shutter.* La Jolla, CA: Film Center for Studies of the Person.

McGuffin, P., & Katz, R. (1989). The genetics of depression and manic-depressive disorder. *British Journal of Psychiatry, 155,* 294–304.

McIntyre, J. J., & Teevan, J. J., Jr. (1972). Television violence and deviant behavior. In G. A. Comstock & E. A. Rubinstein (Eds.), *Television and social behavior* (Vol. 3). *Television and adolescent aggressiveness* (pp. 383–435). Washington, DC: U.S. Government Printing Office.

McKeachie, W. J. (1961). Motivation, teaching methods, and college learning. In M. R. Jones (Ed.), *Nebraska symposium on motivation, 1961* (Vol. 9). Lincoln: University of Nebraska Press.

McKenna v. Fargo. (1978). 451 F. Supp. 1355.

McKenzie, J. (1988). Three superfactors in the 16PF and their relationship to Eysenck's P, E and N. *Personality and Individual Differences, 9,* 843–850.

McKim, W. A. (1986). *Drugs and behavior.* Englewood Cliffs, NJ: Prentice-Hall.

McKusick, L., Coates, T. J., Morin, S. F., Pollack, L., & Hoff, C. (1990). Longitudinal predictors of reductions in high risk sexual behaviors among gay men in San Francisco: The AIDS behavioral research project. *American Journal of Public Health, 80,* 978–983.

Mead, M. (1949). *Male and female.* New York: Morrow.

Mearns, D., & McLeod, J. (1984). A person-centered approach to research. In R. F. Levant & J. M. Shlien (Eds.), *Client-centered therapy and the person-centered approach: New directions in theory, research, and practice* (pp. 370–389). New York: Praeger.

Meichenbaum, D. (1975). Enhancing creativity by modifying what subjects say to themselves. *American Educational Research Journal, 12,* 129–145.

Meichenbaum, D. (1985). *Stress inoculation training.* Elmsford, NY: Pergamon Press.

Meichenbaum, D. (1986). Cognitive-behavior modification. In F. H. Kanfer & A. P. Goldstein (Eds.), *Helping people change: A textbook of methods* (3rd ed., pp. 346–380). Elmsford, NY: Pergamon Press.

Meichenbaum, D. (1991, February-March). *Cognitive behavioral therapy.* Workshop sponsored by the Institute for the Advancement of Human Behavior (Portola Valley, CA), Chicago.

Meichenbaum, D., Gilmore, B., & Fedoravicius, A. (1971). Group insight vs. group desensitization in treating speech anxiety. *Journal of Consulting and Clinical Psychology, 36,* 410–421.

Meichenbaum, D., & Goodman, J. (1971). Training impulsive children to talk to themselves: A means of developing self-control. *Journal of Abnormal Psychology, 77,* 115–126.

Melamed, B. G. (1979). Behavioral approaches to fear in dental settings. In M. Hersen, R. M. Eisler, & P. M. Miller (Eds.), *Progress in behavior modification* (Vol. 7). New York: Academic Press.

Melamed, B. G., & Siegel, L. J. (1975). Reduction of anxiety in children facing hospitalization and surgery by use of filmed modeling. *Journal of Consulting and Clinical Psychology, 43,* 511–521.

Mendelson, M. D. (1991). Transference: Theoretical conceptions and clinical approach. *Contemporary Psychoanalysis, 27,* 189–199.

Merrill, R. M., & Heathers, L. B. (1956). The relation of the MMPI to the Edwards Personal Preference Schedule on a college counseling center sample. *Journal of Consulting Psychology, 20,* 310–314.

Metzler, A. E., & Neimeyer, G. (1988). Vocational hierarchies: How do we count the ways? *International Journal of Personal Construct Psychology, 1,* 205–217.

Meuris, G. (1988). Carl Rogers (1902–1987): Une pedagogie centree sur la personne. [Carl Rogers (1902–1987): Client-centered education.] *Bulletin de Psychologie Scholaire et d'Orientation, 37,* 83–94.

Meyers, A., Mercatoris, M., & Sirota, A. (1976). Use of covert self-instruction for the elimination of psychotic speech. *Journal of Consulting and Clinical Psychology, 44,* 480–483.

Michels, R. (1988). The future of psychoanalysis. *Psychoanalytic Quarterly, 57,* 167–185.

Miller, C. (1991). Self-actualization and the consciousness revolution. [Special Issue: Handbook of self-actualization]. *Journal of Social Behavior and Personality, 6,* 109–126.

Miller, K., & Treacher, A. (1981). Delinquency: A personal construct theory approach. In H. Bonarius, R. Holland, & S. Rosenberg (Eds.), *Personal construct psychology: Recent advances in theory and practice.* New York: St. Martin's Press.

Miller, L. (1989). On the neuropsychology of dreams. *Psychoanalytic Review, 76,* 375–401.

Miller, N. E., & Dollard, J. (1941). *Social learning and imitation.* New Haven, CT: Yale University Press.

Miller, P. C., Lefcourt, H. M., Holmes, J. G., Ware, E. E., & Saleh, W. E. (1986). Marital locus of control and marital problem solving. *Journal of Personality and Social Psychology, 51,* 161–169.

Millis, K. K., & Neimeyer, R. A. (1990). A test of the Dichotomy Corollary: Propositions versus constructs as basic cognitive units. *International Journal of Personal Construct Psychology, 3,* 167–181.

Millon, T. (Ed.). (1967). *Theories of psychopathology.* Philadelphia: Saunders.

Mirin, S. M., & Weiss, R. D. (1989). Genetic factors in the development of alcoholism. *Psychiatric Annals, 19,* 239–242.

Mischel, W. (1966). Theory and research on the antecedents of self-imposed delay of reward. In B. A. Maher (Ed.), *Progress in experimental personality research* (Vol. 3, pp. 85–132). New York: Academic Press.

Mischel, W. (1968). *Personality and assessment.* New York: Wiley.

Mischel, W. (1973). Toward a cognitive social learning reconceptualization of personality. *Psychological Review, 80,* 252–283.

Mischel, W. (1979). On the interface of cognition and personality: Beyond the person–situation debate. *American Psychologist, 34,* 740–754.

Mischel, W. (1980). George Kelly's anticipation of psychology: A personal tribute. In M. J. Mahoney (Ed.), *Psychotherapy Process.* New York: Plenum.

Mischel, W. (1984). Convergences and challenges in the search for consistency. *American Psychologist, 39,* 351–364.

Mischel, W. (1988). Review of conceptual foundations of behavioral assessment. *Behavioral Assessment, 10,* 1125–1128.

Mischel, W., & Baker, N. (1975). Cognitive appraisals and transformations in delay behavior. *Journal of Personality and Social Psychology, 31,* 254–361.

Mischel, W., & Ebbesen, E. (1970). Attention in delay of gratification. *Journal of Personality and Social Psychology, 16,* 329–337.

Mischel, W., Ebbesen, E., & Raskoff, A. (1971). *Cognitive and attentional mechanisms in delay of gratification.* Unpublished manuscript, Stanford University.

Mischel, W., & Moore, B. (1973). Effects of attention to symbolically presented rewards upon self-control. *Journal of Personality and Social Psychology, 28,* 172–179.

Mischel, W., & Moore, B. (1980). The role of ideation in voluntary delay for symbolically presented rewards. *Cognitive Therapy and Research, 4,* 211–221.

Mischel, W., & Peake, P. K. (1982). Beyond deja vu in the search for cross-situational consistency. *Psychological Review, 89,* 730–755.

Mischel, W., Shoda, Y., & Peake, P. K. (1988). The nature of adolescent competencies predicted by delay of gratification. *Journal of Personality and Social Psychology, 54,* 687–696.

Mischel, W., Shoda, Y., & Rodriguez, M. L. (1989). Delay of gratification in children. *Science, 244,* 933–938.

Mitchell, J. (1974a). On Freud and the distinction between the sexes. In J. Strouse (Ed.), *Women & analysis: Dialogues on psychoanalytic views of femininity.* New York: Grossman.

Mitchell, J. (1974b). *Psychoanalysis and feminism.* New York: Pantheon.

Mitroff, I. (1988). Comments on Blight's article. *Journal of Humanistic Psychology, 28,* 67–69.

Mittelman, W. (1991). Maslow's study of self-actualization: A reinterpretation. *Journal of Humanistic Psychology, 31,* 114–135.

Modell, A. H. (1984). *Psychoanalysis in a new context.* New York: International Universities Press.

Modell, A. H. (1988). The centrality of the psychoanalytic setting and the changing aims of treatment. *Psychoanalytic Quarterly, 57,* 577–596.

Moldin, S. O., Reich, T., & Rice, J. P. (1991). Current perspectives on the genetics of unipolar depression. *Behavior Genetics, 21,* 211–242.

Moll, A. (1912). *The sexual life of the child.* New York: Macmillan. (German edition, 1909)

Montague, E. K. (1953). The role of anxiety in serial rote learning. *Journal of Experimental Psychology, 45,* 91–96.

Mooney, S. P., Sherman, M. F., & loPresto, C. T. (1991). Academic locus of control, self-esteem, and perceived distance from home as predictors of college adjustment. *Journal of Counseling and Development, 69,* 445–448.

Moore, J. (1990). On the "causes" of behavior. *The Psychological Record, 40,* 469–480.

Moran, M. G. (1991). Chaos theory and psychoanalysis: The fluidic nature of the mind. *International Review of Psycho-Analysis, 18,* 211–221.

Morris, B. S. (1949). Officer selection in the British Army, 1942–1945. *Occupational Psychology, 23,* 219–234.

Morrison, J. R., & Stewart, A. M. (1971). A family study of the hyperactive child syndrome. *Biological Psychiatry, 3,* 189–195.

Motley, M. T., & Baars, B. J. (1978). Laboratory verification of "Freudian" slips of the tongue as evidence of pre-articulatory semantic editing. In B. Ruken (Ed.), *Communication yearbook 2.* New Brunswick, NJ: Transaction.

Mowrer, O. H., & Mowrer, W. M. (1938). Enuresis: A method for its study and treatment. *American Journal of Orthopsychiatry, 8,* 436–447.

Muller, J. (1987). Lacan's view of sublimation. *American Journal of Psychoanalysis, 47,* 315–323.

Multon, K. D., Brown, S. D., & Lent, R. W. (1991). Relations of self-efficacy beliefs to academic outcomes: A meta-analytic investigation. *Journal of Counseling Psychology, 38,* 30–38.

Muran, J. C. (1991). A reformulation of the ABC model in cognitive psychotherapies: Implications for assessment and treatment. *Clinical Psychology Review, 11,* 399–418.

Murray, H. A. (1951). Uses of the Thematic Apperception Test. *American Journal of Psychiatry, 107,* 577–581.

Murray, H. A. (1962). *Explorations in personality.* New York: Science Editions.

Neale, J. M. (1968). Personal communication.

Neale, J. M., & Liebert, R. M. (1986). *Science and behavior: An introduction to methods of research* (3rd ed.). Englewood Cliffs, NJ: Prentice-Hall.

Neale, J. M., & Weintraub, S. (1977). Personal communication.

Neher, A. (1991). Maslow's theory of motivation: A critique. *Journal of Humanistic Psychology, 31,* 89–112.

Neimeyer, G. J., & Hudson, J. E. (1985). Couples' constructs: Personal systems in marital satisfaction. In D. Bannister (Ed.), *Issues and approaches in personal construct theory* (pp. 127–171). Orlando, FL: Academic Press.

Neimeyer, G. J., & Neimeyer, R. A. (Eds.). (1990). *Advances in personal construct psychology* (Vol. 1). Greewich, CT: JAI Press.

Neimeyer, R. A., Baker, K. D., & Neimeyer, G. J. (1990). The current status of personal construct theory: Some scientometric data. In G. J. Neimeyer & R. A. Neimeyer (Eds.), *Advances in personal construct psychology* (Vol. 1, pp. 3–22). Greewich, CT: JAI Press.

Neisser, U. (1976). *Cognition and reality.* San Francisco: W. H. Freeman.

Neisser, U. (1988). Five kinds of self-knowledge. *Philosophical Psychology, 1,* 35–59.

Neisser, U. (1991). Two perceptually given aspects of the self and their development. *Developmental Review, 11,* 197–209.

Nesse, R. M. (1990). The evolutionary function of repression and the ego defenses. *The Journal of the American Academy of Psychoanalysis, 18,* 260–285.

Nezu, A. M., & D'Zurilla, T. J. (1989). Social problem solving and negative affective conditions. In P. C. Kendall & D. Watson (Eds.), *Anxiety and depression: Distinctive and overlapping features* (pp. 285–315). San Diego, CA: Academic Press.

Nezu, A. M., Nezu, C. M., & Perri, M. G. (1989). *Problem-solving therapy for depression: Theory, research, and clinical guidelines.* New York: Wiley.

Nichols, S. L., & Newman, J. P. (1986). Effects of punishment on response latency in extraverts. *Journal of Personality and Social Psychology, 50,* 624–630.

Nicol, S. E., & Gottesman, I. I. (1983). Clues to the genetics and neurobiology of schizophrenia. *American Scientist, 71,* 398–404.

Nisbett, R. E., & Wilson, T. (1977). Telling more than we can know: Verbal reports on mental processes. *Psychological Review, 84,* 231–259.

Nisenson, S., & DeWitt, W. A. (1949). *Illustrated minute biographies.* New York: Grosset & Dunlap.

Noller, P., Law, H., & Comrey, A. (1987). Cattell, Comrey, and Eysenck personality factors compared: More evidence for the five robust factors? *Journal of Personality and Social Psychology, 53,* 775–782.

Norcross, J. C., & Goldfried, M. R. (Eds.). (1992). *Handbook of psychotherapy integration.* New York: Basic Books.

Norman, W. T. (1963). Toward an adequate taxonomy of personality attributes: Replicated factor structure in peer nomination personality ratings. *Journal of Abnormal and Social Psychology, 66,* 574–583.

Novick, J. (1987). The timing of termination. *International Review of Psycho-Analysis, 14,* 307–318.

Nowicki, S., & Duke, M. P. (1974). A preschool and primary locus of control scale. *Developmental Psychology, 10,* 874–880.

Nowicki, S., & Duke, M. P. (1983). The Nowicki-Strickland life-span locus of control scales: Construct validation. In H. M. Lefcourt (Ed.), *Research with the locus of control construct: Vol. 2. Developments and social problems* (pp. 9–51). New York: Academic Press.

Nowicki, S., & Strickland, B. (1973). A locus of control scale for children. *Journal of Consulting and Clinical Psychology, 40,* 148–154.

O'Connor, D., & Wolfe, D. M. (1991). From crisis to growth at midlife: Changes in personal paradigm. *Journal of Organizational Behavior, 12,* 323–340.

O'Connor, R. D. (1969). Modification of social withdrawal through symbolic modeling. *Journal of Applied Behavior Analysis, 2,* 15–22.

Oei, T. P. S., Evans, L., & Cook, G. M. (1990). Utility and validity of the STAI with anxiety disorder patients. *British Journal of Clinical Psychology, 29,* 429–432.

Ogden, T. (1982). *Projective identification and psychotherapeutic technique.* New York: Jason Aronson.

Ogden, T. H. (1987). The transitional Oedipal relationship in female development. *International Journal of Psycho-Analysis, 68,* 485–498.

Ogilvie, D. M. (1987). The undesired self: A neglected variable in personality research. *Journal of Personality and Social Psychology, 52,* 379–385.

Ogilvie, D. M. (1988, June). *Dreaded states and desired outcomes.* Paper presented at the meeting of the Society for Personology, Durham, NC.

O'Grady, K. E. (1988). The Marlowe-Crowne and Edwards social desirability scales: A psychometric perspective. *Multivariate Behavioral Research, 23,* 87–101.

O'Hare, D. P. A., & Gordon, I. E. (1976). An applicaton of repertory grid technique to aesthetic measurement. *Perceptual and Motor Skills, 42,* 1183–1192.

Oldroyd, D. (1986). *The arch of knowledge.* New York: Methuen.

O'Leary, A. (1992). Self-efficacy and health: Behavioral and stress-physiological mediation. *Cognitive Therapy and Research, 16,* 229–245.

O'Leary, C. J. (1989). The person-centered approach and family therapy: A dialogue between two traditions [Special Issue: Person-centered approaches with families]. *Person-Centered Review, 4,* 308–323.

O'Leary, E. (1989). The expression of disapproval by teachers and the maintenance of unconditional positive regard. *Person-Centered Review, 4,* 420–428.

Orgler, H. (1963). *Alfred Adler: The man and his work.* New York: Putnam (Capricorn Books).

Ormel, J., & Schaufeli, W. B. (1991). Stability and change in psychological distress and their relationship with self-esteem and locus of control: A dynamic equilibrium model. *Journal of Personality and Social Psychology, 60,* 288–299.

Orpen, C. (1991). The work locus of control scale as a predictor of employee attitudes and behaviour: A validity study. *Psychological Studies, 36,* 67–69.

Osgood, C. E., Suci, G. J., & Tannenbaum, P. H. (1957). *The measurement of meaning.* Urbana: University of Illinois Press.

Osman, M. P., & Tabachnick, N. D. (1988). Introduction and survey of some previous views. *Psychoanalytic Review, 75,* 195–215.

OSS Assessment Staff. (1948). *Assessment of men.* New York: Holt, Rinehart & Winston.

Öst, L. G., & Hugdahl, K. (1985). Acquisition of blood and dental phobia and anxiety response patterns in clinical patients. *Behaviour Research and Therapy, 23,* 27–34.

Ozer, E. M., & Bandura, A. (1990). Mechanisms governing empowerment effects: A self-efficacy analysis. *Journal of Personality and Social Psychology, 58,* 472–486.

Padgett, D. K. (1991). Correlates of self-efficacy beliefs among patients with non-insulin dependent diabetes mellitus in Zagreb, Yugoslavia. *Patient Education and Counseling, 18,* 139–147.

Pais, J. (1979). Social-psychological predictors of adjustment for divorced mothers. *Dissertation Abstracts International, 39,* 5165. (University Microfilms No. 79–03460).

Pancoast, D. L., & Archer, R. P. (1988). MMPI adolescent norms: Patterns and trends across 4 decades. *Journal of Personality Assessment, 52,* 691–706.

Pancoast, D. L., & Archer, R. P. (1989). Original adult MMPI norms in normal samples: A review with implications for future developments. *Journal of Personality Assessment, 53,* 376–395.

Pani, M. K. (1991). Differences in locus of control and reading abilities among grade three children. *Psycho-Lingua, 21,* 9–12.

Paprota, M. (1988). *Real/undesired-self discrepancies and depression in male and female high school students.* Unpublished undergraduate honors thesis, Department of Psychology, Rutgers University.

Pardes, H., Kaufmann, C. A., Pincus, H. A., & West, A. (1989). Genetics and psychiatry: Past discoveries, current dilemmas, and future directions. *American Journal of Psychiatry, 146,* 435–443.

Parker, K. C. H., Hanson, R. K., & Hunsley, J. (1988). MMPI, Rorschach, and WAIS: A meta-analytic comparison of reliability, stability, and validity. *Psychological Bulletin, 103,* 367–373.

Parkes, K. R. (1984). Locus of control, cognitive appraisal, and coping in stressful episodes. *Journal of Personality and Social Psychology, 46,* 655–668.

Parkes, K. R. (1986). Coping in stressful episodes: The role of individual differences, environmental factors, and situational characteristics. *Journal of Personality and Social Psychology, 51,* 1277–1292.

Passini, F. T., & Norman, W. T. (1966). A universal conception of personality structure? *Journal of Personality and Social Psychology, 4,* 44–49.

Patterson, C. H. (1990a). Involuntary clients: A person-centered view. *Person-Centered Review, 5,* 316–320.

Patterson, C. H. (1990b). On being client-centered [Special Issue: Fiftieth anniversary of the person-centered approach]. *Person-Centered Review, 5,* 425–432.

Patton, M. Q. (1990). Humanistic psychology and humanistic research [Special Issue: Human inquiry & the person-centered approach]. *Person-Centered Review, 5,* 191–202.

Paul, D. B., & Blumenthal, A. L. (1989). On the trail of little Albert. *The Psychological Record, 39,* 547–553.

Peabody, D., & Goldberg, L. R. (1989). Some determinants of actor structures from trait descriptors. *Journal of Personality and Social Psychology, 57,* 552–567.

Pearce-McCall, D., & Newman, J. P. (1986). Expectations of success following noncontingent punishment in introverts and extraverts. *Journal of Personality and Social Psychology, 50,* 439–446.

Pearson, G. L., & Freeman, F. G. (1991). *Perceptual and Motor Skills, 72,* 1239–1248.

Pederson, L. L., Strickland, C., & DesLauriers, A. (1991). Self-efficacy related to smoking cessation in general practice patients. *International Journal of the Addictions, 26,* 467–485.

Pekarik, E. G., Prinz, R. J., Liebert, D. E., Weintraub, S., & Neale, J. M. (1976). The Pupil Evaluation Inventory: A sociometric technique for assessing children's social behavior. *Journal of Abnormal Child Psychology, 4,* 83–97.

Persky, V. M., Kempthorne-Rawson, J., & Shekele, R. B. (1987). Personality and the risk of cancer: 20–year follow-up of the Western Electric Study. *Psychosomatic Medicine, 49,* 435–449.

Person, E. S. (1988, March). Some differences between men and women: I. The passionate quest. *Atlantic Monthly,* pp. 71–74, 76.

Peters, C. L., & Brown, R. D. (1991). The relationship of high school involvement, high school population size, and gender to college students' self efficacy beliefs. *College Student Journal, 25,* 473–481.

Peterson, L., & Ridley-Johnson, R. (1980). Pediatric hospital response to survey on prehospital preparation for children. *Journal of Pediatric Psychology, 5,* 1–7.

Peterson, L., Schultheis, K., Ridley-Johnson, R., Miller, D. J., & Tracy, K. (1984). Comparison of three modeling procedures on the presurgical and postsurgical reactions of children. *Behavior Therapy, 15,* 197–203.

Phares, E. J. (1978). Locus of control. In H. London & J. E. Exner (Eds.), *Dimensions of personality.* New York: Wiley-Interscience.

Phares, E. J. (1979). Defensiveness and perceived control. In L. C. Perlmuter & R. A. Monty (Eds.), *Choice and perceived control.* Hillsdale, NJ: Erlbaum.

Phares, E. J. (1984). *Introduction to personality.* Columbus, OH: Charles E. Merrill.

Piacentini, J. C., Schaughency, E. A., & Lahey, B. B. (1985). Tantrums. In M. Hersen & C. G. Last (Eds.), *Behavior therapy casebook* (pp. 297–303). New York: Springer.

Pierce, J. V. (1961). *Sex differences in achievement motivation.* Quincy, IL: Quincy Youth Development Project.

Pigott, H. E., & Gonzales, F. P. (1987). The efficacy of videotape self-modeling to treat an electively mute child. *Journal of Clinical Child Psychology, 16,* 106–110.

Pihl, R. O., & Peterson, J. (1990). Inherited predisposition toward alcoholism: Characteristics of sons of male alcoholics. *Journal of Abnormal Psychology, 99,* 291–301.

Pinto, R. P., & Hollandsworth, J. G. Jr. (1989). Using videotape modeling to prepare children psychologically for surgery: Influence of parents and costs versus benefits of providing preparation services. *Health Psychology, 8,* 79–85.

Piper, W. E., Azim, H. F. A., Joyce, A. S., McCallum, M., Nixon, G. W. H., & Segal, P. S. (1991). Quality of object relations versus interpersonal functioning as predictors of therapeutic alliance and psychotherapy outcome. *The Journal of Nervous and Mental Disease, 179,* 432–438.

Pittenger, D. J., & Pavlik, W. B. (1988). Analysis of the partial reinforcement extinction effect in humans using absolute and relative comparisons of schedules. *American Journal of Psychology, 101,* 1–14.

Pittenger, D. J., & Pavlik, W. B. (1989). Resistance to extinction in humans: Analysis of the generalized partial reinforcement effect. *Learning and Motivation, 20,* 60–72.

Pittenger, D. J., Pavlik, W. B., Flora, S. R., & Kontos, J. M. (1988). The persistence of learned behaviors in humans as a function of changes in reinforcement schedule and response. schedules. *Learning and Motivation, 19,* 300–316.

Plaud, J. J. (1992). Should we take the "radical" out of "behaviorism"?: Some comments about behavior therapy and philosophy. *the Behavior Therapist, 15,* 121–122.

Plomin, R. (1986). Behavioral genetic methods. *Journal of Personality, 54,* 226–261.

Plomin, R., & Bergeman, C. S. (1991). The nature of nurture: Genetic influence on "environmental" measures. *Behavioral and Brain Sciences, 14,* 373–427.

Plomin, R., & Nesselroade, J. R. (1990). Behavioral genetics and personality change. *Journal of Personality, 58,* 191–220.

Plomin, R., Pedersen, N. L., McClearn, G. E., Nesselroade, J. R., & Bergman, C. S. (1988). EAS temperament during the last half of the life span: Twins reared apart and twins reared together. *Psychology and Aging, 3,* 43–50.

Poidevant, J. M., Loesch, L. C., & Wittmer, J. (1991). Vocational aspirations and perceived self-efficacy of doctoral students in the counseling professions. *Counselor Education and Supervision, 30,* 289–300.

Polanyi, M. (1959). *The study of man.* Chicago: University of Chicago Press.

Pope, M., Denicolo, P., & de Bernardi, B. (1990). The teaching profession: A comparative view. *International Journal of Personal Construct Psychology, 3,* 313–326.

Popham, S. M., & Holden, R. R. (1991). Psychometric properties of the MMPI factor scales. *Personality and Individual Differences, 12,* 513–517.

Popper, K. R. (1959). *The logic of scientific discovery.* Hutchinson: London.

Porder, M. S. (1987). Projective identification: An alternative hypothesis. *Psychoanalytic Quarterly, 56,* 431–451.

Porter, L. M. (1987). *The interpretation of dreams: Freud's theories revisited.* Boston: Twayne.

Posner, M. (1973). Coordination of internal codes. In W. Chase (Ed.), *Visual information processing.* New York: Academic Press.

Post, P., Stewart, M. A., & Smith, P. L. (1991). Self-efficacy, interest, and consideration of math/science and non-math/science occupations among Black freshmen. *Journal of Vocational Behavior, 38,* 179–186.

Postlethwaite, K., & Jaspars, J. (1986). The experimental use of personal constructs in educational research: The critical triad procedure. *British Journal of Educational Psychology, 56,* 241–254.

Power, M. J. (1991). Cognitive science and behavioural psychotherapy: Where behaviour was, there shall be cognition? *Behavioural Psychotherapy, 19,* 20–41.

Prager, K. J. (1986). Intimacy status: Its relationship to locus of control, self-disclosure, and anxiety in adults. *Personality and Social Psychology Bulletin, 12,* 91–109.

Premack, D. (1965). Reinforcement theory. In D. Levine (Ed.), *Nebraska symposium on motivation* (pp. 123–180). Lincoln: University of Nebraska Press.

Prince, P. N., & Hoffmann, R. F. (1991). Dreams of the dying patient. *Omega, 23,* 1–11.

Prociuk, T. J., & Breen, L. J. (1977). Internal-external control and information-seeking in a college academic situation. *Journal of Social Psychology, 101,* 309–310.

Purton, C. (1989). The person-centered Jungian. *Person-Centered Review, 4,* 403–419.

Putnam, F. W., Guroff, J. J., Sliberman, E. K., Barban, L., & Post, R. M. (1986). The clinical phenomenology of multiple personality disorder: Review of 100 recent cases. *Journal of Clinical Psychiatry, 47,* 285–293.

Quadrel, M. J., & Lau, R. R. (1989). Health promotion, health locus of control, and health behavior: Two field experiments. *Journal of Applied Social Psychology, 19,* 1497–1521.

Rachlin, H. (1977). Review of *Cognition and Behavior Modification* by M. J. Mahoney. *Journal of Applied Behavior Analysis, 10,* 369–374.

Ramond, C. K. (1953). Anxiety and task as determiners of verbal performance. *Journal of Experimental Psychology, 46,* 120–124.

Rangell, L. (1988). The future of psychoanalysis: The scientific crossroads. *Psychoanalytic Quarterly, 57,* 313–340.

Rao, N., Moely, B. E., & Lockman, J. J. (1987). Increasing social participation in preschool social isolates. *Journal of Clinical Child Psychology, 16,* 178–183.

Raskin R., Novacek, J., & Hogan, R. (1991). Narcissistic self-esteem management. *Journal of Personality and Social Psychology, 60,* 911–918.

Rawlings, D., & Carnie, D. (1989). The interaction of EPQ extraversion with WAIS subtest performance under timed and untimed conditions. *Personality and Individual Differences, 10,* 453–458.

Read, P. P. (1974). *Alive: The story of the Andes survivors.* Philadelphia: Lippincott.

Rees, L. (1961). Constitutional factors and abnormal behavior. In H. J. Eysenck (Ed.), *Handbook of abnormal psychology.* New York: Basic Books.

Reisner, M. F. (1989). The future of psychoanalysis in academic psychiatry: Plain talk. *Psychoanalytic Quarterly, 58,* 185–209.

Renik, O. (1990). The concept of transference neurosis and psychoanalytic methodology. *International Journal of Psycho-Analysis, 17,* 197–204.

Rescorla, R. A. (1988). Pavlovian conditioning: It's not what you think it is. *American Psychologist, 43,* 151–160.

Resnik, S. (1987). *The theatre of the dream.* New York: Avistock/Methuen.

Richard, L. S., Wakefield, J. A., & Lewak, R. (1990). *Personality and Individual Differences, 11,* 39–43.

Richard, R. L., & Jex, S. M. (1991). Further evidence for the validity of the Short Index of Self-Actualization [Special Issue: Handbook of self-actualization]. *Journal of Social Behavior and Personality, 6,* 331–338.

Richardson, R. C. (1990). The "tally argument" and the validation of psychoanalysis. *Philosophy of Science, 57,* 668–676.

Richaud de Minzi, M. C. (1991). A new multidimensional children's locus of control scale. *Journal of Psychology, 125,* 109–118.

Riemann, R. (1990). The bipolarity of personal constructs. *International Journal of Personal Construct Psychology, 3,* 149–165.

Riese, M. (1988). Temperament in full-term and preterm infants: Stability over ages 6–24 months. *Journal of Developmental and Behavioral Pediatrics, 9,* 6–11.

Riese, M. L. (1990). Neonatal temperament in monozygotic and dizygotic twins. *Child Development, 61,* 1230–1237.

Rigby, K, & Slee, P. T. (1987). Eysenck's personality factors and orientation toward authority among schoolchildren. *Australian Journal of Psychology, 39,* 151–161.

Ritter, B. (1969). Eliminating excessive fears of the environment through contact desensitization. In J. D. Krumboltz & C. E. Thoresen (Eds.), *Behavioral counseling: Cases and techniques* (pp. 168–178). New York: Holt, Rinehart & Winston.

Rivera, D., & Smith, D. D. (1988). Using a demonstration strategy to teach midschool students with learning disabilities how to compute long division. *Journal of Learning Disabilities, 21,* 77–81.

Roazen, P. (1975). *Freud and his followers.* New York: Knopf.

Robbins, S. B. (1989). Role of contemporary psychoanalysis in counseling psychology. *Journal of Counseling Psychology, 36,* 267–278.

Robert, R., Jansson, B., & Wager, J. (1989). Dreams of pregnant women: A pilot study. *Journal of Psychosomatic Obstetrics and Gynecology, 10,* 21–33.

Robin, A. L., & Foster, S. L. (1989). *Negotiating parent-adolescent conflict: A behavioral family systems approach.* New York: Guilford Press.

Robins, L. N. (1966). *Deviant children grown up: A sociological and psychiatric study of sociopathic personality.* Baltimore, MD: Williams & Wilkins.

Roche, S. M., & McConkey, K. M. (1990). Absorption: Nature, assessment, and correlates. *Journal of Personality and Social Psychology, 59,* 91–101.

Rock, I. (1983). *The logic of perception.* Cambridge, MA: MIT Press.

Rockland, L. H. (1989). Psychoanalytically oriented supportive therapy: Literature review and techniques. *Journal of the American Academy of Psychoanalysis, 17,* 451–462.

Rodriguez, M. L., Mischel, W., & Shoda, Y. (1989). Cognitive person variables in the delay of gratification of older children at risk. *Journal of Personality and Social Psychology, 57,* 358–367.

Roger, D., & Morris, J. (1991). The internal structure of the EPQ scales. *Personality and Individual Differences, 12,* 759–764.

Rogers, C. (1954). Towards a theory of creativity. *ETC: A Review of General Semantics, 11,* 249–260.

Rogers, C. R. (1942). *Counseling and psychotherapy.* Boston: Houghton Mifflin.

Rogers, C. R. (1951). *Client-centered therapy: Its current practice, implications, and theory.* Boston: Houghton Mifflin.

Rogers, C. R. (1959). A theory of therapy, personality, and interpersonal relationships, as developed in the client-centered framework. In S. Koch (Ed.), *Psychology: A study of a science* (Vol. 3, pp. 184–256). New York: McGraw–Hill.

Rogers, C. R. (1961). *On becoming a person.* Boston: Houghton Mifflin.

Rogers, C. R. (1963). The concept of the fully functioning person. *Psychotherapy: Theory, Research, and Practice, 1,* 17–26.

Rogers, C. R. (1965). *Client-centered therapy.* Boston: Houghton Mifflin.

Rogers, C. R. (1973). Some new challenges. *American Psychologist, 28,* 379–387.

Rogers, C. R. (1974). In retrospect: Forty-six years. *American Psychologist, 29,* 115–123.

Rogers, C. R. (1975). Empathic: An unappreciated way of being. *Counseling Psychologist, 5,* 2–10.

Rogers, C. R. (1979). The foundations of the person-centered approach. *Education, 100,* 98–107.

Rogers, C. R. (1980). *A way of being.* Boston: Houghton Mifflin.

Rogers, C. R. (1983). *Freedom to learn for the 80s.* Columbus, OH: Charles E. Merrill.

Rogers, C. R., & Dymond, R. F. (Eds.). (1954). *Psychotherapy and personality change.* Chicago: University of Chicago Press.

Rogers, C. R., & Ryback, D. (1984). One alternative to nuclear planetary suicide. In R. F. Levant & J. M. Shlien (Eds.), *Client-centered therapy and the person-centered approach: New directions in theory, research, and practice* (pp. 400–402). New York: Praeger.

Rohsenow, D. J., & Marlatt, G. A. (1981). The balanced placebo design: Methodological considerations. *Addictive Behaviors, 6,* 107–122.

Rokeach, M., & Kliejunas, P. (1972). Behavior as a function of attitude-toward-object and attitude-toward-situation. *Journal of Personality and Social Psychology, 22,* 194–201.

Rokke, P. A., al-Absi, M., Lall, R., & Oswald, K. (1991). When does a choice of coping strategies help? The interaction of choice and locus of control. *Journal of Behavioral Medicine, 14,* 491–504.

Romi, S., & Itskowitz, R. (1990). The relationship between locus of control and type of aggression in middle-class and culturally deprived children. *Personality and Individual Differences, 11,* 327–333.

Romney, D. M. (1990). Thought disorders in the relatives of schizophrenics: A meta-analytic review of selected published studies. *Journal of Nervous and Mental Disease, 178,* 481–486.

Rorschach, H. (1921). *Psychodiagnostik.* Bern and Leipzig: Ernst Bircher Verlag.

Rose, R. J., Koskenvuo, M., Kaprio, J., Sarna, S., & Langinvainio, H. (1988). Shared genes, shared experiences, and similarity of personality: Data from 14,288 adult Finnish co-twins. *Journal of Personality and Social Psychology, 54,* 161–171.

Rosenberg, S. (1977). New approaches to the analysis of personal constructs in person perception. In J. K. Cole & A. W. Landfield (Eds.), *Nebraska symposium on motivation, 1976* (Vol. 24). Lincoln: University of Nebraska Press.

Rosenblatt, A. D. (1988). Envy, identification, and pride. *Psychoanalytic Quarterly, 57,* 56–71.

Rosenfarb, I. S. (1992). Review of unifying behavior therapy: Contributions of paradigmatic behaviorism by G. H. Eifert & I. M. Evans (Eds.). *Child and Family Behavior Therapy, 13,* 73–75.

Rosenhan, D. L., & Seligman, M. E. P. (1984). *Abnormal psychology.* New York: Norton.

Rosenman, R. H., Brand, R. J., Jenkins, C. D., Friedman, M., Straus, R., & Wurm, M. (1975). Coronary heart disease in the Western Collaborative Group Study: Final follow-up experience of 8½ years. *Journal of the American Medical Association, 233,* 872–877.

Rosenthal, D., Moore, S., & Flynn, I. (1991). Adolescent self-efficacy, self-esteem and sexual risk-taking. *Journal of Community and Applied Social Psychology, 1,* 77–88.

Rosenwald, G. C. (1972). Effectiveness of defenses against anal impulse arousal. *Journal of Consulting and Clinical Psychology, 39,* 292–298.

Rosolack, T. K., & Hampson, S. E. (1991). A new typology of health behaviours for personality-health predictions: The case of locus of control. *European Journal of Personality, 5,* 151–168.

Ross, C. A., Miller, S. D., Reagor, P., Bjornson, L., Fraser, G. A., & Anderson, G. (1990). Structured interview data on 102 cases of multiple personality disorder from four centers. *American Journal of Psychiatry, 147,* 596–601.

Ross, M. (1989). Relation of implicit theories to the construction of personal histories. *Psychological Review, 96,* 341–357.

Rotenberg, V. S. (1988). Functional deficiency of REM sleep and its role in the pathogenesis of neurotic and psychosomatic disturbances. *Pavlovian Journal of Biological Science, 23,* 1–3.

Roth, P. A. (1991). Truth in interpretation: The case of psychoanalysis. *Philosophy of the Social Sciences, 21,* 175–195.

Rotter, J. B. (1954). *Social learning and clinical psychology.* Englewood Cliffs, NJ: Prentice-Hall.

Rotter, J. B. (1966). Generalized expectancies for internal versus external control of reinforcement. *Psychological Monographs, 80,* 1–28.

Rotter, J. B. (1981). The psychological situation in social learning theory. In D. Magnusson (Ed.), *Toward a psychology of situations: An interactional perspective.* Hillsdale, NJ: Erlbaum.

Rotter, J. B. (1982). *The development and application of social learning theory.* New York: Praeger.

Royce, J. R., & Powell, A. (1983). *Theory of personality and individual differences: Factors, systems, and processes.* Englewood Cliffs, NJ: Prentice-Hall.

Rudnytsky, P. L. (1987). *Freud and Oedipus*. New York: Columbia.

Rule, W. R. (1991). Self-actualization: A person in positive movement or simply an esteemed personality characteristic? [Special Issue: Handbook of self-actualization]. *Journal of Social Behavior and Personality*, 6, 249–264.

Runco, M. A., Ebersole, P., & Mraz, W. (1991). Creativity and self-actualization. [Special Issue: Handbook of self-actualization]. *Journal of Social Behavior and Personality*, 6, 161–167.

Runyan, W. M. (1983). Idiographic goals and methods in the study of lives. *Journal of Personality*, 51, 413–437.

Runyan, W. McK. (Ed.). (1988). *Psychology and historical interpretation*. New York: Oxford University Press.

Rushton, J. P., Russell, R. J. H., & Wells, P. A. (1985). Personality and genetic similarity theory. *Journal of Social and Biological Structures*, 8, 63–86.

Russo, D. C. (1990). A requiem for the passing of the three-term contingency. *Behavior Therapy*, 21, 153–165.

Rychlak, J. F. (1990). George Kelly and the concept of construction. *International Journal of Personal Construct Psychology*, 3, 7–19.

Rychlak, J. F. (1991). *Artificial intelligence and human reason: A teleological critique*. New York: Columbia University Press.

Rychlak, J. F., Barnard, S., Williams, R. N., & Wollman, N. (1989). The recognitions and cognitive utiliization of oppositionality. *Journal of Psycholinguistic Research*, 10, 135–152.

Sabbe, B. G. (1991). Clientgerichte partnerrelatietherapie: het model van Auckenthaler. [Client-centered marital therapy: Auckenthaler's model.] *Tijdschrift voor Psychotherapie*, 17, 224–233.

Sackeim, H. A. (1983). Self-deception, self-esteem, and depression: The adaptive value of lying to oneself. In J. Masling (Ed.), *Empirical studies of psychoanalytical theories* (Vol. 1, pp. 101–157). Hillsdale, NJ: Analytic Press.

Safran, J. (1990, November). Cognitive therapy for depression: An examination of the process of change in light of recent developments in interpersonal theory. In A. M. Hayes (Chair), *A comparison of three psychotherapies for depression: The search for mechanisms of change*. Symposium presented at the meeting of the Association for Advancement of Behavior Therapy, San Francisco.

Sagan, E. (1988). *Freud, women, and morality: The psychology of good and evil*. New York: Basic Books.

St. Clair, M. (1986). *Object relations and self psychology: An introduction*. Pacific Grove, CA: Brooks/Cole.

St. Mary, S., & Russo, T. J. (1991). A self-efficacy scale for chemical dependency in adolescence. *Psychology: A Journal of Human Behavior*, 27, 62–68.

Salmon, P. (1988). *Psychology for teachers: An alternative approach*. London: Hutchinson.

Sampson, E. E. (1989). The challenge of social change for psychology: Globalization and psychology's theory of the person. *American Psychologist*, 44, 914–921.

Sand, R. (1988). Early nineteenth century anticipation of Freudian theory. *International Review of Psycho-Analysis*, 15, 465–479.

Sandin, B., Chorot, P., & Fernández-Trespalecios, J. L. (1989). Pavlovian conditioning and phobias: The state of the art. In P. M. G. Emmelkamp, W. T. A. M. Everaerd, F. Kraaimaat, & Y. M. J. M. van Son (Eds.), *Fresh perspectives on anxiety disorders* (pp. 71–85). Amsterdam: Swets & Zeitlinger.

Sappington, A. A. (1990). Recent psychological approaches to the free will versus determinism issue. *Psychological Bulletin*, 108, 1–11.

Sarason, I. G., Sarason, B. R., & Pierce, G. R. (1990). Anxiety, cognitive interference, and performance. *Journal of Social Behavior and Personality*, 5, 1–18.

Sarnoff, C. (1976). *Latency*. New York: Aronson.

Sarnoff, I., & Corwin, S. M. (1959). Castration anxiety and the fear of death. *Journal of Personality*, 27, 374–385.

Sayers, J. (1991). *Mothers of psychoanalysis*. New York: Norton.

Scarr, S., & McCartney, K. (1983). How people make their own environments: A theory of genotype/environment effects. *Child Development*, 54, 424–435.

Schaefer, W. S., & Bayley, N. (1963). Maternal behavior, child behavior, and their intercorrelations from infancy through adolescence. *Monographs of the Society for Research in Child Development*, 28, 1–27.

Schafer, R. (1950). Review of *Introduction to the Szondi Test: Theory and practice* by S. Deri. *Journal of Abnormal and Social Psychology*, 45, 184–188.

Schaffer, H. R., & Emerson, P. E. (1964). Patterns of response to physical contact in early human development. *Journal of Child Psychology and Psychiatry*, 5, 1–13.

Scharff, D. E., & Scharff, J. S. (1987). *Object relations family therapy*. Northvale, NJ: Aronson.

Schiaffino, K. M., Revenson, T. A., & Gibofsky, A. (1991). Assessing the impact of self-efficacy beliefs on adaptation to rheumatoid arthritis. *Arthritis Care and Research*, 4, 150–157.

Schimek, J. G. (1983). The construction of the transference: The relativity of the "here and now" and the "there and then." *Psychoanalysis and Contemporary Thought*, 6, 435–456.

Schlinger, H. D., Jr. (1992). Theory in behavior analysis: An application to child development. *American Psychologist*, 47, 1396–1410.

Schloss, P. J., Smith, M., Santora, C., & Bryant, R. (1989). A respondent conditioning approach to reducing anger responses of a dually diagnosed man with mild mental retardation. *Behavior Therapy*, 20, 459–464.

Schmukler, A. G., & Garcia, E. E. (1989). Special symbols in early female Oedipal development: Fantasies of folds and spaces, protuberances and concavities. *International Journal of Psycho-Analysis*, 71, 297–300.

Schnake, M. E., & Dumler, M. P. (1990). Use of vicarious punishment to offset effects of negative social cues. *Psychological Reports*, 66, 1299–1308.

Schramm, W., Lyle, J., & Parker, E. (1961). *Television in the lives of our children*. Stanford, CA: Stanford University Press.

Schretlen, D. (1988). The use of psychological tests to identify malingered symptoms of mental disorder. *Clinical Psychology Review*, 8, 451–476.

Schretlen, D. (1990). A limitation of using the Wiener and Harmon obvious and subtle scales to detect faking on the MMPI. *Journal of Clinical Psychology, 46*, 782–786.

Schretlen, D., & Arkowitz, H. (1990). A psychological test battery to detect prison inmates who fake insanity or mental retardation. *Behavioral Sciences and the Law, 8*, 75–84.

Schwaber, E. A. (1990). Interpretation and the therapeutic action of psychoanalysis. *International Journal of Psycho-Analysis, 71*, 229–240.

Schwarzer, R. (1992a). Self-efficacy in the adoption and maintenance of health behaviors: Theoretical approaches and a new model. In R. Schwarzer (Ed.), *Self-efficacy: Thought control of action* (pp. 217–243). Washington, DC: Hemisphere.

Schwarzer, R. (Ed.). (1992b). *Self-efficacy: Thought control of action.* Washington, DC: Hemisphere.

Sears, R. R. (1943). *Survey of objective studies of psychoanalytic concepts.* New York: Social Science Research Council, Bulletin 51.

Seeman, J. (1984). The fully functioning person: Theory and research. In R. F. Levant & J. M. Shlien (Eds.), *Client-centered therapy and the person-centered approach: New directions in theory, research, and practice* (pp. 131–152). New York: Praeger.

Seeman, J. (1991). "Person-centered assessment": Reaction. *Journal of Counseling and Development, 69*, 462.

Segall, M. E., & Wynd, C. A. (1990). Health conception, health locus of control, and power as predictors of smoking behavior change. *American Journal of Health Promotion, 4*, 338–344.

Seligman, M. E. P. (1971). Phobias and preparedness. *Behavior Therapy, 2*, 307–320.

Sewell, K. W., Adams-Webber, J., Mitterer, J., & Cromwell, R. L. (1992). Computerized repertory grids: Review of the literature. *International Journal of Personal Construct Psychology, 5*, 1–23.

Shane, M. (1977). A rationale for teaching analytic technique based on a developmental orientation and approach. *International Journal of Psycho-Analysis, 58*, 95–108.

Shannon, B. (1990). Why are dreams cinematographic? *Metaphor and Symbolic Activity, 5*, 235–248.

Shapiro, M. A. (1991). Memory and decision processes in the construction of social reality. *Communication Research, 18*, 3–24.

Shaver, K. G., & Tarpy, R. M. (1993). *Psychology.* New York: Macmillan.

Shear, H. J., & Kundrat, S. L. (1987). Providing conditions to help clients outgrow disturbing dreams. *Psychotherapy, 24*, 363–367.

Sheehy, G. (1976). *Passages: Predictable crises of adult life.* New York: Dutton.

Sheehy, G. (1981). *Pathfinders.* New York: Morrow.

Sheldon, W. H. (1942). *The varieties of temperament: A psychology of constitutional differences.* New York: Harper & Row.

Shell, D. F., Murphy, C. C., Bruning, R. H. (1989). Self-efficacy and outcome expectancy mechanisms in reading and writing achievement. *Journal of Educational Psychology, 81*, 91–100.

Shelton, S. H. (1990). Developing the construct of general self-efficacy. *Psychological Reports, 66*, 987–994.

Sherrill, C., Gench, B., Hinson, M., Gilstrap, T., Richir, K., & Mastro, J. (1990). Self-actualization of elite blind athletes: An exploratory study. *Journal of Visual Impairment and Blindness, 84*, 55–60.

Sherwood, G. G. (1979). Classical and attributive projection: Some new evidence. *Journal of Abnormal Psychology, 88*, 635–640.

Sherwood, M. (1969). *The logic of explanation in psychoanalysis.* New York: Academic Press.

Shimp, T. A., Stuart, E. W., & Engle, R. W. (1991). A program of classical conditioning experiments testing variations in the conditioned stimulus and context. *Journal of Consumer Research, 18*, 1–12.

Shoda, Y., Mischel, W., & Peake, P. K. (1990). Predicting adolescent cognitive and self-regulatory competencies from preschool delay of gratification: Identifying diagnostic conditions. *Developmental Psychology, 26*, 978–986.

Shoda, Y., Mischel, W., & Wright, J. C. (1989). Intuitive interactionism in person perception: Effects of situation-behavior relations on disopositional judgments. *Journal of Personality and Social Psychology, 56*, 41–53.

Shostrom, E. L. (1963). *Personal Orientation Inventory.* San Diego: EdITS/Educational & Industrial Testing Service.

Shostrom, E. L. (1964). An inventory for the measurement of self-actualization. *Educational and Psychological Measurement, 24*, 207–218.

Shostrom, E. L. (1974). *Manual for the Personal Orientation Inventory.* San Diego: EdITS/Educational & Industrial Testing Service.

Shostrom, E. L., Knapp, L. F., & Knapp, R. R. (1976). *Actualizing therapy: Foundations for a scientific ethic.* San Diego: EdITS/Educational & Industrial Testing Service.

Shulman, D. G. (1990). Psychoanalysis and the quantitative research tradition. *The Psychoanalytic Review, 77*, 245–261.

Shulman, D. G. (1990). The investigation of psychoanalytic theory by means of the experimental method. *International Journal of Psycho-Analysis, 71*, 487–498.

Siegel, S. (1985). Drug anticipatory responses in animals. In L. White, B. Tursky, & G. E. Schwartz (Eds.), *Placebo: Theory, research, and mechanisms* (pp. 288–305). New York: Guilford Press.

Siegel, S., & Ellsworth, D. W. (1986). Pavlovian conditioning and death from apparent overdose of medically prescribed morphine: A case report. *Bulletin of the Psychonomic Society, 24*, 278–280.

Siegert, M. B. (1990). Reconstruction, construction, or deconstruction: Perspectives on the limits of psychoanalytic knowledge. *Contemporary Psychoanalysis, 26*, 160–170.

Siegler, I. C., Zonderman, A. B., Barefoot, J. C., Williams, R. B., Costa, P. T., & McCrae, R. R. (1990). Predicting personality in adulthood from college MMPI scores: Implications for follow-up studies in psychosomatic medicine. *Psychosomatic Medicine, 52*, 644–652.

Silverman, L. H. (1983). The subliminal psychodynamic activation method: Overview and comprehensive listing of studies. In J. Masling (Ed.), *Empirical studies in psychoanalysis* (Vol. 1, pp. 69–100). Hillsdale, NJ: Erlbaum.

Simonton, O. C., Mathews-Simonton, S., & Creighton, J. L. (1980). *Getting well again.* New York: Bantam.

Singer, J. L. (1985). Transference and the human condition: A cognitive-affective perspective. *Psychoanalytic Psychology, 2,* 189–219.

Singh, B. G., & Verma, O. P. (1990). Cultural differences in locus of control beliefs in two Indian societies. *Journal of Social Psychology, 130,* 725–729.

Siskind, D. (1987). An example of preverbal determinants in a classical analysis. *Clinical Social Work Journal, 15,* 361–367.

Sitharthan, T., & Kavanagh, D. J. (1991). Role of self-efficacy in predicting outcomes from a programme for controlled drinking. *Drug and Alcohol Dependence, 27,* 87–94.

Sizemore, C. C., & Huber, R. J. (1988). The twenty-two faces of Eve. *Individual Psychology Journal of Adlerian Theory, Research and Practice, 44,* 53–62.

Skinner, B. F. (1953). *Science and human behavior.* New York: Macmillan.

Skinner, B. F. (1956). A case history in scientific method. *American Psychologist, 11,* 221–233.

Skinner, B. F. (1974). *About behaviorism.* New York: Knopf.

Skinner, B. F. (1989). The origins of cognitive thought. *American Psychologist, 44,* 13–18.

Skinner, E. (1992). Perceived control: Motivation, coping, and development. In R. Schwarzer (Ed.), *Self-efficacy: Thought control of action* (pp. 91–106). Washington, DC: Hemisphere.

Slade, L. A., & Rush, M. C. (1991). Achievement motivation and the dynamics of task difficulty choices. *Journal of Personality and Social Psychology, 60,* 165–172.

Slater, M. D. (1989). Social influences and cognitive control as predictors of self-efficacy and eating behavior. *Cognitive Therapy and Research, 13,* 231–245.

Slavin, M. O. (1990). The dual meaning of repression and the adaptive design of the human psyche. *Journal of the Academy of Psychoanalysis, 18,* 307–341.

Slife, B. D., Stoneman, J., & Rychlak, J. F. (1991). The heuristic power of oppositionality in an incidental-memory task: In support of the construing process. *International Journal of Personal Construct Psychology, 4,* 333–346.

Smith, D. A., & Andresen, J. J. (1988). Shadows in dreams. *Contemporary Psychoanalysis, 24,* 46–60.

Smith, J. E., Stefan, C., Kovaleski, M., & Johnson, G. (1991). Recidivism and dependency in a psychiatric population: An investigation with Kelly's dependency grid. *International Journal of Personal Construct Psychology, 4,* 157–173.

Smith, M. B. (1988). The wrong drummer: A reply to Blight. *Journal of Humanistic Psychology, 28,* 62–66.

Smith, M. B. (1990). Humanistic psychology. *Journal of Humanistic Psychology, 30,* 6–21.

Smith, R. E. (1973). The use of humor in the counterconditioning of anger responses: A case study. *Behavior Therapy, 4,* 576–580.

Smith, T. W., & Anderson, N. B. (1986). Models of personality and disease: An interactional approach to Type A behavior and cardiovascular risk. *Journal of Personality and Social Psychology, 50,* 1166–1173.

Smith, T. W., & Pope, M. K. (1990). Cynical hostility as a health risk: Current status and future directions. *Journal of Social Behavior and Personality, 5,* 77–88.

Snyder, C. R., & Larson, G. R. (1972). A further look at student acceptance of general personality interpretations. *Journal of Consulting and Clinical Psychology, 38,* 384–388.

Snyder, F. (1965). The organismic state associated with dreaming. In N. W. Greenfield (Ed.), *Psychoanalysis and current biological thought.* Madison: University of Wisconsin Press.

Snyder, M. (1989). The relationship enhancement model of couple therapy: An integration of Rogers and Bateson [Special Issue: Person-centered approaches with families]. *Person-Centered Review, 4,* 358–383.

Snyder, W. U. (1947). *Casebook of non-directive counseling.* Boston: Houghton Mifflin.

Sokolov, A. N. (1972). *Inner speech and thought.* New York: Plenum.

Solas, J. (1992). Ideological dimension implicit in Kelly's theory of personal constructs. *International Journal of Personal Construct Psychology, 5,* 377–391.

Solomon, K. E., & Annis, H. M. (1990). Outcome and efficacy expectancy in the prediction of post-treatment drinking behaviour. *British Journal of Addiction, 85,* 659–666.

Solomon, L. N. (1988). On being a sociotherapist in policy-land: A commentary on James Blight's article. *Journal of Humanistic Psychology, 28,* 70–72.

Sorrentino, R. M., & Field, N. (1986). Emergent leadership over time: The functional value of positive motivation. *Journal of Personality and Social Psychology, 50,* 1091–1099.

Spector, P. E. (1988). Development of the work locus of control scale. *Journal of Occupational Psychology, 61,* 335–340.

Spence, D. P. (1984). *Narrative truth and historical truth: Meaning and interpretation in psychoanalysis.* New York: Norton.

Spence, J. T., Helmreich, R. L., & Pred, R. S. (1987). Impatience versus achievement strivings in the Type A behavior pattern: Differential effects on students' health and academic achievement. *Journal of Applied Psychology, 72,* 522–528.

Spiegler, M. D. (1983). *Contemporary behavioral therapy.* Palo Alto, CA: Mayfield.

Spiegler, M. D. (1985, August). *Treating guilt within the framework of personal construct theory.* Paper presented at the International Congress on Personal Construct Theory, Cambridge, England.

Spiegler, M. D. (1989). *Transference in everyday life.* Unpublished manuscript, Providence College.

Spiegler, M. D. (1991). Satir's formula for therapeutic endurance: The wonderful human being myth. *Journal of Couples Therapy, 2,* 165–167.

Spiegler, M. D., & Agigian, H. (1977). *The Community Training Center: An educational-behavioral-social systems model for rehabilitating psychiatric patients.* New York: Brunner/Mazel.

Spiegler, M. D., & Davison, G. C. (1989, April). *What therapists tell clients: Implications for psychotherapy integration and ethical practice.* Paper presented at the 5th Annual Conference of the Society for the Exploration of Psychotherapy Integration, Berkeley, CA.

Spiegler, M. D., & Guevremont, D. C. (1993). *Contemporary behavior therapy* (2nd ed.). Pacific Grove, CA: Brooks/Cole.

Spiegler, M. D., & Liebert, R. M. (1970). Some correlates of self-reported fear. *Psychological Reports, 26,* 691–695.

Spiegler, M. D., & Weiland, A. (1976). The effects of written vicarious consequences on observers' willingness to imitate and ability to recall modeling cues. *Journal of Personality, 44,* 260–273.

Spielberger, C. D., & Gorsuch, R. L. (1966). *Mediating processes in verbal conditioning: Report of United States Public Health Service Grants MH-7229, MH-7446, and HD-947.* Unpublished manuscript, Vanderbilt University.

Spielman, A. J., Saskin, P., & Thorpy, M. J. (1987). Treatment of chronic insomnia by restriction of time in bed. *Sleep, 10,* 45–56.

Staats, A. W. (1986). Behaviorism with a personality: The paradigmatic behavioral assessment approach. In R. O. Nelson & S. C. Hayes (Eds.), *Conceptual foundations of behavioral assessment* (pp. 242–296). New York: Guilford.

Staats, A. W. (1989a). Paradigmatic behaviorism's theory of intelligence: A third-generation approach to cognition. *Psicothema, 1,* 7–24.

Staats, A. W. (1989b). Unificationism: Philosophy for the modern disunified science of psychology. *Philosophical Psychology, 2,* 143–164.

Staats, A. W. (1990). Paradigmatic behaviorism and intelligence: Task analysis? Technical plan? or Theory? *Psicothema, 2,* 7–24.

Staats, A. W. (1991). Unified positivism and unification psychology: Fad or new field? *American Psychologist, 46,* 899–912.

Staats, A. W. (1993a). Personality theory, abnormal psychology, and psychological measurement: A psychological behaviorism. *Behavior Modification, 17,* 8–42.

Staats, A. W. (1993b). Why do we need another behaviorism such as paradigmatic behaviorism? *the Behavior Therapist, 3,* 64–68.

Staats, A. W., & Burns, G. L. (1981). Intelligence and child development: What intelligence is and how it is learned and functions. *Genetic Psychology Monographs, 104,* 237–301.

Staats, A. W., & Burns, G. L. (1982). Emotional personality repertoire as cause of behavior: Specification of person-ality and interaction principles. *Journal of Personality and Social Psychology, 43,* 873–881.

Staats, A. W., & Burns, G. L. (1992). The psychological behaviourism theory of personality. *Modern personality psychology: Critical reviews and new directions.* New York: Harvester Whatsheaf.

Staats, A. W., & Eifert, G. H. (1990). The paradigmatic behaviorism theory of emotions: Basis for unification. *Clinical Psychology Review, 10,* 539–566.

Stagner, R. (1976). Traits are relevant: Theoretical analysis and empirical evidence. In N. S. Endler & D. Magnusson (Eds.), *Interactional psychology and personality.* Washington, DC: Hemisphere.

Staw, B. M., & Ross, J. (1985). Stability in the midst of change: A dispositional approach to job attitudes. *Journal of Applied Psychology, 70,* 469–480.

Steele, R. S. (1979). Psychoanalysis and hermeneutics. *International Review of Psycho-Analysis, 6,* 389–411.

Steele, R. S. (1985). Paradigm lost: Psychoanalysis after Freud. In C. E. Buxton (Ed.), *Points of view in the modern history of psychology.* New York: Academic Press.

Steele, R. S. (1986). Deconstructing histories: Toward a systematic criticism of psychological narratives. In T. Sarbin (Ed.), *Psychology and narrative.* New York: Praeger.

Steinmark, S. W., & Borkovec, T. D. (1974). Active and placebo treatment effects on moderate insomnia under counterdemand and positive demand instructions. *Journal of Abnormal Psychology, 83,* 157–163.

Stelmack, R. M. (1990). Biological bases of extraversion: Psychophysiological evidence. *Journal of Personality, 58,* 293–311.

Stelmack, R. M. (1991). Advances in personality theory and research. *Journal of Psychiatric Neuroscience, 16,* 131–138.

Stelmack, R. M., & Stalikas, A. (1991). Galen and the humour theory of temperament. *Personality and Individual Differences, 12,* 255–263.

Stephan, C., & Linder, H. B. (1985). Suicide, an experience of chaos or fatalism: Perspectives from personal construct theory. In D. Bannister (Ed.), *Issues and approaches in personal construct theory*: Orlando, FL: Academic Press.

Stewart, A. E., & Barry, J. R. (1991). Origins of George Kelly's constructivism in the works of Korzybski and Moreno. *International Journal of Personal Construct Psychology, 4,* 121–136.

Stewart, V., & Stewart, A. (1982). *Business applications of repertory grid.* London: McGraw-Hill.

Stiles, T. C., & Götestam, K. G. (1989). The role of automatic negative thoughts in the development of dysphoric mood: An analogue experiment. *Cognitive Therapy and Research, 13,* 161–170.

Stiles, T. C., Schröder, P., & Johansen, T. (1993). The role of automatic thoughts and dysfunctional attitudes in the development and maintenance of experimentally induced dysphoric mood. *Cognitive Therapy and Research, 17,* 71–82.

Stolorow, R. D. (1988). Transference and the therapeutic process. *Psychoanalytic Review, 75,* 245–254.

Storr, A. (1988). *Solitude: A return to the self.* New York: Free Press.

Storr, A., & Kermode, F. (Eds.). (1973). *C. J. Jung.* New York: Viking Press.

Stotland, S., & Zuroff, D. C. (1991). Relations between multiple measures of dieting self-efficacy and weight change in a behavioral weight control program. *Behavior Therapy, 22,* 47–59.

Stotland, S., Zuroff, D. C., & Roy, M. (1991). Situational dieting self-efficacy and short-term regulation of eating. *Appetite, 17,* 81–90.

Strano, D. A., & Dixon, P. N. (1990). The comparative feeling of inferiority index. *Individual Psychology, 46,* 29–42.

Strassburger, L. A., Rosen, L. A., Miller, C. D., & Chavez, E. L. (1990). Hispanic-Anglo differences in academic achievement: The relationship of self-esteem, locus of control and socioeconomic level with grade-point average in the USA. *School Psychology International, 11,* 119–124.

Strean, H. S. (1985). *Resolving resistances in psychotherapy.* New York: Wiley.

Strelau, J. (1987). The concept of temperament in personality research. *European Journal of Personality, 1,* 107–117.

Strickland, B. R. (1977). Internal-external control of reinforcement. In T. Bass (Ed.), *Personality variables in social behavior* (pp. 219–279). Hillsdale, NJ: Erlbaum.

Strickland, B. R. (1978). Internal-external expectancies of health-related behaviors. *Journal of Consulting and Clinical Psychology, 46,* 1192–1211.

Strickland, B. R. (1979). Internal-external expectancies and cardiovascular functioning. In L. C. Perlmuter & R. A. Monty (Eds.), *Choice and perceived control* (pp. 221–231). Hillsdale, NJ: Erlbaum.

Strickland, B. R. (1989). Internal-external control expectancies: From contingency to creativity. *American Psychologist, 44,* 1–12.

Striker, G., & Gold, J. (Eds.). (1993). *Comprehensive handbook of psychotherapy integration.* New York: Plenum.

Strupp, H. H. (1967). *An introduction to Freud and modern psychoanalysis.* Woodbury, NY: Barron's.

Stuart, E. W., Shimp, T. A., & Engle, W. W. (1987). Classical conditioning of consumer attitudes: Four experiments in an advertising context. *Journal of Consumer Research, 14,* 334–349.

Stuart, R. B. (1980). *Helping couples change: A social learning approach to marital therapy.* New York: Guilford.

Stumphauzer, J. S. (1972). Increased delay of gratification in young prison inmates through imitation of high-delay peer-models. *Journal of Personality and Social Psychology, 21,* 10–17.

Sullivan, H. S. (1953). *The interpersonal theory of psychiatry.* New York: Norton.

Sulloway, F. J. (1979). *Freud, biologist of the mind.* New York: Basic Books.

Sutton, W. S. (1991). Hypnocounselling: A client-centered way of tuning into the subconscious. *Australian Journal of Clinical Hypnotherapy and Hypnosis, 12,* 7–20.

Swan, G. E., & MacDonald, M. L. (1978). Behavior therapy in practice: A national survey of behavioral therapists. *Behavior Therapy, 9,* 799–807.

Szasz, T. S. (1960). The myth of mental illness. *American Psychologist, 15,* 113–118.

Tarter, R. E. (1988). Are there inherited behavioral traits that predispose to substance abuse? *Journal of Consulting and Clinical Psychology, 56,* 189–196.

Taylor, J. A. (1953). A personality scale of manifest anxiety. *Journal of Abnormal and Social Psychology, 48,* 285–290.

Taylor, J. A., & Spence, K. W. (1952). The relationship of anxiety level to performance in serial learning. *Journal of Experimental Psychology, 44,* 61–64.

Taylor, S. E., & Brown, J. D. (1988). Illusion and well-being: A social psychological perspective on mental health. *Psychological Bulletin, 103,* 193–210.

Teti, D. M., & Gelfand, D. M. (1991). Behavioral competence among mothers of infants in the first year: The mediational role of maternal self-efficacy. *Child Development, 62,* 918–929.

Thase, M. E., Bowler, K., & Harden, T. (1991). Cognitive behavior therapy of endogenous depression: Part 2: Preliminary findings in 16 unmedicated inpatients. *Behavior Therapy, 22,* 469–477.

Thase, M. E., Simons, A. D., Cahalane, J. F., & McGeary, J. (1991). Cognitive behavior therapy of endogenous depression: Part 1: An outpatient clinical replication series. *Behavior Therapy, 22,* 457–467.

Thigpen, C. H., & Cleckley, H. (1954). A case of multiple personality. *Journal of Abnormal and Social Psychology, 49,* 135–151.

Thigpen, C. H., & Cleckley, H. M. (1957). *The three faces of Eve.* New York: McGraw-Hill.

Thomas, A., & Chess, S. (1977). *Temperament and development.* New York: Brunner/Mazel.

Thomas, A., Chess, S., & Birch, H. G. (1970). The origin of personality. *Scientific American, 223,* 102–109.

Thomas, H. F. (1988). Keeping person-centered education alive in academic settings. *Person-Centered Review, 3,* 337–352.

Thomas, L., & Cooper, P. (1980). Incidence and psychological correlates of intense spiritual experiences. *Journal of Transpersonal Psychology, 12,* 75–85.

Thomaz, M. F., & Gilbert, J. K. (1989). A model for constructivist initial physics teacher education. *International Journal of Science Education, 11,* 35–47.

Thompson, C. M. (1941). The role of women in this culture. *Psychiatry, 4,* 1–8.

Thompson, C. M. (1942). Cultural pressures in the psychology of women. *Psychiatry, 5,* 331–339.

Thompson, C. M. (1943). Penis envy in women. *Psychiatry, 6,* 123–125.

Thompson, C. M. (1950). Cultural pressures in the psychology of women. In P. Mullahy (Ed.), *A study of interpersonal relations.* New York: Hermitage Press.

Thompson, C. M. (1957). *Psychoanalysis: Evolution and development.* New York: Grove.

Thompson, T. (1987). Resistance and preoedipal object relations. *Clinical Social Work Journal, 15,* 342–348.

Throne, J. M. (1992). Understanding Skinner. *American Psychologist, 47,* 1678.

Thurman, P. J., Jones-Saumty, D., & Parsons, O. A. (1990). Locus of control and drinking behavior in American Indian alcoholics and non-alcoholics. *American Indian and Alaska Native Mental Health Research, 4,* 31–39.

Tinsley, B. J., & Holtgrave, D. R. (1989). Maternal health locus of control beliefs, utilization of childhood preventive health services, and infant health. *Journal of Developmental and Behavioral Pediatrics, 10,* 236–241.

Tjeltveit, A. C. (1989). The ubiquity of models of human beings in psychotherapy: The need for rigorous reflection. *Psychotherapy, 26,* 1–10.

Tobin, S. A. (1991). A comparison of psychoanalytic self psychology and Carl Rogers's person-centered therapy. *Journal of Humanistic Psychology, 31,* 9–33.

Torgerson, S. (1990). Comorbidity of major depression and anxiety disorders in twin pairs. *American Journal of Psychiatry, 147,* 1199–1202.

Toshima, M. T., Kaplan, R. M., & Ries, A. L. (1992). Self-efficacy expectancies in chronic obstructive pulmonary disease rehabilitation. In R. Schwarzer (Ed.), *Self-efficacy: Thought control of action* (pp. 325–354). Washington, DC: Hemisphere.

Tracy, L. (1990). Treating factor interpretations as hypotheses. *Social Behavior and Personality, 18,* 309–326.

Trice, A. D. (1990). Adolescents' locus of control and compliance with contingency contracting and counseling interventions. *Psychological Reports, 67,* 233–234.

Trice, A. D., & Hackburt, L. (1989). Academic locus of control, Type A behavior, and college absenteeism. *Psychological Reports, 65,* 337–338.

Tryon, W. W. (1990). Why paradigmatic behaviorism should be retitled psychological behaviorism. *the Behavior Therapist, 13,* 127–128.

Tucker, R. K., & Dyson, R. (1991). Factor structure of the short form measure of self-actualization in a Black sample. *Psychological Reports, 69,* 871–877.

Turk, D., Meichenbaum, D., & Genest, M. (1983). *Pain and behavioral medicine.* New York: Guilford Press.

Turkel, A. R. (1988). Money as a mirror of marriage. *Journal of the American Academy of Psychoanalysis, 16,* 525–535.

Turkkan, J. S. (1989a). Classical conditioning beyond the reflex: An uneasy rebirth. *Behavioral and Brain Sciences, 12,* 161–179.

Turkkan, J. S. (1989b). Classical conditioning: The new hegemony. *Behavioral and Brain Sciences, 12,* 121–179.

Turkkan, J. S., & Brady, J. V. (1985). Mediational theory of the placebo effect: Discussion. In L. White, B. Tursky, & G. E. Schwartz (Eds.), *Placebo: Theory, research, and mechanisms* (pp. 324–331). New York: Guilford Press.

Turkle, S. (1988). Artificial intelligence and psychoanalysis: A new alliance. *Journal of the American Academy of Arts and Sciences, 117,* 241–268.

Turner, R. M. (1990, November). *The utility of psychodynamic techniques in the practice of cognitive behavior therapy.* Workshop presented at the meeting of the Association for Advancement of Behavior Therapy, San Francisco.

Tuttman, S. (1988). Psychoanalytic concepts of "the self." *Journal of the American Academy of Psychoanalysis, 16,* 209–219.

Tversky, A. (1977). Features of similarity. *Psychological Review, 84,* 327–352.

Tyler, F. B., Dhawan, N., & Sinha, Y. (1989). Cultural contributions to constructing locus of control attributions. *Genetic, Social, and General Psychology Monographs, 115,* 205–220.

Ulanov, A., & Ulanov, B. (1987). *The witch and the clown: Two archetypes of human sexuality.* Wilmette, IL: Chiron Publications.

Ulrich, R. E., Stachnik, T. J., & Stainton, N. R. (1963). Student acceptance of generalized personality interpretations. *Psychological Reports, 13,* 831–834.

University of Minnesota. (1982). *User's guide for the Minnesota Report.* Minneapolis: National Computer Systems.

Valliant, G. E. (1971). Theoretical hierarchy of adaptive ego mechanisms. *Archives of General Psychiatry, 24,* 107–118.

Valliant, G. E. (1977). *Adaptation to life.* Boston: Little, Brown.

Valliant, G. E., & Valliant, C. O. (1990). Determinants and consequences of creativity in a cohort of gifted women. *Psychology of Women Quarterly, 14,* 607–616.

Van de Castle, R. L. (1971). *The psychology of dreaming.* Morristown, NJ: General Learning Press.

Van den Hout, M. A., & Merckelbach, H. (1991). Classical conditioning: Still going strong. *Behavioural Psychotherapy, 19,* 59–79.

Vermorel, M. (1990). The drive [*trieb*] from Goethe to Freud. *International Review of Psycho-Analysis, 17,* 249–256.

Vernon, D. T. A. (1974). Modeling and birth order in responses to painful stimuli. *Journal of Personality and Social Psychology, 29,* 794–799.

Veroff, J. (1957). Development and validation of a projective measure of power motivation. *Journal of Abnormal and Social Psychology, 54,* 1–8.

Veroff, J., Atkinson, J. W., Feld, S. C., & Gurin, G. (1960). The use of thematic apperception to assess motivation in a nationwide interview study. *Psychological Monographs, 74* (12, Whole No. 499).

Veroff, J., Reuman, D., & Feld, S. (1984). Motives in American men and women across the adult life span. *Developmental Psychology, 20,* 1142–1158.

Viney, L. L. (1990). Psychotherapy as shared reconstruction. *International Journal of Personal Construct Psychology, 3,* 437–456.

Volkmer, R. E., & Feather, N. T. (1991). Relations between Type A scores, internal locus of control and test anxiety. *Personality and Individual Differences, 12,* 205–209.

Wagner, T. (1988, June 12). Does father always know best? *New York Times Magazine,* pp. 18, 20.

Walker, B. M. (1990). Construing George Kelly's construing of the person-in-relation. *International Journal of Personal Construct Psychology, 3,* 41–50.

Walker, B. M. (1992). Values and Kelly's theory: Becoming a good scientist. *International Journal of Personal Construct Psychology, 5,* 259–269.

Walker, C. E., Milling, L. S., & Bonner, B. L. (1988). Incontinence disorders: Enuresis and encopresis. In D. K. Routh (Ed.), *Handbook of pediatric psychology* (pp. 363–397). New York: Guilford.

Wallace, E. R. (1986). The scientific status of psychoanalysis: A review of Grünbaum's *The foundations of psychoanalysis. The Journal of Nervous and Mental Disease, 174,* 379–386.

Waller, K. V., & Bates, R. C. (1992). Health locus of control and self-efficacy beliefs in a healthy elderly sample. *American Journal of Health Promotion, 6,* 302–309.

Wallerstein, R. S. (1988). One psychoanalysis or many? *International Journal of Psycho-Analysis, 69,* 5–21.

Wallerstein, R. S. (1989). Psychoanalysis and psychotherapy: An historical perspective. *International Journal of Psycho-Analysis, 70,* 563–591.

Walsh, S. M. (1991). Employee assistance and the helping professional: The more things change, the more they stay the same. *Employee Assistance Quarterly, 7,* 113–118.

Walters, G. D., & Greene, R. L. (1988). Differentiating between schizophrenic and manic inpatients by means of the MMPI. *Journal of Personality Assessment, 52,* 91–95.

Wang, A. Y., & Richarde, R. S. (1988). Global versus task-specific measures of self-efficacy. *The Psychological Record, 38,* 533–541.

Ward, S. E., Leventhal, H., & Love, R. (1988). Repression revisited: Tactics used in coping with a severe health threat. *Personality and Social Psychology Bulletin, 14,* 735–746.

Waring, E. M. (1990). Self-disclosure of personal constructs. *Family Process, 29,* 399–416.

Warner, M. S. (1989). Empathy and strategy in the family system [Special Issue: Person-centered approaches with families]. *Person-Centered Review, 4,* 324–343.

Warner, S. L. (1987). Manifest dream analysis in contemporary practice. In M. L. Glucksman & S. L. Warner (Eds.), *Dreams in new perspective: The royal road revisited.* New York: Human Sciences.

Warren, W. (1989). Personal construct theory and general trends in contemporary philosophy. *International Journal of Personal Construct Psychology, 2,* 287–300.

Warren, W. G. (1990). Is personal construct psychology a cognitive psychology? *International Journal of Personal Construct Psychology, 3,* 393–414.

Warren, W. G. (1991). Rising up from down under: A response to Adams-Webber on cognitive psychology and personal construct psychology. *International Journal of Personal Construct Psychology, 4,* 43–49.

Warren, W. G. (1992). Personal construct theory and mental health. *International Journal of Personal Construct Psychology, 5,* 223–237.

Warren, W. G., & Parry, G. (1981). Personal constructs and death: Some clinical refinements. In H. Bonarius, R. Holland, & S. Rosenberg (Eds.), *Personal construct psychology: Recent advances in theory and practice.* New York: St. Martin's Press.

Wasik, B. (1984). *Teaching parents effective problem-solving: A handbook for professionals.* Unpublished manuscript, University of North Carolina, Chapel Hill.

Watson, J. B. (1914). *Behavior: An introduction to comparative psychology.* New York: H. Holt.

Watson, J. B. (1919). *Psychology from the standpoint of a behaviorist.* Philadelphia: Lippincott.

Watson, J. B., & Rayner, R. (1920). Conditioned emotional reactions. *Journal of Experimental Psychology, 3,* 1–14.

Watson, P. J., Morris, R. J., & Hood, R. W. (1990). Intrinsicness, self-actualization, and the ideological surround. *Journal of Psychology and Theology, 18,* 40–53.

Watson, W. E., Doster, J., & Michaelsen, L. K. (1990). Individual and group meaning: Exploring the reciprocal relation. *International Journal of Personal Construct Psychology, 3,* 231–248.

Watzlawick, P. (Ed.). (1984). *The invented reality.* New York: Norton.

Webb, W. B. (1982). Sleep and biological rhythms. In W. B. Webb (Ed.), *Biological rhythms, sleep, and performance.* New York: Wiley.

Weidner, G., & Matthews, K. A. (1978). Reported physical symptoms elicited by unpredictable events and the Type A coronary-prone behavior pattern. *Journal of Personality and Social Psychology, 36,* 1213–1220.

Weinrach, S. G. (1990). Rogers and Gloria: The controversial film and the enduring relationship. *Psychotherapy, 27,* 282–290.

Weisberg, P., & Waldrop, P. B. (1972). Fixed-interval work habits of Congress. *Journal of Applied Behavior Analysis, 5,* 93–97.

Weiss, A. S. (1987). Shostrom's Personal Orientation Inventory: Arguments against its basic validity. *Personality and Individual Differences, 8,* 895–903.

Weiss, A. S. (1991). The measurement of self-actualization: The quest for the test may be as challenging as the search for the self [Special Issue: Handbook of self-actualization]. *Journal of Social Behavior and Personality, 6,* 265–290.

Weitzman, B. (1967). Behavior therapy and psychotherapy. *Psychological Review, 74,* 300–317.

Weitzmann, E. (1961). A note on the EEG and eye movements during behavioral sleep in monkeys. *EEG Clinical Neurophysiology, 13,* 790–794.

Westen, D. (1991a). Cognitive-behavioral interventions in the psychoanalytic psychotherapy of borderline personality disorders. *Clinical Psychology Review, 11,* 211–230.

Westen, D. (1991b). Social cognition and object relations. *Psychological Bulletin, 109,* 429–455.

Wetzler, S., & Marlowe, D. (1990). "Faking bad" on the MMPI, MMPI-2, and Millon-II. *Psychological Reports, 67,* 1117–1118.

White, J., Davison, G. C., Haaga, D. A. F., & White, K. (1992). Cognitive bias in the articulated thoughts of depressed and nondepressed psychiatric patients. *The Journal of Nervous and Mental Disease, 180,* 77–81.

White, L., Tursky, B., & Schwartz, G. E. (Eds.). (1985). *Placebo: Theory, research, and mechanisms.* New York: Guilford Press.

White, R. W. (1959). Motivation reconsidered: The concept of competence. *Psychological Review, 66,* 297–333.

White, R. W. (1960). Competence and the psychosexual stages of development. In M. R. Jones (Ed.), *Nebraska symposium on motivation, 1960* (Vol. 8, pp. 97–141). Lincoln: University of Nebraska Press.

White, R. W. (1963). *Ego and reality in psychoanalytic theory: Psychological issues* (Monograph No. 11). New York: International Universities Press.

White, R. W. (1976). *The enterprise of living: A view of personal growth* (2nd ed.). New York: Holt, Rinehart & Winston.

Whitson, E. R., & Olczak, P. V. (1991). The use of the POI in clinical situations: An evaluation [Special Issue: Handbook of self-actualization]. *Journal of Social Behavior and Personality, 6,* 291–310.

Wicker, A. W. (1971). An examination of the "other variables" explanation of attitude-behavior inconsistency. *Journal of Personality and Social Psychology, 19,* 18–30.

Wickramasekera, I. (1985). A conditioned response model of the placebo effect: Predictions from the model. In L. White, B. Tursky, & G. E. Schwartz (Eds.), *Placebo: Theory, research, and mechanisms* (pp. 255–287). New York: Guilford Press.

Wiedenfeld, S. A., O'Leary, A., Bandura, A., Brown, S., Levine, S., & Raska, K. (1990). Impact of perceived self-efficacy in coping with stressors on components of the immune system. *Journal of Personality and Social Psychology, 59,* 1082–1094.

Wildstein, A. B., & Thompson, D. N. (1989). Locus of control, expectational set, and problem solving. *Perceptual and Motor Skills, 68,* 383–388.

Wilhite, S. C. (1990). Self-efficacy, locus of control, self-assessment of memory ability, and study activities as predictors of college course achievement. *Journal of Educational Psychology, 82,* 696–700.

Wilkinson, S. M. (1991). Penis envy: Libidinal metaphor and experiential metonym. *International Journal of Psycho-Analysis, 72,* 335–346.

Willerman, L. (1975). *Individual and group differences.* New York: Harper's College Press.

Willerman, L., & Plomin, R. (1973). Activity level in children and their parents. *Child Development, 44,* 854–858.

Williams, D. E., & Page, M. M. (1989). A multi-dimensional measure of Maslow's hierarchy of needs. *Journal of Research in Personality, 23,* 192–213.

Williams, R. B., Jr., Friedman, M., Glass, D. C., Herd, J. A., & Schneiderman, N. (1978). Mechanisms linking behavioral and pathophysiological processes. In T. M. Dembroski, S. M. Weiss, J. L. Shields, S. G. Haynes, & M. Feinleib (Eds.), *Coronary-prone behavior.* New York: Springer-Verlag.

Williams, S. L. (1992). Perceived self-efficacy and phobic disability. In R. Schwarzer (Ed.), *Self-efficacy: Thought control of action* (pp. 149–176). Washington, DC: Hemisphere.

Williams, S. L., & Kinney, P. J. (1991). Performance and nonperformance strategies for coping with acute pain: The role of perceived self-efficacy, expected outcomes, and attention. *Cognitive Therapy and Research, 15,* 1–19.

Williams, S. L., & Zane, G. (1989). Guided mastery and stimulus exposure treatments for severe performance anxiety in agoraphobics. *Behaviour Research and Therapy, 27,* 237–245.

Wilson, G. (1986). The behaviour therapy of W. S. Gilbert. *the Behavior Therapist, 2,* 32–34.

Wilson, G. T. (1982). Clinical issues and strategies in the practice of behavior therapy. In C. M. Franks, G. T. Wilson, P. C. Kendall, & K. D. Brownell (Eds.), *Annual review of behavior therapy: Theory and practice* (Vol. 8, pp. 305–345). New York: Guilford Press.

Wilson, G. T. (1984). Fear reduction methods and the treatment of anxiety disorders. In C. M. Franks, G. T. Wilson, P. C. Kendall, & K. D. Brownell (Eds.), *Annual review of behavior therapy: Theory and practice* (Vol. 10, pp. 87–122). New York: Guilford Press.

Wilson, G. T., O'Leary, K. D., & Nathan, P. (1992). *Abnormal psychology.* Englewood Cliffs, NJ: Prentice-Hall.

Wink, P., & Gough, H. G. (1990). New narcissism scales for the California Psychological Inventory and MMPI. *Journal of Personality Assessment, 54,* 446–462.

Winnicott, D. W. (1971). *Playing and reality.* London: Tavistock Publications.

Winson, J. (1985). *Brain and psyche: The biology of the unconscious.* New York: Anchor/Doubleday.

Winter, D., Baker, M., & Goggins, S. (1992). Into the unknown: Transitions in psychiatric services as construed by clients and staff. *International Journal of Personal Construct Psychology, 5,* 323–340.

Winter, D. A. (1990a). *Personal construct theory in clinical practice.* London: Routledge.

Winter, D. A. (1990b). Therapeutic alternatives for psychological disorder: Personal construct psychology investigations in a health service setting. In G. J. Neimeyer & R. A. Neimeyer (Eds.), *Advances in personal construct psychology* (Vol. 1, pp. 89–116). Greewich, CT: JAI Press.

Winter, D. G. (1967). *Power motivation in thought and action.* Unpublished doctoral dissertation, Harvard University.

Winter, D. G. (1968). Need for power in thought and action. In *Proceedings of the 76th Annual Convention of the American Psychological Association, 3,* 429–430.

Winter, D. G. (1972). The need for power in college men: Action correlates and relationship to drinking. In D. C. McClelland, W. N. Davis, R. Kalin, & E. Wanner (Eds.), *The drinking man.* New York: Free Press.

Winter, D. G. (1973). *The power motive.* New York: Free Press.

Winter, D. G. (1987a). Enhancement of an enemy's power motivation as a dynamic of conflict escalation. *Journal of Personality and Social Psychology, 52,* 41–46.

Winter, D. G. (1987b). Leader appeal, leader performance, and the motive profiles of leaders and followers: A study of American presidents and elections. *Journal of Personality and Social Psychology, 52,* 196–202.

Winter, D. G. (1988). The power motive in women and men. *Journal of Personality and Social Psychology, 54,* 510–519.

Winter, D. G., & Barenbaum, N. B. (1985). Responsibility and the power motive in women and men. *Journal of Personality, 53,* 335–355.

Winter, D. G., & Carlson, L. A. (1988). Using motive scores in the psychobiographical study of an individual: The case of Richard Nixon. In D. P. McAdams & R. L. Ochberg (Eds.), *Psychobiography and life narratives.* Durham, NC: Duke University Press.

Winter, D. G., Hermann, M. G., Weintraub, W., & Walker, S. G. (1991). The personalities of Bush and Gorbachev at a distance: Follow-up on predictions. *Political Psychology, 12,* 457–464.

Wolk, S., & Kurtz, J. (1975). Positive adjustment and involvement during aging and expectancy for internal control. *Journal of Consulting and Clinical Psychology, 43,* 173–178.

Wolpe, J. (1958). *Psychotherapy by reciprocal inhibition.* Stanford: Stanford University Press.

Wolpe, J. (1978). Cognition and causation in human behavior and its therapy. *American Psychologist, 33,* 437–446.

Wolpe, J. (1989). The derailment of behavior therapy: A tale of conceptual misdirection. *Journal of Behavior Therapy and Experimental Psychiatry, 20,* 3–15.

Wolpe, J., & Lazarus, A. A. (1966). *Behavior therapy techniques: A guide to the treatment of neurosis.* New York: Pergamon Press.

Wolpe, J., & Rachman, S. (1960). Psychoanalytic "evidence": A critique based on Freud's case of Little Hans. *Journal of Nervous and Mental Diseases, 130,* 135–148

Wolpe, J., & Rowan, V. C. (1988). Panic disorder: A product of classical conditioning. *Behaviour Research and Therapy, 26,* 441–450.

Wolpe, J., & Rowan, V. C. (1989). Classical conditioning and panic disorder: Reply to Sanderson and Beck. *Behaviour Research and Therapy, 27,* 583–584.

Wood, J. V., Taylor, S. E., & Lichtman, R. R. (1985). Social comparison and adjustment to breast cancer. *Journal of Personality and Social Psychology, 49,* 1169–1183.

Wood, R., & Bandura, A. (1989). Impact of conceptions of ability on self-regulatory mechanisms and complex decision making. *Journal of Personality and Social Psychology, 56,* 407–415.

Woodruffe, C. (1985). Consensual validation of personality traits: Additional evidence and individual differences. *Journal of Personality and Social Psychology, 48,* 1240–1252.

Worchel, P. (1955). Anxiety and repression. *Journal of Abnormal and Social Psychology, 51,* 201–205.

Worobey, J. (1986). Convergence among assessments of temperament in the first month. *Child Development, 57,* 47–55.

Wright, J., & Mischel, W. (1982). Influence of affect on cognitive social learning variables. *Journal of Personality and Social Psychology, 43,* 901–914.

Wright, J., & Mischel, W. (1986). *Predicting cross-situational consistency: The role of person variables and situation requirements.* Unpublished manuscript, Columbia University.

Wright, J. C., & Mischel, W. (1987). A conditional approach to dispositional constructs: The local predictability of social behavior. *Journal of Personality and Social Psychology, 53,* 1159–1177.

Wright, L. (1988). The Type A behavior pattern and coronary heart disease. *American Psychologist, 43,* 2–14.

Wrightsman, L. S. (1969). Wallace supporters and adherence to "law and order." *Journal of Personality and Social Psychology, 13,* 17–22.

Wylie, R. C. (1968). The present status of self theory. In E. F. Borgatta & W. W. Lambert (Eds.), *Handbook of personality theory and research* (pp. 728–787). Chicago: Rand McNally.

Yates, B. T., & Mischel, W. (1979). Young children's preferred attentional strategies for delaying gratification. *Journal of Personality and Social Psychology, 37,* 286–300.

Zayas, L. H. (1988). Thematic features in the manifest dreams of expectant fathers. *Clinical Social Work Journal, 16,* 282–296.

Zeldow, P. B., Daugherty, S. R., & McAdams, D. P. (1988). Intimacy, power, and psychological well-being in medical students. *Journal of Nervous and Mental Disease, 176,* 182–187.

Zeller, A. (1950). An experimental analogue of repression, II. The effect of individual failure and success on memory measured by relearning. *Journal of Experimental Psychology, 40,* 411–422.

Zeller, A. (1951). An experimental analogue of repression, III. The effect of induced failure and success on memory measured by recall. *Journal of Experimental Psychology, 42,* 32–38.

Zettle, R. D., & Hayes, S. C. (1987). Component and process analysis of cognitive therapy. *Psychological Reports, 61,* 939–953.

Zetzel, E. (1956). Current concepts of transference. *International Journal of Psycho-Analysis, 37,* 369–376.

Zhurbin, V. I. (1991). The notion of psychological defense in the conceptions of Sigmund Freud and Carl Rogers. *Soviet Psychology, 29,* 58–72.

Zimmerman, B. J. (1990). Self-regulating academic learning and achievement: The emergence of a social cognitive perspective. *Educational Psychology Review, 2,* 173–201.

Zucker, R. A., Manosevitz, M., & Lanyon, R. I. (1968). Birth order, anxiety, and affiliation during a crisis. *Journal of Personality and Social Psychology, 8,* 354–359.

Zuckerman, M. (1983). The distinction between trait and state scales is not arbitrary: Comment on Allen and Potkay's "On the arbitrary distinction between traits and states." *Journal of Personality and Social Psychology, 44,* 1083–1086.

Name Index

Subject Index

Demonstration Materials

The following pages are perforated for
easy removal.

Weight (pounds)

Height (inches)

	I Other person	II Nature of interaction	III Other's behavior	IV Other's intention	V Your evaluation	VI Basis for evaluation
Close relationships						
Distant relationships						

RANK	NAME	NUMBER OF ADJECTIVES USED	PERVASIVENESS				PERCENTAGE OF SIMILARITY
			ALMOST ALWAYS 4	FRE- QUENTLY 3	OCCA- SIONALLY 2	RARELY 1	
	Self						%
Know best 1st							%
2nd							%
3rd							%
4th							%
Know least 5th							%
Σ = Sum (total)		Σ =	Σ =	Σ =	Σ =	Σ =	
		M =	%	%	%	%	

Σ = Sum (total)

M = Mean

	HARDLY AT ALL				A LOT	SCALE SCORE	SUM
ITEM							
How true is this of you?							
1. I make friends easily.	1	2	3	4	5		
2. I tend to be shy. (R)	1	2	3	4	5		
3. I like to be with others.	1	2	3	4	5		
4. I like to be independent of people. (R)	1	2	3	4	5		
5. I usually prefer to do things alone. (R)	1	2	3	4	5		
6. I am always on the go.	1	2	3	4	5		
7. I like to be off and running as soon as I wake up in the morning.	1	2	3	4	5		
8. I like to keep busy all of the time.	1	2	3	4	5		
9. I am very energetic.	1	2	3	4	5		
10. I prefer quiet, inactive pastimes to more active ones. (R)	1	2	3	4	5		
11. I tend to cry easily.	1	2	3	4	5		
12. I am easily frightened.	1	2	3	4	5		
13. I tend to be somewhat emotional.	1	2	3	4	5		
14. I get upset easily.	1	2	3	4	5		
15. I tend to be easily irritated.	1	2	3	4	5		

Attitude number	First sort rank	Second sort rank	Difference	Difference squared
1				
2				
3				
4				
5				
6				
7				
8				
9				
10				
11				
12				
13				
14				
15				
16				
Sum of differences squared =				

1. I like to study.

2. I prefer socializing with people my own age.

3. Success is important to me.

4. I am religious.

5. I dislike crude language.

6. I take good care of my body.

7. I am sensitive to other people's needs.

8. I think it is okay to get drunk occasionally.

9. I prefer to save money than to spend it.

10. I am concerned with how I look.

11. I am organized.

12. I enjoy being alone.

13. I have high standards for my work.

14. I think it is important to obey the law.

15. My family is important to me.

16. I like meeting new people.

Pile 1
STRONGLY AGREE
No. required in pile = 1
Rank = 1.0

Pile 2
MODERATELY AGREE
No. required in pile = 2
Rank = 2.5

Pile 3
SLIGHTLY AGREE
No. required in pile = 3
Rank = 5.0

Pile 4
AMBIVALENT (NEUTRAL)
No. required in pile = 4
Rank = 8.5

Pile 5
SLIGHTLY DISAGREE
No. required in pile = 3
Rank = 12.0

Pile 6
MODERATELY DISAGREE
No. required in pile = 2
Rank = 14.5

Pile 7
STRONGLY DISAGREE
No. required in pile = 1
Rank = 16.0

DEFINITELY AGREE

DEFINITELY DISAGREE

AMBIVALENT

Need category	Examples of recent behavior	Satisfaction rating	Importance rating	Salience rating
Self-actualization	1. 2. 3.			
Esteem	1. 2. 3.			
Belongingness and Love	1. 2. 3.			
Safety	1. 2. 3.			
Physiological	1. 2. 3.			

Description of Peak Experience	General Nature	Feelings
I.		
II.		
III.		

Description	Role	Important to You?	%
_.			
=.			
≡.			

Figure (Name)

Role

1. Self
2. Brother
3. Sister
4. Ex-Pal
5. Rejecting Person
6. Pitied Person
7. Threatening Person
8. Attractive Person
9. Accepted Teacher
10. Happy Person

Sort No.	1. Self	2. Brother	3. Sister	4. Ex-Pal	5. Rejecting Person	6. Pitied Person	7. Threatening Person	8. Attractive Person	9. Accepted Teacher	10. Happy Person	Emergent Pole	Implicit Pole
1			●	●		●						
2	●	●										
3	●						●	●				
4					●			●				
5				●		●						
6		●	●				●					
7		●			●							
8		●				●	●					
9			●			●						
10	●											

TO THE OWNER OF THIS BOOK:

We hope that you have found *Personality: Strategies and Issues*, 7th Edition, useful. So that this book can be improved in a future edition, would you take the time to complete this sheet and return it? Thank you.

School and address: _____

Department: _____

Instructor's name: _____

_____

1. What I like most about this book is: _____

_____

2. What I like least about this book is: _____

_____

_____

3. My general reaction to this book is: _____

_____

4. The name of the course in which I used this book is: _____

_____

5. Were all of the chapters of the book assigned for you to read? _____

    If not, which ones weren't? _____

6. In the space below, or on a separate sheet of paper, please write specific suggestions for improving this book and anything else you'd care to share about your experience in using the book.

_____

_____

_____

_____

_____

_____

_____

Optional:

Your name: _____ Date: _____

May Brooks/Cole quote you, either in promotion for *Personality: Strategies and Issues*, 7th Edition, or in future publishing ventures?

Yes: _____ No: _____

Sincerely,

Robert M. Liebert
Michael D. Spiegler

FOLD HERE

FOLD HERE